Body Memory, Metaphor and Movement

Advances in Consciousness Research (AiCR)

Provides a forum for scholars from different scientific disciplines and fields of knowledge who study consciousness in its multifaceted aspects. Thus the Series includes (but is not limited to) the various areas of cognitive science, including cognitive psychology, brain science, philosophy and linguistics. The orientation of the series is toward developing new interdisciplinary and integrative approaches for the investigation, description and theory of consciousness, as well as the practical consequences of this research for the individual in society.

From 1999 the Series consists of two subseries that cover the most important types of contributions to consciousness studies:

Series A: Theory and Method. Contributions to the development of theory and method in the study of consciousness; Series B: Research in Progress. Experimental, descriptive and clinical research in consciousness.

This book is a contribution to Series B.

For an overview of all books published in this series, please see
http://benjamins.com/catalog/aicr

Volume 84

Body Memory, Metaphor and Movement
Edited by Sabine C. Koch, Thomas Fuchs, Michela Summa and Cornelia Müller

Body Memory, Metaphor and Movement

Edited by

Sabine C. Koch
Thomas Fuchs
Michela Summa
University of Heidelberg

Cornelia Müller
European University Viadrina, Frankfurt (Oder)

John Benjamins Publishing Company

Amsterdam / Philadelphia

The paper used in this publication meets the minimum requirements of the American National Standard for Information Sciences – Permanence of Paper for Printed Library Materials, ANSI z39.48-1984.

Library of Congress Cataloging-in-Publication Data

Body memory, metaphor and movement / edited by Sabine C. Koch, Thomas Fuchs, Michela Summa, Cornelia Müller.
    p. cm. (Advances in Consciousness Research, ISSN 1381-589X ; v. 84)
Includes bibliographical references and index.
1. Muscular sense. 2. Movement, Psychology of. 3. Body schema. 4. Memory. 5. Metaphor.
    I. Koch, Sabine C. II. Fuchs, Thomas. III. Summa, Michela. IV. Müller, Cornelia.
BF285.B63   2012
152.3--dc23   2011039943
ISBN 978 90 272 1350 1   (Hb ; alk. paper)
ISBN 978 90 272 1355 6   (Pb ; alk. paper)
ISBN 978 90 272 8167 8   (Eb)

John Benjamins Publishing Co. · P.O. Box 36224 · 1020 ME Amsterdam · The Netherlands
John Benjamins North America · P.O. Box 27519 · Philadelphia PA 19118-0519 · USA

Table of contents

Introduction   1

Part I. Contributions from phenomenology

1. The phenomenology of body memory   9
    Thomas Fuchs

2. Body memory and the genesis of meaning   23
    Michela Summa

3. Kinesthetic memory: Further critical reflections and constructive analyses   43
    Maxine Sheets-Johnstone

4. Comment on Thomas Fuchs: The time of the explicating process   73
    Eugene T. Gendlin

5. Enduring: A phenomenological investigation   83
    Elizabeth A. Behnke

6. Body memory and dance   105
    Mónica E. Alarcón Dávila

Part II. Contributions from cognitive sciences

7. Implicit body memory   115
    Petra Jansen

8. Embodied concepts   121
    Christina Bermeitinger and Markus Kiefer

9. Cognitive perspectives on embodiment   141
    Christina Jung and Peggy Sparenberg

10. Dynamic embodiment and its functional role: A body
    feedback perspective   155
    Caterina Suitner, Sabine C. Koch, Katharina Bachmeier and Anne Maass

11. Testing Fuchs' taxonomy of body memory: A content analysis
    of interview data   171
    Sabine C. Koch

12. Metaphorical instruction and body memory   187
    Claudia Böger

13. Body memory and the emergence of metaphor in movement
    and speech: An interdisciplinary case study   201
    Astrid Kolter, Silva H. Ladewig, Michela Summa, Cornelia Müller,
    Sabine C. Koch and Thomas Fuchs

14. Moved by God: Performance and memory in the Western Himalayas   227
    William Sax and Karin Polit

15. The memory of the cell   243
    Ralf P. Meyer

Part III. Contributions from embodied therapies

16. Sensation, movement, and emotion: Explicit procedures
    for implicit memories   255
    Christine Caldwell

17. Memory, metaphor, and mirroring in movement therapy
    with trauma patients   267
    Marianne Eberhard-Kaechele

18. Body memory as a part of the body image   289
    Päivi Pylvänäinen

19. The embodied word   307
    Heidrun Panhofer, Helen Payne, Timothy Parke and Bonnie Meekums

20. Emotorics: Development and body memory   327
    Yona Shahar-Levy

21. The emergence of body memory in Authentic Movement   341
    Ilka Konopatsch and Helen Payne

22. Nakedness, hunger, hooks and hearts: Embodied memories
    and movement psychological processes in dance therapy
    and movement pedagogy   353
    Helle Winther

23. Dance/movement therapy with traumatized dissociative patients   369
    Sabine C. Koch and Steve Harvey

24. Focusing, felt sensing and body memory   387
    Elmar Kruithoff

25. Mindfulness, embodiment, and depression   393
    Johannes Michalak, Jan M. Burg and Thomas Heidenreich

Part IV. Conclusions

26. Body memory: An integration   417
    Michela Summa, Sabine C. Koch, Thomas Fuchs and Cornelia Müller

Authors notes   445

Addresses for correspondence   453

Index   459

Introduction

Body memory – Current state of research

This edited volume results from an interdisciplinary collaboration of phenomenologists, cognitive linguists, and psychologists working at the interface of embodiment research.[1] The editors share the interest in the *lived-body* (Merleau-Ponty 1962) and particularly in its *dynamic aspects* (Fuchs 2000, this volume; Koch 2011a, b; Müller 2007, 2008a, b; Sheets-Johnstone 1999; Summa 2011a, b). This brings them to the common ground of body memory and its repercussions in *kinesthesia* which is approached in this book through different disciplinary methods. Part I lays the phenomenological grounds by providing a definition and a taxonomy of body memory, introducing the concept of kinesthetic memory, critically discussing conceptual metaphor theory, and focusing on the particularities of traumatic memory and dance. Part II introduces an embodied perspective on memory within the cognitive sciences, discusses the value and place of the concept of body memory within embodied cognition, and offers an initial testing of Fuchs' taxonomy. Part III contributes clinical theory and applications from a body and movement therapy perspective. In this last part, many authors are motivated by the necessity to address traumatic as well as resourceful body memory in the course of trauma work and healing.

The aim of the book is thus threefold: Firstly, to describe the phenomenon and develop a taxonomy of body memory, to relate it to psychopathology, and to clarify the contributions from the cognitive sciences to an empirically based conceptualization of body memory. Secondly, employing an embodiment perspective to develop dynamic empirical approaches and an according methodology. And thirdly, to integrate approaches to body memory and metaphors from the fields of embodied therapies in clinical practice.

Regarding the overall topic of the book, phenomenologists, cognitive scientists and clinical practitioners are faced with a number of questions:

> What does the *concept* of body memory mean? Is it a useful category? In particular, what is the difference between body memory and implicit memory as conceptualized in the cognitive sciences?

---

1. Thanks to project grant 01UB0390 of the BMBF (German Federal Ministry of Education and Research) to S. Koch, T. Fuchs and C. Müller.

How are we to *empirically measure* and test body memory? Can we capture it in interviews, in movement analysis of video tapes, or by measuring reaction times?

Where are the *constraints* of body memory? What would a differential definition include?

When and how does body memory *become explicit*? Do symbols and metaphors play a role in this process?

And finally, how can practitioners of body and movement therapies *access body memories* in order to efficiently treat individuals in therapy? When is it indicated and promising to access, for example, preverbal memories?

The editors conceptualize memory as embodied; that means, memory is not a set of information stored somewhere in the brain, but the totality of the embodied subject's dispositions, which allow the person to react to present situations and requirements on the basis of past experience. However, we do acknowledge that memory is not monolithic, and any attempt to characterize body memory in terms of a single conceptualization or perspective will certainly not do justice to its heterogeneous aspects. The blind men and the elephant[2] are a suitable metaphor of how it feels when we approach the phenomenon of body memory. Phenomenology is in need of a clear descriptive conceptualization; psychology and the other cognitive sciences have no such concept as body memory and need to carefully approach a first definitional approximation. Movement and body-oriented therapies work with a hitherto rather blurry concept of body memory, and yet they have developed clinical methods to address and access traumatic content and work with it successfully.

All the disciplines involved here have their own reasons and motivations to address the phenomenon. Given their different goals and methods, can we expect to find common ground at this point in time? One common denominator is possibly the view that knowledge is stored in memory not in an *amodal* way, but in a *modality-specific sensorimotor format*, and that any type of recall includes a sensorimotor simulation of the processes involved in the original encoding of the experience (Barsalou, Niedenthal, Barbey & Ruppert 2003; Niedenthal 2007) as a basic assumption of embodied cognition approaches. Following the chapters of the book, the reader might judge whether the different disciplinary perspectives have jointly contributed to an enriched and synoptic understanding of the concept. At the end of the book, we will reassess this question in light of the contributions in this volume.

---

2.   Six blind men are asked to determine what an elephant lookes like. One blind man feels a leg and says the elephant is like a pillar; the next feels the tail and says the elephant is like a rope; the third feels the trunk and says the elephant is like a tree branch; the fourth feels the ear says the elephant is like a hand fan; the fifth who feels the belly says the elephant is like a wall; and the sixth feels the tusk says the elephant is like a solid pipe. This story illustrates the relativity of truth and the dependency on what we think is true on the range of our accessible senory information.

Chapter overview

In the first chapter, Thomas Fuchs provides an overview on body memory from a phenomenological perspective; he introduces his own body memory taxonomy, and relates it to psychopathology. In the second chapter, Michela Summa discusses the relevance of the inquiry into body memory within a phenomenological theory of knowledge. She particularly touches upon the role of body memory in meaning formation by comparing Husserl's theory of *Typus* with the experientialist theory of embodied concepts developed by Lakoff and Johnson (1999). In Chapter 3, Maxine Sheets-Johnstone embeds her description of kinesthetic memory within the current debate on memory in philosophy and the cognitive sciences. Somewhat skeptical regarding the current differentiations of memory types, the author insists on the centrality of kinesthetic memory in everyday life and anchors her account of kinesthetic memory in both phenomenological descriptions and Luria's seminal notion of kinetic melody. Chapter 4 by Elizabeth Behnke introduces the concept of "enduring" to describe a peculiar attitude characterizing traumatic body memory. The phenomenology of 'enduring' describes the bodily and pre-reflective stance to bear and withstand hardships. Yet, it also refers to the temporal spreading out of traumatic experiences, which pervade one's life. In Chapter 5, Monica Alarcon explores the relation between body memory and dance. In doing so, she particularly highlights the interweaving of the spatio-temporal unfolding of body memory in dance, and argues that the lived body shall be quasi-transcendentally considered as the unconstituted condition of both space and time. Commenting on Fuchs' body memory publication from 2003, Eugene Gendlin introduces a new concept of the implicit in Chapter 6. Gendlin particularly contends that the inquiry into implicit memory shall not be exclusively focused on the past, but rather embrace an analysis of our capacity to presently reshape the past and to create something new.

The second part of the book contains chapters of cognitive scientists who took the challenge to anchor the phenomenological conceptualization of body memory in their own empirical work via the recent framework of embodied cognition. The first four chapters are based on a cognitive sciences background from psychology. In Chapter 6 on implicit body memory, Jansen criticizes the cognitive science's methods of conceptualizing and measuring implicit memory as being too narrow for the use of clinical practitioners. In her chapter, she proposes new measurements of body memory analogous to the ones of "classical" memory research. In Chapter 7, Christina Bermeitinger and Markus Kiefer provide an overview of recent empirical embodiment literature, and provide an integration of embodied and classical views on conceptual representation. They particularly discuss embodied processes and the sensorimotor representation perspective of concepts. In Chapter 8, Christina Jung and Peggy Sparenberg summarize recent empirical results in the field of embodied cognition, focusing on the effects of embodiment on emotions and the connections to the human mirror-neuron system. Chapter 9 by Caterina Suitner, Sabine Koch, Katharina Bachmeier and Anne Maass stresses the dynamic aspect of body memory resulting from the inclusion of movement. The authors introduce the spatial agency bias and the dynamic body feedback approach as experimental methods that account for the dynamics of bodily behavior and body memory, with both cultural and universal appearances. A content analysis of interviews by Sabine Koch in Chapter 10 aims to test whether interviewees – when asked about a differentiation of body memory – generate the same categories than assumed in the taxonomy of Fuchs. Results show that Fuchs' categories were all included and were further sub-differentiated by the interviewees.

The next four chapters of part two include the perspective of cognitive linguistics, cognitive anthropology and other fields. Chapter 11 by Claudia Böger provides a perspective from philosophical anthropology and the fields of educational and sport science. Drawing on the background of conceptual metaphor theory (Lakoff & Johnson 1999), the author introduces her empirical work on metaphoric instruction. In two experiments, she showed performance advantages of participants instructed through metaphors versus non-metaphorically instructed participants. In Chapter 12, Astrid Kolter, Silva Ladewig, Michela Summa, Cornelia Müller, Sabine Koch and Thomas Fuchs present a case study on the dynamic emergence of metaphors from body memory in movement. Integrating the perspectives of phenomenology, psychology, cognitive linguistics and movement therapy, the case study shows how verbal and bodily metaphors dynamically emerge from movement, displaying different degrees of activated metaphoricity and different forms of experiencing body memory. This work results from an interdisciplinary methodology to analyze dynamic embodiment, developed by the editors within the BMBF-project "Body Language of Movement and Dance". Chapter 13 by William Sax and Karin Polit provides a dense and rich anthropological perspective on body memory. Conveyed by the examples of ritual possession and a ritual journey in the Himalayas the authors show how memory is to a large part not cognitive but embodied. Chapter 14 by Ralf P. Meyer provides an epigenetic perspective on body memory. The author puts forth that body memory in neurobiological context may be hypothesized as a concept influenced by genetics and epigenetics, environmental input, cultural influence, cognition, and emotion.

The third part of the book provides clinical perspectives of practitioner-researchers from body and movement therapies, who often work with body memories on a daily basis, particularly with regard to trauma treatment. Descriptions from the work with patients of different diagnoses provide a more concrete perspective to understand how body memory emerges from movement, and offers the opportunity to enter into the experiential worlds of the patients. This last part of the book contributes to ground the scientific approaches, and give them purpose by applying them to the clinical work with patients in different fields of embodied therapies that await scientific validation. In Chapter 15, Christine Caldwell integrates a clinical movement therapy perspective with a neuroscientific one, focusing on the fact that neuroscience confirms the crucial role of sensorimotor and affective processing in the neurogenetic shaping and reshaping of human memory, particularly implicit memory. Caldwell emphasizes that the understanding of the phenomenological body's centrality in learning and remembering has profound implications for the psychotherapeutic relationship and methods. Chapter 16 by Marianne Eberhard-Kaechele proposes an integrative model of the trauma process as a common denominator of all therapy schools. She outlines the body's centrality in the development and healing of PTSD and provides a theory of *mirroring* as one of the central methods of assessment and intervention from a movement therapy perspective. In Chapter 17 Paivi Pilvänäinen, on the background of her "tripartite model of body" relating to Casey's (2000) body memory model, provides a comprehensive overview of the theory and works of Eric Kandel and relates them to the concept of body memory. In the second part of her chapter, she describes a movement therapy process of eight women, focusing on the emergence and meaning of body memories in the course of group psychotherapy. In Chapter 18, Yona Shahar-Levy introduces the Emotorics approach she developed in her clinical work in Israel. This approach contains a theory of body memory, which Shahar-Levy also exemplifies using clinical examples from patients. Chapter 19 takes on the challenge to analyze the verbalization and verbalizability of meaning-related processes in movement. Heidrun Panhofer, Helen Payne, Timothy Parke and Bonnie Meekums integrate narrative research and expressive approaches. Their conclusion is that much of the nonverbal therapeutic processes cannot – and in fact need not – be verbalized for healing to occur. In Chapter 20, Ilka Konopatsch and Helen Payne describe the method of authentic movement, a technique in movement therapy to get to truthful, self-congruent, and innovative discoveries by use of movement. Authentic movement often triggers body memories and the emergence of metaphors. Chapter 21 by Helle Winther provides a phenomenological description and detailed analysis of the processes of three patients participating in movement therapy. In Chapter 22, Sabine Koch and Steve Harvey highlight the role of movement therapy for traumatized dissociative patients illustrating their point with a single case study of a child and a group case study with traumatized dissociative identity disorder patients in a clinical setting. They focus on body memories, treatment principles, and methodological options in movement therapy for adults and children. Chapter 23 by Elmar Kruithoff introduces focusing and the felt sense – two core concepts of Eugene Gendlin (1996) – as an aspect of and in relation to body memory. In Chapter 24, Johannes Michalak, Jan Burg and Thomas Heidenreich provide a comprehensive overview of mindfulness-based psychotherapy, the empirical research related to it with a particular focus on the treatment of depression, and their own empirical work in the field. They view body memory as the constant ground on which learning takes place, and emphasize the role of conscious attention toward the body in this process. The final chapter of the editors ties together important research directions that emerge from the book.

For phenomenology as well as for movement therapy, there has been some previous writing, thinking, and predefining the topic, not so for the cognitive sciences. A treatise on body memory from the perspective of the cognitive sciences is an innovative jump into a non-existing field. We have been lucky to find the right kind of open-minded and innovative researchers to put down a foundation of the field from a converging phenomenological, cognitive sciences, and clinical perspective. Independent of their perspective, we would like to thank all authors for their contributions.

Last but not least, we would like to thank the organizing forces behind this edited volume, Teresa Kunz, who more than once formatted the entire set of chapters; Els van Dongen and Jan-Kees van Oord at John Benjamins, and Maxim Stamenov, the series editor of "Advances in consciousness studies" for efficient and reliable editing.

Sabine C. Koch, Thomas Fuchs, Michela Summa and Cornelia Müller
Heidelberg and Frankfurt (Oder), May 2011

References

Barsalou, L. W., Niedenthal, P. M., Barbey, A. K. & Ruppert, J. A. (2003). Social embodiment. In B. H. Ross (Ed.), *The psychology of learning and motivation* (Vol. 43, pp. 43–92). San Diego, CA: Academic Press.

Casey, E. (2000). *Remembering. A phenomenological study.* Bloomington: Indiana University Press.

Fuchs, T. (2000). *Leib, Raum, Person. Entwurf einer phänomenologischen Anthropologie* [Body, space, and the person. An outline of philosophical anthropology]. Stuttgart: Klett-Cotta.

Fuchs, T. (2003). *The memory of the body.* Online at: http://www.klinikum.uni-heidelberg.de/fileadmin/zpm/psychatrie/ppp2004/manuskript/fuchs.pdf.

Fuchs, T. (this volume). The phenomenology of body memory. In S. C. Koch, T. Fuchs, M. Summa & C. Müller (Eds.), *Body memory, metaphor and movement.* Amsterdam: John Benjamins.

Gendlin, E. T. (1996). *Focusing-oriented psychotherapy: A manual of the experiential method.* New York: Guilford.

Koch, S. C. (2011a). *Embodiment: Der Einfluss von Eigenbewegung auf Affekt, Einstellung und Kognition.* [Embodiment: The influence of body movement on affect, attitudes, and cognition]. Berlin: Logos.

Koch, S. C. (2011b). Basic body rhythms and embodied intercorporality: From individual to interpersonal movement feedback. In W. Tschacher & C. Bergomi (Eds.), *The implications of embodiment: Cognition and communication.* Exeter: Imprint Academic.

Lakoff, G. & Johnson, M. (1999). *Philosophy in the flesh. The embodied mind and its challenge to Western thought.* New York: Basic Books.

Merleau-Ponty, M. (1962). *Phenomenology of perception.* London: Routledge.

Müller, C. (2007). A dynamic view on gesture, language and thought. In S. D. Duncan, J. Cassell & E. Levy (Eds.), *Gesture and the dynamic dimension of language. Essays in honor of David McNeill* (pp. 109–116). Amsterdam/Philadelphia: John Benjamins.

Müller, C. (2008a). *Metaphors. Dead and alive, sleeping and waking. A dynamic view.* Chicago: University of Chicago Press.

Müller, C. (2008b). What gestures reveal about the nature of metaphor. In A. Cienki & C. Müller (Eds.), *Metaphor and gesture* (pp. 219–245). Amsterdam/Philadelphia: John Benjamins.

Niedenthal, P. M. (2007). Embodying emotion. *Science, 316,* 1002–1005.

Sheets-Johnstone, M. (1999). *The primacy of movement.* New York: John Benjamins.

Summa, M. (2011a). "Eine Totalität der Perspektive für mich". Das Spannungsfeld der subjektiven Erfahrung zwischen Kompossibilität und Inkompossibilität ["A totality of perspectives for me". The tension-field of subjective experience between compossibility and incompossibility]. In I. Römer (Ed.), *Subjektivität und Intersubjektivität in der Phänomenologie* [Subjectivity and intersubjectivity in phenomenology] (pp. 41–54). Würzburg: Ergon.

Summa, M. (2011b). Das Leibgedächtnis. Ein Beitrag aus der Phänomenologie Husserls. [Body memory. A contribution from Husserl's phenomenology]. *Husserl Studies* (online first).

PART I

Contributions from phenomenology

CHAPTER 1

The phenomenology of body memory

Thomas Fuchs
Heidelberg University

Memory comprises not only one's explicit recollections of the past, but also
the acquired dispositions, skills, and habits that implicitly influence one's present experience and behavior. This implicit memory is based on the habitual
structure of the lived body, which connects us to the world through its *operative intentionality*. The memory of the body appears in different forms, which
are classified as procedural, situational, intercorporeal, incorporative, pain, and
traumatic memory. The life-long plasticity of body memory enables us to adapt
to the natural and social environment, in particular, to become entrenched and
to feel at home in social and cultural space. On the other hand, the structures
accrued in body memory are an essential basis of our experience of self and
identity: The individual history and peculiarity of a person is also expressed by
his or her bodily habits and behavior. Finally, sensations or situations experienced by the lived body may function as implicit *memory cores*, which, under
suitable circumstances, can release their enclosed content, as in Proust's famous
madeleine experience. This unfolding or *explication* of body memory is of particular importance for therapeutic approaches working with bodily experience.

Keywords: lived body, body memory, implicit memory typology, habit,
intercorporeality, trauma

We usually understand memory to indicate our capacity to remember certain events of
our past or to retain and retrieve data and knowledge. But the phenomena of memory
are by no means restricted to explicit recollection. As Descartes already noted, the lute
player must have a memory in his hands, too, in order to play a tune with such skill.[1]
He would certainly be lost should he try to remember the single movements that he

---

1. "Thus, for example, lute players have part of their memory in their hands, because the facility to move and bend their fingers in various ways which they have acquired by habit, helps
them to remember passages that require them to move their fingers in that way in order to
play them." See, *Descartes Lettre à Meyssonnier* 29.01.1940; also, *Lettre à Mersenne* 01.04.1640;
06.08.1640; (Descartes 1996), AT III, pp. 18–21; pp. 47–48; pp. 84–85; pp. 142–144.

once learned deliberately. Obviously there is a memory of the body apart from conscious recollection: Through repetition and exercise, a habit develops. Well-practiced patterns of movement and perception become embodied as skills or capacities that we apply in our everyday lives as a matter of course – the upright gait, the abilities to speak, read, or write, and the handling of instruments such as a bicycle, a keyboard, or a piano. If, following Merleau-Ponty, we regard the body not as the visible, touchable, and moving physical body, but first and foremost as our capacity to see, touch, move, etc., then body memory denotes the totality of these bodily capacities, habits, and dispositions as they have developed in the course of one's life.

In the 19th and 20th centuries, the French philosophers Maine de Biran (1953/1799), Félix Ravaisson (1999/1838), and Henri Bergson (2007/1896) recognized and studied the habitual capacities of the body as an independent kind of memory. For instance, Bergson's distinction between *souvenir-image* and *mémoire habitude* refers to a voluntarily and representative kind of memory, on the one hand, and to an involuntary and mainly enacted kind of memory, on the other hand.

The latter, "this consciousness of a past of efforts stored in the present is certainly a memory as well, but a memory fundamentally different from the first, always directed towards action, based in the present and looking only at the future. (...) Indeed it does not represent our past, but enacts it."[2] Similarly, Merleau-Ponty, in his *Phenomenology of perception*, described the habitual body (*corps habituel*) as the basis of our being-towards-the-world (*être au monde*): The body establishes itself in every situation and attaches us to the world by the invisible threads of its peculiar 'operative intentionality' – threads that have formed already in our earliest contacts with the world (Merleau-Ponty 1962:74, 114).

Merleau-Ponty developed his approach to body memory in particular by considering the role of *operative intentionality* in the formation of habitualities (Merleau-Ponty 1962:122ff.). Considering the cases of a typist and of an organist, he emphasizes the peculiar kind of "knowledge" that allows them to type and play. While they first have to accustom their bodies to the instrument through consciously using the keys, both the typist and the player finally accomplish their tasks spontaneously, without explicitly recollecting the series of movements they have to perform. Their knowledge, as Merleau-Ponty puts it, is in the hands – not in the anatomical hands, of course, but in their lived-body; it comes forth by means of a bodily effort, and cannot be objectively designated:

> Habit expresses our power of dilating our being-in-the-world, or changing our existence by appropriating fresh instruments. If habit is neither a form of

---

2. "...cette conscience de tout un passé d'efforts emmagasiné dans le présent est bien encore une mémoire, mais une mémoire profondément différente de la première, toujours tendue vers l'action, assise dans le présent et ne regardant que l'avenir. (...) À vrai dire, elle ne nous représente plus notre passé, elle le joue." – Bergson (1896/2007:87). *Matière et mémoire* (italics by the author, T.F.).

> knowledge nor an involuntary action, what then is it? It is knowledge in the hands, which is forthcoming only when bodily effort is made, and cannot be formulated in detachment from that effort.   (Merleau-Ponty 1962: 127)

This kind of memory has been discovered and explored by cognitive psychology as *implicit memory* in the last three decades. Research concerning amnesic patients who may still learn simple motor tasks though being unable to retain any new memories has demonstrated the existence of multiple memory systems.[3] As a consequence, explicit or declarative memory has been distinguished from implicit or procedural memory (Schacter 1987). Explicit memory contains single recollections or information that can be reported and described; it may also be called a *knowing that*. By contrast, repeated situations or actions have merged in implicit memory, as it were, which means they have become superimposed on each other and can no longer be retrieved as single past events. They have become a tacit know-how that is difficult to verbalize – we would have some difficulty describing, for example, how to waltz. Thus, explicit recollection is directed from the present back to the past, whereas implicit memory does not represent the past, but re-enacts it through the body's present performance. What we once had acquired as skills, habits, and experience have become what we can do today; hence, body memory is our lived past.

On the other hand, implicit memory is not a mere reflex program realized by the body machine. Merleau-Ponty rightly conceived of body knowledge as a third dimension between merely imagined movement and motor execution. The memory of the body is an impressive refutation of the dualism of pure consciousness and the physical body, for it cannot be attributed to either of them. When I am dancing, the rhythmic movements originate from my body without a need to steer them deliberately – and yet I am living in my movements, I sense them in advance, and I can modulate them according to the rhythm that I feel: I myself am dancing, and not a ghost in a body machine. The movements of my body are at my disposal, I am aware of my capacities, and thus I feel up to my present task as an embodied being. In the last analyses, all capacities acquired earlier in life point to a primordial capacity of the embodied subject, to a basic "I can" (Husserl 1952: 253).

The body is thus the ensemble of organically developed predispositions and capacities to perceive and to act, but also to desire and to communicate. Its experiences, anchored in body memory, spread out and connect with the environment like an invisible network, which relates us to things and to people. It is, as Merleau-Ponty writes, "our permanent means of 'taking up attitudes' and thus constructing virtual presents" (Merleau-Ponty 1962, p.181); in other words, to actualize our past and, with this, to make ourselves feel at home in situations. In a most comprehensive sense,

---

3. Thus, amnesic patients may learn to trace a contour or lay a puzzle and perform better from day to day, without being able to remember having seen the contour or puzzle before (cf. Milner 1962; Corkin 1968).

body memory enables and defines the operative intentionality of the body (Merleau-Ponty 1962).

Forms of body memory

Body memory appears in various forms, which have been elaborated upon in particular by Casey (2000) and Fuchs (2000, 2008a, b, 2011). Casey distinguishes and describes three types: habitual, traumatic, and erotic bodily memory. My own approach includes six forms: procedural, situational, intercorporeal, incorporative, pain, and traumatic memory. They are not strictly separable from each other, but are derived from different dimension of bodily experience – an experience that nevertheless is a unitary "being-towards-the-world."

1. Procedural memory

Procedural memory consists of the sensorimotor and kinesthetic faculties that I have already mentioned before. These can be called procedural as they are realized in dynamic processes: patterned sequences of movement, well-practiced habits, skillful handling of instruments, as well as familiarity with patterns of perception. Without deliberation, my hand and my foot find the gear and the brake of my car, my fingers press the right keys of my keyboard, or I read the black figures on the page as script. My body anticipates the objects in their places, and I am surprised when it doesn't find them there. "It is possible to know how to type without being able to say where the letters which make the words are to be found on the banks of keys" (Merleau-Ponty 1962: 127). My thoughts are immediately converted into patterns of my fingers' movements. Originally, when learning how to type, I had to connect each key to a certain movement explicitly. Through repeated exercise, a unitary temporal pattern or a *Zeitgestalt* of movement formed in my body memory, until I could finally forget the single keys: One does not know anymore how one does what one does. Similarly, when learning to read, the child connects the single letters to the ostensive *Gestalts* of words, which he then recognizes "at a glance," until he finally grasps the meaning of the whole sentence fluently. Through the single letters, which now recede from explicit awareness, the child is intentionally directed toward the meaning of the words.

As we can see, procedural memory unburdens our attention from an abundance of details, thus facilitating our everyday performances. It works in the background without being noticed, remembered, or reflected upon. The body and the senses become a medium through which the world is accessible and available. We are capable of directing our attention toward the *Gestalt* and the meaning of what we encounter. Action is facilitated, as we may intend its goal instead of noticing every single movement. The will becomes free since the bodily means and components of acting recede into the background. A primary goal-directed intention suffices to release the complete arc of action. While his fingers move the keys, the pianist is able to direct himself to the music itself, to listen to his own play. Thus, freedom and art are essentially based on the tacit memory of the body.

Body memory thus mediates the fundamental experience of familiarity and continuity in the succession of events. It unburdens us from the necessity to constantly find our bearings again. Bodily learning means forgetting what we have learned or done explicitly, and letting it sink into implicit unconscious knowing. By this we acquire the skills and dispositions of perceiving and acting that make up our very personal way of being-in-the-world. As William James put it: "It is a general principle in psychology that consciousness deserts all processes where it can no longer be of use" (James 1950: 496). Pointedly, one could also say: What we have forgotten has become what we are.

2. Situational memory

Implicit memory is not confined to the body itself. It extends to the spaces and situations in which we find ourselves. Therefore, it is a spatial memory as well: It helps us to get our bearings in the space of our dwelling, in the neighborhood, in our home town. Bodily experience is particularly linked to interiors, which, over time are imbued with latent references to the past and with an atmosphere of familiarity. Dwelling and habit (in German *Wohnen* and *Gewohnheit*) are both based on the memory of the body. This has been nicely pointed out by Gaston Bachelard in his *Poetics of Space*:

> But over and beyond our memories, the house we were born in is physically inscribed in us. It is a group of organic habits. After twenty years, in spite of all the other anonymous stairways; we would recapture the reflexes of the "first stairway", we would not stumble on that rather high step. The house's entire being would open up, faithful to our own being. We would push the door that creaks with the same gesture, we would find our way in the dark to the distant attic. The feel of the tiniest latch has remained in our hands.
> The successive houses in which we have lived have no doubt made our gestures commonplace. But we are very surprised, when we return to the old house, after an odyssey of many years, to find that the most delicate gestures, the earliest gestures suddenly come alive, are still faultless. In short, the house we were born in has engraved within us the hierarchy of the various functions of inhabiting. (…) all the other houses are but variations on a fundamental theme. The word habit is too worn a word to express this passionate liaison of our bodies, which do not forget, with an unforgettable house.   (Bachelard 1964: 92f.)

Of course, situations are more than spatial entities. They are holistic inseparable units of bodily, sensory, and atmospheric perception: a football game in a roaring stadium, a boat trip on the foaming sea, a night walk through the brightly lit city. The different senses – sight, hearing, touch, taste, and smell – participate in various combinations in situational perception and in the body memory left by it. Above all, intermodal, synaesthetic, and expressive qualities contribute to the atmospheric character of situations (soft contours, swelling noise, bitter defeat, warm welcome, peaceful sea, majestic mountain landscape, etc.). They create the peculiar impression of a situation that is stored as a whole in the intermodal memory of the body.

To be familiar with recurrent situations is what we call experience. Experience is based on the lived body's interaction with the world; it is a practical, not a theoretical knowledge. Experienced persons recognize immediately what is essential or characteristic of a complex situation. They have developed a "sixth sense," a feeling or intuition for it, and recognize familiar patterns where others are just irritated or helpless. In football, for example, the goal-getter has "a nose" for dangerous situations in the penalty area. The sailor senses the faintest signs of the gathering storm. Or to take an example from medicine: The experienced psychiatrist, in her diagnosis, considers not only the single symptoms and anamnestic data, but the entire impression that she gains from the patient and his life situation. And the more her experience grows, the easier will she recognize the illness even during the first contact.

Such knowledge may not be completely expressed in words. The encounter with a depressed patient is characterized by a certain atmospheric perception that is not analyzable in single elements. No textbook can replace one's own experience of a diagnosis and its peculiar coloring. The implicit bodily knowledge may be described only by phrases such as "what it is like" or "how it feels," for example, "what it is like to waltz," "what it is like to talk with a depressed patient," "how the clay should feel when spinning it," "how it smelled at home at Christmas," etc. Therefore, neither the skill of an experienced craftsman nor the diagnostic intuition of a psychiatrist may be conveyed to the learner discursively – he or she has to experience it first-hand, by imitating the teacher and taking up a similar bodily attitude in dealing with the situation.

3. Intercorporeal memory

Among the most important situations are of course our encounters with others. As soon as we have contact with another person, our bodies interact and understand each other, even though we cannot say exactly how this is brought about. Merleau-Ponty termed this sphere of pre-reflective bodily understanding *intercorporeality* (Merleau-Ponty 1960). These embodied interactions are to such a large extent determined by earlier experience that we may speak of an intercorporeal memory, which is implicitly and unconsciously effective in every encounter.

With the progress of developmental research, we can now better comprehend the history of intercorporeal memory. This research has shown that motor, emotional, and social development in early childhood does not proceed on separate tracks, but is integrated through the formation of affective-interactive schemata. From birth on, the infant's procedural memory incorporates an extract of repeated, prototypic experiences with significant others, thus acquiring dyadic patterns of interaction or "schemes of being-with" (Stern 1998), for example, "mamma-feeding-me," "daddy-playing-with-me," etc. This results in what Stern has called *implicit relational knowing* – a bodily knowing of how to interact with others, how to have fun together, how to elicit attention, how to avoid rejection, etc. It is a temporally organized, musical memory for the rhythm, dynamics, and undertones inaudibly present in interactions with others.

This early intercorporeality has far-reaching effects: early interactions turn into implicit relational styles that form one's personality. As a result of learning processes, which are in principle comparable to the acquisition of motor skills, persons later shape and enact their relationships according to the patterns acquired in their primary experiences. These implicit relational styles are also expressed in the habitual posture of the body. Thus, the submissive attitude toward an authority figure implies components of posture and motion (bowed upper body, raised shoulders, inhibited motion), components of interaction (respectful distance, low voice, inclination to consent), and of emotion (respect, embarrassment, humility). All our interactions are based on such integrated bodily, emotional, and behavioral dispositions, which have become second nature, like walking or writing. They are now part of what I call the embodied personality structure (Fuchs 2006). The shy, submissive attitude that we find in dependent persons – their soft voice, childlike facial expression, their indulgence, and anxiousness – belong to an overall pattern of expression and posture that is an essential part of their personality. Our basic attitudes, our typical reactions, and relational patterns – in one word – our entire personality is based on the memory of the body.

To summarize, each body forms an extract of its past history of experiences with others that are stored in intercorporeal memory. In the structures of the lived body, the others are always implied: They are meant in expression and intended in desire. Thus, a person's typical patterns of posture, movement, and expression are only comprehensible when they refer to actually present or imaginary others. Embodied personality structures may be regarded as procedural fields of possibility that are activated in the encounter with others and suggest certain types of behavior. "I do not need to look for the others elsewhere, I find them within my experience, they dwell in the niches which contain what is hidden from me but visible to them" (Merleau-Ponty 1974: 166). The embodied structure of one's personality is therefore most accessible in the actual intercorporeal encounter: The lived body can be understood by other bodies only.

4. Incorporative memory

The development of embodied personality structures in early childhood does not proceed through pre-reflective interactions alone. Starting with the second year of life, it increasingly includes what I call incorporations, which means the shaping of bodily habits by attitudes and roles taken over from others. This happens mostly by bodily imitation and identification: In adults, too, one can observe subordinates adopting the characteristic facial expressions, gestures, or attitudes of their superiors. Similarly, by mimetic identification, for example, in their play, toddlers already adopt attitudes and roles from others, including the gender role, and incorporate them. With this, the body gains an external side; it becomes a body-for-others, a carrier of social roles and symbols, be it in deliberate poses, in clothing, adornment, or cosmetics. One learns to act or to pose, but also to play-act and to inhibit one's spontaneous expressions.

Thus, body memory becomes the carrier of what has been called the *habitus* in sociology (Bourdieu 1990). It may be understood as a set of socially learned dispositions, skills, styles, tastes, and ways of acting, which are often taken for granted or "go without saying," and which are acquired through the activities and experiences of everyday life. According to Bourdieu (1990), the habitus denotes the entire social appearance of a person including his or her posture, manners, taste, clothing, attitudes and general way of life. As a "system of internalized patterns," it produces a selection of culture- or class-specific styles of thought, perception, and action that the individuals take to be their own, but they actually share with the members of their class. "The habitus – embodied history, internalized as a second nature and so forgotten as history – is the active presence of the whole past of which it is the product" (Bourdieu 1990: 56).

Incorporations may be a germ of neurotic developments since they can cause a rupture in the spontaneous bodily performance. To become conscious of one's own appearance in the gaze of the other gives rise to central self-conscious affects such as shame, embarrassment, and pride. They can lead to permanent dispositions such as shyness, sensitivity, vanity, or dramatic tendencies. Narcissistic or histrionic disorders may thus be regarded as an alienating adoption of roles and images that undermine the authenticity of the primary bodily self. Other internalized attitudes serve to inhibit spontaneous, but unwanted impulses. Norbert Elias has shown how the body has been subjected, in the "civilizing process," to a growing disciplining of posture and movement in order to increase individual affect control (Elias 1969). Education, school, and the army were the classical institutions of a painful restriction of the body. Heinrich Heine (1997) has caricatured a historical example of such incorporations when writing that the Prussian soldiers seemed to have swallowed the cane they were once beaten with. Similarly, in today's anancastic personalities, we often find a rigid fixation of body posture, an inhibition of abdominal breathing and of expressive movements, all serving as a means of self-control against unwanted or threatening impulses.

5. Pain memory

This leads us to the next type of body memory, namely, pain memory. It is well-known that painful experiences are taken into the memory of the body; think of the proverb "The burnt child dreads the fire." And the adult, too, may well become aware of this connection when entering his dentist's room. Instinctively, one tenses up, withdraws, or dodges when pain is threatening. It is not only conscious recollection that establishes such impressive associations. In 1911, the French neurologist Claparède described the case of an amnesic patient who could not store any new information because of a brain injury (Claparède 1911). Each day he had to introduce himself to her anew; she could never remember him. One day he covered a tack in his hand when greeting her and the patient with a startle quickly withdrew her hand. The next day she refused to greet him, but couldn't explain why. Her body had learned that the doctor's hand meant danger without herself knowing it.

Thus, experiences of pain are effectively inscribed into body memory. Therefore, an education that is based on pressure, constraint, and deterrence has always known to use pain as a disciplining means. "A thing must be burnt in so that it stays in memory: only something that continues *to hurt* stays in the memory. [...] When man decided he had to make a memory for himself, it never happened without blood, torments, and sacrifices" (Nietzsche 1994: 38). So Nietzsche wrote pointedly in the second essay of his *Genealogy of morality*. Even the word *pain* is derived from the Latin *poena*, which means *punishment*.

Painful experiences have not only accompanied the development of morality, but may also lead to psychosomatic illness. Nearly half of all patients with somatoform pain disorders have suffered severe pain or violence in their childhoods; for example, they may have been frequently physically punished (Egle et al. 1991; Fillingim et al. 1999). The reactivation of pain memory may occur even after a long period of latency. Experiences of humiliation or failure in later life may then trigger acute pain syndromes, which remain unexplainable to the patients themselves. This is an effect not only of implicit pain memory, but also of relational memory. Through the constant alternation between punishment and affection, children may learn that pain and suffering are at least connected with the parent's attention (Engel 1959). Psychogenic pains may later become chronic because patients have unconsciously learned that their expressions of pain are rewarded with attention by their family members. Thus, not only is the pain inscribed into the body, but also the situations and relationships that were connected to its first occurrence.

6. Traumatic memory

The most indelible impression in body memory is caused by trauma, that is, the experience of a serious accident, of rape, torture, or threat of death. The traumatic event is an experience that may not be appropriated and integrated into a meaningful context. As in pain memory, mechanisms of avoidance or denial are installed in order to isolate, forget, or repress the painful content of memory. The trauma withdraws from conscious recollection, but remains all the more virulent in the memory of the lived body, as if it were a foreign body. At every turn, the traumatized person may come across something that evokes the trauma. It is re-actualized in situations that are threatening, shameful, or in some other way similar to the trauma, even if the person is not aware of this similarity. Victims of accidents may panic when the present traffic situation somehow resembles the former traumatic circumstances. Women who have been raped while sleeping may always awaken at the time when the assault took place. The former pains of a torture victim may reappear in a present conflict and correspond exactly to the body parts that were exposed to the torture. The body recollects the trauma as if it were happening anew.

Thus, the victim re-experiences feelings of pain, anxiety, and terror again and again, combined with fragments of intense images. Most of all, the intercorporeal memory of the traumatized person has changed deeply: He or she retains a sense of being defenseless, always exposed to a possible assault. The felt memory of an alien intrusion into the body has irreversibly shaken the primary trust into the world. Every person is turned into a potential threat. Jean Améry writes that the survivor of the torture will no more be able to feel at home, secure, and familiar anywhere in the world (Amery 1966:58). An impressive example of traumatic memory can also be found in the autobiography of the Jewish writer Aharon Appelfeld who as a young boy survived only by hiding in the woods of Ukraine for five years:

> Since the second world war, over 50 years have passed. Much have I forgotten, above all places, dates and names of people, and yet I sense this period with my whole body. Always when it rains, when it gets cold or stormy, I return into the ghetto, the camp or the woods where I have spent such a long time. Memory obviously has longstanding roots in the body. Sometimes the smell of scroungy straw or the cry of a bird suffices to throw me far away and deeply into myself. – All that has happened then has been imprinted into the cells of my body. Not into my memory. The cells of the body seem to remember better than memory although it is assigned for that. Even years after the war I did not walk in the middle of the pavement or lane, but always close to the wall, always in a hurry, like someone who flees. (…) I said "I don't remember", and yet there are thousands of details. Sometimes the smell of food, dampness in the shoes or a sudden noise suffices to take me right back into the war … The war has gripped me to the marrow.
> (Appelfeld 2005:57, 95f.)

Here, it is a whole phase of life that has left its traces in body memory, and these traces are even more durable than autobiographic memories can be: bodily sensations, the senses of taste, smell, or hearing, even certain weather conditions may suffice to suddenly revive the past, and the haunted style of walking along the walls still reflects the behavior of the fugitive.

Final considerations

Having provided an overview on the most important forms of body memory, let me return once again to the polarity of explicit and implicit memory. It has become obvious that there is no strict separation between these memory systems. Body memory does not represent the past but re-enacts it. But precisely through this, it also establishes an access to the past itself, not through images or words, but through immediate experience and action. Thus, it may unexpectedly open a door to explicit memory and resuscitate the past as if it were present as such.

Sensations or situations experienced by the lived body may function as implicit memory cores which, under suitable circumstances, can release their enclosed memories; we may call this an *explication*. It is well known that a forgotten intention can often be retrieved when returning to the place where it had been formed. In particular, sensations of smell or taste, well-known melodies, or the atmospheres of familiar places possess the capacity to revive the past. They are loaded, as it were, with the most intense recollections that we know. If I return to the place of my childhood many years later, my former seeing reappears and my former feelings re-emerge. At the same time, I am seized by a peculiar alienation and bewilderment because the revived past strangely concurs with my present-day life. Thus, recognition reveals a particular temporality: Whereas explicit memory enters the memories in a schedule of the past, in recognition, past and present literally coincide, which comes close to a mystical experience. In the famous "*madeleine*" episode of Proust's *Remembrance of Things Past*, the narrator recognizes the taste of a tea-soaked cake known to him from his childhood, and an overwhelming feeling suffuses him:

> No sooner had the warm liquid mixed with the crumbs touched my palate than a shudder ran through me and I stopped, intent upon the extraordinary thing that was happening to me. An exquisite pleasure had invaded my senses, something isolated, detached, with no suggestion of its origin. (…) Whence could it have come to me, this all-powerful joy?[4]

The narrator strives to explicate the autobiographic content of this implicit memory, but at first in vain: There is just the immediate and overwhelming familiarity of the taste, no recollection of its origin.

> Undoubtedly what is thus palpitating in the depths of my being must be the image, the visual memory which, being linked to that taste, is trying to follow it into my conscious mind (…) Will it ultimately reach the clear surface of my consciousness …?

Finally, after several attempts, the core of the implicit bodily experience opens up and its autobiographic content appears.

---

4. This and the following passages are quoted from Proust (1913–1927:48–51).

> And suddenly the memory revealed itself. The taste was that of the little piece of madeleine which on Sunday mornings at Combray (because on those mornings I did not go out before mass), when I went to say good morning to her in her bedroom, my aunt Léonie used to give me, dipping it first in her own cup of tea or tisane.

This retrieved memory now triggers a cascade of childhood memories, and all at once an entire world awakens:

> … in that moment all the flowers in our garden and in M. Swann's park, and the water-lilies on the Vivonne and the good folk of the village and their little dwellings and the parish church and the whole of Combray and its surroundings, taking shape and solidity, sprang into being, town and gardens alike, from my cup of tea.

Proust's *madeleine*-memory thus hides within a complex of bodily sensations and implicit, only intuited recollections and meanings. I would like to call such a complex a *meaning core*. It is a nodal point of bodily recollection into which the lived past has condensed, as it were, and from which new meanings may unfold. Vaguely felt emotions and impulses may take shape in the sensing of the body, implying reverberations of forgotten or repressed contents as well as forebodings and anticipations of a possible future. In this way, body memory also opens a way to what is latently present in one's own life and sometimes already known on a deeper level. Therapeutic approaches that focus on this "felt sense" of the body such as Focusing (Gendlin 1982), concentrative movement therapy, dance/movement therapy, and others, may help the clients to open the meaning cores of body memory and untangle their latent motives and feelings.

In sum, the body is not just a structure of limbs and organs, nor merely a realm of sensations and movements. It is also a historically formed body whose experiences have left their traces in its invisible dispositions. By installing itself in every situation, the body always carries its own past into the surroundings as a procedural field of possibilities. His experiences and dispositions permeate the environment like an invisible net that spreads out from its senses and limbs, connects us with the world and renders it familiar to us. Each perception, each situation is permeated by implicit bodily recollections. "What we call reality," as Proust writes, "is a relation between those sensations and those memories which simultaneously encircle us" (Proust 1934: 1008).

Body memory is the underlying carrier of our life history, and eventually of our whole being-in-the-world. It comprises not only the evolved dispositions of our perceiving and behaving, but also the memory cores that connect us most intimately with our biographical past. And even when dementia deprives a person of all of her explicit recollections, she still retains her bodily memory: The history of her life remains present in the familiar sights, smells, feel, and handling of things, even when she is no more capable of accounting for the origin of this familiarity and of telling her life history. Her senses become the carriers of personal continuity, of a more felt than known recollection – the tacit, but enduring memory of the body:

> But when from a long-distant past nothing subsists, after the people are dead, after the things are broken and scattered, still, alone, more fragile, but with more vitality, more unsubstantial, more persistent, more faithful, the smell and taste of things remain poised a long time, like souls, ready to remind us, waiting and hoping for their moment, amid the ruins of all the rest; and bear unfaltering, in the tiny and almost impalpable drop of their essence, the vast structure of recollection.   (Proust 1981:48–51)

References

Améry, J. (1977). *Jenseits von Schuld und Sühne. Bewältigungsversuche eines Überwältigten* [Beyond guilt and expiation]. München: dtv.

Appelfeld, A. (2005). *Geschichte eines Lebens* [The story of a life]. Reinbek: Rowohlt.

Bachelard, G. (1964). *The poetics of space.* Translated by D. Russell; originally published 1960. Boston, Massachusetts: Beacon Press.

Bergson, H. (2007). *Matière et mémoire. Essai sur la relation du corps à l'esprit* [Matter and memory. Essay on the relation of body and spirit; originally published 1896]. Paris: PUF.

Bourdieu, P. (1990). *The logic of practice.* Translated by R. Nice. Stanford: Stanford University Press.

Claparède, E. (1911). Reconnaissance et moitié [Recognition and me-ness]. *Archives de Psychologie, 11,* 79–90.

Casey, E. (2000). *Remembering. A phenomenological study.* Bloomington: Indiana University Press.

Corkin, S. (1968). Acquisition of a motor skill after bilateral medial temporal lobe excision. *Neuropsychologia, 6,* 225–265.

De Biran, M. (1953). *Influence de l'habitude sur la faculté de penser* [The influence of habits on the faculty of thinking; originally published 1799]. Paris: PUF.

Descartes, R. (1996). *Œuvres de Descartes* [Descartes' collected works], Edited by C. Adam and P. Tannery. Paris: Vrin.

Egle, U. T., Kissinger, D. & Schwab, R. (1991). Eltern-Kind-Beziehungen als Voraussetzung psychogener Schmerzsyndrome bei Erwachsenen [Parent-child relations as precondition of pain-syndromes in adults]. *Psychotherapie, Psychosomatik und Medizinische Psychologie, 41,* 247–256.

Elias, N. (1969). *The Civilizing Process, Vol. I. The History of Manners.* Oxford: Blackwell.

Engel, G. L. (1959). "Psychogenic" pain and the pain prone patient. *American Journal of Medicine, 26,* 899–918.

Fillingim, R. B., Wilkinson, T. S. & Powell, T. (1999). Self-reported abuse history and pain complaints among young adults. *Clinical Journal of Pain, 15,* 85–91.

Gendlin, E. T. (1982). *Focusing, Second edition.* New York: Bantam Books.

Fuchs, T. (2000). Das Gedächtnis des Leibes [The memory of the body]. *Phänomenologische Forschungen, 5,* 71–89.

Fuchs, T. (2006). Gibt es eine leibliche Persönlichkeitsstruktur? Ein phänomenologisch-psychodynamischer Ansatz [Is there a bodily structure of personality? A phenomenological-psychodynamical approach]. *Psychodynamische Psychotherapie, 5,* 109–117.

Fuchs, T. (2008a). *Leib und Lebenswelt. Neue philosophisch-psychiatrische Essays* [The lived body and the life-world. New philosophical-psychiatric essays]. Kusterdingen: Die Graue Edition.

Fuchs, T. (2008b). Leibgedächtnis und Lebensgeschichte (2006). [Body memory and life history] In F. A. Friedrich, T. Fuchs, J. Koll, B. Krondorfer & G. M. Martin (Eds.), *Der Text im Körper. Leibgedächtnis, Inkarnation und Bibliodrama* [The text in the body. Body-memory, incarnation, and bibliodrama] (pp. 10–40). Hamburg: EB-Verlag.

Fuchs, T. (2011). Body memory and the unconscious. In D. Lohmar & J. Brudzinska (Eds.), *Founding Psychoanalysis. Phenomenological Theory of Subjectivity and the Psychoanalytical Experience* (pp. 69–82). Dordrecht: Kluwer.

Heine, H. (1997). *Deutschland. Ein Wintermärchen* [Germany. A winter's tale]. München: dtv.

Husserl, E. (1952). *Ideen zu einer reinen Phänomenologie und phänomenologischen Philosophie. II. Phänomenologische Untersuchungen zur Konstitution. Vol. IV, Husserliana* [Ideas pertaining to a pure phenomenology and to a phenomenological philosophy. Studies in the phenomenology of constitution]. Den Haag: Martinus Nijhoff.

James, W. (1950/1890). *The principles of psychology. Vol. 2.* New York: Dover.

Merleau-Ponty, M. (1962). Phenomenology of perception. English translation C. Smith. London: Routledge & Kegan Paul.

Merleau-Ponty, M. (1960). *Le philosophe et son ombre* [The philosopher and his shadow]. In *Signes* [Signes]. Paris: Gallimard.

Merleau-Ponty, M. (1974). *Die Abenteuer der Dialektik* [Adventures of the dialectic; Original published 1955]. Frankfurt: Suhrkamp.

Milner, B. (1962). Les troubles de la mémoire accompagnant des lésions hippocampiques bilaterales [Memory troubles that accompany bilateral damages of the hippocampus]. In P. Passquant (Ed.), *Physiologie de l'hippocampe* [The physiology of the hippocampus] (pp. 257–272). Paris: Centre National de la Recherche Scientifique.

Nietzsche, F. (1994). *On the genealogy of morality.* Translated by C. Diethe. Cambridge: Cambridge University Press.

Proust, M. (1981). *Remembrance of things past. Volume 1: Swann's Way: Within a Budding Grove.* (First French Edition 1913–1927) Translation by C. K. Scott Moncrieff and T. Kilmartin. New York: Vintage.

Proust, M. (1934). *Remembrance of things past. Volume 7: Time regained.* (First French Edition 1913–1923) Translation by C. K. Scott Moncrieff and T. Kilmartin (1934, vol. 2). New York: Random House.

Ravaisson, F. (1999). *De l'habitude* [On habitude; originally published 1838]. Paris: PUF.

Schacter, D. (1987). Implicit memory: History and current status. *Journal of Experimental Psychology, 13*(3), 501–518.

Schacter, D. (1996). *Searching for memory. The brain, the mind, and the past.* New York: Basic Books.

CHAPTER 2

Body memory and the genesis of meaning

Michela Summa
Heidelberg University

This chapter aims to provide a phenomenological account of the role of body memory in the formation of meaning. To this aim, the theory of embodied meaning put forward by experientialism and the phenomenological account of *Typoi* and typological constitution are comparatively considered. First the difficulties in the experientialist theory of embodied meaning are discussed. Second Husserl's phenomenology of typological apprehension is presented as offering a more appropriate account of the genesis of meaning in relation to implicit body memory. Third it is argued that the refined conceptual background in contemporary cognitive linguistics opens up the field for a fruitful dialogue between phenomenology and cognitive linguistics regarding the constitution of meaning.

Keywords: phenomenology, experientialism, body memory, meaning formation, basic-level categories, image schemas, *Typus*

In recent years, substantial research has been devoted to the phenomenology of implicit body memory (Casey 2000; Fuchs 2000, 2008a, 2008b, 2011, this volume). Often engaging in a dialogue with the cognitive sciences, these studies thematize the difference between explicit and implicit forms of memory and define body memory as the pre-thematic yet operative "consciousness" of the past, as it displays itself to a bodily subject. Different from explicit memory, implicit body memory does not represent the past by means of an act of recollection. Through body memory, rather, the past impacts the subject's present and future, it is enacted in his/her performances, and it informs the unfolding of the subject's experience without him/her being explicitly aware of this process. In a most comprehensive sense, thus, body memory defines a form of operative intentionality (Merleau-Ponty 1945), which entails the totality of acquired perceptual and behavioral subjective dispositions.

Notably, previous phenomenological studies have highlighted the role of implicit body memory in shaping the most basic layers of subjective and intersubjective experience. Notwithstanding the relevance of this research within the phenomenological and interdisciplinary debate on memory and (inter-)subjectivity, I believe that further analysis regarding the role of implicit body memory within a phenomenological theory of knowledge is still required. More precisely, I wish to show that body memory participates in the constitution of perceptual meaning, which defines the basic layer for the genesis of higher order meaning formations.

The aim of this chapter is to explore this key issue by discussing two approaches to the genesis of meaning: the phenomenological and the experientialist. Founded by Edmund Husserl at the beginning of the 20th Century,[1] phenomenology primarily designates the systematic descriptive analysis of experience and of the intentional correlation between consciousness and the world. Motivated by the urgency to return to the things themselves, phenomenology aims to provide a new ground for scientific knowledge, which has its *alpha* and *omega* in the structures and dynamics of lived experience. The notions of experientialism and embodied realism,[2] on the other hand, designate the theory of embodied cognition originally put forward by George Lakoff and Mark Johnson (Johnson 1987; Lakoff & Johnson 1980, 1999). The challenge of experientialism is in a way as radical as the phenomenological one. In contrast with both the computational or formal-symbolic account of cognition and with an unspecified "mainstream Western philosophy" (Lakoff & Johnson 1999:21), experientialists claim to give shape to a novel empirically grounded philosophy, which is supposed to undermine the alleged metaphysical background of the traditional approaches to cognition and experience.

The appeal to experience as the testing ground of all scientific theories, entailed by the very notion of experientialism, is clearly reminiscent of phenomenology. However, a closer analysis of both projects shows that there is more methodological and theoretical incongruousness than similarity between them.[3] In what follows, I seek to disentangle the moments of this tension regarding the role of the body in the formation of meaning. In doing this, I will adopt a phenomenological stance, thereby using phenomenology primarily as descriptive method grounded in experience rather than as an established doctrine. From this perspective, I challenge the theory put forward by embodied realism and its consistency with the appeal to the primacy of experience. In the first section, I discuss some controversial issues in the experientialist theory of embodied meaning and highlight the internal tensions that characterize it. I further argue that these tensions, which ultimately imply some basic inconsistencies in the theory, prevent experientialism from providing a proper phenomenological account of the role of body memory in the constitution of meaning. In the second section, I examine the phenomenology of typological constitution and apprehension. Here,

---

1.   See notably Husserl (1984a, 1984b).

2.   In the following, I will use these two notions interchangeably.

3.   Indeed, the occasional references to phenomenology in the above mentioned texts are often unclear and sometimes even contradictory. In spite of recognizing the role of phenomenology in defining a proper approach to experience, the authors criticize Husserl's philosophy as representative of the objectivist tradition of Western thought (Lakoff & Johnson 1980: 180–182, 195).

I particularly wish to shed light on the role of implicit body memory in the formation of perceptual meaning and thus to reformulate the notion of embodied meaning from a phenomenological standpoint. Finally, in the third section, I more closely consider the analogies and the differences between Husserl's phenomenology of *Typus* and the experientialist approach to basic-level categories and image schemas, thereby aiming to open up a field for further inquiry on the relation between meaning and embodiment.

Experientialism on embodiment and meaning

Embodied concepts are the keystone of the experientialist theory of meaning. Thus, the first question we shall ask of experientialism concerns the nature of these concepts. I submit that, far from being obvious, the notion of "embodied concept" can be understood in at least three ways. First, it can refer to the fact that perception, movement, and sensations, which dynamically make up our bodily experience, play a major role in the constitution of concepts. Second, it can be related to the instantiation of meanings in signs, whereby the sign would be metaphorically conceived as the "body of meaning." Third, it can mean that concepts directly originate from some material structures in the body. Whereas the first and the second connotations can be phenomenologically addressed as based on lived subjective and intersubjective experience (Sonesson 2007), this may not be true for the third one. Nevertheless, in spite of its appeal to the primacy of experience, experientialism eventually endorses this third option by defining embodied concepts as "a neural structure that is actually part of, or makes use of, the sensorimotor system of our brains" (Lakoff & Johnson 1999:20).

One does not need to be a Husserl specialist to see that this definition deeply conflicts with the phenomenological theory of meaning. This not only because, by neglecting the ideality of meaning, it makes a mistake analogous to the one made by psychologism with respect to pure logic, but also because it goes a step further than psychologism by reducing meaning to the factual and material structure of the human brain. However, my strategy in this chapter is not to adapt Husserl's psychologism critique in the *Prolegomena* (Husserl 1975) to what we might call a more modern form of physicalism or neurobiologism because this might be contested as stemming from a supposedly idealist and disembodied approach to meaning. Rather, I discuss the discrepancies between the given definition and the appeal to the primacy of experience and subsequently present a phenomenological alternative that remains faithful to both the irreducibility of meaning to physicality and its bodily relatedness.

The first difficulty we encounter in approaching the definition of embodied concepts – and the experientialist theory of meaning in general – is a methodological one. On the one hand, indeed, experientialism appeals to "descriptive or empirical phenomenology" (Johnson 1987:XXXVII) and to an "informal phenomenological analysis" (Johnson 2005:21), which supposedly has its roots in lived experience. On the other hand, however, this description is considered unsatisfactory and inadequate for giving a comprehensive theory of meaning formation so that the "standard explanatory methods of linguistics, psychology and neuroscience" (Johnson 2005:21) are required to complement it. The methodological *mélange* of "quasi-phenomenological" descriptions from the first-person perspective and naturalistic (mostly neuroscientific)[4] statements from the third-person perspective risks being inconsistent and generating some confusion between the levels of explanation that are experientially accessible and those that are not, as the latter ultimately represents theoretical constructs within a given epistemological paradigm. Seeing the blue of the sky, perceiving a chair, and moving in a room – respectively presented as the experiential basis of color concepts, basic-level categories, and spatial-relation concepts (Lakoff & Johnson 1999:16) – are unquestionably experiences. Yet the physical laws and the neural structures that underlie them are not. Let us make this point clearer by referring to color concepts, that is to one of the three just-mentioned sets of concepts the authors refer to in order to show how embodied concepts are "shaped by our bodies and brains, especially by our sensorimotor system" (Lakoff & Johnson 1999:22).[5] Against our allegedly illusionary perceptual belief, upon which sentences such as "the sky is blue" are grounded, the authors emphasize the truth of the physical and neurobiological explanations of color perception, showing that colors do not exist in the external world and that our experience of colors results from the combination of physical (the wavelength of reflected light, lighting conditions) and neurobiological factors (the three kinds of color cones in our retinas, which respectively absorb the light of long, medium, and short wavelengths, and the neural circuitry connected to those cones). Without questioning the validity of the physical theory of colors, I believe there must be a reason why, even if anyone who has a middle-secondary education degree at school *knows* that color is actually not a property of things, people still say that blood is red and that the sun is yellow. And there must be a reason why even a physicist, waking up on a Sunday morning in June, may rejoice that the sun is shining in the blue sky, and express his/her disappointment if this is not the case. This reason, I submit, is experience. Pace Lakoff and Johnson, indeed, I *do see* the blue sky, even though I *know* that the sky is not a surface and as such cannot reflect the wavelength of reflective light. Yet the wavelength of reflective light itself, the lighting conditions, the color cones in my retina, and the neural circuitry connecting them may well be the physical and neurobiological conditions of my experiencing, but they are definitely not experientially given themselves (Lakoff & Johnson 1999:23).[6]

---

4. Regarding this "neurological turn," see notably Dodge and Lakoff (2005); Gallese and Lakoff (2005); Lakoff and Johnson (1999).

5. I will examine the two other sets of embodied concepts (basic-level categories and spatial-relation concepts) in the last section of this chapter.

6. The analogy the authors make with astronomy is also instructive. Just as astronomy tells us that the earth is not a stationary planet at the center of the universe, but rather turns around the

As Jordan Zlatev (2007, 2010) has convincingly shown, even skirting the prob-lems related to what I called the methodological *mélange* of description and explana-tion, the experientialist view of embodied concepts still entails some incongruence. The latter particularly concerns the notion of embodiment, and, more precisely, the discussion of this notion in *Philosophy in the Flesh*. In this book, Lakoff and Johnson distinguish three levels of embodiment: the phenomenological level, the neural level, and the level of the cognitive unconscious (Lakoff & Johnson 1999:101). The first problem in this trisection is that the relation between the different levels is not closely examined. Occasionally, the authors seem to purport that the three levels are con-nected by a foundational relation. Thus, the level of the cognitive unconscious would make up the bottom of the pyramid and be followed in successive order by the neural and by the phenomenological levels. Yet it remains unclear whether the authors claim that the neural level of embodiment is the *cause* of the phenomenological or instead its material *condition*. To prevent reductionism, and to provide a solid theory of the mind-body relation, a thoughtful analysis of this relation would be required. Besides this architectural problem, some aspects in the very definition of these three levels might also be questionable if considered from a phenomenological perspective. Let us see why.

1. What we would expect from a theory called experientialism is first of all a thoughtful and consistent examination of the phenomenological level of embodi-ment. Still, surprisingly enough, the analysis of this level of embodiment is the least developed of the three. In spite of recognizing that phenomenological reflection (er-roneously equalized with introspection)[7] may allow us to "examine many of the back-ground pre-reflexive structures that lie beneath our conscious experience" (Lakoff & Johnson 1999:12), the authors eventually equate the phenomenological embodi-ment with conscious experience (Lakoff & Johnson 1999:103). The same approach also characterizes Lakoff's and Johnson's more recent research. Indeed, if the former

---

sun, in the same way, cognitive science tells us that colors do not exist in the external world. Yet the astronomical truth, which we certainly recognize as being based on empirical and techni-cal discoveries, does not coincide with the givenness of the earth as the universal soil of all our experiences. And the tension between these two ways of considering the earth does not mean that we have to give up one or the other, but rather that we have to understand their relation and genealogically consider the development of scientific thought from the most basic layers of lived experience. Particularly relevant in this sense is one of the later manuscripts of Husserl's, which refers to the overthrow [*Umsturz*] of the Copernican theory in the usual interpretation of a world view. By stressing the irreducibility of the earth as the soil from which all our experi-ences depart, Husserl – and with him Merleau-Ponty – by no means intends to question the astronomical truth of Copernicanism, nor would he defend some sort of geocentric model. On the contrary, he stresses the irrevocability of our bodily, spatio-temporal, world experience of the earth as soil, with respect to which all scientific world-views are genealogically derivative. See Husserl (1940) and Merleau-Ponty (1960:294, 1964:306–307, 1994:102).

7.   See Husserl (1984a, 1984b, 1987:102) and Gallagher and Zahavi (2008:19).

eminently focuses his studies on the role of the sensorimotor system in conceptual formation,[8] the latter develops his "informal" phenomenological approach in his philosophical writings. Nevertheless, in doing this, he constantly stresses that the phenomenological description can tell only part of the story regarding human cognition. As such it must be complemented, or maybe even rectified, by appealing to the discoveries of the contemporary science of mind, notably neurobiology, cognitive neuroscience, and cognitive linguistics (Johnson 2007, 2010).

In principle, I do not believe there is something wrong with the idea that phenomenology and cognitive science should complement and enlighten one another. This collaboration, though, may become theoretically dangerous if the respective domains of inquiry are not clarified from the very beginning. The risk, as I mentioned, is a curious *mélange* of a description of what is experientially given and an explanation of the mechanisms that are supposed to underlie our lived experience. Finally, such an approach entails the fatal reduction of all phenomenological givenness to *explicit* consciousness, without further thematizing *from a phenomenological perspective* the different modalities of *implicit* (bodily, temporal, etc.) awareness.[9] The phenomenology of body memory is meant precisely to offer a contribution to the investigation of this domain of implicit bodily experience.

2. In the above mentioned definition of embodied concepts, we already encountered the neural level of embodiment. This level was presented there as being in a way the *locus* of conceptual formation. The definition, as we have seen, is questionable with respect to two points: first, it reduces concepts to material reality; second, it eventually conflicts with the appeal to the primacy of experience by giving more merit to scientific explanations than to phenomenological descriptions. Yet, even bracketing these problems, we need to ask whether, by basically conceiving of the body and the neural system as interchangeable, the authors do not risk committing a *pars pro toto* mistake. If one assumes this equivalence – and the definition of the neural embodiment seems to imply it – the experience of the body is not different from the supposed "experience" of a brain in a vat (Gallagher & Zahavi 2008; Zlatev 2007). As a consequence, experientialism either neglects the idea that sensorimotor interactions are performed with the sensory organs, or it reduces the latter to mere transducers of neural impulses. Moreover, it underestimates the roles of other corporeal systems, for instance, the hormonal, in interacting with the environment (Zlatev 2007).

3. Finally, the level of the cognitive unconscious is considered to be "the massive portion of the iceberg that lies below the surface, below the visible tip that is consciousness" (Lakoff & Johnson 1999: 103). The authors recognize that the only empirical evidence we have of the cognitive unconscious is related to its efficaciousness, namely, to the role it supposedly plays in conceptualization and reasoning, that is, in

---

8.   See, notably Dodge and Lakoff (2005); Gallese and Lakoff (2005).

9.   This is a central issue in the current phenomenological literature. See, notably Gallagher (2005); Zahavi (1999, 2005).

the activities that already belong to the conscious level. The cognitive unconscious is neither experientially given nor is its existence empirically demonstrated. Rather, it defines a level of embodiment that must be hypothesized or postulated (Lakoff & Johnson 1999: 103, 115) as being the ultimate ground of meaning formation. As such, the cognitive unconscious presumably entails all the operations that are "completely and irrevocably inaccessible to direct conscious introspection" (Lakoff & Johnson 1999: 12). More concretely, the cognitive unconscious includes "all our automatic cognitive operations," but also "all our implicit knowledge," and it deeply shapes our "automatic" comprehension of what we experience (Lakoff & Johnson 1999: 12).[10]

The radical inaccessibility of the cognitive unconscious makes it hardly compatible with phenomenology. First, phenomenology tends to conceive of the unconscious as latency, or as the basic "subsoil" of consciousness, which can, in principle, be reflexively addressed. Second, the cognitive unconscious does not even fall under the category of the alien, which, according to Husserl defines the peculiar *experiential accessibility* of that which is originally inaccessible.[11] Regarding bodily experience, this latter, apparently cryptic formulation refers to the fact that the body is never completely at our disposal, since belonging after all to the material world, it often opposes resistance to the unfolding of our voluntary activities. Being both the organ of perception or movement and a potential obstacle to its unfolding, the body essentially has an ambiguous status, and, consequently, it cannot be constituted in the same way as other things are.[12] In other words, the alienness entailed by bodily experience is connected to the ambiguity of the body as the "turning-point" (*Umschlagstelle*) between sense and natural causality (Husserl 1952: 286). This alienness, however, is experientially given: I do experience the resistance of my body when I am tired or sick, when I try to hold my breath longer than I can, or when I am ashamed and seek in vain to control the redness of my cheeks. On the contrary, the cognitive unconscious, according to Lakoff and Johnson, cannot be experientially given at all. But if this is true, how can we avoid considering it a mere theoretical construct?

Additionally, the definition of the cognitive unconscious as opposed to the phenomenological and the neural level of embodiment is not consistently developed in the text. On the one hand, indeed, Lakoff and Johnson stress the differences between these three levels arguing that, as opposed to the phenomenological level, the cognitive unconscious is not directly accessible to conscious awareness and, as opposed

---

10. For a partial and explanatory list of the accomplishments of the cognitive unconscious, see Lakoff and Johnson (1999).

11. See Husserl (1950: 144); Husserl (1973: 631). Here, Husserl defines alienness (*Fremdheit*) as "bewährbare Zugänglichkeit des original Unzugänglichen" and as "Zugänglichkeit in der eigentlichen Unzugänglichkeit."

12. "Derselbe Leib, der mir als Mittel aller Wahrnehmungen dient, steht mir bei der Wahrnehmung seiner selbst im Wege und ist ein merkwürdig unvollkommen konstituiertes Ding" (Husserl 1952: 159).

to the neural level, it entails not only the automatic neural operations, but also "implicit knowledge" in the form of habitualities (Lakoff & Johnson 1999: 10). On the other hand, as Zlatev (2007) points out, the notion of the cognitive unconscious risks becoming superfluous as it either coincides with the phenomenological or with the neural level of embodiment. Indeed, two different kinds of entities are conflated in the cognitive unconscious: (a) structures such as domain-to-domain mappings and neural computations, i.e., unconscious neurophysiologic causal mechanisms, which we are not aware of; (b) entities such as nouns, verbs, basic-level categories, etc. If the former applies, then the difference between the cognitive unconscious and the neural level of embodiment is not clear anymore. But if the latter applies, then the cognitive unconscious can be brought to consciousness and can thus become the object of phenomenological description: nouns, verbs, and basic-level categories, in fact, are consciously accessible since their intentional constitution can be reflectively addressed. This option, of course, is incompatible with the claim that the cognitive unconscious in principle escapes all conscious awareness.

In exposing this theory, Lakoff and Johnson do not explicitly use the concept of body memory. Nevertheless, they refer to "implicit knowledge" (Lakoff & Johnson 1999: 13), to "memories relevant to what is being said" in a situation, and to the "noticing and interpreting your interlocutor's body language" (Lakoff & Johnson 1999: 10–11) as resulting from the activity of the cognitive unconscious. Consequently, these bodily attitudes and behaviors, which would fall under the phenomenological notion of body memory, supposedly stem from an experientially inaccessible level of embodiment. If this is true, then no room seems to be left for body memory as operative *intentionality* giving shape to subjective lived experience.

Addressing the phenomenological account of *Typus* and typological apprehension, I intend to show in the next section how perceptual meaning formation presupposes the operative intentionality of body memory. In doing this, I seek to provide a view of the embodiment of meaning that remains faithful to the primacy of experience.

Typoi and body memory

Having excluded that embodiment merely refers to processes taking placed in the brain, we still have two possible ways of considering the relation between meaning and embodiment: Embodiment can refer either to the genesis of meaning in the experience of a bodily subject or to function of signs as peculiar "bodies" in which meaning is instantiated. In my argument here, I will follow only the first way. By addressing the basic constitution of perceptual meaning as it is developed in Husserl's genetic phenomenology, I wish to provide an alternative to the previously presented theory of embodied concepts. In particular, I will show that such a constitution is based on the operative intentionality of implicit body memory as it has been defined in the introduction to this chapter.

To begin with, in spite of all developments debated in the literature,[13] two distinctive moments of Husserl's early theory of meaning in the *Logical Investigations* remain unaltered in the later texts. First, different from the psychologistic approaches, Husserl stresses the irreducibility of meaning to mental representations, and consequently remains committed to the thesis of the ideality of meaning. Ideality here shall not be conceived as resulting from a new form of Platonism, which would end up in a split of the ideal and the real world. Ideality, instead, is related to the irreducibility of meaning to a mere factual occurrence, but this does not exclude that the very constitution of meaningful idealities has its roots in experience. And this is the second keystone of Husserl's theory of meaning. As opposed to the formalistic interpretation of meaning, indeed, Husserl constantly stresses the relation between lived experience and meaning, and progressively comes to thematize not only the peculiar temporal-genetic constitution of meaning, but also its historical roots in life-world experience.[14] Husserl's account of *Typoi* and typological apprehension is particularly connected with the latter point. Yet what is a *Typus*? And which function does it fulfill in the process of constitution?

The most basic form of *Typus* consists of the synthetic connection of sensible data, characterized by a peculiar internal regularity. So, for instance, the simultaneous presentation of visual, tactile, taste, and smell sensations in drinking of a cup of coffee, and the reiteration of such presentation in different contexts, allow us to implicitly constitute the *Typus* "coffee" out of a synthesis of similarity between the different experiences. By the repetition of our experiences with different coffees, we will notice that there is a common core, even if we will probably taste different coffee blends, and we will drink coffee sometimes with and sometimes without sugar or milk. Thus, we will progressively constitute *Typoi* of different levels, refining our senses and becoming able to immediately distinguish the *Typus* German coffee, from the *Typus* Italian *espresso*, *caffè macchiato*, and *cappuccino*. By each new experience with this drink, then, we will implicitly reactivate our fund of experience, and recognize (or typologically apprehend) the kind of coffee we are drinking by the first sip. Moreover, we will progressively learn the adequate attitude to assume in the different social and interactional contexts in which we drink a cup of coffee. In other words, we will not only acquire a certain familiarity with coffee on the cognitive level, but also shape our individual practical style of dealing with cups of coffee in the different situations.

As the example shows, the phenomenology of the *Typus* and typological apprehension refers to the vague morphological pre-knowledge [*Vorbekanntheit*] implied in all perceptual experience (Husserl 1999: 32, 136). We mostly recognize things as being of a certain type, and even when we are measured with unknown entities, we always tend to trace them back to familiar patterns. In the same way, we typologically

---

13. See, for instance, the two following recent volumes on meaning, language, and expression: Mattens (2008) and Rizzoli (2008).

14. See, notably, Husserl (1976a, 1999); Welton (1983).

recognize situations, and each of us has an individual style to adapt himself/herself to the given circumstances. Considered as the pre-form of the concept, the *Typus* is a synthetically constituted, yet pre-categorial, function that allows us to perceive something *as* something (Husserl 1999: 32; Lohmar 2008: 103). *Typoi* are morphological or vague idealities,[15] which stem from the basic passive synthetic accomplishments of lived experience, but nonetheless remain irreducible to the factual moments of this or that experience.

As shown by Dieter Lohmar, *Typoi* in Husserl's phenomenology have an analogous function as Kant's schemas of empirical concepts (Lohmar 2008: 119).[16] The schema of an empirical concept is defined by Kant as the sensible concept of an object, in agreement with the category ["*der sinnliche Begriff eines Gegenstandes, in Überein-stimmungmit der Kategorie*"] (KrV B 186/A146). As such, it meanwhile realizes the category and restricts it to the empirical conditions of sensible experience. As this definition shows, the schema has a "mediating" function between the particular sense data given in this concrete experience and a general concept: for example, the schema of an empirical concept, such as "dog", properly defines a *rule* according to which we can *see a dog* on the basis of a manifold of sense data. As such, the schema is not restricted to this or that empirical experience, it is synthetic (it brings a manifold into a unity), and it has a rule-like structure (KrV B 180/A141).

Like Kant's schema, Husserl's *Typus* is synthetic, it has a rule-like structure, and it allows us to perceive something as something. Yet, different from Kant's theory of the schematism in the first *Critique*, the focus in Husserl's later texts is not the question of the applicability of general concepts to experience, but rather the genetic constitution of *Typoi* in and through experience.[17] The phenomenology of the *Typus* and typological apprehension, in other words, aims at defining the processes that make possible the institution, the sedimentation, and the reactivation of familiar perceptual patterns.

I submit that such constitution is based on the passive synthetic accomplishments of what we have previously defined as implicit body memory. As noted when referring to the coffee example, a *Typus* is constituted thanks to the reiteration of similar experiences. Yet in order for such a constitution to be possible, the sensuous and perceptual

---

15. Regarding the distinction between exact (i.e., mathematical) and vague, morphological, or descriptive essences, see Husserl (1976b: 155).

16. It must be stressed, though, that Kant's priority in the chapter on the "Schematism of Pure Concepts of the Understanding" in the first *Critique* is to determine the a priori conditions of the possibility of knowledge by defining the applicability of pure intellectual concepts to experience. Consequently, he conceives of schemas as being both logically and temporally subordinate to concepts and is not primarily concerned with the issue of the emergence of schemas (and in particular of empirical concepts' schemas) themselves.

17. In the *Critique of Pure Reason*, indeed, Kant is not primarily interested in the genesis of empirical concepts, but rather seeks to show how concepts in general are applied to experience. A more detailed inquiry into the formation of empirical concepts, realized by the cooperation of imagination and the understanding, is to be found in the *Critique of Judgment*.

experiences cannot simply occur in a punctuated manner, they cannot flow without leaving any trace. Rather, implicit temporal and associative syntheses must be operative in and through such repetition (Husserl 1999: 36, 126, 2008: 463). The constitution of *Typoi* is thus based on these passive synthetic accomplishments, which presuppose the fundamental correlation between our bodily subjective experience and the world-appearance (Husserl 1966). Precisely the temporal and associative synthetic process of habitualization, making possible the constitution and the sedimentation of *Typoi*, defines the *Leistung* of implicit memory. Moreover, since perception is accomplished by a bodily subject, and since kinaesthetic experience plays a major motivational role in the constitution of a perceptual sense (Husserl 1952: 164, 1962: 390), we can legitimately consider the process of habitualization as a form of *bodily* memory.

Implicit body memory is not only relevant for the *Stiftung* of perceptual, typological meaning, it is also responsible for its implicit preservation, for the motivated expectation of future appearance of the same object, and eventually for the reactivation or the "awakening" [*Weckung*] of *Typoi* in different contexts and situations. Through this temporal and associative process, the *Typus* progressively becomes a familiar and pre-conceptual pattern of experience, which sediments in our individual "archive" of experience and is associatively reactivated in similar perceptual contexts or with respect to similar perceptual objects.[18]

As we noted, *Typoi* make possible a form of cognition on the threshold between theoretical and practical knowledge. On the one hand, they make theoretical descriptions possible and define the basis for the formation of general and abstract concepts. On the other hand, they are acquired through habitualization, and become part of one's individual "heritage" or style of experiencing the world, such as practical attitudes. Moreover, they are actualized and adapted to different concrete perceptual situations in accordance not only with the objective style of appearance, but also with the subjective dispositions toward the world. The typological apprehension, thus, is by no means an inferential process; it does not imply any explicit act of recognition. It rather defines the proper "usage of" or the proper "dealing with" morphological *Typoi* and empirical concepts in the given situational context. As such, this process opens up the field for new possibilities of situation-related cognition.

Typoi, basic-level categories, and image schemas

Let us now more closely consider the phenomenology of the *Typus* in relation to the experientialist view of embodied concepts. At first sight, *Typoi* present some similarities with both the basic-level categories and the image schemas. Once again, though, a closer comparison shows that there are more points of disagreement than convergences between the two theories.

---

18. Husserl (1999: 26, 136). For further discussion of these issues, see Summa (2011).

Let us first consider the so-called basic-level categories. Drawing from the theory of Berlin and Rosch, Lakoff and Johnson (1999:27) define basic-level categories according to the following four conditions. Basic-level categories are (a) the highest level at which a single mental image can represent an entire category; (b) the highest level at which category members have similarly perceived shapes; (c) the highest level at which a person uses similar motor actions for interacting with category members; and (d) the level at which most of our knowledge is organized. Examples of basic-level categories are: chair, car, or cat, i.e., categories located in between general concepts (respectively: furniture, vehicle, animal) and more specific categories that can be hardly accessible to the average perceiver (respectively: rocking chair, sports car, Siamese cat). Concerning this definition, we shall first point out that the criteria for identifying such basic-level categories might be very different from individual to individual; therefore, it would be worthwhile to further thematize the notion of perception assumed here. Thus, to return to our coffee example, an Italian coffee drinker would immediately perceive an *espresso lungo* as different from an *espresso ristretto*. Both would be for him basic-level categories according to the mentioned criteria. Yet this might not be the case for consumers who are less familiar with the different tastes of Italian coffees.

Phenomenologically restated, basic-level categories derive from the primary generalization of the individualities that are concretely given in perceptual experience. As we have seen, it is precisely to account for this first level of generalization (which, as the coffee example shows, is differentiated according to the experiential background of each individual subject) that Husserl introduces the notion of *Typus*. Yet the analogy between *Typoi* and basic-level categories ends here. Consistent with their approach to embodiment, indeed, experientialists trace the formation of basic-level categories uniquely back to "the fact that we are neural beings" (Lakoff & Johnson 1999:30). Different from phenomenology, experientialism does not retrace the transcendental conditions of possibility of categorization, not does it properly investigate its being grounded on the structures of lived experience; it is rather assumed as a fact resulting from the evolution of the species.

It is more complex to draw a comparison between *Typoi* and image schemas. At least partially, this is due to the ambiguities entailed by the notion of image schema, which we shall now try to disentangle. The concept of image schema was jointly introduced by Lakoff and Johnson (Johnson 1987; Lakoff 1987) to designate the recurring, dynamic patterns of perceptual interaction that give coherence and structure to experience. As such, image schemas are considered to be meaningful, yet pre-conceptual and non-propositional, structures that "organise our mental representations at a level more general and abstract than that at which we form particular mental images" (Johnson 1987:23–24). This general definition, as a recent collective volume shows (Hampe 2005b), has been subject to different and sometimes even conflicting interpretations. In summing up some of these readings, Zlatev (Zlatev 2005, 2010) shows that images schemas are differently conceived as (a) abstract structures (Johnson

1987); (b) basic levels of experience types (Gibbs 2005); (c) representational structures (Grady 2005; Lakoff 1987); (d) non-representational structures (Gibbs 2005; Johnson 2005); (e) part of the cognitive unconscious, thus non-consciously accessible (Johnson 2005; Lakoff & Johnson 1999); and (f) phenomenal structures, thus consciously accessible (Gibbs 2005). To this list, we can add Zlatev's own view, which, replacing image schemas with mimetic schemas, stresses the relevance of intersubjective experience in the formation of meaning (Zlatev 2005, 2007). As we can see from this summary, the disagreement about image schemas entails at least four aspects, namely: (a) their representational versus non-representational status; (b) their accessibility versus non-accessibility to consciousness; (c) their level of abstractness; and (d) their private versus intersubjective status.

Yet, if we stick to the standard view on image schemas, and follow Beate Hampe's (2005a) cross-reading of Lakoff's and Johnsons's definitions, we can further characterize image schemas on the basis of the following four criteria. (a) Image schemas are meaningful pre-conceptual structures arising from recurrent human bodily movement in space, perceptual interactions, and ways of object manipulation; (b) their schematic character is due to the fact that they catch the contours or the morphological structure of sensorimotor experience; (c) they are analogous patterns beneath conscious awareness; and (d) they are both internally structured, as they are made up by few related parts, and highly flexible, as they can be adapted to different experiential contexts. Even if the image schema list provided by the authors has never constituted a closed set (and may even be in principle open), for the sake of clarification, we can mention some examples of image schemas: container/containment; path/source-path/goal; link; part-whole; center-periphery; force; surface, process; full-empty; process; cycle; iteration; object; collection, etc. (Johnson 1987).

In what sense can these patterns be compared with Husserl's *Typoi*? And what are the differences between them? Let us start with the analogies. Like Husserl's *Typus* and Kant's schemata, the experientialist image schema is a pre-categorial structure organizing our experience. And indeed, even though the phenomenology of typological constitution and apprehension is not mentioned in the texts, Johnson admittedly recognizes in Kant's theory of the schematism a precursor of his own account of image schemas, thereby particularly stressing the role of the imagination as a mediator between the concepts of the understanding and sensible intuition (Johnson 1987, 2005). Besides, neither *Typoi* nor image schemas can be equated to mental images, which, in a way, would reduplicate the intended object in a mental representation. Moreover, like *Typoi*, image schemata are strictly related to the dynamics of our perceptual interaction with the surrounding world. Finally, the flexibility of image schemas and their adaptation to different situations also recall the vague or morphological structure of *Typoi*.

There are, however, also important differences between *Typoi* and image schemas. First, whereas the constitution of *Typoi* is mainly based on perception and presupposes the phenomenology of noetic-noematic correlation, image schemas are almost uniquely identified by resorting to the forms of bodily movement. These forms, as it were, are then transposed to objects of experience (e.g., in the case of the container schema), or to more comprehensive experiential contexts (e.g., in the case of the schema center-periphery). As a consequence, image schemas seem to define highly formal structures, as they are considered independently of any specific sensible content. The latter is not true for *Typoi*, which, as we have seen, are deeply rooted in the synthetic connection of sensible data. Certainly, *Typoi*, such as image schemas, are also the basis for further levels of abstraction and even for formalization. In themselves, however, *Typoi* necessarily entail the reference to particular sensible contents. The most crucial difference between body schemas and *Typoi*, however, is again related to the notion of embodiment. Saying that image schemas are embodied eventually means that they are sensorimotor structures and that they are part of the cognitive unconscious and thus not accessible to consciousness and reflection. Consequently, the same critique we have previously raised regarding embodiment applies to image schemas. Husserl's *Typoi* (and even more so, Kant's schemata) are not neural sensorimotor structures of our brains, nor are they *caused* by those structures, nor are they part of a supposed cognitive unconscious. Rather, they are experiential patterns stemming from our intentional relatedness to the world, and their intentional constitution can be reflectively brought to consciousness and be thematized.

Notwithstanding these crucial differences, we can still try to address image schemas from a phenomenological point of view. To this aim, we shall ask experientialism the same questions we have asked the phenomenology of *Typoi*; namely: (a) how are image schemas constituted for the experiencing subject? (b) To which level of generality do they correspond? (c) What is their concrete function in lived experience?

As for the first point, the identification of image schemas is achieved through the cross-linguistic analysis of motion and spatial relation concepts (Dodge & Lakoff 2005; Lakoff & Johnson 1999) and by resorting to the so-called "informal phenomenological analysis" of every day experience (Johnson 1987, 2005). The recurrent patterns of categorization discovered thanks to this twofold inquiry concern not only perceptual things, but also the reciprocal relations between things and the apprehension of perceptual contexts. Moreover, the sensorimotor realm of image schemas is also the basis for the formation of more abstract and more general concepts, which are achieved thanks to the capacity of conceptual metaphor (Johnson 2010; Lakoff & Johnson 1980). Considered apart from the background we have critically addressed, the inquiry into this process of metaphorization appears much more promising, as it potentially opens up a field of phenomenological investigation concerning the role of body memory in embodied cognition. This could emerge, for instance, from the phenomenological analysis of the connection between linguistic and gestural expression, and of the so-called multimodal metaphors, that is, those metaphors that are expressed both linguistically and by means of corporeal gestures. The dynamic interaction and the temporal shifts between the linguistic and the gestural expression of the same metaphor may indeed help us to further explore the dynamics of bodily based cognition (Müller 2008; Kolter, Ladewig, Summa, Müller, Koch & Fuchs, this

volume). However, if one assumes that image schemas exclusively stem from sensorimotor neural structures and that eventually they are part of the cognitive unconscious, there will be little room for developing an inquiry into the specific role of body
memory (as operative intentionality) in this process.

As for the second point, image schemas apparently correspond to different levels of generality. This might be confusing if one seeks to grasp their specificity with
respect to basic-level categories. The schema "container", for example, could also
match the four mentioned criteria that define basic-level categories. Moreover, from
a phenomenological point of view, a closer inquiry into the intentional process of
variation and the synthesis of similarity, which allows us to constitute generalities out
of the singular experiences (Husserl 1962, 1999), is required. Thus, a challenge for
further research may also be the closer analysis of the relation between the phenomenological theory of generalization and the above mentioned process of conceptual
metaphorization.

As for the third point, image schemas are fundamentally introduced to ground
categorization and to aid the formation of abstract meaning and the capacity of reasoning. The study of image schemas is consequently supposed to show how meaning,
imagination, and reason emerge from organic bodily interactions with the environment. This is based on the dynamic account of experience, as image schemas are primarily "structures of an activity by which we organise our experiences in ways we can
comprehend" and as they are flexible and malleable, so that they can be instantiated
in different contexts and situations (Johnson 1987: 29–30). However, given the lack of
a proper analysis of the intentional aspect of meaning constitution, it is not clear how
image schemas, once they are formed, are applied or activated in lived experience.
Nor does the theory explain how we can possibly recognize objects with concrete
properties, and act according to the situation. Thus, saying that I have the schema of
a container as a sensorimotor structure operating in my cognitive unconscious still
does not explain how I may (or may not) immediately recognize a burning hot cup of
tea and consequently be able to manipulate this object in the proper way (e.g., to avoid
drinking the contents of this container in just one sip or to pour it on my hand). This
form of practical knowledge can be mediated only by some form of morphological
or typological recognition of the particular object I have in front of me, which, as we
have seen, presupposes a certain familiarity (acquired through body memory) with
objects and situations of the same kind (*Typus*).[19]

---

19. Some more specific remarks concerning the container schema and its application to spatial
relations is required here. Occasionally, the authors claim that lived spatial relation expressed
by the preposition "in" can be traced back to this schema. However, this approach risks missing
the specificity of the different spatial experiences as bearers of meaning. Particularly, from a
phenomenological perspective, our being "in the world" cannot be reduced to the containment
schema: The subject is not in the world in the same way as the tea is in the cup. Rather, its being
in the world implies a meaningful relation to the horizonal givenness of things in its dynamic
unfolding. Our spatial experience of the world, thus, is not reducible to that of a container, but

Conclusions

The aim of this chapter was to shed light on the role of body memory in the process of meaning formation and thereby to provide some clarity regarding the notion of embodied meaning. Adopting a phenomenological approach, I first showed why the notion of embodiment put forward by experientialism is unsatisfactory. Appealing to the phenomenological account of *Typus* and typological apprehension, I further highlighted that the constitution of perceptual meaning is deeply rooted in the experience of a bodily subject and that it presupposes the operative intentionality of body memory. Finally, the comparison between the phenomenology of perceptual meaning formation and the experientialist account of basic-level categories and image schemas has in a way enhanced the distance between phenomenology and experientialism. Nevertheless, considered apart from the theoretical background of experientialism, the function of image-schemas and of metaphorization in the formation of concepts may be more closely considered in connection with the phenomenological account of lived experience. This can be done by assuming that image schemas result from the situatedness of the subject in the life-world (Sonesson 2007; Zlatev 2010) and by developing in particular the intersubjective character of meaningful experience.[20]

References

Casey, E. (2000). *Remembering. A phenomenological study.* Bloomington: Indiana University Press.

Dodge, E. & Lakoff, G. (2005). Image schemas: From linguistic analysis to neural grounding. In B. Hampe (Ed.), *From perception to meaning: Image schemas in cognitive linguistics* (pp. 57–91). Berlin: Mouton de Gruyter.

Fuchs, T. (2000). Das Gedächtnis des Leibes [The memory of the body]. *Phänomenologische Forschungen, 5*, 71–89.

Fuchs, T. (2008a). *Leib und Lebenswelt. Neue philosophisch-psychiatrische Essays* [The body and the life-world. New philosophical-psychiatric essays]. Kusterdingen: Die Graue Edition.

Fuchs, T. (2008b). Leibgedächtnis und Lebensgeschichte [Body memory and life history]. In F. A. Friedrich, T. Fuchs, J. Koll, B. Krondorfer & G. M. Martin (Eds.), *Der Text im Körper. Leibgedächtnis, Inkarnation und Bibliodrama* [The text in the body. Body memory, incarnation, and bibliodrama] (pp. 10–40). Hamburg: EB-Verlag.

---

shall rather be described through the metaphor of the horizon and connected to the meaningfulness of all experiential givenness.

20. From this perspective, an important contribution is given by Zlatev's analysis of mimesis and mimetic schemas as mediator between the lived-body and collective language (Zlatev 2005, 2007). With respect to the phenomenology of body memory (Fuchs 2008b), this approach is particularly promising as it allows one to highlight the role not only of habitual, but also of intercorporeal and incorporative body memory in the process of meaning formation.

Fuchs, T. (2011). Body memory and the unconscious. In D. Lohmar & J. Brudzinska (Eds.), *Founding psychoanalysis. Phenomenological theory of subjectivity and the psychoanalitical experience* (pp. 69–82). Dordrecht: Kluwer.

Fuchs, T. (this volume). The phenomenology of body memory. In S. C. Koch, T. Fuchs, M. Summa & C. Müller (Eds.), *Body memory, metaphor and movement*. Amsterdam: John Benjamins.

Gallagher, S. (2005). *How the body shapes the mind*. Oxford: Oxford University Press.

Gallagher, S. & Zahavi, D. (2008). *The phenomenological mind. An introduction to philosophy of mind and cognitive Science*. London and New York: Routledge.

Gallese, V. & Lakoff, G. (2005). The brain's concepts: The role of the sensori-motor system in conceptual knowledge. *Cognitive Neuropsychology, 22*(3/4), 455–479.

Gibbs, R. W. J. (2005). The psychological status of image schemas. In B. Hampe (Ed.), *From perception to meaning. Image schemas in cognitive linguistics* (pp. 113–136). Berlin: Mouton de Gruyter.

Grady, J. E. (2005). Image schemas and perception. Refining a definition. In B. Hampe (Ed.), *From perception to meaning. Image schemas in cognitive linguistics* (pp. 35–56). Berlin: Mouton de Gruyter.

Hampe, B. (2005a). Image schemas in cognitive linguistics: Introduction. In B. Hampe (Ed.), *From perception to meaning. Image schemas in cognitive linguistics* (pp. 1–12). Berlin: Mouton de Gruyter.

Hampe, B. (Ed.). (2005b). *From perception to meaning. Image schemas in cognitive linguistics*. Berlin: Mouton De Gruyter.

Husserl, E. (1940). Grundlegende Untersuchungen zum phänomenologischen Ursprung der Räumlichkeit der Natur [Fundamental investigations on the phenomenological origin of the space of nature]. In M. Farber (Ed.), *Philosophical essays in memory of Edmund Husserl* (pp. 307–325). Cambridge, MA: Harvard University Press.

Husserl, E. (1950). *Cartesianische Meditationen und Pariser Vorträge*. [Cartesian meditations and the Paris lectures]. Den Haag: Martinus Nijhoff.

Husserl, E. (1952). *Ideen zu einer reinen Phänomenologie und phänomenologischen Philosophie. Phänomenologische Untersuchungen zur Konstitution*. [Ideas pertaining to a pure phenomenology and to a phenomenological philosophy. Studies in the phenomenology of constitution]. Den Haag: MartinusNijhoff.

Husserl, E. (1962). *Phänomenologische Psychologie. Vorlesungen Sommersemester 1925* [Phenomenological psychology. Lectures summer semester 1925]. Den Haag: Martinus Nijhoff.

Husserl, E. (1966). *Analysen zur passiven Synthesis*. [Analyses concerning active and passive synthesis]. Den Haag: Martinus Nijhoff.

Husserl, E. (1973). *Zur Phänomenologie der Intersubjektivität. Dritter Teil (1929–1935)* [On the phenomenology of intersubjectivity. Third part 1929–1935]. Den Haag: Martinus Nijhoff.

Husserl, E. (1975). *Prolegomena zurreinen Logik* [Prolegomena to pure logic]. Den Haag: MartinusNijhoff.

Husserl, E. (1976a). *Die Krisis der europäischen Wissenschaften und die transzendentale Phänomenologie* [The crisis of the European sciences and transcendental phenomenology]. Den Haag: Martinus Nijhoff.

Husserl, E. (1976b). *Ideen zu einer reinen Phänomenologie und phänomenologischen Philosophie. Allgemeine Einführung in die reine Phänomenologie* [Ideas pertaining to a pure phenomenology and to a phenomenological philosophy. General introduction to pure phenomenology]. Den Haag: MartinusNijhoff.

Husserl, E. (1984a). *Logische Untersuchungen. Untersuchungen zur Phänomenologie und Theorie der Erkenntnis* [Logical investigations. Investigations in phenomenology and theory of knowledge]. Den Haag: Martinus Nijhoff.

Husserl, E. (1984b). *Logische Untersuchungen. Elemente einer phänomenologischen Aufkärung der Erkenntnis* [Logical investigations. Elements of a phenomenological elucidations of knowledge]. Den Haag: Martinus Nijhoff.

Husserl, E. (1987). *Aufsätze und Vorträge (1911–1921)* [Essays and speeches]. Den Haag: Martinus Nijhoff.

Husserl, E. (1999). *Erfahrung und Urteil. Untersuchungen zur Genealogie der Logik* [Experience and judgement. Investigations in a genealogy of logic]. Hamburg: Mainer.

Husserl, E. (2008). *Die Lebenswelt* [The life-world]. Dordrecht: Springer.

Johnson, M. (1987). *The body in the mind.* Chicago IL: University of Chicago Press.

Johnson, M. (2005). The philosophical significance of image schemas. In B. Hampe (Ed.), *Fromperception to meaning. Image schemas in cognitive linguistics* (pp. 15–34). Berlin: Mouton de Gruyter.

Johnson, M. (2007). *The meaning of the body. Aesthetics of the human understanding.* Chicago & London: Chicago University Press.

Johnson, M. (2010). Metaphor and cognition. In D. Schmicking & S. Gallagher (Eds.), *Handbook of phenomenology and cognitive sciences* (pp. 401–414). Dordrecht: Springer.

Kant, I. (1903). *Kritik der reinen Vernunft.* Königlich Preußische Akademie der Wissenschaften. Erste Auflage 1781 Vol. IV, Kant's gesammelte Schriften. Berlin: De Gruyter & Co.

Kant, I. (1904). *Kritik der reinen Vernunft.* Königlich Preußische Akademie der Wissenschaften. Zweite Auflage 1787 Vol. III, Kant's gesammelte Schriften. Berlin und Leipzig: De Gruyter & Co.

Kolter, A., Ladewig, S., Summa, M., Müller, C., Koch, S. C. & Fuchs, T. (this volume). Body memory and the emergence of metaphor in movement and speech. An interdisciplinary case study. In S. C. Koch, T. Fuchs, M. Summa & C. Müller (Eds.), *Body memory, metaphor and movement.* Amsterdam: John Benjamins.

Lakoff, G. (1987). *Women, fire and dangerous Things. What categories reveal about the mind.* Chicago: University of Chicago Press.

Lakoff, G. & Johnson, M. (1980). *Metaphors we live by.* Chicago IL: University of Chicago Press.

Lakoff, G. & Johnson, M. (1999). *Philosophy in the flesh. The embodied mind and its challenges to Western thought.* New York: Basic Books.

Lohmar, D. (2008). *Phänomenologie der schwachen Phantasie. Untersuchungen der Psychologie, Cognitive Science, Neurologie und Phänomenologie zur Funktion der Phantasie in der Wahrnehmung.* [Phenomenology of weak fantasy. Investigations in psychology, cognitive sciences, neurology, and phenomenology on the function of fantasy in perception]. Dordrecht: Springer.

Mattens, F. (Ed.). (2008). *Meaning and language: Phenomenological perspectives.* Dordrecht: Springer.

Merleau-Ponty, M. (1945). *Phénoménologie de la perception* [Phenomenology of perception]. Paris: Gallimard.

Merleau-Ponty, M. (1960). *Signes*. [Signs]. Paris: Gallimard.

Merleau-Ponty, M. (1964). *Le visible et l'invisible. Suivi de notes de travail.* [The visible and the invisible. Followed by working notes]. Paris: Gallimard.

Merleau-Ponty, M. (1994). *La nature. Notes. Cours du Collège de France* [On nature. Notes. Lecture course at Collège de France]. Paris: Seuil.

Müller, C. (2008). *Metaphors dead and alive, sleeping and waking. A dynamical view.* Chicago/London: University of Chicago Press.

Rizzoli, L. (2008). *Erkenntnis und Reduktion. Die operative Entfaltung der phänomenologischen Reduktion im Denken Husserls* [Knowledge and reduction. The operative unfolding of the phenomenological reduction in Husserl's thought]. Dordrecht: Springer.

Sonesson, G. (2007). From the meaning of embodiment to the embodiment of meaning: A study in phenomenological semiotics. In T. Ziemke, J. Zlatev & R. M. Frank (Eds.), *Body, language, mind: 1. Embodiment* (Vol. 1, pp. 85–128). Berlin: Mouton de Gruyter.

Summa, M. (2011). *Das Leibgedächtnis. Ein Beitrag aus der Phänomenologie Husserls* [Body memory. A contribution from Husserl's phenomenology]. *Husserl Studies, 27*(3): 173–196.

Welton, D. (1983). *The origins of meaning. A critical study of the thresholds of husserlian phenomenology.* Den Haag: Martinus Nijhoff.

Zahavi, D. (1999). *Self-awareness and alterity. A phenomenological investigation.* Evanston, IL: Northwestern University Press.

Zahavi, D. (2005). *Subjectivity and selfhood: Investigating the first-person perspective.* Cambridge, MA: The MIT Press.

Zlatev, J. (2005). What is a schema? Bodily mimesis and the grounding of language. In B. Hampe (Ed.), *From perception to meaning. Image schemas in cognitive linguistics* (pp. 313–343). Berlin: De Gruyter.

Zlatev, J. (2007). Embodiment, language, and mimesis. In T. Ziemke, J. Zlatev & R. M. Frank (Eds.), *Body, Language, and Mind: 1. Embodiment* (Vol. 1, pp. 297–338). Berlin: Mouton de Gruyter.

Zlatev, J. (2010). Phenomenology and cognitive linguistics. In D. Schmicking & S. Gallagher (Eds.), *Handbook of Phenomenology and Cognitive Sciences* (pp. 415–443). Dordrecht: Springer.

CHAPTER 3

Kinesthetic memory

Further critical reflections and constructive analyses

Maxine Sheets-Johnstone
University of Oregon

This essay expands and broadens a 2003 article on kinesthetic memory.[1] It does so by critically examining currently favored taxonomies of memory as put forward by scientists, philosophers, and neuroscientists, and, in turn, by presenting a phenomenological perspective on body memory based on investigations by a Jungian analyst/phenomenological philosopher. The perspective brings to light highly complex and subtle dimensions of body memory, thus challenging us to enrich our understanding of body memory by turning studious attention to experience and actively investigating living experiences of body memory.

Keywords: taxonomies of memory, either/or contraries, kinesthesia, habit, kinesthetic/kinetic melodies, kinetic dynamics, pointillist conceptions of movement, tactile-kinesthetic/affective bodies, body memory

To put kinesthetic memory in the perspective of present-day cognitive science and philosophy and of present-day neuroscience is to take into account the flourishing of taxonomies of memory. Though not in substantive ways documented as such, the many categorizations of memory according to "type" are seemingly based on the firm ground of "observation" if not "experience." In other words, they are put forth not as speculative entities, but entities one can point to as it were, as one would point to morphological traits that taxonomically characterize a species. Yet this seeming

---

1. The article "Kinesthetic Memory" originally appeared in 2003 in a special issue of *Theoria et Historia Scientiarum* dedicated to the theme of "Embodiment and Awareness: Perspectives from Phenomenology and Cognitive Science" (Sheets-Johnstone 2003). I thank the journal's editor Tomasz Komendzinski for permission to use my original article here, where it has been put in the expanded perspective of present-day cognitive science and philosophy and in the broader context of a trenchant and provocative phenomenological study of remembering. The expanded perspective is set forth in the opening section that follows; the broader context is set forth in the concluding section titled "A Phenomenological Afterword."

authoritative empiricism may be questioned. Indeed, what is particularly interesting about these categorizations is their dichotomous nature. Whatever the type of memory, it is conceived in each instance in terms of an opposite. It has a contrary in the specific sense in which Aristotle (1963) limned contraries (*Categories* 11b15–14a25). Though the contraries may be related (e.g., see Baars & Gage 2010:327–329 on episodic and semantic memory), they are in the most basic sense without intermediates. They are "either/or's" – either this or that, like black and white, without greys.

Thus we read about procedural memory as distinct from declarative memory, explicit memory as distinct from implicit memory, semantic memory as distinct from episodic memory, short-term memory as distinct from long-term memory, and so on. The contraries themselves appear quite straightforwardly to be the offspring of a more fundamental contrary, an incontrovertible oppositional pair that conceptually parents its progeny: the mind/body dichotomy or the mental/physical dichotomy, for example, the conscious/unconscious dichotomy, the verbal/nonverbal dichotomy, and so on. What is passed over in this enterprise, in this pursuit of oppositional taxonomic distinctions, is an understanding of what we might describe as the whole animal itself, the basic phenomenon of memory. Just what are we referencing when we speak or write of memory? When it comes to "body memory" in particular, just what are we talking about and trying to understand? We might indeed ask: "What are we naming?" (see Sheets-Johnstone 2005).

Thomas Fuchs states that there is "[o]bviously ... a memory of the body apart from conscious recollection." He identifies such memory as habits developed through "repetition and exercise." Such habits, he says, "have become a tacit know-how, hardly to be verbalised," adding as example that "we would have some difficulty in describing ... how to waltz" (Fuchs 2003:1–2). He goes on to state that "procedural memory," which he defines as a form of "implicit memory," is "in the background without being noticed" and that "[b]odily learning means to forget what we have learned or done explicitly, and to let it sink into implicit, unconscious knowing" (ibid.:3).

What I hope to show in the following critical reflections and amplified discussion of kinesthetic memory are quite different understandings of "body memory," a memory that is first of all grounded in the qualitative dynamics of movement, and that is far more readily understood experientially and even neurologically in terms of "kinaesthetic/kinetic melodies" rather than in terms of "implicit knowing," "procedural memory," "tacit know-how," and so on, and this precisely because kinaesthetic/kinetic melodies hew to the realities of experience as well as to neurology, as the investigations of neuropsychologist Alexsandr Romanovich Luria show so well (see further this text for a detailed exposition of same). In short, when we attend to the qualitative dynamics of movement – whether sweeping the floor or brushing our teeth, winding our way down a series of steps or making our way down the street and around a corner, hammering a nail or threading a needle, getting into our car or stretching to the fullest on getting out of bed – we realize that the complexities and subtleties of our movement are grounded in kinetic qualities that structure our movement and constitute its particular dynamics. In turn, we realize not only that we are most commonly marginally aware of these dynamics in the process of our every-day habitual movements, but that unless we were just so marginally aware, we would hardly recognize slip-ups of one kind and another in the course of doing what we do; that is, we would hardly recognize that, as Heidegger and a variety of personages have famously since put it, "something has gone wrong" (Heidegger 1962: 102–105; Searle 1992: 184). Moreover – and perhaps most significantly – we realize or have the possibility of realizing that at any time we wish, we can bring the dynamics of these habitual movements to the fore. We can thus indeed pay attention once again to the kinesthetic dynamics of waltzing and describe how to waltz. We can do so because we ourselves once learned how to waltz, and now, if we wish, we can turn our attention to what we once learned and analyze the components of the kinesthetically felt dynam-ics of a waltz: its tensional, linear, areal, and projectional qualities (Sheets-Johnstone 1966 [1979/1980], 1999/expanded 2nd ed. 2011; see also Sheets-Johnstone 2011a, b).

Fuchs actually validates this fact implicitly when, in writing of the fact that "memory of the body is an impressive refutation of the dualism of consciousness and the physical body," he states, "For when I am dancing, the rhythmic movements are released by my body without a need to make them deliberately – and yet I am guid-ing my movements according to the gesture and rhythm that I feel" (Fuchs 2003: 2). Precisely: "*according to the gesture and rhythm that I feel.*" Indeed, the dynamics of movement are *felt* as they unfold. They are felt kinesthetically. How in fact could I possibly "guide" "the gesture and rhythm" of my movements when dancing unless gesture and rhythm – what is more exactingly and properly described as the *qualita-tively structured dynamics of movement* – were experienced? An essential truth war-rants highlighting in this context. It in fact warrants underscoring since its import is everywhere overlooked.

Neurologist Marc Jeannerod observes – much to his disappointment from the viewpoint of being able to design an experiment to resolve the "Wundt/James" prob-lem of whether "conscious knowledge about one's actions" is *a posteriori* or *a priori*, that is, whether it is based on "efferent information of a central origin" or "informa-tion from sensory organs," hence the impossibility of determining accurately whether it is Wundt or James who is correct – that it is impossible to shut off kinesthesia (Jeannerod 2006: 56). Jeannerod's observation is clearly not just of passing inter-est, but of seminal, irrefutable significance. Unlike vision, hearing, taste, and smell, kinesthesia cannot be closed off or dampened except pathologically: we cannot shut out our kinesthetically-felt bodies as we can shut out vision by closing our eyes, shut out noise by clamping our ears, shut out smells by pinching our nose, shut off tastes by closing our mouths. Our primordial animation is with us from the beginning to the end of our lives, and with it, our kinesthetic sense modality. As I have else-where shown at length, we come into the world moving; we are precisely not stillborn (Sheets-Johnstone 1999/expanded 2nd ed. 2011). That "[t]here are no reliable meth-ods for suppressing kinesthetic information arising during the execution of a move-ment" (Jeannerod 2006: 56) means that however focally attentive we are or might be elsewhere, kinesthesia cannot be totally suppressed. Pathology apart, the dynamics of our own movement, an awareness of our own body-in-motion is an insuppressible fact of life.

Surely the fact that we cannot block out kinesthesia calls into question black and white taxonomic contraries regarding body memory. The conscious/unconscious dichotomy is no longer tenable; neither is the implicit/explicit or the procedural/declarative. The episodic/semantic dichotomy is similarly at the very least suspect if not untenable. Moreover untenability not infrequently rests on an additional dichotomous conceptual foundation, what is taken as an incontrovertible oppositional pairing generated by the mind/body dichotomy or other such parental form mentioned above. In particular, the fact that we cannot block out kinesthesia calls into question the underlying epistemic taxonomic contrary "knowing how" and "knowing that." To appreciate this conceptual liability, we have only to consider what Husserl terms if/then relationships, what infant psychiatrist Daniel Stern terms "consequential relationships" (Stern 1985: 80–81), and what infant psychologist Lois Bloom terms "relational concepts" (Bloom 1993: 50). We all learn early on, for example, that *if* we close our eyes, *then* it gets dark. We in other words *know that* if we do such and such, such and such will happen. Our adult animate lives are replete with awarenesses of if/then relationships, relationships that we *know how* to instantiate and *know how* to avoid.

Many scientists have propounded taxonomies of memory and written at length about the particulars of each type. Psychologists Bernard Baars and Nicole Gage, for example, following the classification of D. L. Schacter and E. Tulving, describe types of memory in terms of an over-arching dichotomy: "declarative (conscious) memory" and "non-declarative (non-conscious) memory" (Baars & Gage 2010: 326). The former is broken down into semantic or factual memory as opposed to episodic or event memory. Non-declarative is broken down into four types – skills, priming, dispositions, nonassociative (ibid.; see also ibid.: 311: "*memory is not unitary, but consists of different types*"; italics in original). Baars and Gage earlier describe "a functional framework for learning and memory" (ibid.: 309) in which long-term memory is broken down into explicit and implicit learning: "perceptual," "episodic," and "semantic" types of memory on the "explicit learning and retrieval" side; "implicit memory," "habits and motor skills," and "primed biases and goals" types or aspects of memory on the "implicit learning and retrieval" side. Operating between working memory – of "relatively small capacity" and "limited duration" – and long-term memory is a "central executive," who – or that – is involved only in learning and retrieval on the explicit side.

Now with all due respect to these and like-minded scientists and their efforts not only to distinguish and analyze different types of memory taxonomically, but to locate them functionally in different areas of the brain, it is nonetheless relevant to recall the cautionary admonitions of Socrates who, in speaking of kinds of knowledge, observed that "division into species [should be] according to the natural formation, where the joint is, not breaking any part as a bad carver might" (Plato 1937a, *Phaedrus* 265E). Moreover, as he elsewhere admonished, "we certainly should divide everything into as few parts as possible" (Plato 1937b, *Statesman* 287). In finer terms, then, instead of taking up a preeminently taxonomic stance in relation to memory and attempting to hone it to match if not encompass completely the realities of life itself, we might turn our attention to the realities of life itself to begin with. We might thereby discover that we are indeed movement-born, that the faculty of kinesthesia is insuppressible, and that we might therefore do well to begin our investigations of memory with an examination of movement itself. We might thereby be led to bypass linguistic practices that conceptually disfigure the truths of experience by encasing them in a motorology, as in talk of motor intentionality, motor control (Merleau-Ponty 1962), motor schema, motor intention (Gallagher 2005), and more broadly, talk of sensorimotor subjectivity (Hanna & Thompson 2003; Thompson 2007; Zahavi 2005), sensorimotor profiles (Noë 2004), and the like. In a word, we would realize the fundamental fact of animation that integrally and explicitly informs the evolution of animate forms of life, that indeed constitutes the basic evolutionary fact of animate life, and the fundamental fact that the faculties of kinesthesia and proprioception are its inextinguishable phylogenetic and ontogenetic correlates. In following through in this manner, we would realize that kinesthetic memory is a staple of life and that focal attention on kinesthetic memory constitutes precisely a holistic rather than divisionary enterprise.

The aim of the sections that follow is to elucidate the nature of kinesthetic memory, demonstrate its centrality to everyday human movement, and thereby promote fresh cognitive and phenomenological understandings of movement in everyday life. Prominent topics in this undertaking include kinesthesia, dynamics, and habit. The endeavor has both a critical and constructive dimension. The constructive dimension is anchored in Luria's seminal notion of a kinetic melody and in related phenomenological analyses of movement. The dual anchorage stems from the general fact that kinesthetic memory is based on kinesthetic experience, hence on the bodily felt dynamics of movement, and on the particular fact that any movement creates a distinctive kinetic dynamics in virtue of its spatio-temporal-energic qualities. The critical dimension focuses on constructs that commonly anchor discussions of movement but bypass the reality of a kinetic dynamics, notably, Merleau-Ponty's "motor intentionality," and the notions of a body schema and body image. The pointillist conception of movement and the Western metaphysics that undergird these constructs is examined in the succeeding section of the paper, and, as noted above, the concluding section offers a particularly relevant phenomenological perspective on "remembering."

Luria's kinetic- and kinesthetically-informed neuropsychology

Russian neuropsychologist Aleksandr Romanovich Luria is regarded "a founding father of neuropsychology" (Goldberg 1990), lauded for his insights and meticulous clinical research (e.g., Teuber 1966, 1980; Pribram 1966, 1980). He describes movement pathologies as disturbed kinetic melodies; everyday movement no longer flows forth in effortless ways, or indeed, is no longer even a possibility for patients with brain lesions. In *The Working Brain*, Luria describes how kinetic melodies are constituted, using writing as an example. "In the initial stages," he observes, "*writing* depends on memorizing the graphic form of every letter. It takes place through a chain of isolated motor impulses, each of which is responsible for the performance of only one element of the graphic structure; with practice, this structure of the process is radically altered and writing is converted into a single 'kinetic melody', no longer requiring the memorizing of the visual form of each isolated letter or individual motor impulses for making every stroke" (Luria 1973: 32).

He later specifies how voluntary movement is a "complex functional system," fulfilled in "the perfect performance of a movement" on the basis of four fundamental conditions: (1) "*kinaesthetic afferentation,* (2) a system of "*spatial coordinates*" centered on "the visual and vestibular systems and the system of cutaneous kinaesthetic sensation," (3) a "*chain of consecutive movements,* each element of which must be denervated after its completion so as to allow the next element to take its place," and (4) a "motor task" which at more complex levels of conscious action "*are dictated by intentions*" (ibid.: 35–37). At the neurological level, voluntary movement is thus the orchestrated result of "completely different brain systems" (ibid.: 37) that work together in such a way that a kinetic melody unfolds.

Of singular significance is Luria's recognition that voluntary movement is not just a spatial phenomenon but a *temporal* phenomenon. Luria in fact distinguishes between the temporal and spatial distribution of motor impulses in terms of the premotor and postcentral cortical zones, respectively, noting specifically that the premotor zones of the brain "are responsible for the "*conversion of individual motor impulses into consecutive kinetic melodies*" (ibid.: 179). Earlier, he pointedly emphasizes that "Movement is always a process with a *temporal course*" that "requires a continuous *chain of interchanging impulses*" (ibid.: 176). In this context, he reiterates in more general terms his descriptive account of the origin of kinetic melodies: "In the initial stages of formation of any movement this chain must consist of a series of isolated impulses; with the development of motor skills the individual impulses are synthesized and combined into *integral kinaesthetic structures* or *kinetic melodies* when a single impulse is sufficient to activate a complete *dynamic stereotype* of automatically interchanging elements" (ibid.: 176). He later specifies that the construction and performance of any complex movement depend on:

1.   an intact frontal lobe, or what he designates an intentional "brain zone";
2.   kinesthesia, or what he designates an "*integrity of its [the movement's] kinaesthetic afferentation*";
3.   a temporal organization, or what he designates a "constant regulation of *muscle tone* ... and a sufficiently rapid and smooth *changeover* from one system of motor innervations to another, with the formation of complete *kinaesthetic melodies* in the final stages of development of skilled movement" (ibid.: 251–253).

With respect to the latter requirement, Luria emphasizes the necessity of the second requirement – kinesthetic afference – citing physiologist Nicholas Bernstein's detailed studies of movement and its fundamental "degrees of freedom" (Bernstein

1984, 1996). As he points out, the degrees of freedom in human movement and the constantly changing tone of the muscles "explain why it is that, in the performance of a voluntary movement or action, although the motor task preserves its regulatory role, the highest responsibility is transferred *from efferent to afferent impulses*" (Luria 1973:249). Kinesthesia is thus of maximal significance; successful voluntary movement and the formation of "a complete dynamic stereotype" depend on it.

Though not explicitly specified in this way, kinetic melodies are inscribed in the body. They are "*integral kinaesthetic structures*" (Luria 1973:176) and are thus essentially, i.e., in a living, experiential sense, not brain events but corporeally resonant ones, in-the-flesh dynamic patterns of movement that are *initiated* – and run off. The most basic of kinetic melodies, ones that might be called fundamental melodies of life – if not fundamental melodies *for* life – are forged in the course of infancy and childhood, some of them beginning in pre-natal life (Luria 1980:192). In each instance, they are kept alive by kinesthetic memory; their inscription in the body is by way of kinesthetic memory, which is to say by way of distinctive movement dynamics. Thus, in normal everyday adult life, a kinetic dynamics unfolds that is at once familiar and yet quintessentially tailored kinetically to the particular situation at hand: a familiar but distinctive kinetic dynamics unfolds in articulatory gestures as we speak, in repetitive downward swoops of our arm as we hammer, in subtle, varying shifts of direction and bendings of our body as we move quickly forward along a crowded sidewalk. The familiarity of these dynamics is grounded in invariants, invariants of speech, of hammering, of weaving a path around obstacles. Their tailoring is grounded in the particular situational vagaries found in the present experience: feeling ill at ease speaking to this particular person, hammering with this new hammer, weaving our way on this icy sidewalk.

Kinetic melodies that are inscribed in our bodies are dynamic patterns of movement. They constitute that basic, vast, and potentially ever-expandable repertoire of "I cans" (Husserl 1970, 1973, 1980, 1989) permeating human life: walking, speaking, reaching, hugging, throwing, carrying, opening, closing, brushing, running, wiping, leaping, pulling, pushing. The basic kinetic repertoire is indeed virtually limitless, being constrained only by age, inclination – and pathology. Its sequential complexity and intricacy are similarly virtually limitless, not only with respect to everyday "I cans" such as writing and tying knots, for example, but with respect to dancing, diving, skiing, performing surgical procedures, administering medical courses of action, learning artistic modes of applying paint and of sculpting a piece of wood, and so on. In each instance, knowledgeability is not simply a know-*how*, a lesser form of knowledge that is "merely physical." Kinetic melodies are saturated in cognitive and affective acuities that both anchor invariants and color and individualize the manner in which any particular melody runs off.

Luria's concept of kinetic melodies is an experientially-based concept rooted in the kinetic dynamics of life as normally lived. "Kinetic melody" thus describes *an experienced kinetic event*: writing one's name fluently, reciting the months of the year, solving an arithmetical problem (Luria, e.g. 1966:226; see also below). What is ruptured by tumors, hemorrhages, or brain lesions ruptures a normally *dynamic* life, a life of meaningful movement and of ease in movement. When Luria at one point characterizes a wounded patient as suffering an "*adynamia* of psychological process- es" (ibid.: 224–226), he quotes the patient's own reflections on his wound, reflections that show clearly that the patient's psychological *adynamia* is played out kinetically. The patient withdrew for weeks into idleness – "[I] just lay idly in bed" – and social indifference, not writing or speaking but "behav[ing] as if I were alone, or by myself, and with nothing to care about" (Luria 1966: 225). "My comrades," he remarks, "even took me for a deaf-mute" (ibid.: 224). In the most fundamental sense, his adynamia is corporeally represented (for more on corporeal representation, see Sheets-Johnstone 1990). It is in fact significant that his adynamia begins to lift only with a resumption of movement: "Only after six weeks, when I began to do exercises, did I write my first letter" (ibid.: 225). It is as if he needed to reawaken himself *kinetically* – to his tactile- kinesthetic body and to *kinesthetically felt dynamics* – before he could rekindle the "kinetic melody" of writing.

Smooth kinetic melodies nevertheless proved beyond this patient. In particular, he was not able to carry out serially coordinated movement. In Luria's words, "The formation of a skilled movement in the form of a smooth 'kinetic melody' met with insuperable difficulties" (ibid.: 231). What is more, arithmetical calculations, which were formerly within his province, were no longer so. Luria notes that "Despite the differences between these [arithmetical] disturbances and the disturbances of skilled movements described above, they have one common feature: In both cases we are dealing with a disturbance of the smooth, automatized performance of complex op- erations" (ibid.: 256). In short, what was beyond this patient was *complex sequential activity*, including not only arithmetical calculations but coherent narrative speech. The effects of the lesion were thus spread out over a variety of activities – "com- plex, smooth *skilled movements*," "*intellectual operations*," coherent narrative speech (ibid.: 290) – but all were rooted in a common thematic: complex sequential activity. It bears emphasizing that Luria's concern with complex sequential activity, hence with the *temporality* of movement, pervades his detailed neurological studies, and that, in consequence, animate movement is recognized not merely as a spatial phenomenon – movement with respect to a particular situation – but as a spatio-*temporal* one.

Luria's descriptive accounts of disturbances in kinetic melodies and of their link- age to pathologies in *brain zones* (Luria 1973) constitute the basis for fundamental neurological understandings of human movement, that is, understandings of how pathologies impede or obliterate dynamic patterns of movement that are the bedrock of everyday human life activities. Given the acuity of his observations, his extraor- dinarily comprehensive clinical and experimental studies, and his central concern with movement, it is curious that his work is not mentioned in present-day studies of movement, if not by cognitivists, then by dynamic systems theorists. Although the latter's perspective is broader – ecological kinetics of organism-environment rela- tions – and their aim narrower or reductive – mathematical formulations of move- ment or "law-based" principles (Kugler & Turvey 1987, e.g., p. 6) – and although kinesthesia is totally eclipsed by "information" and an experiencing subject virtually discounted (cf. Wilberg 1983), there is nonetheless a basic kinship. Dynamic systems theorist J. A. Scott Kelso's "dynamic patterns," for example, in spite of being analyzed in radically different terms (Kelso 1995), are descriptively riveted on movement in the same way Luria's kinetic melodies are; both centralize attention not on objects in motion but on movement itself, and, in particular, on coordinated movement. Moreover Luria would agree with dynamic systems theorists Peter Kugler and Michael Turvey that movement is not "a complex *thing* put together from simpler things" like a reflex (Kugler & Turvey 1987: 405); it is heterarchically, not hierarchically, organized. Luria's dynamic understanding of neurology and neuropsychology are in fact a model exemplification of how investigations of movement can be anchored in what many dynamic systems theorists term "real-time" phenomena (van Gelder & Port 1995; Thelen & Smith 1994) rather than exclusively in studies of *the* brain, in the kinetic artificialities of movement laboratories, or in computer modeling.

A critical commonality is notable as well, however. Neither Luria nor dynamic system theorists recognize the fact that movement creates its own distinctive temporal-spatial-energic qualities, and that this formative process results in the creation of a distinctive dynamics – precisely as "kinetic melody" and "dynamic pattern" so aptly suggest but do not specify. The dynamics are not only behaviorally observable; they are experienced by the self-moving body creating them and thereby potentially the basis of kinesthetic memory. In effect, through self-movement, there is always potentially a form to remember, a form not of sensations as such, but of a movement dynamic.

Kinesthetic memory

Animation is of the nature of life. Being animate beings, we move, and in moving articulate a kinetic dynamics. We do so as adults in virtue of kinesthetic memory, and, to begin with, in virtue of our having learned our bodies and learned to move ourselves (Sheets-Johnstone 1999/expanded 2nd ed. 2011). Because dynamic patterns of movement have distinctive spatial, temporal, and energic qualities,[2] they each have a distinctive spatio-temporal-energic dynamic form that is potentially invariant, depending upon whether we practice the pattern, and through repetition, learn it. Kinetic dynamics are thus of the essence of kinesthetic memory in precisely the way they are of the essence of kinetic melodies. Melody and memory are in fact dynamic images of one another – as Luria indicates when he identifies kinetic melodies as "*integral kinaesthetic structures*." In effect, being dynamically patterned, kinesthetic memories are not vague, abstract kinetic phantoms but are inscribed in the body as

---

2. The qualities of movement – tensional, linear, amplitudinal, and projectional – are analyzed in detail in Sheets-Johnstone (1980 [1966]). The qualitative nature of movement is discussed in detail in Sheets-Johnstone (1999/expanded 2nd ed. 2011).

specific bodily dynamics, dynamics that, as enacted, are at once familiar and tailored distinctively to the particular situation at hand. Familiarity and distinctive tailoring were briefly specified earlier in the examples of speaking, hammering, and weaving one's way along a crowded sidewalk. A more detailed example will bring finer dimensions of both aspects to light.

Writing one's name is commonly thought of as an act rather than as a coordinated series of movements. Yet a coordinated series of movements defines more accurately "the act" of writing one's name. More specifically still, to write one's name is to move through a dynamic series of coordinated movements that is kinesthetically felt *both* as dynamic and as dynamically familiar. What makes the series familiar are invariant dynamic features common to all instances of writing one's name: greater and lesser moments of force occur at certain moments in the flow, moments where one accentuates a letter or part of a letter, for example; changes in direction take place smoothly or abruptly at certain places, and in a jagged or rounded manner; pauses occur at certain moments in the writing, perhaps with a felt sense of suspension as when one dots an *i* or crosses a *t*; the beginning of the signature and its end are clearly marked in some way. In short, in the writing of one's name, a distinctive spatio-temporal-energic dynamic plays itself out, and with it, a certain dynamic is experienced that is both familiar and unique. The uniqueness of the dynamics is first and foremost a kinesthetic uniqueness, not a visual uniqueness. In fact, it is fundamentally the kinetic and kinesthetically-felt dynamics that make the signature both visually unique and visually familiar.

At the same time, however, one's signature is tailored to present particularities: the writing implement one is using, for example, the surface on which one is writing, and the importance of the signature are variables capable of generating variations on a theme, as when, for example, one is writing one's name on a blackboard, or writing with a pen that is running dry, or signing a document such as a marriage license or a will. The dynamics of writing one's name – the ease, rhythm, size of one's movements, and so on – vary in proportion to the particularities of the immediate situation. A basically invariant and familiar dynamics adjusts itself to the situation at hand.

One can readily see how the dynamic series of coordinated movements unfolds as a kinetic melody: *once initiated*, the movement flows on by itself. Assuming one has learned to write one's name, and barring pathological disturbances, one does not need to oversee the drawing of each letter, for example, as one did when learning to write; one does not get lost somewhere in the process, as one might if suffering from a brain lesion. A coordinated series of movements whose dynamics are engrained in kinesthetic memory is run off and recognized kinesthetically. As it runs off, it is unified by retentions and protentions (Husserl 1964) until the series and its familiar and unique dynamics come to an end. When Luria speaks of the *automatization* of movement, it is important to point out that he is describing the way in which a single impulse is sufficient to activate a kinetic melody, and not asserting that one is unaware of writing one's name, that one is unconscious of doing so, or that one can nod off while the process continues by itself. Furthermore, it is not merely that beginning a kinetic melody is sufficient to generate its entire performance; it is that the movement that flows forth effortlessly in a coherent dynamic does so because we know and remember the flow in a corporeally felt sense: *we kinetically instantiate what we know kinesthetically*. What is automatic is, in effect, kinesthetic memory. The melody runs off by itself because a familiar dynamics is awakened in kinesthetic memory and generated by it.

The point warrants further clarification, notably because the initial impulse is significant beyond the fact that it generates a kinetic dynamics on the basis of kinesthetic memory. The initial impulse is volitional. Unless we suffer from dementia or some similar malady, we do not find ourselves out of the blue brushing our teeth, for example, or walking on a street ten blocks from home. We initiate brushing and walking. We initiate them by initiating a certain kinetic dynamics that includes a certain bodily orientation, a certain environmental setting, a certain interaction with certain implements or items – a toothbrush or shoes, for example – and so on. Similarly, we do not suddenly find ourselves *not* brushing our teeth anymore but eating breakfast, or *not* walking anymore but sitting on a park bench. We are kinesthetically aware of a certain kinetic dynamics coming to an end. In short, our tactile-kinesthetic body is always present, and present along a gamut of possible awarenesses from marginal to maximal. Any time we wish to pay *closer* attention to it, there it is.

The relationship between voluntary action and kinesthesia has important implications with regard to attention, familiarity, and something "going wrong." The relationship is put in ironically sharp relief in a commonly used textbook, *Scientific Bases of Human Movement*. In a chapter titled "The Proprioceptors and Their Associated Reflexes," Gowitzke and Milner (1988: 193) write that "The voluntary contribution to movement is almost entirely limited to initiation, regulation of speed, force, range, and direction, and termination of the movement." Kinetic "limitations" are in fact sizable freedoms, precisely as Bernstein originally demonstrated by way of *degrees of freedom* in his studies of human movement and as any attempt by any normal person to duplicate a movement sequence with pinpoint exactitude readily indicates. Initiation, termination, speed, force, range, and direction of movement may in fact be "regulated," the last four "limitations" in particular specifying in an abbreviated and incomplete way spatio-temporal-energic qualities of movement, qualities we can voluntarily change in myriad ways virtually any time we wish and in so doing, change the dynamics of any movement we perform. We can, for example, change resolute movements into hesitant ones by changing the force, range, and speed of our movement. We might thereby radically alter the way in which we customarily write our name, brush our teeth, or walk – and thereby nullify a familiar dynamic.

Turning attention to our own movement in continuation of an initial volitional impulse, we attend to a kinetic melody in progress: as noted, any time we care to pay closer attention to our tactile-kinesthetic body, there it is. Turning attention elsewhere but continuing on with the melody, we marginalize tactile-kinesthetic sensitivities but are not totally unaware of ourselves in the process of moving. Thus, to say that we are aware of ourselves moving only when something goes wrong is misguided. Noticing that something is wrong necessarily assumes the familiar dynamic feel of that same or similar something going right. Indeed, we can be aware that something goes wrong only if we already know what commonly goes right. To insist otherwise is illogical.

Now to acknowledge that we can be aware that something is amiss only if we already know a familiar kinetic dynamics is to acknowledge that we can be aware of something going wrong only on the basis of kinesthetic memory. *Kinesthetic memory is the foundation of familiar kinetic dynamics.* It is thus not without reason that Luria at one point speaks of "*kinaesthetic* melodies" (Luria 1973:253; italics added). Kinesthetic memory is structured along the lines of "kinaesthetic melodies," and *familiar* "kinaesthetic melodies" are inscribed in kinesthetic memory.

The term "motor"

Motor skills are not properly "motor" phenomena, and the term "motor" is in fact wayward. The skills are kinetic, and they are learned through sensory-kinetic experience. Moreover complex concepts are generated in the course of sensory-kinetic learnings, concepts having to do with the dynamics created by self-movement, i.e., with spatio-temporal-energic qualities of movement.[3] "Motor" skills do not generate such concepts because no sentient moving person is present who is moving skillfully or learning to move skillfully: the erstwhile sentient moving person has been reduced to an operative motor.

The above broad criticisms of a "motor" vocabulary to describe organic movement need tempering in recognition of researchers not misled by the term, researchers who, being implicitly or explicitly aware of how a purely motor vocabulary effaces living subjects, justly take a sentient moving person into account.[4] Luria, for example, does not compromise the reality of sentient moving persons in his neurological investigations of "motor" tasks and "motor programmes" (Luria 1973). His non-mechanization of self-movement stems from his dual conception of science, a conception neuropsychologist Oliver Sacks eloquently eulogizes in his foreword to Luria's *The Man with a Shattered World* (Sacks 1972) and a conception Luria himself eloquently puts forth in *The Making of Mind*. In essence, Luria distinguishes between classical and romantic science, the former being geared to a reductionist perspective, computer simulations, "mathematical schemas," and the like (Luria 1979:176); the latter being geared to observation and description – "phenomenological description" (ibid.:177) – that is neither "superficial" nor "incomplete" (ibid.), but that traces out relationships among things and events in such a way that multiple perspectives are

---

3.   What the textbook names as voluntary aspects of movement – "speed, force, range, and direction" – are created qualities of self-movement; measurements of these aspects constitute third-person assessments.

4.   As Merleau-Ponty might say, such researchers, unlike others, do not simply "manipulate things and give up living in them" (Merleau-Ponty 1964:159).

gained and "we come to the essence of the object, to an understanding of its qualities and the rules of its existence" (ibid.: 178). Given Luria's equal esteem for both sciences, it is not surprising that kinetic/kinesthetic melodies figure centrally in his neurological investigations: they are vital to a veridical account of neurological normalities and pathologies. His combined classical and romantic neuroscience contrasts markedly with the austere landscape of today's cognitive neuroscience where kinetic/kinesthetic melodies figure as alien, flimsy bodies lacking sturdy credentials and localization.

Unlike analyses of "motor behavior," however, analyses of kinetic/kinesthetic melodies open the way to commonly overlooked aspects of movement, in part, just those "limited" aspects of movement designated "voluntary." In opening toward these foundational aspects of self-movement, analyses of kinetic melodies readily defuse typically mechanical concepts underpinning motor analyses in the same way that they defuse typically mechanical understandings of automatization. This is because kinetic/kinesthetic melodies are descriptive of the dynamic phenomena themselves, not a mechanical reduction of them. More concretely, they pinpoint the nature of self-movement in a living sense; they *language kinetic experience*.[5] The term *motor* is no match for this experientially-descriptive language. The term, after all, names a mechanical device, a man-made machine, and is not a term whose genesis lies in observations of living organisms. Darwin, whose round-the-world observations of life would authorize use of the term were it accurate, does not use it. In fact, the term has no evolutionary foundations. It is not difficult to appreciate why: "motor" does not describe the dynamics of living bodies but purportedly specifies something inside, something hidden from view, a "driving force" that gets the larger object in which it inheres moving in some way, *its* movement providing energies for the object to move or to do work. We can thus appreciate why neither dynamics nor volition are of topical, not to say strategic, "motor" concern: a real-life kinetics and kinesthesia are nowhere to be found. Kelso documents this lack from a dynamic systems perspective when, in writing of "traditional approaches" to motor learning, he concludes that "The organism, to put it bluntly, is treated like a machine whose task is to associate inputs and outputs" (Kelso 1995: 160).[6]

---

5. For more on the concept and challenge of *languaging experience*, see Sheets-Johnstone (1999, 2002).

6. The opening statement of a review of a recent neuroscience book on "motor learning" testifies to the preoccupation with something "inside": "Motor learning can be defined as a set of neural processes associated with practice that lead to changes in performance and capabilities" (Flash 2001: 1612). The book – *The Acquisition of Motor Behavior in Vertebrates* – is amply instructive in this regard: brain structures and neural networks are the focal concerns; eye-blink conditioning is a major topic (e.g., "Eyeblink conditioning is recognized as a form of motor learning" [Hallett, Pascual-Leone & Topka 1996: 291]); ablation studies constitute a major form of investigation; verbal communication, communication that obviously requires sequential articulatory movement, is not recognized as "procedural" knowledge – knowledge that "refers to sequential behavior and usually relates to motor performance" – but is naively categorized as

In sum, to continue to refer to sentient moving bodies in terms of motor behavior, motor memory, and so on, without balancing the ledger to include dynamic and voluntary aspects of movement, is to continue to think of animate forms as mechanical things that are capable neither of generating kinetic melodies nor of voluntarily initiating movement or of voluntarily shaping it by changing its dynamics. The point is of critical importance not only in light of the manner in which movement is commonly studied in today's scientific world, but in light of the manner in which uncritical usage skews understandings to the point that kinetic melodies are occluded even as they appear to be recognized. Merleau-Ponty's "motor intentionality" is a classic instance. It warrants extended discussion because it furnishes insights into veridical understandings of movement, kinesthetic memory, and habit.

Merleau-Ponty's "motor intentionality"

Merleau-Ponty's motor intentionality verges on Luria's kinetic melodies not only in offering an explanation of pathological disturbances, but in emphasizing the importance of the first instant of a movement: "being the active initiative, [the first movement] institutes the link between a here and a yonder, a now and a future which the remainder of the instants will merely develop" (Merleau-Ponty 1962: 140). Because Merleau-Ponty does not examine *the experience* of movement, however, he never arrives at its dynamic kinetic structure. Moreover because he does not recognize kinesthetic experience, he does not recognize kinesthetic memory and the kinetically/kinesthetically forged sense of familiarity that is the basis of habit. He appears to believe that to recognize kinesthetic experience is to fall into the empiricists' trap of "a mosaic of 'extensive sensations'" (ibid.: 143n) and that the truth of movement lies rather in the fact that the body "is a system which is open on to the world, and correlative with it" (ibid.). In brief, he appears to believe that to admit kinesthetic experience into his account would tether him to a subject in exclusion of a world. In effect, though he speaks specifically of "a kinetic melody" (ibid.: 134), of the "melodic character" of a gesture (ibid.: 105), of how a patient's movments have lost their "melodic flow" (ibid.: 116), and of how the same patient fails to grasp a story "as a melodic whole" (ibid.: 132), the experiential nature and history of the melody, and its dynamic character elude him. What structures kinetic melodies is in the end "ambiguated"[7]

"declarative" knowledge – knowledge that "refers to facts and includes all information about which we think and that we communicate verbally" (ibid.: 289). Knowledge about "sequential tasks" lags behind knowledge about conditioned response. In fact, knowledge about living movement – kinetic melodies – is far in arrears of knowledge about laboratory-induced movement.

7. Johnstone (2001) uses the term "disambiguator" to designate a notational device that distinguishes two different meanings of an otherwise ambiguous sentence. I am borrowing and converting his term.

rather than phenomenologically analyzed. The 'motor' of "motor intentionality" is, in other words, hidden from view, as in classical science, located in "autonomous" and "anonymous" "functions" (ibid., e.g., pp. 84, 86, 160), or equivalently, inheres in a "prepersonal *I* who provides the basis for the phenomenon of movement" (ibid.: 276, Note 1). There is neither a tactile-kinesthetic body nor kinesthetic memory in these functions or prepersonal *I*, nor a kinetic history, a history not only of learning the kinetic melody of a new movement sequence, but of learning one's body and learning to move oneself to begin with (Sheets-Johnstone 1999/expanded 2nd ed. 2011), self-directed learnings that each and every human initiates and carries out from birth. The essential familiarity of habit – its kinetic dynamics – has in turn no experiential foundations.

Yet *habit* is of central moment to Merleau-Ponty's "motor intentionality." Because "a movement is learned when the body has understood it" (Merleau-Ponty 1962: 139)[8] and because it is the understanding, competent body and not the learning or practicing body that defines Merleau-Ponty's "motor intentionality," motor intentionality is easily conceived to be fundamentally the work of a "habit body," *a body that already knows*. Indeed, it becomes ironically clear how and why a habit body holds a privileged position in Merleau-Ponty's account of movement. A habit body already knows how to move, and its movement is already all of a piece: a habit body is both already "expressive" and a readily "expressive" storehouse of "kinetic melodies" (ibid.: 146). Accordingly, there is no need to dwell on *just how the body comes to be a habit body or what kinesthetically structures its understandings*. In a "prepersonal" kinesthetic-less world, habit has no experiential precursors and no need of such. The body "which is open on to the world and correlative with it" is a ready-made. Thus, when Merleau-Ponty defines habit as "knowledge in the hands, which is forthcoming ... when bodily effort is made" (ibid.: 144), he passes over a tactilely and kinesthetically resonant body that is the source of knowledge "in the hands," a body that has *learned* its way in the world from the beginning by moving, gaining knowledge "in the hands" and elsewhere in the process. He thereby misses *the familiar kinetic dynamics that fundamentally constitutes habit*, in this instance, the habit that is there in person "in the hands." Moreover although he points out with respect to movement of one's body that "[t]he synthesis of both time and space is a task that always has to be performed afresh," thus indicating that the habit body is flexible, adjusting itself to the kinetic demands of the moment, the task "that always has to be performed afresh" never makes an appeal to kinetic knowledge or to kinesthetic memory. On the contrary, Merleau-Ponty affirms that "Our bodily experience of movement is not a particular case of knowledge [but] provides us with a way of access to the world and the object, with a 'praktognosia'" (ibid.: 140). Clearly, the very stuff of habits – their foundational kinesthetic familiarity,

---

8. Cf. Bergson, whose writings were well-known to Merleau-Ponty and who, speaking specifically of how repetition "teaches" the body in the course of learning a new coordination, stated, "A movement is learned when the body has been made to understand it" (Bergson [1896] 1991: 112).

a familiarity renewed by way of kinesthetic memory each time they are reactivated – is nowhere recognized.

Merleau-Ponty's *habit body* is not only without kinesthesia but is also preeminently an adult body without a history, a body that thereby rings false neurologically as well as existentially. In both a neurological and existential sense, kinesthesia and kinesthetic memory are essential to progressive developmental achievements and capacities, and to the formation of habits on the basis of those achievements and capacities. Adultist views of oneself in the world, perhaps particularly ontologically-oriented "phenomenological" views,[9] ignore the complex nature of infancy and its intricate developmental history, a history without which one could not attain adult habits, let alone adultist views of oneself in the world. While Merleau-Ponty's "motor intentionality" and habit body rightly prominence the body, they ignore a previous and ongoing lifetime of kinesthetic learning and memory at the same time that they presuppose it at every step.

In sum, so strong is Merleau-Ponty's driving thematic of an indissoluble body-world relationship that it overrules an investigation of movement and in consequence effectively squelches a phenomenological account of self-movement, i.e., of kinesthetic experience. While it is true that Merleau-Ponty avoids the representations of the intellectuals and the "extensive sensations" of the empiricists by tying subject and object – body and world – together through a "motor intentionality" that "cease[s] to draw a distinction between the body as a mechanism in itself and consciousness as being for itself" (ibid.: 139), the move is not without hazard. Kinetic melodies demand kinetic explanations. Merleau-Ponty can speak of "melodic flows" devoid of kinesthesia and kinesthetic memory only by explaining the body's ready access to the world as "autonomous" and "anonymous" functions of a prepersonal *I*, in essence, as "motor" functions defined by classical science. But we must note that he also specifies another "motor" phenomenon, one that appears to be a subrogate for kinesthesia, namely, the body image (*schéma corporel*).[10]

Body image

Merleau-Ponty is not the only person to invoke a body image to explain corporeal-kinetic phenomena, but his writings on the subject are a good place to begin since he takes up the term from its original coinage in neurology, and since his "existential analysis" (ibid.: 136) of it readily demonstrates how kinesthesia and kinesthetic memory may be trivialized or passed over altogether. He begins by considering the original definition of body image – in his words, "a *compendium* of our bodily

---

9.   One could cite Heidegger as well.

10. See Gallagher (1986, 1995) for discussions of the confusion of body image and body schema.

experience" (ibid.: 98) – and goes on to improve on it, defining body image rather as "a total awareness of my posture in the intersensory world" (ibid.: 100). But he improves on this definition too, enlarging it, citing the fact that "Psychologists often say that the body image is *dynamic*" (ibid.). He makes "total postural awareness" *dynamic* by making it a bodily "attitude" rather than a bodily "form": "Brought down to a precise sense, this term means that my body appears to me as an attitude directed towards a certain existing or possible task" (ibid.). He discusses this bodily attitude essentially in terms of space, specifically, "a *spatiality of situation*" (ibid.). One looks in vain, however, in the examples he subsequently gives and in the discussions that follow, of a veritable *dynamic*: "the situation of the body in face of its tasks" (ibid.) nowhere spells out a *dynamic* beyond the rather commonplace fact that the body moves in face of its tasks.

Merleau-Ponty's re-definition of the body image as "a spatiality of situation" coincides with the self-description of the patient whose case study constitutes the basis for his reformulation of the term. The patient – Schneider – is capable of kinetic melodies only in concrete situations, where specific objects calling for specific movements are present – for example, scissors, leather, needle, and thread – and not in abstract situations where he is requested to perform certain movements – for example, pointing to a part of his body. Of the former movements, Schneider states that "I experience the movements as being a result of the situation, of the sequence of events themselves; myself and my movements are, so to speak, merely a link in the whole process and I am scarcely aware of any voluntary initiative… It all happens independently of me" (ibid.: 105). The statement is a conceptual blueprint of the "third term" – *existence* – that Merleau-Ponty wishes to instantiate between the rationalists' representations – "the psychic" – and the empiricists' sensations – "the physiological" (ibid.: 122). With respect to kinesthesia and kinesthetic memory, the self-description is crucially telling: movement is simply "a result of the situation"; and the moving subject is "scarcely aware of any voluntary initiative." It is no wonder, then, that in Merleau-Ponty's correlative autonomous, anonymous, prepersonal body-world nexus, kinesthesia and kinesthetic memory are replaced by a body image whose dynamics consist simply in the fact that the body moves.[11] Being a power that projects the body into the world, the body image creates an "'intentional arc'" (ibid.: 136) that existentially links it to the world. In the patient's case, the arc is truncated and otherwise damaged. To paraphrase Merleau-Ponty, the arc no longer "projects round about Schneider his past, his future, his human setting, his physical, ideological, and moral situation; it no longer brings about the unity of his senses, of intelligence, of sensibility and motility" (ibid.).

Body image and intentional arcs notwithstanding, Merleau-Ponty remarks pointedly on the extraordinary way in which Schneider uses movement to get his bearings with respect to a task he is asked to do or to an object he is asked to recognize. "If a part of his body is touched and he is asked to locate the point of contact, he first of all

---

11. Ostensibly, Merleau-Ponty has reduced normal, everyday movement to its most elementary level, but that level in fact fails to account for the dynamics of movement – the basis of habit – and the ontogenetical realities of infant life.

sets his whole body in motion and thus narrows down the problem of location, then he comes still nearer by moving the limb in question" (ibid.: 107); "If the subject's arm is extended horizontally, he cannot describe its position until he has performed a set of pendular movements which convey to him the arm position in relation to the trunk" (ibid.); "The patient himself neither seeks nor finds his movement, but moves his body about until the movement comes" (ibid.: 110). Later, as if in summation of these facts, Merleau-Ponty comments that "concrete movements, which are preserved by the patient as are those imitative movements, whereby he compensates for his paucity of visual data, arise from kinaesthetic or tactile sense, *which incidentally was remarkably exploited by Schneider*" (ibid.: 113, italics added). In short, it is through moving, through "active movements" (ibid.: 107), that Schneider tries to find his way, follow an order, respond to a request, and so on. Merleau-Ponty thus appears to recognize kinesthesia, but only in the pathological instance when no kinetic melody is forthcoming, or more generally, "only when something goes wrong." Kinesthesia might thus seem to be something like the proverbial tree falling in the forest: unless we sense it, it does not exist. Indeed, Merleau-Ponty's solution is to relegate "consciousness of movement" to an amorphous *background*:

> [F]or the normal person every movement is, indissolubly, movement and consciousness of movement. This can be expressed by saying that for the normal person every movement has a *background*.... The background to the movement is not a representation associated or linked externally with the movement itself, but is immanent in the movement inspiring and sustaining it at every moment.
>
> (ibid.: 110)

The term "background" is both an expeditious and ambiguous way of reckoning with "consciousness of movement": it effectively nullifies kinesthetic experience and kinesthetic memory, and thereby makes "consciousness of movement" literally, logically, and experientially unintelligible. By invoking a "background," Merleau-Ponty recognizes what must be recognized – "consciousness of movement" – but cuts short its actual experience, nature, and significance. Certainly we are not ordinarily attentive kinesthetically in a *focal* way when brushing our teeth or weaving our way quickly through a crowd; we are concentrated on the task at hand. Our kinesthetic awareness of ourselves *is* in the "background." But being in the background does not mean that it is altogether outside awareness. It is not only that any time we care to pay *focal* attention to our "consciousness of movement," there it is, but that *the familiarity of our movement in the form of a certain kinetic dynamics undergirds our brushing, weaving, and so on, and is marginally or pre-reflectively in our awareness even as we focally attend to what we will have for breakfast as we brush or to the appointment to which we are rushing as we weave.* A kinetic dynamics is sensuously present at the lower end of the continuum that describes the intensity – or focal to marginal – gradient of consciousness. In fact, if as Merleau-Ponty writes, the background "is immanent in the movement inspiring and sustaining it at every moment," then a certain kinetic dynamics is undeniably underway that is familiar as well as self-propelling, a dynamics that is not there only if we notice it *focally*, but a dynamic that is present as a familiar, ongoing, and particular kinesthetic melody. How otherwise might one legitimately speak of a "consciousness of movement"?

In sum, a veritable kinetic dynamics is not reducible to a "[bodily] attitude directed towards a certain existing or possible task." Merleau-Ponty's reformulated body image falls short of fulfilling its dynamic promise. A veritable kinetic dynamics is kinesthetically felt, which is to say it is experienced in the flow of movement itself, and with a sense of familiarity (supposing the movement is not novel) generated through kinesthetic memory.

Body image and body schema

The term body image is actually misleading since it conjures up not only something preeminently *visual*, but something not actually perceived, i.e., something *imaginary*. Philosopher Shaun Gallagher and neurophysiologist Jonathan Cole try to correct these false impressions by specifying body image in exacting terms and by distinguishing it from body schema (see also Gallagher 1986, 1995). In their joint article on a "deafferented subject" – a man who lost virtually all kinesthetic awareness – they attempt to document just what is missing in the way of a body image and body schema, and how the subject – referred to as IW – compensates for the loss and learns to move anew. In the process, and unlike Merleau-Ponty, Gallagher and Cole do not trivialize or pass over kinesthesia. On the contrary, using the broader term "proprioception," they specify both a neurological informational system and a system of experiential awareness. They thereby distinguish body image from body schema: body image is "a complex set of intentional states" that includes perceptual experience, conceptual understandings, and emotional attitudes; body schema is "a system of motor capacities, abilities, and habits that enable movement and the maintenance of posture," a system that operates "preconsciously" and "subpersonally" (Gallagher & Cole 1998:132). They implicitly vindicate Luria's neurological diagnostic and his emphasis on the quintessential significance of kinesthetic afferents to intention or "will" when they state, "At the earliest stage of his illness IW had no control over his movements and was unable to put intention into action. There was, one might say, a disconnection of will from the specifics of movement" (ibid.:135). The implicit vindication, however, is short-lived: neither body schema nor body image approximate to the neurological and experiential dynamics of a kinetic melody.

To begin with, a body schema has no basis in experience. It is at best an explanatory convenience, a hypothetical entity in the brain (or central nervous system as a whole) that is conjured to do the work of putting movement together, furnishing a kinetic blueprint for neurological eyes only, as it were. In contrast, a kinetic melody describes both what is constructed neurologically in the course of learning – a distinctive temporal course of innervations and denervations, as in learning to walk, to brush one's teeth, to make an abdominal incision, to do the tarantella – and what is experienced – a distinctive dynamic flow of movement. A kinetic melody is not a *thing* in the brain (or in the central nervous system) but a particular neurological and experiential dynamic. Each melody is in fact a *neuromuscular dynamic* whose innervations and denervations, together with the constantly changing muscle tone they generate, constitute a particular temporal organization. Kinetic melodies thus straddle two worlds; unlike a body schema, they describe inherently dynamic patterns that are at once neurological and experiential.

A body image suffers from the same lack of experiential grounding and dynamic resonance as a body schema. The identification of "the perception of movement" with body image (Gallagher & Cole 1998: 134) not uncommonly reduces to a *positional* awareness of the body – e.g., "I can tell you where my legs are even with my eyes closed"; "Proprioceptive awareness is a felt experience of bodily position that helps to constitute the perceptual aspect of the body image" (ibid.: 137). While the perception of movement certainly includes positional awarenesses, it is quintessentially a *dynamic* awareness, and to overlook the kinetic/kinesthetic dynamics that are its source is to distort the account of "the perception of movement."

The problem with the body image might be judged to be basically a methodological problem: beginning with a construct instead of experience. Unless one begins with and hews to experience, the very thing one wants to explain eludes one, in this instance, the experience of an unfolding dynamics, the perception of one's own body in motion. The first question is properly not "How is such an experience possible?," but "What is the nature of kinetic experience?" In turn, the first task is not to come up with an explanatory entity but with a descriptive account of the phenomenon in question.[12] Methodology is thus of critical importance. Turning toward "the thing itself" – *self-movement* – one realizes that a body image is not up to the task set for it. The phenomenology of self-movement cannot be deduced from pathology. Certainly one may infer the normal from the pathological, but inference is not phenomenology.

The importance of hewing to experience may be highlighted by noting a correspondence between Schneider and IW: IW too "exploits" movement to trigger movement. He exploits it not by actively initiating movement as Schneider does, but through his ready ideational access to earlier experiences of normal movement. IW already knows fundamental kinetic melodies; he knows "how they go," so to speak, and even how they are supposed to go. Thus, when Gallagher and Cole write that "IW's success in recovering useful movement function has depended primarily on his finite mental concentration, and to a much lessor (sic) degree on reaccessing or relearning motor programs which are, so far, poorly understood" (ibid.: 138), they neglect to consider that IW knows the movement he intends or "wills": he has a kinetic memory of what it is to reach, to grasp, to sit, to stand. He knows these movements in his bones, even though he can no longer move these bones except by visual initiation and monitoring.

---

12. One might cite neurophysiologist Kurt Goldstein (1939) as well as Husserl: "[I]t is the first task of biology to *describe carefully all living beings as they actually are*" (p. 6); *What do the phenomena … teach us about the 'essence' (the intrinsic nature) of an organism?*" (p. 7).

Thus, although he cannot call forth kinetic melodies from kinesthetic memory, he can structure his present visually guided movement on the basis of his kinetic knowledge of them. In fact, short of this dynamic memory of movement, he would not even know how to begin moving. To appreciate this, one need only consider what it would be like *to be born* as a "deafferented subject." IW's visual re-creation of movement does not begin from scratch but from a previous body of knowledge of such mundane kinetic melodies as walking, buttoning, and picking up an egg.

In sum, kinetic melodies describe the reality of movement in neurological and experiential ways that neither body schema nor body image can approximate. They do so because they explicitly recognize a bodily-kinetic dynamic. More explicitly still, they recognize a vast range of bodily-kinetic dynamics "in face of the world," each melody being distinctly analyzable as a dynamic pattern of movement. Body image and body schema are no match for this bodily-kinetic dynamic. Indeed, they are recalcitrant to Gallagher and Cole's noble clarifying efforts and should be jettisoned in favor of a veridical phenomenology of self-movement, one that recognizes the foundationally dynamic character of movement from the start.

The pointillist conception of movement: Its conceptual underpinnings and liabilities

Motion, Descartes stated, "[is] the transfer of one piece of matter, or one body, from the vicinity of the other bodies which are in immediate contact with it, and which are regarded as being at rest, to the vicinity of other bodies" (Descartes [1644] 1985: 233). With respect to a body in face of its task – sitting down, lifting a suitcase, cutting a swath of grass – point A and point B are typically the points of interest. They mark the place of departure and arrival of a moving body, and thereby the beginning and end of its task. The points say nothing of the dynamics of movement. They describe a basically static spatial world intermittently interrupted by bodies changing position.

The spatial concordance of body and world described by Merleau-Ponty is rooted in a pointillist conception of movement: individuals move from point A to point B, following along the lines of an intentional arc. In privileging *position*, the conception neglects to account for and virtually effaces movement itself. The neglect and virtual effacement are straightaway evident in Merleau-Ponty's concluding analysis of Schneider: "[T]he normal subject has his body not only as a system of present positions, but besides, and thereby, as an open system of an infinite number of equivalent positions directed to other ends. What we have called the body image is precisely this system of equivalents, this immediately given invariant whereby the different motor tasks are instantaneously transferable" (Merleau-Ponty 1962: 141).[13] Movement – what putatively

---

13. The temporality of movement is of notable significance in this context. As Luria points out, voluntary movement demands not only kinesthetic afference but an ever-changing series

should make the body image *dynamic* – is nowhere in evidence because in fact there is no dynamic, but only a pointillist conception of "motricité."

The pointillist conception is similarly exemplified in the earlier quotations from Gallagher and Cole: knowing where one's legs are when one's eyes are closed, for example. The conception clearly leads one erroneously to believe that movement is simply a change of position, and in turn to conceive a kinesthetic awareness of movement to be an awareness of changed positions. The conception is actually spatially deficient in its non-recognition of the spatial qualities of movement and correlative kinesthetic awarenesses. In fact, however persuasive the notion of "a spatiality of situation" – "know[ing] indubitably where my pipe is" (Merleau-Ponty 1962: 100) – its explanatory referents – body image and body schema – effectively suppress the essential insight that *movement creates its own space, time, and force, and thereby the dynamics that are movement itself*. If movement did not create its own space, time, and force, there would be no such thing as habit: no specific kinetic dynamic would exist to repeat, to practice, to learn. Equally, there would be nothing to remember, hence, no kinesthetic memory.

The pointillist conception of movement that body schema and body image implicitly support emanates from a bias of Western thought that anchors reality in the spatiality of things to the exclusion of their temporality, i.e., their impermanence, their flow, their temporal dynamics. A Western predilection for mechanics over dynamics, for mass – *things* – over flow – *dynamics* (e.g., Yates 1987; Kelso 1995) – testifies to this bias. Traditional views of motor behavior, motor memory, motor control, motor habits, and so on, exemplify a further dimension of the bias in their Cartesian reduction of movement to objects in motion, quantifiable *things* tied to positions in space and moments in time, and either by nature not kinesthetically attuned or by manner of study not recognized as being kinesthetically attuned. Not only is it easier to explain conditioned eye-blinking (see Note 5) by way of objects in motion than to describe dynamic processes like piano-playing by way of kinesthesia and kinesthetic memory, but it is less perilous ontologically: like mechanisms, objects in motion are spatially-localized, stable entities that anchor functions. Correlatively, distinct units in the brain dedicated to short-term storage and long-term storage, and opposing species of memory – e.g., fact, declarative, and representational as against skill, procedural, and dispositional, respectively (Goethals & Soloman 1989: 5]) – specify solid, well-defined memory repositories and categories as the kinetic dynamics of kinesthetic memory do not. Clearly, a motorized mechanics-over-dynamics goes hand in hand with a conception of movement that eschews the temporal in favor of the spatial.

---

of innervations and denervations. What he terms the "dynamic stereotype" is habit, a basically invariant but still kinetically variable phenomenon: "*the invariant motor task is fulfilled not by a constant, fixed set, but by a varying set of movements which, however, lead to the constant, invariant effect*" (1973: 248). Transferability is thus grounded not in a body image but in dynamic sedimentations constituting a familiar dynamics anchored in kinesthetic memory.

Being temporal by nature, kinesthetic memories, like kinetic melodies, subsume not only rhythmicities within their compass, but temporally unfolding postural and orientational relations, kinetic protentions and retentions, and so on. Kinesthetic memory is thus not a pointillist system of remembered *sensations*, but a remembered spatio-temporal-energic dynamics. Indeed, kinesthetic memory is not memory of sensations of one's body, but of perceptions of the dynamics of self-movement. The point warrants elaboration.

Kinetic melodies are subtended by kinetic harmonies. Everyday movement involves the whole body; coordinated movement is the result of global kinetic orchestrations. Kinetic melodies are thus grounded in a *kinetic harmonics* that is the whole moving body. In turn, the experience of movement is not a matter of localized and discrete bodily sensations, but of a felt harmonious whole where particular areas may be tonally dominant, as when one kicks a ball, moves a fork to one's mouth, or stands up. Discrete, localized bodily sensations – sensations *as such* – are not dynamic awarenesses but preeminently positional ones like itchings and ticklings. Neurophysiologists Jonathan Cole and Jacques Paillard's (1995: 256) perspicuous but kinetically unelaborated distinction between "topokinetic" movement (e.g., pointing to a place on the body where one was touched) and "morphokinetic" movement (e.g., drawing figure eights in the air in front of one) adumbrates the difference between positional and dynamic awarenesses of movement. To be topokinetically attuned – to attend to or remember positional sensations *as such* – is to reduce movement to an object in motion in the manner of Descartes and thereby forego the sense of a dynamic kinetic harmonics. (It is significant that Cole and Paillard describe the *gestural language* of deafferented subjects as a "morphokinetic melody," while otherwise explaining the subjects' movement in terms of body image and body schema [ibid.: 259].) The kinesthetic memory of walking – *not a visual image but a morphokinetic recollection* – subsumes a kinetic harmonics; the memory is not a memory of positions but of a whole body dynamic, which is based not on bodily sensations – localized, positional happenings – but on the perception of movement. In short, kinesthetic memories are constituted through and through by dynamic, not sensational, sedimentations. There is in fact no position that the body is *in* in walking.[14]

The liabilities of a pointillist conception of movement point toward a challenging methodological question: what justifies starting with pathology, i.e., the loss of kinetic melodies? If the purpose is to understand everyday self-movement, why not start with a magnification of such movement rather than with its diminishment? Why, for example, not begin with dance, and ask whether motor theories, body schemas, and body images are up to the task of explaining how such intricate and complicated ongoing movement is learned and remembered. Merleau-Ponty spoke of dancing as a "motor habit" and said that "forming the habit of dancing is discovering, by analysis,

---

14. – any more than there is a position that the wind is *in* in blowing, or that a wave is *in* in rolling forward.

the formula of the movement in question" (Merleau-Ponty 1962: 146, 142, respectively). Of his dance "Untitled Solo," Merce Cunningham wrote,

> A large gamut of movements, separate for each of the three dances, was devised, movements for the arms, the legs, the head and the torso which were separate and essentially tensile in character, and off the normal or tranquil body-balance. The separate movements were arranged in continuity by random means, allowing for the superimposition (addition) of one or more, each having its own rhythm and time-length. But each succeeded in becoming continuous if I could wear it long enough, like a suit of clothes.   (Cunningham: undated, unpaginated)

Untitled Solo is hardly a motor habit and learning it was hardly learning "by analysis, the formula of the movement." Through practice, the dance became a kinesthetically crystallized whole, etched in kinesthetic memory and articulated by way of kinesthetic memory. Were one to take Cunningham's description as a transcendental clue to coordinated movement, one might say that if one "wears movement long enough," it can become a kinetic dynamic that spins continuously out of one's body like the web of a web-spinning spider.

Beginning with extraordinary rather than diminished kinetic capacities means beginning with "the thing itself" and gaining direct knowledge about the inherent dynamics of movement.[15] While in one sense extraordinary movement is at the other extreme of pathological movement, the idea of a linking continuum is methodologically misleading, for precisely by beginning with the extraordinary, one begins with the neurological and experiential reality of a kinetic melody and a kinetic harmonics, and goes from there to foundational dynamic understandings. A methodological focus on the extraordinary has the power to bring these dynamic understandings to light because it magnifies rather than constricts subtleties and complexities inherent in kinesthetic experience and kinesthetic memory.

A phenomenological afterword

To say that our tactile-kinesthetic/affective bodies are at the core of our being resonates with infant psychiatrist Daniel Stern's descriptive account of the development of a "core self." In particular, infant life is grounded experientially in what Stern identifies and describes as "self-agency," "self-coherence," "self-affectivity," and "self-history" (Stern 1985; for a detailed analysis and discussion of our tactile-kinesthetic bodies

---

15. Such knowledge depends on a qualified observer. If cognitive science is to make use of experiential reports, it should insure that reportees are trained if not in phenomenological methodology, then in "auto-sensory observation" (Jacobson 1967, 1970). IW's report of "a 'crude' sense of effort" (Gallagher and Cole 1998: 137) is tantalizing in this respect. What is this "crude" sense?

in infancy and their integral relationship to Stern's designation of a "core self," see Sheets-Johnstone 1999/expanded 2nd ed. 2011: Chapter V). An infant's experiential-ly-grounded core self is of course "situated"; in descriptively apt Husserlian terms, it is the zero point of a surrounding world, a world of other living beings as well as objects. Moreover it should be obvious that self-other and subject-world relationships develop from infancy onward; that is, our intercorporeal and surrounding world relationships are developmentally elaborated not simply in the course of infancy, but in childhood, and in adulthood. Accordingly, no more than our tactile-kinesthetic/affective bodies does our "core self" need to be "embedded" in the world, "situated" here or there; it is always and already at the zero point of orientation toward whoever or whatever is sensuously present. Realizing this fact, one readily realizes that movement – precisely as in *self-agency* – and affectivity – precisely as in *self-affectivity* – are basic aspects of human life, hence basic aspects of human memory involving "self-coherence" and "self-history" as well. One readily realizes in turn that cognitive-based taxonomies of memory that omit in particular the experienced bodily complexities and subtleties of self-movement and self-affectivity are clearly amiss. Indeed, perhaps the most surpris-ing aspect of cognitive taxonomies of memory is not only the absence of movement *as such*, i.e., of *kinesthetic memory*, but the absence of emotions in any substantive expe-riential sense. Fuchs mentions "traumatic memory" in his taxonomic scheme (Fuchs 2003: 7–8) and neuropsychological studies are replete with case histories of amnesic patients (see, for example, Broadbent, Clark, Zola & Squire 2002), for example, but the broad experiential palette of emotional life and its memorial resonances, rever-berations, and repercussions are missing. Edward Casey's acute and trenchant phe-nomenological insights into *body memory* in his penetrating study of remembering is a palliative to these absences (Casey 1987). Casey, it should be noted, is a Jungian psychoanalyst in addition to being a philosopher. It bears notice too that with respect to 'bodily remembering', Casey explicitly states that his concern is not with "memory of the body," but precisely with *body memory* (ibid.: 147). I turn to his chapter on body memory in this brief but hopefully substantive Afterword to highlight both his insights on the topic and the possible paths of inquiry we might gainfully think about, ponder, and explore in response to his analysis.

Prior to his experiential exemplification and discussion of "three major types of body memory" (ibid.), Casey makes several general observations that merit direct quotation:

1. "Body memory alludes to memory that is intrinsic to the body, to its own ways of remembering, how we remember in and by and through the body. Memory *of* the body refers to those manifold manners whereby we remember the body as the accusative object of our awareness.... [A]t a number of points in the present chapter I fall prey to the all too natural temptation to substitute a recollective con-sciousness of the body as I remember it 'objectively' for the way the body itself, in its sinews and on its surfacc, remembers is own activity" (ibid.).

2. "Bergson is the first philosopher to have devoted concerted attention to [memory]; but he took a part of such memory (i.e., 'habit memory') for the whole of it. Merleau-Ponty, very much inspired by the example of Bergson, speaks of the body as 'habitual' ... [but] fails to underline the importance of body *memory* as such. If Merleau-Ponty fills the void left gaping in Heidegger's *Being and Time* [with respect to 'something going wrong'] ... his own text exhibits a no less glaring lacuna in its bypassing of body memory" (ibid.).
3. I am proposing that the body is of centralmost concern in any adequate assessment of the range of remembering's powers.... If the body is indeed 'the natural subject of perception' and the 'point of view on points of view' [quotes from Merleau-Ponty], body memory is in turn the natural center of any sensitive account of remembering. It is a privileged point of view from which other memorial points of view can be regarded and by which they can be illuminated" (ibid.: 147–148).

Casey tests and documents just such observations and claims in descriptively exact examples he gives within the three major types of memory that he analyzes: habitual memory, traumatic (exemplifying painful) memory, and erotic (exemplifying pleasurable) memory. In each instance, his examples testify to his observation that body memory is a matter of memory "in and by and through the body," not memory of an object-body. His ensuing discussion of the *marginality* of body memory in each of the major types of body memory challenges us to think about the different temporal modes in which body memory is peripheral to, or at a remove from the actual present, not only as in moving through habitual everyday engrained patterns of movement, but as in blocking out the past to avoid pain and in inclining toward the future when, as a possibility, we think or imagine ourselves enjoying what we might call "more of the same." His discussion of the *depth and density* of body memory is equally provocative in illuminating spatial dimensions of body memory as is his discussion of the *co-immanence of past and present* that illuminates further temporal dimensions. With respect to depth and density, for example, Casey observes that "Body memories manifest themselves as continually vanishing into the depths of our corporeal existence – and just as continually welling up from the same depths" (ibid.: 166); with respect to co-immanence of past and present, he observes that "[W]e should speak of *immanence* rather than of 'intersection' between past and present. Instead of taking up a perspective on the past ... in body memories we allow the past to enter actively into the very present in which our remembering is taking place" (ibid.: 168). He goes on actually to demonstrate how spatial and temporal aspects of body memory are in reality intertwined, that is, how they are inseparably interconnected.

After stating "baldly" that "*there is no memory without body memory*" at the beginning of his penultimate section of the chapter (ibid.: 172; italics in original), Casey proceeds to perhaps the most provocative questions: "How can body memory, which is typically so reticent and so submerged, be so basic for all memory? In what does its peculiar importance consist?" (ibid.). His follow-up explication, which draws on philosopher Alfred North Whitehead's *Process and Reality,* is challenging and impels us precisely to ponder the questions more and more deeply: if there is indeed no memory without body memory, what is the basis of the anchoring import of body memory and how is it that it plays such a typically recessive role in what we deem "memory"?

The questions can readily prompt us to recall the insuppressibility of kinesthesia. In turn, we might initially ask whether it is possible to connect Jeannerod's passing but seminally significant comment about our ever-present awareness of our moving bodies, however marginalized that awareness might be, with the foundational status of body memory, however marginalized that foundational status might be? If a connection can be made, then the fact that *body memory* is at the core of memory correlates in exacting ways with the fact that *kinesthesia* is at the core of our being, or in broader terms, that animation defines the nature of life. Indeed, from the beginning to the end of our lives, we humans, like other species within the Kingdom Animalia, are *animate* forms – in Husserlian terms, "*animate organisms.*" Kinesthesia and kinesthetic memory are from this perspective natural built-ins of life. Casey's phenomenological exemplifications and probings of body memory challenge us to think along these lines. His insights about the experiential nature and scope of body memory clearly confront us with questions warranting our studious attention and active investigation.

References

Aristotle (1963). *Categories.* Trans. J. L. Ackrill. In J. Barnes (Ed.), *The complete works of Aristotle,* Vol. 1 (pp. 3–24), Princeton: Princeton University Press.

Baars, B. J. & Gage, N. M. (2010). *Cognition, brain, and consciousness: Introduction to cognitive neuroscience* (2nd ed.). San Diego, CA US: Elsevier Academic Press.

Bergson, H. (1991). *Matter and memory,* Trans. N. M. Paul & W. S. Palmer. New York: Zone Books.

Bernstein, N. (1984). Biodynamics of locomotion. In H. T. A. Whiting (Ed.), *Human motor actions: Bernstein reassessed* (pp. 171–222). Amsterdam: North-Holland.

Bernstein, N. (1996). On dexterity and its development. In M. L. Latash & M. T. Turvey (Eds.), *Dexterity and its development* (pp. 3–244). Norwood, NJ: Lawrence Erlbaum.

Bloom, L. (1993). *The transition from infancy to language: Acquiring the power of expression.* New York: Cambridge University Press.

Broadbent, N. J., Clark, R. E., Zola, S. & Squire, L. R. (2002). The medial temporal lobe and memory. In L. R. Squire & D. K. Schacter (Eds.), *Neuropsychology of memory.* New York/London: Guilford Press.

Casey, E. S. (1987). *Remembering: A phenomenological study.* Bloomington: Indiana University Press.

Cole, J. & Paillard, J. (1995). Living without touch and information about body position and movement. Studies on deafferented subjects. In J. Bermudez, A. Marcel & N. Iylan (Eds.), *The body and the self* (pp. 245–266). Cambridge, MA: MIT Press.

Cunningham, M. (undated). *Changes: Notes on choreography*. In F. Starr (Ed.). New York: Something Else Press.

Descartes, R. (1985) [1644]. *Principles of philosophy. The philosophical writings of Descartes* (1st ed). Trans. J. Cottingham, R. Stoothoff & D. Murdoch. Cambridge: Cambridge University Press.

Flash, T. (2001). Motor learning. *Science, 275*, 1612–1613.

Fuchs, T. (2003). *The memory of the body*, http://www.klinikum.uni-heidelberg.de/fileadmin/zpm/psychatrie/ppp2004/manuskript/fuchs.pdf.

Gallagher, S. (1986). Body image and body schema: A conceptual clarification. *Journal of Mind and Behavior, 7*(4), 541–554.

Gallagher, S. (1995). Body schema and intentionality. In J. Bermúdez, A. J. Marcel, N. Eilan, J. Bermúdez, A. J. Marcel & N. Eilan (Eds.), *The body and the self* (pp. 225–244). Cambridge, MA: MIT Press.

Gallagher, S. (2005). *How the body shapes the mind*. Oxford: Oxford University Press.

Gallagher, S. & Cole, J. (1998). Body image and body schema in a deafferented subject. In D. Welton (Ed.), *Body and flesh* (pp. 131–147). Oxford: Blackwell.

Goethals, G. R. & Soloman, P. R. (1989). Interdisciplinary perspectives on the study of memory. In P. R. Soloman, G. R. Goethals, C. M. Kelley & B. R. Stephens (Eds.), *Memory: Interdisciplinary approaches*. New York: Springer-Verlag.

Goldberg, E. (1990). Tribute to A. R. Luria. In E. Goldberg (Ed.), *Contemporary neuropsychology and the legacy of Luria* (pp. 1–9). Hillsdale, NJ: Lawrence Erlbaum.

Goldstein, K. (1939). *The organism: A holistic approach to biology derived from pathological data in man*. New York: American Book Company.

Gowitzke, B. A. & Milner, M. (1988). *Scientific bases of human movement (3rd ed.)*. Baltimore: Williams and Wilkins.

Hallett, M., Pascual-Leone, A. & Topka, H. (1996). Adaptation and skill learning: Evidence for different neural substrates. In J. R. Bloedel, T. J. Ebner & S. P. Wise (Eds.), *The acquisition of motor behavior in vertebrates*. Cambridge: Bradford Book, MIT Press.

Hanna, R., & Thompson, E. (2003). Neurophenomenology and the spontaneity of consciousness. In E. Thompson (Ed.), *The problem of ponsciousness* (pp. 133–162). Calgary, Alberta, CA: University of Calgary Press.

Heidegger, M. (1962). *Being and time*. Trans. J. Macquarrie & E. Robinson. New York: Harper & Row.

Husserl, E. (1964). *The phenomenology of internal time consciousness*. Trans. J. S. Churchill. Bloomington: Indiana University Press.

Husserl, E. (1970). *The crisis of the Euroepean sciences and transcendental phenomenology*. Trans. D. Carr. Evanston, IL: Northwestern University Press.

Husserl, E. (1973). *Cartesian meditations*, Trans. Dorion Cairns. The Hague: Martinus Nijhoff.

Husserl, E. (1980). *Ideas pertaining to a pure phenomenology and to a phenomenological philosophy, Book 3*. Trans. T. E. Klein & W. E. Pohl. The Hague: Martinus Nijhoff.

Husserl, E. (1989). *Ideas pertaining to a pure phenomenology and to a phenomenological philosophy, Book 2*. Trans. R. Rojcewicz & A. Schuwer. Boston: Kluwer Academic.

Jacobson, E. (1967). *Biology of emotions*. Springfield, IL: Charles C. Thomas.

Jacobson, E. (1970). *Modern treatment of tense patients*. Springfield, IL: Charles C. Thomas.

Jeannerod, Marc. (2006). *Motor cognition: What actions tell the self*. Oxford: Oxford University Press.

Johnstone, A. (2001). *The liar syndrome*. Unpublished paper.

Kelso, J. A. S. (1995). *Dynamic patterns*. Cambridge: Bradford Book/MIT Press.

Kugler, P. N. & Turvey, M. T. (1987). *Information, natural law, and the self-assembly of rhythmic movement*. Hillsdale, NJ: Lawrence Erlbaum.

Luria, A. R. (1966). *Human brain and psychological processes*, Trans. Basil Haigh. New York: Harper & Row.

Luria, A. R. (1973). *The working brain*, Trans. B. Haigh. Harmondsworth, Middlesex, England: Penguin Books.

Luria, A. R. (1979). *The making of mind*, In M. Cole & S. Cole (Eds). Cambridge: Harvard University Press.

Luria, A. R. (1980). *Higher cortical functions in man* (2nd ed.). Trans. B. Haigh. New York: Basic Books.

Merleau-Ponty, M. (1962). *Phenomenology of perception*. Trans. Colin Smith. London: Routledge & Kegan Paul.

Merleau-Ponty, M. (1964). Eye and mind. In J. M. Edie (Ed.), *The primacy of perception* (pp.159–90). Evanston: Northwestern University Press.

Noë, A. (2004). *Action in perception*. Cambridge, MA: MIT Press.

Plato (1937a). *Phaedrus*. Trans. B. Jowett. In *The dialogues of Plato*, Vol. 1 (pp. 233–282). New York: Random House.

Plato (1937b). *Statesman*. Trans. B. Jowett. In *The dialogues of Plato*, Vol. 2 (pp. 283–340). New York: Random House.

Pribram, K. (1966). *Preface to A. R. Luria's human brain and psychological processes* (pp. xiii–xv). New York: Harper & Row.

Pribram, K. (1980). *Preface to A. R. Luria's higher cortical functions in man* (2nd ed.) (pp. xv–xvi). New York: Basic Books.

Sacks, O. (1972). *Foreword to A. Luria's 'The man with a shattered world'*. Trans. L. Solotaroff. Cambridge: Harvard University Press.

Searle, J. (1992). *The rediscovery of the mind*. Cambridge, MA: Bradford Books/MIT Press.

Sheets-Johnstone, M. (1966) [1979/1980]. *The phenomenology of dance*. Madison, WI: University of Wisconsin Press. [Second editions: London: Dance Books Ltd. 1979; New York: Arno Press, 1980].

Sheets-Johnstone, M. (1990). *The roots of thinking*. Philadelphia: Temple University Press.

Sheets-Johnstone, M. (1999/expanded 2nd ed. 2011). *The primacy of movement*. Philadelphia: John Benjamins.

Sheets-Johnstone, M. (2002). Descriptive foundations. *Interdisciplinary Studies in Literature and Environment, 9*(1), 165–179.

Sheets-Johnstone, M. (2003). Kinesthetic Memory. In S. Gallagher & N. Depraz (Eds.), *Theoria et Historia Scientiarum*, Vol. VII, No. 1 (pp. 69–92), special issue on "Embodiment and Awareness".

Sheets-Johnstone, M. (2005). What sre we naming? In H. De Preester & V. Knockaert (Eds.), *Body image and body schema* (pp. 211–231). Amsterdam: John Benjamins.

Sheets-Johnstone, M. (2011a). From movement to dance, forthcoming in special issue of *Phenomenology and the Cognitive Sciences* on dance (ed. Ivar Hagendoorn & Tomasz Komendinzski).

Sheets-Johnstone, M. (2011b). Fundamental and inherently related aspects of animation. Forthcoming in A. Foolen, U. Ludtke, J. Zlatcv & T. Racine (Eds.), *Moving ourselves, moving others: The role of e(motion) for intersubjectivity, consciousness, and language*. Amsterdam: John Benjamins.

Stern, D. N. (1985). *The interpersonal world of the infant: A view from psychoanalysis and developmental psychology*. New York: Basic Books.

Teuber, H.-L. (1966). *Preface to A. R. Luria's 'Human brain and psychological processes'* (pp. vii–xi). New York: Harper & Row.

Teuber, H.-L. (1980). *Preface to A. R. Luria's 'Higher cortical functions in man'* (2nd ed) (pp. xi–xiv). New York: Basic Books.

Thelen, E. & Smith, L. B. (1994). *A dynamic systems approach to the development of cognition and action*. Cambridge: Bradford/MIT Press.

Thompson, E. (2007). *Mind in life: Biology, phenomenology, and the sciences of mind*. Cambridge, MA: Harvard University Press/Belknap Press.

van Gelder, T. & Port, R. F. (1995). It's about time: An overview of the dynamical approach to cognition. In T. van Gelder & R. F. Port (Eds.), *Mind as motion: Explorations in the dynamics of cognition* (pp. 1–43). Cambridge: Bradford Books/MIT Press.

Wilberg, R. B. (1983). Memory for movement. In R. A. Magill (Ed.), *Memory and control of action* (pp. 39–46). Amsterdam: North-Holland.

Yates, F. E. (1987). *Foreword to P. N. Kugler and M. T. Turvey's 'Information, natural law, and the self-assembly of self-movement'*. Hillsdale, NJ: Lawrence Erlbaum.

Zahavi, D. (2005). *Subjectivity and selfhood: Investigating the first-person perspective*. Cambridge, MA: MIT Press.

CHAPTER 4

Comment on Thomas Fuchs*

The time of the explicating process

Eugene T. Gendlin
University of Chicago

The body has at last entered our current intellectual discourse. Fuchs provides another advance in that development. Until recently the most common question my philosophy would elicit was "But why the body?" Fuchs systematically describes how the body's memory functions in all present living. He brings its ubiquitous performances together and classifies them. I will comment on this valuable treatise, and extend its import. I will add a distinction. I propose concepts of a different kind for some of his major terms.

Keywords: body memory, implicit processes, explicating process, creative processes of body memory

I

I certainly agree with what Fuchs vividly and directly points to. I do have one objection: He tells it all as if the body's performances consisted only of the learn*ed*, automat*ed*, repeat*ed*, "-ed," only habits, repetitions, *re*-enactments, as if the body could only *repeat* its past, as if it were incapable of anything new.

> Through repetition and exercise, a habit has developed. Long-trained patterns of movement and perception have been embodied …[I]mplicit memory … does not re-present the past, but re-enacts it in the course of the body's performance. What we have acquired as skills, habits and experience, has become what we are today; implicit knowing is our *lived past*. (Fuchs 2003: 1)

What Fuchs doesn't quite say but shows throughout is that the past reshapes itself in the course of the body's present performance. Of course the past exists and functions

---

* This comment refers to the online article of Thomas Fuchs from 2003, available at: http://www.klinikum.uni-heidelberg.de/fileadmin/zpm/psychatrie/ppp2004/manuskript/fuchs.pdf.

in and as our new present. But the present must be capable of something new, otherwise past experience could not have happened either. The past might have been based on a previous past, but at some point it had to be new. And not only at an earlier point. Present experiencing is always capable of something new that reshapes the past.

The present living process *reshapes its past by reshaping itself*, reshaping what it was. In every living process each next bit reshapes the previous. We could say that the past reshapes itself as present living. Or, we could say that present living *generates* a "past" *by* reshaping itself.

The past is not past because an observer determines that it happened at an earlier position on Newton's absolute time line. The past is the living process's own past, *made past* by its new present. Or, we can say the past makes itself past by functioning to shape a new present. If one living process is both (and I agree it is), we have to say that it is a constantly self-reshaping process.

But this regenerative living process does not fit the familiar conceptual models; it fits neither the model of separate single unit-events, nor the usual holism. Fuchs uses both although the body's performance points beyond them.

He speaks of *explicit* memory as recording "single events," as if the objective environment consisted of single events. And he calls *implicit* memory "holistic:"

> ... skills that have been formed by repetition and automation. They integrate *single elements* into *holistic* temporal patterns ...   (Fuchs 2003: 2, my emphasis)

I don't think Fuchs wants to *assume the old model of environmental reality as meaningless singles that have to be integrated into meaningful patterns and wholes.*

In my view, there is a more original tie between body and environment. Living process *is* body-environment interaction, always already organized and patterned, not first meaningless separate events that have to be integrated. The earlier patterns function implicitly in the development of more complex patterns.

It is true, however, that we first learn many things in separate singles, so I need to make a distinction: The separate singles that we learn are made later, after a new pattern emerges. Civilization is passed on by dividing creative innovations into single parts so that everyone can learn them. The singles are made from a creative innovation after it has come.

Quite different from singles, Fuchs shows something more profound: the natural process of a living body building upon itself. This *natural* building upon itself is not an integration of prior singles.

To view the living process as beginning with singles is a case of the traditional Western model which always assumes that nature consists of the units which logical analysis separates and combines. The recent analytic creations are read back into all the earlier, more basic processes. But we can honor and use the immense contributions of the analytic unit model and still also have the new science of living bodies which is developing right here. *How the living process reshapes itself need not be reduced to later-made singles.*

Take Fuchs' example of learning how to waltz. Certainly it is a *learned* rhythm, but we could not learn it if the body's living process didn't already have some rhythms or the capacity for rhythm. Some person's body process *first generated* the waltz pattern. Then it was divided into parts, so that now others can learn part-moves until the rhythm emerges for them too. It emerges as a new form reshaping the human body's rhythms. And because it can emerge from human bodies, therefore everyone *can* learn it.

Dancing is not just the learned steps. Dancing is the original body process now further developed.

We learn reading and writing like we learn the waltz. As individuals we learn the letters first, but letters are a "recent" Phoenician innovation after writing was in word-pictures for thousands of years. They broke the sound-patterns of words up into separate sound parts so that letters could stand for sound-parts.

Like the waltz rhythm, the word-sound patterns developed first. And what we recognize when we read is still the words, the *pattern* of letters, not letter by letter. We recognize the words just as we used to recognize them in picture writing. Well, of course. This is how we recognize cats and dogs, and all objects. We recognize them by their patterns, not by integrating single parts. Breaking things up into units for analysis, teaching, automation, and technology is a later development, not the beginning of living processes.

The significance of what Fuchs describes goes further. Understanding what the body provides takes one beyond the current conceptual models. It can reshape the current conceptual models. As he says,

> The memory of the body is an impressive refutation of the dualism of consciousness and the physical body.   (Fuchs 2003: 2)

If what Fuchs points to is the case – and it is – then it also instances a very different overall conceptual model. The body's performances go beyond single units or holism. I will now try to show an alternative model in a few instances.

II

I will reformulate a few terms Fuchs uses, so that they don't fall back into either of the old models. Seeing the performances of the body can liberate us from them if we have an alternative. Elsewhere I have developed a model of process (Gendlin 1997, in press). I will use it to reformulate four terms: "holism," "time," "space," and "intercorporeal memory" (emotion, affect-motor schema).

"Melted" and "holism"

Developing previous patterns into higher order patterns is characteristic of all living process, even the most primitive kind. Animals also generate new behavior, and human bodies generate new cognitive patterns as well. All living process constantly reshapes itself.

But all living is internally complex. Even a single cell does many things at once. These are not separate singles, but they always remain many *specific* events. They happen in an interrelated way. These unseparated specifics are not "holistic," not merged or melted. They remain precise and rigorously specific.

In Fuchs' example, each of the piano player's fingers functions specifically with its own sequence of acts. No "holistic" merger could play the piece. Fuchs certainly doesn't deny the specific precision of each finger. He uses the old word "holistic" only to say that the player plays without retrieving the single finger movements. Similarly, his word "melted" is meant to describe how they are in the player's awareness, not how they function.

This kind of "specificity" goes beyond the old models according to which everything must be either separate or merged. To conceptualize this kind of specificity we need a new kind of concept. We can create the concept right here from how each finger performs its specific actions. Let us allow this way of functioning to define a concept. How we name it is less important. I propose *"functional specificity," "unseparated multiplicity"* and *"implicit precision"* (see Gendlin 1997, in press).[1]

But what is in the player's consciousness is not at all indeterminate. It is *more determined* than a fixed pattern because it is *both* finely specific *and* open to being enacted in a new way.

For example, a musical composition first comes to the composer as an improvisation directly from the body. Then it is written down because the composer deems it worth keeping. Composers first *play* (in both meanings of the word), then there is something to write in notes and measures. But a great score is an opportunity for fresh unique expression. If just the score is repeated, critics complain that the performance was pointless. And even the performer's unique way of playing can lose its exciting effect if it is played as something repeatable. The performer strives to let it come as a fresh expression (see Gendlin 1993).

In the old models it would be paradoxical to speak of a bodily sense that is both finely determined and is also an open implying of fresh further coming. But we can allow this to define a concept. I call it a "felt sense."[2]

"Unseparated multiplicity" and "felt sense" begin to tell this different kind of order, the order of implicit process, more order than the fixed patterns of a static "is."

---

1.   Hegel's holism refers only to thought. The body is assumed to be purely mechanical. Hegel dismissed actual experiencing as indeterminate in the first few pages of his *Phenomenology* (see Schoeller, in press). So his view was nothing like the bodily experiential differentiation.

2.   A *felt sense* can always form and come if one invites it. With a little training people can learn to put their attention into the body and invite the *physical quality* of right now (expansive, constricted, heavy, jumpy, or no word for it, just … *this* quality). The quality changes with each thing, however large or tiny. If the unique quality actually comes, then further steps come *from it*. We call this practice "focusing" (Gendlin 1978/2009, 1997).

Temporal patterns – Zeitgestalten

If we think the words, our fingers type the letters. Fuchs very revealingly points out that we can do a complex action if we aim at the result we want. We cannot do it if we aim first at one part, and then the next. This is familiar, but it can be quite startling when we have to do something that is new. We move ahead with just the aim, not knowing what we will actually do. The body has to find the actual doing, and quite often it does! Letting the body do it may bring more into the new doing than we know.

How the envisioned future can imply and shape the ensuing present shows vividly that the living process doesn't happen only in linear time, now now now. Nor is it enough to say with Husserl that each moment has a "protension" to the next. *The whole sequence is always implied*, although nothing like it may ever have happened before. But also in ordinary actions the whole sequence is implied. The aim is present throughout. The enacting *happens into* the implied sequence. The now now now *occurs into* the implying.

I propose an expanded model of time. Time does not consist only of nows. The now now now *occurs into* the implying which is thereby *carried forward*.[3]

Linear time consists merely of positions on an observer's time line. The positions are supposed to be external and independent of what happens. Linear time is an empty frame. The time patterns (Zeitgestalten) of a living process are its own, the body carrying itself forward.

The future that is present now is not a time-position, not what will be past later. The future that is here now is the implying that is here now. The past is not an earlier position but the now implicitly functioning past. (For this more intricate model of time in detail, see Gendlin 1997: IVB.)

Getting our bearings in space

We don't live in empty abstract geometric space either, as Fuchs points out. "Situations … are more than abstract entities." He cites for example "a roaring soccer game." He points to the inherent relation of "wohnen" (inhabiting) and "Gewohnheit" (habit). I would add only that the living activity comes before the repetition.

We don't want to assume that empty geometric space is the reality, as if the space that living generates were only subjective, only due to repetition of separable units. Let us not assume a universe of separated units in empty space. Such units are essential for technology and making things. But nothing living consists of separated units. A universe consisting of separated units could not have living processes in it.

---

3. "*Carrying forward*" relates back as well as forward. Its time is retroactive. It is a further development which now says what "*was*" there then (see Gendlin & Lemke 1983). We predicted that time symmetry would be violated, which has recently come about. We predicted that relativity limitations on quantum equations would be loosened, which has not yet happened.

The featureless space comes from human making (*homo faber*). Humans make new things and fill the world with them. We make furniture from trees. Making things requires making separate parts which we can glue together, or analytic parts which we logically connect. We move separated parts *from here to there* and combine them. Human making happens in seemingly featureless here-there space. It is a space just of motion, changes in locations. It is an abstract frame of points and mathematics, a wonderful human creation.[4]

Fuchs rightly speaks of "a procedural field of possibility." I add that we live in the space of developing tissues, behavior possibilities, cognition, and felt senses. The body's performances could not happen if the featureless space of mere locations were the nature of the universe.

Interaction

Fuchs says:

> ... the motor, emotional and social development in early childhood does not run on separate tracks, but is tightly connected through integrated affect-motor schemata.   (Fuchs 2003: 4)

He cites

> what Daniel Stern calls implicit relational knowing – a bodily knowing of how to deal with others, how to have fun with them...   (Fuchs 2003: 5)

In the context of the body's relational knowing, words such as "affect," "motor," and "emotion" no longer say what we want to say. These old words involve the assumption that our situations and interactions are subjective epiphenomena in a universe of separate parts. In what way motor and emotional and social development are "not on separate tracks" points to something else, not just to a combination of them.

Fuchs points out that someone's cowed posture tells us a lot about that person. The posture is not just the spatial relation of shoulders and limbs.

We can build on what Fuchs says. The body's understanding of others is *prior* to our understanding of ourselves. G. H. Mead (1934: 138) argued that self-knowledge develops from prior empathy with others. Wittgenstein wrote: "Think, too, how one can imitate someone's face without seeing one's own in a mirror" (1953: 285). Our bodies can produce the other person's face and posture because they respond *directly* to each other's expressions.

This prior interconnection is one strand of the larger fact that every living body *is* body-environment interaction. The body consists of body-environment interaction

---

4. Quantum physics has taken a big step beyond featureless space. Featureless space still persists because it is built into most of our concepts.

long before there is a separate body distinct from a separate environment around it. Living bodies and their environment are a much more original interaction, long before perception and sentience (consciousness) develop so that we perceive a body here separate from an environment there.

We *are* body-environment interaction. Other people are an essential part of the environmental interaction which we are. We live our situations with our bodies. We do a lot more with our bodies than we know about. That is why others can sense what we ourselves don't know in ourselves. Our bodies live directly in our situations. That is why focusing works (see Note 2).

When I attend directly to the body-sense that can come about any situation, a whole field of detail opens. I hear from the *"me"* that *"I"* don't know so well.[5]

Human situations and interactions involve expressive patterns, but these living patterns do not lock us in as fixed patterns do. Rather than allowing only what fits within fixed patterns, we develop them by living *further*. In the continuation of living process a pattern *is* a further *implying*.

We can see the different kind of order that is characteristic of implicit functioning in the surprising fact that everyone becomes understandable if they keep going "on in," if they keep differentiating their experience further and further. At first they are often closed puzzles, even to themselves.

We are learning how to listen to each other, to say back what we understand so as to check it, to accept correction after correction until at last the person exhales a "Yes, that's what I mean." Then a characteristic little silence ensues. In that little silence the person tends to go deeper. The next saying is often from a deeper level, eventually to felt sensing.

Our bodies can feel-understand anyone who differentiates from *felt sense* to *felt sense* far enough. Experiential differentiation has a different kind of "*universality*," just as it is precisely the performer's "unique" musical expression which reaches our bodies. The body can empathically generate this universal uniqueness, even when it is utterly foreign to how we ourselves actually live and think. There is no universality whatever in human content. But experiential differentiation is understandable to everyone who listens; it has a superordinate kind of universality.

III

In conclusion

a.   We are learning how to move beyond the old determinism. We are at the beginning of a new science of living process, a more open culture, and a new development of the individual.

---

5.   This is similar but not the same as G. H. Mead's theory of the "I" and the "me" (1934: 173).

Freud found an impossibility of change on many dimensions. Character was unchangeable; children and psychotics couldn't be worked with at all; infantile sexuality and early childhood events were never modifiable; everything was explained by "repetition compulsion." Some things are still unchangeable, but the fact that so many of his impossibles have begun to give way hints that perhaps none of them are inherently impossible. But this has only been the first 100 years, a little more than one lifetime. We are still near the beginning of this human development.

b.   Experiences build upon previous experiences. What once was new becomes an old tool in the formation of a newer new. And this is true of the species and the individual. Each kind of living body is genetically able to do at birth what ancestors slowly developed. And for each of us what we acquired with difficulty is now functioning implicitly in new situations and new developments.

The body's digestion and circulation work reliably and repetitiously although they also produce important effects in each new situation. The body structure is never finished constituting itself. It is not like machines which we first make, and only turn on when completed. The living body constitutes itself from the first cell, and never stops constituting itself further. And so also do new behaviors and cognitions function implicitly in the formation of still newer behaviors and cognitions.

c.   The very power of logic to determine "necessary" implications that explain some puzzle also provides the possibility of going further in a way that exceeds the logic. This seeming paradox is explained if we consider not only the pattern and its logical implications, but also the experiential understanding which the explaining brought. It is not from the flat pattern that we develop beyond it, but from the bodily understanding process. "Aha!" we exclaim as we understand the logical explanation. The bodily aha! involves much more than what can follow from the logic that brought it.

Therefore we need to go back and forth between logic and bodily-felt understanding. They build upon each other. It would be wrong to make an ideology of lauding one and pretending to do without the other.

We see clearly that dividing something into units and explaining it logically can bring a new clarity that is not only the explanation itself, but also a wider bodily carrying forward. New clarity continues the living process. That is why it can be so exciting. Thinking is not just *about* something; thinking *is* a mode of the living process.

Living process does not consist of fixed patterns; it generates the patterns by which it carries itself forward.

d.   There is one living process which continues the past into the new present, in which the past functions. This is not a paradox. In every present living process its past functions implicitly in going beyond itself. The continuing process has a greater kind of order leading to concepts of a new kind. These begin to explain what Fuchs points to, and carry our understanding forward.

References

Fuchs, T. (2003). The memory of the body. http://www.klinikum.uni-heidelberg.de/fileadmin/
     zpm/psychatrie/ppp2004/manuskript/fuchs.pdf.
Gendlin, E. T. (1978/2009). *Focusing.* New York: Bantam Books.
Gendlin, E. T. (1993). *Improvisation provides.* Paper presented at a panel on "Improvisation,"
     organized by Robert Crease at the Society for Phenomenology and Existential Philosophy
     in New Orleans, October 24, 1993. Available at http://www.focusing.org/gendlin/docs/
     gol_2223.html.
Gendlin, E. T. (1997). *A process model.* New York: The Focusing Institute. Also available at
     http://www.focusing.org/process.html.
Gendlin, E. T. (in press). Implicit precision. In Z. Radman (Ed.), *Knowing without thinking:
     The theory of the background in philosophy of mind.* Basingstoke: Palgrave Macmillan. Also
     available at http://www.focusing.org/gendlin/pdf/gendlin_implicit_precision.pdf.
Gendlin, E. T. & J. Lemke (1983). A critique of relativity and localization. *Mathematical Model-
     ing, 4,* 61–72. Also available at http://www.focusing.org/gendlin/docs/gol_2153.html.
Mead, G. H. (1934). *Mind, self, and society.* Chicago: University of Chicago Press.
Schoeller, D. (under review). Experiencing and expressing.
Wittgenstein, L. (1953/2001). *Philosophical investigations.* Blackwell Publishing.

CHAPTER 5

Enduring

A phenomenological investigation

Elizabeth A. Behnke
Study Project in Phenomenology of the Body

This investigation describes a particular form of traumatic body memory that I term "enduring." This is an inner bodily gesture that allows us to endure (withstand, survive) difficult experiences while we are undergoing them, yet may continue to endure (in the temporal sense) long after these experiences are over, whether we are aware of its effect on our ongoing style of embodiment or not. I use a Husserlian phenomenological approach to elucidate the kinaesthetic structure of "enduring," linking it with boundary violation and examining its temporal structure before suggesting some ways in which movement and awareness practices can help to restore a more open, fluid relation to the world in the here and now.

Keywords: Husserl, phenomenology, embodiment, boundary violation, traumatic body memory

> Und man ist dazu da, daß man's ertragt.
> Und in dem "Wie,"
> da liegt der Ganze Unterschied.
> > Die Marschallin, Act One, *Der Rosenkavalier* (1909–1910)
> > Hugo von Hofmannsthal / Richard Strauss

My aim in this paper is to document and describe a specific inner gesture[1] that I shall call "enduring," a term that has a double sense: enduring something means undergoing it in such a way that one is somehow able to bear what one is suffering (German *aushalten, ertragen*), while at the same time, this experience of withstanding what one is enduring is lasting rather than momentary (German *andauern, fortdauern*), demanding persistence and perseverance (German *anhalten, ausdauern*). This double

---

1. For more on the notion of an "inner gesture," see Appendix below.

sense is also expressed in the Latin word from which the English word "endure" derives, for although *indūrāre* – 'to make hard' – can be traced to the Proto-Indo-European root *deru-* ('to be firm, solid, steadfast'), it is also informed by a semantic cross
with the Latin *dūrāre,* 'to last long,' which stems from the Proto-Indo-European *deue-*
('of long duration'). Thus to endure something requires that one become firm and
strong enough to last it out, standing up to it and surviving it rather than succumbing
to it, by offering sustained and solid resistance to it. And I shall explore these themes
in kinaesthetic terms by identifying a persisting style of lived movement that enables
us to endure traumatic events while they are happening, yet may itself endure long
after these events are past, continuing to shape our own lived bodily engagement in
the here and now whether we are aware of it or not.[2]

The present investigation of "enduring" draws upon Husserlian phenomenological methods and research findings.[3] Among other things, this means that I shall be
offering descriptions, not arguments; the aim is to bring to light a particular phenomenon and/or style of experiencing so as to explicate its structures and explore
its implications. In what follows, however, I shall simply report some of the results of
my investigation without discussing the methods employed or the broader phenomenological account of embodiment serving as the context of the investigation.[4] And
in the spirit of the phenomenological turn to the experiential evidence itself, I shall
begin with a turn to 'body-feeling' (*Leibgefühl*), identifying – for the sake of the exposition – four stages in a process that in actual practice can flow more continuously,
skip steps, etc.

Finding the phenomenon: An initial description

(a) Let us say that I become aware of a certain salience within the somaesthetic
field as a whole (and especially in its depths, rather than its merely surface tactile

2.   "Enduring" (which will always be given in quotation marks when I am referring to the
inner gesture under investigation) can be the response to many sorts of adverse or traumatic
events, including not only extremes of torture, abuse, or sexual assault, but other difficult circumstances (e.g., war, forced migration or internal displacement, enemy occupation, terrorist
threat, natural disasters) and emotional situations (e.g., profound loss). Moreover, "enduring"
can have an intercorporeal dimension: a dying woman may be wracked by physical pain, but
the inner gesture of "enduring" may also be found in the son looking into her eyes and trying to
be strong for her, or in the family members listening to evidence in the trial of the man accused
of abducting, torturing, and murdering a child.

3.   References to Husserl are illustrative rather than exhaustive. My approach is particularly
influenced by the late (1929–1934) "C-manuscripts" on time-constitution.

4.   For more on a Husserlian approach to embodiment and kinaesthetic consciousness, see the
discussions and the sources cited in Behnke (1997, 2008a, 2009a, 2009b).

sensitivities): an obscure zone of tension stands out against a more undifferentiated global body-feeling. In contrast to, for example, the sudden onset of a sharp and clearly localized pain, the tension has a certain (though not clearly defined) intensity; it occupies a more or less vaguely circumscribed 'spread' (*Ausbreitung*); and it is given as "continuing," both in the sense of "already underway" (rather than having just begun)[5] and in the sense of "persisting" (rather than ceasing). Thus, for example, while lying quietly on my back in a warm, safe place where I am free from interruptions, I may gradually sense "something" in my upper left torso. However, I may not yet feel this clearly. For example, I may be unsure where the "edges" of what I am feeling are; the vaguely felt sensation may seem to involve part of my upper left arm and part of the left side of my neck as well as my left upper chest, but its mode of givenness may still be nebulous. In fact, I may hardly be certain that I am feeling anything at all. (b) Now, however, comes the crucial move of "yielding" to the feeling, "inhabiting" it – 'being there with it, and remaining with it, in the manner peculiar to feeling' (*fühlendes Dabei-Sein, Dabei-Bleiben*), *undergoing* it, living it from within as something that is happening to me rather than having it over-against me as an object I am observing.[6] In other words, I let go of what I have elsewhere termed a "separative" style of experience (Behnke 1984) in which the experiencer identifies with an ideal "vanishing point" in one's head, behind one's eyes, while the vaguely felt tension is "down there" somewhere "in one's body." Instead, I allow myself to live this very area of my body from within and experiment with opening myself up to the feeling more fully (cf. Behnke 2007:80) in somewhat the same spirit as when one is guided to "relax around the pain" in recuperating from injury. (c) If the tension I am now living-through is indeed an example of the inner gesture of "enduring,"[7] I will now be able to appreciate the distinctive feature of this gesture: it displays a double vector, simultaneously enacting a centripetal move (pulling back inward) and a centrifugal move (pushing outward). In the case of the vaguely felt upper left torso tension, I may now be able to realize that I am simultaneously contracting back toward the core of my body and expanding outward in my upper chest. And (d) the very recognition of the "tension" as an ongoing tens*ing* will often allow a shift to occur – one that may well allow the local, doubly-directed tensing to release a bit, but may also involve changes in other kinaesthetic systems, and above all, in breathing. Thus, for example,

---

5. Cf. Husserl (2001b:285) where Husserl's example is becoming aware not only that his feet are cold, but that they have been cold for some time.

6. See Husserl (2006:351–352), discussed in Behnke (2008b:50), and cf., e.g., Husserl (2006:198, 273, 319–320, 323–324, 340–341; 2008:358–359). Note that while Husserl often speaks of "*Dabei-Sein*" and "*Dabei-Bleiben*" in the context of affective saliences motivating external perception, the accent here is on subjectively living-through the very feeling of "undergoing" itself, including its affective valence.

7. Naturally, not every tension has this structure; for some other types of inner gestures, see Behnke (1997).

experiencing the simultaneous push-pull structure of the kinaesthetic activity I have been ongoingly maintaining in my upper left torso may immediately liberate a fuller breath in my belly (as well as changes in the tension in question). It is, however, important to note that this type of inner gesture – one characterized by the fact that centripetal and centrifugal directions are simultaneously in play in the very same area of the body – can occur in many different areas of the body, and where the release is felt will differ as well. I thus take "enduring" as an experiential pattern or possibility that can be exemplified in numerous ways.

Further explication: "Enduring" as a mode of "undergoing"

How may the initial description of this process be further elucidated? First of all, thematizing what I am directly feeling, bodily, not only allows that which I am undergoing – here, ambient patterns of tension – to come to fuller awareness in general, but can also allow me to appreciate "undergoing" itself as a lived subjective process. In other words, I am not merely sensing myself rather than something else, but am taking the "how" of this very sensing as a theme for phenomenological exploration as well, so that I am not only aware of what the experience is "about," but attuned to the experiential process itself. Thus it is not simply a matter of noticing certain phenomena (bodily tensions) in terms of the "how" of their givenness (as vaguely localized, temporally ongoing, etc.), but of appreciating an essential correlational complicity between my own comportment – my mode of experienc*ing,* which we might term the "how" of my "receiving" what is "given" – and that which is given in the experience. This, however, shifts the accent from ascertaining something factual about the state of an object (e.g., my own lived body as a unique experiential "object," presented to "me" via certain somaesthetic sensations) to undergoing the ongoing immediacy of a subjective process that I myself am continuing to live-through from within.[8] And as I begin to yield to the experience, inhabiting it more fully, I may begin to sense quite directly that the "how" of the sensing involves a subtle *kinaesthetic* activity, whether I am "welcoming" or "refusing" what I am experiencing. For example, if I am experiencing something painful, there is a tendency to try to close myself off, clamping down so the feeling is muted, but if it is comfortable or pleasant, I may find myself opening up so that I am undergoing what I am experiencing more fully. In this way the moment of yielding to the vaguely felt tension brings a kinaesthetic consciousness into play and allows me to experience the structure of the inner gesture through which I am living-through what I am undergoing. In the present case, this structure – its

---

8. Husserl emphasizes that the mode of original awareness proper to the egoic and kinaesthetic differs in general from the mode of awareness of appearances – see, e.g., Husserl (1973b: 500, 529) – and further distinguishes a "becoming" that is not simply given as "something is happening," but is experienced as "I am doing" or (as in the present case) "I am undergoing" (Husserl 2001b: 278); cf. also Behnke (2007: 68–69; 2008a: 146, 149; 2008b: 49–50).

kinaesthetic "signature," if you will, recognizable even if inscribed in different kinaesthetic systems – involves, as already indicated, two simultaneous kinaesthetic vectors, one pulling inward, as if retreating from something, and the other pushing outward, as if to fend it off. In this way *"enduring" is itself a distinctive mode of undergoing.* And although I have been emphasizing the possibility of suffusing my own experiencing with awareness rather than having-something-over-against-"me"-as-an-object, here it is appropriate to recall the relationality of kinaesthetic life so that these vectors can be understood in correlation with their transitive object, which is simultaneously that-from-which I am withdrawing and that-against-which I am defending myself. Thus I am simultaneously pulling away from something (a centripetal move, toward the core, as when one flinches away from something painful) and pushing back at it (an outward, centrifugal move – as when one senses the hands around one's neck and tries frantically to make one's neck bigger as well as stronger, so the hands cannot choke off one's breath completely). Yet this double kinaesthetic vector is neither a mere helpless shrinking into oneself nor a way of being able to fight back effectively after all. Instead, it creates a zone of tension whose lived meaning is that of attempting to establish and maintain a boundary, not just for a moment, but in a sustained effort of self-preservation. It is, in short, an ongoing inner gesture of "enduring" what can most appropriately be termed *boundary violation.* By linking "enduring" with boundary violation, however, I am addressing it in terms of traumatic bodily memory. Thus I shall first clarify how I am understanding "boundary violation" here; then I shall provisionally sketch out the temporal structure of several different types of traumatic bodily memories and of ordinary (non-traumatic) experience before discussing the temporal structure(s) proper to the inner gesture of "enduring."

The temporality of "enduring"

The inaugural "moment": Boundary violation

I am using the notion of "boundary violation" in the extended sense developed by Kirkengen (2001, 2010), a sense that can be approached by considering the contrasts between two constellations of meaning: on the one hand, the notions of boundaries, integrity, dignity, and respect; and on the other hand, the notions of violation, transgression, humiliation, and reification. One familiar sense of the term 'boundaries' has to do with (male) testing of (female) sexual boundaries: What are the limits? What is unacceptable? Who has to right to decide? (Kirkengen 2001: 208, 211, 428 n. 212). But Kirkengen takes the term more broadly:

> I have spoken with many adults whose childhood was spent in what I would call "unboundaried" families. With that, I mean families in which the adults did not respect closed doors, personal letters, diaries, or drawers, where none of the children's body parts were off limits to adult hands, where all secrets were

broadcast, where children were ridiculed and laughed at in front of others, where physical punishment was meted out indiscriminately, where adults used lies and excuses – in other words, these were homes where the child got no respect and the child's personal integrity was scorned.   (Kirkengen 2010:54)

Thus the notion of boundary violation goes beyond the specific issue of having one's limits transgressed in sexual violation to encompass any way in which a person's dignity is violated through being humiliated, harassed, stigmatized, marginalized, rejected, neglected, abandoned, or abused (Kirkengen 2010:40, 86–87). This includes not only physical and sexual assault along with emotional abuse, but also socially embedded ways of denying respect to individuals or groups in patterns of racism or sexism (Kirkengen 2001:390–392; 2010:15–16, 154–156, 194–198). What is ultimately at stake is the principle of human integrity – and the ways in which the lived experience of being made a thing, being humiliated, being used can be *"embodied as sickness and death"* (Kirkengen 2010:193; cf. 16–22 et passim).

Kirkengen's notion of boundary violation as integrity violation, then, is ultimately an ethical notion of human wholeness – one explicitly meant to replace the Cartesian dualism that still dominates mainstream medicine (Kirkengen 2001:1–8, 22–24; 2010:18–20, 118–120, 234–235). It furnishes a principle according to which we must not be reduced to mere means for others' ends, since "each person, by being human, leads a life. No one can be displaced from that position" (Gendlin 1986:35). Or perhaps we must say: no one *should* be displaced in this way, because such expropriation does in fact occur. And being "invaded," as it were, by having one's boundaries disregarded (Kirkengen 2001:247) is deeply disruptive not only to one's integrity at that moment, but to the integrity of one's ongoing life; it effects an "existential trauma" with a "web of consequences" for one's personal development "in terms of self-esteem, confidence, trust and health" (Kirkengen 2001:15). In this way the "moment" of boundary violation is not merely a matter of the temporal onset of an assault to one's integrity, but names a distinguishable yet inseparable thread that is henceforth woven into our existence as a whole.[9] Let us accordingly turn to the effect of traumatic events on the ongoing flow of lived experience, beginning with a brief account of three possibilities.

Trauma and temporality: Three models[10]

A limit case (*Grenzfall*) might be provided by a model of complete *resilience:* I may experience something traumatic, but once it is over, I let it go, and the past is the past,

---

9. On the technical Husserlian sense of a non-independent (*unselbständig*) "moment" as a distinguishable but inseparable part of a whole, see Husserl (1984:231–233, 272–274).

10. Here it is not possible to provide a complete typology of the varieties of traumatic bodily memory documented in phenomenological investigation. On body memory in general, see

reachable by memory but exercising little influence on the course of a kinaesthetic life that has returned to normal without visible – or invisible – scars. In contrast, a second model might be termed the model of associational *reactivation*. As Husserl has shown, the most fundamental modes of temporal association are the simultaneous and the successive: two things are associated because they happened at the same time (for example, simultaneously being beaten and smelling the attacker's alcoholic breath) or because they stand in a before-after relation (for example, a soldier on active duty seeing a pile of debris by the roadside and being injured by an improvised explosive device seconds later). And the most fundamental principle of reactivation is similarity, with the added principle that the original situation as a whole may be reactivated by the current presence of part of it – when a similar smell comes again, the fear and the pain are conjured up again; the soldier on leave may panic on seeing similar trash.[11] Thus reactivation typically displays an episodic temporality, occurring whenever what triggers it is encountered. A third model, however, involves the continual *reiteration* of a style of coping that is rooted in the original traumatic episode(s), but becomes one's ongoing style of experiencing per se. For example, one may have survived

---

Casey (1987: Ch. 8); on traumatic body memory in particular, see, e.g., Kirkengen (2001: 230–260), for a number of examples illustrating the theme of "recognized memories," as well as for some discussion of the difficulties of addressing this topic in biomedical research (and cf. 55–66, 130, 163 on the importance of narrative in ordering the confused times of traumatic memories; 105, 338–339 on sensorimotor embodiment of trauma as a special form of body memory; and 6, 248, 393 on the limits of generic typologies in understanding the lived experiences of individuals). In this section I merely offer a preliminary sketch, and it is, of course, incomplete. For example, I omit a model of "recalibration" where from now on my tacit "normal" expectations have shifted ("the world is no longer a safe place"), and see also the model of "reintegration" suggested below. Moreover, not all of the models mentioned are mutually exclusive (e.g., an individual might experience moments of "reactivation" within a more encompassing style of "reiteration"); the point here is simply to contrast the temporal structures concerned. It is similarly outside the scope of this paper to specify the relation of "enduring" to other types of traumatic bodily memory, since the relevant phenomenological research has not yet been carried out – a fact that illustrates one of the most annoying yet exciting aspects of concrete phenomenological work: namely, that whenever one sets out to describe a particular phenomenon, one finds oneself confronted not only with a number of received presuppositions in need of critique, but also with a constellation of related phenomena that can only be fully distinguished from the target phenomenon when these phenomena too have been described in detail. Thus every concrete phenomenological description is haunted by a host of further descriptive projects yet to be carried out, and the present paper is no exception.

11. On the phenomenology of association see, e.g., Husserl (1966: 122, 175, 179–180; 2006: 251–254, 308); on the examples mentioned, cf. Kirkengen (2010: 106, 148); for further case studies, see Kirkengen (2001: 290–317). Note that Kirkengen, a family physician, compiled these case histories in the course of a phenomenological investigation of the bodily consequences of boundary violation – thus the examples she presents do not come from the world of clinical psychology.

traumatic experiences by dissociating, radically "spacing out" so that one does not feel what is going on at all; the body keeps going, but there is nobody home, and one lives in "inner exile" (Kirkengen 2010: 263–264), no longer living-through the familiar feel and variegated textures of one's own kinaesthetic life (cf. Behnke 2002). "Enduring" has the same temporal structure: in order to survive circumstances one has no power to change, one has to find a way to endure/withstand them – which then becomes the enduring/lasting style of experience as a whole. How does this come about?

The temporal structure of normal (non-traumatic) experience

As Husserl emphasizes, in the ongoing course of experience in general, the past casts a shadow over the future, as it were (Husserl 1966: 289, 323). For example, my initial encounter with a new object is not merely a singular event I may subsequently remember, but serves as the 'primal institution' (Urstiftung) – the inaugural instance – of this type of object per se, and I will henceforth recognize similar objects as objects of this type (see, e.g., Husserl 1950a: 141; 1974: 317; 2001a: 144–145; 2008: 437). Yet at the same time, the very experience of acquiring such new possibilities is carried forward into a future in which the world as a whole remains an open horizon for the institution of further new forms of experience. Moreover, in normal non-traumatic experience, whatever is given here and now constantly predelineates "more" that could be experienced when I bring the appropriate kinaesthetic capabilities into play (see, e.g., Husserl 1954: 160; 1966: 10–15; 1974: 240–241; 2008: 112–115). For example, in seeing "this side" of the green box, I am not only recognizing it as a physical object with "other sides" that will come into view when I move around it (or turn it around), but am already anticipating that the as yet unseen sides of the green box are indeed green. Similarly, appreciating the panorama from here already predelineates further views that will emerge as I continue to walk down the path. Thus I experience the world as a whole as an open horizon of variegated possibilities to-be-explored, and the general style of what is to come is predelineated without ever guaranteeing that a particular predelineation will in fact be fulfilled – perhaps the green box is not green all over after all (cf., e.g., Husserl 1966: 211–212; 1974: 164, 288).

Now if we inquire more closely into the structure of such predelineation of a determinable indeterminacy, we find that more is at stake than the anticipation of sensuous content of some sort, for the latter moment is inseparable from its *affective valence* and a corresponding *kinaesthetic vector*: the affective valences of what attracts or repels are always already pervaded with the kinaesthetic vectors of "toward" or "away," of seeking and lingering with the pleasant or avoiding the unpleasant (cf., e.g., Husserl 1973a: 450; Husserl 2006: 318–319, 351; Behnke 2007: 69). And these three interwoven moments are accompanied by a fourth for which Husserl uses the technical term *Geltung*, which carries the nuance of 'holding good' 'being in force,' or 'being accepted' – including accepting the being or reality of that which is being experienced. But here too there is a predelineation in play, a *Vorgeltung* such that what is predelineated *holds good in advance;* it is accepted as a reality before it even arrives.[12] Finally, all of this not only presupposes that the situated experiencer who is experiencing this really existing, physiognomic world from a particular standpoint has a certain 'leeway' (*Spielraum*) of kinaesthetic freedom, but rests upon the tacit predelineation of this kinaesthetic capability itself as ongoingly available, holding good in advance as a realm of possibilities freely at my disposal (see, e.g., Husserl 1954: 163–167; 1966: 428; 2003: 96 n. 1; 2006: 229–230, 346). How are things different in the case of traumatic experiences?

The temporal structure of "enduring"

One key is that in the type of traumatic experience involved in the genesis of the traumatic bodily memory I am terming "enduring," the situation is radically unpleasant, but the kinaesthetic possibilities typically summarized as "fight" or "flight" are no longer available; one's kinaesthetic freedom is significantly restricted, whether one is physically restrained, powerless in face of an overwhelming threat, or simply frozen in terror (cf. Husserl 2002b: 262–263; 2008: 316). Equally important, however, is the temporal structure of the type of traumatic situation in question, which is not a momentary event, but has a duration of its own: it "lasts," and one must "outlast" it without knowing how much longer it will last. In such an experience, the open world may collapse into a here and now from which I cannot escape – all that is left of the temporal horizon is the leading edge of the now (in Husserl's terms, the "protentional" dimension of the living present), the very moment where the violation is ongoingly maintained. And this is no longer an open horizon of variegated possibilities; instead, what is protentionally predelineated as "what will come in the most immediate, just-coming new now" is completely dominated by the effective force of what Husserl terms the immediate retentional horizon, the "comet's tail" of immediate past moments (just-past, just-just-past, etc.), so that all that is accepted in advance is "more of the same," which holds good as "ineluctably ongoing without respite." In such a case, one is affected not only by what one is currently actually undergoing, but also

---

12. Although Husserl sometimes speaks of *Geltung* in conjunction with logical 'validity' (*Gültigkeit*), his use of the term typically carries the connotation of 'accepted as holding good' in a broader sense; much of the time it refers to 'ontic acceptance' (*Seinsgeltung*), i.e., claims to being (see, e.g., Husserl 2006: 348–350), but the broader sense also includes acceptance of other sorts of "general assumptions" (cf. Husserl 2001c: 184–185) as well as of something's 'being-thus' (*Sosein*) or even of the automatic availability of my own capabilities (cf., e.g., Husserl 2002b: 280). Husserl uses the term *Vorgeltung* (and similar locutions referring to what is 'accepted in advance') with a variety of nuances – see, e.g., Husserl (1954: 157; 1973b: 353; 2002b: 222, 302, 392, 433, 437, 444; 2006: 225, 314). What is important here, however, is that passive predelineations of content co-involve a 'belief in advance' (*Vorglaube*) in its reality (see, e.g., Husserl 2006: 96) – all taking place in a pre-predicative 'life of acceptance' (*Geltungsleben*) whose performances can be explicated phenomenologically (Husserl 1974: 241).

by one's own immediate affective anticipation, continually motivating one to brace in advance for what is already accepted in advance as the inevitable continuation of the current violation.[13] There is no longer an open horizon to-be-explored, but only the inexorable and immediate prolongation of that which is to-be-endured: the violation is predelineated as enduring (continuing); my survival depends on my enduring (withstanding) it. Husserl speaks of the continued efficacy of the past in terms of the metaphor of "sedimentation" (see, e.g., Husserl 1954: 152, 371–372; 1966: 178, 181, 183–184; 1974: 252, 257; 2006: 56, 59, 160, 345–346). What is sedimented here, however, is not merely the content of one's predicament (the source of the details that can be associatively reawakened and reactivated), but the dynamic self-prolongation of the very gesture of "enduring" as a global style of experience to be continually renewed in my kinaesthetic life here and now, holding good as "necessary" even if there is no current boundary violation to endure.[14] In this way what is instituted is not a type of experienceable object, but an obligatory mode of subjective existence.

"Enduring" is accordingly a form of traumatic bodily memory in which what is "remembered," in the sense of being "memorialized," kept constantly alive, is not that which one had to undergo, but *how* one managed to undergo it.[15] Yet I – the active, waking I – may not be consciously aware either of this persisting style of comportment or of its connection with the events that initially motivated it. Thus the past that is trapped in these frozen gestures of defense – of protection against boundary violation, of self-preservation – makes me into its unwitting accomplice, turning me into a living cenotaph, a continual re-enactment and reminder of something that happened somewhere else: the incessant reiteration of a kinaesthetic style that was originally mobilized as an emergency measure, a way of bearing the unbearable, has become a permanent part of my very bearing, my stance in the world.

This, however, inevitably affects my style of world-engagement as well, since by ongoingly hardening myself here and now, in the living present, I simultaneously seal myself off from this present to a greater or lesser degree (cf. Behnke 2007: 72). Hanna (2004–2005, 2008) has addressed this issue in terms of the metaphor of "somatic osmosis," understanding somatic experience as a whole according to the model of a cell whose membrane both defines its individual integrity and mediates its ongoing relational interchange with what lies beyond the membrane. Thus in the case of

---

13. See Husserl (2006: 322–323), where, however, Husserl's example is being affected by anticipating the continuation of the pleasurable; cf. Casey (1987: 160–161).

14. Cf. the case history recounted in Kirkengen (2001: 253–255), where a woman describes her chronically tense stomach muscles as her constant "readiness" to be hit, arising from her attempts to make herself a "wall" between her violent father and her battered mother.

15. Bodily tensions can, of course, also arise when one is anxious about one's future. However, "enduring" relates to the already 'settled' (*erledigt*) past (cf. n. 19 below), where the worst has already happened (and is continuing to occur); the task is now to survive it, and the will to do so becomes a "settled," abiding aim with its own temporal ongoingness (see Husserl 2006: 100 n. 1).

"enduring," the problem is not that I am attempting to maintain the integrity of my own boundaries, but that I have become frozen and fixed, with my style of somatic osmosis no longer shifting in response to changing situations. What could restore the fluid dynamics through which I maintain appropriate boundaries that are appropriately permeable to each situation? Here what is needed is a model of *reintegration* in which past patterns are neither automatically reactivated whenever certain associations are triggered nor automatically reiterated no matter what the occasion. And although various modalities of somatic psychotherapy address this problem in their own ways, I would like to identify some general principles of restorative embodiment work that may help to release the inner gesture of "enduring" from its obligatory reiteration and reintegrate it into the richer nexus of possibilities pertaining to the kinaesthetic system as a whole.

Restorative embodiment work: Regaining healthy rapport with the world through bodily awareness

What follows is not drawn from the asymmetric sphere of dyadic therapy in which an "expert" is consulted by a "client" or "patient," but belongs instead to the tradition of "giving therapy away" by empowering people to consult their own experience and become their own "authorities" (Gendlin 1984, especially 297–300). More specifically, it is meant as a mode of somatic education (not "therapy") in which people can move toward techniques of bodily authenticity rather than being subsumed in social/institutional dynamics of alienation in which the dictates of experts outrank and erase what is directly available to us in lived bodily experience (see Johnson 1983:79–83, 142–145, 152–154, 167–171, 181–184; cf. Kirkengen 2001:59–60). Here, however, I can only present several principles informing such restorative embodiment work – principles that could, of course, be fleshed out through many sorts of experiential experiments.[16]

First is the principle of *retrieval from anonymity*. But this involves more than tapping into the texture of my own experience and becoming aware, for example, of previously unnoticed tensions. Instead, what must be recovered is my own kinaesthetic complicity with what I am living-through.[17] This not only means becoming more affectively available for what I am undergoing (the "yielding" already described), so

---

16. I have given these principles names that form the acronym "RAPPORT" (Retrieval from Anonymity; Possibilizing; Protentional Openness; Relational Trust) in order to facilitate presenting the principles in the form of an experiential workshop.

17. Typically, we are not directly concerned with kinaesthetic activity in its own right, but with what it makes possible (perceiving a thing, performing a practical action, etc.), so these tacit means-'through'-which experience proceeds (Husserl's term is *Durchgang*) must be explicitly thematized – see, e.g., Husserl (2006:329; 2008:14, 365, 629).

that, for example, the intensity of a vague tension is more clearly felt, but also involves appreciating the double efficacy of the kinaesthetic patterns that come into play in the act of "undergoing." On the one hand, bracing against what I am enduring functions as the style of kinaesthetic receptivity correlative to the boundary violation I originally had to survive. On the other hand, however, like all styles and patterns of lived move-ment, these too are accompanied by the corresponding somaesthetic sensations – the feel of the movement concerned.[18] A transformative shift begins when I recognize that the tension I am currently sensing is not an external assault from which I must protect myself here and now, but the feel of my own ongoing inner gesture of tensing. In other words, when the inner gesture of "enduring" was originally instituted, what I was undergoing was boundary violation; as "enduring" endures, however, what I am undergoing is the feeling of maintaining my own defenses against violation. But why is the retrieval of the kinaesthetic dimension of the experience as an ongoing activity of tensing so crucial?

Like any currently actualized kinaesthetic configuration, this tensing is surround-ed by its own unique halo of further moves immediately possible "from here" (see Behnke 2009a: 206; 2009b: 21). For example, a movement pushing away from center can push a little further or release a bit back toward center; a movement pulling back toward center can do so more strongly or release into becoming a bit less contracted. This, however, brings a second principle into play, the principle of "*possibilizing*" (see Zaner 1981: 175–180). What this means here is that the currently actual kinaesthetic patterns are recast as possibilities – possibilities that happen to be actualized at the moment, but horizonally indicate other possibilities: it could be otherwise. Thus, for example, it is possible to defend myself even more emphatically against what I am undergoing, or else to make more room for what I am feeling, thereby reinstating a range of possible modes of undergoing what I am experiencing, running from "en-during" it to simply "being-there-for" it to "enjoying" it. And even if the tensing I am concerned with is initially experienced as a local tension, any shift in the local gesture can allow a further release to ripple out to other kinaesthetic systems, since enacting this particular tensing entails its own ancillary adjustments that are free to readjust when the tensing in question is altered: just as it is ultimately the kinaesthetic system as a whole that says "no" to violation, so also is it the whole that shifts when the previ-ously obligatory gesture loses its automatic efficacy and becomes merely one gesture among many other possible gestures.

Now in some cases, the very act of becoming more affectively available for a vague tension can motivate a release, while in other cases the practical act of "possibilizing" can be accomplished by deliberately "matching" the tensing that has been retrieved from anonymity. Here "matching" names an experiential move of aligning my "I can" with what is already going on anyway, inhabiting it as something that I, the active wak-ing I, am now doing. For example, I may recast a tension in my shoulder and upper

---

18. For more on the localization of kinaesthetic capability in somaesthetic sensibility, see Behnke (2002).

chest as a gesture I am currently making – holding myself in exactly this position, with precisely this degree of contraction – so that it is a matter of actualizing certain kinaesthetic possibilities rather than others, which then allows further possibilities to become horizonally available as well (see Behnke 1988; 2009a: 206–207). In yet other cases, however, the inner gesture of "enduring" is so deeply sedimented that we must invoke an additional principle of *protentional openness*. Recall that in the original, founding experience, the temporal horizon shrinks to the most immediate protentional continuation of the current now, and the emerging present is already anticipated as an extension of the already settled past[19] in the ceaseless prolongation of the necessity of surviving the ongoing violation. To transform the kinaesthetics of "enduring" into the kinaesthetics of trust and safety it is helpful to return, experientially, to the leading edge of the now as it spills over into the next now in such a way as to recover the essential openness whereby what is predelineated may be fulfilled *or* disappointed and a new sense-formation (rather than "more of the same") may still emerge. Here the radical reduction to the living present must suspend the acceptance-in-advance of a future whose style of sensuous content and affective valence is already presumed. But as I have already indicated, the affective valence permeating and inseparable from the sensuous content of what we are undergoing is equally inseparable from the kinaesthetic style of receptivity in play.[20] Thus staying with the microstructure of time – the immediate welling up of the new now – and adopting an attitude of "not-knowing" what will come next simultaneously involves a certain deactivation of the kinaesthetic anticipations already in place (cf. Behnke 2009a: 194–197, 208–210). More precisely, what is deactivated is the automatic acceptance-in-advance of the necessity of "enduring": the inner gesture in question is still available if needed, still part of the repertoire, but no longer holds good as the obligatory style of all kinaesthetic life.

And what is thereby restored might be addressed in terms of a principle of *relational trust*, a more responsive style of self-temporalization that is able to trust the unknown without subjecting it in advance to the rule of the already settled past. This does not imply that the past never happened or that its lessons are not valuable, nor does it guarantee that all future situations will be safe. Instead, it means learning to trust my own kinaesthetic style(s) of receptivity as they partner the shifting situation with an appropriate degree of permeability and self-preservation (cf. Behnke

---

19. For Husserl, the 'settled' (*erledigt*) is the realm of the already determined, in contrast to the open future of determinable indeterminacy; see, e.g., Husserl (2001b: 148; 2002b: 166, 170 n. 1, 171; 2006: 30–31, 44, 285, 395, 403).

20. Cf. the discussion and the sources cited in Behnke (2008b: 48). We may see styles of kinaesthetic receptivity as proceeding along a spectrum running between the two main possibilities mentioned earlier ("welcoming" and "refusing" what I am experiencing), possibilities that might fruitfully be compared with Laban's notion of attitudes of "accepting"/indulging or "resisting"/fighting; see, e.g., Maletic (1987: 101, 179, and cf. 162–163, Appendix I, for an introduction to convergences between Laban's work and the phenomenological tradition in general).

2007:78–81). In this way restorative embodiment work becomes a practice not only of (re)inhabiting my own streaming life in its living immediacy and (re)appropriating my most immediate horizon of possibilities, but of participating in the play of a world that is not fixed in advance. The inner gesture of "enduring," then, is a form of traumatic bodily memory that has forgotten its own situated origins while at the same time memorializing them in the persistent re-enactment of a style of surviving an unendurable past. Recovering from this painful amnesia does not disown the past that originally motivated it, but restores a more open future into which we as streaming beings experiencing a streaming world[21] can more freely move.

Appendix: The sense of the term "inner gesture"[22]

How is the notion of an "inner gesture" used in this paper? Since it is meant in a distinctively phenomenological sense, it must first be presented in phenomenological terms.

Methodological points

Descriptive phenomenological work proceeds in terms of demonstration, not definition (cf. Husserl 1976:191; 2002a:326). Moreover, the writer who presents the result of descriptive phenomenological investigation assumes that a reader who is geared into a phenomenological attitude will participate as an active partner in the investigation by "cashing in" or "redeeming" (Husserl 1950b:62; 1987:32; 2002a:322) the words on the page for the phenomena themselves (Husserl 1950b:60; 1954:123; 1973c:9). Husserl is quite clear on this requirement: "phenomenology demands a direct personal production of the pertinent phenomenon" (Husserl 2002a:326), and if a reader has not "actively produced the phenomenon" in him/herself "in a spirit of unprejudiced cooperation such as this work after all requires" (Husserl 2002a:319), then anything such a reader may say about the work "is just so much hot air" (Husserl 2002a:322). In other words, a phenomenological description is like a musical score that each reader must perform for him/herself by turning to the relevant experiential evidence.

Doing this successfully, however, requires developing an "appropriate sensibility" (Sokolowski 1974:108–109) for the dimension of experience in question (here, embodied experience, lived kinaesthetically "from within" by the movers themselves, rather than observed "from the outside"). In addition, one must develop a sensitivity

---

21. See Husserl (2006:58): "Wir haben (wir, die strömend seienden) diese Welt selbst in strömender Gegebenheitsweise als strömend gegenwärtige Welt ..." (and cf. also, e.g., Husserl 2008:565–570).

22. I would like to thank an anonymous referee for inviting me to discuss the notion of "inner gesture" in more detail.

to the degree of universality the description aims at. Not all phenomenological investigations strive toward establishing findings that might be expressed in a statement taking the form, "For any conceivable X whatsoever, it holds that y." Instead, an investigation such as the one conducted here attempts to delineate what might be termed a repeatable or shareable experiential "pattern" or "possibility" that transcends the "facts" in any given case (cf. Behnke 1997: 185–186), yet is not automatically a necessary feature of all human experience per se.[23] Thus I cannot assume that all of the phenomenologically attuned readers who come upon this essay will have had a life history leaving them with a vivid firsthand experience of the inner gesture of "enduring." But there can be various sorts of inner gestures, and I shall follow Husserl's procedure for terminological control (Husserl 1976: 9, 139–140, 190–191) by using experiential examples to introduce the type of phenomenon that is at stake here.

Experiential examples

1. Let us say that your hand (or other body part) is resting on a surface of some sort. Can you let the weight of your hand (or lower arm, foot, etc.) settle more fully into the surface that supports you? Or to take another example, let us say that you have a small stone (or other object) in the palm of your hand, or perhaps a living being (e.g., a child or a pet) on your lap; can you more fully accept the weight of the stone (etc.), receiving and welcoming the weight as it settles into your hand (etc.)?[24] Practice with such "inner gestures" can lead us to appreciate many nuances of embodied life that are palpable to the experiencer even if they are hardly noticeable to a casual observer.
2. Choose somewhere in your body to experiment with (your neck? stomach? one ankle? etc.), and increase the muscle tension ever so slightly, without actually changing the position of your body in space (and then, of course, feel free to release the tension once again). This "inner gesture" too is a matter of a micromovement immediately accessible to the mover, rather than an overt movement traversing objective space.
3. Here I shall use a story to get at an experiential possibility (one that was already mentioned on pp. 94–95 above). Imagine that a photographer has entered the room, and is telling you that your current pose is just perfect, asking you to hold it, just as it is (e.g., with your head at just this angle, with this precise degree of tension in your shoulders, etc.). As you "hold still" for the photographer, you are

---

23. Determining the distribution of the type of experience in question within a given population is, of course, a different task calling for different research tools; here, the point is that what is technically called "eidetic" phenomenological investigation can take place at different levels.

24. Experiential experiments with giving and receiving weight are often used in Sensory Awareness practices, based on the work of Elsa Gindler (1885–1961) and Heinrich Jacoby (1889–1964) and their students.

now "maintaining" certain kinaesthetic possibilities rather than others (on bodily stillness as a mode of kinaesthetic movement, cf. Husserl 1954: 108; 1973c: 300–301), and there is a sense in which what was previously just a habitual posture with a habitual degree of tonus has now become an "inner gesture" of holding your head or shoulders in a particular way. Moreover, the very act of "matching" (Behnke 1988) what is already going on anyway, suffusing it with my *fiat* (cf. Husserl 1952: 257–259) so that it is something I am kinaesthetically doing, could also be taken as an "inner gesture" in a less literal sense.

4. Finally, if we continue along a spectrum of metaphorical senses, we find a group of phenomenologists who use the notion of "gesture" as a way of describing phenomenological practice itself, speaking of the phenomenological methods technically known as epochē and reduction in terms of a gesture of awareness (cf. Depraz, Varela & Vermersch 2003) with three main phases: a gesture of interrupting our usual engagement with the world – a "suspending move" (Depraz 2002: 123); a gesture of redirecting one's attention to the how of one's own experience (Depraz, Varela & Vermersch 2000: 171–172); and a gesture of "letting go" and "allowing," of receptively welcoming whatever emerges, letting it come (Depraz et al. 2000: 175; Depraz 2002: 124). In this example a "gesture" is simply a move that can be made, whether or not this results in any literal deployment of my kinaesthetic capabilities. It is nevertheless a style of mobilizing my "I can," e.g., setting aside what I think I already know, establishing a zone of silence free from the language already at my disposal, and opening my awareness without trying to become aware of anything in particular (Depraz et al. 2000: 179–180) – experiential moves that are not always easy to make, but that make sense as "moves" when one actually attempts to try them out.

Discussion

This initial phenomenological approach to the notion of an inner gesture emphasizes *movement*, not as displacement across extended space, but as kinaesthetic deployment; correlatively, the emphasis lies not on external observation, but on the immediacy (and "invisibility") of the lived "I can" (its "inwardness," if you will).[25] However, the notion of an "inner gesture" cuts across the voluntary-involuntary distinction, as can be seen from the example of bringing to light a habitual postural configuration as an

---

25. The metaphorical use of the term 'inner' to mean something like 'considered from the standpoint of the experiencer' (for the locutions 'von inner her' and 'von innen gesehen,' see, e.g., Husserl 2006: 158, 167, 170, 423, and cf. ibid.: 169 for 'von außen her' and 'von außen gesehen') cannot be examined here. However, for a philosophical discussion of the "inner" as the intimate autonomy of a non-objectified, "own" life whose dynamic movement is continually ahead of itself, see Patočka (2007); cf. also Behnke (1984: Appendix B).

"inner gesture" that had been proceeding on its own before "I" consciously "matched" it, inhabiting it from within as something that I am currently lucidly doing.

This in turn raises the question of how to distinguish "gesture" from "posture." One way of looking at the difference between "gesture" and "posture" would take gesture as local and posture as global. Yet as useful as this distinction is, it obscures the interarticulation of the various kinaesthetic systems that comprise the kinaesthetic system as a whole: the enactment of what seems to be a particular, isolated gesture such as raising one arm actually entails many ancillary adjustments in the body as a whole in order to keep one's balance and maintain stability elsewhere (Juhan 1987: 114, cf. 279). Thus each local gesture mobilizes the entire body as its support. Another key to the difference between "gesture" and "posture," however, is a temporal process I have termed the sedimentation of motility in materiality. The kinaesthetic system as a whole offers myriad possibilities both for making specific moves in individual kinaesthetic systems and for supporting this movement by stabilizing ourselves elsewhere in the body. However, our life experiences may lead us to favor certain fixed positions over others:

> Over the years, it is the habitual repetition of these preferred fixations which creates the individualized tension patterns in our musculatures, and eventually even alters the thickness of our fascia and the shape of our bones in order to more efficiently accommodate a limited number of positions. ... Indeed, my favorite fixed positions eventually cease to be *something I am doing* and become to a large degree what I am. (Juhan 1987: 220, cf. 103)

In this way "experimentation becomes gesture, gesture becomes posture, and posture becomes structure" (Juhan 1987: 231), and our movement settles into well-worn channels that both testify to our kinaesthetic history and shape our ability to make new moves.

Seen in terms of considerations drawn from a phenomenology of lived movement, then, a "gesture" in the more literal / less metaphorical sense is a move that can be made kinaesthetically – typically, a local move that is nevertheless supported in and by the body as a whole, while the notion of an "inner" gesture refers to gestures (including micromovements) that may not be overt or visible (cf. Behnke 1997: 188), and may not be initially appreciated as such by the embodied experiencer in question, but can become lucidly lived from within precisely as a type of lived movement (even if the move in question is a sedimented "holding pattern" ongoingly maintaining the same bodily configuration and tonus, and thus shaping our posture and structure as well). What happens, however, if we shift our focus away from the phenomenological tradition and inquire into the ordinary language sense of 'gesture' as a mode of expressive comportment?

The question of expression

The *American Heritage Dictionary* defines the central meaning shared by 'gesture' and related terms as "an expressive, meaningful bodily motion," noting that a gesture in the literal sense of "a motion of the limbs or body" serves "to express or help express thought or to emphasize speech." But we must not take this definition too narrowly, for one's entire postural style may make its own expressive gesture of wariness and defiance or weariness and defeat, of radiant buoyancy or serene confidence, and so on (cf. Juhan 1987: 232–233). Moreover, although we may deliberately perform a particular bodily gesture in order to underscore something we are saying, there are also expressive gestures that escape us inadvertently, as it were, perhaps even betraying something we may not want to communicate. Thus as with the phenomenological sense, which emphasizes gestures as kinaesthetic events, the expressive sense too encompasses both sides of the voluntary-involuntary distinction and cannot be fully divorced from the notion of posture. Finally, the dictionary definition is unduly cognitive in defining 'gesture' in terms of 'thought' and 'speech,' which ignores the affective dimension of expressive gestures. Bearing these considerations in mind, let us inquire in what way an "inner gesture" can be an expressive gesture, using the inner gesture of "enduring" as an example.

Two intertwined distinctions are of help here. The first is temporal – "enduring" as it is lived out during the original violation in contrast to "enduring" as an ongoing inner gesture later in life; the second has to do with standpoint, and can be illustrated in terms of both temporal possibilities: the inner gesture of "enduring" as perceived by the victim and by the violator during the original trauma, and as perceived by the survivor and by others later. For the victim at the time of the original trauma, "enduring" is not primarily meant as an expressive gesture. Instead, it is a practical action rooted in the instinct of self-preservation. Now for Husserl, the "practical" and the "affective" are not mutually exclusive; in concrete experience, the affective dimension suffuses the practical, and neither can be considered a separate category. Thus from the side of the victim, the lived experience of "enduring" is shot through with the sense that what one is undergoing is very bad indeed. It is nevertheless the violator who not only experiences the victim's comportment as expressive of pain (including the pain of all sorts of boundary violation as well as literal physical pain), but deliberately elicits this expression:

> The pain shall force the victim to become subservient. The pain shall show the force and power of the one and the weakness and powerlessness of the other. The pain is meant to demonstrate that the abuser dominates and the abused is subjugated, physically and literally. The pain shall document who is in control through fortune, action, and active position – with the social rank connected to these phenomena. Through its power, the pain documents who is the weak one, with low status, unable to resist, and passively obedient. The pain is an expression

of the fact that someone has willfully made another the object of his or her scorn. The pain is the result of having been made an object – a thing.

(Kirkengen 2010:85)

In other words, the perpetrators of violation need to *see* the experiential suffering they are causing, and what I have termed "enduring" is one form the expression of this suffering can take.

What about the standpoint of the survivor later in life? Kirkengen (2001:2, 5, 59–60, 233–236, 270, 321–322, 335, 375, 390–394, et passim) emphasizes that many institutional and social practices have contributed to silencing the lived experience of abuse, ensuring that it remains both unsaid and unheard. Instead, the experience is inscribed in the body in numerous ways, making it a "mutely testifying" body whose expressions serve as "valid, unspoken messages for silenced, unspeakable experiences" (Kirkengen 2001:5, 407 n. 2). From the standpoint of the survivor, this sort of experience might be summed up in the silent cry, "Can't you *see* that there's something wrong?" (cf. Kirkengen 2001:122, 132, and especially 260–266), and according to Kirkengen, mainstream medicine has singularly failed to see "the lived impact of silenced violation" (2001:287) or to respond to its "unheard messages" (2001:289). In contrast, psychotherapists attuned to the play of micromovements (cf. Depraz et al. 2000:178) and professionals working in the field of somatics (body work and body/movement awareness approaches) are more likely to take, for example, "differences in muscle tone in different parts of the body" (Kirkengen 2010:263; cf. 2001:48–49, 60, 286–287, 413 n. 102) as meaningful – if unspoken – expressions. The inner gesture of "enduring," then, can truly only function as an expressive gesture for those who have learned to see its traces, hear its message, and understand its meaning; then it shines through the flesh, and demands an ethical response.

References

Behnke, E. A. (1984). *World without opposite / Flesh of the world (A carnal introduction)*. Felton, CA: California Center for Jean Gebser Studies; rpt. www.lifwynnfoundation.org.

Behnke, E. A. (1988). Matching. *Somatics*, 6(4), 24–32; rpt. in D. H. Johnson (Ed.), *Bone, breath, and gesture: Practices of embodiment* (pp. 317–337). Berkeley: North Atlantic Books, 1995; partially trans. as Faire un avec la sensation. *3ᵉ millénaire, 56* (2000), 60–63, 81.

Behnke, E. A. (1997). Ghost gestures: Phenomenological investigations of bodily micromovements and their intercorporeal implications. *Human Studies, 20,* 181–201.

Behnke, E. A. (2002). Embodiment work for the victims of violation: In solidarity with the community of the shaken. Prague: Organization of Phenomenological Organizations, www.o-p-o.net; Il lavoro somatico per le vittime della violenza: In solidarità con la comunità degli scampati. Trans. A. Bruzazzi & A. Licinio. *Biblioteca Husserliana, 1* (2009), http://biblioteca-husserliana.com/krisis/Behnke_Krisis2.pdf.

Behnke, E. A. (2007). Bodily relationality: An experiment in phenomenological practice (VII). In L. Embree & T. Nenon (Eds.), *Selected essays from North America* (pp. 67–97). Vol. 5 of *Phenomenology 2005*. Bucharest: Zeta Books.

Behnke, E. A. (2008a). Interkinaesthetic affectivity: A phenomenological approach. *Continental Philosophy Review, 41,* 143–161.

Behnke, E. A. (2008b). Husserl's protean concept of affectivity: From the texts to the phenomena themselves. *Philosophy Today, 52* (SPEP Supplement), 46–53; El concepto proteico de afectividad en Husserl: De los textos a los fenómenos mismos. Trans. G. Vargas Guillén & H. P. Reeder. *Anuario Colombiano de Fenomenología, 3* (2009), 55–68.

Behnke, E. A. (2009a). Bodily protentionality. *Husserl Studies, 25,* 185–217.

Behnke, E. A. (2009b). The human science of somatics and transcendental phenomenology. *Žmogus ir Žodis, 11*(4), 10–26.

Casey, E. S. (1987). *Remembering: A phenomenological study.* Bloomington, IN: Indiana University Press.

Depraz, N. (2002). What about the *praxis* of reduction: Between Husserl and Merleau-Ponty. In T. Toadvine & L. Embree (Eds.), *Merleau-Ponty's reading of Husserl* (pp. 115–125). Dordrecht: Kluwer.

Depraz, N., Varela, F. J. & Vermersch, P. (2000). La réduction à l'épreuve de l'expérience. *Études Phénoménologiques, 31–32,* 165–184.

Depraz, N., Varela, F. J. & Vermersch, P. (2003). *On becoming aware: The pragmatics of experiencing.* Amsterdam: John Benjamins.

Gendlin, E. T. (1984). The politics of giving therapy away: Listening and focusing. In D. Larsen (Ed.), *Teaching psychological skills: Models for giving psychotherapy away* (pp. 287–305). Monterey, CA: Brooks/Cole.

Gendlin, E. T. (1986). *Let your body interpret your dreams.* Wilmette, IL: Chiron.

Hanna, T. (2004–2005). What is somatics? Part IV. *Somatics, 15*(1), 52–56.

Hanna, T. (2008). Somatology: Part III. *Somatics, 15*(4), 10–16, 53–54.

Husserl, E. (1950a). *Cartesianische Meditationen und Pariser Vorträge.* S. Strasser (Ed.). *Husserliana* I. Den Haag: Martinus Nijhoff.

Husserl, E. (1950b). *Die Idee der Phänomenologie. Fünf Vorlesungen.* W. Biemel (Ed.). *Husserliana* II. Den Haag: Martinus Nijhoff.

Husserl, E. (1952). *Ideen zu einer reinen Phänomenologie und phänomenologischen Philosophie. Zweites Buch. Phänomenologische Untersuchungen zur Konstitution.* M. Biemel (Ed.). *Husserliana* IV. Den Haag: Martinus Nijhoff.

Husserl, E. (1954). *Die Krisis der europäischen Wissenschaften und die transzendentale Phänomenologie. Eine Einleitung in die phänomenologische Philosophie.* W. Biemel (Ed.). *Husserliana* VI. Den Haag: Martinus Nijhoff.

Husserl, E. (1966). *Analysen zur passiven Synthesis. Aus Vorlesungs- und Forschungsmanuskripten 1918–1926.* M. Fleischer (Ed.). *Husserliana* XI. Den Haag: Martinus Nijhoff.

Husserl, E. (1973a). *Zur Phänomenologie der Intersubjektivität. Zweiter Teil (1921–1928).* I. Kern (Ed.). *Husserliana* XIV. Den Haag: Martinus Nijhoff.

Husserl, E. (1973b). *Zur Phänomenologie der Intersubjektivität. Dritter Teil (1929–1935).* I. Kern (Ed.). *Husserliana* XV. Den Haag: Martinus Nijhoff.

Husserl, E. (1973c). *Ding und Raum. Vorlesungen 1907.* U. Claesges (Ed.). *Husserliana* XVI. Den Haag: Martinus Nijhoff.

Husserl, E. (1974). *Formale und transzendentale Logik. Versuch einer Kritik der logischen Vernunft.* P. Janssen (Ed.). *Husserliana* XVII. Den Haag: Martinus Nijhoff.

Husserl, E. (1976). *Ideen zu einer reinen Phänomenologie und phänomenologischen Philosophie. Erstes Buch. Allgemeine Einführung in die reine Phänomenologie.* K. Schuhmann (Ed.). *Husserliana* III/1. Den Haag: Martinus Nijhoff.

Husserl, E. (1984). *Logische Untersuchungen. Zweiter Band. I. Teil. Untersuchungen zur Phänomenologie und Theorie der Erkenntnis.* U. Panzer (Ed.). *Husserliana* XIX/1. Den Haag: Martinus Nijhoff.

Husserl, E. (1987). *Aufsätze und Vorträge (1911–1921).* T. Nenon & H. R. Sepp (Eds.). *Husserliana* XXV. Dordrecht: Martinus Nijhoff.

Husserl, E. (2001a). *Natur und Geist. Vorlesungen Sommersemester 1927.* M. Weiler (Ed.). *Husserliana* XXXII. Dordrecht: Kluwer.

Husserl, E. (2001b). *Die Bernauer Manuskripte über das Zeitbewusstsein (1917/18).* R. Bernet & D. Lohmar (Eds.). *Husserliana* XXXIII. Dordrecht: Kluwer.

Husserl, E. (2001c). *Logik. Vorlesungen 1896.* E. Schuhmann (Ed.). *Materialien* I. Dordrecht: Kluwer.

Husserl, E. (2002a). *Logische Untersuchungen. Ergänzungsband. Erster Teil. Entwürfe zur Umarbeitung der VI. Untersuchung und zur Vorrede für die Neuauflage der Logischen Untersuchungen (Sommer 1913).* U. Melle (Ed.). *Husserliana* XX/1. Dordrecht: Kluwer.

Husserl, E. (2002b). *Zur phänomenologischen Reduktion. Texte aus dem Nachlass (1926–1935).* S. Luft (Ed.). *Husserliana* XXXIV. Dordrecht: Kluwer.

Husserl, E. (2003). *Transzendentaler Idealismus. Texte aus dem Nachlass (1908–1921).* R. D. Rollinger & R. Sowa (Eds.). *Husserliana* XXXVI. Dordrecht: Kluwer.

Husserl, E. (2006). *Späte Texte über Zeitkonstitution (1929–1934). Die C-Manuskripte.* D. Lohmar (Ed.). *Materialien* VIII. Dordrecht: Springer.

Husserl, E. (2008). *Die Lebenswelt. Auslegungen der vorgegebenen Welt und ihrer Konstitution. Texte aus dem Nachlass (1916–1937).* R. Sowa (Ed.). *Husserliana* XXXIX. Dordrecht: Springer.

Johnson, D. H. (1983). *Body.* Boston: Beacon Press.

Juhan, D. (1987). *Job's body: A handbook for bodywork.* Barrytown, NY: Station Hill Press.

Kirkengen, A. L. (2001). *Inscribed bodies: Health impact of childhood sexual abuse.* Dordrecht: Kluwer.

Kirkengen, A. L. (2010). *The lived experience of violation: How abused children become unhealthy adults.* Trans. E. S. Shaw. Bucharest: Zeta Books.

Maletic, V. (1987). *Body – Space – Expression: The development of Rudolf Laban's movement and dance concepts.* Berlin: Mouton de Gruyter.

Patočka, J. (2007). Das Innere und die Welt. Trans. S. Lehmann. Intro. A. C. Santos. *Studia Phaenomenologica, 7,* 15–70.

Sokolowski, R. (1974). *Husserlian meditations: How words present things.* Evanston, IL: Northwestern University Press.

Zaner, R. M. (1981). *The context of self: A phenomenological inquiry using medicine as a clue.* Athens, OH: Ohio University Press.

CHAPTER 6

Body memory and dance

Mónica E. Alarcón Dávila

Hochschule Furtwangen, mBody, Artistic Research

Memory implies the retention of the present as well as the expectation of future events, even though these, as soon as they are perceived, pass by and belong to the past. This article investigates the possibility of a subjective *bodily* experience of time as a form of body memory. In dialog with Husserl's later phenomenology of the body and with the phenomenology of dance, it will be argued that the body is the unconstituted condition of the constitution of time and space.

Keywords: phenomenology, body memory, dance, time and space, consciousness

The body has become a very important topic since the '80s, not just for philosophy, but also for other disciplines like sociology, literature, and dramatics (see Alarcón 2009: 1–5). Although the body is understood in different ways, it can be said that in current philosophical discussion, the prevailing interpretation of the body is that of a *border zone* between 'having' and 'being', matter and the soul, subjectivity and objectivity. The German language distinguishes between *Körper* and *Leib*. *Körper* means the physical, organic body, which can be seen as an object. *Leib* means the body as center of experience, the 'lived', subject body.[1] The outcome of such an interpretation of the body leads up to the recognition that the human being is not just a thinking entity, but also an embodied one. This issue can be pinpointed in the terms of Gabriel Marcel, as follows: My own body, which I have, cannot be reduced to a thing among others. The thinking subject does not simply have a body, but rather *is* his or her body. One's own body is the condition for all further kinds of *having* and would not be of the same nature as the things that we can have (see Marcel 1954).[2] Far from

---

1. *Leib* and *Körper* are two perspectives from which to consider the human body; they are useful for analytical approaches, but in reality they belong together (see Gugutzer 2006: 30–31).

2. It is not only Gabriel Marcel who emphasizes the double reality of the body, but also thinkers like Edmund Husserl, Maurice Merleau-Ponty, and Bernhard Waldenfels, among others. Husserl, for example, calls the body *Leibkörper*. As *Körper*, the body is part of nature and, as

Descartes' reduction of the body to a *res extensa*, the body is now acknowledged as a complex reality with a variety of different aspects that may be taken into consideration. This complexity is clearly envisaged if the interdependency and correlative influence among theory, culture, and our bodily experience are adequately considered (see Gugutzer 2006: 9–53).

The concept of body memory owes its actuality to this general philosophical and cultural interest in the body. Publications over the last 20 years have shown a growing interest in this concept (see, among others: Assmann 2009; Bannasch & Butzer (Eds.) 2007; Bauer 2010; Clastres 1976: 175; Duden & Weigel 1989; Kandel 2006; Öhlschläger & Wiens (Eds.) 1997; Sheldrake 1991; Uehlein 1982: 76–93; Wenzel 1997), which has meanwhile become recognized and applied in various ways: The traumatic memory and the casual remembrance, a memory triggered by a souvenir or a monument revisited, all may be labeled as such.[3] Body memory, at the very least, is used as a complement to mental memory. Thomas Fuchs (2003) explains the difference between mental and body memory in terms of 'explicit' and 'implicit' memory. Whereas explicit memory is conscious, recalling facts and events of the past, implicit memory occurs without assistance from our consciousness. The latter form of memory, i.e. *body memory*, comprises automatic acts that can be performed without thinking and that may occur spontaneously. All our habits and motor skills such as dancing, swimming, and walking fall into this category (see Casey 1987).

Phenomenology and dance

Memory implies the retention of the present as well as the expectation of future events, even though these, as soon as they are perceived, pass by and belong to the past. The capacity to 'extend' the duration of events beyond their objective temporal extension provides not only the opportunity to contemplate them, but also to experience both oneself and the world as being ordered and meaningful. We are able to distinguish one thing from another in much the same way as we are able to recognize, in the very midst of change, certain relationships and the continuities among them. Otherwise, we would be dealing with an unmanageable jumble of meaningless things. Discontinuity

---

such, follows the interdependency of cause and effect. As *Leib*, the body is the root of one's own experience, even the bearer of an 'I' (see Husserl 1973: 161–162). For Merleau-Ponty, not only does the human body avoid the dualism of thing and consciousness, but rather the whole relation with the world is grounded in bodily mediation (see Merleau-Ponty 2002). Waldenfels described the difference between body and mind as a later dissociation of moments that in truth belong together. The body (*Leib*) eludes this dualism and is, through an ambivalent sensibility, active and passive at the same time (see Waldenfels 2006).

3.   Arnd Beise, in his article *Körpergedächtnis als Kulturwissenschaftliches Konzept*, gives a very good critical summary of the different meanings of this concept in the cultural sciences (2007: 9–25).

and chance, like a pause within movement and a moment of silence within sound, can occur, too, within that order.

An art like dance – which has the human body as subject and object of its performance – is a suitable example to consider some questions about body memory. The phenomenological consideration of dance allows considering the body in the full exercise of its *ergon* and acts, like a magnifying glass making visible some aspects of our bodily experience that in daily life can be easily overlooked. The body acts mostly as a medium and alludes to something other than itself: We walk to the office, drink coffee and phone our friends, drive a car, etc. The body is the silent companion of all our activities and is commonly perceived only when it doesn't 'work'; for example, because of discomfort, pain, or sickness. In dance, on the contrary, the movements of the body are in the foreground; the dancer is at the same time the mover and the moved. The double reality of the body as a physical thing and as a subjective sensuous experience rises to the surface in dance and can be understood as a non-reifying experience of the physical body (see Legrand & Ravn 2009: 389–408).

Dance shows not only a body, but also a body in movement, which, with its fleetingness, seems to forestall a reification of itself. A dancing body demands the understanding of the body as *self-aware* and able to move by itself (Waldenfels 2008: 13–22). Body memory asks about the relationship between body and time.

The point addressed by this paper is whether we are capable of a subjective *bodily experience* of time. If the body is understood as able *to move by itself* and steadily changing, it is clear that the body is not just a spatial but also a temporal 'thing'. In a dialog between Husserl's later phenomenology of the body and a phenomenology of dance, it will be argued that the body is the unconstituted condition of the constitution of time and space.[4]

Spaciousness of time: The dancing body

Every act of dancing still has to do with the following physical forces: gravity, inertia, and acceleration. The body is attracted to the center of the earth. It tends to continue in stillness or in movement, as well as to augment or reduce the speed of its movements. The exchange among these forces and the dancing body requires an inherent muscular force of the body that goes along with or against the tendency of these

---

4. The togetherness of time and space in the experience of the moving body has been treated, among others, by Erwin Straus in his interpretation of distance (*Ferne*) as a spatial-temporal form of sensation (*Empfinden*) (Straus 1956); by Alexander Lurija with his concept of kinetic melodies (1973: 176); and by Maxine Sheets-Johnstone with her concept of kinesthetic memory (2003: 89).

physical forces.[5] If we compare dance with music, for example, it could be said that the dancer's instrument is able to play itself, and it would thus not be understood as an instrument like any other. All dancing still embodies a determinate relation of the dancer with his or her own body, with time and space, and with the other dancers. At first sight, one would think that the rhythm of dance is exclusively predetermined by the rhythm of the music. That is true for many styles of dance, but dancers have their own bodily rhythm and can dance with, against, or without music. Over the course of time, the independence of dance from music has been expressed in different ways. Especially interesting for the approach of this paper is the technique of Merce Cunningham, to which I want to refer briefly.

Cunningham's dance style is deemed the culmination of modern dance aesthetics and the beginning of post-modern dance. His dances are termed *abstract* because they do not express some topic of the soul or tell a story. He considers dance a physical-aesthetic manner of movement, and points out that every movement can be an instance of dancing. His choreographies generally begin with a question or problem to be solved through movement; for example, how does a body fall? He uses fortuity in his choreographies in order to find new movements. Chance in the guise of the I-Ching, for example, or his choreographic software, Lifeforms decides the sequence of movements. In fact, Cunningham broke with most modern dance principles. The main perspective of the stage was replaced by a multi-perspective relating to the viewer's position. The multi-perspective corresponds to a decentralization of the movement of different parts of the body: each part of the body can move in different directions and different rhythms at the same time. One of his major innovations is his approach to the independence of dance and music. He developed this conception with John Cage and further applied it to other facets of art, such as stage lighting and costumes. Dance and music are independent forms of art; they only have their temporality in common. Dancers listen to music first at the premiere and dance with their own independent rhythm. For Cunningham, it is not just the sequence of the steps that count, but also the moment of transition between one step and the other, the moment in which one step is ending and the next is coming into being. Whereas the steps, the sequence, and the time (measured by stopwatch) are predetermined, it is the dancers' responsibility to transform these different and separate steps into one dance: to join one step to another in a danced rhythm. Cunningham breaks the immediate connection between the movement of the dancers and its expression. The dancer must learn to dance absolutely new and strange movements that are chosen by chance and pitted against their kinetic sense. These movements do not belong to a known style or personal preferences. In the process of learning and producing dance from these initially isolated and randomly selected forms and steps, the dancer has

---

5.   This goes, of course, not only for dance but also for all our movements. The difference is that in dance, these sensible structures of our experience are in the foreground and, therefore, noticeable.

the opportunity to experience his or her 'own' body and the act of dancing as if for the first time (see Alarcón 2009: 96–119).

The fleetingness of dance as soon it appears, it disappears seems to reveal the spaciousness of time. Like architecture, dance deals with the handling of space; like music, it is strictly bound to time. In dance, time and space are confluent; they belong to each other (see Laban 1991). As a dancer moves, the movement is passing. The dancer goes from one movement to the next and, in doing so, one step leads to the next into unified movements that become a continuous process of dancing. As in listening to a melody, a dancer needs to hold the past (*retention*) and project into the future (*protention*).[6] Dancing involves being aware of one's own action while sensing oneself in all one's movements, which have a rhythm and a form. This self-awareness makes an art like dance possible. It is not a conceptual reflection by the artist about the body and its movements; rather, it is a tactile, kinesthetic, conscious experience of the body as one's own. Tactile, kinesthetic, bodily self-reference is not just an ever-changing *now*, but rather the experience of self-continuity in the midst of change.

The body as special *res extensa* and *res temporalis*

Husserl acknowledged the haptic-kinesthetic constitution of the body (*Leibkörper*) as body consciousness and his analysis of the kinesthetic system[7] to the constitution of perceptual reality makes his philosophy especially attractive for a theory of dance. But Husserl's insistence on his transcendental-phenomenological project seems to be in opposition to a phenomenology of dance that presupposes the body. If, however, the transcendental subject is an embodied one, then he/she belongs to an order that is a presupposition that cannot be constituted, but an order to which the transcendental embodied subject belongs: the world. This *aporia* concerns not just the theory of the body, but rather involves the whole of transcendental phenomenology as such. The explanation of Husserl's phenomenology of the body goes beyond

---

6. "Er [der Ton] fängt an und hört auf, und seine ganze Dauereinheit, die Einheit des ganzen Vorgangs, in dem er anfängt und endet, 'rückt' nach dem Enden in die immer fernere Vergangenheit. In diesem Zurücksinken 'halte' ich ihn noch fest, habe ihn in einer 'Retention', und solange sie anhält, hat er seine eigene Zeitlichkeit, ist er derselbe, seine Dauer ist dieselbe" (Husserl 1966: 385).

7. The kinesthetic system is for Husserl: "[…] ein System möglicher subjektiver Bewegungen, das durch vielfältiges, sei es auch regelloses Durchlaufen verschmolzen ist zu einem vertrauten habituellen Bewegungssystem (jede mögliche Bewegung also eine bekannte und praktisch zu intendierende). Durch Übung ist Herrschaft über dieses System erwachsen, jede intendierte Bewegung 'kann ich' also, und darin liegt, sie ist jederzeit für mich ausführbar und als das in eins mit ihrer Vorstellung bewusst." E. Husserl, Ms. D 13 IV (1921), 4 (quoted by Claesges 1964: 76).

the scope of this article. Consequently, I will only mention the key arguments (see Alarcón 2009: 143–187).

The solution to this opposition is founded on the double reality of the body as *res extensa* (*Körper*) and as the organ of perception and action (*Leib*) (Husserl 1956: 145). Husserl distinguishes between the conscious thematization of the body as a thing among others, on the one hand, and the body as a system of possibilities for the constitution of things on the other hand. In this latter case, an unthematized body consciousness, also called *kinesthetic consciousness*, accompanies and enables the constitution of things and space. The body, by virtue of kinesthetic consciousness, differentiates itself and constitutes the body as a *res extensa*. Thus, for the transcendental subject, the body appears as both constituted (*Körper*) and as constituting (*Leib*). The body is the *conditio sine qua non* of the experience of objects and, as such, belongs to the *ego-cogito*. As constituted *res extensa*, the body belongs to the *cogitata*. The body objectifies itself thanks to the kinesthetic system and the double structure of touch; for example, one hand touching the other.[8] The self-objectivation of the live body, thus, requires an embodied subject. The body is consequently the unconstituted condition of constitution (see Alarcón 2009: 187).

In his later writings, Husserl succeeded in reconciling his transcendental-phenomenological philosophy with a theory of the body (see among others: Claesges 1964; Dos Reis Piedade 2002; Staudigl 2003). Nevertheless, Husserl's theory of the body is always related to the constitution of things and space: the constitution of the latter, indeed, presupposes the body's activity and localization in space (Husserl 1973). The body is a unique *res extensa* and, as such, an *apriori* for the constitution of space (see Claesges 1964). However, at least from the perspective of the kinesthetic system, the body cannot be considered as a unique *res extensa* only, but also as a special *res temporalis* and, as such, an *apriori* for the constitution of time. Thanks to the kinesthetic system, movement plays a very important role in the constitution of things and space. It is a *moving* body which is an *apriori* of constitution and not just a body.

Although Husserl's kinesthetic system doesn't dance – but it is necessarily moving – it could be said that the moving/living subject is capable of dancing. Thus, the experience of time in dance also applies to all our movements. This would mean that

---

8. Die linke Hand abtastend habe ich Tasterscheinungen, d.h. ich empfinde nicht nur, sondern ich nehme wahr und habe Erscheinungen von einer weichen, so und so geformten, glatten Hand. Die anzeigenden Bewegungsempfindungen und die repräsentierenden Tastempfindungen, die an dem Ding 'linke Hand' zu Merkmalen objektiviert werden, gehören der rechten Hand zu. Aber die linke Hand betastend finde ich auch in ihr Serien von Tastempfindungen, sie werden in ihr 'lokalisiert', sind aber nicht Eigenschaften konstituierend [...]. Spreche ich vom physischen Ding 'linke Hand', so abstrahiere ich von diesen Empfindungen[...]. Nehme ich sie mit dazu, so bereichert sich nicht das physische Ding, sondern es wird Leib, es empfindet. [...] Der Leib konstituiert sich also ursprünglich auf doppelte Weise: einerseits ist er physisches Ding, Materie, er hat seine Extension, in die seine realen Eigenschaften [...] eingehen; andererseits finde ich auf ihm, und empfinde ich 'auf' ihm und 'in' ihm [...]" (Husserl 1952: 144–145).

one's own body is the necessary condition of the constitution of time and space. As we saw previously, time and space cannot be considered independently of each other in dance. Rhythm in dance is the rhythm of the movement of the body. This is possible thanks to a perceived continuity in the process of dance (change), which means that the consciousness of the body is also a bodily consciousness of time. The tactile, kinesthetic self-reference of the body is not just a *now* that always changes, but has a duration (*durée*) (see Spateneder 2007): the sensation of this body as mine (as 'I') is always with me. This enables me to distinguish between movements I made myself and movements external to my own body, even as I am steadily changing my movements and perceiving other things. Consequently, the concept of body memory demands an understanding of the body as a unique *res extensa* and *res temporalis* at one and the same time. The relation between body and time and its consequence for an understanding of the body within Husserl's transcendental phenomenology remains an object for further examination.

References

Alarcón, M. (2009). *Die Ordnung des Leibes. Eine tanzphilosophische Betrachtung.* [The order of the body. A dance-philosophical account]. Würzburg: Königshausen & Neumann.

Assmann, A. (2009). *Erinnerungsräume: Formen und Wandlungen des kulturellen Gedächtnisses.* [Space of remembering. Forms and transformations of cultural memory]. München: Beck.

Beise, A. (2007). Körpergedächtnis als kulturwissenschaftliches Konzept. [Body memory as a cultural-studies concept]. In B. Bannasch & G. Butzer (Eds.), *Übung und Affekt. Formen des Körpergedächtnisses* (pp. 9–25). Berlin: de Gruyter.

Bannasch, B. & Butzer, G. (Eds.) (2007). *Übung und Affekt. Formen des Körpergedächtnisses.* [Exercise and affection. Forms of body memory]. Berlin: de Gruyter.

Bauer, J. (2010). *Das Gedächtnis des Körpers: wie Beziehungen und Lebensstile unsere Gene steuern.* [The memory of the body. How relations and lifestyle regulate our genes]. New edition. Frankfurt am Main: Eichborn.

Casey, E. (1987). *Remembering. A Phenomenological Study.* Bloomington: Indiana University Press.

Claesges, U. (1964). *Edmund Husserls Theorie der Raumkonstitution.* [Edmund Husserl's theory of space constitution]. Den Haag: Nijhoff.

Clastres, P. (1976). *Staatsfeinde: Studien zur politischen Anthropologie.* [The enemies of the state. Studies in political anthropology]. Frankfurt am Main: Suhrkamp.

Dos Reis Piedade, J. I. (2002). *Der Bewegte Leib. Kinästhesen bei Husserl im Spannungsfeld von Intention und Erfüllung.* [The moved body. Husserl's Kinesthesia between intention and fulfillment]. Wien: Passagen Verlag.

Duden, A. & Weigel, S. (1989). Schrei und Körper. [Shriek and body]. In T. Koebner (Ed.), *Lakoon und kein Ende: Der Wettstreit der Künste* [Lakoon and no end: The contest of the arts] (pp. 113–141). München: Edition Text + Kritik.

Fuchs, T. (2003). *The Memory of the Body.* http://www.klinikum.uni-heidelberg.de/fileadmin/zpm/psychatrie/ppp2004/manuskript/fuchs.pdf.

Gugutzer, R. (2006). Der Body Turn in der Soziologie. [The body turn in sociology]. In R. Gugutzer (Ed.), *Body turn: Perspektiven der Soziologie des Körpers und des Sports* [Body turn: Perspectives in the sociology of the body and sport.] (pp. 9–53). Bielefeld: Transcript.

Husserl, E. (1973). *Ding und Raum. Vorlesungen 1907.* [Thing and space. Lectures 1907]. Den Haag: Nijhoff.

Husserl, E. (1966). *Zur Phänomenologie des inneren Zeitbewußtseins* (1893–1917). [On the phenomenology of the consciousness of internal time]. Den Haag: Nijhoff.

Husserl, E. (1952). *Ideen zur einen reinen Phänomenologie und phänomenologischen Philosophie. Zweites Buch. Phänomenologische Untersuchungen zur Konstitution.* [Ideas pertaining to a pure phenomenology and to a phenomenological philosophy. Studies in the phenomenology of constitution]. Den Haag: Nijhoff.

Kandel, E. (2006). *In search of memory. The emergence of a new science of mind.* New York: W. W. Norton.

Laban, R. von (1991). *Grundlagen der Raumharmonielehre des Tanzes.* [Foundations of the theory of spatial harmony in dance]. Wilhelmshaven: Florian Noetze.

Legrand, D. & Ravn, S. (2009). Perceiving subjectivity in bodily movement: the case of dancers. *Phenomenology and the Cognitive Sciences,* 8(3), 389–408.

Marcel, G. (1954). *Sein und Haben.* Übers. Ernst Behler. Paderborn: Schöningh.

Merleau-Ponty, M. (2002). *Phenomenology of perception.* Translated by Colin Smith rev. Forrest Williams. London: Routledge & Kegan Paul.

Öhlschläger, C. & Wiens, B. (Eds.) (1997). *Körper – Gedächtnis – Schrift: der Körper als Medium kultureller Erinnerung.* [Body – Memory – Writing: The body as a medium of cultural memory] Berlin: Erich Schmidt.

Spateneder, P. (2007). *Leibhaftige Zeit. Die Verteidigung des Wirklichen bei Henri Bergson.* [Bodily time. The defense of the real in Henri Bergson]. Stuttgart: Kohlhammer.

Staudigl, M. (2003). *Die Grenzen der Intentionalität. Zur Kritik der Phänomenalität nach Husserl.* [The limits of intentionality. For a critique of phenomenality in Husserl]. Würzburg: Königshausen & Neumann.

Sheldrake, R. (1991). *Das Gedächtnis der Natur: das Geheimnis der Entstehung der Formen in der Natur.* [The memory of nature. The secret of the emergence of forms in nature]. Bern: Scherz.

Straus, E. (1956). *Vom Sinn der Sinne: ein Beitrag zur Grundlegung der Psychologie.* [The Primary World of Senses: A Vindication of Sensory Experience]. Berlin: Springer.

Sheets-Johnstone, M. (2003). Kinesthetik memory. *Theoria et Historia Scientiarum,* 7, 69–92.

Lurija, A. (1973). *The working brain.* New York: Basic Books.

Uehlein, F. (1982). *Die Manifestation des Selbstbewußtseins im konkreten 'Ich bin'. Endliches und Unendliches Ich im Denken S. T. Coleridges.* [The manifestation of self-consciousness in the concrete "I am". The finite and the infinite I in the thought of S. T. Coleridges.] Hamburg: Felix Meiner.

Waldenfels, B. (2008). Der Leib und der Tanz. [The body and dance.] In A. Aurnhammer & G. Schnitzler. (Eds.), *Der Tanz in den Künsten 1770–1914* [Dance in the arts 1770–1914] (pp. 13–22). Freiburg: Rombach.

Waldenfels, B. (2006). *Das leibliche Selbst: Vorlesungen zur Phänomenologie des Leibes.* [The bodily self. Lectures on the phenomenology of the body.] Frankfurt am Main: Suhrkamp.

Wenzel, H. (1997). *Gespräche – Boten – Briefe: Körpergedächtnis und Schriftgedächtnis im Mittelalter.* [Speeches – messengers – letters: Body memory and the memory of writings in the Middle Ages.] Berlin: Erich Schmidt.

PART II

Contributions from cognitive sciences

CHAPTER 7

Implicit body memory

Petra Jansen
Institute of Sport Science, University of Regensburg

The dichotomy between explicit and implicit memory systems or memory processes seems to be prominent in cognitive psychology literature. Recently it was discussed that this dichotomy is due to different measurement methods (Buchner & Jansen-Osmann 2006; Reder, Park, & Kieffaber 2009) and does not provide directly evidence for two different processes or even systems. Graf and Schacter (1985) used the term "implicit memory" for describing a situation where a task performance is influenced by a prior experience without the necessity of becoming aware of that prior experience. In this sense, "implicit body memory" does not mean in any case *unconsciousness*. From a cognitive psychology point of view, it means that implicit measurements are used. In "classical" memory tasks implicit memory measurements are category production, word identification or word fragmentation. But what are the explicit and implicit measurements of body memory? It is the goal of this chapter to propose new insights in different measurements of body memory analogous to "classical" memory research.

Keywords: cognitive psychology, memory structure and processes, dichotomy of explicit and implicit memory

Implicit memory from a cognitive psychology view

In cognitive psychology, memory research is a wide field. Theories of memory are concerned with the structure of memory as well as the processes which operate within this structure. An example for a memory process theory is the "levels of processing theory" of Craik and Lockhart (1972). These author assume that the "depth" how a stimuli is processed accounts for the strength of memory traces. Structure and processes depend on each other and can't be viewed separately even theorists concentrate on one of them. Furthermore, there is also a relation between memory and learning. The learned material must be encoded, stored in a memory system and then retrieved.

Concerning the structure of memory systems, theorists agree that working memory and long term memory are two different memory systems. Baddeley and Hitch

(1974) replaced the long existing assumption of a short-term store with the concept of working memory. This working memory exists of a central executive, a phonological loop and a visuo-spatial sketchpad (VSSP) and is expanded by an episodic buffer (Baddeley 2003). Furthermore, Baddely (2003) differentiated between the above mentioned fluid systems (phonological loop, visuo-spatial sketchpad, central executive and episodic buffer) and the crystallized systems (visual semantics, episodic LTM and language). Whereas the VSSP deals with the storage of visual and spatial information, the phonological loop processes verbal information. The central executive has a controlling function, the episodic buffer a more linking one between long term and working memory.

Concerning the research on long term memory there are several theories describing dichotomies of long-term memory systems, as it is for example the dichotomy of episodic and semantic memory (Tulving 1972). According to Tulving and as it is reflected by the name "Episodic memory" describe the storage of information which occurred in a particular time in a particular place (see Eysenck & Keane 2000). If you remember the loveparade tragedy in Duisburg on the 25th of July 2010 you retrieve this information from your episodic memory system. In contrast to that general knowledge of the world is stored in a semantic memory system. Next to this dichotomy, Cohen and Squire (1980) propose a memory system, which distinct between two different knowledge systems, a declarative and a procedural one. This means the distinction between "knowing that" and "knowing how". Thereby, declarative knowledge seems to cover semantic and episodic memory storage, whereas procedural knowledge refers to the performance of skilled actions.

Beside these dichotomies the one between explicit and implicit memory exists. Graf and Schacter (1985) used the term "implicit memory" for describing a situation where a task performance is influenced by a prior experience without the necessity of becoming aware of that prior experience. Explicit memory seems to require conscious thinking. Today it is discussed that implicit memory is not a specific memory system but this term is used for a specific measurement of experience (Reder, Park, & Kieffaber 2009). One can differentiate between implicit and explicit memory tests. Two typical explicit memory tests are the recognition of persons, places and others and the free recall of persons, objects etc. Implicit memory test do not rely on a learning phase but the aftereffect on a specific experience is measured indirectly. One measurement of implicit memory is the *Word Fragment Completion task*. Participants were presented words which they were not able to rehearse because they were often misled by irrelevant items. Then the words were presented again but with missing letters. Results show that participants could easier complete the words when they were presented before even they were not consciously learned.

Using implicit memory tests some behavioral dissociation in patients and older and younger adults could be shown. In 1970 Warrington and Weiskrantz investigated that amnestic patients showed a worse performance in an explicit memory measurement but not in an implicit one. The same research pattern was shown with younger and older adults. Light and Singh (1987) reported a worse recognition of words by the older adults compared to the younger adults, but not a worse performance in the word completion test. Those dissociations exist but this does not prove that there are two different memory systems, because there might be a methodological bias with implicit measurements. Implicit tests are not as reliable as explicit tests (Buchner & Wippich 2000). One might resume that implicit memory tests were used every time when explicit tests could not be applied, as might be the case with the investigation of patients processing information during an operation or any other condition where their consciousness is temporarily "switched off".

Reder, Park, and Kieffaber (2009) summarize that the same memory representation is used regardless whether information is tested explicitly or implicitly. The developed a computational model called SAC with a memory representation in nodes and the connection to other nodes via experience. The strength of the nodes and of the binding between nodes is based on their history that means the context within they are experienced during encoding. Implicit and explicit tasks do retrieve the same memory representation.

Body memory: A new psychological concept?

The former explanations have shown that in cognitive psychology implicit memory is more a question of a specific measurement than a specific memory system or process. But what does this mean for research in body memory and movement? First of all, body memory is not a commonly used concept within cognitive psychology. Most of researchers in this area would judge the term "body memory" as something strange and maybe as an esoteric concept! This does not hold true for a cognitive approach on body perception. Quite recently it was shown that the presence of the head in point-light figures plays a dominant role in body perception. Headless bodies are processed completely different from bodies with heads (Yovel, Pelc, & Lubetzky 2010). Furthermore neuroscientific research in this area has concentrated on the cortical areas for body awareness (Berlucchi & Aglioti 2010). It relies on a large neural network where the posterior parietal cortex, the extrastriate body area and anterior insula play an important role (see Figure 1).

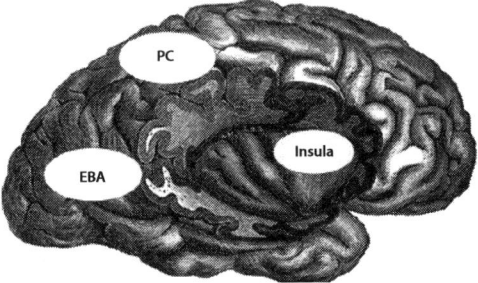

Figure 1. Different cortical areas spezialized for different aspects of bodily awareness (figure from Berlucchi & Aglioti 2010)

As it was stated above cognitive psychologist are not used to the term of body memory/cognitive psychology so far has no concept of body memory (even though some of its recent "embodiment" research is addressing the phenomenon in the way that it is conceptualized by phenomenology). Body schema as a sensorimotor map of the body, and body image as a pictorial description do exist (Paillard 1999; Joraschky, Loew, & Röhricht 2008). But regardless of this, the term "body memory" is used outside the field of cognitive psychology. Fuchs (2003) stated that the "experiences have left their traces in its invisible dispositions". He distinguished between procedural, situational, intercorporeal, incorporative and traumatic memory (see Figure 2). Procedural body memory contains the storage of the patterns of movement in a holistic design. Situational body memory means that the body stores much more than you can see, it stores the atmosphere of a situation. Intercorporeal memory emphasize the interactions, incorporative body memory means the integration of structures and roles of others, traumatic memory refers to the storage of intense negative body experience.

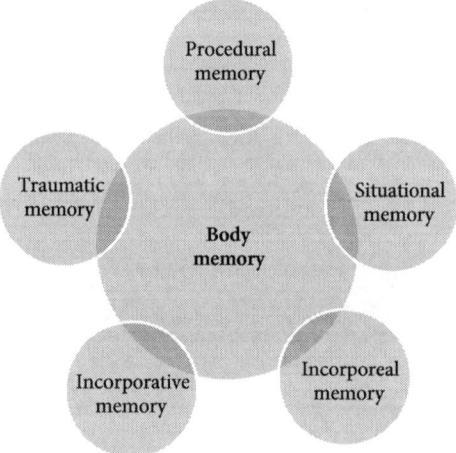

Figure 2. Body memory according to Fuchs (2003)

None of us might doubt that our previous experience is stored in our body. But from a cognitive psychologist point of view one has to ask how we can measure such implicit body memory? In one sense it means that we can't adopt explicit tests/testing. We can't show some body pictures and ask the participants whether they remember these pictures or not. Measuring implicit body memory from a cognitive psychologist perspective means to construct a test where the participants are not aware that their body memory is retrieved. Next to word completion tasks, perceptual priming is often used in implicit body memory and might be adopted in/applied to body memory research.

Perceptual priming is studied in situations in which we know that stimuli have been learned in some way before. For example, when participants have recently learned some pictures, they will recognize them faster when these pictures appear on a monitor screen compared to new pictures. Furthermore, conceptual priming must be taken into account. *Conceptual priming* is based upon the activation of related concepts in memory (Lloyd & Newcombe 2009). It was shown that even children show better conceptual priming than adults when the stimuli are relevant to their lives.

From a cognitive psychology perspective, body memory might be investigated with perceptual and conceptual priming of body pictures. It has already been shown, that there was no priming effect for body poses/postures that are impossible to be performed with the human body (Daems & Verfaillie 1999). It will be due to the co-operation of researchers on embodiment and cognitive psychology to develop pictures from the human body also in a conceptual and procedural situation. Participants in an experiment will react faster on "known" body pictures compared to new ones. But according to Reeder, Park, and Kieffaber's (2009) assumption that information is encoded in connection to other information it might also be essential to present varying contextual information with this body pictures. It will be a challenging task to establish the experimental procedure of implicit body measurement – but it is absolutely essential when "implicit body memory" should not only be a philosophic but also an empirical concept.

References

Baddeley, A. (2003). Working memory: looking back and looking forward. *Nature Reviews Neuroscience, 4,* 829–839.

Baddeley, A. D., & Hitch, G. (1974). Working memory. In G. H. Bower (Ed.), *The psychology of learning and motivation: Advances in research and theory* (Vol. 8, pp. 47–89). New York: Academic Press.

Berlucchi, G., & Aglioti, S. M. (2010). The body in the brain revisited. *Experimental Brain Research, 200,* 25–35.

Buchner, A., & Jansen-Osmann, P. (2006). Implizites Gedächtnis [Implicit memory]. In J. Funke & P. A. Frensch (Hrsg.), *Handbuch der Allgemeinen Psychologie: Kognition* [Handbook of general psychology: Cognition] (pp. 356–362). Göttingen: Hogrefe.

Buchner A., & Wippich W. (2000). On the reliability of implicit and explicit memory measures. *Cognitive Psychology, 40,* 227–259.

Cohen, N. J., & Squire, L. R. (1980). Preserved learning and retention of pattern analysing skill in amnesia: Dissociation of knowing how and knowing that. *Science, 210,* 207–210.

Craik, F. I. M., & Lockhart, R. S. (1972). Levels of processing: A framework for memory research. *Journal of Verbal Learning and Verbal Behavior, 11,* 671–684.

Daems, A., & Verfaillie, K. (1999). Viewpoint dependent priming effects in the perception of human actions and body postures. *Visual cognition, 6,* 665–693.

Eysenck, M. W., & Keane, M. T. (2000). *Cognitive psychology*. Hove: Psychology Press Ltd.

Fuchs, T. (2003). *The memory of the body.* http://www.klinikum.uni-heidelberg.de/fileadmin/zpm/psychatrie/ppp2004/manuskript/fuchs.pdf.

Graf, P., & Schacter, D. L. (1985). Implicit and explicit memory for new associations in normal and amnesic subjects. *Journal of Experimental Psychology: Learning, Memory, and Cognition, 11,* 501–518.

Joraschky, P., Loew, T., & Röhricht, F. (2008). Körpererleben und Körperbild [Body experience and body image]. Stuttgart: Schattauer.

Light, L. L., & Singh, A. (1987). Implicit and explicit memory in young and older adults. *Journal of Experimental Psychology: Learning, Memory and Cognition, 13,* 531–541.

Lloyd, M. E., & Newcombe, N. S. (2009). Implicit memory in childhood: Reassessing developmental invariance. In M. L. Courage & N. Cowan (Eds), *The development of memory in childhood* (pp. 93–114). Hove: Psychology Press.

Paillard, J. (1999). Body schema and body image. A double dissociation in deafferented patient. In G. N. Gantchev, S. Mori & J. Massion (Eds), *Motor control. Today and tomorrow* (pp. 197–214). Sofia: Academic Publishing House "Prof. M. Drinov".

Reder, L. M., Park, H., & Kieffaber, P. (2009). Memory systems do not divide on consciousness: Reinterpreting memory in terms of activation and binding. *Psychological Bulletin, 135,* 23–49.

Tulving, E. (1972). Episodic and semantic memory. In E. Tulving & W. Donaldson (Eds.), *Organization of memory* (pp. 381–403). New York: Academic Press.

Warrington, E. K., & Weiskrantz, L. (1970). Amnesic Syndrome: consolidation or retrieval? *Nature, 228,* 628–630.

Yovel, G., Pelc, T., & Lubetzky, I. (2010). It's all in your head: Why is the body inversion effect abolished for headless bodies? *Journal of Experimental Psychology: Human Perception and Performance, 36,* 759–767.

CHAPTER 8

Embodied concepts

Christina Bermeitinger and Markus Kiefer
University of Hildesheim, Institute for Psychology, Hildesheim, Germany /
University of Ulm, Department of Psychiatry, Ulm, Germany

There is a long-standing debate within philosophy and psychology on the question whether concepts are abstract mental entities or based on reactivation of sensory and motor representations. The chapter reviews what concepts are and what they are for. The relation of concepts and semantic memory is pointed out. The classical views on conceptual representations proposing an amodal representation of concepts are contrasted with recent embodiment theories, which assume that concepts are essentially grounded in perception and action. Different sources of evidence from behavioral psychology and neuropsychology foster the view that concepts are represented in the sensory and motor systems. We attempt an integration of embodied and classical views on conceptual representation and discuss embodied processes in related areas of cognitive psychology.

Keywords: concept representation, category representation, classic view, embodied view, sensory and motor reenactment, situational dependency, concepts as action supporting

Imagine (human) beings without body, just mind. How do they think, how do they process words, what meaning have concepts to them? For example, what is a chair to them? Does it have any meaning at all? The nature of conceptual representation is controversially debated since several hundreds of years within philosophy and psychology, and during the last few decades also within neuroscience and computational science. Classically, an amodal view was predominant. According to this view, the body as well as the sensory and motor systems are not relevant for higher-level cognition. Thus, conceptual representations, which are the constituents of thought, are assumed to be based on abstract symbols and relations between these symbols (e.g., Fodor & Pylyshyn 1988; Minsky 1975; Newell & Simon 1976). In this view, a mind without body can easily be imagined and hypothetical creatures without body vs. creatures with body should not differ with regard to their cognitive abilities.

In contrast, there is a growing number of researchers within the field of human cognition who assume that mental processes are based on bodily interactions with one's environment (e.g., Clark 1999; Pecher & Zwaan 2005; Glenberg 1997), that is "The mind is inherently embodied" (Lakoff & Johnson 1999:1). Regarding to this view, the body and basic sensory-motor structures do not represent a "support system for a mind that needs to be fueled and transported" (Pecher & Zwaan 2005:1) but, in contrast and depicted in extreme manner, are thought to constitute the mind. Cognitive processes do not represent a software that can run independently from the hardware (i.e., the human brain and body) in which they were acquired. Thus, the body typifies the basis for cognition and the same processes that are used for bodily interactions (i.e., for perception and action) support mental processes. Therefore, it seems not possible to think of a mind without body or to imagine how a mind without body would think or feel because the entire basis for developing and maintaining cognitive structures and processes is lacking.

In this chapter, we will argue that concepts are essentially grounded in perception and action. Before we present evidence demonstrating that concepts are represented in an embodied mind, we will first introduce the term 'concept' and will then give a short overview of traditional theories on conceptual representations.

Concepts – What they are and what they are for

There are several theoretical approaches on what concepts are. Pre-theoretically, concepts represent the constituents of thoughts. Within philosophy, the term 'concept' is used for diverse projects and things (e.g., Goguen 2005; Margolis & Laurence 2006). Thus, a common definition is lacking (Zalta 2001). However, most psychological theoretical accounts assume that concepts constitute the meaning of objects, events, and abstract ideas. Concepts refer to categories of exemplars because conceptual representations generalize across specific instances and situations, in which we have encountered the referent in the past (e.g., specific exemplars of birds; e.g., Kiefer & Pulvermüller, in press). Traditionally, concepts are thought to be stored in semantic long-term memory (Tulving 1972). The term 'semantics' refers to the elementary meaning of concepts and objects. Therefore, within semantic memory, individuals have represented facts and knowledge about the world without referring to a particular or personal spatiotemporal experience (Tulving 1972). With the help of our semantic knowledge we can answer questions like: What is the capital of Sweden? What does the binomial theorem says? What does a bulb look like? What is the basic color of a Ferrari? According to traditional theories, metaphorically, semantic memory can be compared to a dictionary with information regarding a concept's identity, spelling, and pronunciation, to an encyclopedia with information about the meaning of a concept, and to a thesaurus with information about words or things with similar meanings (e.g., Hutchison 2003).

Meanwhile somewhat outdated memory theories presuppose that memory is for memorizing (see e.g., Glenberg 1997, who discussed the function of memory for human cognition). However, only few people would deny the importance of (semantic) memory for our everyday life. This fact could be seen as tentative evidence that there have to be more functions and deeper reasons for memory than pure 'memorizing'. Thus, more recent theories assume that memory is not only for simple memorizing but instead, memory is supposed to facilitate essentially interaction and action with and in the environment (e.g., Glenberg 1997; Kiefer & Pulvermüller 2011). Semantic memory also plays a crucial role for verbal communication because concepts provide the meaning of words to which they are linked (e.g., Levelt, Roelofs & Meyer 1999). Since antiquity, philosophers such as Aristotle have been interested in the question of how we should think about concepts. In the following 2500 years, philosophy, linguistics, computer sciences, science of education, and psychology have been engaged in the study of semantic memory in one way or another (e.g., Baddeley 1997; Rogers & McClelland 2004). However, although it is an old topic to understand the organization and representation of semantic memory, it is nevertheless a prevailing theme and probably one of the most debated topics of contemporary cognitive science (e.g., Canessa et al. 2008; Laiacona, Barbarotto & Capitani 2006; Mahon & Caramazza 2003; Matsuka, Sakamoto & Chouchourelou 2008; McMullen & Purdy 2006; Mechelli, Sartori, Orlandi & Price 2006).

As we have already pointed out above, a concept is the mental representation of a category which forms a class of different objects, events or ideas (e.g., Murphy 2004). For example, the concept 'bird' includes different examples of birds. Thus, concepts represent categories. In turn, "Categories are great simplifiers" (Blair & Homa 2003: 1293) because properties attributed to the category can be generalized to the exemplars. Furthermore, knowledge can be transferred to new objects and predictions are optimized. The advantages are evident (e.g., Murphy 2004; see also Waldmann 2008, who described some more advantages and functions of categories). For instance, one does not have to describe or memorize each single property of a specific category exemplar if he or she knows from which category the exemplar is derived. For example, a bird is characterized by being bipedal, having wings, having a beak, having feathers, being an animal, it flies, lays eggs, builds a nest, and so on. If someone tells you about a specific bird, for instance a kori bustard, he or she has to say only that this is a bird and most often you will have a good first impression of the exemplar 'kori bustard' and how you can (or cannot) interact with it. With respect to general cognitive economy, a good categorization considers that the exemplars within a specific category (although they differ in detail) are more similar than a specific exemplar of that category with an exemplar of a different category (e.g., Rosch 1977; Zayan & Vauclair 1998). So, if one becomes acquainted with a new exemplar of the category bird, for instance again the kori bustard, one must only keep in mind that kori bustards are birds and in addition the specific properties of kori bustards (e.g., they are extremely large and mostly grey in color). But it is not necessary to memorize the single properties of a kori bustard which also hold for birds. Thus, simplifying through categorization is one of the most basic, general, and universal processes of creatures' nature and of every neural system (e.g., Feldman 2006). The process of simplifying prevents the cognitive system from being overloaded or from suffering a 'run-time error' due to the overabundance of stimuli which stream over and into us in every second of life (e.g., Zayan & Vauclair 1998). Categorization is therefore a very basic principle also in humans. Even in the most chaotic of circumstances, humans search for a subjacent organizing principle (e.g., Schnabel 2008).

Traditional amodal theories on categorization and conceptual representation

The first set of theories, which we review here, mainly focus on the issue of how a concept is assigned to a given object or event, or in other words of how objects or events are categorized. In a meanwhile outdated view, each concept is exactly described by a definition including necessary and sufficient conditions as in Aristotelian logic (e.g., Bruner, Goodnow & Austin 1956), for instance, a bird may be defined as an entity consisting of elements with the features [+feathers], [+beak], [+wings], [+lays eggs] and [+ability to fly]. Thereby, each object can be classified as being a representative of a given concept or as no representative of a given concept. However, due to some theoretical considerations and numerous empirical results (especially the finding of graded memberships and inter- and intraindividual variability of the classification of one object as being a member of a specific category, e.g., Hampton 1979; McCloskey & Glucksberg 1978; Rosch 1975) this view (which is most often simply termed *classical view*) is generally thought of as being unfounded and antiquated (e.g., Waldmann 2008) or even as being "a total flop" (Murphy 2004: 483).

Three more recent alternative theories have been developed to explain the categorization process (see e.g., Waldmann 2008), namely the prototype, exemplar, and knowledge approaches. Central to *prototype approaches* (e.g., Lakoff 1987; Rosch 1973) is the assumption that a specific set of features characteristic or typical to a specific concept is represented – either as an ideal exemplar/best example, or as the average of exemplars, or simply as accumulation of different characterizing features. However, it is possible that no real exemplar of a category exists which actually has all of these features or matches perfectly the ideal exemplar. Some prototype approaches further assume that features within such a feature set are weighted according to their relevance for a given concept or category (e.g., Komatsu 1992). On the contrary, the *exemplar approaches* (e.g., Murphy 1993; Nosofsky & Palmeri 1997; Ross 2000; Ross & Spalding 1994) assume that single exemplars, or even each single encounter with an exemplar, are stored and represented together with the category's name or the concept's label. However, exemplar approaches also assume that categories are set up by creating a rule for a typical exemplar (e.g., the prototypical songbird: is small, flies, builds nests, sings, and so on) and by storing exceptions of this rule as exemplars. A new exemplar is then compared with the rule and (all) stored things. An exemplar is classified as member of a specific category when it is more similar to instances which are stored with the specific category label compared to instances which are stored with other category labels.

Besides these theories which are mainly based on the principles of similarity and the comparison of features or exemplars, there is one theory that takes the general knowledge about the world into account by including the view that things or features are not unrelated but do have several relationships to other things or features in the world (e.g., Markman 2003; see also Bruner 1957). The theory further assumes that such correlations are part of category representations and generally part of our knowledge. This theory is therefore termed *knowledge approach or simply theory theory* and is especially corroborated by evidence showing that (the difficulty of) categorization interacts with previous knowledge (e.g., Wattenmaker, Dewey, Murphy & Medin 1986).

As stated by Murphy (2004), "there is no clear, dominant winner" (p. 488) in the field of theories on categorization and the most reasonable approach would be to assume an involvement of different approaches or mechanisms to explain all data and phenomena (e.g., Sternberg 2009; for an overview of findings which are problematic for each account and of findings which can corroborate each account see e.g., Murphy 2004; Waldmann 2008). For example, before a prototype can be established (this would be the case if a person has only one or a few encounter[s] with exemplars of a specific category), a concept is mainly based on a single or few exemplar(s). Furthermore, there are several theories which assume multiple systems. These systems can act jointly but it is also assumed that interindividual and intraindividual differences exist (see e.g., Waldmann 2008).

Besides these above mentioned theories on categorization, a different class of theories is aimed to explain the structure of conceptual memory.[1] Kiefer and Pulvermüller (in press) introduced four important dimensions to classify different theoretical accounts on the structure of conceptual representations: The amodal/modality-specific dimension (amodal: conceptual representations are independent and distinct from representations in perceptual and motor areas; modality-specific: conceptual representations are grounded in perceptual and motor representations, embodiment approach), the local/distributed dimension (local: a concept is coded by one node; distributed: a concept is coded across several nodes), the flexible/stable dimension (flexible: concepts are flexibly tailored to the current context and are constituted of dynamically recruited features; stable: concepts represent situational invariant mental knowledge entities), and the experience-dependent/innate dimension (experience-dependent: concepts are formed by experience; innate: concepts represent innate a priori categorical specializations).

Regarding conceptual memory structure, an early view assumes that each concept is represented as a single node within a unitary semantic network (Collins & Loftus 1975; Collins & Quillian 1969; Quillian 1968). The nodes are linked to meaningfully related other concepts. In summary, this early account is a prototypical exemplar of

---

1.   Although both classes of theories are not completely independent from each other, we first present them here in a side-by-side manner.

local and amodal theories which assume that concepts are developed by experience but then represent stable and situational invariant abstract entries.[2]

Some findings challenging the traditional amodal view

Situational dependency. Meanwhile, there is cumulative evidence that concepts are represented dynamically and variably across situations (e.g., Hoenig, Sim, Bochev, Herrnberger & Kiefer 2008; Pecher & Raaijmakers 2004; Raposo, Moss, Stamatakis & Tyler 2009; Yeh & Barsalou 2006) which clearly contradicts the above mentioned assumption that concepts or word meanings are like more or less fixed dictionary entries (Badre & Wagner 2002; McRae, de Sa & Seidenberg 1997) and are coded in local (or single) nodes. For example, Greenspan (1986) presented spoken sentences and participants concurrently made lexical decisions on visually presented words (e.g., music or heavy). Different sentences activated different properties of the same sentence-final word (e.g., 'The young man played the piano' or 'The young man lifted the piano.'). Facilitating effects on the lexical decision were only found if the target words matched the activated property. A further example for flexible recruitment of different features was presented from Barsalou (1982, Experiment 2). He presented word pairs and participants had to decide how similar the objects (to which the words referred) were. Either, the words were accompanied by their common category (e.g., furniture, birds, etc.), by an ad-hoc category (e.g., possible gifts, taken on camping trips, etc.), or by no category. The author found that participants rated category coordinates (e.g., sofa – desk, robin – eagle) as equally similar independent of whether a common category name or no category accompanied the word pairs. However, word pairs of the ad-hoc categories (e.g., record album – necklace, flashlight – rope) were rated significantly more similar when they were accompanied by the ad-hoc category compared to no category. Barsalou (1982) concluded that some features are activated independent of context whereas other features are activated only when a specific context (which activates the overlapping features) is given. Furthermore, he interpreted his results as evidence that not all features that may be represented in concepts are active whenever a word is encoded.

These initial findings could be replicated with different measures and methods. For instance, recent experiments by Bermeitinger and colleagues (Bermeitinger 2009; Bermeitinger, Wentura & Frings 2008, 2011) used the semantic priming paradigm to contribute to this issue. The semantic priming paradigm represents the most utilized paradigm in cognitive psychology for studying the organization and processing of semantic knowledge (for reviews see, e.g., McNamara 2005; Neely 1991). In a typical version of this paradigm, participants judge whether or not targets are real words, and a prime word – which is completely irrelevant to the participants' task – precedes

---

2. The last point is a necessary consequence from the local representation format.

each target. This prime word can either be semantically related (e.g., flower-rose) or semantically unrelated (e.g., bird-rose) to the target. Although primes do not predict the correct target response, participants usually respond faster in related as compared to unrelated trials. Bermeitinger et al. used this paradigm and investigated differences between natural categories (i.e., biological or living objects such as predators, vegetables, etc.) and artifactual categories (i.e., man-made or non-living objects such as tools, dishes, etc.). That is, they presented category labels as primes and category exemplars as targets on which participants made word-nonword decisions. Additionally, Bermeitinger et al. interspersed these category priming task with a second task requiring subjects to react to either perceptual or action features of objects which are completely independent of the priming task, for example, simple geometric shapes. Focusing on perceptual features enhanced semantic priming effects for natural categories, whereas focusing on action features enhanced semantic priming effects for artifactual categories. In fact, significant priming effects emerged only for those categories which are thought to rely on the features (visual vs. action) activated by the second task.

Such context-dependent or second-task-dependent activations of features (see also e.g., Kiefer & Martens 2010) cannot be explained by traditional theories, especially not by theories assuming a local conceptual representation. To implement more flexibility in concept representation, distributed semantic memory models were developed (e.g., the parallel distributed processing framework by Rumelhart & McClelland 1986). Therein, concepts are coded by several representational units which were assumed, for instance, as representing different (semantic) features (e.g., Devlin, Gonnerman, Andersen & Seidenberg 1998; Tyler & Moss 2001). Thus, for a current representation of a concept, the configuration of activation across these several units can differ from that of past or future representations. The different representations can vary as a function of situational constraints and change over time by experience. According to these distributed network theories (e.g., Rogers et al. 2004), conceptual knowledge is represented independently and distinct from perception and action in an amodal format within a unitary semantic system. This unitary system is assumed to be located in the anterior temporal lobe structures.

Category-specificity. Challenging for theories assuming a unitary semantic system are findings that different categories (e.g., animals, furniture, fruit, and tools) are associated with activation in different brain regions (e.g., Spitzer, Kwong, Kennedy, Rosen & Belliveau 1995; for reviews and/or meta-analysis see Bookheimer 2002; Humphreys & Forde 2001; Joseph 2001; Martin & Chao 2001). Further evidence for, at least partially, different brain areas involved in processing natural versus artifactual categories comes from studies with brain damaged patients. The reviews of Forde and Humphreys (1999) and Capitani, Laiacona, Mahon, and Caramazza (2003) point out that the most reliable form of category-specific deficits can be observed for biological objects. The reviews suggest that the representation of artifacts is the other global subtype that can be damaged independently from the biological categories. There is also some evidence from behavioral studies that natural and artifactual objects (or categories) were processed in different ways or at least with a different time course. One basic finding is that superordinate categorization of living objects seems to be faster and more accurate as the superordinate categorization of nonliving objects. This pattern was found in the majority of studies (for the opposite pattern with basic-level naming see e.g., Lloyd-Jones & Humphreys 1997), as indicated by several tasks, for example, by a living versus nonliving decision task (e.g., Allen, Goldstein, Madden & Mitchell 1997; Gold, Beauregard, Lecours & Chertkow 2003), by naming pictured objects (using matched stimuli regarding, for example, concept familiarity and visual complexity; e.g., Laws, Leeson & Gale 2002), by semantic classification tasks (e.g., Marques 2002, Experiment 1) or by an auditory lexical decision task (e.g., Wurm, Whitman, Seaman, Hill & Ulstad 2007).

Such findings suggest that there is not a single unitary system but, perhaps, several semantic subsystems. To explain such findings, domain-specific theories were developed (e.g., Caramazza & Mahon 2003; Caramazza & Shelton 1998). These theories assume distinct innate semantic subsystems dissecting the semantic space into, for example animals (it is suggested that animals are represented in left anterior temporal cortex), vegetables, tools (it is suggested that tools are represented more dorsally in parietal areas) etc. The different semantic subsystems are assumed to be a consequence of evolutionary pressure which has formed specialized brain circuits containing knowledge of one categorical/conceptual domain. However, as in theories on a unitary semantic system, in these domain-specific theories, concepts are thought to be represented in local and most probably stable manner. Thus, in contrast to distributed memory models, these domain-specific theories have again difficulties to explain context dependencies.

Modality specificity. Challenging for assumptions regarding a unitary semantic system or innate domain-specific semantic subsystems also is evidence especially from brain imaging studies and studies using electrophysiological measures, which support the view that concepts are represented in the sensory and motor systems in a modality-specific fashion (for review, see e.g., Kiefer & Pulvermüller, in press; Meteyard & Vigliocco 2008). Modality-specific theories are also favored by evidence from behavioral studies (for review, see e.g., Bergen & Feldman 2008) and from studies with brain damaged patients (e.g., Neininger & Pulvermüller 2001). Over the last years, there is growing evidence for different brain activations in the sensory and motor systems when dealing with different types of concepts, for example, from different categories as tools versus vegetables (see above). As activation for different categories is most often found in sensory or motor areas, this sort of evidence is difficult to reconcile with domain-specific theories. For example, access to artifactual categories such as tools, for which action-related information is highly relevant and processing of action-related conceptual representations (e.g., action words) is impaired in patients with lesions encompassing the motor cortex (e.g., Gainotti 2004; Gainotti, Silveri, Daniele & Giustolisi 1995; Neininger & Pulvermüller 2001, 2003). In contrast, deficits for natural objects, for which perceptual (especially visual) information is highly relevant, are most often consequences after lesions in the visual association cortex (Tranel, Damasio & Damasio 1997).

Martin and Chao (2001) summarized in their review on fMRI studies regarding category specific activations that the overall data suggested an activation cluster in the more lateral region of the fusiform gyrus for living objects and a cluster in the more medial region of the fusiform gyrus for nonliving things. This means that a region – the fusiform gyrus (lying in the ventral occipitotemporal cortex) – that was thought to be responsible especially for the processing of shape responds differently dependent on the category type. In parallel to findings from brain damaged patients, a further common finding is that manipulable objects (especially tools) activate brain regions usually associated with motion perception or with grasping. For instance, in the picture naming task, artifacts (compared to natural objects) have been reported to evoke more activation in the left ventral premotor cortex, a brain area involved in action representation (e.g., Bookheimer 2002; Damasio, Grabowski, Tranel, Hichwa & Damasio 1996; Martin & Chao 2001; Martin, Wiggs, Ungerleider & Haxby 1996). Additionally, for different action words slightly different regions were activated depending on the body part involved in carrying out the action (e.g., foot – "kick"; mouth – "lick"; Boulenger, Hauk & Pulvermüller 2009; Hauk, Johnsrude & Pulvermuller 2004; Hauk & Pulvermüller 2004).

Further evidence for modality-specific activations comes from studies using event-related potentials (ERPs) (e.g., Kiefer 2001, 2005; Kiefer, Sim, Liebich, Hauk & Tanaka 2007; Pulvermüller, Lutzenberger & Preissl 1999). For example, using repetition priming, a semantic decision task, or a classification task, different waves, and a different topography for the activation of artifactual versus natural categories have been found (Kiefer 2001, 2005; Paz-Caballero, Cuetos & Dobarro 2006; Sim & Kiefer 2005; but see Hinojosa, Martín-Loeches, Muñoz, Casado, Fernández-Frías & Pozo 2001). The different topography of the ERP effects over visual and motor cortex is in line with the suggestion that visual conceptual features are more relevant for representing natural categories whereas action-related conceptual features are more relevant for representing artifact categories. For example, Paz-Caballero et al. (2006) found bilaterally more positive ERPs from about 300 ms up to about 600 ms for natural compared to artifactual line drawings with a semantic categorization task. Kiefer, Sim, Herrnberger, Grothe, and Hoenig (2008) found in their combined EEG/fMRI study that recognizing words denoting objects, for which acoustic features are highly relevant (e.g., "dog", "telephone"), suffices to ignite cell assemblies in the posterior superior and middle temporal gyrus. These cell assemblies were also activated by listening to real sounds. Due to the early onset (at about 150 ms after word onset) of activation in this region, the activity most likely reflects rapid access to acoustic conceptual features in auditory cortex instead of later post-conceptual processes (e.g., imagery).

In summary, these results provide evidence for direct links between perceptual and conceptual processing and between motor and conceptual processing. Furthermore, perceptual and motor brain regions seem to be essentially involved in accessing conceptual representations. In consequence, a lot of traditional assumptions regarding category representation have to be reconsidered.

Embodiment accounts of conceptual representation

Especially findings on situational dependency and modality specificity support the view that concepts are grounded in perception and action (e.g., Barsalou, Simmons, Barbey & C. D. Wilson 2003; Gallese & Lakoff 2005; Glenberg 1997; Humphreys & Forde 2001; Kiefer & Spitzer 2001; Lakoff & Johnson 1999; Martin & Chao 2001). Concepts are supposed to be embodied in the modality-specific sensory and motor systems, and representations are context dependent. However, a unified theory on embodied cognition is still missing as well as a unitary term for that what is meant. For example, whether "situated cognition" includes "embodied cognition" or vice versa and whether "embedded cognition" or "enacted cognition" should be the term encompassing all other aspects depends on individual preferences and emphases (e.g., Robbins & Aydede 2009). Until now, there are some diverse claims on embodied cognition, for example, M. Wilson (2002) identified six claims:

> 1st cognition is situated,
> 2nd cognition is time-pressured,
> 3rd we off-load cognitive work onto the environment,
> 4th the environment is part of the cognitive system,
> 5th cognition is for action (and communication),
> 6th offline cognition is body-based or based on reenactment.

We have already presented several pieces of evidence in support of an embodiment view. Therefore, we here want to highlight three aspects which seem especially noteworthy for such an embodiment view of conceptual representation.

First, concepts are based on reenactment of perception, action, and interoception. As presented above, there is several evidence that motor and perceptual processing is not only closely linked to conceptual processing (e.g., Pulvermüller 2005; Kiefer et al. 2008) but represents the crucial basis for conceptual processing (e.g., Gallese & Lakoff 2005). Also interoceptive states are thought to be reenacted when concepts are processed (e.g., Barsalou 2009). Sensory and motor processes and functions developed for perception and action are also acting during off-line thought processes that do not refer on the immediate environment (e.g., Pecher & Zwaan 2005; Kiefer et al. 2007, 2008). Zwaan and Madden (2005) argued that meaning is construed by activating and integrating sensorimotor representations in simulations of specific situations (for an account on simulation and simulators see e.g., Barsalou 2009). During the process of reenactment, first, modality-specific states are stored, second, at later times these states (or biased versions of these states) are partially reenacted.

Second, concepts are situated. Barsalou (1982) was one of the first who postulated that concepts are situated. He extensively investigated this issue and offered some theoretical contributions. According to him (e.g., Barsalou 2009), during retrieval, first and always, only a small subset of the features stored for a category becomes active in a given situation. Second, when a concept becomes active, accompanying representations of associated situations become active as well (e.g., Barsalou 2003; Yeh & Barsalou 2006). Thus, a concept is not a situation-invariant representation of a category but is a context dependent representation produced out of many possibilities (Hoenig et al. 2008). Not only concrete things or objects, but also abstract concepts like truth or freedom (e.g., Barsalou & Wiemer-Hastings 2005; Gibbs 2005) seem to be represented situated and with strong re-reference to sensorimotor systems (but see e.g., Bickerton 1995).

Third, concepts are for action (and communication). In contrast to the view that memory is for memorizing and that concepts are seen as detached databases (as it is implicitly assumed in traditional semantic memory theories), concepts can be seen as "agent-dependent instruction manuals" (Barsalou 2009:244). Thus, a concept is seen as ability to create different situation-dependent representations supporting goal pursuit in the current setting including instructions for interacting with the current category exemplar. As concepts ties "our past experiences to our present interactions with the environment" (Murphy 2004, outside back cover) they are supposed to essentially enhance our interactions with objects in the environment (see e.g., Clark 1999; Glenberg 1997) ultimately assuring survival (e.g., Borghi 2005). As concepts can be linked with words, they constitute the meaning of language and are one important prerequisite of verbal communication. One precondition is again the flexible adjustment of a concept to the current situation. Borghi (2005) goes one step further by assuming that not only perception and action are the basis of conceptual processing but that perception is (instead of the recording of sensorial messages) influenced and filtered by action. Evidence comes, for instance, from recent research: using an action priming paradigm, Kiefer, Sim, Helbig, and Graf (2011) showed that action representations rapidly activated within 100 ms are able to influence the ongoing visual object recognition process. Thus, conceptual knowledge makes it possible for us to "extract information from the object so that we are able to interact with it successfully" (Borghi 2005:10).

Integrations, junctions, relations

First of all, traditional theories on categorization (e.g., the prototype approach, the exemplar approach, the knowledge approach) can be accomplished with accounts on the structure of semantic memory (e.g., neural models which represent a more micro view on concept representation, see above; e.g., Chalmers 1990; Matsuka et al. 2008). For example, one integrative model would assume a (distributed) storage of particular exemplars. Abstraction from these particular exemplars can occur in a flexible manner. That is, no single abstraction is stored (as it is assumed in prototype theories) but a specific abstraction can be generated by demand. This abstraction is temporally instable, can include various features, and can depend on, for example, expectancy, a particular reference point, a specific situation, or a global focus (see e.g., Bermeitinger 2009; Barsalou 1982, 1983; Wentura 1995).

Second, as shown above, behavioral, electrophysiological, neuroimaging and neuropsychological evidence strongly support embodiment approaches to conceptual representations (for a classification of theories in stronger and weaker versions of embodiment see e.g., Meteyard & Vigliocco 2008). However, there are also accounts which assume (additionally) an amodal conceptual system with a *pure* semantic region or some kind of abstraction. A possibility of integrating amodal and modal representations is tapped by Barsalou (2009) who assumed that "patterns of active neurons in association areas constitute amodal recodings of activation in modality-specific areas". However, he also assumed that these patterns are actually not amodal because of modality-specific tunings. In recent theoretical approaches hybrid models were proposed, envisaging a conceptual system comprised of modality-specific systems in sensory and motor areas plus an amodal "conceptual hub", which integrates the distributed modality-specific representations (Simmons & Barsalou 2003; Kiefer, Schuch, Schenk & Fiedler 2007; Patterson, Nestor & Rogers 2007; Mahon & Caramazza 2008; Pulvermüller, Cooper-Pye, Dine, Hauk, Nestor & Patterson 2010). Vigliocco, Vinson, Lewis, and Garrett (2004) state that semantic or concept representations are based on modality dependent features. Additionally, in their account, conceptual representations are thought to be supra-modal and their function is to bind together modality dependent features. Such binding areas are part of several theoretical accounts, originally developed from neuroscientific ideas. For example, Damasio (1989; Damasio & Damasio 1994) assumed a convergence zone (located in higher order association areas in frontal and temporal cortices) in which features (as parts, shape, color, movement, etc.) contained in primary sensory cortices were combined to codes of more complex events (e.g., temporal relationships). Thus, these convergence zones synchronize and coordinate activation over primary cortices.

In sum, there is strong evidence for conceptual representations grounded in the sensory and motor systems. Thus, concepts are to a considerable degree embodied, that is, based on reenactment of modality-specific regions, situation dependent, and built in support of appropriate interaction with the environment. However, the pattern of findings regarding the relationship between semantic and perceptual information is overall rather complex. Thus, some kind of convergence zone or even more abstract representations are still under debate (e.g., Arbib 2008; Bickerton 1995; Kiefer & Pulvermüller, in press; Meteyard & Vigliocco 2008).

Similar to conceptual knowledge held in semantic memory, which is essential for goal-directed interaction within the environment and verbal communication, other cognitive phenomena have also been demonstrated to be based on a reactivation of sensory and motor representations and as situation dependent. For example, emotion (e.g., Griffith & Scarantino 2009; Niedenthal 2007; Sheets-Johnstone 2008), consciousness (e.g., J. Prinz 2009; Sheets-Johnstone 2008), problem solving (e.g., Kirsh 2009; Thomas & Lleras 2009), spatial cognition (e.g., Tversky 2009), selective attention and action planning (e.g., Leboe, Whittlesea & Milliken 2005; Hommel, Müsseler, Aschersleben & W. Prinz 2001), and even mathematics (e.g., Lakoff & Núñez 2000; Núñez 2008) have been recently described as embodied processes. This suggests that embodiment represents a principle that generalizes across a variety of phenomena in many areas of cognition and emotion.

In conclusion, the embodiment approach seems to be fruitful for fostering an integrative view on cognition as a whole. In this integrative view, concepts might play an important role as links between past experiences and present situations, in which problems have to be solved and for which selective attention is needed. In such a constellation, concepts can be possibly seen as a guide depending on experience and situation for directing attention to features that are relevant in the present situation and for choosing actions that are appropriate for the current problem. Thus, embodied concepts that are grounded in perception and action are essential tools for successful behavior in a dynamically changing world with various situations and their affordances.

References

Allen, P. A., Goldstein, B., Madden, D. J. & Mitchell, D. B. (1997). Adult age differences in long-term semantic priming. *Experimental Aging Research, 23*, 107–135.

Arbib, M. A. (2008). From grasp to language: Embodied concepts and the challenge of abstraction. *Journal of Physiology, 102*, 4–20.

Baddeley, A. (1997). *Human memory: Theory and practice*. East Sussex, England: Psychology Press.

Badre, D. & Wagner, A. D. (2002). Semantic retrieval, mnemonic control, and prefrontal cortex. *Behavioral & Cognitive Neuroscience Reviews, 1*, 206–218.

Barsalou, L. W. (1982). Context-independent and context-dependent information in concepts. *Memory & Cognition, 10*, 82–93.

Barsalou, L. W. (1983). Ad hoc categories. *Memory & Cognition, 11*, 211–227.

Barsalou, L. W. (2003). Situated simulation in the human conceptual system. *Language and Cognitive Processes, 18*, 513–562.

Barsalou, L. W. (2009). Situating concepts. In P. Robbins & M. Aydede, *The Cambridge handbook of situated cognition* (pp. 236–263). New York: Cambridge University Press.

Barsalou, L. W., Simmons, W. K., Barbey, A. K. & Wilson, C. D. (2003). Grounding conceptual knowledge in modality-specific systems. *Trends in Cognitive Sciences, 7*, 84–91.

Barsalou, L. W. & Wiemer-Hastings, K. (2005). Situating abstract concepts. In D. Pecher & R. Zwaan (Eds.), *Grounding cognition: The role of perception and action in memory, language, and thought* (pp. 129–163). New York: Cambridge University Press.

Bergen, B. & Feldmann, J. (2008). Embodied concept learning. In P. Calvo & A. Gomila, *Handbook of cognitive science: An embodied approach* (pp. 313–331). Amsterdam: Elsevier.

Bermeitinger, C. (2009). *Facts and artifacts about tureens and artichokes: Natural and artifactual categories investigated with semantic priming*. Göttingen: Cuvillier.

Bermeitinger, C., Wentura, D. & Frings, C. (2008). Nature and facts about natural and artifactual categories: Sex differences in the semantic priming paradigm. *Brain & Language, 106*, 153–163.

Bermeitinger, C., Wentura, D. & Frings, D. (2011). How to switch on and switch off semantic priming effects: Activation processes in category memory depend on focusing specific feature dimensions. *Psychonomic Bulletin & Review, 18*, 579–585.

Bickerton, D. (1995). *Language and human behavior*. Seattle: University of Washington Press.

Blair, M. & Homa, D. (2003). As easy to memorize as they are to classifiy: The 5–4 categories and the category advantage. *Memory & Cognition, 31*, 1293–1301.

Bookheimer, S. (2002). Functional MRI of language: New approaches to understanding the cortical organization of semantic processing. *Annual Review of Neuroscience, 25*, 151–188.

Borghi, A. M. (2005). Object concepts and action. In D. Pecher & R. A. Zwaan (Eds.), *Grounding cognition: The role of perception and action in memory, language, and thought* (pp. 8–34). New York: Cambridge University Press.

Boulenger, V., Hauk, O. & Pulvermüller, F. (2009). Grasping ideas with the motor system: Semantic somatotopy in idiom comprehension. *Cerebral Cortex, 19*, 1905–1914.

Bruner, J. S. (1957). Going beyond the information given. In J. S. Bruner, E. Brunswik, L. Festinger, F. Heider, K. F. Muenzinger, C. E. Osgood & D. Rapport (Eds.), *Contemporary approaches to cognition* (pp. 41–69). Cambridge, MA: Harvard University Press.

Bruner, J. S., Goodnow, J. J. & Austin, G. A. (1956). *A study of thinking*. New York: Wiley.

Canessa, N., Borgo, F., Cappa, S. F., Perani, D., Falini, A., Buccino, G., et al. (2008). The different neural correlates of action and functional knowledge in semantic memory: An fMRI study. *Cerebral Cortex, 18*, 740–751.

Capitani, E., Laiacona, M., Mahon, B. & Caramazza, A. (2003). What are the facts of semantic category-specific deficits? A critical review of the clinical evidence. *Cognitive Neuropsychology, 20*, 213–261.

Caramazza, A. & Mahon, B. Z. (2003). The organization of conceptual knowledge: The evidence from category-specific semantic deficits. *Trends in Cognitive Sciences, 7*, 354–361.

Caramazza, A. & Shelton, J. R. (1998). Domain-specific knowledge systems in the brain: The animate-inanimate distinction. *Journal of Cognitive Neuroscience, 10*, 1–34.

Chalmers, D. J. (1990). Why Fodor and Pylyshyn were wrong: The simplest refutation. In *Proceedings of the Twelfth Annual Conference of the Cognitive Science Society* (pp. 340–347). Hillsdale, NJ: Lawrence Erlbaum.

Clark, A. (1999). An embodied cognitive science? *Trends in Cognitive Sciences, 3*, 345–351.

Collins, A. M. & Loftus, E. F. (1975). A spreading-activation theory of semantic processing. *Psychological Review, 82*, 407–428.

Collins, A. M. & Quillian, M. R. (1969). Retrieval time from semantic memory. *Journal of Verbal Learning and Verbal Behavior, 8*, 240–247.

Damasio, A. R. (1989). The brain binds entities and events by multiregional activation from convergence zones. *Neural Computation, 1*, 123–132.

Damasio, A. R. & Damasio, H. (1994). Cortical systems for retrieval of concrete knowledge: The convergence zone framework (pp. 61–74). In C. Koch & J. L. Davis (Eds.), *Large-scale neuronal theories of the brain*. London, UK: MIT Press.

Damasio, H., Grabowski, T. J., Tranel, D., Hichwa, R. D. & Damasio, A. R. (1996). A neural basis for lexical retrieval. *Nature, 380*, 499–505.

Devlin, J. T., Gonnerman, L. M., Andersen, E. S. & Seidenberg, M. S. (1998). Category-specific semantic deficits in focal and widespread brain damage: A computational account. *Journal of Cognitive Neuroscience, 10*, 77–94.

Feldmann, J. A. (2006). *From molecule to metaphor: A neural theory of language.* Seattle: MIT Press.

Fodor, J. & Pylyshyn, Z. (1988). Connectionism and cognitive architecture: A critical analysis. *Cognition, 28*, 3–71.

Forde, E. M. E. & Humphreys, G. W. (1999). Category-specific recognition impairments: A review of important case studies and influential theories. *Aphasiology, 13*, 169–193.

Gainotti, G. (2004). A metanalysis of impaired and spared naming for different categories of knowledge in patients with a visuo-verbal disconnection. *Neuropsychologia, 42*, 299–319.

Gainotti, G., Silveri, M. C., Daniele, A. & Giustolisi, L. (1995). Neuroanatomical correlates of category-specific semantic disorders: A critical survey. *Memory, 3*, 247–264.

Gallese, V. & Lakoff, G. (2005). The brain's concepts: The role of the sensory-motor system in conceptual knowledge. *Cognitive Neuropsychology, 22*, 455–479.

Gibbs, R. W. (2005). Metaphor interpretation as embodied simulation. *Mind & Language, 21*, 434–458.

Glenberg, A. M. (1997). What memory is for. *Behavioral and Brain Sciences, 20*, 1–55.

Goguen, J. (2005). What is a concept? In F. Dau, M. L. Mugnier & G. Stumme (Eds.), *ICCS 2005, LNAI 3596* (pp. 52–77). Berlin: Springer.

Gold, D., Beauregard, M., Lecours, A. R. & Chertkow, H. (2003). Semantic category differences in cross-form priming. *Journal of the International Neuropsychological Society, 9*, 796–805.

Greenspan, S. L. (1986). Semantic flexibility and referential specificity of concrete nouns. *Journal of Memory and Language, 25*, 539–557.

Griffith, P. & Scarantino, A. (2009). Emotions in the wild: The situated perspective on emotion. In P. Robbins & M. Aydede, *The Cambridge handbook of situated cognition* (pp. 437–453). New York: Cambridge University Press.

Hampton, J. A. (1979). Polymorphous concepts in semantic memory. *Journal of Verbal Learning and Verbal Behavior, 18*, 441–461.

Hauk, O. & Pulvermüller, F. (2004). Neurophysiological distinction of action words in the fronto-central cortex. *Human Brain Mapping, 21*, 191–201.

Hauk, O., Johnsrude, I. & Pulvermuller, F. (2004). Somatotopic representation of action words in human motor and premotor cortex. *Neuron, 41*, 301–307.

Hinojosa, J. A., Martín-Loeches, M., Muñoz, F., Casado, P., Fernández-Frías, C. & Pozo, M. A. (2001). Electrophysiological evidence of a semantic system commonly accessed by animals and tools categories. *Cognitive Brain Research, 12*, 321–328.

Hoenig, K., Sim, E.-J., Bochev, V., Herrnberger, B. & Kiefer, M. (2008). Conceptual flexibility in the human brain: Dynamic recruitment of semantic maps from visual, motion and motor-related areas. *Journal of Cognitive Neuroscience, 20*, 1799–1814.

Hommel, B., Müsseler, J., Aschersleben, G. & Prinz, W. (2001). The theory of event coding (TEC): A framework for perception and action planning. *Behavioral and Brain Sciences, 24*, 849–937.

Humphreys, G. W. & Forde, E. M. E. (2001). Hierarchies, similarity, and interactivity in object recognition: 'Category-specific' neuropsychological deficits. *Behavioral and Brain Sciences, 24*, 453–509.

Hutchison, K. A. (2003). Is semantic priming due to association strength or feature overlap? *Psychonomic Bulletin & Review, 10,* 785–813.

Joseph, J. E. (2001). Functional neuroimaging studies of category specificity in object recognition: A critical review and meta-analysis. *Cognitive, Affective & Behavioral Neuroscience, 1,* 119–136.

Kiefer, M. (2001). Perceptual and semantic sources of category-specific effects: Event-related potentials during picture and word categorization. *Memory & Cognition, 29,* 100–116.

Kiefer, M. (2005). Repetition-priming modulates category-related effects on event-related potentials: Further evidence for multiple cortical semantic systems. *Journal of Cognitive Neuroscience, 17,* 199–211.

Kiefer, M. & Martens, U. (2010). Attentional sensitization of unconscious cognition: Task sets modulate subsequent masked semantic priming. *Journal of Experimental Psychology: General, 139,* 464–489.

Kiefer, M. & Pulvermüller, F. (in press). Conceptual representations in mind and brain: Theoretical developments, current evidence and future directions. *Cortex.*

Kiefer, M. & Spitzer, M. (2001). The limits of a distributed account of conceptual knowledge. *Trends in Cognitive Sciences, 5,* 469–471.

Kiefer, M., Schuch, S., Schenck, W. & Fiedler, K. (2007). Mood states modulate activity in semantic brain areas during emotional word encoding. *Cerebral Cortex, 17,* 1516–1530.

Kiefer, M., Sim, E. J., Helbig, H. B. & Graf, M. (2011). Tracking the time course of action priming on object recognition: Evidence for fast and slow influences of action on perception. *Journal of Cognitive Neuroscience, 23,* 1864–1874.

Kiefer, M., Sim, E. J., Herrnberger, B., Grothe, J. & Hoenig, K. (2008). The sound of concepts: Four markers for a link between auditory and conceptual brain systems. *The Journal of Neuroscience, 28,* 12224–12230.

Kiefer, M., Sim, E. J., Liebich, S., Hauk, O. & Tanaka, J. (2007). Experience-dependent plasticity of conceptual representations in human sensory-motor areas. *Journal of Cognitive Neuroscience, 19,* 525–542.

Kirsh, D. (2009). Problem solving and situated cognition. In P. Robbins & M. Aydede, *The Cambridge handbook of situated cognition* (pp. 265–306). New York: Cambridge University Press.

Komatsu, L. K. (1992). Recent views on conceptual structure. *Psychological Bulletin, 112,* 500–526.

Laiacona, M., Barbarotto, R. & Capitani, E. (2006). Human evolution and the brain representation of semantic knowledge: Is there a role for sex differences? *Evolution and Human Behavior, 27,* 158–168.

Lakoff, G. (1987). *Women, fire and dangerous things: What categories reveal about the mind.* Chicago: University of Chicago Press.

Lakoff, G. & Johnson, M. (1999). *Philosophy in the Flesh: The embodied mind and its challenge to Western thought.* New York: Basic Books.

Lakoff, G. & Núñez, R. (2000). *Where mathematics comes from: How the embodied mind brings mathematics into being.* New York: Basic Books.

Laws, K. R., Leeson, V. C. & Gale, T. M. (2002). The effect of 'masking' on picture naming. *Cortex, 38,* 137–148.

Leboe, J. P., Whittlesea, B. W. A. & Milliken, B. (2005). Selective and nonselective transfer: Positive and negative priming in a multiple-task environment. *Journal of Experimental Psychology: Learning, Memory, and Cognition, 31,* 1001–1029.

Levelt, W. J., Roelofs, A. & Meyer, A. S. (1999). A theory of lexical access in speech production. *Behavioral and Brain Sciences, 22,* 1–75.

Lloyd-Jones, T. J. & Humphreys, G. W. (1997). Categorizing pears and naming chairs: Category differences in object processing as a function of task and priming. *Memory & Cognition, 25,* 606–624.

Mahon, B. Z. & Caramazza, A. (2003). Constraining questions about the organisation and representation of conceptual knowledge. *Cognitive Neuropsychology, 20,* 433–450.

Mahon, B. Z. & Caramazza, A. (2008). A critical look at the embodied cognition hypothesis and a new proposal for grounding conceptual content. *Journal of Physiology (Paris), 102,* 59–70.

Margolis, E. & Laurence, S. (2006). Concepts. In E. N. Zalta (Ed.), *Stanford Encyclopedia of Philosophy.* URL=<http://plato.stanford.edu/entries/concepts>.

Markman, A. B. (2003). Conceptual representations in psychology. In L. Nadel (Ed.), *Encyclopedia of cognitive science* (Vol. 1, pp. 670–673). London: Nature Publishing Group.

Marques, J. F. (2002). An attribute is worth more than a category: Testing different semantic memory organisation hypotheses in relation to the living/nonliving things dissociation. *Cognitive Neuropsychology, 19,* 436–478.

Martin, A. & Chao, L. L. (2001). Semantic memory and the brain: Structure and processes. *Current Opinion in Neurobiology, 11,* 194–201.

Martin, A., Wiggs, C. L., Ungerleider, L. G. & Haxby, J. V. (1996). Neural correlates of category-specific knowledge. *Nature, 379,* 649–652.

Matsuka, T., Sakamoto, Y. & Chouchourelou, A. (2008). Modeling a flexible representation machinery of human concept learning. *Neural Networks, 21,* 289–302.

McCloskey, M. & Glucksberg, S. (1978). Natural categories: Well defined or fuzzy sets? *Memory & Cognition, 6,* 462–472.

McMullen, P. A. & Purdy, K. S. (2006). Category-specific effects on the identification of non-manipulable objects. *Brain & Cognition, 62,* 228–240.

McNamara, T. P. (2005). *Semantic priming: Perspectives from memory and word recognition.* New York: Psychology Press.

McRae, K., de Sa, V. R. & Seidenberg, M. S. (1997). On the nature and scope of featural representations of word meaning. *Journal of Experimental Psychology: General, 126,* 99–130.

Mechelli, A., Sartori, G., Orlandi, P. & Price, C. J. (2006). Semantic relevance explains category effects in medial fusiform gyri. *Neuroimage, 30,* 992–1002.

Meteyard, L. & Vigliocco, G. (2008). The role of sensory and motor information in semantic representation: A review. In P. Calvo & A. Gomila, *Handbook of cognitive science: An embodied approach* (pp. 291–312). Amsterdam: Elsevier.

Minsky, M. (1975). A framework for representing knowledge. In P. H. Winston (Ed.), *The psychology of computer vision* (pp. 211–277). New York: McGraw-Hill.

Murphy, G. L. (1993). Theories and concept formation. In I. van Mechelen, J. A. Hampton, R. S. Michalski & P. Theuns (Eds.), *Categories and concepts: Theoretical views and inductive data analysis* (pp. 173–200). London: Academic Press.

Murphy, G. L. (2004). *The big book of concepts.* Cambridge, MA: MIT Press.

Neely, J. H. (1991). Semantic priming effects in visual word recognition: A selective review of current findings and theories. In D. Besner & G. W. Humphreys (Eds.), *Basic processes in reading: Visual word recognition* (pp. 264–336). Hillsdale, NJ: Erlbaum.

Neininger, B. & Pulvermüller, F. (2001). The right hemisphere's role in action word processing: A double case study. *Neurocase, 7,* 303–317.

Neininger, B. & Pulvermüller, F. (2003). Word-category specific deficits after lesions in the right hemisphere. *Neuropsychologia, 41*, 53–70.

Newell, A. & Simon, H. (1976). Computer science as empirical inquiry: Symbols and search. *Communication of ACM, 19*, 113–126.

Niedenthal, P. M. (2007). Embodying emotion. *Science, 316*, 1002–1005.

Nosofsky, R. M. & Palmeri, T. J. (1997). An exemplar-based random walk model of speeded classification. *Psychological Review, 104*, 266–300.

Núñez, R. E. (2008). Mathematics, the ultimate challenge to embodiment: Truth and the grounding of axiomatic systems. In P. Calvo & A. Gomila, *Handbook of cognitive science: An embodied approach* (pp. 333–353). Amsterdam: Elsevier.

Patterson, K., Nestor, P. J. & Rogers, T. T. (2007). Where do you know what you know? The representation of semantic knowledge in the human brain. *Nature Reviews Neuroscience, 8*, 976–987.

Paz-Caballero, D., Cuetos, F. & Dobarro, A. (2006). Electrophysiological evidence for a natural/artifactual dissociation. *Brain Research, 1067*, 189–200.

Pecher, D. & Raaijmakers, J. G. W. (2004). Priming for new associations in animacy decision: Evidence for context dependency. *Quarterly Journal of Experimental Psychology, 57A*, 1211–1231.

Pecher, D. & Zwaan, R. A. (2005). Introduction to grounding cognition: The role of perception and action in memory, language, and thinking. In D. Pecher & R. A. Zwaan (Eds.), *Grounding cognition: The role of perception and action in memory, language, and thought* (pp. 1–7). New York: Cambridge University Press.

Prinz, J. (2009). Is consciousness embodied? In P. Robbins & M. Aydede, *The Cambridge handbook of situated cognition* (pp. 419–436). New York: Cambridge University Press.

Pulvermüller, F. (2005). Brain mechanisms linking language and action. *Nature, 6*, 576–582.

Pulvermüller, F., Cooper-Pye, E., Dine, C., Hauk, O., Nestor, P. & Patterson, K. (2010). The word processing deficit in Semantic Dementia: All categories are equal but some categories are more equal than others. *Journal of Cognitive Neuroscience, 22*, 2027–2041.

Pulvermüller, F., Lutzenberger, W. & Preissl, H. (1999). Nouns and verbs in the intact brain: Evidence from event-related potentials and high-frequency cortical responses. *Cerebral Cortex, 9*, 497–506.

Quillian, M. R. (1968). Semantic memory. In M. Minsky (Ed.), *Semantic information processing* (pp. 227–270). Cambridge, MA: MIT Press.

Raposo, A., Moss, H. E., Stamatakis, E. A. & Tyler, L. K. (2009). Modulation of motor and premotor cortices by actions, action words and action sentences. *Neuropsychologia, 47*, 388–396.

Robbins, P. & Aydede, M. (2009). A short primer on situated cognition. In P. Robbins & M. Aydede, *The Cambridge handbook of situated cognition* (pp. 3–10). New York: Cambridge University Press.

Rogers, T. T. & McClelland, J. L. (2004). *Semantic cognition: A parallel distributed processing approach*. Cambridge, MA: MIT Press.

Rogers, T. T., Lambon Ralph, M. A., Garrard, P., Bozeat, S., McClelland, J. L., Hodges, J. R. et al. (2004). Structure and deterioration of semantic memory: A neuropsychological and computational investigation. *Psychological Review, 111*, 205–235.

Rosch, E. H. (1973). Natural categories. *Cognitive Psychology, 4*, 328–350.

Rosch, E. (1975). Cognitive representations of semantic categories. *Journal of Experimental Psychology: General, 104*, 192–233.

Rosch, E. (1977). Human categorization. In N. Warren (Ed.), *Studies in cross-cultural psychol-ogy* (pp. 1–49). London: Academic Press.

Ross, B. H. (2000). The effects of category use on learned categories. *Memory & Cognition, 28,* 51–63.

Ross, B. H. & Spalding, T. L. (1994). Concepts and categories. In R. J. Sternberg (Ed.), *Thinking and problem solving* (pp. 119–148). San Diego: Academic Press.

Rumelhart, D. E. & McClelland, J. L. (Eds.). (1986). *Parallel distributed processing: Explorations in the microstrucutre of cognition* (Vol. I and II). Cambridge, MA: MIT Press.

Schnabel, U. (2008, August 14). Der sanfte Atheist [The gentle atheist]. *Zeit, 63,* p. 14.

Sheets-Johnstone, M. (2008). Getting to the heart of emotions and consciousness. In P. Calvo & A. Gomila, *Handbook of cognitive science: An embodied approach* (pp. 453–465). Amsterdam: Elsevier.

Sim, E. J. & Kiefer, M. (2005). Category-related brain activity to natural categories is associated with the retrieval of visual features: Evidence from repetition effects during visual and functional judgments. *Cognitive Brain Research, 24,* 260–273.

Simmons, W. K. & Barsalou, L. W. (2003). The similarity-in-topography principle: Reconciling theories of conceptual deficits. *Cognitive Neuropsychology, 20,* 451–486.

Spitzer, M., Kwong, K. K., Kennedy, W., Rosen, B. R. & Belliveau, J. W. (1995). Category-specific brain activation in fMRI during picture naming. *Neuroreport, 6,* 2109–2112.

Sternberg, R. J. (2009). *Cognitive psychology.* Belmont: Wadsworth Cengage Learning.

Thomas, L. E. & Lleras, A. (2009). Swinging into thought: Directed movement guides insight in problem solving. *Psychonomic Bulletin & Review, 16,* 719–723.

Tranel, D., Damasio, H. & Damasio, A. R. (1997). A neural basis for the retrieval of conceptual knowledge. *Neuropsychologia, 35,* 1319–1327.

Tulving, E. (1972). Episodic and semantic memory. In E. Tulving & W. Donaldson (Eds.), *Organization of memory* (pp. 381–403). New York: Academic Press.

Tversky, B. (2009). Spatial cognition: Embodied and situated. In P. Robbins & M. Aydede, *The Cambridge handbook of situated cognition* (pp. 201–216). New York: Cambridge University Press.

Tyler, L. K. & Moss, H. E. (2001). Towards a distributed account of conceptual knowledge. *Trends in Cognitive Science, 5,* 244–252.

Vigliocco, G., Vinson, D. P., Lewis, W. & Garrett, M. F. (2004). Representing the meaning of object and action words: The featural and unitary semantic space hypothesis. *Cognitive Psychology, 48,* 422–488.

Waldmann, M. R. (2008). Kategorisierung und Wissenserwerb [Categorization and knowledge acquisition]. In J. Müsseler (Ed.), *Lehrbuch Allgemeine Psychologie* [Textbook on general psychology] (pp. 376–427). Heidelberg, Germany: Spektrum.

Wattenmaker, W. D., Dewey, G. I., Murphy, T. D. & Medin, D. L. (1986). Linear separability and concept learning: Context, relational properties, and concept naturalness. *Cognitive Psychology, 18,* 158–194.

Wentura, D. (1995). *Verfügbarkeit entlastender Kognitionen* [Accessibility of exculpating cognitions]. Weinheim, Germany: Beltz.

Wilson, M. (2002). Six views of embodied cognition. *Psychonomic Bulletin & Review, 9,* 625–636.

Wurm, L. H., Whitman, R. D., Seaman, S. R., Hill, L. & Ulstad, H. M. (2007). Semantic processing in auditory lexical decision: Ear-of-presentation and sex differences. *Cognition & Emotion, 21,* 1470–1495.

Yeh, W. & Barsalou, L. W. (2006). The situated nature of concepts. *Journal of American psychology*, *119*, 349–384.

Zalta, E. (2001). Fregean senses, modes of presentation, and concepts. *Philosophical Perspectives*, *15*, 335–359.

Zayan, R. & Vauclair, J. (1998). Categories as paradigms for comparative cognition. *Behavioural Processes*, *42*, 87–99.

Zwaan, R. A. & Madden, C. (2005). Embodied sentence comprehension. In D. Pecher & R. A. Zwaan (Eds.), *Grounding cognition: The role of perception and action in memory, language, and thought* (pp. 224–245). New York: Cambridge University Press.

CHAPTER 9

Cognitive perspectives on embodiment

Christina Jung and Peggy Sparenberg

Max Planck Institute for Human Cognitive and Brain Sciences, Leipzig

This chapter focuses on theories of embodiment and relevant empirical findings. The embodied approach in cognitive science claims that cognition is based on action. It argues that external stimuli evoke sensorimotor activations in the observer. Specially, it has been suggested that during action observation, corresponding motor programs are activated in the observer. This is supported by the discovery of mirror neurons and evidence of interactions between perception and action production. Moreover, it has been argued that humans represent other people's intentions and beliefs in an interpersonal setting. Humans seem to be able to automatically integrate other individuals' (anticipated) behaviour into their own (re-)actions, which allows the prediction of other people's actions and fast and flexible reactions in social situations.

Keywords: embodiment, emotion, imitation, prediction, social interaction, action simulation

Embodiment in cognitive science – A definition

Our body is always with us. Except for in neurological disorders like, for example, the loss of proprioception (as described in the patient Ian Waterman by Cole 1995) or the alien hand syndrome (a disorder where the patient experiences the sensation of a limb – mostly the hand – as not belonging and/or as not controlled by themselves) (for an overview see Biran & Chatterjee 2004), experiencing our bodies is an everyday experience. Accordingly, it is reasonable to assume that the body and the way human beings experience it shapes perception and cognition. In cognitive science, the embodied approach claims that cognition is based on action (Wilson 2002). That is, the sight and sound of external stimuli evoke sensorimotor activations in the observer. Empirical research has provided evidence that several types of external stimuli are represented in terms of sensory and motor aspects in the observer. It is known that object perception is embodied. For example, looking at a cup automatically activates the motor programs of a grasping movement towards this cup (Tucker & Ellis 1998). Furthermore, language is also an external stimulus which is suggested to be embodied

(Arbib 2005; Liberman & Mattingly 1985). It has been shown that while reading or listening to sentences, humans seem to internally simulate the action which is described in the sentences (Glenberg & Kaschak 2002). For example, participants are faster at judging whether a sentence makes sense while making a simultaneous hand-reaching movement when the direction of this movement corresponds to the direction of the movement described in the sentence (e.g., closing a drawer and a hand-reaching movement away from the body) (Glenberg & Kaschak 2002). In line with this finding, concepts can also influence action production on a more general level and after a time delay. Bargh and colleagues showed that participants walked more slowly after an experiment when they were primed with an elderly stereotype as compared to control participants (Bargh, Chen & Burrows 1996).

Finally, a large number of studies have addressed the question of how other individuals' actions are represented and processed. The action of another person is a special external stimulus because it is a highly complex, dynamic stimulus. This is not only because the body contains a number of body parts and limbs, which can be moved separately from each other, and these movements can have a different quality (smooth versus sharp) or speed (fast versus slow), but also because the movements of different body parts can be combined in several ways and there are also biomechanical constraints. Altogether, this makes the perception and understanding of another person's action quite a challenging task. Nevertheless, humans fulfill this task easily and without exerting any particular effort. The next section deals with the mechanisms which may underlie the representation and processing of one of the most interesting classes of stimuli: other individuals' actions.

Mirrors in action: Mechanisms of action understanding, imitation and action prediction

Humans can easily perceive, understand and even anticipate other individuals' actions although these are highly complex and highly dynamic social stimuli. This might be because the observed action can be directly mapped onto the observer's motor representations. Moreover, the perception of actions seems to automatically activate corresponding motor programs in the observer.

Evidence of such an automatic activation of corresponding motor programs in the observer comes from the "chameleon effect" (Chartrand & Bargh 1999). The chameleon effect describes how partners in a conversation imitate each other automatically and unconsciously. For example, incidental foot-shaking and face-rubbing is imitated by the conversation partner. The explanation for this phenomenon is that observing these body movements automatically activates the motor system in the same way as performing the action(s), and is often labelled "covert imitation" or "action simulation".

It has been proposed that there is a close link between the mental representation of the posture and the movement of one's own body, and the mental representation of the posture and movement of another person's body (see ideomotor theory of action by James 1890), and that both domains might share a common coding system (see Common Coding Principle by Prinz 1990, 1997; TEC by Hommel et al. 2001). The fact that a large number of studies show "action congruency effects" provides evidence of a close behavioral link between action perception and action production. Action congruency effects refer to findings of a facilitation effect showing that action execution is faster and more precise when the same action is observed concurrently or prior to action execution as compared to when a different action is observed, even when the observed action is not relevant for the reaction time task (Brass, Bekkering & Prinz 2001; Brass, Bekkering, Wohlschlager & Prinz 2000; Stürmer, Aschersleben & Prinz 2000). For example, Brass and colleagues (2000) showed that the observation of a lifting movement of the index finger led to faster execution of a lifting movement with the index finger relative to the middle finger, even when the observed movement was irrelevant to the task. This indicates that the observation of a movement automatically activates corresponding motor programs in the observer and prepares the observer's motor system for the execution of the same movement. This leads in turn to faster initiation times.

In extension to this influence of action observation on the speed of the initiation of action execution, there is also evidence of an influence on how precisely an action is performed. Kilner and colleagues (2003) demonstrated that participants show increased variance in arm movement execution when they observe a human model executing a qualitatively different arm movement as compared to the same arm movement. This difference does not appear when participants watch a robot performing similar movements. Similar results were found in the auditory domain. Participants are faster at reading a written syllable aloud when they see a mouth pronouncing the same syllable as compared to when they watch a mouth pronouncing a different syllable (Kerzel & Bekkering 2000). Altogether, these findings support the assumption that the observation of a certain action activates the corresponding motor programs in the observer, and it seems that this covert action imitation is a fast and automatic process.

One can even go one step further: If action perception and action execution draw on the same representations, training one process should have a positive influence on the performance of the other process. Such an influence was shown by Casile and Giese (2006). The authors showed that motor learning without vision can influence later perceptual performance. In this study, blindfolded participants were motor trained with novel arm movements that would normally not be observed or executed by the participants. After this motor training, participants showed improved visual recognition performance for trained arm movements, while no improvement in visual recognition performance was present for untrained arm movements. Moreover, a strong correlation was found between the individual performance in arm movement execution and the improvement in visual recognition performance (Casile & Giese 2006). This suggests a direct and specific action perception-execution link.

As a neural correlate of such a perception-action link the so called mirror neurons were obtained. These neurons are located in area F5 in the macaque monkey brain (Gallese, Fadiga, Fogassi & Rizzolatti 1996) and fire both when the monkey observes an action and when it performs this action on its own. Studies using functional magnet resonance imaging (fMRI) and transcranial magnetic stimulation (TMS) have provided evidence that such a mirror neuron system also exists in the human brain. Several premotor and parietal brain regions in the human brain are active during the observation of other people's actions and action execution (Fadiga, Fogassi, Pavesi & Rizzolatti 1995; Grezes, Armony, Rowe & Passingham 2003; Rizzolatti & Craighero 2004). Moreover, this activity during action observation is greater when the observer has the intention to imitate the observed action later in comparison to when simply recognizing it (Grezes, Costes & Decety 1999).

However, covert imitation not only allows us to prepare for action imitation, rather it also allows action understanding (Jeannerod 2001). It enables the observer to access the underlying intentions and goals of another person's action and literally allows us to put ourselves in the shoes of another person and to see the world through another person's eyes. Liepelt and colleagues showed that the underlying intention of the person observed modulates action congruency effects (Liepelt, Cramon & Brass 2008). The authors visually presented an action (finger lifting movement) which was intentionally performed, unintentionally performed (by a machine), or intentionally initiated, but not performed (due to a force against the finger which suppressed the execution). They showed that action congruency effects were significantly smaller when the same action was performed unintentionally by a machine as compared to when it was performed intentionally. No significant difference was found between the action congruency effect in an intentionally performed action and an intentional, but suppressed, action (by force). These findings suggest that it is not the movement kinematics that are important for motor priming, but rather the underlying intention of the movement. Accordingly, the anticipated movement which would result from the underlying intention (and not the observed movement pattern itself) might be represented in the observer.

But why does the visual system "need" the motor system in order to fulfill the function of action understanding and action prediction? Thornton and Knoblich (2006) suggest that the answer is "time". They argue that action representations have a temporal and a spatial component. It is suggested that action perception uses both spatial and temporal components and that the mental representations of this perception also involve a dynamic (i.e., temporal) dimension (Freyd 1987). The motor system might provide the temporal dimension and the change-over-time for the perceptual system (Viviani 2002). This is in line with the arguments by Schütz-Bosbach and Prinz (2007) that the visual system uses the predictive properties of the motor system.

Prediction is an essential ability for human beings, because it allows the selection of an appropriate response in advance of an anticipated event and is therefore more advantageous than simply reacting to upcoming events. Perception of an external stimulus (object, odor, noise, etc.) takes a certain amount of time from arrival at the sense organ to being processed at high level cognitive functions (e.g. identification, response programming, and memory retrieval). Therefore, there is a time delay which needs to be bridged by prediction (Schütz-Bosbach & Prinz 2007) allowing an individual to react quickly and successfully in our environment.

The fact that perception is a predictive process is supported by studies identifying the representational momentum (Bertamini 1993; Finke & Freyd 1985; Freyd & Finke 1984). Representational momentum is a visual phenomenon in which a movement or an implied movement of an object is automatically and unconsciously extrapolated in its trajectory beyond the actual movement on the screen. Representational momentum has been also demonstrated for human movements (Jarraya, Amorim & Bardy 2005). Participants watched a point-light character performing a gymnastic movement and they were required to memorize the final orientation of the point-light character from the initial viewpoint and to match it to a test posture. A representational momentum effect was observed, suggesting that the point-light movement is automatically extrapolated in time and that the action is represented in its future states (i.e., the action is anticipated). Physiological support for predictive action perception also comes from studies using eye tracking (Falck-Ytter, Gredeback & von Hofsten 2006; Flanagan & Johansson 2003). For example, Flanagan and Johansson showed that during action observation, eye movements are ahead of the observed motion. This proactive eye-gaze behavior is highly similar to eye-gaze behavior during action execution, indicating that action perception is predictive and that participants anticipated the upcoming action states rather than simply following present states.

In sum, action perception is highly embodied. The perception of an action (or even the intention of another person to act) is represented in the body of the observer by the activation of corresponding motor programs. This allows action understanding and action prediction. Such a "mirroring" mechanism is also suggested to be present in the perception and understanding of another class of special social stimuli: emotions.

Embodied emotion

If someone smiles at us, we are more likely to smile back than if someone looks at us with an angry expression. Yawning is contagious for humans not only when they observe other humans yawning, but also when they see apes and dogs doing so. When we see someone suffering from pain or in a depressed mood, we are able to empathize or feel with him. These events all provide evidence that we mirror each other's emotions. We also know that mimicry and bodily states are closely connected to specific emotional states, and that we indeed feel more self-confident if we adopt an upright position and speak with a loud, firm voice. In the following part of the chapter, we will discuss mechanisms of embodied emotion.

As we have described previously, it is now widely accepted that cognition is embodied, although there are still different views of this topic under discussion (Wilson 2002). This concept seems to work not only for cognitive processes like action perception and production or language understanding but could be also be applied to affective states and sensations. The theory of embodied emotion suggests that the experience of a given emotional state involves perceptual, somatovisceral and related motor activation (Niedenthal 2007).

In the past, there was debate about the relationship between bodily states and the ascribed emotion in a given situation. Some researchers argued that emotion comes first and our body starts to react to this emotion while in the emotional state (Cannon 1927). In contrast, James (1884) and Lange (1885, 1912) both came to the conclusion that in fact the relationship must be the inverse of this. James proposed that "the bodily changes follow directly the perception of the exciting fact, and that our feeling of the same changes as they occur IS the emotion."

Almost 100 years later, Ekman, Levenson & Friesen (1983) provided the first empirical evidence for the James-Lange theory of emotion. They asked their subjects to contract specific facial muscles which are known to be involved in one of the six facial expressions related to basic emotions (Ekman & Friesen 1971). They measured physiological parameters and compared these to a relived emotion task in which participants were asked to experience each of the six emotions by putting themselves in the emotional state. They found that just by contracting the facial muscles, emotion-specific autonomic activity was triggered. Strack, Martin and Stepper (1988) showed that people judged a cartoon as being funnier when they held a pen between their teeth that led to the contraction of a facial muscle that is essential for smiling in contrast to holding the pen between their teeth in a way that prevented smiling, ruling out the possibility that cognitive factors (e.g., induction of emotional state could have been recognized by the subjects) might have been responsible for the effect. This 'facial induction method' was replicated and has recently been used in an EEG experiment (Wiswede, Münte, Krämer & Rüsseler 2009) showing that this unconscious emotion induction caused by activating different facial muscles led to a change in the dopaminergic system which influences positive affect and performance monitoring.

It is also worth noting that the facial expressions related to the six basic emotions (Donato, Bartlett, Hager, Ekman & Sejnowski 1999) are not culturally determined. They are biological determined and are reliably identified by people across all cultures (Matsumoto 1992). It has also recently been shown that neonates already exhibit some of the facial expression related to disgust when exposed to unpleasant olfactory stimuli (Soussignan, Schaal, Marlier & Jiang 1997).

While most research has focused on facial expressions in emotion research, different emotional states are also strongly associated with certain postures. This has been shown reliably with point-light walkers, where minimal information about a body is given (Chouchourelou, Matsuka, Harber & Shiffrar 2006). Stepper and Strack (1993) showed that people who received a test result while adopting an upright or working position felt more proud and in a better mood than the ones who adopted a slumped posture. It was also shown that autobiographical memories are embodied (Dijkstra, Kaschak & Zwaan 2007). Dijkstra et al. showed faster response times and better free recall of autobiographical events when body positions during prompted retrieval of the events were similar to the body positions in the original events as compared to when the body position was incongruent. Similarly, recent findings show that retrieval of biographical memories was modulated by the direction of simple arm movements (Casasanto & Dijkstra 2010; Koch, Glawe & Holt, in press). In the study of Casasanto and Dijkstra, participants recalled more positive memories when they moved their arm upwards and more negative memories with a downward arm movement. The authors concluded that positive and negative life experiences are implicitly associated with schematic representations of upward and downward motion, consistent with theories of metaphorical mental representation (Casasanto & Dijkstra 2010).

Analogous to action simulation processes, it is likely that mechanisms of emotion simulation exist. The reverse simulation model suggests that people recognize facial expressions by mimicking observed expressions which in turn generates the corresponding emotional experience in the observer (Lipps 1907; Oberman, Winklelman & Ramachandran 2007). Dimberg and colleagues showed that exposure to pictures with happy and angry faces evoked increased activity in muscles related to smiling (zygomatic major) or frowning of the eyebrows (corrugators supercilii) in the observer, in congruence with the emotional state of the picture shown (Dimberg & Thunberg 1998). The same results were obtained when they controlled for conscious awareness of the emotions by using a backward masking method (Dimberg, Thunberg & Elmehed 2000).

The neural mechanism responsible for this facial mimicry and simulation of emotions could be mirror neurons. This would imply that neurons which are active either if someone is in an emotional state or sees someone in the same emotional state exist. Recent evidence was provided by fMRI experiments showing that such a mechanism does exist for both actions and also for somatosensory and emotional mirroring (Keysers & Gazzola 2009). The specific brain areas that are active if we are touched by an object are also active when we see someone being touched on the same body part (Blakemore, Bristow, Bird, Frith & Ward 2005; Keysers et al. 2004). Evidence for mirror mechanisms related to different emotional states was found for disgust (Jabbi, Swart & Keysers 2007; Wicker et al. 2003), happiness (Hennenlotter et al. 2005; Jabbi et al. 2007), pain (Botvinick et al. 2005) and combinations of different emotions (Carr, Iacoboni, Dubeau, Mazziotta & Lenzi 2003). Mirror mechanisms for action, somatosensation and emotion allow us to understand others' feelings and needs quickly and easily. Presumably, these mechanisms were beneficial during the evolutionary process. It is possible that they allowed humans to establish social bonding, to take care of their group and/or family members, and involvement in social interactions needed for hunting or gathering.

Looking into each other's mirror: Mechanisms of social interaction

In the past decade, researchers were not only interested in how single individuals perceived and acted on their environment but were also interested in how humans interacted with people like them. In the early stages of this research, they investigated how the sight and/or sound of others' actions facilitated or inhibited an individual's own action (Burnham 1910; Triplett 1898). Theories of motor contagion and the ideo-motor principle were discussed as alternative hypotheses. When Zajonc (1965) came up with his theory of social facilitation, it was then widely accepted that unspecific arousal elicited by the mere presence of other individuals accounted for performance enhancement or loss depending on task difficulty. As theories of embodied cognition and the common coding principle with mirror neurons as a possible neural substrate became increasingly accepted in the last twenty years, it was self-evident that these accounts could also hold for many aspects of interpersonal communication and social interaction. These considerations resulted in the concept of shared representations (Decety & Sommerville 2003), meaning that an individual cannot be conceptualized independently of a conceptualization of others. Through interactions with others, individuals internalize other people's perspectives. These representations of the self and other are overlapping but also distinct. At present there are diverse approaches and theories about small group (mostly studied in dyadic settings) interactions, each of them focusing on different aspects of interaction between two or more individuals. In this section, we will introduce the most prominent approaches and terms; mimicry, joint action, task sharing and unintentional synchronization.

We have already introduced the chameleon effect in this chapter. This behavioral matching or mimicry is the tendency to mimic an interaction partner in speech patterns, facial expressions, affective states (via facial feedback) and body posture. Mimicry is here seen as being unconscious and happening automatically; it leads to liking and rapport (Chartrand & Dalton 2009).

Joint action is defined as "any form of social interaction whereby two or more individuals coordinate their actions in space and time to bring about a change in the environment" (Sebanz, Bekkering & Knoblich 2006). What becomes clear from this definition is that interaction between individuals takes place in the time domain as well as in the spatial domain. In contrast, it is less clear whether the two individuals need to have a common goal (Bekkering et al. 2009) or whether the definition also includes automatic, unconscious coordination (e.g., avoiding bumping into other people in a crowded environment (Garrod & Pickering 2009)). When studying interpersonal interactions, there are the three central parameters which can be measured or need to be controlled for: firstly, their alignment in time, secondly, their alignment in space, and thirdly, whether they are goal-directed or incidental in purpose.

One of the most widely used frameworks for studying joint action in experimental cognitive psychology is the following well-known paradigm: A task is divided between two participants in a way that each of them is responsible for one part of the complete task. Performance in such a joint task is then compared to performance in the classical setting (one individual is responsible for the complete task) and to a single setting in which one subject performs only the partial task alone with no one sitting next to him/her. This paradigm has been tested with several paradigms, for example, the Simon task (Sebanz, Knoblich & Prinz 2003), the SNARC effect (Atmaca, Sebanz, Prinz & Knoblich 2008), inhibition of return task (Welsh et al. 2005), and a stop-signal task (Schuch & Tipper 2007). The results of all these studies show that effects observed in the joint setting are more or less equivalent to the ones observed in the classical setting but differ from the results observed in the single setting. Thus far, the scientific debate has not reached consensus on the interpretation of these joint effects. One interpretation is 'that people have a strong tendency to form shared task representations, taking into account what those around them need to be doing, and [...] there is a level at which one's own and the co-actor's actions are represented in a functionally equivalent way' (Natalie Sebanz & Knoblich 2009). Another, more universal interpretation is that the representation of the task set is changed by the social context in a way that individuals represent the complete task if they work side-by-side with a conspecific in comparison to working alone. That is to say, being in a social setting modifies our cognition in order to enable us to communicate and interact with the humans beings around us. Further research has to specify which particular cognitive functions are modulated by the social context.

Social interactions are often rhythmic. Imagine the first days of a baby's life: The parents cradle the baby in their arms, nursery rhymes are sung, when the child gets older she takes part in playground games and might learn to play in an orchestra or learn how to dance. It seems remarkably easy for us humans to find a common rhythm with the people we are interacting with. If we walk side-by-side, we easily fall in step, although our legs might differ in length. There is no need to expend effort on these activities; we easily find this common rhythm. This pull to coordinate with other individuals was proven experimentally by Richardson, Marsh and Schmidt (2005). They asked their subjects to solve an interpersonal puzzle task while swinging a handheld pendulum and manipulated whether visual or verbal interactions were emphasized. By measuring the amount of time during which the pendulums of the two actors were swinging in phase, they showed that unintentional synchronization only emerged if pairs were visually coupled but not when they were allowed to interact verbally with each other. However, there is little research concerning the underlying mechanism of unintentional synchronization. It seems clear that coordination of movement timing requires fairly exact anticipation of others' actions in order to synchronize with the other, suggesting that the mechanisms involved rely on tight perception-action links between the two individuals.

Conclusions

This chapter has focused on the cognitive perspectives of embodiment. The examples we described provide a short overview over the fast progress that has been made in research in the field of embodied cognition, in particular, in the area of action understanding and social interactions. The idea that perception and action share a system and are not distinct, and the detection of a neuronal correlate, mirror neurons, brought about a major change in cognitive psychology. We cannot be sure that the findings and theories provided here will still hold in ten or thirty years but it is a snapshot of what has happened in the twenty years since this change.

Our cognitive system has evolved for social interactions and action understanding. The key to understanding how we perceive and interact with others, are affected by their moods, and help them in a fast, predictive and flexible way seems to be given in our physical selves.

References

Arbib, M. A. (2005). From monkey-like action recognition to human language: An evolutionary framework for neurolinguistics. *Behavioral and Brain Sciences, 28*(2), 105–124.

Atmaca, S., Sebanz, N., Prinz, W. & Knoblich, G. (2008). Action co-representation: The joint SNARC effect. *Social Neuroscience, 3*(3–4), 410–420.

Bargh, J. A., Chen, M. & Burrows, L. (1996). Automaticity of social behavior: Direct effects of trait construct and stereotype activation on action. *Journal of Personality and Social Psychology, 71*(2), 230–244.

Bekkering, H., de Bruijn, E. R. A., Cuijpers, R. H., Newman-Norlund, R., van Schie, H. T. & Meulenbroek, R. (2009). Joint action: Neurocognitive mechanisms supporting human interaction. *Topics in Cognitive Science, 1*(1), 340–352.

Bertamini, M. (1993). Memory for position and dynamic representations. *Memory & Cognition, 21*(4), 449–457.

Biran, I. & Chatterjee, A. (2004). Alien hand syndrome. *Archives of Neurology, 61*(2), 292–294.

Blakemore, S., Bristow, D., Bird, G., Frith, C. & Ward, J. (2005). Somatosensory activations during the observation of touch and a case of vision-touch synaesthesia. *Brain, 128*(Pt 7), 1571–1583.

Botvinick, M., Jha, A., Bylsma, L., Fabian, S., Solomon, P. & Prkachin, K. (2005). Viewing facial expressions of pain engages cortical areas involved in the direct experience of pain. *Neuroimage, 25*(1), 312–319.

Brass, M., Bekkering, H. & Prinz, W. (2001). Movement observation affects movement execution in a simple response task. *Acta Psychologica, 106*(1–2), 3–22.

Brass, M., Bekkering, H., Wohlschlager, A. & Prinz, W. (2000). Compatibility between observed and executed finger movements: comparing symbolic, spatial, and imitative cues. *Brain and Cognition, 44*(2), 124–143.

Burnham, W. H. (1910). The Group as a Stimulus to Mental Activity. *Science, 31*(803), 761.

Cannon, W. B. (1927). The James-Lange theory of emotion: A critical examination and an alternative theory. *American Journal of Psychology 39*, 10–124.

Carr, L., Iacoboni, M., Dubeau, M., Mazziotta, J. & Lenzi, G. (2003). Neural mechanisms of empathy in humans: a relay from neural systems for imitation to limbic areas. *Proc Natl Acad Sci U S A, 100*(9), 5497–5502.

Casasanto, D. & Dijkstra, K. (2010). Motor action and emotional memory. [Article]. *Cognition, 115*(1), 179–185.

Casile, A. & Giese, M. A. (2006). Nonvisual motor training influences biological motion perception. *Current Biology, 16*(1), 69–74.

Chartrand, T. L. & Bargh, J. A. (1999). The chameleon effect: the perception-behavior link and social interaction. *Journal of Personality and Social Psychology, 76*(6), 893–910.

Chartrand, T. L. & Dalton, A. N. (2009). Mimicry: Its Ubiquity, Importance, and Functionality. In E. Morsella, J. A. Bargh & P. M. Gollwitzer (Eds.), *Oxford Handbook of Human Action* (pp. 458–483). New York: Oxford University Press, Inc.

Chouchourelou, A., Matsuka, T., Harber, K. & Shiffrar, M. (2006). The visual analysis of emotional actions. *Social Neuroscience, 1*(1), 63–74.

Cole, J. (1995). *Pride and the daily marathon*. Cambridge, MA: MIT Press.

Decety, J. & Sommerville, J. A. (2003). Shared representations between self and other: a social cognitive neuroscience view. *Trends in Cognitive Sciences, 7*(12), 527–533.

Dijkstra, K., Kaschak, M. P. & Zwaan, R. A. (2007). Body posture facilitates retrieval of autobiographical memories. *Cognition, 102*(1), 139–149.

Dimberg, U. & Thunberg, M. (1998). Rapid facial reactions to emotional facial expressions. *Scandinavian Journal of Psychology, 39*(1), 39–45.

Dimberg, U., Thunberg, M. & Elmehed, K. (2000). Unconscious facial reactions to emotional facial expressions. *Psychological Science, 11*(1), 86–89.

Donato, G., Bartlett, M. S., Hager, J. C., Ekman, P. & Sejnowski, T. J. (1999). Classifying facial actions. *Ieee Transactions on Pattern Analysis and Machine Intelligence, 21*(10), 974–989.

Ekman, P. & Friesen, W. V. (1971). Constants across cultures in face and emotion. *Journal of Personality and Social Psychology, 17*(2), 124–129.

Ekman, P., Levenson, R. & Friesen, W. (1983). Autonomic nervous system activity distinguishes among emotions. *Science, 221*(4616), 1208–1210.

Fadiga, L., Fogassi, L., Pavesi, G. & Rizzolatti, G. (1995). Motor facilitation during action observation: a magnetic stimulation study. *J Neurophysiol, 73*(6), 2608–2611.

Falck-Ytter, T., Gredeback, G. & von Hofsten, C. (2006). Infants predict other people's action goals. *Nature Neuroscience, 9*(7), 878–879.

Finke, R. A. & Freyd, J. J. (1985). Transformations of visual memory induced by implied motions of pattern elements. *Journal of Experimental Psychology-Learning Memory and Cognition, 11*(4), 780–794.

Flanagan, J. R. & Johansson, R. S. (2003). Action plans used in action observation. *Nature, 424*(6950), 769–771.

Freyd, J. J. (1987). Dynamic mental representations. *Psychological Review, 94*(4), 427–438.

Freyd, J. J. & Finke, R. A. (1984). Representational momentum. *Journal of Experimental Psychology-Learning Memory and Cognition, 10*(1), 126–132.

Gallese, V., Fadiga, L., Fogassi, L. & Rizzolatti, G. (1996). Action recognition in the premotor cortex. *Brain, 119*(Pt 2), 593–609.

Garrod, S. & Pickering, M. J. (2009). Joint action, interactive alignment, and dialog. *Topics in Cognitive Science, 1*(1), 292–304.

Glenberg, A. M. & Kaschak, M. P. (2002). Grounding language in action. *Psychon Bull Rev, 9*(3), 558–565.

Grezes, J., Armony, J. L., Rowe, J. & Passingham, R. E. (2003). Activations related to "mirror" and "canonical" neurones in the human brain: an fMRI study. *Neuroimage, 18*(4), 928–937.

Grezes, J., Costes, N. & Decety, J. (1999). The effects of learning and intention on the neural network involved in the perception of meaningless actions. *Brain, 122*(Pt 10), 1875–1887.

Hennenlotter, A., Schroeder, U., Erhard, P., Castrop, F., Haslinger, B., Stoecker, D. et al. (2005). A common neural basis for receptive and expressive communication of pleasant facial affect. *Neuroimage, 26*(2), 581–591.

Hommel, B., Musseler, J., Aschersleben, G. & Prinz, W. (2001). The Theory of Event Coding (TEC): a framework for perception and action planning. *Behav Brain Sci, 24*(5), 849–878; discussion 878–937.

Jabbi, M., Swart, M. & Keysers, C. (2007). Empathy for positive and negative emotions in the gustatory cortex. *Neuroimage, 34*(4), 1744–1753.

James, W. (1884). What is an emotion? *Mind, 9*, 188–205.

James, W. (1890). *Principles of pschology.* New York, NY.

Jarraya, M., Amorim, M. A. & Bardy, B. G. (2005). Optical flow and viewpoint change modulate the perception and memorization of complex motion. *Perception & Psychophysics, 67*(6), 951–961.

Jeannerod, M. (2001). Neural simulation of action: a unifying mechanism for motor cognition. *Neuroimage, 14*(1 Pt 2), 103–109.

Kerzel, D. & Bekkering, H. (2000). Motor activation from visible speech: Evidence from stimulus response compatibility. *Journal of Experimental Psychology-Human Perception and Performance, 26*(2), 634–647.

Keysers, C. & Gazzola, V. (2009). Expanding the mirror: vicarious activity for actions, emotions, and sensations. *Curr Opin Neurobiol, 19*(6), 666–671.

Keysers, C., Wicker, B., Gazzola, V., Anton, J., Fogassi, L. & Gallese, V. (2004). A touching sight: SII/PV activation during the observation and experience of touch. *Neuron, 42*(2), 335–346.

Kilner, J. M., Paulignan, Y. & Blakemore, S. J. (2003). An interference effect of observed biological movement on action. *Curr Biol, 13*(6), 522–525.

Lange, C. G. (1885/1912). The mechanism of the emotion. In B. Rand (Ed.), *The classical Psychologist* (pp. 672–684). Boston: Houghton Mifflin.

Liberman, A. M. & Mattingly, I. G. (1985). The motor theory of speech-perception revised. *Cognition, 21*(1), 1–36.

Liepelt, R., Cramon, D. Y. & Brass, M. (2008). What is matched in direct matching? Intention attribution modulates motor priming. *Journal of Experimental Psychology: Human Perception and Performance, 34*(3), 578–591.

Lipps, T. (1907). Das Wissen von fremden Ichen [The knowledge of foreign Is]. In T. Lipps (Ed.), *Psychologische Untersuchungen [Psychological Research]* (pp. 694–722). Leipzig, Germany: Engelmann.

Matsumoto, D. (1992). More Evidence for the Universality of a Contempt Expression. *Motivation and Emotion, 16*(4), 363–368.

Niedenthal, P. (2007). Embodying emotion. *Science, 316*(5827), 1002–1005.

Oberman, L. M., Winklelman, P. & Ramachandran, V. S. (2007). Face to face: Blocking facial mimicry can selectively impair recognition of emotional expressions. *Social Neuroscience, 2*(3–4), 167–178.

Prinz, W. (1990). A common coding approach to perception and action. In O. Neumann & W. Prinz (Eds.), *Relationships between perception and action: Current approaches* (pp. 167–201). New York: Springer.

Prinz, W. (1997). Perception and action planning. *European Journal of Cognitive Psychology, 9*, 129–154.

Richardson, M. J., Marsh, K. L. & Schmidt, R. C. (2005). Effects of visual and verbal interaction on unintentional interpersonal coordination. *Journal of Experimental Psychology-Human Perception and Performance, 31*(1), 62–79.

Rizzolatti, G. & Craighero, L. (2004). The mirror-neuron system. *Annu Rev Neurosci, 27*, 169–192.

Schuch, S. & Tipper, S. P. (2007). On observing another person's actions: Influences of observed inhibition and errors. *Perception & Psychophysics, 69*(5), 828–837.

Schütz-Bosbach, S. & Prinz, W. (2007). Prospective coding in event representation. *Cogn Process, 8*(2), 93–102.

Sebanz, N., Bekkering, H. & Knoblich, G. (2006). Joint action: bodies and minds moving together. *Trends in Cognitive Sciences, 10*(2), 70–76.

Sebanz, N. & Knoblich, G. (2009). Predicition in joint action: What, when, and where. *Topics in Cognitive Science, 1*(1), 353–367.

Sebanz, N., Knoblich, G. & Prinz, W. (2003). *Your task is my task: Shared task representations in dyadic interactions.* Mahwah: Lawrence Erlbaum Assoc Publ.

Soussignan, R., Schaal, B., Marlier, L. & Jiang, T. (1997). Facial and autonomic responses to biological and artificial olfactory stimuli in human neonates: Re-examining early hedonic discrimination of odors. *Physiology & Behavior, 62*(4), 745–758.

Stepper, S. & Strack, F. (1993). Proprioceptive determinants of emotional and nonemotional feelings. *Journal of Personality and Social Psychology, 64*(2), 211–220.

Strack, F., Martin, L. & Stepper, S. (1988). Inhibiting and facilitating conditions of the human smile: a nonobtrusive test of the facial feedback hypothesis. *J Pers Soc Psychol, 54*(5), 768–777.

Stürmer, B., Aschersleben, G. & Prinz, W. (2000). Correspondence effects with manual gestures and postures: a study of imitation. *Journal of Experimental Psychology: Human Perception and Performance, 26*(6), 1746–1759.

Thornton, I. M. & Knoblich, G. (2006). Action perception: Seeing the world through a moving body. *Current Biology, 16*(1), R27–R29.

Triplett, N. (1898). The dynamogenic factors in pacemaking and competition. *The American Journal of Psychology, 9*(4), 507–533.

Tucker, M. & Ellis, R. (1998). On the relations between seen objects and components of potential actions. *Journal of Experimental Psychology: Human Perception and Performance, 24*(3), 830–846.

Viviani, P. (2002). Motor competence in perception of dynamic events: a tutorial. In W. Prinz & B. Hommel (Eds.), *Attention and Performance XIX: Common Mechnanisms in Perception and Action* (pp. 406–443). Oxford: University Press.

Welsh, T. N., Elliott, D., Anson, J. G., Dhillon, V., Weeks, D. J., Lyons, J. L., et al. (2005). Does Joe influence Fred's action? – Inhibition of return across different nervous systems. *Neuroscience Letters, 385*(2), 99–104.

Wicker, B., Keysers, C., Plailly, J., Royet, J., Gallese, V. & Rizzolatti, G. (2003). Both of us disgusted in My insula: the common neural basis of seeing and feeling disgust. *Neuron, 40*(3), 655–664.

Wilson, M. (2002). Six views of embodied cognition. *Psychon Bull Rev, 9*(4), 625–636.

Wiswede, D., Münte, T., Krämer, U. & Rüsseler, J. (2009). Embodied emotion modulates neural signature of performance monitoring. *PLoS One, 4*(6), e5754.

Zajonc, R. B. (1965). Social facilitation. *Science, 149*(3681), 269–274.

Dynamic embodiment and its functional role

A body feedback perspective

Caterina Suitner,* Sabine C. Koch,** Katharina Bachmeier[#] and Anne Maass*

*University of Padova / **University of Heidelberg / [#]University of Jena

The situated nature of memory is here discussed with a specific focus on body memory. The chapter describes two studies on the effects of dynamic movement qualities on memory and one study on the Spatial Agency Bias, that is the tendency to envisage action as evolving in the same direction in which we habitually read and write. In addition to showing the situated nature of memory, we will for the first time provide evidence for its dynamic aspect. Situated memory will be discussed as functional in the interaction with the environment and body feedback as a key underlying mechanism.

Keywords: dynamic embodiment, body feedback, spatial agency bias, movement rhythms, body memory

Dynamic embodiment and body memory

Philosophical, neuro-scientific, cognitive, linguistic, and clinical perspectives are urging that body and mind are so strongly intertwined that it is difficult to even argue for a mental process that is not in some way grounded in physical experience. Even if, at a theoretical level, this relation has been acknowledged at both on-line and off-line levels (Niedenthal, Barsalou, Winkielman, Krauth-Gruber & Ric 2005), the role of the body in memory processes has received less attention. In the present chapter, we want to emphasize the situated nature of memory, focusing on body memory (Glenberg 1997) and investigating off-line embodiment phenomena as evidence for it. We will address the following issues: First, we will discuss the situated nature of memory as not only resulting from but also aiming at the interaction with the environment. Then, we will discuss ways to investigate body memory via dynamic body feedback (Koch 2011), particularly body feedback from movement qualities. Second, we will illustrate this point with the Spatial Agency Bias (Maass, Suitner, Favaretto & Cignacchi 2009), that is the tendency to envisage action as evolving in the same direction in which we habitually read and write (e.g., from left to right in Western cultures). Body feedback refers to afferent feedback from the muscles to the central nervous system (e.g., from facial expressions, posture and movement) that has been shown to have a crucial influence on perception, emotional experience, formation of attitudes, and regulation of behavior (Adelmann & Zajonc 1987; Zajonc & Markus 1984). Whereas much previous research has focused on static aspects of embodied cognition, we foreground its dynamic aspects. Two studies on memory effects from dynamic movement qualities are described. Finally, we will provide some preliminary conclusions on dynamic embodied memory.

Cognition ultimately rests on body experience (Semin & Smith 2008). According to this theoretical perspective, mental schemata have a profound motor component and action representations are automatically activated during conceptual processing. Far from being an abstract process, intelligence emerges from the interaction of the body with the physical environment and hence our sensory-motor activity becomes the basis of cognitive processes (Smith 2005). For example, Song and Schwarz (2008) have shown that participants evaluated a task as more difficult when its instructions were presented in a difficult (vs. easy) to read print font. People apparently use their (seemingly unimportant and logically irrelevant) visuo-motor experiences as a source of information in this decisional process.

Importantly, bodily experiences play a role not only at initial encoding but also later on as these experiences are re-enacted during decoding of new information. Cognition is therefore conceptualized as a modality-specific process that initially uses the bodily states involved in a given experience in order to create knowledge (on-line embodiment) and subsequently re-enacts these bodily states during processes that are decoupled from that experience (off-line embodiment) (Niedenthal et al. 2005; Wilson 2002). Mental representations (regardless of whether they are concrete or abstract) are therefore rooted in the body as sensori-motor information is recorded in the encoding phase of information. When such representations are recalled later on, their embodied characteristics are revived through simulation and irrupt while decoding new information (Barsalou 2005). Therefore, cognition simultaneously (a) uses sensori-motor information to process the information at hand during knowledge creation and (b) uses and integrates re-enacted bodily states from earlier experiences while decoding new information. It is this second type of embodiment that can be related to the concept of body memory.

In his seminal article "What memory is for", Arthur Glenberg (1997) lays out an embodied theory of memory, reminding us that memory is in the service of perception and action (similar to the "cognition is for action" accounts of Fiske 1992; or Mussweiler 2006). According to Glenberg (1997: 1), *conceptualization is the encoding of patterns of possible physical inter-action with a three-dimensional world (…) determined by the types of bodies we have*. Glenberg's quasi-evolutionary, functional embodiment perspective provides important clues about the process behind meaning-making. Moreover, it points out the constraints memory is bound to, as the body and its interaction with the physical environment works as tangible bases of the mnemonic system, with stored information being strongly intertwined with the cor-poreal experience through which it is acquired (see also the concept of motor reso-nance proposed by Zwaan & Taylor 2006).

Memory is therefore bound to the constraints of the environment and the body, as it serves the system's needs for spatial coherence, self-coherence, and temporal co-herence. Glenberg (1997) claims that previous memory theories have treated internal representations as meaningless symbols for the encoding of features (e.g., Harnad 1990; Hintzman 1986) or as propositions relating meaningless symbols. Interestingly, the predominant methods of studying memory have heavily relied on laboratory stud-ies providing arbitrary word lists and measuring recall, recognition, priming effects, etc. mostly through reaction time measures, errors, and hits as their dependent vari-ables. These measurements become less convincing, if memory is not conceptualized as embodied and in the service of interaction in a three-dimensional environment.

Although great emphasis has been put on the body in the scenario of grounded cognition (Barsalou 2008), experiments have mainly focused on static bodily states, neglecting the main characteristic of bodies, namely movement. In the present chap-ter we propose that the patterns of movement that we have acquired throughout our lives leave their traces in memory and we show how dynamic body feedback mecha-nisms affect both concurrent cognition and memory retrieval.

Building on Glenberg (1997), we *also* take the stance that symbols are not only grounded in our bodies, but that they also adjust to the way our bodies interact with the environment that surrounds us. The emergence of such embodied symbols is in-deed situated and context-dependent, proving that memory ultimately is for action. For example, when we ride a bike our body re-enacts the already acquired movements without the need of a rationale planning of our behavior, however, if the path is un-usually slippery and steep, different movements are necessary to adjust our behavior to the situation. We therefore use our body memory in a selective and adaptive way, in line with the actions we are about to conduct. These arguments will be addressed below, together with concrete research examples that illustrate each point.

Dynamic body feedback

The first part of this chapter is dealing with the phenomenon of how kinesthetic body feedback affects concurrent cognition and attitude formation. The influence of dy-namic movement can re-activate body memory, a fact that also has important impli-cations for psychotherapy.

In the panorama of situated cognition, what Glenberg (1997) defines as body memory may, in part, be equated to the concept of off-line embodiment, defined as an embodiment effect that arises during memory-retrieval and that is de-coupled from real-world environments. Such off-line embodiment is quite distinct from on-line embodiment denoting a situated embodiment effect in which cognitive activity oper-ates directly in a real-world environment. For instance, sitting in the classroom being called upon by the teacher and not knowing the answer to any of her questions might cause cold sweat, a dry throat, gaze aversion, and an increased pulse frequency (on-line embodiment). The mere imagination of this situation may have the same bodily effects (off-line embodiment; cf. Niedenthal et al. 2005).

On the empirical side, Glenberg and Kaschak (2002) found that participants were faster at judging the meaning of a sentence when it was compatible with the hand movement required for the response (e.g., "close the drawer" with forward movement; "open the drawer" with backward movement). This action-sentence compatibility effect occurred even when the sentences referred to abstract actions that involved directional communication (i.e., participants were fastest in judging the sentence "You told Liz the story" with a forward movement and "Liz told you the story" with a backward movement). These findings are consistent with the claim that language comprehension is grounded in bodily action and provide evidence for the action-oriented nature of embodied processes. However, they cannot easily be reconciled with abstract symbol theories of meaning.

The underlying assumption of embodiment approaches is that all memories are stored in our body as perceptual symbols that can be re-activated via sensory-motor simulations (Barsalou 1999; Niedenthal et al. 2005). Given memories have such a format it should be possible to access them via body feedback mechanisms (Ping & Goldin-Meadow 2010). Such body feedback mechanisms are, for example, facial feedback, postural feedback, and other more dynamic bodily feedback effects (for example from the voice or body rhythms). Body feedback experiments have shown that the way in which we hold our body can change our perceptions, emotions, cognitions, or reaction times in certain tasks (for a systematic overview see Hatfield, Cacioppo & Rapson 1994). Strack, Martin and Stepper (1988), for example, had their participants hold a pen either between their teeth or between their lips and found that participants holding the pen between their teeth rated a cartoon as funnier than participants who held the pen between their lips. The authors see the reason for this effect in the fact that the facial muscles one uses for smiling are inhibited in the lip condition. When planning Botox injections, that paralyze facial muscles, one should therefore take into account that they may reduce the capacity of feeling mild emotions (Davis, Senghas, Brandt & Ochsner 2010).

Most of these experiments, however, have used static manipulations of bodily postures or gestures (LaFrance 1985; Laird 1984; Riskind 1984; Rossberg-Gempton & Poole 1992) and have not included *dynamic movement*. Acknowledging that we are moving beings, the challenge in embodiment research is to operationally integrate *dynamic body feedback* as an independent variable and to extend the definition of embodiment to the dynamic realm. In the following sections we will outline how *dynamic body feedback* affects concurrent cognition (on-line effect) and body memory (off-line effect).

On-line attitudes deriving from movement qualities (smooth vs. sharp rhythms)

In order to test the influence of dynamic movement feedback on affect, attitudes and cognition under ecologically valid conditions, Koch (2011) induced actual movement instead of static postures in experimental settings. In everyday life, it is rather artificial to hold a certain posture for more than a minute. The manipulation of movement makes the designs more realistic, but also more complex. Theories of body philosophy (Merleau-Ponty 1962; Sheets-Johnstone 1999) and movement analysis (Laban 1960; Kestenberg 1995) suggest that next to the movement shape (e.g., approach vs. avoidance) the movement quality (i.e., the muscular tension flow producing kinesthetic qualities) must be taken into account as an additional important factor in such designs. We therefore investigated the influence of movement qualities, and we specifically focused on those qualities that have been described in clinical and developmental movement analysis, namely movement rhythms with smooth vs. sharp transitions (Kestenberg 1995; Loman 2007) and efforts, a concept denoting movement impetus or actuation (Laban 1960; Kestenberg Amighi et al. 1999). Movement qualities – rhythms as well as efforts – can be categorized into fighting (e.g., sharp, strong) and indulgent types (e.g., smooth, light). Efforts are the most conscious forms of movement qualities, rhythms the most unconscious (Kestenberg 1995). Movement rhythms are periodic alternations in tension and relaxation of the muscles, such as when somebody chews on a pencil, curls their hair, or taps their foot. Smooth vs. sharp movements denominate the transitions (reversals) between tension and relaxation. They play a role in (individual) body feedback, but also in human communication. Here we focus on their kinesthetic function.

Cacioppo, Priester, and Berntson (1993) investigated a held directional movement toward (approach) or away from the body (avoidance) in their experiments on the influence of arm flexion and extension on rudimentary attitudes. Building on their research, Koch (2011) applied factual approach and avoidance movements and varied movement qualities (smooth versus sharp movement rhythms), thus creating four movement conditions: an approach movement with smooth rhythms, an approach movement with sharp rhythms, an avoidance movement with smooth rhythms, and an avoidance movement with sharp rhythms. These movements were displayed from a video-clip and participants were instructed to follow the movements from the video-clip until they felt they could sustain the movement for themselves. The movements were carried out with alternating arms moving either smoothly or sharply towards the body (in a "bring-it-toward-me" mill-like approach movement) or away from their body (in a "push-it-away-from-me" mill-like avoidance movement) while participants watched valence-free Chinese ideographs on a projector. Participants' evaluation of the ideographs was the dependent variable, with higher values indicating a positive attitude. Results suggested a main effect of approach/avoidance with participants in the approach movement condition rating the ideographs as significantly more positive than participants in the avoidance condition. This effect was further qualified by movement quality (interaction effect): the most positive evaluation resulted from

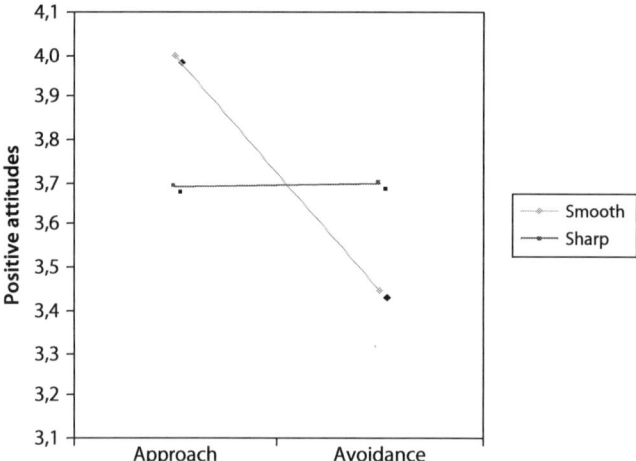

Figure 1. Positive attitudes in functions of movement shape (approach vs. avoidance) and movement quality (smooth vs. sharp)

smooth approach movements, and the least positive from smooth avoidance movements. Sharp movements canceled out the effects of approach and avoidance motor behavior on attitudes (see Figure 1).

The author explains the main effect of approach/avoidance on attitudes similarly to Cacioppo et al. (1993) by pointing out the ontogenetic and phylogenetic functional value of bringing good things (such as good food and benevolent people) toward the body and pushing bad things (such as bad food and malevolent people) away from the body, emphasizing the lifelong practice of these actions. Such lifelong practices enter into and form our body memory. The author interprets the influence of movement qualities (smooth vs. sharp movement) arguing that in both sharp as well as smooth movements the body feedback gets to the person, but only in smooth condition, where the organismic system is in an indulging, relaxed state, can the meaning of the movement be attached to the ideographs, since then the system has a higher permeability, than in the fighting, more tense state of the sharp rhythms, where the person is ready to defend, follow through with a goal, and focus on something without getting distracted by an external stimulus or body feedback effects. Future research is therefore needed to verify whether, only in the smooth, indulgent state will the body feedback actually get to the person and "sink in", and the person can then accommodate to the situation, whereas in the sharp, fighting mode, the person is mostly in a defensive state where body feedback will be suppressed, since its conscious perception could be a danger to disturbing the person's action plans. In this case, assimilation of the environment should be more likely to occur (both accommodation and assimilation understood in terms of Piaget here).

In clinical movement analysis, the basic distinction of smooth vs. sharp movement rhythms is assumed to correspond to different psychological needs (Kestenberg

1995). The round, smooth transitions can be observed in playful exploration and indulgent situation, where one yields into the pleasure of the movement, such as jumping for the joy of jumping, and twisting for the joy of twisting. The sharp rhythms can be observed in situations where fighting, controlling, and vigilant behavior is functional. Sharp rhythms serve the readiness to intentionally follow through with one's goals. An example would be tapping one's fingers or patting one's hand, expressing the need to go ahead.

In her study, Koch (2011) has demonstrated that movement qualities are related to positive and negative valence and influence attitudes of participants. In sum, the findings of Koch (2011) show that movement quality, and specifically smooth vs. sharp movement rhythms, are important dimensions of meaning making and have specific implications for cognition and affect. Specifically, smooth rhythms have a more positive valence than sharp rhythms. Furthermore, movement quality had similar effect-sizes than approach and avoidance motor behavior on attitudes and interacted with the approach and avoidance motor behavior dimension. Such findings have several interpersonal implications, suggesting that movement qualities (e.g., movement rhythms implemented via handshakes) may affect person perception in affect and judgment of personality characteristics (for more details, see Koch 2011). The next study tested whether movement qualities in body feedback also work at an off-line level, influencing memory retrieval.

Body memory evoked from movement qualities (light vs. strong efforts)

That memory is under the influence of body feedback mechanisms was shown in a study of Kasper and Koch (2010) where body and movement therapists (N = 66) moved for about three minutes in either a light ("as if floating or drifting") or a strong movement quality ("as if pulling or pushing something heavy") as the specification of fighting and indulgent movement qualities in the force or gravity dimension (Laban & Lawrence 1974) and were then asked about their affect and memory retrieval. Affect was measured with the *Brief KMP Affect Questionnaire* (Koch & Müller 2007), and memories were generated in a two-step procedure. First, participants were asked to generate as many life events as possible, then they were asked to rate the valence of those events on a 4-point-scale according to how pleasant or unpleasant they had been for them.

In accordance with the hypotheses, participants in the condition of light movements remembered more positive life events, activities and persons than participants in the condition of strong movements. They further reported more positive affect after light than after strong movements. Figure 2 shows the effects on memory retrieval and affect.

Similar results were obtained when participants held an open hand position (palms toward the ceiling, hands resting on the knees in a sitting position on a chair) vs. making a fist in the same position (Kasper & Koch 2010). Interestingly, results for

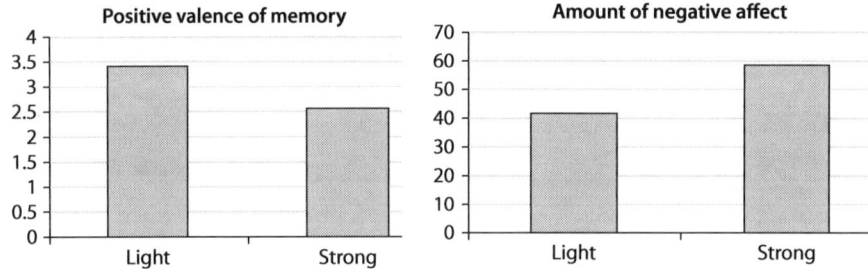

Figure 2. Effects of movement quality (light vs. strong) on valence of memories and affect. Valence of memory and affect were more positive after light movement (y-axis$_{valence}$ = means of positive valence; memory for life events in free recall; y-axis$_{affect}$ = means of negative affect)

these merely static postures were not as pronounced as for the ones where dynamic movement was employed, showing the stronger impact of dynamic movement.

In sum, the research reported so far suggests that carrying out specific movements may influence how we perceive and evaluate others, what we recall and how we feel, providing converging evidence for the importance of dynamic body feedback on cognition, affect, and attitudes. From an ecological point of view, we enact movements of many types during the day, depending on the situation, but we also repeat usual movements (e.g., while using a fork or typing on a keyboard). It is unclear how long-term effects of habitual activities (i.e., off-line embodied effects or body memory) interact with movements driven by the situation on shaping our cognitive processes. This issue will be addressed in the following paragraph.

Memory is embodied to facilitate the interaction with the environment: Evidence from research on spatial agency bias

So far we have shown that movements are encoded during knowledge creation and that dynamic body feedback is a source of information for both impression formation and memory retrieval. Therefore not only bodily states but also bodily movements are able to affect both on-line and off-line cognition, showing the importance of dynamism in the panorama of the embodiment research. A second issue we want to address here is the functional role of such dynamic mechanisms. In his embodied approach to memory, Arthur Glenberg (1997: 1) conceptualizes memory as a functional human capacity that has "evolved in service of perception and action in a three-dimensional environment, and that (…) is embodied to facilitate interaction with the environment". Thus, memory primarily serves a survival function and is channeled by possible interactions of the body with its surrounding environment. In line with this reasoning, we argue that dynamic body feedback is adaptive and functional. We will show that off-line processing is under the influence of contextual variables presenting another dynamic embodied effect, namely the Spatial Agency Bias (SAB).

The SAB consists of the systematic tendency to depict events in line with the trajectory of the predominant writing direction in a given culture. For instance, when asked to draw an aggressive scene, English or Italian speakers tend to position the aggressor to the left and the victim to the right, with action evolving from left to right, whereas Arabic or Urdu speakers tend to draw the same scene from right to left. According to the SAB model, this bias derives from the habitual repetition of directed hand and eye movements during writing and reading. The consistent trajectories experienced during these actions are the bodily base for the mental representation of actions in general. This embodied representation of action is later recalled and simulated while representing new actions, whose direction end up being consistent with the writing direction even in situations that require no writing. For example, Italian speakers preferentially envisage social interactions with the agent to the left of the recipient. To the contrary, Arabic speaking participants envisage the agent to the right of the recipient, re-enacting a leftward motion, in line with the writing direction of their language (Maass & Russo 2003). Presumably, the direction of the language in a given culture creates a mental schema for action, which is generated by visual scanning during reading and by the motor activity of writing (a cultural embodiment effect). The schema, initially originating from a practical behavior, is later applied to the abstract domain of symbolic representations. The physical action and the resulting bodily coordination, therefore, promote a preferential direction that is strongly associated with the concept of agency and with target persons who represent this concept, namely active or agentic targets. For example in Western countries, stereotypically agentic targets (e.g., males or young people) tend to be envisaged to the left of less agentic targets (e.g., females or old people) (Maass et al. 2009).

Importantly, this preferential direction is expected to prevail even in the absence of any bodily action such as writing or drawing. For instance, when asking participants to estimate the relative speed of moving objects, rightward directed cars, soccer balls, or runners are perceived as faster than their leftward directed mirror images (e.g., Maass, Pagani & Berta 2007; also Suitner 2009). Similarly, when asked to choose between two mirror representations of the same event (e.g., a target person offering a gift or kicking somebody else) people generally prefer scenes in which the actor is positioned to the left of the recipient (Suitner 2009). Finally, in one study we presented face profiles of women and men that were either oriented towards the right or towards the left from the participants' perspective. The participants' task was to decide as fast as possible whether the target person was male or female. In line with widely held stereotypes that associate men with greater agency, participants made fewer mistakes in identifying males that were rightward (rather than leftward) oriented whereas the opposite tendency was observed for female targets (Suitner & Maass 2010). Thus, the trajectory used for writing and reading becomes the "default" representation of actions, and of agentic people, even on tasks that do not involve writing or reading. Although the spatial bias clearly originates in scanning and writing habits, it goes well beyond writing or reading tasks, including all kinds of tasks such as recognition, mental imaging, or preference.

The direction of written language can be considered the off-line bodily foundation (or body memory) in which the embodied representation of agency is grounded. Our hypothesis is that body memory not only derives from previous interaction with the environment, but that it is also activated or inhibited as a function of momentary situational constraints, showing its action-oriented nature. For instance, an Italian student is likely to prefer a rightward oriented representation of action and to perceive a soccer ball as faster when going into the net from the left, unless she is on her way home from her Hebrew class or has just opened her Japanese cartoon booklet with the intention to read it. As this example shows, we expect that the off-line simulation corresponding to habitual bodily foundation (such as writing from left to right) will be inhibited whenever momentary constraints intervene (such as looking at a Japanese cartoon in a right to left fashion). The reason for this prediction is simple: Off-line simulations that are incoherent with current environmental demands would simply be maladaptive.

In order to test this hypothesis, three of the authors (i.e., Suitner, Maass & Bachmeier) had Italian participants perform a right- or left-moving pseudo-writing task (see also Suitner & Maass in press; and Suitner 2009). The pseudo-writing task consisted in simple pre-writing exercises such as those used in pre-school education in many countries, showing letters (such as h or I) either on the left or on the right side of the sheet. The letters had then to be copied by participants throughout the entire line (either from left-to-right or from right-to-left). The rightward priming procedure was assumed to activate the conventional writing/reading direction in Italian culture and was therefore expected to lead to a strong spatial bias. Leftward priming was thought to create a completely new situation, which was expected to momentarily replace the culturally determined writing/reading habit, thus eliminating the usual spatial bias. After the pseudo-writing task, participants viewed a series of stimulus pairs representing two identical targets (either male or both female) running in opposite direction (one rightward, the other leftward). The participants' task was to choose, for each stimulus pair, the person who seemed to be more masculine/feminine. To avoid a gender bias due to instructions, half of the participants were asked to identify the person who seemed more masculine, half the person who seemed more feminine. The responses were recoded so that higher scores indicated a greater number of rightward running targets rated as more masculine.

According to the SAB literature (Maass et al. 2009), the rightward direction is associated with the target that is stereotypically more masculine. We therefore expected the rightward moving target to be chosen as the more masculine target, but only after the rightward pseudo-writing task. This SAB was not expected after a leftward pseudo-writing task, because we assumed that the standard rightward representation of agency would be simulated only when relevant to the context. Hence, we expected the right-to-left exercise to inhibit the activation of the body memory that is usually activated in the SAB context. The effect of the pseudo-writing task was in line with

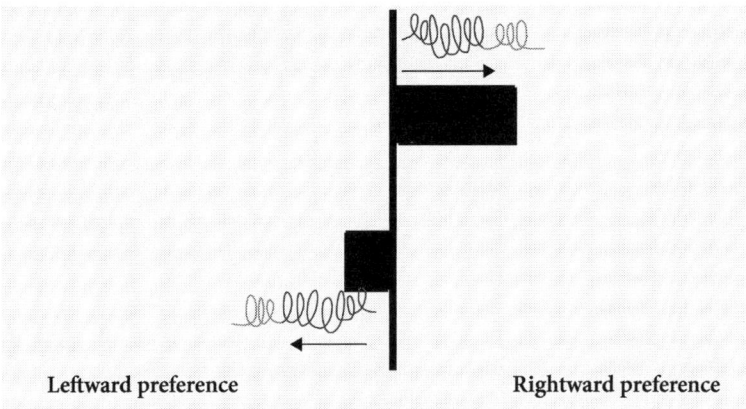

Leftward preference   Rightward preference

Figure 3. Evaluation of rightward (vs. leftward) moving targets as more masculine after a rightward (vs. leftward) writing exercise

our hypotheses: Participants perceived the right-running target as more masculine after having done a left-right writing exercise but not after an opposite (right-left) writing task (see Figure 3).

In addition, we assessed the degree to which participants endorsed traditional gender stereotypes administering an Italian adaptation of the Personal Attributes Questionnaire (Spence, Helmreich & Stapp 1974). Participants were asked to judge adjectives and clauses describing stereotypically masculine (e.g., "aggressive", "competitive", "resists well under pressure") or feminine (e.g. "ready to help others") characteristics and behaviors, and to indicate for each whether the statement was more typical of men or women. The scale was coded so that higher values indicated traditional gender stereotypes (with more masculine and fewer feminine traits being attributed to males than to females). We expected that the SAB would increase with increasing stereotype endorsement, except for those participants who had previously performed a right-to-left writing exercise likely to inhibit the SAB.

In line with this idea, the endorsement of traditional stereotypes was positively associated with the SAB effect such that with increasing gender stereotyping (PAQ) the spatial bias increased. Important, however this occurred only after a (culturally congruent) rightward writing exercise (see regression slopes presented in Figure 4).

In sum, right-moving targets were perceived as more masculine only after participants had performed a writing task that corresponded to the usual direction in which language is written in their culture. This effect disappeared (and even slightly reversed) after participants had been engaged in a motor activity opposite to their normal writing habit. Moreover, after rightward writing, the more participants shared traditional gender stereotypes, the more masculine they perceived the right-moving target to be. This relation was absent after leftward writing.

Together, these findings indicate that dynamic embodiment effects, attributable to rightward writing and reading in Western cultures, is not always activated, but

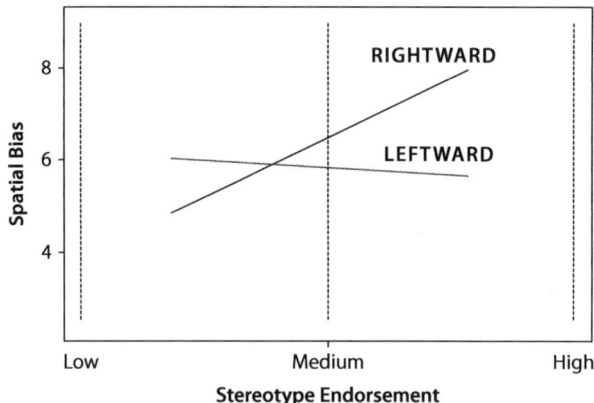

Figure 4. Number of times the rightward-oriented target was selected as the more masculine as a function of stereotype endorsement and activated direction. Chance level = 6

rather subject to context-specific variations in visuo-motor activity. Therefore, the contextual situation is extremely relevant and may indeed determine whether culturally grounded preferences for the left-right trajectory do or do not emerge as offline embodiment. Our findings add to the existing literature showing that the left-right trajectory has a privileged status in our cultural context but that the bias is flexible and sensitive to a large amount of daily activities that are unrelated to writing or reading, thus providing evidence for an interaction of online and offline embodied effects.

Conclusions: Dynamic embodiment in social psychology

In this chapter, we have been showing that there is a potentially huge basin of embodied phenomena still under-investigated in the literature: namely dynamic embodiment. Situated cognition has acknowledged the role of bodies in human cognition. We propose that it is time to move on and to consider bodies in motion. The ability to move, plan movements, and interpret them is a key component of our everyday life, and has a powerful effect on cognition. We could even argue that it provides the grounding for cognition (Glenberg 1997).

The body provides strong feedback to guide our thinking. We have shown here that the quality of movement is an important feature of such body feedback, affecting attitude formation towards neutral objects or social targets. A smooth approach movement makes an ideograph more pleasant than a sharp approach movement, a rightward movement makes a moving target appear more masculine. This effect of movement on cognition is not only evident at the on-line level, it is also palpable at the off-line level. On one side, actual movement influences what we recall from memory, as shown with the effect of light vs. strong movement on the pleasantness of recollections. On the other side, previously experienced movements affect the way we construct actual reality, as evident in the case of the SAB effect, in which writing direction affects the way we envisage agency. We can therefore conclude that dynamism is an important aspect of embodiment. As previously advanced, it is likely that the impact of dynamic embodiment effects is even stronger than the effects of static embodiment. This has important implications and could be applied in various contexts. For example, dynamic body feedback may have a strong impact of attitude change and may therefore be used in political campaigns, advertisement, or social communication. Furthermore, the way our body experiences its movements in a certain situation can be re-traced and the respective memories can be re-activated and accessed by moving in the exact same qualities and shapes no matter whether the memory was implicit or explicit, conscious or unconscious to us in that moment. These processes can be helpful in body psychotherapy (see part three of this edited volume). For traumatized persons, for example, next to building the verbal narrative of their trauma, it is important to build the nonverbal narrative as well. Since most traumata happen to persons directly on the body level, the body needs to tell a coherent story before the verbal narrative can even be started to be built or parallel to it (Caldwell 2010; Koch & Weidinger von der Recke 2009).

A second important issue raised in this chapter concerns the functional and contextualized role of embodiment. We have shown that even if movements that had been experienced repeatedly in the past (e.g., writing) may form a relatively stable mental schema, contextually experienced movements can reduce the availability of such schema, proposing a new situated schema. In fact, performing a counter-directed movement reduced the SAB, probably because participants' mental schema was momentarily influenced by (and adjusted to) the contextually experienced direction.

Importantly, our research on SAB also shows that embodied processes are, at least in part, subject to social and cultural influences. Although human bodies are substantially the same around the world and although the large majority of human beings are right-handed, languages are written in very different ways. Scripts may proceed from left-to-right (e.g., European languages), from right-to-left (e.g., Hebrew, Arabic), or they may alternate left-ward and right-ward. Other scripts move in a vertical manner, as in the case of many idiographic languages (e.g., Japanese or Chinese) that are written from top-to-bottom with rows proceeding from right to left. To complicate things further, the same languages (such as Kurdish, Azeri, or Japanese) may be written with different scripts in different parts of the world, attesting to the great variability of one of the prime activities of modern human beings: writing and reading. If script direction creates a generalized scheme for action that affects off-line cognition well beyond the act of writing and reading, then one should not expect such schemata to be universal. This suggests that embodied cognition, both online and offline, should be investigated under a social and cross-cultural perspective.

From a social psychological perspective, it also becomes relevant to understand the social grounding of embodied processes. Given that we use our own bodies as the primary source for embodied cognition, it is likely that – via mapping mechanisms –

we are also able to construct cognition by observing others (Wilson & Knoblich 2005). For example, if I see my conversation partner suddenly turns motionless and with the eyes turned upward (as if to look into her forehead), I can readily infer that she is thinking and does not want to be disturbed. Similarly, even if I am not able to use a gun and I have never touched one, I can still recognize it by virtue that I have see others using it (likely in movies) and I will probably be affected by the elaboration of its functional properties. The spatial orientation of familiar objects, such as a cup, affects the time we need to elaborate them: it is easier to elaborate objects that are oriented congruently with their potential use. For example, Tucker and Ellis (2001) showed that participants are faster to categorize a cup when the handle is on the same side of the response hand (making it graspable). Similarly to what happens with a cup, we might expect that participants will more easily process a gun when its orientation is congruent with its potential use, even if its use has only been observed and not directly experienced. Thus, embodied cognition may vary greatly because different cultures allow for different bodily experiences (such as writing), no matter whether personally experienced or indirectly observed in others.

In sum, it seems timely, that embodiment research is further developed to include (a) the dynamic aspects of online and off-line cognition, and (b) the situational variables (environmental and social) affecting such phenomena. This chapter is meant as a contribution in this direction.

References

Adelmann, P. K. & Zajonc, R. B. (1987). Facial efference and the experience of emotion. *Annual Review of Psychology, 40,* 249–280.

Barsalou, L. W. (2005). Abstraction as dynamic interpretation in perceptual symbol systems. In L. Gershkoff-Stowe & D. Rakison (Eds.), *Building object categories* (pp. 389–431). Mahwah, NJ: Erlbaum.

Barsalou, L.W. (1999). Perceptual symbol systems. *Behavioral & Brain Sciences, 22,* 577–609.

Barsalou, L. W. (2008). Grounded cognition. *Annual Review of Psychology, 59,* 617–645.

Cacioppo, J. T., Priester, J. R. & Berntson, G. (1993). Rudimentary determinants of attitudes II: Arm flexion and extension have differential effects on attitudes. *Journal of Personality and Social Psychology, 65,* 5–17.

Caldwell, C. (2010). Personal communication.

Davis, J. I., Senghas, A., Brandt, F. & Ochsner, K. N. (2010). The effects of BOTOX injections on emotional experience. *Emotion, 10*(3), 433–440.

Fiske, S. T. (1992). Thinking is for doing: Portraits of social cognition from daguerrotype to laserphoto. *Journal of Personality and Social Psychology, 63,* 877–889.

Glenberg, A. M. (1997). What memory is for. *Behavioral and Brain Sciences, 20*(1), 1–55.

Glenberg, A. M. & Kaschak, M. P. (2002). Grounding language in action. *Psychonomic Bulletin & Review, 9*(3), 558–565.

Harnad, S. (1990). The symbol grounding problem. *Physica D, 42,* 335–346.

Hatfield, E., Cacioppo, J. T. & Rapson, R. L. (1994). *Emotional contagion.* Paris: Cambridge University Press.

Hintzman, D. L. (1986). "Schema abstraction" in a multiple-trace memory model. *Psychological Review, 93,* 411–428.

Kasper, D. & Koch, S. C. (2010). *Body Memory: Empirical investigations of a phenomenological concept.* Poster presented at the International Small Group Meeting on Body Memory, Metaphor and Movement, March 01–03, 2010, in Heidelberg, Germany.

Kestenberg, J. S. (1995). *Sexuality, body movement and rhythms of development.* Northvale: Jason Aronson. (Originally published in 1975 under the title *Parents and Children*).

Kestenberg Amighi, J., Loman, S., Lewis, P. & Sossin, K. M. (1999). *The meaning of movement. Developmental and clinical perspectives of the Kestenberg Movement Profile.* Amsterdam: Gordon & Breach.

Koch, S. C. (2011). Basic body rhythms and embodied intercorporality: From individual to interpersonal movement feedback. In W. Tschacher & C. Bergomi (Eds.), *The implications of embodiment: Cognition and communication.* Exeter: Imprint Academic.

Koch, S. C. & Müller, S. M. (2007). The KMP-questionnaire and the brief KMP-based affect scale. In S. C. Koch & S. Bender (Eds.), *Movement Analysis – Bewegungsanalyse. The Legacy of Laban, Bartenieff, Lamb and Kestenberg* (pp. 195–202). Berlin: Logos.

Koch, S. C. & Weidinger-von der Recke, B. (2009). Traumatized refugees: An integrated dance and verbal therapy approach. *The Arts in Psychotherapy, 36,* 289–296.

Laban, R. (1960). *The mastery of movement.* London: MacDonald & Evans.

Laban, R. & Lawrence, F. C. (1974). *Effort: Economy in body movement.* Boston, MA: Plays. (Originally published in 1947).

LaFrance, M. (1985). Postural mirroring and intergroup relations. *Personality and Social Psychology Bulletin, 11,* 207–217.

Laird, J. D. (1984). The real role of facial response in the experience of emotion: a response to Tourangeau and Ellsworth, and others. *Journal of Personality and Social Psychology, 47,* 909–917.

Loman, S. (2007). The KMP and pregnancy: Developing early empathy through notating fetal movement. In S. C. Koch & S. Bender (Eds.), *Movement analysis – Bewegungsanalyse. The legacy of Laban, Bartenieff, Lamb and Kestenberg* (pp. 187–194). Berlin: Logos.

Maass, A., Pagani, D. & Berta, E. (2007). How beautiful is the goal and how violent is the fistfight? Spatial bias in the interpretation of human behavior. *Social Cognition, 25,* 833–852.

Maass, A. & Russo, A. (2003). Directional bias in the mental representation of spatial events: Nature or culture? *Psychological Science, 14*(4), 296–301.

Maass, A., Suitner, C., Favaretto, X. & Cignacchi, M. (2009). Groups in space: Stereotypes and the spatial agency bias. *Journal of Experimental Social Psychology, 45,* 496–504.

Merleau-Ponty, M. (1962). *Phenomenology of perception.* London: Routledge.

Mussweiler, T. (2006). Doing Is for Thinking! Stereotype activation by stereotypic movements. *Psychological Science, 17*(1), 17–21.

Niedenthal, P. M., Barsalou, L. W., Winkelman, P., Krath-Gruber, S. & Ric, F. (2005). Embodiment in attitudes, social perception, and emotion. *Personality and Social Psychology, 9*(3), 184–211.

Ping, R. & Goldin-Meadow, S. (2010). Gesturing saves cognitive resources when talking about nonpresent objects. *Cognitive Science, 34,* 602–619.

Riskind, J. H. (1984). They stoop to conquer: Guiding and self-regulatory functions of physical posture after success and failure. *Journal of Personality and Social Psychology, 47*, 479–493.

Rossberg-Gempton, I. & Poole, G. D. (1992). The relationship between body movement and affect: From historical and current perspectives. *The Arts in Psychotherapy, 19*, 39–46.

Semin, G. S. & Smith, E. R. (Eds.). (2008). *Embodied grounding.* Cambridge: Cambridge University Press.

Sheets-Johnstone, M. (1999). *The primacy of movement.* Philadelphia: John Benjamin.

Smith, L. B. (2005). Cognition as a dynamic system: Principles from embodiment. *Developmental Review, 25*, 278–298.

Song, H. & Schwarz, N. (2008). If It's Hard to Read, It's Hard to Do. *Psychological Science, 19*(10), 986–988.

Spence, J. T., Helmreich, R. & Stapp, J. (1974). The Personal Attributes Questionnaire: A measure of sex role stereotypes and masculinity-femininity. *JSAS Catalog of Selected Document in Psychology, 4*, 43–44.

Strack, F., Martin, L. & Stepper, S. (1988). Inhibiting and facilitating conditions of the human smile: A non-obtrusive test of the facial feedback hypothesis. *Journal of Personality and Social Psychology, 54*, 768–777.

Suitner, C. (2009). Where to place social targets? Stereotyping and spatial agency bias. Doctoral Thesis, University of Padova.

Suitner, C. & Maass, A. (in press). Writing direction, agency and gender stereotyping: An embodied connection. In T. Schubert & A. Maass (Eds), *Spatial dimensions of social thought.* Berlin: Mouton de Gruyter.

Tucker, M. & Ellis, R. (2001). The potentiation of grasp types during visual object categorization. *Visual Cognition, 8*(6), 769–800.

Wilson, M. (2002). Six views of embodied cognition. *Psychonomic Bulletin & Review, 9*(4), 625–636.

Wilson, M. & Knoblich, G. (2005). The case for motor involvement in perceiving conspecifics. *Psychological Bulletin, 131*, 460–473.

Zajonc, R. B. & Markus, H. (1984). Affect and cognition: The hard interface. In C. Izard, J. Kagan & R. B. Zajonc (Eds.), *Emotions, cognition and behavior* (pp. 73–102). Cambridge: Cambridge University Press.

Zwaan, R. & Taylor, L. J. (2006). Seeing, acting, understanding: Motor resonance in language comprehension. *Journal of Experimental Psychology: General, 135*, 1–11.

CHAPTER 11

Testing Fuchs' taxonomy of body memory

A content analysis of interview data

Sabine C. Koch
Heidelberg University

In this chapter, we tested the body memory taxonomy of Fuchs (2003) using content analysis of interviews and questionnaire data – a widely used method for approaching a new concept or phenomenon in the cognitive or social sciences (Mayring 1995; Merten 1995). We conducted interviews on body memory with 61 experienced and inexperienced movers (Study 1) and analyzed questionnaire data of 77 participants (Study 2) in order to find out whether Fuchs' taxonomy encompasses all relevant aspects of what comes to peoples' minds when they think about the phenomenon of body memory. As a result, all of Fuchs' categories emerged in participants' narratives. Some categories were further differentiated, such as traumatic memories related to a physical or a psychic insult. In particular, situational memory was identified as an overarching category that can be differentiated into various sense modalities (haptic, auditive, olfactory, kinaesthetic, visual). Fuchs' taxonomy of body memory was thus further validated on the basis of this first qualitative empirical test.

Keywords: body memory, content analysis, phenomenology, psychology

In the perspective of Fuchs (2003) with its predecessors in French philosophy (e.g., Bergson 1991), body memory is conceptualized as implicit, nonconscious memory (knowing how) as opposed to explicit, conscious recollection (knowing that).

> Obviously there is a memory of the body apart from conscious recollection: Through repetition and exercise, a habit has developed. Long-trained patterns of movement and perception have been embodied as skills or faculties that we practice as a matter-of-course in our everyday life – the upright gait, the ability of speaking, reading or writing, and the handling of instruments such as a bicycle or a piano. (Fuchs 2003: 1)

This implicit form of memory has been investigated in psychology as procedural memory. However, Fuchs' conceptualization contains more than procedural memory

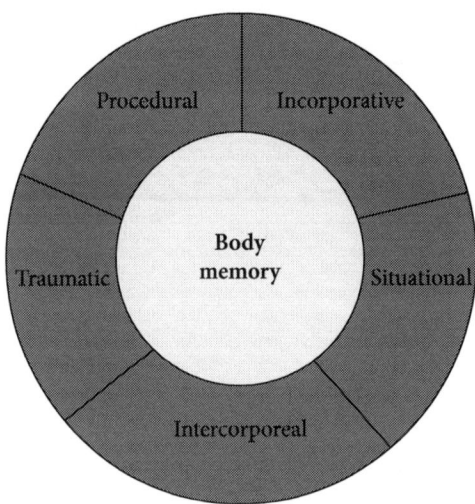

Figure 1. Body memory model of Fuchs (2003)

or a differentiation of procedural memory. Altogether, Fuchs distinguishes five forms of body memory (see Figure 1).

1. Habitual/procedural body memory: Skill memory for motor processes; driving a car, playing an instrument, etc.
    "When reading, I am directed towards the meaning of the sentence through the single letters that recede from my awareness. As we can see, procedural memory unburdens our attention from an abundance of details, thus facilitating our everyday performance. (...) Through moving the keys the pianist is able to direct himself to the music itself, to listen to his own play. Thus freedom and art are essentially based on the tacit memory of the body" (Fuchs 2003: 2–3).
    Psychopathology demonstrates to us that there are multiple memory systems: "Research into amnesic patients who may still learn simple motor skills though not being able to retain new explicit recollections has demonstrated the existence of multiple memory systems" (Fuchs 2003: 1).
2. Situational body memory: Spatial familiarity memory (for interior and exterior spaces), atmospheric perception. "Bodily experience is particularly connected to interiors which over time are filled with latent references to the past and with an atmosphere of familiarity" (Fuchs 2003: 3).
3. Intercorporeal body memory: Our early bodily encounters provide an implicit template for our somatic reactions in encounters with others; "It is a temporally organised, musical memory for the rhythm, dynamics and undertones inaudibly present in the interaction with others" (Fuchs 2003: 5); it turns into implicit relational knowing – a bodily knowing of how to deal with others (cf. Stern 1985); "The lived body may only be understood by another body" (Fuchs 2003: 6).

4. Incorporative body memory: Family and cultural habitus; "the reshaping of primary bodily structures by attitudes and roles taken over from others. This happens mostly by bodily imitation and identification" (Fuchs 2003:6). Examples are the adoption of poses, manners, or gender roles.

5. Traumatic body memory: Severely painful experiences, such as accidents, neglect, abuse, torture, and threat of death are stored in the body and often suppressed from consciousness; they can lead to psychosomatic diseases. "The trauma withdraws from conscious recollection, but remains all the more virulent in the memory of the body, as a foreign body, as it were. At every step the traumatised person may come across something that revokes the trauma" (Fuchs 2003:7). In trauma, the feeling of "at-homeness" is often lost and needs to be regained. Research on post traumatic stress disorder teaches us about the specific significance and the rules of this memory system.

Fuchs attributes the primary role for the *experiences of identity* and *the self* to body memory.

> Autobiographic memory only represents the past *as* the past. The memory of the body, on the contrary, mediates the real, living presence of the past. Thus it is also the essential basis of the self.   (Fuchs 2003:8)

Since the taxonomy of Fuchs (2003) offers a theoretical model – with deductively and experientially/phenomenologically derived categories – that has not yet been tested empirically, we approached a first test of the theory via the use of content analysis of interview data and questionnaire data. The comparison of this inductively derived interview corpus and the written material with the deductively derived categories of Fuchs' taxonomy allowed a first test of the theoretical model using the experience of the participants of our studies.

Method

Sample

Study 1
In a structured interview, 61 participants including 45 experienced (39 women and 6 men; mean age: 38.40; $SD = 11.80$; range: 24–56; all White) and 16 inexperienced movers (15 women and 1 man; mean age: 23.00, $SD = 4.60$; range 19–31; all White) were administered 10 questions (Appendix A) on and related to the topic of body memory. Since we wanted to start with a group that had easy access to corporeal memories, the 45 experienced movers were recruited in six different groups of body psychotherapy and movement therapy professional trainings in middle and southern Germany (in the context of the study "influence of movement qualities on memory"). They had not yet covered the topic of body memories in their trainings. The

16 inexperienced participants were students of psychology recruited in the context of the study "dance your life."[1] Thus, both groups were not naïve regarding the topic of body memory. The experienced groups were contacted via their leaders, and participants received a snack for their participation. The inexperienced group was recruited at our home university and received either five Euros or course credit for their participation.

Study 2

In Study 2, 77 participants, all inexperienced (56 women and 21 men; mean age: 24.10; $SD = 8.04$; range: 18–56; all White), with 92% students (63% psychology) completed a questionnaire with items taken from Study 1. This group of participants had not read about body memory and thus was naïve regarding the topic. Participants were recruited at the University of Heidelberg in and around the psychology campus and received seven euros and fifty cents or course credit for their participation in this as well as another study that was combined with this study. We followed the APA ethical guidelines when conducting both studies.

Procedure

Study 1

Participants were administered 10 structured questions on the topic of body memory after they had done some improvisational movement (3 to 10 min). The interview on body memory took 5 min. Fife interviewers (four female, one male; ages 25 to 45) conducted the interviews that were digitally audiotaped. Two female coders (one having also conducted interviews; the other not) then transcribed and analyzed the interviews. The coding procedure is further specified in the next paragraph (and in Figure 2).

Study 2

Participants completed a questionnaire as the first part of a two part study. They were asked to rate the 40 most prototypical body memories of the sample of Study 1 according to whether and to what degree they knew similar situations. For each rating they were provided space to write down the corresponding similar situation. In the

1.   We would like to thank Nicole Parusel, Detlef Kasper, Eva Hentz and Verena Braun for gathering the data of this content analysis; the German Federal Ministry of Research and Education (BMBF) for support in the context of the grant 01UB0930A to S. Koch, T. Fuchs, and C. Müller. This interdisciplinary cooperation is fruitful in that psychology and cognitive linguistics can add empirical data in support of Fuchs' taxonomy, and phenomenology can thus profit from empirical differentiations; cognitive science in turn can profit from the differentiations made in the theory of Fuchs, and movement therapy can refer to a theoretical model when investigating its clinical practice and the resulting hypotheses about body memory.

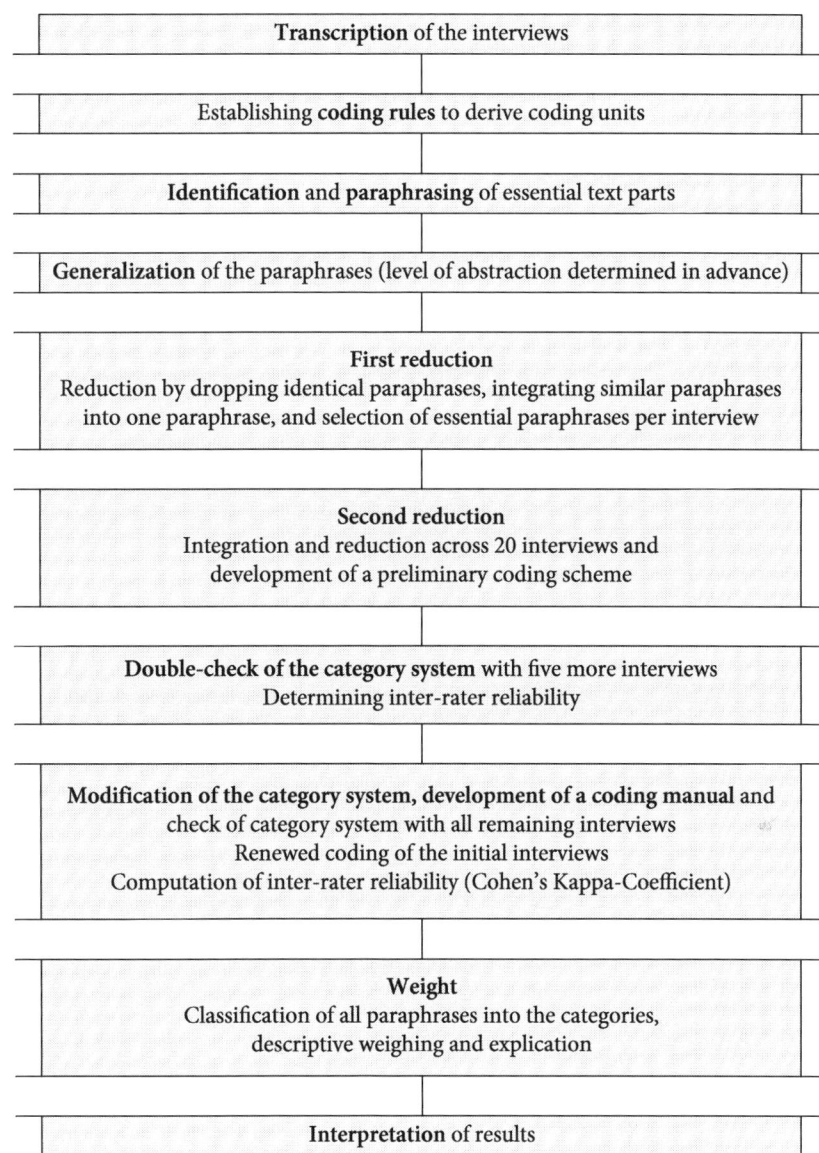

| Transcription of the interviews |

| Establishing coding rules to derive coding units |

| Identification and paraphrasing of essential text parts |

| Generalization of the paraphrases (level of abstraction determined in advance) |

| First reduction |
Reduction by dropping identical paraphrases, integrating similar paraphrases into one paraphrase, and selection of essential paraphrases per interview

| Second reduction |
Integration and reduction across 20 interviews and development of a preliminary coding scheme

| Double-check of the category system with five more interviews |
Determining inter-rater reliability

| Modification of the category system, development of a coding manual and |
check of category system with all remaining interviews
Renewed coding of the initial interviews
Computation of inter-rater reliability (Cohen's Kappa-Coefficient)

| Weight |
Classification of all paraphrases into the categories, descriptive weighing and explication

| Interpretation of results |

Figure 2. Schema of treatment of the interview data according to Mayring (1995:56)

end, they were asked to additionally report one of their own body memories. From all the open answers in the questionnaire, the categories of Fuchs were once again derived with an inter-rater reliability between two female independent coders of 100% (Braun 2011).

Content analysis

The procedure of the content analysis is described for Study 1. The open answers in Study 2 were treated accordingly. We chose to follow the quantitative content analysis method of Mayring (1995) and additionally used the method of category formation suggested by Merten (1995: 98: 147). Both methods assured an economic and systematic, rule- and theory-guided reduction of the interview data with the possibility of intersubjective control at each step.

We used mainly summative content analysis (Mayring 1995: 56), the goal being the reduction of the material in such a way that the essence of the content would be contained and the abstraction would still reflect the basic material (Mayring 1995). The single steps of the procedure were:

1. Transcription: Complete transcriptions were done on the interview data of the experienced movers; the lay interviews were then only transcribed in the relevant parts oriented at the already developed categorization scheme. Transcripts contained nonverbal and paraverbal utterances (such as smiles, sighs, etc.) as far as they seemed relevant for the analysis.
2. Establishing coding rules: We had a female main coder (Coder 1), who established the coding rules and coded all of the 45 interviews with the experienced movers (Parusel 2010); another female coder (Coder 2) coded the 16 interviews with the inexperienced movers after the coding scheme was already established.
3. First reduction: paraphrasing and generalizing (Mayring 1995).
4. Second reduction: construction and integration (Mayring 1995).
   4.1 Formation of theory-derived complete and independent categories
   4.2 Category formation and development of the coding scheme (Appendix B)
   4.3 Double-checking of the category system with a second coder

For the purpose of determining the observer agreement, Coder 2 coded eight interviews of the 45 experienced movers' data (28 codes/categorizations; > 10% of the corpus). The resulting inter-rater reliability of the two independent female coders was *Cohen's Kappa* = .86 (agreement of 94.7%), which is very good for interpretative categories (Cohen 1960; Landis & Koch 1977).

Results

Exemplary definitions of body memory

Regarding the definition of body memory, it was striking that participants more often mentioned negative or painful experiences than positive ones. Habitual memory from automatic movement such as riding one's bike was also a familiar concept to participants. They further seemed to be quite aware of the connections between physical and psychic well-being; they knew that they could raise their psychic well-being by bodily activity or that feeling bad on a psychic level would often correspond to feeling bad physically as well.

The definitions they generated for the concept of body memory spanned a broad range (translation by author):

> "Body memory is a form of memory that is realized in the cells of the body" (Vp 1)

> "Body memory is the inner motion that joins the affect (it generates) to become a gradually ever more conscious phenomenon" (Vp 38)

> "The phenomenon that mind also results from body/bodily stuff, ... and that therefore memories, pertaining to the realm of the mind, are not only present in the brain but maybe also in the posture or body attitude" (Vp 4)

> "Body memory is my recollection of specific movements or body sensations, that is, things that happened in my body or that I express with my body" (Vp 29)

> "Body memory is the memory content that my body carries to the outside, which was formerly cognitively stored" (Vp 30)

> "Body memory means that next to the brain, the muscles and the skeleton store experiences" (Vp M02)

> "Body memory means that the body stores every experience one has made and the feeling that is connected with that experience by transforming it, for example, in bodily tension, which is higher tension for negative emotion and more relaxation for positive emotion" (Vp M03)

Types of body memory

The first thing that stands out is the fact that all categories of Fuchs were covered by the participants no matter whether the participants were experienced or inexperienced (Table 1). The category of traumatic memory contained two subcategories that were always clearly distinct: (a) body memories related to *physical pain*, and (b) body memories related to *psychological trauma*.

One new category was observed in addition: the *instrumental use of body feedback* (e.g., every time this stressful thing happens, I take on this posture and take a deep breath and it helps me get over it). This is a particularly interesting category since body feedback is one major way to activate/access body memories, and it obviously serves the goal of activating psychophysical *resources* in all 18 cases of its occurrence. Whereas it is not directly a subcategory of body memory (among other reasons, because it is too explicit), it has an important function in the use of body memory as a resource to activate resiliency and recovery.

Table 1. Frequency of type of body memory by participant group in Study 1 (and Study 2)

Type of body memory	Frequency experienced n = 45	Frequency inexperienced n = 16 (n = 77)	Total Study 1 (+ Study 2)
1 Procedural body memory	8	7 (5)	15 (20)
2 Situational body memory	109	10 (35)	119 (154)
3 Intercorporeal body memory	8	2 (5)	10 (15)
4 Incorporative body memory	9	2 (2)	11 (13)
5a Traumatic body memory	6	7 (2)	13 (15)
5b Pain-related body memory	12	2 (4)	14 (18)
6 Instrumental use of body / resource-related body memory	13	5 (4)	18 (22)
Total BM	152	30 (49)	182 (231)

One of the most outstanding aspects is probably the extremely high number of *situational body memories*. This high frequency points to two problems: (a) Situational body memory seems to pervade all the other categories; there is an aspect of situational body memory that makes it a meta-category for all the other categories, and (b) situational body memory is very hard to distinguish from autobiographic memory when it is explicitly talked about in an interview or written about in a questionnaire context. The data suggest that situational body memory is a category separate from the other subcategories of body memory that are all quite homogeneous in frequency and independent of each other. Finally, *inexperienced movers generated fewer body memories* overall.

Situational body memory: Substructure by senses

Since situational body memory has this overarching role within the taxonomy, results of the content analysis suggest further differentiating it; this was possible by sense modality and fell naturally into the resulting categories (Table 2).

Interestingly, the kinaesthetic channel was most often named as responsible for triggering body memories in Study 1. This may be due to the fact that we worked predominantly with movement experts as underlined by the fact that the kinaesthetic channel was less pronounced in Study 2. Olfactory memories were the most frequent trigger of body memories in Study 2. Visual memories were exclusively named in Study 2. The fact that visual memories played almost no role is particularly striking because the visual sense usually dominates a major percentage of our perception. The last category is the situational memory (encompassing all senses) that cannot be

Table 2. Frequency of sense modalities of body memory by participant group in Study 1 (and Study 2)

Sense modality of stimulus	Frequency experienced n = 45	Frequency inexperienced n = 16 (n = 77)	Total Study 1 (+ Study 2)
1 Kinaesthetic	47	2 (4)	49 (53)
2 Olfactory	40	2 (16)	42 (58)
3 Auditory	10	0 (3)	10 (13)
4 Haptic	2	0 (4)	2 (6)
5 Gustatory	1	0 (1)	1 (2)
6 Visual	0	0 (3)	0 (3)
7 Atmospheric (situational, all senses)	9	6 (5)	15 (20)
Total	109	10 (36)	119 (155)

differentiated into sense modalities, but rather mirrors an atmospheric influence on memory resulting from the entire situation. This category was filled with 15 utterances in Study 1 and 5 utterances in Study 2.

Apart from differentiating situational body memory into sense modalities, it is also possible to narrow its definition down to *spatial memory* for interior and exterior spaces. Research on autism would support the formation of such a distinct category.

Examples of the single categories (generalized level)

This section will provide a number of representative examples for each of the body memory categories.

The formation of the new category of "instrumental use of body feedback," employing body memory as a resource, was supported by many utterances, among them these three quotes from three different training groups (translation by the author):

> "...in principle, I can use body memory in order to influence the body actively... in decelerating I think of ...ahhh... resting and finding inner peace, and then I can open an entire hierarchical pattern of negative and positive emotions (...) and help to remember, ...hey, the positive, ...yield into the deceleration and give the energy into it..." (FM08, f, 40)

> "... you can do a postural shift, (...) I can take on a specific body posture, and through this posture those strong specific feelings can come out again (...) after the death of my father I was in this mourning attitude, ... if I now take on that bodily posture I can re-activate the mourning (...) or this upward-posture that I

Table 3. Selected generalized examples by type of body memory in Study 1

	Frequency
1. Procedural body memory	
Automatic movement process while dancing	1
To play the violin, childhood memory	1
Automatic motor process while driving a car/red light/siren	3
Automatic motor processes from primary school time	1
Automatic motor process while riding a bike	1
Memories of a no longer existing object	1
2. Situational body memory	
Smell → childhood memories	14
Movement/posture → childhood memories	20
Situation → negative memories	4
Same situation → same thoughts/deja-vu	2
3. Intercorporeal body memory	
Encounters with others determine/influence one's own feelings, childhood memories	3
Encounter with others, first impression	1
Name of the person/memory	1
4. Incorporative body memory	
Panic attacks due to experiences of the mother	1
Identification over generations	1
Body attitude of another/memory	4
Fear of blizzards from grandmother	1
To see somebody activate body memory	1
5a. Traumatic body memory	
Sounds/abuse	1
Situation/car accident	2
Voice/negative childhood memory/drunk father	1
Fear of dogs	1
Posture/grief	1
5b. Pain-related body memory	
Medication/situation/fear of dentist	2
Posture/movement/pain memory	3
Situation/fainting, falling	1
Situation/experience of pain	2
Stress/tension/stomach ache	1
6. Instrumental use of body feedback	
Movement/positive effect	6
Posture/positive effect	4
Body work/exercise for relief/relaxation	2
Posture/supportive in situation	1

gradually assume, that I ...wow...a wonderful feeling... and I just need to stand like this and ...wow... there it is again." (E12, f)

"...certain mind-states can bring about certain body-symptoms (...), if I raise my gaze, my sternum, and my chest then something opens and I can feel that different thoughts arise (...) or if I want certain things in life, then I can attune and prepare myself through bodily exercises/body work, this is an inner option for self-help." (F04, f)

Body feedback mechanisms have been described, systematized, and empirically investigated by Hatfield, Cacioppo, and Rapson (1994), and more recently by Koch (2011) and Suitner et al. (this volume).

Resulting extended taxonomy

On the basis of the content analysis, the taxonomy of Fuchs needs to be extended into a model that includes a "closer to the core layer" of the four basic types of body memories: procedural, intercorporeal, incorporative, and traumatic; the more external

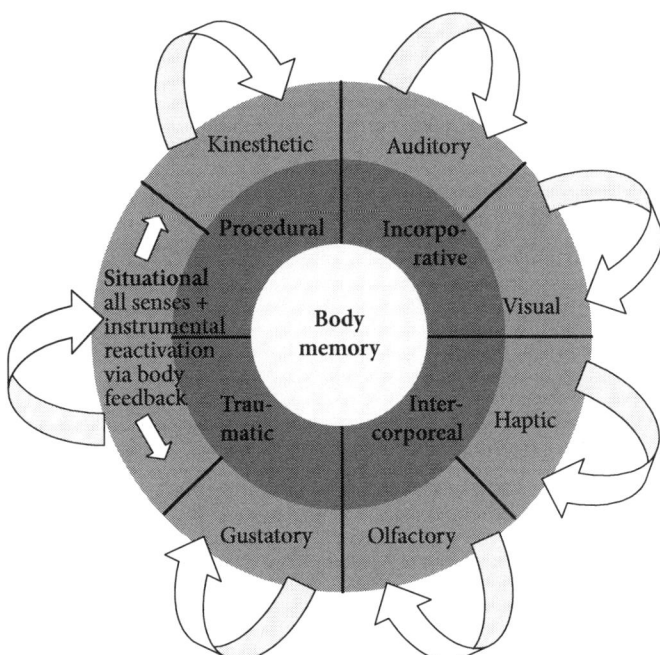

Note. Situational body memory is an overarching category now subdivided into the specific senses: Arc-like arrows indicate the possibility of accessing body memory via body feedback mechanisms.

Figure 3. Body memory model resulting from the content analysis of interview data

layer of situational body memory, sometimes quite explicit and autobiographical, that needs to be differentiated into the sense modalities of visual, auditory, haptic, olfactory, gustatory, and kinaesthetic; on the basis of the content analysis, we recommend differentiating *all* utterances into the corresponding sense modalities so that situational body memory will in fact dissolve as a subcategory and rather become a functional dimension related to situational triggers of body memories, providing clues for how to access them via body feedback in therapy (Figure 3). This outmost layer of the resulting model thus bears important pieces of information, for instance, for trauma therapy.

Discussion

In sum, the content analysis suggests minor extensions of the taxonomie of Fuchs and generates further research questions. The content analysis suggests important – but minor – extensions and has generated further research questions. Examples of such questions are: Are we treating situational body memory in the appropriate way now in the extended model? How do we differentiate true recalled body memories from autobiographical memories, if they are to be explicated in an interview situation? How do we best integrate the functional use of body memory as a resource?

In this first analysis, we developed new subcategories and identified new related categories. The analysis further suggests dropping a category that was too broad to be useful: situational body memory. The overarching situational memory category was differentiated into the different sense modalities and dissolved into the second level of analysis. Instead of dissolving the situational body memory aspect entirely into the sense modality specification for all categories of the taxonomy, there are reasons for keeping the spatial memory aspect of it in the taxonomy. Particularly, the impairment of spatial memory in autism is an argument for such a separate body memory subsystem. There are also quotes in the corpus of the interview data that support keeping the spatial memory aspect of situational memory in the taxonomy, for example, "this is one form of body memory, when I have for example changed the interior of my living space; then I walk through the corridor and want to turn around and then I think, oh no, it has already been 10 years that there was the mirror, now it is no longer there..." (FM10). We could thus alternatively narrow the situational memory category down to spatial memory and recode the interview corpus accordingly.

Limitations of our study include that we cannot exclude that the experienced movers in Study 1 in particular had been reading about body memory before participating in our study. Thus, their reporting about their inductive experiencing may have been mixed with deductive knowledge from the literature and from clinical practice. The experienced and the inexperienced groups were not comparable in terms of age, gender, and potential motivation to participate: The use of different reward systems for participation may have been responsible for motivational effects between the groups. However, these group differences are not a threat to the integrity of the study, since (a) we did not analyze the data by the experience of participants, and (b) the results of the entire sample yielded the same results as the data of the experienced group when inexperienced participants were added to the experienced group. Limitations of Study 1 further include the use of five interviewers who had interviewed only parts of the sample. There were two interviewers for the experienced movers, two others for the inexperienced movers, and one interviewer for both groups. Since interactional processes are always different depending on the dyad, we cannot exclude effects of single interviewers and dyadic constellations in Study 1 – as is true in any interview situation. Study 2, however, gathered body memory experiences in written form and can thus claim greater objectivity – making utterances less subject to social desirability or reactance phenomena, in this respect. The convergent evidence of Study 1 and Study 2 is a strong argument for the validity of the body memory taxonomy of Fuchs. Both studies in combination furthermore account for the mono-method bias by providing two different ways of assessing body memory.

To continue our work, situational body memory as a meta-category is taken into the phenomenological analysis of Summa (2011) at this point in time. Moreover, encouraged by a first experimental study on the effects of movement qualities on body memory (Kasper & Koch 2010), in which we tested person-related, activities-related, and life-event-related memory retrieval, and found that memories were more positive when participants moved in a light quality and less positive when they moved in a strong quality, experimental studies resulting from these first qualitative investigations are planned.

Conclusions

In this first empirical investigation, we were able to validate and extend the taxonomy of Fuchs (2003). Participants of our studies demonstrated similar conceptions and similar differentiations of body memory that were reflected in their utterances throughout. They were able to access and differentiate certain forms of body memory that corresponded to the taxonomy of Fuchs (2003). No category was left out. All categories can be kept for developing the model further.

The relations of the body memory concept to cognitive science research need to be further specified. Habitual/procedural memory corresponds to the procedural memory of cognitive psychology. The other forms of body memory have not been addressed explicitly in psychological memory research. One could say that they are included in situational memory and thus also have their habitual aspects. However, we believe that it is useful to differentiate them properly for the benefit of cognitive sciences. To differentiate *intercorporeal* aspects that include "our basic attitudes, our typical reactions and relational patterns, in one word: our personality itself" (Fuchs 2003:5), would move memory research more closely to developmental research, but also to personality and social psychology as well as communication research and movement analysis. "I do not need to search for the others, I find them within my own experience, they inhabit the niches which contain what is hidden to me, but visible to them" (Merleau-Ponty 1974: 166). The inclusion of *incorporative memory*, on the other hand, would move psychological memory research closer to the sociological concept of "habitus," an important embodiment perspective, and would build bridges to cognitive and cultural anthropology. And finally, the specific research on *traumatic but also resource-oriented body memory* could do a great service to developmental, clinical, and health psychology. It is thus worth while to continue with the efforts to integrate the concept of body memory into clinical and cognitive science research.

References

Bergson, H. (1991). *Materie und Gedächtnis. Eine Abhandlung über die Beziehung zwischen Körper und Geist.* [Translation of *„Matière et mémoire"* von J. Frankenberger]. Hamburg: Felix Meiner.

Braun, V. (2011). Das Leibgedächtnis. *Eine faktorenanalytische Überprüfung der Leibgedächtniskategorien von Fuchs* [Body memory – a factoranalytic test of the categories of Fuchs]. University of Heidelberg: Unpublished Thesis.

Cohen, J. (1960). A coefficient of agreement for nominal scales. *Education and Psychological Measurement, 20,* 37–46.

Fuchs, T. (2003). *The memory of the body.* http://www.klinikum.uni-heidelberg.de/fileadmin/ zpm/psychatrie/ppp2004/manuskript/fuchs.pdf

Hatfield, E., Cacioppo, J. & Rapson, R. L. (1994). *Emotional contagion.* New York: Cambridge University Press.

Kasper, D. & Koch, S. C. (2010). *Body Memory – A pilot study.* Poster presented at the Conference "Embodiment, Intersubjectivity and Psychopathology", Heidelberg September, 30th to October, 2nd 2010.

Koch, S. C. (2011). Basic body rhythms and embodied intercorporality: From individual to interpersonal movement feedback. In W. Tschacher & C. Bergomi (Eds.), *The implications of embodiment: Cognition and communication* (pp. 151–171). Exeter: Imprint Academic.

Landis, J. R. & Koch, G. G. (1977). The measurement of observer agreement for categorical data. *Biometrics, 33,* 159–174.

Mayring, P. (1995). *Qualitative Inhaltsanalyse. Grundlagen und Techniken* [Qualitative content analysis. Foundations and techniques]. Weinheim: Deutscher Studien Verlag.

Merten, K. (1995). *Inhaltsanalyse* [Content analysis]. Opladen: Westdeutscher Verlag.

Parusel, N. (2010). *Body Memory. Eine Inhaltsanalyse von Interviewdaten* [Body memory. A content analysis of interview data]. Heidelberg: Unpublished Thesis.

Stern, D. N. (1985). *The interpersonal world of the infant. A view from psychoanalysis and developmental psychology.* New York: Basic Books.

Suitner, C., Koch, S. C., Bachmeier, K. & Maass, A. (this volume). Dynamic embodiment and its functional role: A body feedback perspective. In S. C. Koch, T. Fuchs, M. Summa & C. Müller (Eds.), *Body memory, metaphor and movement.* Amsterdam: John Benjamins.

Summa, M. (2011). Das Leibgedächtnis. Ein Beitrag aus der Phänomenologie Husserls. [Body memory. A contribution from Husserl's phenomenology]. *Husserl Studies* (online first).

Appendix A

Interview questions from Study 1

---

1. *Do you know the term "body memory"? What does it mean to you?* [Kennen Sie den Begriff „Körpergedächtnis"/„Leibgedächtnis"? Was verstehen Sie darunter?]

---

2. *Can you give me an example from your own experience?* [Können Sie mir ein Beispiel aus Ihrer eigenen Erfahrung nennen?]

---

3. *Do you have easy access to your body memory? How frequent are your experiences with it?* [Ist Ihnen das Körpergedächtnis gut zugänglich? Wie häufig machen Sie damit Erfahrungen?]

---

4. *How would you define "body memory" in one sentence?* [Wenn Sie das Körpergedächtnis in einem Satz definieren müssten, wie würde dieser Satz lauten?]

---

5. *Do certain body postures or other bodily experiences trigger certain memories for you?* [Gibt es Körperhaltungen oder andere körperliche Erfahrungen, die bestimmte Erinnerung bei Ihnen auslösen?]

---

6. *What is your explanation for how "body memory" works? (You do not need to put it in sophisticated wording...)* [Haben Sie eine Erklärung über den Wirkmechanismus des Körpergedächtnisses? Wie stellen Sie sich vor, dass das funktioniert? (Sie können es ruhig laienhaft ausdrücken).]

---

7. *Are you familiar with the movement qualities of Laban?* [Sind Sie mit den Bewegungsqualitäten nach Laban vertraut?]

---

8. *Are you familiar with the concept of "body memory" through your professional training?* [Sind Sie mit dem Konzept des Körpergedächtnisses durch Ihre Ausbildung vertraut?]

---

9. *Our questions so far have mainly referred to postures and movements. Do you have other experiences with body memories from sounds, smells, or situations as well? Examples?* [Unsere Fragen bezüglich des Körpergedächtnisses richteten sich insbesondere auf Haltung und Bewegung. Gibt es weitere Bereiche, in denen das Körpergedächtnis eine wichtige Rolle spielt? Können Sie Beispiele nennen, z. B. in Bezug auf Geräusche, Gerüche oder Situationen?]

---

10. *Have I missed asking you anything that you would like to report about "body memory" in addition to what was already discussed?* [Denken Sie, dass ich es versäumt habe nach etwas Bestimmtem zu fragen? Gibt es etwas über das Thema Körpergedächtnis, das sie mir gerne noch erzählen möchten?]

Thank you for your participation!

Appendix B

Coding scheme: Categories

1 = **procedural** (sensorimotor – automatic motor processes)
2 = **situational**
    a.   kinaesthetic (movement/posture)
        i.   negative/positive emotions
        ii.   negative/positive memories
        iii.   negative/positive childhood memories
        iv.   memories of repeated situations
    b.   olfactory (smell)
        i.   neutral/positive/negative memory
        ii.   neutral/positive/negative childhood memory
    c.   auditory (sounds/music)
        i.   childhood memories
        ii.   positive/negative emotions
    d.   gustatory (taste)
    e.   haptic (touch)
        i.   negative/positive childhood memories
    f.   atmospheric (situational, all senses)
        i.   negative childhood memories
        ii.   "same" situation (same thoughts/feelings/deja-vu – "everytime, when")
    g.   visual
3 = **intercorporeal**
    a.   encounter with others → first impression
    b.   identification with others → negative childhood experiences
4 = **incorporative**
    body attitude of another person (e.g., activates body memory)
5 = **traumatic/pain-related**
    a.   traumatic
        i.   voice → negative childhood memories
    b.   pain-related
        i.   situation → pain memory
6 = **instrumental**
    movement/posture → positive effect

CHAPTER 12

Metaphorical instruction and body memory

Claudia Böger
Bundeswehr University of Munich

The aim of this chapter is to discuss how and why metaphorical instructions work during movement learning. The claim of subject-oriented research in movement science and cognitive semantics is that meaning articulation is grounded in movement execution. Movement is considered as a transmodal meaning-articulation, which is important for the relationship between the environment and the subject. Image schematic processes of meaning generation will be examined in detail. At the level of image schemata there are explicit interferences between the contents of natural language and movement, because language is bodily anchored. Experimental evidence suggests that semantic processing of metaphoric information within a dynamic agent-environment interaction is more efficient than processing of non-metaphorical information.

Keywords: metaphorical instruction, movement, body memory, sport science

Metaphorical instruction in the fields of sports science and embodiment

Metaphorical instruction is frequently used in sports praxis. But there is no common theory regarding the mechanisms through which metaphorical instruction works within the learning process. There is certainly an abundance of research in sports science about the utilization of metaphorical instruction, but the semantic core meaning of metaphorical instructions in movement execution is not well understood.

The aim of this contribution, and the leading question, is to clarify (a) why metaphorical instructions are often much more efficient than classical forms of instruction and (b) what interdependency exists between the meaning of the linguistic information and the meaning of the movement. In order to investigate metaphorical instruction during movement learning, it is necessary to describe the interacting factors such as language, movement, and meaning and to specify their reciprocity.

Philosophical anthropology, and its use in sports education pedagogy (Grupe 1969; Grupe & Krüger 2002; Meinberg 1981; Prohl 2006), as well as the approach of embodied cognition, provide the theoretical framework of this research. The common ground of both of these theories stems from a specific understanding of cognition and the body. According to theorists of philosophical anthropology such as Plessner (1975), Gehlen (1958), and Plügge (1967), the body can be understood as a "medium" or an "agent to the world" ["Mittler zur Welt"]. Embodied cognitive science further makes reference to Maurice Merleau-Ponty (1966/1974), another theorist of philosophical anthropology. Merleau-Ponty assumed that the living body (corps vivante; Leib) has a mediative function between body (corps propre; Körper) and mind (Plügge 1967). This understanding of the body implies that individuals cannot be analyzed separately from their environment (von Weizsäcker 1973; Gibson 1979). Tamboer (1991, 1997) renews this idea for sport science by focusing on the meaningful relation between man and environment at the moment in which a person experiences. Next to embodied ordinary experiences, athletic and active movement also leaves an imprint on the so-called body memory (Fuchs 2000). Using such body memories (activated by metaphoric instruction) for teaching and learning movements, two perspectives can be distinguished:

1.   The meaningful experience arises between an individual and the environment. This could be the basis for initiating a learning process about meanings that comes from the embodied experience of the subject. In this context, it is important to remark that learning could not be stimulated with physical parameters, because it is not part of the experience of human acting. Specifying this argument, we have to admit that physical parameters are always content of the movement, but are always translated into conceptual metaphor, when talking about the experience of the movement. The conceptual metaphor translates abstract concepts into concrete terms, which are grounded in the sensory-motor-system (Lakoff & Nunez 2000). This means that embodied experiences in movements of the individual can build the basis of a learning process (Panhofer 2009).
2.   The experience of the movement could first be verbalized through the instructor. This suggestion provides more space for the teacher to pick up experiences creating new learning situations and bring the learner to a reciprocal process of learning and teaching. In other words, the overlap between language, perception, movement and meaning arises, as findings from newer embodiment research suggest (e.g. Bergen & Feldmann 2008; Dantzig, Pecher, Zeelenberg & Barsalou 2008; Fischer & Zwaan 2008). This will be shown in the following section.

Embodied movement in sport science

Sports science is dominated by different theoretical approaches for the learning of movements. Anthropology-oriented theories and methods (e.g. Laging 2006; Loibl 2001; Scherer & Bietz in press; Volger 1999, 2004) draw upon the man-environment relation, to visualize the embedding of the moving individual in the environment and to pick up the resulting experience for the learning process, in contrast to methods that draw upon cybernetic-oriented theories (Roth 2003; Daugs 1989). This theoretical view maintains that the teaching and learning of movement does not only rest upon the principles of physics, but is also based on the phenomenological background of the subject-formed movement execution. Both physical and anthropological conditions constitute the movement and in this way we have to think about movement (Loosch 2004; Böger 2006a; Scherer & Bietz in press). The more important point from the anthropology-orientated stance on movement signifies that the moving person is acting in a man-environment context and this context is characterized by relational acting of the person (e.g. von Weizsäcker 1973; Metzger 1975; Buytendijk 1956). Working with metaphorical instructions during practical movement learning is one possibility to make use of the relation between man and environment. The question is why and how metaphorical instructions operate. Including this theoretical background, and with the help of metaphorical instruction, I want to take a look at the connection between language, movement, and meaning on a semantic level (Böger & Skilters 2006; Skilters & Böger 2008; Skilters & Böger in press; Böger 2011). But first, I want to describe the surrounding context within which instructions can obtain their desired effect.

There are three more variables that influence the movement experience of a person.

1. The situational context that develops when a person starts to move (Scherer 1998; Trebels 1990) and proportionately causes the execution of the movement.
2. Perception always comes along with movement. It is impossible to separate oneself from perception during action but also during inactivity (Böger 2006a). This fact is relevant for the understanding of any kind of instruction. Therefore, the perceived meaning of the instruction is working during movement execution.
3. Embodied movement patterns determine the movement execution. The manner in which a person receives the movement-relevant information contained in language, and uses it for movement execution, will be examined in relation to cognitive semantics, movement theories and to the theory of embodiment (Skilters & Böger in press).

Even though theoretical arguments of metaphor in cognitive linguistics ascribe to "static" linguistic roots, it seems useful to explain semantics with real body movement and to observe the influence of metaphor during movement execution.

Embodied cognitive science and body memory

Herein are located the similarities to the theory of embodiment. In the "embodiment premise" (Gibbs 2006; Johnson 1987), one can read that subjectively felt experiences, from the acting body, are the point of origin of action, just as cognition cannot be considered separately from man and his/her environment. This statement leads to the guiding assumption for the approach to a theory of embodied metaphoric structures, used for movement learning: that language and perception have common roots (Böger & Skilters 2006) and can be activated through the body (Merleau-Ponty 1966/1974). The following findings served the assumption in several ways: there is also evidence that any kind of perception is embodied, that language and perception are anchored in bodily experience (Gibbs 2003; Gibbs, Lima & Francozo 2004; Glenberg 2007; Johnson 1987; Lakoff & Johnson 1999) and that there are reciprocal dependencies between visual perception and movement execution, as well as language comprehension and movement execution (e.g. Barsalou 1999; Bergen & Feldmann 2008; Bergen, Lau, Narayan, Stojanovic & Wheeler 2010; Dantzig, Pecher, Zeelenberg & Barsalou 2008; Gallese & Lakoff 2005; Glenberg & Kaschak 2002; Glenberg, Sato, Cattaneo, Riggio, Palumbo & Buccino 2008; Zwaan & Taylor 2006; Fischer & Zwaan 2008).

Previous work by Böger and Skilters (2006), and Skilters and Böger (in press) described the similarities between language, movement, and meaning, with the help of cognitive semantics. The focus of this contribution is basically on image schemas in movement execution (e.g. Gibbs & Colston 1995/2006), whereas another contribution of Skilters and Böger (2008) focuses on other aspects of cognitive semantics, such as the action-sentence compatibility effect (Glenberg & Kaschak 2002) and the Indexical Hypothesis (Glenberg 1997; Glenberg 1999; Kaschak & Glenberg 2000).

One assumption is that meaning and meaning assignment are generated by reciprocal interactions between language and movement. The implicit and unconscious principles of cognitive processing, structure movement execution and language and are rooted on a bodily level. In relation to metaphor, empirical research in psychology shows that embodied experiences provide an information basis for the development of concepts of understanding (Gibbs 2003:7). I claim that the mode of action of the metaphorical instruction is to be found in these similarities, that the meaning of a metaphor is a guiding principle in the execution of movement, and also that the individual interpretation of a metaphor is a guiding principle in the execution of movement.

Two experiments shall support this thought. The first experiment I want to discuss (Böger 2006a, 2006b), laid the ground for the idea to study the problem of metaphoric instruction and its semantic meaning and to look for the shared roots of language and movement. The experimental design (fully developed in Böger 2006a) used in the empirical part of this study, is different and even somewhat contrary to classical movement research on the phenomenon of negative asynchrony (e.g., Aschersleben 1994; Dunlap 1910; Miedreich 2000; Stevens 1886). However, the experimental design makes it possible to investigate the phenomenon of negative asynchrony under the focus of the subjective determination of meaning and the phenomenological experience in general.

With this experimental design, several experiments on the interaction of movement perception and meaning assignment and the perception of differences during the performance of action have been carried out (Böger 2006a). The experiments were guided by the hypothesis that metaphorical instructions reduce the degree of negative asynchrony. A series of experiments was conducted under identical test conditions: In every experimental set a metronome generated an acoustic "click", whereas the subject produced a "tap" with a castanet. In the experiment, the test persons were first instructed to "tap the castanet at the same time as the metronome clicks" with

the metronome click. The second, metaphorical instruction asked the test persons to "merge with the sound" or to "identify with the click". Within the experiment, one can measure the delay difference produced by the test persons. It is the so-called negative asynchrony, a delay of about 20 to 50 ms between the click of the metronome and the tap of the test person. The subjects (n = 8) were not informed about producing negative asynchrony while they were tapping and also did not know whether their action was modified through the instructions. Using the Wilcoxon paired-samples test (t = 3.00, p = .020; 1-tailed), we found that it is possible to reduce the rate of negative asynchrony significantly with the second type of instruction (the metaphoric one). The results of the experiment suggest that the test persons use environmental information for their action, but handle it at a subjective level. What kind of resource supports them? On the one hand, movement execution exploits the environmental, situation-based contextual information. On the other hand, the subjective level of articulation catalyzes movement execution. The main results lead to the assumption that the self-active processes inherent the active subject direct the execution of the action (Böger 2006a). Moreover, instructions including metaphorical components decrease negative asynchrony during the execution of an action.

The second experiment should support these assumptions. For the experimental design, I used the two-hand coordination test of the Vienna Test System where the subjects (n = 17) have to move a point along a line on the screen with the help of two joysticks. The positions of the joysticks were fixed, one in the horizontal and the other in the vertical direction. First, the subjects were allowed to have one run-through under the screen instruction: "It is important that the point is moved as precisely and as fast as possible. Take care that the point does not leave the trace. Should it happen, try to move the point back on the trace as fast as possible." Then the experiment started with four trials for the metaphorical instruction: "Imagine, you are the ball and have the feeling of being absorbed by point B." and after a break continued with four trials for the non-metaphorical instruction: "Please focus your attention on the coordination of your hands." One half of the group started with the metaphorical instruction and the other with the non-metaphorical instruction. The results are shown in Figure 1 and Figure 2. Figure 1 shows the mean of the processing time obtained with the instructions (see Figure 1). With the paired samples t-test the significant result (p = .025; 1-tailed) show that the subjects were acting faster under the metaphorical instruction (M = 21.6; SD = 7.80) than under the non-metaphorical instruction (M = 25.59; SD = 7.55). Figure 2 shows another interesting result. According to the processing time an error rate of variations from the given line was detected. The mean shows less errors with the non-metaphorical instruction (M = 3.88; SD = 2.16), but participants made significantly more errors under the metaphorical instruction (M = 4.98; SD = 3.27).

To provide a deeper insight into the effect of metaphorical instruction (see Figure 3) the sequence of instructions was also tested. The test demonstrates how the test persons react to the different sequence of instructions. The results show that there is no significant difference within the first sequence (metaphorical instruction

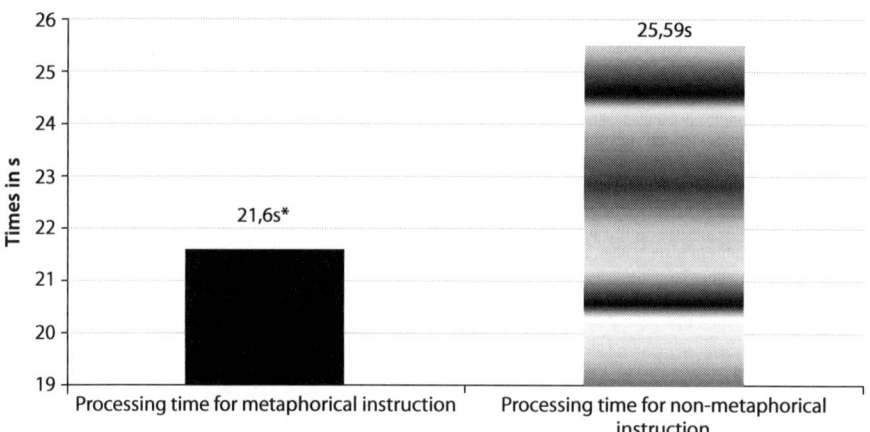

Figure 1. Processing time for both forms of instruction

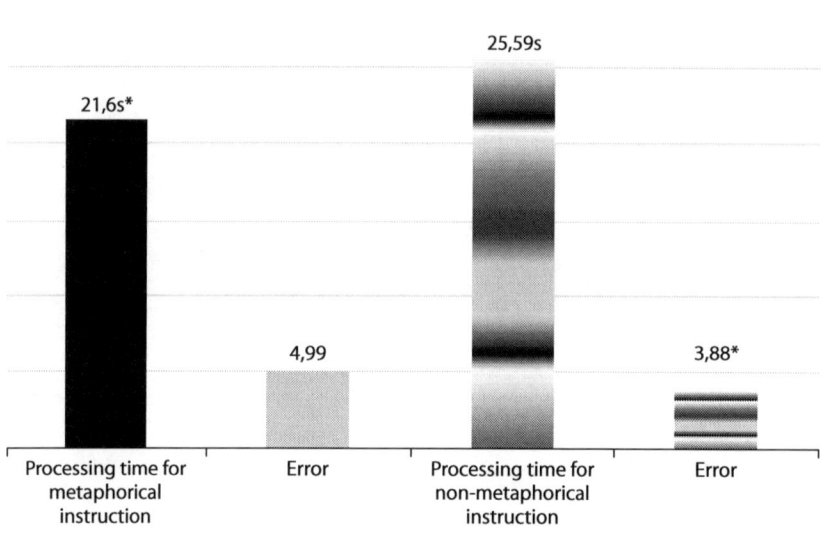

Figure 2. Processing time and error rates for both forms of instruction

(M = 22.03; SD = 8,38) first, non-metaphorical instruction: (M = 22.92; SD = 6.03) afterwards). But the group which received the metaphorical instruction as their second instruction was significantly faster (non-metaphorical instruction: (M = 28.59; SD = 8,33) first, metaphorical instruction: (M = 21.11; SD = 7.64) afterwards). The paired samples t-test realizes another significant result from the second sequence of instructions (p = .027). The statistical result allows us to conclude that the test persons

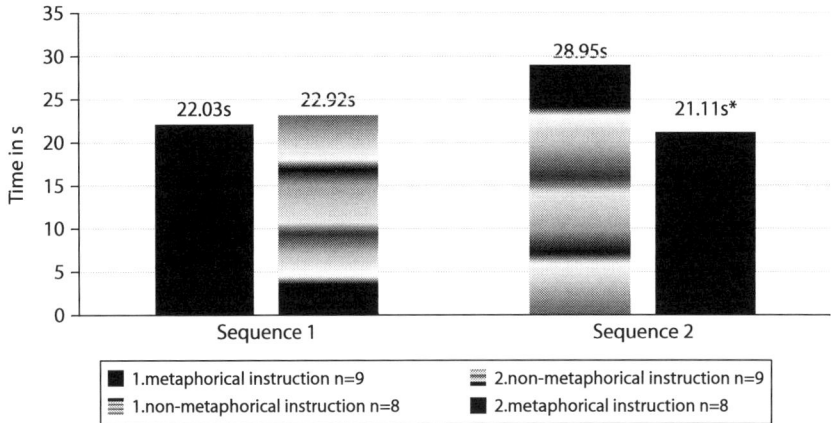

Figure 3. Sequence of instruction

react much better to the combination of non-metaphorical instruction first and metaphorical instruction second than vice versa (see Figure 3).

The results suggest that metaphorical instructions support the movement execution due to the linkage between language and movement execution generated by experience. Metaphorical instructions primarily refer to experiential factors. The non-metaphorical instructions are in contrast experientially poorer and concern the link between language and movement without significantly involving the additional metaphorical domain. The agents are faster and more precise in using the environmental information in the case where the instruction correlates with their experiential background.

Conclusion for movement, meaning, and language

The theory of cognitive semantics supports this argument: 'Metaphorical instructions' or 'metaphorical components in instructions' correlate with the individual and subjective semantic domain of the test person and points out that metaphor is fundamentally grounded in embodiment (Gibbs, Lima & Francozo 2004). This must be taken into account in order to achieve the expected action.

A definition of metaphor (Lakoff & Johnson 1999) shows that we have to describe metaphor on different mechanisti levels. Metaphor consists of two asymmetric experiential domains. The first is non-metaphorical and the second, which is derived from the first, is metaphorical. This means that, if we do understand the source of the experiential domain, we are able to capture the meaning of the resulting metaphorical experiential domain, but not vice versa. Within this approach, they point out different dimensions of experience, integrating perception and motor activity (Lakoff & Johnson 1999; Zwaan & Madden 2005). Transferring this thought into sports means that movement contains semantics at a bodily level. Gibbs (2005) said that embodiment plays a crucial role in the determination of meaning processes. Meaning is always present at the level of bodily perception and language can be understood as one possibility of meaning determination. This interpretation of language, movement, and meaning is to be distinguished from the position of understanding meaning as semantically autonomous and purely linguistic, and relies upon classical experiments in cognitive semantics (Lakoff 1987; Lakoff & Johnson 1999; Johnson 1987).

In respect to metaphor, an interesting emerging question is now, what kinds of meanings are existent in separate paraphrases for separate individuals. Within this context language, movement, and meaning are interpreted in the following way:

- Language is a non-autonomous and non-modular system
- Movement is a relational and reciprocal process between the subject and the environment
- Meaning is a complex relational cognitive structure within a subject- (or agent-) situation basis influenced by perception. This means that meaning is always articulated in a concrete situation and by a concrete agent.
- The possibility of analyzing meaning is given by movement execution.

Assuming that experience is gained and previous experience is accessed during movement learning, it must be possible to communicate these experiences in metaphorical instruction. In this case, we have to realize that the sportsmen are acting upon their own subjective base of experience. The subject modifies and interprets an instruction during movement execution. A pure objective instruction is not executable in a common dynamic agent-environment interaction. For this reason, one can distinguish between two effects of embodiment: Namely that action is based on aspects concerning the subject and is intersubjective – because different individuals react in a similar way under certain situations. Barsalou speaks of "shared embodiment" (Barsalou 1999).

This can be said about the processing of instructions during the movement execution tasks, but another fact should be discussed. This kind of semantic processing is consistent with the image schematic approach to metaphors. Image schemas emerge experientially from the sensori-motor activity in manipulating objects, orientating ourselves spatially and temporally or directing the perceptual focus (cf. Gibbs & Colston 1995/2006: 239). Image schemata are inherently dynamic and are modified during a lifetime – both naturally and artificially. In different stages of development of our body morphology (during the process of growing) we implement slightly different image schemata. Image schemata are the format (but not the content) for executing movement and articulating meaning. The same image schema can contain several different movements and meaning assignments. Image schemata are dynamic structural invariants common to our bodily articulation, semantics (also metaphor) and language comprehension.

As such image schemata are multi-sensorial forms to be filled with different contents (in different situations and by different agents), but they are not the content itself. The origins of image schemata are in the bodily action, but image schemata can contain both perceptual, concrete information (e.g., "balanced weights") and more abstract, metaphorical material ("balanced personalities", "balanced views", "balanced systems"). The important point is that both experiential domains contain the same image schematic structure although they differ in the content.

There are two aspects to be distinguished in thinking about image schemata:

1. Image schemata are first cognitive patterns, developed before language is learned by a person, and in this sense image schemata are a precondition for a wide range of cognitive processes (including language processing). Image schemata arise in the bodily experience of every individual and thus are primarily grounded in the first-person perspective (cp. Gärdenfors 2007:70).
2. Equally important is the fact that image schemata are modified during life, both perceptually in action and in simulation processes (in respect to imagined bodily action).

One and the same image schema is implemented differently for different persons, depending on the environmental and experiential factors of the agent and also on the bodily configuration of the agent. This is unavoidable since image schemata arise and are often implemented via perception. But perception is determined by the types of bodies we have (Glenberg 1997). In respect to movement execution and semantic articulation, it is possible to formulate a common shared image schematic structure both in linguistic instructions (metaphorical or not) and in the according movement execution act (see Figure 4).

In that case, we are allowed to say that meaning is constitutive of the set of actions available to an agent in a given situation. The set of actions are derived from integrating "affordances to accomplish action-based goals" (Glenberg & Kaschak 2002:558). The affordances are derived from situational and experiential information and correspond to the bodily morphology of an agent. Finally, the results and related empirical

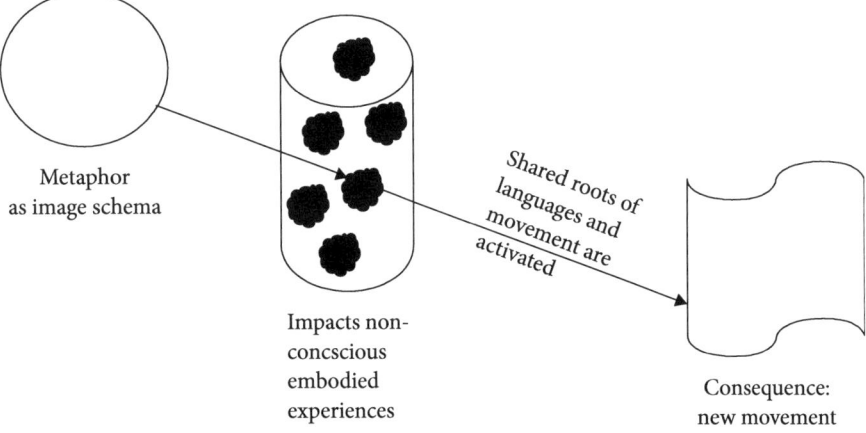

Figure 4. Process of meaning articulation in movement (Böger 2010)

evidence suggests that language is not distinct from the rest of cognition: Language comprehension is based on the same cognitive systems that are used for perception, action, planning, and interaction with the environment (Kaschak, Madden, Therriault, Yaxley, Aveyard, Blanchard & Zwaan 2005; Zwaan & Kaschak 2008).

A more detailed analysis of the metaphorical instructions and the corresponding correlation of movement and meaning is needed. Accordingly, a more careful analysis of how to classify metaphors, or the interaction between metaphors and of the context in which they appear should be provided (see also Gibbs & Perlman 2006: 215).

References

Aschersleben, G. (1994). *Afferente Informationen und die Synchronisation von Ereignissen* [Afferent information and the synchronisation of events]. Europäische Hochschulschriften [European Academic Publications]. Reihe VI. Psychologie, 456. Frankfurt am Main: Lang.

Barsalou, L. W. (1999). Perceptual symbol systems. *Behavioral and Brain Sciences, 22*, 577–609.

Bergen, B. K. & Feldman, J. (2008). Embodied concept learning. In P. Calvo & T. Gomila (Eds.), *Handbook of Cognitive Science: An Embodied Approach* (pp. 313–331). Amsterdam: Elsevier.

Bergen, B., Lau, A., Narayan, S., Stojanovic, D. & Wheeler, K. (2010). *Body part representations in verbal semantics.* Unpublished Manuscript.

Böger, C. (2006a). *Subjekt und Eigenaktivität. Aspekte einer Theorie der subjektiven Handlungsstrukturierung bei der Synchronisation von Ereignissen* [Subject and Eigen-activity. Aspects of a theory of the subjective structure of action in the synchronisation of events]. Dissertation Universitätsbibliothek Erfurt, urn:nbn:de:gbv:547-200601317.

Böger, C. (2006b). Non-conscious self activity of the acting person. In I. Martinkova, L. Dastlik & M. Pelis (Eds.), *The art of life II* (pp. 9–16). Prague: The Karolinum Press.

Böger, C. & Skilters, J. (2006). *Semantic articulation and movement execution.* Annual Meeting, European Society for Philosophy and Psychology, Queens-University-Belfast, Abstracts (pp. 6–7), Available at: www.psych.qub.ac.uk/eurospp2006/programme/papersandposters/abstracts.pdf.

Böger, C. (2010). Embodiment und metaphorische Instruktion. In G. Amesberger, Th. Finkenzeller & S. Würth (Eds.), *Psychophysiologie im Sport – zwischen Experiment und Handlungsoptimierung* (pp. 61). Feldhaus: Czwalina.

Böger, C. (2011). Formgenese und metaphorische Instruktion: Zur Wechselwirkung von Bedeutung und Bewegung [Genesis of form and metaphoric instruction: On the interplay of meaning and movement]. In J. Bietz & M. Roscher (Eds.), *Form und Bewegung – Prozesse der Ordnungsbildung und ihre wirklichkeitskonstituierende Bedeutung* [Form and movement. Processes of order-formation and their reality-constituting meaning]. Lehmanns media: Berlin.

Buytendijk, F. J. J. (1956). *Allgemeine Theorie der menschlichen Haltung und Bewegung.* [General theory of the human posture and movement] Berlin: Springer.

Dantzig, S., Pecher, D., Zeelenberg, R. & Barsalou, L. W. (2008). Perceptual processing affects conceptual processing. *Cognitive Science, 32*, 579–590.

Daugs, R. (1989). *Beiträge zum visuomotorischen Lernen im Sport* [Contributions to visual-motor learning in sports]. Schorndorf: Hofmann.

Dunlap, K. (1910). Reactions to rhythmic stimuli, with attempt to synchronize. *Psychological Review, 17*, 399–416.

Fischer, M. H. & Zwaan, R. A. (2008). Embodied language: a review of the role of the motor system in language comprehension. *The quarterly journal of experimental psychology, 61* (6), 825–850.

Fuchs, T. (2000). *Leib, Raum, Person. Entwurf einer phänomenologischen Anthropologie* [Body, space, and the person. Outline of a phenomenological anthropology]. Stuttgart: Klett-Cotta.

Gallese, W. & Lakoff, G. (2005). The brain's concepts: The role of the sensory-motor system in conceptual knowledge. *Cognitive Neuropsychology, 22* (3/4), 455–479.

Gärdenfors, P. (2007). Cognitive semantics and image schemas with embodied forces. In J. M. Krois, M. Rosengren, A. Steidele & Westerkamp D. (Eds.), *Embodiment in Cognition and Culture* (pp. 57–76). Amsterdam, Philadelphia: John Benjamins.

Gehlen, A. (1958). *Der Mensch. Seine Natur und seine Stellung in der Welt* [The human being. His nature and position in the world]. Bonn: Athenäum.

Gibbs, R. W. Jr. (2003). Embodied experience and linguistic meaning. *Brain and Language, 84*, 1–15.

Gibbs, R. W. Jr., Lima, P. C. & Francozo, E. (2004). Metaphor is grounded in embodied experience. *Journal of Pragmatics, 36*, 1189–1210.

Gibbs, R. W. Jr. (2005). The psychological status of image schemas. In B. Hampe (Ed.), *From perception to meaning: Image schemas in cognitive linguistics* (pp. 113–135). Berlin: De Gruyter.

Gibbs, R. W. Jr. (2006). *Embodiment and cognitive science.* Cambridge: Cambridge University Press.

Gibbs, R. W. Jr. & Colston, H. L. (1995/2006). The cognitive psychological reality of image schemas and their transformations (originally published in: Cognitive Linguistics 1995, 6(4), 347–378). In D. Geeraerts (Ed.), *Cognitive linguistics: Basic readings* (pp. 239–268). New York: De Gruyter.

Gibbs, R. W. Jr. & Perlman, M. (2006). The contested impact of cognitive linguistic research on the psycholinguistics of metaphor understanding. In G. Kristiansen, M. Achard, R. Dirven & F. J. Ruiz de Mendoza Ibáñez (Eds.), *Cognitive linguistics: Current applications and future perspectives* (pp. 211–228). New York: De Gruyter.

Gibson, J. J. (1979). *The ecological approach to visual perception.* Boston: Houghton Mifflin.

Glenberg, A. M. (1997). What memory is for. *Behavioral and Brain Sciences, 20*, 1–55.

Glenberg, A. (1999). Why mental models need to be embodied. In G. Rickert & C. Habel (Eds.), *Mental models in discourse processing* (pp. 77–90). Amsterdam: Elsevier.

Glenberg, A. M. & Kaschak, M. P. (2002). Grounding language in action. *Psychonomic Bulletin & Review, 9*(3), 558–565.

Glenberg, A. M. (2007). Language and action: creating sensible combinations of ideas. In G. Gaskell (Ed.), *The Oxford handbook of psycholinguistics* (pp. 361–370). Oxford, UK: Oxford University Press.

Glenberg A. M., Sato, M., Cattaneo, L., Riggio, L., Palumbo, D. & Buccino, G. (2008). Processing abstract language modulates motor system activity. In M. H. Fischer & R. A. Zwaan (Eds.), Grounding cognition in perception and action. *A Special Issue of the Quarterly Journal of Experimental Psychology* (pp. 905–919).

Grupe, O. (1969). *Grundlagen der Sportpädagogik* [Foundation of sport pedagogy]. Barth: München.

Grupe, O. & Krüger, M. (2002). Sportpädagogik [Sport pedagogy]. In G. Bäumler, J. Court & W. Hollmann (Eds.), *Sportmedizin und Sportwissenschaft* [Sport medicine and the sport science] (pp. 373–412). Academia: Sankt Augustin.

Johnson, M. (1987). *The body in the mind.* Chicago, London: The University of Chicago Press.

Kaschak, M. P. & Glenberg, A. M. (2000). Constructing meaning: The role of affordances and grammatical constructions in sentence comprehension. *Journal of Memory & Language, 43*(3), 508–529.

Kaschak, M. P., Madden, C. J., Therriault, D. J., Yaxley, R. H., Aveyard, M., Blanchard, A. A. & Zwaan, R. A. (2005). Perception of motion affects language processing. *Cognition, 94,* B79–B89.

Laging, R. (2006). *Methodisches Handeln im Sportunterricht. Grundzüge einer bewegungspädagogischen Unterrichtslehre* [Methodological acting in sports education. Outline of a movement-pedagogic theory of teaching]. Seelze-Velber: Kallmeyersche Verlagsbuchhandlung.

Lakoff, G. & Johnson, M. (1999). *Philosophy in the flesh: The embodied mind and its challenge to western thought.* New York: Basic Books.

Lakoff, G. & Núñez, R. (2000). *Where mathematics comes from: How the embodied mind brings mathematics into beings.* New York: Basic Books.

Loibl, J. (2001). *Basketball – genetisches Lehren und Lernen: spielen – erfinden – erleben – verstehen* [Basketball – genetic teaching and learning: playing, inventing, experiencing, understanding]. Schorndorf: Hofmann.

Loosch, E. (2004). Widersprüche und Paradoxien in der Bewegungsforschung: Dilemma und Chance für den Erkenntnisfortschritt [Contradictions and paradoxes in the research on movement: Dilemma and possibilities for the progress of knowledge]. *Leipziger Sportwissenschaftliche Beiträge, 2,* 1–21.

Merleau-Ponty, M. (1966/1974). *Phänomenologie der Wahrnehmung.* [The phenomenology of perception]. Berlin: De Gruyter.

Metzger, W. (1975). *Gesetze des Sehens* [Laws of seeing/vision]. Frankfurt am Main: Kramer.

Miedreich, F. (2000). *Zeitliche Steuerung von Handlungen. Empirischer Test des Wing-Kristofferson Modells* [Temporal control of actions. Empirical testing of Wing-Kristofferson's model]. Aachen: Shaker Verlag.

Meinberg, E. (1981). *Sportpädagogik* [Sport-pedagogy]. Stuttgart: Kohlhammer.

Panhofer, H. (2009). *New approaches to communicate the embodied experience in Dance Movement Psychotherapy.* Unpublished thesis submitted in partial fulfillment of the requirements of the University of Hertfordshire for the degree doctor of philosophy.

Plessner, H. (1975). *Die Stufen des Organischen und der Mensch. Einleitung in die Philosophische Anthropologie* [The levels of the organic and the human being. Introduction to philosophical anthropology]. Berlin: De Gruyter.

Plügge, H. (1967). *Der Mensch und sein Leib* [The human being and the lived-body]. Tübingen: Niemeyer.

Prohl, R. (2006). *Grundriss der Sportpädagogik* [Outline of sport pedagogy]. Wiebelsheim: Limpert

Roth, K. (2003). Wie lehrt man schwierige geschlossene Fertigkeiten? [How do we learn difficult special skills?] In Bielefelder Sportpädagogen, *Methoden im Sportunterricht* [Methods in sports education] (pp. 27–46). Schorndorf: Hofmann.

Skilters, J. & Böger, C. (2008). *Semantic grounding of movement: Effects of movement execution on the semantic processing.* 9th Conference on Conceptual Structure, Discourse, and Language (CSDL9). Available at SSRN: http://ssrn.com/abstract=1292853.

Skilters, J. & Böger, C. (in press). Embodied semantic structures in movement execution and language. In J. Luchjenbroers & M. Aldridge (Eds.), *Conceptual Structure and Linguistics Research*, Vol. 1: Grammar, Blending and Metaphor. John Benjamins: Amsterdam, Philadelphia.

Stevens, L. T. (1886). On the time-sense. *Mind, 11,* 393–404.

Scherer, H.-G. (1998). Ein situationsorientiertes Lernmodell für eine situative Sportart [A situational learning model for situational sports]. In G. Schoder (Ed.), *Skilauf und Snowboard in Lehre und Forschung* [Skiing and snowboard in teaching and research] (pp. 9–33). Hamburg: Verlag.

Scherer, H.-G. & Bietz, J. (in press). *Lehren und Lernen von Bewegung* [Teaching and learning in movement] Baltmannsweiler: Schneider.

Tamboer, J. W. J. (1991). Relationsmodalitäten statt Leib-Seele-Verhältnisse [Modalities of relation instead of body-mind relations]. *Integrative Therapie, 1–2,* 58–84.

Tamboer, J. W. J. (1997). Die menschliche Bewegung in der Bewegungsforschung. Über den Zusammenhang von Menschenbild, Bewegungsauffassung und Untersuchungsmethoden [The human movement in the research on movement. On the connection of the idea of man, the conception of movement, and methods of investigation]. In E. Loosch & M. Tamme (Eds.), *Motorik-Struktur und Funktion* [The structure and function of motor behavior] (pp. 23–37). Hamburg: Czwalina.

Trebels, A. H. (1990). Bewegung sehen und beurteilen [Seeing and evaluating movement]. *Sportpädagogik, 14* (1), 12–20.

Volger, B. (1999). Über den Umgang mit Metaphern beim Lehren und Lernen von Bewegungen [On the use of metaphors in learning and teaching movements]. In B. Heinz & R. Laging (Eds.), *Bewegungslernen in Erziehung und Bildung* [Movement learning in education and formation] (pp. 121–129). Hamburg: Czwalina.

Volger, B. (2004). Der Weg zum Brunnen muss so gut sein wie der Trunk. [The way to the fountain must be as good as the drink] In M. Sukale & S. Treitz (Hrsg.), *Philosophie und Bewegung. Interdisziplinäre Betrachtungen* [Philosophy and movement. Interdisciplinary perspectives] (pp. 261–291). Münster: Lit Verlag.

Weizsäcker, V. von (1973). *Der Gestaltkreis.* [The Gestalt-circle]. Stuttgart: Suhrkamp.

Zwaan, R. A. & Madden, C. J. (2005). Embodied sentence comprehension. In D. Pecher & R. A. Zwaan (Eds.), *Grounding cognition: The role of perception and action in memory, language, and thinking* (pp. 224–245). Cambridge, UK: Cambridge University Press.

Zwaan, R. A. & Taylor, L. J. (2006). Seeing, Acting, Understanding: Motor Resonance in Language Comprehension. *Journal of Experimental Psychology: General, 135*(1), 1–11.

Zwaan, R. A. & Kaschak, M. P. (2008; in press). Language in the brain, body, and world. In P. Robbins & M. Aydede (Eds.), *Cambridge handbook of situated cognition* (pp. 368–381). Cambridge University Press: Cambridge UK.

CHAPTER 13

Body memory and the emergence of metaphor in movement and speech

An interdisciplinary case study

Astrid Kolter,* Silva H. Ladewig,** Michela Summa,*
Cornelia Müller,** Sabine C. Koch* and Thomas Fuchs*
*University of Heidelberg / **Viadrina University, Frankfurt/Oder

The present study is an empirical documentation of body memory and the transition from implicit to explicit memory from the cognitive-linguistic, movement analytic, and philosophical perspectives in a therapeutic application. The transition from implicit memory to explicit memory is described using the concept of activated metaphoricity. It is argued that body movements executed in the absence of speech may provide the experiential source for multimodal metaphors. Tracing these bodily movements from speechless contexts to contexts encompassing speech and body movement allows for the empirical documentation of the transition from implicit body memory to explicit verbalized memory. In this chapter, these theoretical claims are substantiated from the results of an interdisciplinary case study in a dance/movement therapy context.

Keywords: emergence and activation of metaphors, multimodal metaphors, body memory, from implicit to explicit memory, movement qualities, dance/movement therapy

Body memory is a currently debated issue in the cognitive sciences, in phenomenology as well as in dance/movement therapy. The present paper adopted the phenomenological stance and considered body memory as an implicitly operating form of intentionality through which the past is presently experienced. Yet, different from explicit memory, the past is not voluntarily represented in implicit body memory; it rather pre-thematically exerts an impact on present experience. Thus, body memory cannot be reduced simply to subpersonal processes. Instead, it designates a form of experiential latency, which, however, accompanies all experiences and can, in principle, become explicit (Fuchs 2000, 2008a, 2008b, in print; Summa 2011). Nevertheless, the process of explication does not reach a complete conscious self-transparency: Implicit and explicit moments, both considered as modes of intentionality, rather seem to be constantly interwoven in the complex unity of experience. In our study, we tested this hypothesis on the basis of a concrete case study. By addressing the process of explication of body memory as an emergence of metaphors in movement and speech, we aimed to provide further evidence for the assumption of a dynamic relation between explicit and implicit moments of lived experience.

One of the most important expressions of body memory is movement. It has a primary role for human experience and communication. Before children even start to speak, they are already able to cope with the environment and communicate in complex ways without words (Kestenberg 1995; Sheets-Johnstone 1999; Stern 1985). Movement has an important function for individual and interpersonal affect regulation (Zajonc & Markus 1984), and as expressive movement, can have important healing functions (Chaiklin & Wengrower 2009; Levy 1992; McNiff 2009). Expressive movements have been argued to provide the experiential bases of multimodal metaphors in face-to-face conversations as well as in the reception of films (Kappelhoff & Müller 2011).

In order to investigate the phenomenon of body memory in relation to the emergence of metaphors in movement and speech, an explorative study was conducted at the University of Heidelberg. A context was created in which participants were encouraged to express themselves of their lives by moving and following their inner impulses or images. The case analysis presented in this chapter features one of the participants. It is based on the interdisciplinary integration of three perspectives of research: the cognitive linguistic, the psychological, and the phenomenological. The first part of the chapter introduces the theoretical background of each perspective. In the second part, the setting of data collection and the joint case analysis with applications to therapy is presented. The concluding part discusses the relevant outcomes of the study and their impact on the interdisciplinary theoretical approach.

Theoretical background

First, we provide a short introduction to the theoretical backgrounds of (1) cognitive linguistics, (2) Kestenberg movement analysis, and (3) phenomenology.

(1) Investigating body memory from a linguistic perspective means to examine how bodily experiences are realized in speech and gesture. More specifically, the relation between implicit and explicit memory is investigated in terms of the dynamic activation of metaphors (Müller 2008a, 2008b; Müller & Tag 2011). Metaphoricity is regarded as grounded in embodied experiences and believed to have the potential to be activated to different degrees over time in a discourse (from sleeping to waking, from minimal activation to extremely high activation; see Table 1). Metaphoricity is therefore considered to be inherently dynamic: It is both a process that unfolds over time in the course of a conversation and a gradable form of meaning activated at different points in time within a discourse. Activation of verbal metaphoric

Table 1. Dynamic category of metaphors (Müller 2008a)

	Activation of metaphoricity is low (backgrounding of metaphoricity)	Metaphoricity is activated (foregrounding of metaphoricity)	Metaphoricity is highly activated (foregrounding of metaphoricity, conscious awareness)
Multimodal metaphor (with elaboration and metacommunication)			Waking (explicit meaning)
Multimodal metaphor (with elaboration)		Waking (implicit meaning)	
Monomodal metaphor (without elaboration)	Sleeping (implicit meaning)		

meaning, however, presupposes transparency of the metaphoric meaning for the respective speaker and hearer. An opaque metaphor cannot be activated by an average speaker in a naturalistic context (Müller 2008a).

Different degrees of metaphor activation are achieved through foregrounding techniques employed by the participants of a conversation such as elaboration, specification, or multimodal construction. These strategies can be empirically documented by applying "a sequential and cognitive-linguistic Metaphor Foregrounding Analysis (MFA)" (Müller & Tag 2011). If metaphoricity is foregrounded, it is considered to be activated in the interaction (i.e., a given speaker addresses a co-participant by foregrounding metaphoricity).

A dynamic view on metaphors goes along with a dynamic approach to attention (Chafe 1994), assuming that attention flows selectively from one attentional focus to another. It also goes along with an interactive understanding of the flow of attention. Speakers organize their speech for an attending co-participant (*recipient design*; Garfinkel 1967), and it is assumed that the flow of attention in a conversation is shared by speaker and hearer. Foregrounding strategies show where a speaker/hearer's focus of attention is located, it uncovers whether a given metaphorically used word or gesture is inactive (sleeping), activated (awake), or highly activated in his/her conscious awareness (awake; Müller 2008a, 2008b, 2011; Müller & Tag 2011).

As metaphors show different degrees of activation, the question can be raised regarding whether the emergence and activation of metaphoricity shows transfers of implicit to explicit memory. The analysis presented in our paper aims to provide an answer to this question.

(2) The psychological assessment of body memory sets upon certain movement parameters indicating implicit or explicit awareness of a bodily experience. Analyzing the data from the point of view of psychology means applying methods that allow for a differentiation of movement and meaning on explicit and implicit levels. The method of the Kestenberg Movement Profile (KMP; Kestenberg 1995; Kestenberg Amighi et al. 1999) uses a system of approximately 120 parameters and combinations of them

Table 2. Scheme of unconscious, preconscious, and conscious parameters of movement according the Kestenberg Movement Profile (KMP)

	Unconscious	Preconscious	Conscious
Quality of movement	Rhythms, attributes	Pre-efforts	Efforts
Shape of movement	Bipolar and unipolar shape flow	Shaping in directions	Shaping in planes

serving to describe dynamic movements and their semantics in the communication process. Basic dimensions are the qualities of movement (System I) and the shapes of movement (System II). Qualities of movement originate from the rhythmical alternation of tension and relaxation in the muscles. They can be differentiated into either the "indulgent, libidinal" or the "fighting, aggressive" type (Laban 1960; A. Freud 1965). Shapes of movement can be differentiated into "growing and shrinking" and can be traced back to the alternation of "inhaling and exhaling." Both qualities of movement and shaping can manifest themselves on an unconscious, a preconscious, and a conscious level (Kestenberg 1995; Kestenberg Amighi et al. 1999; Kestenberg & Sossin 1979; Koch 2011). The reliability between observers using the KMP has been acceptable as investigated by Koch, Cruz and Goodill (2002), Koch (2006), and Sossin (1987). One hypothesis of this interdisciplinary analysis is that the unconscious is related to implicit (sleeping metaphors), the preconscious to implicit/explicit (sleeping/waking metaphors), and the conscious to explicit (waking metaphors) meta-communicative awareness. Table 2 provides an overview of the categories of the KMP.

Therapists work to make the implicit conscious, but they also work with the implicit itself. In dance/movement therapy, making implicit content conscious is one of the treatment goals. Moments in which this "making the implicit conscious" happens are often called significant moments in therapy. Those moments are usually difficult to capture and depend widely on subjective interpretation. Significant moments are here defined as "that part of the session where the therapist believed there was an event which significantly developed the therapeutic relationship or pushed the therapy forward in some way" (Campbell, Bianco, Dowling, Godberg, McNab & Pentecost 2003: 420). A significant moment is further defined as a moment in therapy when some insight is reached (Elliott, Saphiro, Firth-Cozens, Stiles, Hardy, Llewelyn & Margison 1994: 450), which consists of four elements: the metaphorical vision, the connection making, the suddenness, and the newness (Elliott et al. 1994).

(3) Addressing body memory, phenomenology primarily aims to descriptively differentiate its concrete modes of manifestation as well as to investigate its inner structure and dynamics. Thus, the inquiry into the different forms of body memory and the taxonomic definitions stem from the description of the modalities in which body memory concretely manifests itself in lived experience. Consistently, body memory cannot be reduced to a mere subpersonal process, but shall rather be considered as a form of "operative intentionality" (Merleau-Ponty 1945). As such, body memory plays a role in the constant shaping of one's (inter)subjective experience and

Table 3. Implicit and explicit memory

	Implicit	Explicit
Way of knowing	Knowing how	Knowing that
Verbalizability	Cannot easily be verbalized	Implicit declarative
Form of awareness	Pre-thematic unconscious	Thematic conscious
Relation between present and past	(Past →) present	Present → past

in the process of basic meaning formation (Casey 2000; Fuchs 2000, 2008a, 2008b; Summa 2011, this volume).

From a phenomenological perspective, the first general distinction to be made regarding memory concerns the different forms of awareness of the past. The distinction between implicit and explicit memory, developed in cognitive psychology (see Schacter 1996) can thus be reformulated in phenomenological terms (Fuchs 2008a, 2008b). Explicit memory entails both the autobiographic recollections of the episodes of one's own past (autobiographic memory) and the presentification [Vergegenwärtigung] of knowledge acquired from other sources (semantic memory). These recollections are explicitly conscious and declarative. Resorting to the distinction put forward by Ryle, it could be said that explicit memory coincides with our "knowing that," whereas implicit memory refers to our pre-reflective and pre-thematic "knowing how" (Ryle 2000). In implicit memory, indeed, the past is not properly re-presented; it rather operates latently and is enacted in our present experience. In his recent works, Fuchs has developed a thoughtful description of the different manifestations of body memory. On the basis of careful phenomenological analyses, he typologically distinguishes five forms of body memory: habitual, situational, intercorporeal, incorporative, and traumatic body memory. The different phenomena that fall under each of these categories are further considered as to their specificity (Fuchs 2008a, 2008b).

In sum, the three viewpoints converge in considering experience as a complex whole that entails both implicit and explicit moments. Fuchs' typological differentiation of body memory phenomena makes the analysis of the relation between these moments possible. Applying a sequential and cognitive-linguistic approach to the investigation of activated metaphoricity allows for an empirical account of these moments and captures the dynamic and gradual aspects of body memory. The KMP describes the transformation from implicit rhythms and shape-flow, via pre-efforts and shaping in directions, to explicit efforts and shaping in planes. This transformation is gradual but observed in a categorical way with the possibility of mixed categories (e.g., one element of efforts and one of pre-efforts mixed in one action such as later seen in the case analysis (spiral movement down with light and flexible dynamics)).

The goal of the following case analysis was to investigate the process of the emergence of contents of body memory in movement and speech from the three disciplinary perspectives. Finally, an integration of the results of these perspectives was intended.

Joint case analysis

The aim of this research was to find out whether implicit memory and explicit memory are discontinuously juxtaposed, or whether continuous processes of transition between them should be assumed. Documenting how metaphors in movement and speech emerge over time in a discourse offers an empirical access to this question. Therefore, the central objectives of our analysis were to investigate the emergence of body memory and metaphors from movement – that is, the investigation of bodily movement – and to describe the "languaging" of movement – that is, the translation of body movement into words.

The data collection setting

In the exploratory study conducted at the Department of Psychology at the University of Heidelberg, video data were gathered from 35 participants (psychology students, dance/movement therapists in training, and clinical patients). These data show the processes of emerging metaphoricity in movement and speech and the interplay of implicit and explicit experiential processes.

    Participants were instructed to move with their eyes closed. Their movements were not accompanied by music. They were asked to improvise aspects of their lives within a time frame of 10 min.[1] Subsequently, participants were asked to select one aspect of their movement sequence and to repeat the selected movements several times.[2] Finally, in the third phase, participants were asked to repeat the selected movement sequence and verbalize while moving.[3] Following the three movement parts, an interview was conducted focusing on important aspects of the performance and on particular images that arose as well as memories of the person during and after moving.

The analyzed movement patterns

The person chosen for the case study was a woman in her 40s who was diagnosed with bipolar affective disorder. She participated in the exploratory study in July of 2010,

---

1.   The instructions were as follows: "In our research project, we will analyze the translation of embodied contents in speech. In order to do so, we would like you to express an important aspect of your life in movement. You have ten minutes to move around freely and to follow your inner impulses. Please choose personally meaningful moments. If it helps you to focus on your imaginations, you can close your eyes. In a second part, you will be asked to choose some of these movements and to repeat them. Afterwards, a short interview will be conducted."

2.   "Now, we would like you to choose one part of this movement sequence and repeat it."

3.   "Please repeat the selected sequence again and verbalize while you do it."

when she expressed important aspects of her life in the presence of a dance/movement therapist.

The transfer from implicit memory to explicit memory and the activation of metaphors in movement and speech were analyzed in particular with respect to the third phase of the study (i.e., the one encompassing both movement and verbalization). Two alternated movement patterns in the patient's performance were the objects of the joint analysis. One observed pattern was a swinging movement of the patient's body and hands from right to left and vice versa. Another pattern was a spiral movement executed with the left hand from the highest peak above the head down to the waist and the other way around. The patient performed these two alternating patterns for the entire period (3.48 min). While performing the swinging movement several times, she conceptualized her life situation as a wave that sometimes goes up and sometimes down. This conceptualization was also traceable in her verbalization when performing the spiral movement downward. After several repetitions of the spiral movement from up to down, the patient realized that her movement was only directed downward. From that moment on, she tried to modify the spiral movement from the waist up to the peak above the head and noticed that this attempt broached a central problem of hers.

Procedure of the analysis

The presentation of the linguistic analysis follows the dynamic emergence and unfolding of metaphors, traceable as the therapeutic session progressed. As metaphoricity can be expressed in speech or gesture only or in both speech and gesture, the research discriminates between monomodal and multimodal metaphors (Cienki & Müller 2008a, 2008b; Müller 2008a, 2008b; Müller & Cienki 2009). To be able to follow the analytical steps reconstructing the emergence and activation of metaphoricity in speech and gestures, illustrations are included, which document the progression of the different facets of metaphoric meaning (see Figures 1 to 7). This type of analysis that includes graphic presentation has been developed in an interdisciplinary project on multimodal metaphors, (bodily and cinematic) expressive movements, and affective processes (Kappelhoff & Müller 2011).[4] Metaphoric expressions are shown as boxes on a timeline. The size of these boxes corresponds roughly to the length of a verbal, gestural, or verbo-gestural metaphoric expressions as identified in the ELAN-Software;[5] the graphic patterns of the boxes correspond to the different metaphoric

---

4. The project was funded by the Cluster of Excellence "Languages of Emotion" at the Freie Universität Berlin. For further information see: www.languages-of-emotion.de/en/expressive-movement.html.

5. ELAN (Eudico Linguistic Annotator) was developed at the Max Planck Institute for Psycholinguistics in Nijmegen (www.mpi.nl/tools).

meanings. The investigation from a cognitive-linguistic perspective provides the basis for the psychological and phenomenological analyses.

The psychological analysis is based upon the psychological perspective that focuses on the connection of body movement and affect examined by the movement analysis (KMP). The quality and shape of movements are categorized into unconscious rhythms and shape flow, pre-efforts and shaping in directions as a step between unconsciousness and consciousness, and conscious efforts and shaping in planes. In this manner, significant moments for the patient can be recognized.

The phenomenological analysis is focused on the relation between implicit and explicit moments of experience, while integrating the cognitive-linguistic and the psychological perspectives. In doing so, this analysis takes a descriptive stance toward the experiences and the expressions of the patient. The complex of these experiences and expressions defines, on the one hand, the explanandum of phenomenological inquiry and, on the other hand, the final criterion for testing the theoretical-categorical background, and possibly the ability to refine it. Thus, consistent with the basic principles of phenomenology, experience is assumed not only as the starting point of all theoretical inquiry, but also as the ultimate reference point for the validation of a theory. Aiming at uncovering the meaningful structures of experience as it is lived through from the 1st- and from the 2nd-person perspective, all objectifying assumptions regarding movement, memory, implicit processes, and explications from the 3rd-person perspective are bracketed here, in a way analogous to the phenomenological epoché. This means, specifically, that both the movements and the linguistic expressions of the patient are taken as modes of meaningful interaction with the world, as it is concretized in the very specific situation of the study.

The joint analysis documented the transformation process of implicit memory to explicit knowledge, which presented itself as a temporally orchestrated and unfolding process. The aim was to show that this process becomes empirically traceable in the emergence and activation of metaphoricity. This undertaking is presented in a sequence of seven stages of emergent and activated meaning. Note however, that the seven stages are stages within a continuous process of metaphor emergence; not seven discrete steps.

Stage 1. Emerging metaphor: "Life feels like waves moving up and down"

In the movement phases without verbalization, the patient alternates between executing a swinging movement with the arms and the upper body and a spiral movement performed downward with the left arm while walking through the room in a circle. The same movements are executed in the context encompassing speech while standing frontally to the camera. The patient begins by swinging her upper body and her arms to the right and to the left. After performing this movement pattern three times, the patient starts verbalizing using a simile comparing her life situation with a wave ("*mein Leben ist wie 'ne Welle*" / "my life's like a wave"). While doing so, the patient performs the swinging movement. Accordingly, the experiential base of the simile (i.e., the swinging movement) is expressed in both speech and gesture. Therefore, the simile can be considered to be multimodally construed.

In the following, the patient elaborates this multimodal simile. She carries on moving in a swing-like fashion but now verbalizes different qualities of the movement (Figure 1). When reaching the endpoint of the swinging movement, which is directed upward, she says: "*mal geht's auf*" ("sometimes it goes up"). When going backward and reaching the lowest point of the swinging movement, she says: "*mal geht's ab*" ("sometimes it goes down"). It appears that the felt qualities of the swinging movement have provided the experiential base or source domain for the patient's metaphoric utterances. In particular, the different directions of the swinging movement seem to have triggered her metaphoric understanding of life as an upward and downward movement. It is through the patient's verbalization that the metaphor "life feels like moving up and down" emerges. Now the bodily movement (i.e., the gestures) along with the verbal expressions form a multimodal metaphor (Cienki & Müller 2009). In this metaphor, directionality is foregrounded as the patient's verbalization of upwardness and downwardness is accompanied by upward and downward movements. Note that zooming in on directionality implies a choice on the side of the speaker. She could as well have departed from the manner of the movement as an experiential source for a metaphoric verbalization of her feelings about her life situation. She could have said something like: "I feel like a boat in a heavy storm." In such a metaphoric expression the wave-like pattern of the movement would have been foregrounded and hence activated. However, this is not what she does. From the experience of walking around in a room and performing wave-like movements with her upper body and her hands, she singles out a contrastive directionality: the up and down path of her movements.

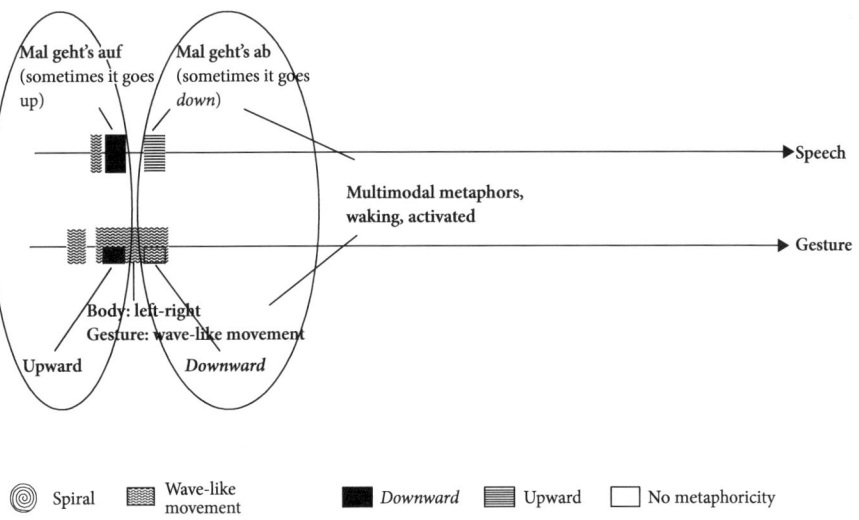

Figure 1. Emerging metaphor "life feels like waves moving up and down"

Accordingly, a multimodal metaphor (an idiomatic expression) has emerged, which is foregrounded (because it has been expressed in two modalities at the same time) and whose metaphoricity can be considered to be awake and activated (Müller 2008; Müller & Tag 2011). With regard to memory, it appears that a transition from implicit (body memory) to explicit (declarative) memory is on its way. However, since it does not receive meta-communicative awareness, it can be considered only activated, not highly activated.

Analyzing the action from a psychological perspective of dance/movement therapy (movement analysis with the KMP), the horizontal side-to-side movement includes a vertical up-down movement. This bipolar (horizontal and vertical) shape-flow is a symmetrical growing and shrinking of the body. Bipolar shape-flow structures the patient's discharge of fighting and indulging drives, and is assumed to inform us about the patient's self-feelings and general affect. The movement is generally conducted as smooth, round, without strength, and without much inner participation as indicated by the bound center (chest) and the peripheral movements. The patient uses a mixture of oral sucking rhythm and inner genital swaying rhythm, which can provide hypotheses about an early need for being held combined with a need for holding others. These needs are implicit (unconscious).[6] In addition, the patient is using preconscious directional movements (sideways and across), paired with the pre-efforts of gentle and gradual. By the use of both of these pre-efforts, a prevalent insecurity of the patient can be inferred.

If a psychological view of the cognitive-linguistic part is taken, the smooth, repetitive movement of growing and shrinking encourages the patient's metaphoric utterance as upwardness and downwardness. It is assumed that continuously repeating this movement helps to conserve the affect of the moment. This conservation facilitates the emerging metaphor of upwardness and downwardness.

In order to understand the "emerging" character of the metaphor presented above from a phenomenological standpoint, the context of such emergence must be kept in mind. At this point, the patient has already been asked to stage some relevant aspects of her life twice. In the first and longer sequence, the patient still has a searching attitude, trying out different kinds of bodily movements. The spectrum of these movements, with their forms and qualities, shall be considered as belonging to the patient's implicit body memory, as it describes a habitually developed and individual style of rhythmic bodily action and situated interaction. As the psychological (KMP) analysis reveals, these patterns of movement reveal unreflected characters of the patient's dispositions. It is during this longer sequence that the swinging movement is performed for the first time. Yet its meaning remains at this stage implicit. A first step toward explication is accomplished in the second phase when the patient is asked to repeat one moment of the previous sequence in front of the camera. The formulation of the task here clearly invites the patient to adopt a self-reflective and self-explicating attitude

---

6. If the KMP speaks of unconscious, preconscious, or conscious, it refers to the Freudian concepts.

toward the previously spontaneous movement performance. Thus, it is argued that the swinging movement through this primary process of explication progressively becomes a wave-like movement. And this wave-like movement subsequently becomes the experiential source of the explicitly verbalized simile "my life's like a wave." This explication has itself an impact on the performance of the bodily movement, which, in the next stages, is more thoughtfully accomplished in its wave-like articulation.

Stage 2. Body movement: Point of initialization – the spiral movement

The second aspect under consideration is the patient's performance of a spiral movement oriented downward, accomplished with the left arm (Figure 2). The patient has shown this movement pattern in the movement phases without verbalization before. While executing the spiral movement, the patient talks about feeling mostly good ("*und meistens bin ich sehr manisch. Dann geht's ganz gut.*" / "and mostly I am very manic. Then it's going quite well."). Contrary to the previous action, the patient does not verbalize the directions of gestural performance. While talking about positive circumstances of her life, a downward movement is performed. Directionality that was foregrounded through the use of speech and gesture in the previous action is visible only in the gestural movement. Accordingly, the metaphor "life feels like moving up and down" is only monomodally construed in the bodily movement. Metaphoricity, in this case, can be considered to be asleep and minimally active.

The clockwise spiral movement, which is executed for the first time in this instance, is not verbalized at all. However, being fully aware of the whole sample and arguing from a retrospective perspective that takes the stepwise evolvement of meta-

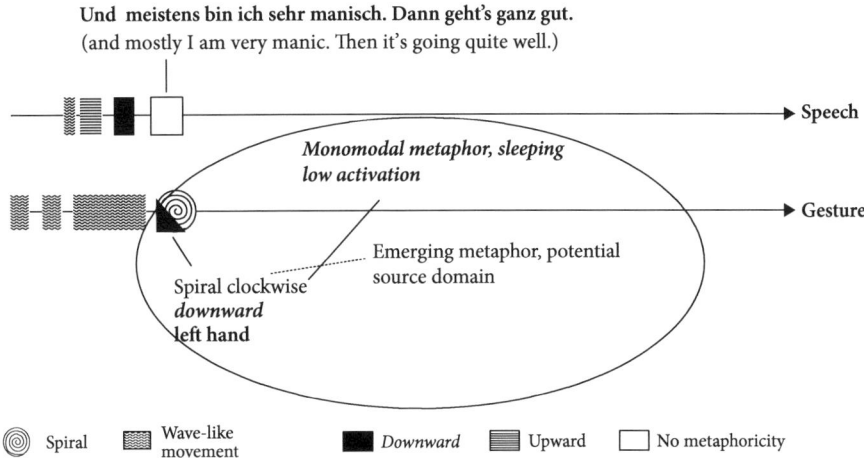

Figure 2. Body movement: Point of initialization – the spiral movement

phors in speech and gesture into account, this gestural movement can be considered to be a potential source domain for a metaphor emerging in later stages (see Stage 5).

From a KMP perspective, the loop is conducted with light and flexible movements downward. The spiral movement is a shape in direction up to down as well as a three dimensional circular movement. The shape formed by the up-down direction is a line and is associated both with defenses against external stimuli and with a link between internal and external. The circular movement is associated with an integrating connection between the right and the left cerebral hemispheres. The patient acts at the stage of pre-efforts and therefore on a pre-conscious level. In addition, there are unconscious elements such as the mixture of sucking and swaying rhythms alluding to a need for being held and holding others. Moreover, the use of the "light" movement quality (efforts) is indicative of the patient being in control of the movements and a higher level of consciousness.

As noticed from both a linguistic and a psychological point of view, a first contrast between movement and linguistic expression emerges at this stage. The verbal expression, indeed, has a positive valence ("*Dann geht's ganz gut*" / "Then it's going quite well"), whereas the spiral movement is oriented downward, which rather entails a negative valence for the patient that will be specified later on. At this point, the meaning of the downward spiral movement, thus, is still implicit, and becomes explicit only at a second stage. Moreover, the positive expression "*Dann geht's ganz gut*" / "Then it's going quite well" could also be considered to be a further explication of the previous wave-like movement, which is fluctuating and horizontal. In the immediately following slide, corresponding to the next movement-speech sequence, the patient linguistically explicates the downward spiral movement previously accomplished ("*bin sehr oft tief gefallen*" / "I plummeted very often"). In this short sequence, therefore, movement precedes verbal expression. These phenomena are indicative of a certain retroactiveness (*Nachträglichkeit*), which is constitutive of the reflective explication with respect to the spontaneous performances.

Eventually, the presence of sleeping and minimally activated metaphoricity, preconscious, and conscious aspects in the sequence, which has been highlighted in the linguistic and psychological analysis, bears witness to the interweaving of explicit and implicit moments in the whole complex of lived experience. Explication, as it will be shown more clearly with respect to other phases of the movement-speech sequence, is neither a sudden break, nor is it unidirectional.

Stage 3. From body movement to foregrounding aspects of metaphoric meaning "life goes up and down"

The patient performs a spiral movement downward with her left arm while saying that her life has always gone up and down (Figure 3). When saying "*und ab bei mir*" / "and down with me," this movement pattern is performed. As in the first action, the patient's bodily movement provides the source for the metaphor "life feels like moving

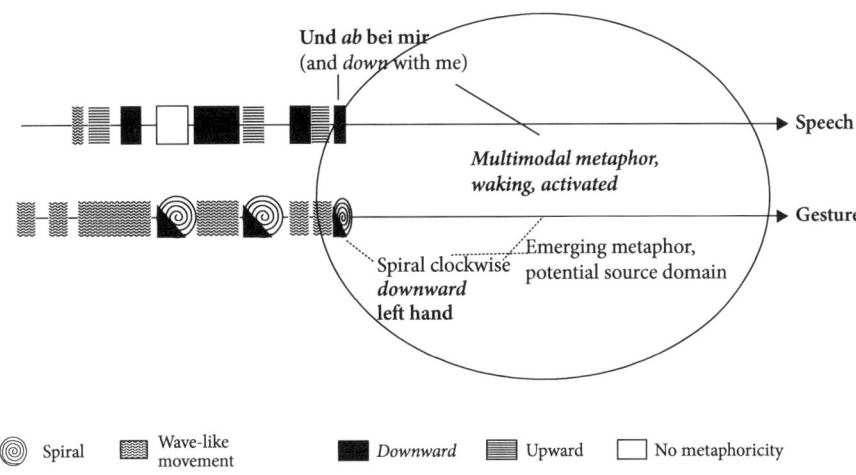

Figure 3. From body movement to foregrounding aspects of metaphoric meaning "life goes up and down"

up and down," which is multimodally construed. It can be considered to be an awake and activated metaphor since both modalities are involved in their construction. Once again, it is only the aspect of downwardness that is being foregrounded. The gestural movement pattern of the clockwise spiral movement is taken up verbally and remains therefore in the background of shared attention within the conversational interaction. It is not activated meaning the bodily movement is implicit at this moment in time, but will later be taken up by the speaker. We therefore suggest that what we see here is the experiential source of an emerging metaphor involving the spiral movement.

From the KMP perspective, the loop is conducted with flexible and light downward movements (pre-efforts and efforts); curiously, the patient generally uses only indulging and no fighting tension-flow qualities, indicating difficulties with separation and moving on. Although "downward" is the corresponding shape of the tension-flow quality of "strength," the patient does not show any strength during the downward movements. The gesture of the spiral movement is preceded by an arc-like movement to the top at all moments of its occurrence (not depicted in the graphics). According to KMP-theory, these phases in which movement begins can indicate the search for guidance, but can also indicate a mere bridging of two points. Yet, more importantly, this arc-like movement, from the second spiral movement on, is accompanied by and in fact followed by "upward"-verbalizations. This observed sequence points again to a retroactiveness (*Nachträglichkeit*) of the verbal expression compared to the according arc-like upward movement. Generally, the repetition of the movement sequence seems to help the patient first to conserve the affective quality, and in a second step to verbalize the affect. A second aspect is also related to the retroactiveness of the verbal expression: Verbalization and congruency of verbalization and movement is shown only after the movement or gesture has previously been repeatedly shown in movement only.

Phenomenologically relevant, at this stage, is the convergence between linguistic expression and a specific aspect of the main part of the movement: The patient is saying "down," and the movement is going downward (congruency of speech and gesture). This means that, after some repetitions of the up and down movements, the patient has become explicitly conscious of the meaning of her expressive movements. Yet, again, the process of explication is not unidirectional and is not to be conceived as an interpretation that would be superimposed on the otherwise neutral and unaltered movement. Rather, the process of metaphorical explication has an impact on the formation of the movement itself, which is progressively formed and experienced as being the metaphor of life. The awareness of this "as-structure" and its impact on the unfolding of movement itself belong to the process of explication.

Stage 4. Multimodal metaphor "life is a downward movement"

While executing a downward spiral movement, the patient continues to talk about the course of life as being up and down ("*ja also dieses Auf und Ab*" / "well this up and down"). Although both upward and downward directions are being verbalized, now it is only the quality of downwardness that is being multimodally construed. Along with speech, the downward spiral movement foregrounds "downwardness" and accordingly the metaphor "life is a downward movement" is activated and awake. The spiral movement has not been verbalized or activated yet. It remains backgrounded but we suggest that it serves as an experiential source domain for an emerging metaphor in the following example. The aspect of upwardness is only monomodally construed through speech and is to be considered asleep and only minimally active.

While the efforts and the tension-flow qualities of the patient do not change in the downward spiral movement (light and flexible), it can be argued that at this point the patient's speech entails an ambivalence ("*ja also dieses Auf und Ab*" / "well this up and down") that is not mirrored in the movements (spiral movement clockwise and downward). Following KMP-theory, the downward shaping gesture points to simple (the line from up to down) as well as complex relations (the spiral movement as a three-dimensional movement) in a person's life: Descending is used as a shape that is related to downward communication and presentation (shaping in planes), the line from up to down (shaping in directions) is related to learning by explication but also to putting somebody or something down in the sense of devaluation. The moment of concordance between movement and linguistic expression (spiral movement downward and "*Ab*" / "down") mirrors the patient's explicit intentions. Both the downward spiral movement and the correlative verbalization "down" (*ab*) have a negative connotation, which at this stage begins to become explicit. The patient's speech, however, betrays some implicit positive connotations that are absent in her self-presentation in movement: Life is not only "*Ab*" ("down") but also "*Auf*" ("up"), even if the lat-

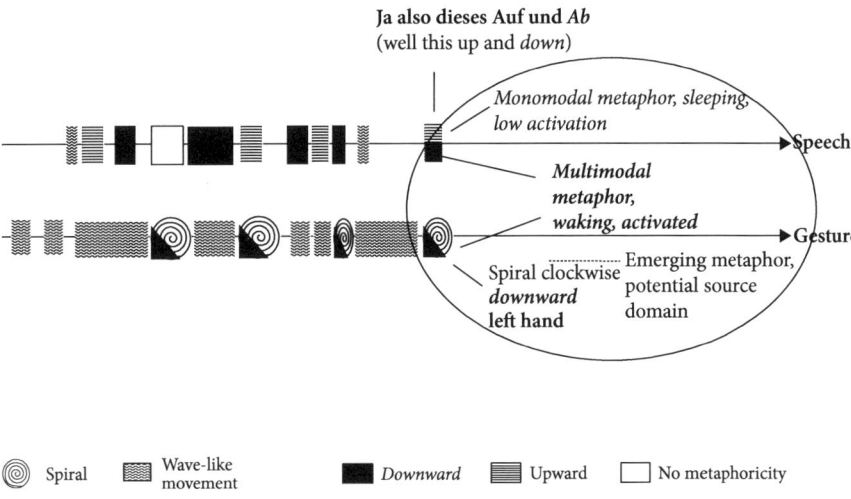

Figure 4. Multimodal metaphor "life is a downward movement"

ter is not expressed in the self-presentation through movement. This discrepancy is phenomenologically understood as a sign of the complexity of linguistic expression, where implicit and explicit moments are intertwined. Language and speech, thus, not only deliberately express explicit contents of consciousness. Rather, they also entail moments of expression that can be considered to be stemming from the latent intentional work of implicit memory.

Stage 5. Emerged metaphor "the course of life feels like a spiral moving downward"

A few moments later (in Stage 5), the patient verbalizes not only the bodily quality of downwardness but also the spiral movement pattern (Figure 5). She says "*und die Spirale nach unten*" / "and the spiral downward" while executing this movement. Now the spiral movement, which has been performed several times before without verbalization, is being "translated" into speech. We can see now that multimodal metaphors may emerge in a process in which bodily experiences provide the dynamic grounds for the emergence of metaphoric meaning. What we have regarded as a potential source for a metaphor in previous actions has now become a source domain for a multimodal (verbo-gestural) metaphor. These observations suggest that the metaphor capturing "the course of life feels like a spiral moving downward" has emerged. Compared to the previous actions, more aspects of the experiential source are being foregrounded through speech and gesture – downwardness and the spiral movement. Accordingly, the activation of metaphoricity has increased and activated metaphoricity presents itself as dynamic and temporally orchestrated process.

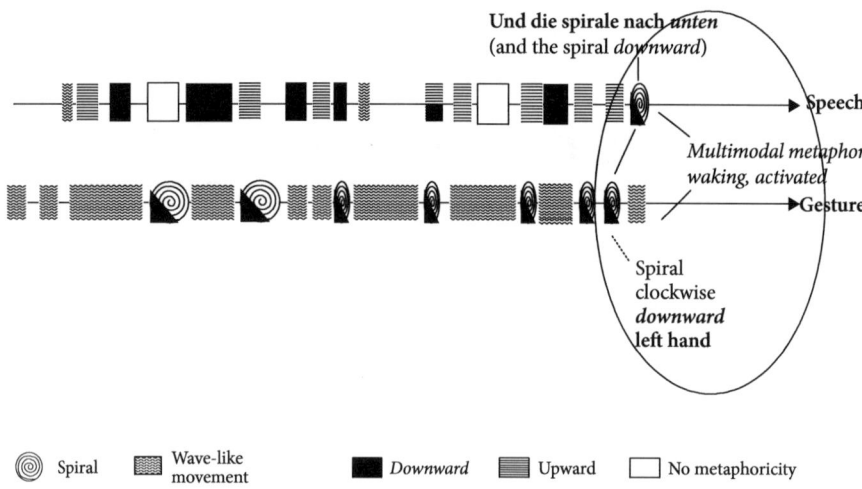

Figure 5. Emerged metaphor – "the course of life feels like a spiral moving downward"

According to the KMP analysis, the spiral movement is performed with indirect and light movement downward (efforts), and thus moves more into explicit consciousness. The patient generally uses shaping in planes, indicating the ability to relate complexly and maturely to others. However, the patient is not using the corresponding strong movement quality for the descending movements. The preferred use of "descending" is possibly a manifestation of the patient's preference to learn by explaining to others (related to giving), while the upward movement would indicate an intention of learning through explication from others (related to taking). Nevertheless, the spiral movement includes not only a downward movement, but also a twisting movement. With twisting movements, a person generally expresses the need for certain playfulness, flirtatiousness and coyness, but also ambivalence.

At this stage, metaphoric expression begins to "inform" the transition from implicit to explicit awareness: Metaphors are activated even if they are not yet reflected upon. This concerns both the direction (downward) and the form (spiral) of the accomplished movement. The KMP analysis, however, shows that the downward spiral does not have, as it should be expected, the strong quality that corresponds to descending movements but rather a lighter twisting-playful quality. This seems to reveal a certain ambivalence in the movement pattern. Considered together, thus, the linguistic and the KMP analyses show that, even when metaphoricity is activated, the patient's body memory still operates implicitly (here, with respect to the qualities of movements), so that the fully transparent self-experience is never achieved.

Stage 6. Conscious awareness of metaphoricity – "the course of life feels like a spiral moving downward"

As the therapeutic session moves on, the temporally orchestrated waking metaphor reaches a high degree of activation. In Stage 6, the increase of metaphor activation reaches its climax as the patient refers to her own gestures with a meta-commentary. This indicates that she has now become consciously aware of metaphoricity. She zooms in on one aspect of the experiential source domain, namely the aspect of downwardness. While performing once again a spiral movement downward she says "*ja geht eigentlich immer nur von oben nach unten merk ich grad*" / "it always goes from up to down, only I've just noticed." Her meta-commentary: "*merk ich grad*" / "I've just noticed" indicates retrospective explicit awareness of the aspect of the experiential source domain (the spiral movement downward), which appears to be the significant one for the speaker.

The spiral movement pattern is not verbalized. Accordingly, this aspect of the metaphor "the course of life feels like a spiral moving downward" is considered to be backgrounded, implicit, and hence asleep.

Again, the spiral movement is conducted with flexible and light movements downward (pre-efforts and efforts). Following KMP-theory, the pre-effort of flexibility can indicate a tendency toward "winding out of the issues" as a motor manifestation of the defense mechanism of avoidance, but also of learning by association. The latter possibility would fit with the patient's diagnosis and further observations. Yet the use of flexibility (pre-effort) could also indicate that there is a danger present for the patient in the moment of this movement; possibly the patient wants to avoid the "going down" with the flexible movement, but can only decelerate the timing of the process by doing so. The retroactiveness (*Nachträglichkeit*) of the speech (upward verbalizations) to the arc-like upward movement still persists in this phase (not depicted in the graphics). The step from Stage 5 to Stage 6 (the metaphor "the course of life feels like a spiral moving downward" moves to the background – the metaphor is asleep and implicit (see Figure 6) – while the metaphor downward is activated and explicit) shows that the patient realizes this subordinating preference in her movements during the therapeutic process.

At this stage, linguistic expression acquires an even starker explicatory role. The patient, indeed, not only explicates the meaning of her own movements, but also takes an explicit stance and positions herself on a meta-level with respect to the very process of explication. Yet, as the patterns and the temporal notation show, the explication again follows the spontaneous accomplishment of movement. This bears witness to the previously mentioned retroactiveness (*Nachträglichkeit*) of the explication with respect to the implicit accomplishment of movement.

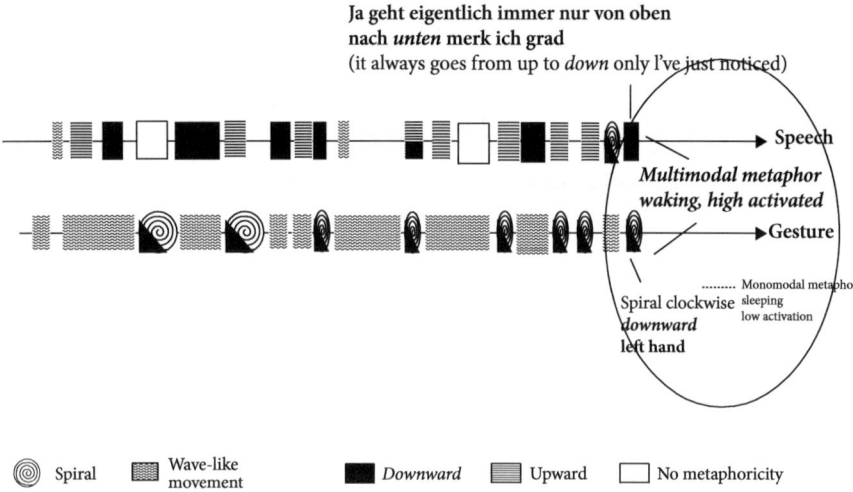

Figure 6. Conscious awareness of metaphoricity – "the course of life feels like a spiral moving downward"

Stage 7. Conscious awareness of an alternative – "the course of life feels like a spiral moving upward"

In the last stage to be presented, a spiral movement directed upward is executed (Figure 7). While performing this bodily movement the patient realizes that moving the spiral in the opposite upward direction poses a major problem for herself ("*geht nicht von unten nach hoch*" / "doesn't go from down to up"). Again the patient becomes consciously aware of the movement's direction. As opposed to this, the movement pattern of the spiral is not verbalized at all and remains therefore backgrounded. We may conclude therefore that at the end of the process of metaphor emergence and elaboration, the direction of the movement remains at center stage. Neither the wave-like nor the spiral movement patterns ever reach conscious awareness. Although we may assume that their bodily performance ensures a felt sense of movement and is part of the experiential source domain of the multimodal metaphor: "the course of life feels like a spiral moving upward," upwardness is massively foregrounded through verbal meta-commentary on the verbo-gestural metaphor. It has reached a high degree of activation. From a therapeutic viewpoint, this can be called a significant moment.

The observation of a strong activation of the metaphor "the course of life feels like a spiral moving upward" is consistent with the results of the KMP, even though the KMP perspective sees the patient more consciously (in movement) from the beginning. The upward spiral movement is performed with pre-efforts that are gentle and gradual; the movement is no longer flowing but appears clumsy: The patient steps back to the use of pre-efforts. The use of pre-efforts is related to higher incertitude,

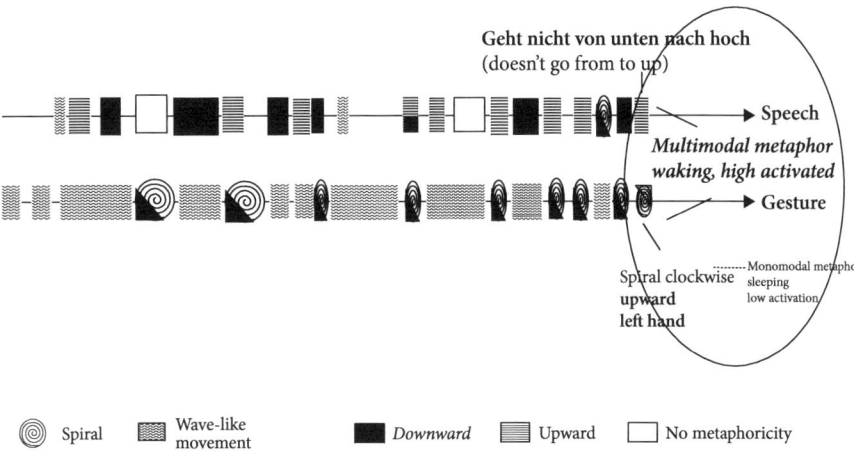

Figure 7. Conscious awareness of an alternative – "the course of life feels like a spiral moving upward"

movements still to be learned (upward learning style indicates search for guidance), and movements that are unfamiliar and probably even threatening (upward defense mechanisms of reaction formation indicated by gentle movement and procrastination indicated by gradual movement). The qualities of movement show a high level of self-awareness, particularly toward the end of the sequence. The patient's movement expresses her wish to move upward and to find a way to liberate herself from the subordinating attitude. Thus, a learning process has been started on the movement level. Therapeutic support of this upward movement and the exploration of its implications are now warranted. Support is important, first, on the level of movement by enriching the repertoire; later, concerning the transference into daily life and attitude.

The linguistic analysis shows that the sequence entails a contrast between the spontaneous accomplishment of movement and its explicit interpretation. Reflectively addressing her movements, indeed, the patient observes that the spiral movement does not proceed in a bottom-up fashion, but rather, precisely in the same moment she accomplishes the spiral movement upward. Thus, even if this is neglected in the patient's speech (*"geht nicht von unten nach hoch"* / "doesn't go from down to up"), the spiral can be, and indeed the movement is, oriented upward. This is pragmatically demonstrated by the very accomplishment of the movement, even if the meaning of this change of orientation at that stage is still implicit. This contrast further testifies to the ambiguous character of lived experience, whereby implicit and explicit moments are always already intertwined. Through therapeutic meta-discourse, contrasts such as the one presented here might be further developed in a more conscious change of the prevailing negative attitude. The next part of the present paper discusses applications to therapy.

Applications to therapy

In the interview immediately after the movement sequences, the patient provides a verbal summary of the meaning of the movement: Pessimism (*"pessimistisch eingestellt bin"* / "have a pessimistic attitude") is related to downward movement. Ascending (*"aufsteigen ist schwieriger"* / "ascending is more difficult") is related to upward movement, which is new. Using the metaphor of the client, ascendance is the therapeutic step toward changing important present problems.

The metaphor is a central possibility for the start of an efficient therapeutic process, the validation of important therapeutic milestones, and the formulation and accomplishment of the main therapeutic goals. It provides the client and the therapist with a joint image in speech and movement that can at any point in the therapeutic process readily be drawn upon.

The patient found the metaphor autonomously in movement. The therapist in fact is often only approached for validation. In the process, the therapist may ask questions about missing aspects, feelings, and thoughts. The metaphor helps with re-framing issues, and with working playfully, creatively, and in a goal-directed manner on therapeutic problem solving. It contains the main therapeutic interests of the client (*"es soll aufwärts gehen und ich soll die Kontrolle darüber haben"* / "I want to move upward and I should be in control") and enables major advances in the therapeutic process.

Dance/movement therapists have tried to describe such important moments of metaphoricity or bodily understanding in therapy as "significant moments" (Hill 2006; Panhofer 2009), or as "moments of heightened synchrony" (Adler 1970) with respect to interaction situations. However, it has been difficult to move the analysis of such "significant moments" beyond the descriptive level. The case analysis here offers the opportunity to investigate the micro-level structures and sequencing of movement and language and thus to take a closer look at such "significant moments" in therapy with an interdisciplinary empirical method.

Conclusion

The present case analysis was focused on the process of explication of implicit memory in the experience of a patient within a setting inspired from dance/movement therapy. The joint analysis showed that in most cases, meaning is first expressed through movement, and only subsequently verbalized. This sequence indicates retroactiveness (*Nachträglichkeit*) (see Stages 2 to 7) of linguistic explication with respect to movement in the meaning making processes. However, it is possible that this retroactiveness is based on an instructional artifact. One critical point is that the instructions to first move and then verbalize provide a clue to this succession by instructional demands. In future studies, the retroactiveness could be verified by a countercheck with instructions to first verbalize and then move or to do both at the same time from the start.

The analysis of the activation of metaphors, the KMP analysis of movement, and the phenomenological description of the explication processes mirror the patient's development in the therapeutic process. In the beginning of the analyzed sequence she performed movements of waves and downward spirals, and subsequently described or interpreted them. The metaphors were activated, yet many issues pertaining to the metaphors were backgrounded, implicit, and did not reach conscious awareness (see Stages 1 and 2). More precisely, even if some of the metaphors were multimodally activated quite early in the sequence (e.g., Stages 1, 3) there were other aspects that remained implicit (e.g., Stages 2, 4). The presence of contrasts at some stages shows how implicit and explicit moments as well as sleeping and waking metaphors are deeply intertwined (e.g., Stages 5, 7). This sequence furthermore shows that rather than conceiving of metaphors as discrete units they should be regarded as a process of meaning construal in which new metaphoric expressions dynamically emerge, are elaborated, and are selectively activated over the course of a conversation.

Assuming the distinction between "knowing how" and "knowing that" formulated by Ryle (2000) and following the phenomenological analyses of body memory developed by Fuchs (2000, 2008a, 2008b) and Summa (2011, this volume), it may be argued that the patient's movements are expressions of learned behavioral patterns and attitudes, which are sedimented in her body memory. In the beginning of the present performance, this repertoire was only latently significant and could not be easily verbalized or made explicit. The task of verbalizing significant meanings of movement brought the patient to direct her attention to the implicit aspects of her experience. In the course of the analyzed period, some sleeping (monomodal) metaphors (see Stage 2) were awakened (multimodal; see Stage 5), with the highest degree of activation of specific metaphors in Stages 6 and 7. Yet, as we have argued, even in the phases of highest activation, the latent impact of the implicit moments of experience was observable, particularly through the emerging contrasts between the spontaneous performance and the explication. Finally, the patient explicitly verbalized the difficulty of performing the spiral movement in a bottom-up manner (*"geht nicht von unten nach hoch"* / "doesn't go from down to up"), which equals the highest point of metaphor activation (see Stage 7).

The integration of the three research perspectives (cognitive linguistic, psychological, and phenomenological) thus proves to be fruitful for the analysis of the explication of implicit body memory and of the interplay between implicit and explicit experiential moments in the process. In particular, the prevalence of expressive movements[7] shows the relation between body memory and the most basic experience of meaning. Even if the tasks the patient is supposed to accomplish mainly entail

---

7.   In this chapter, we do not use the notion of expressive movement in the specific sense adopted by Müller and Kappelhof (in press). We rather refer to the analyses of expressive movement developed in the philosophical anthropology of the 20th century, notably Plessner and Buytendijk. According to these authors, expressive movements are not instrumentally oriented toward an external aim. As such they are distinguished from actions, the meaning of which

self-reflective moments, it has been shown that implicit moments constantly affect the process of explication. This particularly emerges with respect to the contrasts and the tensions between movements, gestures, and the self-explicatory statements of the patient. Thus, the implicit and the explicit moments of lived experience are not to be considered within a linear and progressive process, nor do they symmetrically mirror one another. Rather, they are entangled in the complexity of the concrete lived experience, and can even conflict with each other.

Yet, the concrete analysis of the case study has also enriched the theoretical background of each singular approach and therefore underlines the value of interdisciplinarity in related questions. The joint analysis of the case study, indeed, has been able to show the convergences between metaphorical activation (cognitive linguistics) and the dynamic explication of implicit experience (phenomenology). Transfers from implicit to explicit memory can be traced using the linguistic concepts: Implicit memory is described in terms of sleeping metaphors, which are not or only minimally activated. Explicit memory is captured using the concepts of waking and activated metaphors (if they receive meta-communicative awareness). Moreover, the application of these notions demands a specification of the conception of "(body) memory." Thus, the transfer from implicit to explicit memory has to be regarded as gradable. Furthermore, explicit memory is not only expressed in speech but also in gestures. These findings suggest that explicit and declarative memory is not restricted to language or verbalization but can also be expressed in a bodily manner.

In the "grey zone" between the two polarities (sleeping metaphors can be qualified as implicit whereas awake metaphors can be qualified as explicit), a dynamic of interwoven implicit-explicit experiential processes unfolds and can be phenomenologically addressed as the manifestation of the constitutive ambiguity of experience. Moreover, the couple "explicit/implicit" can be phenomenologically considered in relation to the couple "conscious/unconscious." The latter, together with the intermediate level of the preconscious, notably belongs to the conceptual background of the KMP. Even if a detailed comparison between the phenomenological approach to the unconscious with particular regard to body memory (Fuchs, in print) and the analytic structure adopted by the KMP cannot be further thematized here, some hints regarding the proper way of understanding the relation between conscious and unconscious moments of experience are provided by the interdisciplinary inquiry. More exactly, the three descriptive approaches have shown that the transition from implicit memory to explication, from sleeping metaphors to waking metaphors, and from the unconscious through the preconscious to consciousness, has a procedural unfolding that does not necessarily proceed one way. Consciousness and the unconscious, explicitness and implicitness can certainly be analytically distinguished and described, yet they are always already intertwined and jointly inform the complex structure of lived experience.

---

derives precisely from the aim. Expressive movements rather have an immanent and symbolically expressed meaning (see Buytendijk 1964; Plessner 2003).

The interdisciplinary integration resulting from the study can be schematically represented as follows:

Table 4. Transformation of implicitness to explicitness

	Implicitness	Transformation	Explicitness
	Implicit memory	→	Explicit memory
Experience	"Knowing how"	Transformation through movement and verbalization of movement	"Knowing that"
	Body memory		As object of explicit memory
		→	
Metaphoric meaning	Sleeping metaphor ↓ Monomodal metaphor	Activation of metaphoricity → Is transformed into →	Waking metaphor ↓ Multimodal metaphor
Body movement	Movement gestalt, gesture, expressive movement	Movement as experiential domain triggers emergence of metaphor →	Emerging metaphor (monomodal and multimodal)
Quality of movement	Rhythms, attributes (affect-related tension-/ shape-flow changes)	Pre-efforts (movements of uncertainty and becoming aware)	Efforts (movements of awareness and mastery)
Shape of movement	Bipolar and unipolar shape flow	Shaping in directions	Shaping in planes

The process of explicating implicit body memory through movement and speech has also some crucial implications regarding therapeutic practice. Therapists emphasize that most patients who have not completely lost their ability to symbolize (as is the case, for instance, in patients affected by dementia) will readily seek a central metaphor (such as a decline, a steep path, a peak experience, a deep valley) to indirectly designate their illnesses; an example would be a schizophrenic patient who speaks of "feeling like a prisoner locked inside my body." This indirect reference to one's own life and illness marks one of the first steps of the explication of implicit memory and may help the patients to learn how to deal with their problems. On the other hand, for those patients who have lost their ability to symbolize, body memories often remain entirely on the implicit level. Embodied knowledge and recognition will then be reflected in the patient's heightened positive affect, a heartfelt smile, a shimmer in his/her eyes, and even in some explicit fragments such as the ability to remember a step of a dance, a line of a song, a caress of their parents, an image, or a tune. Dance/

movement therapy can be particularly rewarding because it relies on and stimulates the resources of the patients no matter whether they are still able to explicitly symbolize and remember or not.

The case study suggests that the conflation of movement and speech (such as in dance/movement therapy) can be helpful for the therapeutic process. Implicit contents of body memory, which latently and unconsciously shape our present behavior and attitudes can be made explicit, and the patients can become aware of the complex interweaving of explicit and implicit moments (i.e., of transparency and opaqueness that make up their experience). The analysis of gesture and speech facilitates the disclosure of discrepancies, inconsistencies, and retroactive relations between movement and speech, also in the context of verbal therapies, pointing to the centrality of self-synchrony and the primacy of movement. The analysis of multimodal meaning, metaphors, and body memory can thus be helpful in any therapeutic context, no matter what therapeutic perspective is employed.

Acknowledgements

The chapter was written within the project "Körpersprache von Tanz und Bewegung. Bedeutungsemergenz, Versprachlichung und therapeutische Nutzung" funded by the German Federal Ministry of Education and Research (BMBF; see http://www.psychologie.uni-heidelberg.de/projekte/bewegung/index_engl.shtml). We would like to thank Jane Thompson, Esther Weiss, and Nikolai Kaufmann for translations and proofreading; Teresa Kunz for the layout, and Annabelle Humm for providing the transcription of the interview. Special thanks go to all psychology students, dance/movement therapists in training, and patients who took the time to participate in the study and tell us about various aspects of their lives.

References

Adler, J. (1970). Looking for me. Video available at: http://www.berkeleymedia.com/catalog/berkeleymedia/films/arts_humanities/looking_for_me

Adler, J. (2002). Offering from the conscious body. The discipline of authentic movement. Rochester, VT: Inner Traditions.

Buytendijk, F. J. J. (1964). Algemene theorie der menselijke houding en beweging [General Theory of Human Posture and Human Movement] Utrecht/Antwerp: Spectrum.

Campbell, D., Bianco, V., Dowling, E. Godberg, H., McNab & Pentecost, D. (2003). Family therapy for childhood depression: researching significant moments. Journal of Family Therapy, 25, 417–435.

Casey, E. (2000). Remembering. A phenomenological Study. Bloomington: Indiana University Press.

Chafe, W. (1994). *Discourse, consciousness, and time. The flow and displacement of conscious experience in speaking and writing*. Chicago and London: University of Chicago Press.

Chaiklin, S. & Wengrower, H. (2009). *The art and science of dance/movement therapy: Life is dance*. New York: Routledge.

Cienki, A. & Müller, C. (Eds.). (2008a). *Metaphor and gesture*. Amsterdam/Philadelphia: John Benjamins.

Cienki, A. & Müller, C. (2008b). Metaphor, gesture and thought. In R. W. Gibbs, Jr. (Eds.), *The Cambridge handbook of metaphor and thought* (pp. 484–501). Cambridge: Cambridge University Press.

Elliot, R., Saphiro, D., Firth-Cozens, J., Stiles, W., Hardy, G., Llewelyn, S. & Margison, F. (1994). Comprehensive Process of Insight Events in Cognitive-Behavioural and Psychodynamic-Interpersonal Psychotherapies. *Journal of Counselling Psychology, 41*(4), 449–463.

Fuchs, T. (2000). Das Gedächtnis des Leibes [The memory of the body]. *Phänomenologische Forschungen, 5,* 71–89.

Fuchs, T. (2008). Leibgedächtnis und Unbewusstes. Zur Phänomenologie der Selbstverborgenheit des Subjekts [*Body memory and the unconscious. Phenomenology of the subject's self-concealment*]. *Psycho-Logik. Jahrbuch für Psychotherapie, Philosophie und Kultur, 3,* 33–50.

Fuchs, T. (2008a). *Leib und Lebenswelt. Neue philosophisch-psychiatrische Essays* [Body and the life-world. New philosophical-psychiatric essays]. Kusterdingen: Die Graue Edition.

Fuchs, T. (2008b). Leibgedächtnis und Lebensgeschichte [Body memory and life history]. In F. A. Friedrich, T. Fuchs, J. Koll, B. Krondorfer & G. M. Martin (Eds.), *Der Text im Körper. Leibgedächtnis, Inkarnation und Bibliodrama* [The text in the body. Body memory, incarnation and bibliodrama] (pp. 10–40). Hamburg: EB-Verlag.

Fuchs, T. (in print). Body memory and the unconscious. In D. Lohmar & J. Brudzinska (Eds.), *Founding psychoanalysis. Phenomenological theory of subjectivity and the psychoanalytical experience*. Dordrecht: Kluwer.

Freud, A. (1965). *Normality and pathology in childhood*. New York: International Universities Press, Inc.

Garfinkel, H. (1967). *Studies in ethnomethodology*. London: Prentice Hall.

Hill, H. (2006). Dance therapy as person centered care. In S. C. Koch & I. Bräuninger (Eds.), *Advances in Dance/Movement Therapy. Theoretical perspectives and empirical findings* (pp. 166–176). Berlin: Logos.

Kappelhoff, H. & Müller, C. (2011). Embodied meaning construction. Multimodal metaphor and expressive movement in speech, gesture, and in feature film. In *Metaphor in the Social World,* 6.

Kestenberg, J. S. & Sossin, K. M. (1979). The role of movement patterns in development, Vol. 2. New York: Dance Notation Bureau Press.

Kestenberg, J. S. (1995). *Sexuality, body movement and rhythms of development*. Northvale: Jason Aronson. (Originally published in 1975 under the title Children and Parents).

Kestenberg Amighi, J., Loman, S., Lewis, P. & Sossin, K. M. (1999). *The Meaning of Movement: Development and clinical perspectives of the Kestenberg Movement Profile*. New York, NY: Brunner-Routledge.

Koch, S. C., Cruz, R. & Goodill, S. (2002). The Kestenberg Movement Profile (KMP): Reliability of novice raters. *American Journal of Dance Therapy, 23*(2), 71–88.

Koch, S. C. (2006). Gender at work: Differences in use of rhythms, efforts, and preefforts. In S. C. Koch & I. Bräuninger (Eds.), *Advances in Dance/Movement Therapy. Theoretical perspectives and empirical findings* (pp. 116–127). Berlin: Logos.

Koch, S. C. (2011). Movement analysis in dance therapy: Semantics of movement qualities, rhythm and shape according to Laban and Kestenberg. *Acta Universitatis Carolinae – Kinanthropologica, 47, 2.*

Koch, S. C. (this volume). Testing Fuchs' taxonomy of body memory – A content analysis. In T. Fuchs, S. C. Koch, M. Summa & C. Müller (Eds.), *Body memory, metaphor and movement.* New York: John Benjamins.

Laban, R. v. (1960). *The mastery of movement.* London: MacDonald & Evans.

Levy, F. J. (1992). *Dance/Movement Therapy. A healing art.* Reston, VA: American Alliance for Health, Physical Education, Recreation and Dance.

McNiff, S. (2009). *Integrating the arts in therapy. History, theory, and practice.* Sprinfield, IL: Charles C. Thomas.

Merleau-Ponty, M. (1945). *Phénoménologie de la perception* [Phenomenology of perception]. Paris: Gallimard.

Müller, C. (2008a). *Metaphors. Dead and alive, sleeping and waking. A dynamic view.* Chicago: University of Chicago Press.

Müller, C. (2008b). What gestures reveal about the nature of metaphor. In A. Cienki & C. Müller (Eds.), *Metaphor and gesture* (pp. 219–245). Amsterdam/Philadelphia: John Benjamins.

Müller, C. (2011). Reaction paper. Raymond Gibbs. Are 'deliberate' metaphors really deliberate. A question of human consciousness and action. *Metaphor in the Social World, 1*(1), 61–66.

Müller, C. & Cienki, A. (2009). When speech and gesture come together. Forms of multimodal metaphor in the use of spoken language. In C. Forceville & E. Urios-Aparisi (Eds.), *Multimodal metaphor* (pp. 299–332). Amsterdam/Philadelphia: John Benjamins.

Müller, C. & Tag, S. (2011). The dynamics of metaphor. Foregrounding and activating metaphoricity in conversational interaction. *Cognitive Semiotics, 6.*

Panhofer, H. (2009). *New approaches to communicate the embodied experience in Dance Movement Psychotherapy.* Unpublished doctoral dissertation: University of Hertfordshire.

Plessner H. (2003). *Ausdruck und menschliche Natur* [Expression and Human Nature]. Frankfurt a. M.: Suhrkamp.

Ryle, G. (2000). *The concept of mind. Chicago*: The University of Chicago Press.

Schacter, D. (1996). *Searching for memory. The brain, the mind, and the past.* New York: Basic Books.

Sheets-Johnstone, M. (1999). *The primacy of movement.* New York: John Benjamins.

Sossin, K. M. (1987). Reliability of the Kestenberg Movement Profile, *Movement Studies, 2,* 23–28.

Stern, D. N. (1985). *The interpersonal world of the infant.* New York: Basic Books.

Summa, M. (2011). Das Leibgedächtnis. Ein Beitrag aus der Phänomenologie Husserls [Body memory. A contribution from Husserl's phenomenology]. *Husserl Studies* (online first).

Summa, M. (this volume). Body memory and the genesis of meaning. In T. Fuchs, S. C. Koch, M. Summa & C. Müller (eds.), *Body memory, metaphor and movement.* New York: John Benjamins.

Zajonc, R. B. & Markus, H. (1984). Affect and cognition: The hard interface. In C. Izard, J. Kagan & R. B. Zajonc (Eds.), *Emotions, cognition and behavior* (pp. 73–102). Cambridge: Cambridge University Press.

CHAPTER 14

Moved by God

Performance and memory in the Western Himalayas

William Sax and Karin Polit
University of Heidelberg

We review the history of the anthropological study of "body memory" and argue that it was developed in a fruitful way only with the advent of practice theory and performance studies, which focused on embodied meanings in addition to purely linguistic ones. We provide two case studies of embodied memory. In the first, collective memories of oppression and exploitation are activated by the recitation of particular stories, sometimes resulting in mass possession. In the second, practices associated with the periodic processions of a Western Himalayan deity are shown to be based on local forms of embodied memory.

Keywords: anthropology, collective memory, performance, ritual, India

In this chapter, we wish to explore several aspects of ritual practices connected to body memory. We will argue that it is clearly exemplified by certain kinds of ritual performances, understood as forms of practice. This kind of memory is not cognitive in the narrow sense; that is, it is not a matter of representations or language; rather, it is best understood as a dimension of people's embodied experience, including their belonging to a particular place and social group, a particular context.[1] Presenting two case studies from the Western Himalayas in North India, we will argue that in both cases, ritual performance plays an important role in creating and preserving memories, and in reinforcing social hierarchy and dealing with social suffering. We want to advance the "hermeneutics of the body" proposed by Connerton (1989; cf. Sax 2006), a hermeneutics that will enable us to examine and understand meaning not only in its linguistic but also in its embodied dimensions.

---

1. It makes little sense to talk of cultural differences here, as many differences we observe actually occur just as frequently within a group of people who share the same language, religion and nationality. When we speak of a particular „culture," we mean a local context with its environment, history, religion(s), language(s), etc.

The anthropology of the body has long focused on diverse forms of embodied experience. The discussion began with Mauss' classic essay *Les Techniques du corps* (1934) in which he pointed out that the body is not a naturally given object, nor do people from different cultures experience their bodies in the same way. According to Mauss everyday activities such as eating, washing, or swimming, differ not only according to culture, but also according to gender and class. Such body techniques are thus a 'craft' (Latin: *habilis*), that is taught.

However, this approach was not immediately followed up by other scholars, and Mauss's essay was only "rediscovered" in the 1980s. Before that, American Cultural Anthropology focused on the idea of culture as a *meaningful system*, in terms of which the world was experienced and interpreted by individual persons. One of the most prominent figures, Clifford Geertz, insisted that culture did not consist merely of "ideas in the head" but was essentially public, and therefore to be found in the kinds of public institutions that had earlier been analyzed by the British Structural-Functionalists in terms of their social functions. During the same period, the French anthropologist Claude Levi-Strauss developed a unique social theory that he called "structuralism", which focused on formal relations among meaningful elements in a cultural system. According to Levi-Strauss, the meaning of a structure lies in its form, not its content; and moreover this "meaning" is abstract and theoretical, with only an indirect relationship to personal experience. In general, during the 60s and 70s, anthropologists worked with a notion of meaning that viewed "cultures" as semiotic or symbolic systems whose elements (ritual, language, dress, food) were formally related to each other. The idea was that a description and analysis of such formal relations (which were characterized by some, in a rather vague way, as "structure," by others as systems of rules, and by still others along linguistic lines) was, *pari passu*, a description of the "culture" under investigation. But whichever school one adhered to, it was assumed that meaning was essentially linguistic, or at least that it could be expressed linguistically, typically in a propositional statement of the form, "X is (or 'means') Y."

In the late 1970s and continuing in the 1980s, the anthropology of the body received a new impetus, the phenomenological approach of Merleau-Ponty (1966) attracted new attention, and at the same time performance theory made some striking advances. It seems to us that these paradigms, taken together, provide a useful way of thinking about "body memory." The anthropology of the body had never really died; it had only been temporarily forgotten. The Heidelberg Sociologist Norbert Elias, for example, had taken up Mauss's idea of *habitus* and used it to explain how Europe's noble classes, in a process lasting centuries, distinguished themselves from the common people in matters of taste, cuisine, deportment, language, etc., thus "naturalizing" a class-based difference. Later, the French sociologist Pierre Bourdieu developed the notion of *habitus* into the master concept of what came to be called "practice theory," where *habitus* meant something like the unreflective and thoroughly naturalized set of tendencies and dispositions characteristic of a particular class, ethnic group, occupation, etc. (see Bourdieu 1990). The important point to note is that Bourdieu deliberately set out to refute those structuralists, linguistically-oriented theorists, and others who had attempted to reduce culture to a set of explicit rules that can or should be formulated in language.

An example from the study of ritual will suffice to make the point. In a famous (1979) article, Frits Staal argued that ritual was "meaningless" because participants in a ritual are seldom able to interpret it, and even when they do so, their interpretation is usually naive and/or inadequate. Ritual, according to Staal, is pure, rule-governed activity "without meaning or goal" (Staal 1979: 9), and its rules, like those of language, are not normally available for critical reflection. Later in the same article, Staal discussed the *mantras* of Vedic ritual, which are conceived of as inherently powerful sonic equivalents of deities and other cosmic forces. Because some of these *mantras* have no indexical referents, Staal concluded that they, too, were devoid of meaning.

But in light of Bourdieu's practice theory (of which Staal was probably unaware when he wrote his article), we might ask if and to what degree rituals inscribe values and indeed forms of knowledge into the bodies of participants (for example, the initi- and who is scarred or beaten before being allowed to see the holy of holies of his tribe; the Christian who is taught when to stand and when to kneel in relation to scripture or to the sacred host; the Muslim who dramatically experiences the radical egalitar- ianism of Islam while kneeling next to others in the mosque), without necessarily reducing them to sets of rules that can be formalized in language, memorized and applied. This is indeed one of Bourdieu's central claims: that regularized, standardized behavior is not normally learned by memorizing sets of rules, but rather by mimesis or imitation. He has for example famously observed that kneeling in church does not so much express subordination as it produces subordinated kneelers. In other words, to understand the meaning of kneeling in church, one need not imagine that the kneeler formulates a propositional phrase in his head, to the effect that, "I am lower than God, therefore I should kneel," nor that he follows a rule of the form, "When before the altar, one should kneel." It is enough to suppose that, through a process of observation and mimesis, he has learned to kneel in church at particular times, and that this learning involves far more an *inscription* of the rules *in his body* than it does a linguistic formulation and acceptance of them. In other words, kneeling is neither the bodily expression of a propositional statement, nor is it the physical implementa- tion of a semantic rule. Rather, it is a meaningful form of bodily expression. "Practical belief," wrote Bourdieu, "is a state of the body" (1990: 68).

Is memory also a state of the body? Performance studies have answered this ques- tion in the affirmative. As Diana Taylor (2003) has argued, performances themselves are practices of memory in the sense that they are forms of social knowledge. Perfor- mance can sustain, transform, and transfer complex embodied knowledge. Perhaps this makes it less powerful in certain contemporary contexts, since it cannot be stored in an archive or digitalized and broadcast, thus reaching a (potentially very) large au- dience. However the immediacy and sensuous impact of an effective, live performance makes it an extremely powerful medium for reinforcing body memory. For example, spectacular rituals and performances may facilitate powerful collective experiences, and instigate enduring, collective memories (see below; also Connerton 1989).

The rituals in our case studies are performances in Richard Schechner's sense, since they are clearly demarcated from everyday behavior and their particulars – gestures, movements, body postures – are conventionalized, and authored by someone other than the performer.[2] In fact, the particulars of these rituals are practices developed in and through the history of the performance itself, shaped, transmitted and transformed by generations of worshippers. These bodily positions and movements transport information connected, for example, to the identity of a deity, its mythical story, the history of its worship and of the group, but also more complex meanings of social norms and moral obligations. This kind of information is such that only insiders are able to grasp its full content. And even this understanding is based on intuitive, habitual, and embodied knowledge rather than on cognitive functioning and symbolic decoding. In this way, rituals enable many people to have a similar bodily experience, to share an embodied memory. Memory based on individual experience and everyday interactions, in Assmann's (1997) now famous work on cultural memory identified as communicative memory and a more sustainable and institutionalized social and public culture of memory, fuse during such performances. It is in Merleau-Ponty's sense the simultaneous experience of being present as a body and the sensual experience of being in the world in which the body is medium and producer of meanings at the same time.

Unlike theatrical performances, the body memory of participants in the rituals discussed below depends, not on rehearsal, but on *habitus* and mimesis. The ritual requires and assumes that those who perform it already possess the (embodied) skills to do so competently, and at the same time it transmits this knowledge to those in the audience. We understand ritual movements such as dance and possession as ways of experiencing and transmitting cultural knowledge and collective memory. They are vehicles for forms of embodied knowledge, which are different from language-based knowledge. The persons involved know how to move to a certain rhythm, and how to hold their bodies so as to signify a certain deity; in other words they exhibit what the ritual theorist Bell (1992), in her influential book *Ritual Theory, Ritual Practice*, calls "ritual mastery."

Consider, for example the cult of *Kachiya Bhairav*, practiced by people of the lower castes in the Western Himalayas, and described at length by Sax (2009). The major narratives associated with this god tell of their (sometimes brutal) oppression by their high-caste neighbors. In one song, a proud and defiant young man is imprisoned in a subterranean pit; in another, a young boy's hands are amputated; in another, two innocent girls are sold into slavery by high-caste men. In each case, the god *Kachiya* incarnates, literally 'becomes embodied,' in order to save the low-caste people from their oppressors and restore justice. As Sax shows, these stories are above all performances, involving singing, recitation, dancing, and possession. Indeed, the singing of

---

2.   As Schechner puts it, "performances mark identities, bend and remake time, adorn the body with costumes, and provide people with behavior that is "twice-behaved," not-for-the-first time, rehearsed, cooked, prepared" (1995: 1).

these songs is one of the most powerful techniques for making the god incarnate, for causing him to become embodied. This is usually done during extensive rituals involving several nights of music, animal sacrifice, and the presence of numerous family members and villagers invited as guests.

When the sun has set and dinner has been eaten, drums summon human guests to gather in the courtyard in front of the host's house. The music is familiar, and exciting: the high-pitched clanging of the inverted metal platter rapidly beaten with two wooden sticks, the voice of the guru reaching out above the sounds of his two-headed drum with its unmistakable sound, the hypnotic echo of the third musician, a singer who echoes the final words of every line sung by the guru. When the performance is effective, the atmosphere is charged. Supernatural power (*siddhi*) fills the courtyard with an electrifying presence, and the singing of the line "I have no one" can result in mass possession. Many listeners fall into trance; people roll about on the floor, grimacing and writhing in pain, their hands twisted into the shape of a bird-like claw, the characteristic sign of possession by Kachiya (see Figure 1). This is the most persuasive and powerful appearance of the god, more compelling than any iconographic description, more immediate than any story. When Kachiya possesses a person, s/he is visibly transformed: bared teeth, bent waist, dancing on her knees on the floor, cramped and claw-like hands. This is the appearance of Kachiya in its two most important senses: it is *how* he manifests himself, and it is *what* he looks like. It is his physical embodiment, seen by devotees often enough to persuade them that he is quite real. Indeed, when Sax asked his friends if they "really believed" in Kachiya, their most common response was, "Of course I do. How could I not believe in him? He comes and dances, and you can see him right there in front of you!"

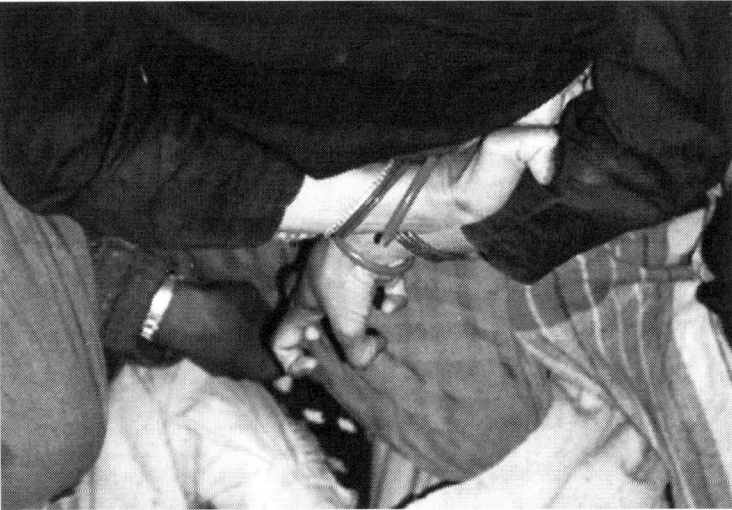

Figure 1. Hands of a person possessed by Kachiya, photo by W. Sax

It is also the most crucial moment in the cult rituals, the moment when myth and iconography, context and social memory, power and morality, all come together; the moment when, as Geertz puts it, ritual fuses "the world as lived and the world as imagined" together (1973:112). From local people's point of view, such ritual possession confirms the power and presence of the god. If it does not occur, the ritual has failed.

Kachiya Bhairav appears *in the body* of a possessed person: this is not a matter of "symbolism" or language. Drawing on Connerton (1989), Sax argues that it is also a matter of collective memory. The stories whose recitation brings about mass possession are understood as founding events in the collective and religious history of the lower castes which, when recited in the context of a ritual, cause a profound change in the consciousness of the (largely or exclusively) low-caste audience, resulting in possession. But the possessed body is contorted and in pain, because what is being remembered is not merely an historical event, but rather the embodied experience of suffering and affliction that is the mutual bond of the lower castes. This is why the song is almost never performed in front of the higher castes.

The social suffering of the lower castes derives from their membership in a social category. Discrimination against them is pervasive, deeply rooted in everyday practice, as well as in understandings of human relationships as substantial and continuous exchanges, where the body itself remembers contact with other people, places, and objects. Higher caste people experience the bodies of low caste people as distorted and repulsive. This, too, is a product of embodied memory, since it is related to the fact that most people in the Western Himalayas do not experience their bodies as a self-contained entity with a clear-cut boundary – the human skin. Rather, a singular human body is part of a system in which persons, places, animals and supernatural beings are constantly involved in substantive relationships with each other. As Marriott (1976) and Inden (Mariott & Inden 1977) point out, everyday Indian practices reflect the assumption that persons have more or less open boundaries and may therefore affect each other's natures through transactions of food, services, words, bodily substances, and the like.

The example of Kachiya Bhairav's rituals clearly shows that embodied practices can serve as reminders of social suffering, and bring long-past events (including, perhaps, mythical or imagined events) into the emotional present. In this case, the embodied memory of paradigmatic events contributes to the solidarity of the group, thus reinforcing their collective identity. This is another example of the relationship between collective memory and public acts of "reminding" (cf. Casey 1987; Csordas 1997). And this memory is based not only on narratives but also upon embodied experience. In his study of charismatic healing, Csordas rightly connected this to Bourdieu's concept of *habitus*, remarking that revelatory reminders and remindands are not only thoughts and words, but sensuous embodied images, and the memory invoked is not necessarily a reliving in the sense of watching a 'videotape' copy, but one that evokes concrete self presence. Second, revelation collapses the duality of self and other by the intersubjective interplay of themes and elements shared within a habitus (1997:148).

The experience of the lower castes of Chamoli district triggers the memory of certain events, while the ritual described actually produces memories as well. Such rituals are part of a larger system of cultural memory that is deeply rooted in bodily experience and manifests itself in emotions during these dramatic actions of possession as well as in cultural norms and values. Since many of these are naturalized and not reflected upon, they differ profoundly from explicit and narrative memories.

The most important thing about these sorts of memories for the current discussion is that they are both collective and embodied. Paul Connerton (1989) has shown that this is not a contradiction, since most memories are in fact socially constructed and practically embodied. Here memories are understood as mindful representations, and integral parts of being in the world in a physical body. Similarly, Casey (1987) argues that memory is situated neither in the individual body nor in society at large, but somewhere in between. For example, commemorative rituals maintain memory by referring to a community's "master narrative", itself a product of commemorative events (ibid.: 224–225). While an event requires performers and audience, and thus impacts their bodies and memories, its effect is usually much larger, since it reaches all participants as a community. While such events usually refer to particular memories connected to certain groups, they also recreate these memories in the event itself. In this context, memory is at the same time the product and the producer of practices, located in space as well as time, collective as well as individual.

At this point it is useful to take on board some findings of performance studies, mainly the ideas of Diana Taylor, who claims that (c)ultural memory is, among other things, a practice, an act of imagination and interconnection. [...] Memory is embodied and sensual, that is conjured through the senses; it links the deeply private with social, even official, practices. Sometimes memory is difficult to invoke, yet, it is highly efficient; it's always operating in conjunction with other memories [...] (2003:82).

Therefore, we need to acknowledge the narratives in cultural memories as well as non-verbal practices. Performances are important precisely because, at least in rural India, they often transmit primarily non-verbal, non-narrative knowledge. They can also be crucial for communal identity, as we have shown above. Memories can be sustained, reproduced and created through performances. And memories can, in turn, maintain and produce communal identity. In order to understand how this works, we need to look at events as producers of meaning or as Taylor puts it, at "scenarios as meaning-making paradigms that structure social environments, behaviors, and potential outcomes" (2003:28), rather than privileging texts and narratives. If we take performances (including rituals) seriously as practices of cultural production, then we may be able to understand how traditions can be stored in the body. Movements, gestures, dances, music, and aromas can be mnemonic devices which, especially in the context of rituals, transmit traditions such as the way a person should relate to a deity, how the hand should be held when interacting with divine beings, how one is to sit showing respect, gendered and caste divisions of space, but also myths and stories of the past. Since all of this is performed before a live audience, spatial and temporal dimensions are changed in the process. Ritual performances are, among other things, pasts experienced as present. Therefore, Taylor claims that it is impossible to think about cultural memory and identity as disembodied. For her, the bodies participating in the transmission of knowledge and memory are themselves a product of certain taxonomic, disciplinary, and mnemonic systems. Gender impacts how these bodies participate, as does ethnicity. The techniques of transmission vary from group to group. The mental frameworks – which include images, stories, and behaviors – constitute a specific archive and repertoire (2003: 86).

The rituals of Bhairav should be seen in this context. In order to highlight the argument that narrative and embodied memory work hand in hand when it comes to collective memories, we want to take a closer look at another case study from the same area – a local deity on pilgrimage. The deity, Jakh, is a local deity like Bhairav, however he is not the god of the lower castes but rather of the high-caste Rajputs, who are the traditional landholding families of the region. Jakh is at the same time their god and their mythical ancestor. In mythical times the great warrior Babhru Bahan was tricked by Krishna[3] and lost his head before he could reverse the course of the great Mahabharata[4] battle. As compensation for this injustice, Krishna offered him the status of a divine king. As a local expert on Jakh's ritual songs and myths, Govind Singh Rawat, explained:

> Krishna said to Jakh: Hey Babhru Bahan! None of this is your fault! It is all my doing! I had my reasons for cutting off your head! In the future, in the age of Kaliyug[5] and through all the coming ages I will make you the god of the land. You will be anointed as a deity in many places. Your people will carry you for six months. All the people who belong to the village where your temple stands will take you on a pilgrimage for six months. You will be worshiped in every home. They will give you sacrifice and take you to holy places and pilgrimage sites. They will take you to all places that can be reached in six months.

---

3.   Krishna is a subordinate manifestation of Vishnu, one of the high gods of Hinduism. His speech to the reluctant Arjuna at the merge of the great battle in the Mahabharata is better known as the Bhagavat Gita (cf. Michaels 2004: 211–215).

4.   The *Mahabharata* is India's great epic of war and tragedy. It tells the tale of the five Panadava brothers who fight for their rightful throne against their cousins, the ninety-nine Kauravas. It culminates in the great battle at Kurukshetra (cf. Sax 2002).

5.   Kali Yuga is the last of four ages within the Yuga cycle of Hindism. In this cosmological model, time follows a and endless cycle of creation and destruction where the yugs follow each other like the seasons (cf. Michaels 2004: 335).

Figure 2. Jakh's mask in the temple of Okimath, photo by K. Polit

According to the local story, this satisfied *Jakh*, and he became a divine king in the Western Himalayas (see Figure 2).[6] Since that time, claim his devotees, he is periodically taken on a pilgrimage. Many forms of Jakh reside in the area around the town of Gopeshwar, in Chamoli district in the Indian state of Uttarakhand (see Figure 3). He has numerous temples, and each temple has a village responsible for satisfying the form of Jakh that resides in it. According to his disciples, if Jakh has not been taken on pilgrimage for a long time, the village will suffer. The women will have difficulties conceiving male offspring, children will die, cows will stop giving milk, the fields will dry up, and men will start fighting. According to Govind Singh Rawat, this began to happen in the village Maikot Kujaum, since villagers had not taken their divine king on his pilgrimage for more than sixty years. The villagers finally consulted the god's medium and his priest, and decided to begin the pilgrimage in October, 2007. After sixty-nine years, the divine king Jakh of Maikot Kujaum visited his land and his

---

6. For a detailed discussion on divine kings in the Western Himalays, see Sax (2003).

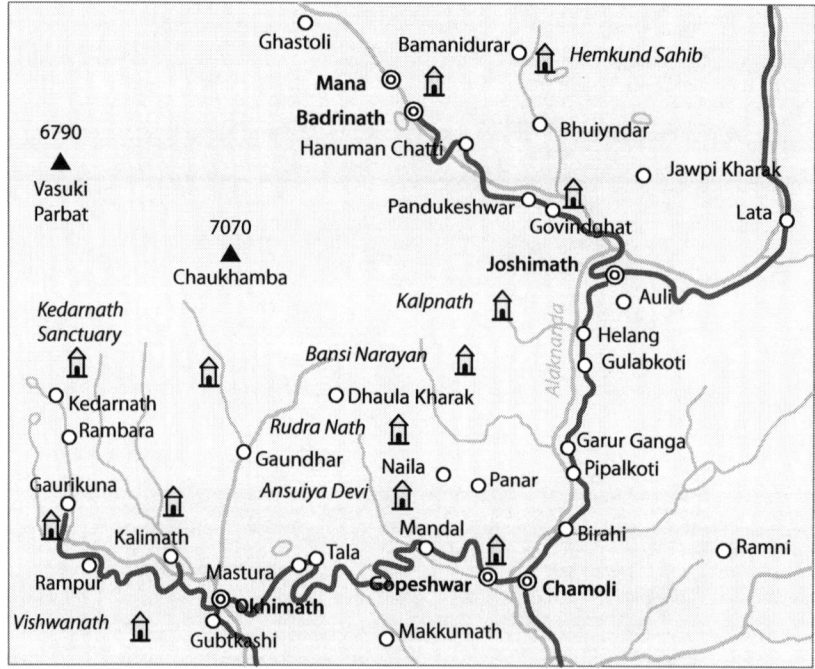

Figure 3. Map of Gopeshwar and surrounding area, map by Nils Harm, Department of Geography, South Asia Institute, University of Heidelberg

out-married sisters.[7] Three young men were chosen to be his servants during the pilgrimage. One of them, Mohan Singh Bandari, described the process of being chosen:

> Usually I work with cars. The other villagers chose three of us to dance the deity[8] – Jakh *devta* (god) – for six months, who now, after sixty-nine years,

---

7.   Women who have married and left their parents' home to live with their husband and his family, called *dhyanis,* play an important role in the social relations and ritual practices of Garhwal (Sax 1990). On occasions when she visits her natal home, she has all sorts of privileges compared to unmarried sisters and in-married sisters-in-law. Rights and obligations are mostly linked to practices that uphold her father's and mother's honour in her *sauryas.* It is, for example, considered highly shameful if an outmarried woman's parents let their daughter work in their house. With marriage a daughter has been given to another family with all her productive powers, and she should never again be productive in her father's house (Polit 2011). The importance of the *mait* for the *dhyanis* is sung about in many songs all over Garhwal. Many rituals require her presence.

8.   People in the region typically use the transitive form *nacana* for ritual occasions where they 'cause the god to dance' (i.e. where people are made to be possessed, after which the god dances in their bodies). We have translated this common locution here as 'dancing the deity'.

has emerged again. He emerged for a six-month pilgrimage. He started on October 2nd and we went from here to Badrinath via Rudranath. When the people first proposed that I do this, I did not want to, because I had to think of my family. I refused to come at first, but then the god, king Jakh, appeared twice in my dreams. He told me not to refuse. Because I had danced him for two days, in my dreams. In the dream I went and carried him to the village down there and then back up here! I refused on the third and fourth day. But he came to my dreams again. Jakh *devta*. He danced on my shoulders. We went down there below the village to another *devta*. We call that place Lam Dunga. We went there in my dreams. Then we came here to the temple. And on that day I said, "May my house be as it is, for six months, I will serve the *devta*." That is how I changed my mind. But the *devta* has also looked after me! I have no regrets.

The three Rajput servants from Maikot Kujaum village became temporary ascetics who had to undergo several purifying rituals before the pilgrimage and follow certain rules to maintain their purity during the journey. They were not allowed to shave or cut their hair and nails, and they bathed twice a day and ate only pure food (also twice a day). They needed to maintain physical and mental purity, since they were in regular, bodily contact with the god. As the *devta* moved from village to village, he danced in their bodies (see Figure 4). This dancing is crucial for divine power to unfold. As the low caste bard and drummer Ram Das put it, "During the day, the *devta* needs to be danced… we make him dance (with the drum rhythms). The *devta* dances to ten rhythms. In some villages he needs two, in others three. This is how Jakh *devta* dances to ten rhythms." While the servants said that they needed to learn some of the basic dance steps, they also claimed that they did not move by their own will across the land, or through a village or a crowd of worshippers. Instead, they claimed that the deity stirred them, that he made them move in the desired direction.[9] The three servants also woke the divine king in the morning, sang him songs of worship (*jagar*), fed him, attended to him during the day, and put him to bed. Anasuya Singh Bishth, another servant of the god, described their duties as follows:

> We travel everywhere! After eating and asking for food at every house, we let the *devta* stand in the evening. Then we sing him a song (*jagar*) to put him to sleep. After that, the *devta* goes to sleep. We untie all the saris and cloths, everything that has been tied to the *devta* during the day. We free him from this. And then we carefully put him to sleep. Then we worship him and do his ritual illumination (*arati*). After that, all the people involved in the rituals eat.

---

9. This detail is, of course, crucial for worshippers and servants alike, since when the agency lies with the deity, there can be no favoritism.

Figure 4. The godking Jakh dancing, he is carried by one of his servants,
photo by K. Polit

At night these men have yet another duty. As soon as the sun sets, Jakh must be en-
tertained. For this purpose, his entourage carries sacred masks, which are supposed
to contain the power of ancient gods, who dance at night for the entertainment of the
divine king. "Then," says Ansuya Prasad,

> Narad Muni emerges. He emerges from the place of the god! Where the god
> sleeps. Narad means the night's Shankar Bhagwan – which means Shiva.[10] He
> comes in the form of Shiva. As long as Narad Muni is outside, nobody, no vil-
> lager or onlooker will have any problem! As long as this power roams outside,
> Narad Muni's power, God will also keep watching over us from inside!

---

10. Shiva is one of the great gods of Hinduism. As an ascetic he resides on Mt. Kailash. Both
potent and chaste, he is the world's creator as well as its destroyer (cf. Michaels 2004).

The bard Ram Lal explained Narad's role in the divine pilgrimage of Jakh and why the performance at night is so important:

> When *Jakh devta*'s head was cut off, our king Daksh Prajapati (as he is also called) had to be pacified. To pacify him, to make him happy, he (Narad) participates in a play, he starts playing around. To invite all the gods, Narad goes to *Hun Desh* (Tibet), where he also lives. Therefore he can invite the others. So he invites the gods, and he makes jokes! That is Narad's role.

During the night's performances Narad, who is always embodied by one of the three servants, does several things. First, he recalls the events of the pilgrimage. In a stylized conversation with the low-caste bard, he tells the audience about the villages visited, the food received, the offerings given and the number of masks danced in each respective village, all the time mocking the people he has met, making jokes about their homes, their habits, their appearance, their animals and livestock. Next, he invites a number of other important deities by means of a dance, and they in turn dance to their special rhythms and songs. The songs narrate these gods' stories, but are in archaic Garhwali so that most people claim not to understand them. After they are sung, Narad comically re-enacts his life as a Himalayan villager. He ploughs his fields, tries to perform a ritual, looks for one and finds two wives, fights with the Brahmin priest about the latter's fees, and raises his children. All this he does with great difficulty and clumsiness, humorously reminding the villagers of their own lives and the collective fate they share (cf. Purohit 1993).

This sequence was repeated for six months every day and in every village. In the mornings, the divine king was ritually awakened by his servants, made a round through the village, blessed his subjects and tributaries, and then left for the next village, where he was greeted, given a place for a temporary temple, worshipped, fed, and eventually put to bed. Then, in the courtyard of his temple, the other gods emerged and danced for his and the villagers' entertainment. In all of these activities the servants were crucially involved. As their hair and beards grew, and their bare feet hardened, their relationship to the god changed and grew ever more intimate, so much that, when the time came to part from the deity, they were devastated. As one of them, Mohan Singh Bandari said,

> Now, slowly, the *devta* is getting ready to go back to his place! I mean, his departure is near. And we expect that boredom will overcome us. How will we be able to live at home? For six months we have spent all our time with the *devta*! So how will we … we won't be able to live in our houses without our Jakh *devta*! We have come to regard the *devta* as our mother and father. We have carried him for six months! And now, when the *devta* returns to his place, we will feel very lonely. For days, we will not be able to eat. Because the one we have carried on our shoulders will leave us! It will be very sad!

Jakh's devotees connect their actions and ritual practices to events in the age of India's ancient epic of war and disaster, *Mahabharata*. To them the events of the *Mahabharata* are not "mythical," but instead quite real. The pilgrimage of their king Jakh is an event connecting Rajput villagers to their own history. In this sense, the servants are a product of cultural memory. Their bodies are marked by practices related to caste and gender, and their practices during the pilgrimage tend to fuse individual and collective identities. Once they are chosen to become servants, they merge with their institutionalised position. Throughout their earlier lives, they will have seen other servants pass by their village with their deities. And now, like all those men before, and like their ancestors, they become the god's servants. In assuming this position they are re-enacting Krishna's boon to Jakh as much as they are re-enacting the position of their own Rajput community within the wider network of Garhwal. After all, they are the proud descendants of a great warrior. Interestingly however, their appearance in the night as Narad embodies a different identity. In truth, nearly all participants are peasants, and the divine play of Narad portrays him as a peasant, connecting the mythical Narad's life to the life of a peasant.

When asked, the servants said that they could not narrate the myth of their divine king. At least they felt they could not do it accurately enough for the anthropologist to record it. Yet, they perform most of the rituals that reflect this narrative, and simultaneously remind Jakh's subjects of their connection to him and with each other. Embedded in the ritual practices is a cultural identity – descendants of the ancient warrior and divine king Jakh – that clearly is a product of their history, both as it is understood by the anthropologist, and in their own terms. The dance of the god carries cultural norms and values connected to this identity. The servants create networks among themselves as individuals, as well as among people, places, different deities, and multiple temporalities. Their divine dance and their night-long performances bring the past into a living present, enabling their audiences to share commonalities of mythical times and places in present times and village places through embodied experience.

In our view, a theoretical language privileging "structure," "function," or "symbols" cannot neither capture adequately how the rituals of Bhairav and Jakh's journeys are experienced, nor what they mean. Performance is a prime example of how, in social life, all sorts of meanings occur simultaneously. The embodied cultural practices introduced in this chapter are a way of knowing that is possible only because people experience similar performances throughout their lives, so that knowledge is inscribed in their bodies and thus their memories. What they remember not only lets them move in the appropriate way, and take postures that are immediately recognizable by everyone in the audience as belonging to a certain deity, it also contains knowledge about this deity, the history of the group, memories of social suffering, and practices of social hierarchy. In this way, ritual actors are involved in fusing the past with the present, producing a memory that is both embodied and meaningful. It is important to note that this form of body memory is not an exotic product of the North Indian

Himalayas but a feature of most or all human groups. While we have chosen traditions of possession and ritual to exemplify local phenomena, the processes described are, we believe, universal, because memory is never exclusively cognitive but always, at least partly, embodied.

References

Assmann, J. (1997). *Das kulturelle Gedächtnis: Schrift, Erinnerung und politische Identität in frühen Hochkulturen* [Cultural memory: Writing, remembering, and political identity in early civilizations]. München: C.H. Beck.

Bell, C. (1992). *Ritual theory, ritual practice*. Oxford and New York: Oxford University Press.

Bourdieu, P. (1990). *The logic of practice*. Stanford, CA: Stanford University Press.

Casey, E. (1987). *Remembering. A phenomenological study*. Bloomington: Indiana University Press.

Connerton, P. (1989). *How societies remember*. Cambridge: Cambridge University Press.

Csordas, T. (1997). *The sacred self: a cultural phenomenology of charismatic Healing*. Berkely and Los Angeles: University of California Press.

Geertz, C. (1973). *The interpretation of cultures*. New York: Basic Books.

Mariott, M. & Inden, R. (1977). Towards an ethnosociology of South Asian caste systems. In K. David (Ed.), *The new wind: Changing identities in South Asia* (pp. 227–238). The Hague: Mouton.

Marriott, M. (1976). Hindu transactions: Diversity without dualism. In B. Kapferer (Ed.), *Transaction and meaning* (pp. 109–142). Philadelphia: ISHI.

Mauss, M. (1934). Les Techniques du corps [The techniques of the body]. *Journal de Psychologie, 32*, 3–4.

Merleau-Ponty, M. (1966). *Phänomenologie der Wahrnehmung* [Phenomenology of perception]. Übersetzt und mit einem Vorwort versehen von Rudolf Boehm. Berlin: de Gruyter.

Michaels, A. (2004). *Hinduism: past and presence*. Princeton: Princeton University Press.

Polit, K. M. (2011). *Good women: practices of gender and agency among Dalit women in the Himalayas*. Orient Longman: Hyderabad, India.

Purohit, D. R. (1993). *Medieval English folk drama and Garhwali folk theatre: A comparative study*. PhD Thesis, H.N.B. Garhwal University.

Sax, W. S. (1990). Village daughter, village goddess: residence, gender, and politics in a Himalayan pilgrimage. *American Ethnologist, 17*, 491–512.

Sax, W. S. (2002). *Dancing the self: personhood and performance in the pandav lila of Garhwal*. New York: OUP.

Sax, W. S. (2009). *God of justice: ritual healing in the central Himalaya*. New York: Oxford University Press.

Sax, W. S. (2003). Divine kingdoms in the Central Himalayas. In N. Gutschow et al. (Eds.), *Sacred landscapes of the Himalaya* (pp. 177–194). Vienna: Verlag der Österreichischen Akademie der Wissenschaften.

Sax, W. S. (2006). At the borders of morality: Rituals of aggression. In Henrik Jungaberle, Rolf Verres & Fletcher DuBois (Eds.), *Rituale erneuern: Ritualdynamik und Grenzerfahrung aus interdisziplinärer Perspektive* (pp. 297–314). Gießen: Psychosozial Verlag.

Schechner, R. (1995). 2nd DRAFT, July 95, *Performance Studies Textbook*. http://www.nyu.edu/classes/bkg/schechner. Last access: 27.01. 2011.

Staal, J. F. (1979). The meaninglessness of ritual. *Numen, 26*, 2–22.

Taylor, D. (2003). *The archive and the repertoire. Performing cultural memory in the Americas.* Durham and London: Duke University Press.

CHAPTER 15

The memory of the cell

Ralf P. Meyer
University of Freiburg

Body memory and neurobiology – two faces of the same coin? Our genome serves as a basis for cellular development. Ensuing proliferation and differentiation of the cells are regulated by epigenetic factors and specific hormones, and are characterized by external influence like nutrition, environment, and education. This is an important process in adoption. The brain cells further integrate into a complex and stressable network by synaptogenesis and plasticity – a prerequisite in higher brain function. Brain's limbic system conducts memory, cognition, and emotion and interacts with the visual and prefrontal cortex, the frontal and temporal lobes. Perception and imitation are main factors in learning, memory, and emotional reaction. Body memory in neurobiological context may be hypothesized as a concept influenced by (epi)genetics, environmental input (hormones), cultural influence (network building), cognition, and emotion.

Keywords: body memory, brain, cell memory, epigenetics, neurobiology, neuronal network, steroid hormones

Brain research or – more general – the neurosciences can be characterized by the attempt of a cognitive system trying to uncover itself, using the methodology of the life sciences. Many efforts have been made during the last decades to investigate sensory and motor systems as well as neuron-to-neuron connectivities inside the brain. Especially the understanding of pathological malfunctions occurring in brain tumors, neurodegeneration, dementia, or epilepsy has rapidly progressed and led to a series of new strategies of therapy and disease control (Wieloch & Nikolich 2006; Berg 2008; Meyer et al. 2010).

However, if we aim to enlighten our mental or psychic properties, hence those functions which depict who human beings really are, the life science approach gives rise to strong and controversial discussion. Is it admissible to associate existential orientation or mental state with organic procedures in specific cells of the brain or even the whole body? Is cellular memory connected to body memory? In other words, can body memory be drawn back to conservative evolutionary processes in mechanisms

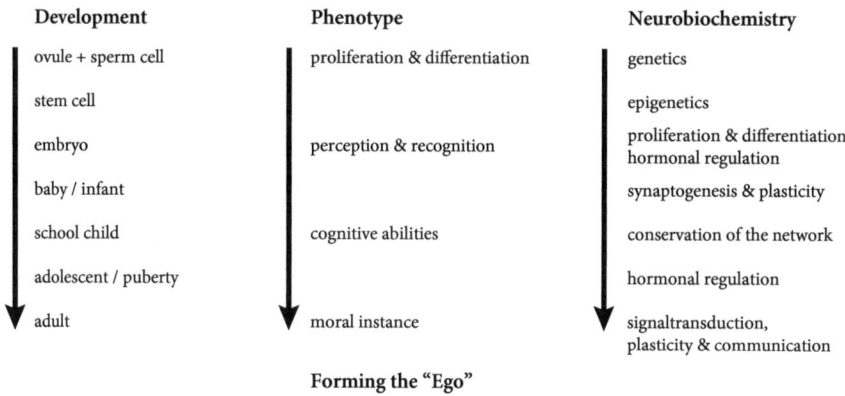

Development	Phenotype	Neurobiochemistry
ovule + sperm cell	proliferation & differentiation	genetics
stem cell		epigenetics
embryo	perception & recognition	proliferation & differentiation, hormonal regulation
baby / infant		synaptogenesis & plasticity
school child	cognitive abilities	conservation of the network
adolescent / puberty		hormonal regulation
adult	moral instance	signaltransduction, plasticity & communication

Forming the "Ego"

Figure 1. Overview on human development from the ovule to adulthood in comparison to the mental phenotype and the neurobiochemical action

such as cell-to-cell communication or cellular network building? And, last but not least, would the interpretation of the neuroscientific results lead to the dissociation of the old dichotomy of body and memory or body and mind (Singer 2002)?

Up to now, a satisfying answer to these questions is not possible. In the present chapter, some new results and novel concepts of brain research are presented in order to enforce and continue the necessary discussion on the interplay of body memory and neurobiology: Are both two faces of the same coin?

Life span can be roughly characterized by procreation, evolving in the embryo and perinatal phase, recognizing in early childhood, and the development of cognition and memory to a moral authority during puberty up to adulthood. These processes are induced and/or accompanied by in part dramatic changes in brain cell development, architecture, and action which may influence our psyche, mental states, and situative behavior (see Figure 1).

The genome serves as the basis for cellular development

In terms of neurobiology, our genome, based on evolutionary input, serves as a basis for further cell and body development. Our genome is a product of a certain amount of combination of four molecules, the deoxyribonucleic acids (DNA) adenine (A), guanine (G), thymidine (T), and cytosine (C), arranged in base pairs of two correlated complementary strands. Major parts of this DNA, the so called genes, code for specific proteins. These proteins are the major building blocks of the cells.

Interestingly, the size of the genome and the complexity of the organism do not necessarily correlate. The genome of the common newt *triturus vulgaris* expands that of the humans by the ten-fold [$2,5 \times 10^{10}$ (newt) to $3,27 \times 10^9$ (humans)] (Mainz 2010). Furthermore, a similar amount of genes can lead to completely different species. The human genome codes for about 20,000 to 25,000 genes (Consortium 2004) and differs from the amount of genes in the mouse to only ~1% and in the chimpanzee to ~0,1% (Reymond et al. 2002). Taken together, even smallest differences in gene amount or DNA base pair sequence can cause major differences in the phenotype. The aggregation of relatively simple building blocks, the four DNA bases, produces increasingly complex structures and, along with these, increasingly complex physical and cognitive performance. But can these arrangements of DNA base-pairs explain the differences between humans in mental stability, cognitive abilities, and situative handling? To step forward in understanding cellular memory, we have to enlighten the processes occurring in the regulation of gene expression.

Cellular identity

Starting from the ovule, growth and development of the human body during the embryo and perinatal phase go along with the generation of a multitude of different, highly specialized cells with different function all creating a functional body. Bone cells, liver cells, kidney cells, epithelial and endothelial cells, several different nerve and glial cells, and many other cell types evolute from the ovule. All of them are based on the same genome, but their development leads to a different cellular phenotype. Obviously each cell type follows a specialized either innate or acquired cellular proliferation and differentiation program to develop into the designated final cell (Levenson & Sweatt 2005). Moreover, once a specified cell type has reached its final destination and designation – its so called mature state – it will preserve life spanning. A liver cell will reproduce as liver cell, a bone cell as bone cell, etc.

This proliferation and differentiation process from the ovule to the final target cell is regulated by epigenetic factors and the action of specific hormones. Depending on the designated cell type, different genes at specified time points come to expression. Along the way of processing from DNA over the translating molecules ribonucleic acid (RNA) and precursor proteins to the final protein several steps of regulation and modification are included to ensure that the correct proteins are formed, which guarantee the development of the intended cell type. Epigenetic regulation of gene expression is a process to ensure cellular diversity with respect to form, shape, localization, and function.

In the so called *in utero* stage of human development predominantly environmental stimuli like nutrition, maternal supply and behavior have an influence on gene regulation. With respect to neuronal development, individually altered histone acetylation, methylation, phosphorylation, and ubiquitinylation cause changes in gene expression and lead to individual neuronal and synaptic function in the brain (Levenson & Sweatt 2005). The process of epigenetic gene regulation is also stimulated by specific hormones, namely by steroid hormones like testosterone and estrogen. These hormones play a crucial role in brain development in the embryonic phase in order to ensure correct neuronal proliferation, differentiation, and nerve cell integration into the developing brain architecture (see Figure 1) (McEwen 1992; Hagemeyer et al. 2000; Wang et al. 2003; Baron-Cohen et al. 2005; Fu et al. 2006). The differentiation of an embryonic or neuronal stem cell to a mature neuron appears to be a self-sustaining mechanism and persists through segmentation (Levenson & Sweatt 2005). It is characterized by the expression of specific marker proteins at specified time frames during neuronal development (Knoth et al. 2010).

The importance of epigenetic regulation becomes evident when studying several diseases coming along with pathologically altered histone acetylation or DNA methylation. In schizophrenia, DNA methylation is increased around the reelin gene, which is an extracellular matrix protein involved in synapse development (Levenson & Sweatt 2005; Heinrich et al. 2006). In Alzheimer's disease, histone acetylation of the APP gene is decreased. APP, the (beta)-amyloid precursor protein, acts as essential transcription factor (Levenson & Sweatt 2005). Taken together, epigenetic regulation of gene expression is crucial for correct cellular maturation and appears as a major part of the implementation and determination of cellular memory.

Network formation

As mentioned above, in the prenatal phase of development external influence on the human central nerve system is restricted to those sparse effects which can be absorbed *in utero*. The nerve system and its cell-to-cell contacts have reached a premature state.

Finally, the fetus is born and is now called "baby". This event is accompanied by a dramatic step forward in brain development. Visual, acoustic, and haptic inputs promote neuronal interaction in order to form a stressable and functional cell network in the brain. These developmental processes will last at least to puberty. Finally, around 100 billion neurons and a ten-fold manifold of glial cells form a network which is engraved by a permanent cooperation of genetic and epigenetic factors (Kold et al. 1996). Brain development is assigned by a steady-state modification of nerve cell contacts by which only one third of the original contacts will persist (Singer 2002). Brain architecture is influenced by experience and external signals in extraordinary ways. The resulting „primed cells" integrate into a complex network of brain cells characterized by synaptogenesis and plasticity. Repeated signal pathways are confirmed, incidental events are considered less. The binding of different neurons to a stressable network appears as a prerequisite in higher brain function.

Neuronal binding is an important step in adaptation to different events. It is reported that an initial or incidental event causes a group of neurons to fire nerve signals. The signals of those neurons within this group which are similar in frequency and amplitude will superimpose to a signal which is significantly beyond the signal-to-noise ratio of the other nerve cells. These neurons are "bound" together and form a network with respect to a particular event or stressor. These neuronal binding appears conservative for further events of the same type, which means that henceforth obviously the same neurons bind together to react on the designated stressor or external activator (Singer 1999; Engel et al. 2001; Engel & Singer 2001). The neurons memorize their connection.

It becomes evident that network formation in the brain is largely dependent on external influences, life experiences, and educational or cultural influences. This is extremely important during early childhood up to puberty and adolescence. Traumatic incidents in the early life span may have dramatic effects on brain development and architecture. In patients suffering from post-traumatic stress disorder symptoms (PTSD), the medical history very often reveals traumatic incidents during early childhood (De Kloet et al. 2005). Interestingly, PTSD is often correlated with a life-spanning impaired expression of glucocorticoid receptors in the limbic system of the brain, coming along with a reduced ability to deactivate the stress hormone cortisol and therefore to handle stress effects (Rostene et al. 1995; De Kloet et al. 2005). Hence mental behavior finds its molecular correlate.

Cognition, perception, and emotion

On an anatomic level, we can separate the brain firstly into four main structures: the neocortex, the cerebellum, the brainstem, and the limibic system (see Figure 2).

The cortex and its major lobes (frontal, parietal, occipital, and temporal lobes) is correlated to the higher brain functions such as language, cognition, perception, and imitation (see Figure 2A). The limbic system represents a complex core structure in the old phylogenetic part(s) of the mammalian brain. It consists of a set of brain structures including the hippocampus, amygdala, anterior thalamic nuclei, hypothalamus, and limbic cortex (see Figure 2B) (Conn & Freeman 2000). The limbic system nowadays can be regarded as a balancing structure in processing input from and to external and internal environment (McLachlan 2009). Especially, memory and cognition,

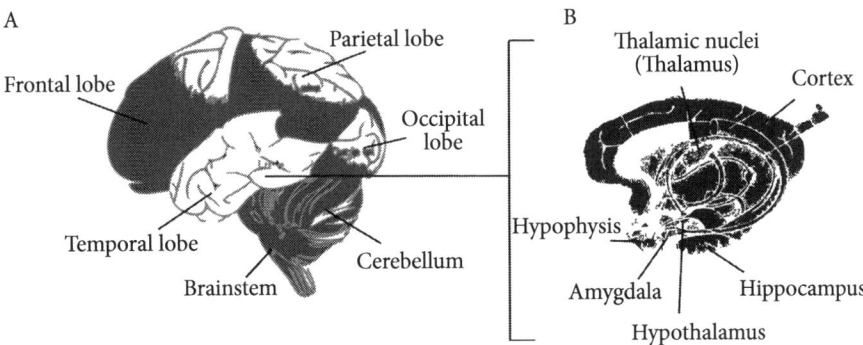

Figure 2. Overview on the anatomical sections of the human brain (A) and the limbic system (B). The limbic system is located above the brainstem and beneath the temporal lobes

sexual behavior, and also stress and fear are processed, weighed, and balanced by the limbic system (McLachlan 2009; Roozendaal et al. 2009). The limbic system is also a major target for the action of steroid hormones like testosterone or oestrogen (Killer et al. 2009; Meyer et al. 2009).

The coordinate interplay between structures of the neocortex and the limbic system appears crucial in building our own identity. This can be exemplified in examining the network connections active in memory and emotion. There are strong network connectivities between the subcortical areas of the limbic system, namely the amygdala, hippocampus and the thalamic regions, and some specified areas of the neocortex, the visual and prefrontal cortex, the frontal lobe, the parietal lobe, and the temporal lobe (Pessoa 2008). With respect to memory and emotion, the amygdala and the steroid hormone system appear to be (the most) important regulators.

The mirror neuron system may serve as another example of building highly individual network connections in the brain. Learning by imitation as conducted by the mirror neuron system has several advantages. It saves time and is economic in order to aquire motoric skills and social competence (Newman-Norlund et al. 2007; Rizzolatti & Fabbri-Destro 2008). The mirror neurons are premotoric parietal cells (cells of the parietal cortex), that get activated if a targeted action is executed or the same or similar action is observed, but performed by others (Iacoboni & Dapretto 2006). The „cylce of imitation" includes information input from the superior temporal sulcus (STS) to the frontoparietal mirror neuron system (MNS), subsequent processing and evaluation of sense and meaning in the MNS, and a backflow of information to the STS in order to perform imitation (see Figure 3) (Iacoboni & Dapretto 2006).

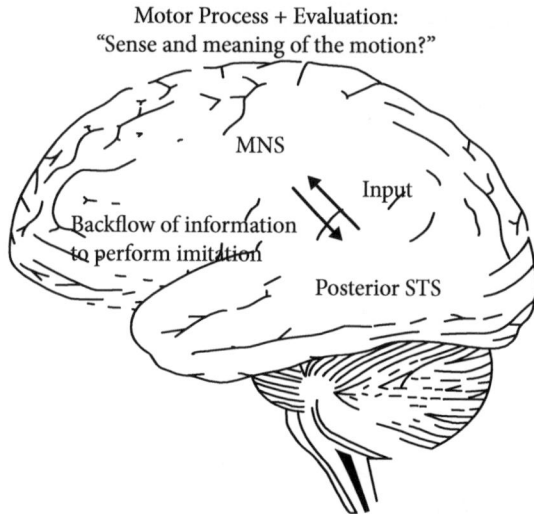

Figure 3. The "cycle of imitation" in the mirror neuron system of the brain. MNS: frontoparietal mirror neuron system, STS: superior temporal sulcus (Iacoboni & Dapretto 2006)

Perception and imitation appear to be main factors in individual learning, memory, and emotional reaction.

Conclusion: Body memory and neurosciences

Especially through the technology and the strategies of modern neurosciences, neurobiology and brain research have begun to expand to the inner spheres of the self. This approach may have far-reaching consequences for our idea of man. The neurosciences have started to stride along the path to explain mind and mental or psychic properties in neurobiochemical context. The first steps include models and concepts to approach the memory of the cell. In other words, neurobiology opens a field of stimulating interdisciplinary discussion on body or cellular memory.

Memory and emotion, as well as perception and imitation are influenced or strongly affected by brain networks, predominantly between neuronal structures of the limbic system, the amygdala, the hippocampus, and the hypothalamus with cortical structures of the prefrontal, temporal, and parietal cortex. Within those areas, specific neuronal populations fulfill specific functions, getting imprinted by evolution, but also by personal experience, cultural or educational background of the person. Humans have a long evolutionary history. Size and anatomical functional diversity of the brain predominantly determine cognitive abilities. Genetic and epigenetic factors are important for cellular memory. Genetics, epigenetics, and external stimuli are the basis for cell-to-cell connectivities of our individual neuronal network.

In conclusion, body memory in neurobiological context maybe hypothesized as a concept influenced by genetics and epigenetics, environmental input, cultural influence, cognition, and emotion.

References

Baron-Cohen, S., Knickmeyer, R. C. & Belmonte, M. K. (2005). Sex differences in the brain: implications for explaining autism. *Science, 310*, 819–823.

Berg, D. (2008). Biomarkers for the early detection of Parkinson's and Alzheimer's disease. *Neurodegenerative Diseases, 5*, 133–136.

Conn, P. M. & Freeman, M. E. (2000). *Neuroendocrinology in physiology and medicine.* Totowa, NJ: Humana Press.

Consortium, I. H. G. S. (2004). Finishing the euchromatic sequence of the human genome. *Nature, 431*, 931–945.

De Kloet, E. R., Joels, M. & Holsboer, F., (2005). Stress and the brain: from adaptation to disease. *Nature Reviews Neuroscience, 6*, 463–475.

Engel, A. K., Fries, P. & Singer, W. (2001). Dynamic predictions: oscillations and synchrony in top-down processing. *Nature Reviews Neuroscience, 2*, 704–716.

Engel, A. K. & Singer, W. (2001). Temporal binding and the neural correlates of sensory awareness. *Trends Cognitive Science, 5*, 16–25.

Fu, M., Liu, M., Sauve, A. A., Jiao, X., Zhang, X., Wu, X., Powell, M. J., Yang, T., Gu, W., Avantaggiati, M. L., Pattabiraman, N., Pestell, T. G., Wang, F., Quong, A. A., Wang, C. & Pestell, R. G. (2006). Hormonal control of androgen receptor function through SIRT1. *Molecular Cell Biology, 26*, 8122–8135.

Hagemeyer, C. E., Rosenbrock, H., Singec, I., Knoth, R. & Volk, B. (2000). Different testosterone metabolism by immortalized embryonic and postnatal hippocampal neurons from C57BL/6 mice: a crucial role for androstenedione. *Journal of Neuroscience Research, 60*, 106–115.

Heinrich, C., Nitta, N., Flubacher, A., Muller, M., Fahrner, A., Kirsch, M., Freiman, T., Suzuki, F., Depaulis, A., Frotscher, M. & Haas, C. A. (2006). Reelin deficiency and displacement of mature neurons, but not neurogenesis, underlie the formation of granule cell dispersion in the epileptic hippocampus. *Journal of Neuroscience, 26*, 4701–4713.

Iacoboni, M. & Dapretto, M. (2006). The mirror neuron system and the consequences of its dysfunction. *Nature Reviews Neuroscience, 7*, 942–951.

Killer, N., Hock, M., Gehlhaus, M., Capetian, P., Knoth, R., Pantazis, G., Volk, B. & Meyer, R. P. (2009). Modulation of androgen and estrogen receptor expression by antiepileptic drugs and steroids in hippocampus of patients with temporal lobe epilepsy. *Epilepsia, 50*, 1875–1890.

Knoth, R., Singec, I., Ditter, M., Pantazis, G., Capetian, P., Meyer, R. P., Horvat, V., Volk, B. & Kempermann, G. (2010). Murine features of neurogenesis in the human hippocampus across the lifespan from 0 to 100 years. *PLoS One, 5*, e8809.

Kold, B., Whishaw, J. Q., Atkinson, R. A., Lindzey, G. & Thompson, R. F. (1996). Fundamentals of human neuropsychology. New York: Worth Publishers.

Levenson, J. M. & Sweatt, J. D. (2005). Epigenetic mechanisms in memory formation. *Nature Reviews Neuroscience, 6*, 108–118.

Mainz, U. (2010). Molekulargenetik der Eukaryoten. [Molecular genetics of the eukatyote] available at: http://molgen.biologie.uni-mainz.de/Downloads/PDFs/Molekulargenetik%20der%20Eukaryoten/Molgen3.pdf. (last accessed date: 15.09.2010).

McEwen, B. S. (1992). Steroid hormones: effect on brain development and function. *Hormone Research, 3*, 1–10.

McLachlan, R. S. (2009). A brief review of the anatomy and physiology of the limbic system. *Canadian Journal of Neurological Sciences, 36, Supplement 2*, 84–87.

Meyer, R. P., Gehlhaus, M., Schwab, R., Burck, C., Knoth, R. & Hagemeyer, C. E. (2009). Concordant up-regulation of cytochrome P450 Cyp3a11, testosterone oxidation and androgen receptor expression in mouse brain after xenobiotic treatment. *Journal of Neurochemistry, 109*, 670–681.

Meyer, R. P., Pantazis, G., Killer, N., Burck, C., Schwab, R., Brandt, M., Knoth, R. & Gehlhaus, M. (2010). Xenobiotics in the limbic system – affecting brain's network function. *Vitamines and Hormones, 82*, 87–106.

Newman-Norlund, R. D., van Schie, H. T., van Zuijlen, A. M. & Bekkering, H. (2007). The mirror neuron system is more active during complementary compared with imitative action. *Nature Neuroscience, 10*, 817–818.

Pessoa, L. (2008). On the relationship between emotion and cognition. *Nature Reviews Neuroscience, 9*, 148–158.

Reymond, A., Marigo, V., Yaylaoglu, M. B., Leoni, A., Ucla, C., Scamuffa, N., Caccioppoli, C., Dermitzakis, E. T., Lyle, R., Banfi, S., Eichele, G., Antonarakis, S. E. & Ballabio, A. (2002). Human chromosome 21 gene expression atlas in the mouse. *Nature, 420*, 582–586.

Rizzolatti, G. & Fabbri-Destro, M. (2008). The mirror system and its role in social cognition. *Current Opinions in Neurobiology, 18*, 179–184.

Roozendaal, B., McEwen, B. S. & Chattarji, S. (2009). Stress, memory and the amygdala. *Nature Reviews Neuroscience, 10*, 423–433.

Rostene, W., Sarrieau, A., Nicot, A., Scarceriaux, V., Betancur, C., Gully, D., Meaney, M., Rowe, W., De Kloet, R. & Pelaprat, D. (1995). Steroid effects on brain functions: an example of the action of glucocorticoids on central dopaminergic and neurotensinergic systems. *Journal of Psychiatry & Neuroscience, 20*, 349–356.

Singer, W. (1999). Neuronal synchrony: a versatile code for the definition of relations? *Neuron, 24*, 49–65, 111–125.

Singer, W. (2002). *Der Beobachter im Gehirn – Essays zur Hirnforschung* [The observer in the brain. Essays in brain research]. Frankfurt: Suhrkamp.

Wang, L., Andersson, S., Warner, M. & Gustafsson, J. A. (2003). Estrogen receptor (ER)beta knockout mice reveal a role for ERbeta in migration of cortical neurons in the developing brain. *Proceedings of the National Academy of Sciences U.S.A, 100*, 703–708.

Wieloch, T. & Nikolich, K. (2006). Mechanisms of neural plasticity following brain injury. *Current Opinions in Neurobiology, 16*, 258–264.

PART III

Contributions from embodied therapies

Sensation, movement, and emotion

Explicit procedures for implicit memories

Christine Caldwell
Naropa University

Though cognitive neuroscience locates all memory systems in the brain and has gone to great lengths to understand the issues involved in the various forms that memory takes, where these forms are stored, and how they interact, it may be 'neurocentric' to think of memory as only occurring in and mediated by the brain. Undoubtedly, neural networks for memory abound in many different areas of the brain, and are absolutely essential hubs for the encoding, storage, and retrieval of human experience. Yet emerging work in neuroscience also confirms the crucial role of sensorimotor and affective processing in the shaping and reshaping of human memory. A case for 'body memory' can be made, and the role of the moving, sensing, feeling, and emoting body can now be seen as fundamental to the developmental structuring of and subsequent neurogenetic changing of memory, particularly implicit memory. This understanding of the phenomenological body's centrality in the navigation of non-verbal and affect-laden learning and remembering has profound impacts for our understanding of attachment, enactment, the therapeutic relationship, and psychotherapeutic procedures.

Keywords: movement, emotion, implicit memory, neuroscience, somatic psychology, psychotherapy

As much as some scientists and academics would like it to be so, our bodies do not exist in the discrete categories that our minds (our left hemispheres, to be exact) tend to create for purposes of clarity and organization. The brain is not separate from the rest of the body, and the body's systems are not isolated from each other. All parts of the body form a network of mutual influence and interdependence, and together they produce the mind. This 'interbeing' is at no place more evident than in the structure and function of memory systems. For instance, as far as the body is concerned, learning and memory are the same thing; something that you remember is something you have learned. In order to demonstrate what you have learned, you 'recall' it.

Memory tends to be seen almost exclusively as a function of brain processes, and memories are generally accepted as being located in neural networks inside the brain (Squire & Schacter 2002). While the evidence for this is overwhelming, these networks in the central nervous system (brain and spinal cord) cannot be divorced from the operations of the peripheral nervous system (the networks in the rest of the body). By beginning with this fundamental assumption, we can better understand the phenomenon known as 'body memory.'

The term body memory has been in popular use for some time, and has been used to describe the fact that once you learn how to ride a bike you never again have to think consciously about how to do it – your body just does it – and you never forget how to do it. Dancers speak of it when they perform complex choreographed steps they have worked hard to learn but now can enact without cognitive effort. These body phenomena might be partially understood as sensory 'engrams' (Juhan 1987). More recently, the term body memory has been used by mental health professionals to explain why a client's postures, gestures, movements, and states of arousal change when they remember instances of trauma or other intense events (Elzinga & Bremner 2002). It is as if the body is remembering (re-membering) the past, just as much as the mind does, and is even re-experiencing the event in the present moment.

This chapter, along with other chapters in this volume, attempts the tricky task of articulating the concept of body memory neuroscientifically, but without resorting to reductionistic neurocentrism. It also endeavors to use an interdependence perspective to inform various methods of psychotherapy, with the hope that working directly with body memories can facilitate more effective healing.

Conceptual overview of body memory

Many different types of memory exist, and are distributed throughout the brain as well as being networked with the rest of the body. "Human memory is not a unitary faculty, but rather an ensemble of various forms of learning that differ in their uses, their operating characteristics, and the neural networks that mediate their processing" (Gabrieli et al. 1995:76). Different types of memory tend to be stored in the parts of the brain where the information they are based on is processed (Gabrieli 1998; Gabrieli et al. 1995; Garrett 2009; Squire 1992). Thus, visual memories are located at visual processing areas, etc.

Most all memories originate as sensory impressions, an observation that is fraught with somatic significance that will be discussed later. They form as a result of a three-stage process that begins with *encoding* sensory events into meaningful schemas, *consolidating* them into storage, then *retrieving* them when we want to remember them. Different types of memory have been identified because of observed differences in how events are encoded, consolidated, and retrieved.

The two main divisions of memory are named because they involve separate systems and operations (Squire 1992). Declarative memory, or recall of facts and events, is conscious and *explicit*. In this system I remember that I rode my bike to work yesterday. Nondeclarative memory involves *implicit,* or nonconscious activities such as how to perform actions (like riding a bike), habit formation, and classical conditioning. Declarative memories tend to be located in time, whether something happened yesterday or a decade ago. They begin to form somewhere in our second or third year of life, when we have mastered the rudiments of language and our hippocampi have matured enough to store our personal historical narratives (Cozolino 2002; Lambert & Kinsley 2005).

Nondeclarative memories, on the other hand, have no words and no time stamp – as with riding my bike, *remembering is also doing* – the memory IS the action in the present moment, and past and present are therefore not different from one another. This functional sameness of action and remembering, past and present, emerges as highly significant for a nuanced understanding of many behaviors (Calvin 1998).

When I consciously observe and track my experience of riding the bike, the combination of moving and witnessing the sensory detail of my movements may lay down both declarative and nondeclarative memories. Both declarative and nondeclarative encoding relies on bodily sensations. In the former, the sensations and movement merge with my time stamped tracking of what occurred when, and would be recalled via words and images. In the latter, the sensations and movements become sensory engrams that can be recalled through enacting the same or similar activities. The explicit and implicit memory systems, though structurally separate, can be recalled either separately, or together. In the crucible of remembering a traumatic event, for instance, the scene might be recounted verbally while the body enacts the reactions that were encoded at the same time.

Enactment becomes highly relevant for a nuanced understanding of memory, because early experiences, especially interactions with caregivers, lay down largely unconscious 'maps' for making movements in both sides of the brain. These motor maps generate output signals to the muscles that produce complex movements and positions. Blakeslee and Blakeslee (2007) stress the significance of these motoric forms of memory, because our sense of meaning and our appraisal process is rooted in agency (the ability to act and choose), and agency, they noted, depends on embodiment.

Our motoric maps can be thought of as encoded body memories of how well we have moved through past experiences with a sense of agency. These movement memory maps then shape motoric responses (actions and choices) to current events. But because the recreated action patterns are mixed in with current embodied states, therapy that attends to our current embodied states may be able to influence and restructure these largely implicit maps via careful enactment sequencing.

Enactment relies on sensorimotor experiences. If we go back to Juhan's concept of a sensory engram, for instance, we find that:

> Each discrete sensory record of a particular movement is called a sensory engram and once the feeling of it is established as a clear, recallable memory, this engram is like a template. When we want to accomplish an act, we first recall the sensory

> engram associated with past repetitions of that act – remembering how it felt to do it. Motor systems are then set into motion to reproduce the remembered sequence of sensations laid down in the engram. The sensory cortex has memorized the feel of a movement and each time it's recalled for the purpose of repeating the action. The proprioceptive feedback of all the body parts is compared against that memory for each step of the intended repetition, and cerebellar corrections are made automatically and unconsciosuly. Learning of a new motor skill is a process of establishing a new series of sensory engrams, and the ability to repeat skill depends on the preservation of an intact sensory engram.   (Juhan 1987:266)

This memory for the feel of a movement, and the ability to replicate it in the present moment by blending the sensory engram with present bodily states may be the structural basis for what we are deeming body memory (Doyon & Ungerleider 2002). At the same time, we are building up to the idea that memories are not really representations of something that happened, but are schemas and engrams that form as a result of the mixing together of events with their social context, our physiological state, our mood and emotions, the environmental context, and our interactions with others.

In this way, we could say that most memory is inherently an associative process. Encoding, retention/consolidation, and retrieval all happen via association – if one sensory element of a memory is currently present, a whole network of associations will be called up along with it, and the new situation will be deemed a match to that memory. This can cause significant errors in our perceptions of the world and our current behavioral enactments in the context of those perceptions, as is often the case in unresolved trauma. This may also help us to understand why therapeutic modalities that involve the moving of memory, or bodily re-enactment, have such power to access the unresolved material that many therapy clients want to explore and resolve (Gabbard 2000).

It is within the framework of implicit, nonconscious enactment that we can understand body memory, because implicit memory contains stored patterns of bodily and emotional interaction with others, as well as personal experience. It begins to record our nonverbal body narratives, via the amygdalae, as early as our third trimester in utero. Implicit memories are often nonconsciously activated by nonverbal cues from others, as well as our own bodily sensations and explicit remembering (Cozolino 2002; Lambert & Kinsley 2005).

Body memory and emotion

The amygdalae, located in the limbic area, evaluate the emotional meaning of incoming stimuli, and stamp sensory events with emotional associations (especially fearful ones) as an intrinsic part of the creation of implicit memory. Enacting an implicit memory, functionally the same as retrieving it, will call up the emotions that were encoded with it. The emotion will be experienced as a present moment event, but is equally an act of emotional remembering (Feldman Barrett, Niedenthal & Winkielman 2005; LeDoux 1996). This point becomes critical in the depth of a psychotherapy session, when a client may confuse an emotional memory with what is happening right now. Sorting that out often hallmarks healing and recovery.

Thus, explicit systems stamp time as the relevant reference points for memory, and implicit systems stamp emotion as salient markers of an event. Emotions are central to implicit encoding, storage, and retrieval, and therefore are thought to shape perception via our selective attention to what our implicit schema have deemed emotionally significant. After assigning meaning to sensory information, the amygdalae shape emotional behavior by projections to the hypothalamus, hippocampus, and basal forebrain (Van der Kolk 1994). Van der Kolk has noted that in animals, strong stimulation of the amygdala interferes with hippocampal functioning, and that this implies that intense emotion may inhibit accurate evaluation and categorization of experience. It may also reflect the central nervous system's privileging of affect-based bodily experience over the verbal narratives we create, when in an intense situation. Again, this has strong implications for how psychotherapy might most effectively proceed.

LeDoux terms this process 'emotional memory' (1996, 2002). One of his most significant findings is that classical conditioning can cause fear to be permanently associated to a neutral event (such as a bell sound), causing a body memory to be enacted (such as shaking and cowering). Also via classical conditioning, one can train the bodily response to diminish (a process called extinction). But LeDoux asserts that this behavioral extinction is the result of the brain's controlling the fear response rather than the elimination of the emotional memory. The emotional memory does not extinguish; we can just manage not to re-enact it.

Body memory and attachment

In our first few years of life, memory is laid down via sensorimotor processes – the bodily interactions we have with our caregivers, our environment, and our body. These encoded interactions are implicit, and governed by affective states (Schore 2001). In the midst of our early bodily experiences of being held and put down, touched, gazed at, and played with, we form attachment bonds that can unconsciously drive most our future relational interactions. This attachment bond governs how our bodies come to know, trust, and care for the bodies of others. Mental models of who we are and who others are come later, and are constructed from the body models we have laid down earlier. Badenoch notes that:

> Implicit memories of first year are encoded without conscious awareness – the memories contain behavioral impulses, affective experience, perceptions, sensations, and images. With repeated experience they cluster into mental models (generalized nonverbal conclusions about the way life works). The conclusions

create anticipations of how life will unfold and remain largely below consciousness, guiding ongoing perceptions and actions in ways that reinforce the fore-
gone conclusions. We often experience these as "The Truth" or "The Way Things
Are" and when we do find words for them they sound like axiomatic realities.

(2008: 16)

Schore (2001) pioneered this understanding of the role of bodily states in attachment
when he reported that early emotional exchanges are encoded in the form of *representations* of the self interacting with caregivers. These representations are not verbal
or even pictorial, but are stored as psychophysiological arousal and affective states.
He concludes that our early sense of self is constructed bodily. Van der Kolk (1994)
adds that these early representations of experience include procedural memories,
which can be understood as motor skills and body memories of the felt sense of early
experiences.

A type of implicit memory called imprinting is used by humans and other mam-
mals from late fetal development through early childhood. It involves quick, strong,
global associations that do not fade over time, and is the basis for an infant's capacity to know and attach to its primary caregivers. These associations are experienced
bodily, linking, for instance, a warm visceral feeling of pleasure with mother and with
being fed and soothed, a tensing of muscles with repeatedly being startled by an aunt,
and excitement tinged with a bit of fear with father and physical play.

These imprinted, basic relational scenarios are important for us to figure out the
rules of engagement of in our primary relationships. Because of this, imprinting is
most prominent at or around birth, and then tapers off as a learning/memory strategy.
However, we remain capable of using imprinting under intense or stressful circumstances for the rest of our lives. In these circumstances it underlies the formation of
post traumatic stress disorder, strongly linking all the different internal and external stimuli that are present during a traumatic event (called state bound learning),
whether they are actually related to the trauma or not.

Whether attachment develops as secure or insecure rides on bodily experiences
that are memorized below the level of conscious awareness, are stored as body maps,
and retrieved as bodily actions. In order to positively influence attachment styles,
therapists are likely to need to use their own bodies as vehicles for relational repair
(Lyons-Ruth et al. 1998).

Body memory and trauma

Both chronic stress and unresolved trauma (PTSD) adversely affect memory systems.
Declarative memory is particularly compromised. Van der Kolk (1994) explains that
not only do chronic stress and PTSD interfere with hippocampal functioning (therefore declarative memories), but that they also cause deficits in the medial prefrontal
cortex, a structure that exerts back pressure against the fears and panic generated by

the amygdala. This lack of a prefrontal braking mechanism may be the structural underpinning of trauma survivors' experiences of the increasing frequency and intensity of overwhelming traumatic memories. Perversely, deficits in these brain areas can also result in strong emotional reactions occurring alongside a compromised ability to recall the emotional event.

Trauma memories are also encoded in body maps, and can be retrieved in bodily enactments. Our current physiological arousal can trigger traumatic memories, as well as those same memories precipitating bodily arousal. The stress hormones that are released in these arousal states may further imprint and strengthen unresolved traumatic memories. People with PTSD tend to over-interpret present moment sensory experiences as a recurrence of past trauma (Van der Kolk 1994), demonstrating the power of implicit memory, which is retrieved without any time stamp, to confuse and disrupt current perceptions of what is happening and how to deal with it.

It can be said that the goal of trauma therapy is to help clients live in the present moment, unencumbered by dictates from past events. It might also be said that trauma therapy seeks to unravel old sensory engrams and motoric maps that distort present experience and behaviors. However, the literature on trauma and memory also points to the fact that many trauma survivors experience their bodies as unregulated and untrustworthy, largely due to dysfunctional memory systems (Parson 1999). If my body shakes and sweats and cannot move every time I remember a past trauma, I am unlikely to want to pay attention to it. Paying attention to it might even make things worse.

Current trauma therapies that understand the body's role in healing and recovery tend to begin with facilitating a client's ability to stay within a physiological 'window of tolerance' (Ogden, Minton & Pain 2006; Rothschild 2000; Levine 1997), where arousal is kept to manageable levels, enabling the client to track her state in the present moment, and *experientially* distinguish between then and now. In this environment, the client can then gradually combine narrative recall with carefully enacted movement sequences that can re-pattern sensory engrams and motor plans so that a sense of agency, recovery, and embodiment is generated (Caldwell 2009, 2002).

Body memory and psychotherapy

Therapy that acknowledges and works with body memories may give therapists and their clients their best chance at facilitating change that lasts. This likely involves remembering or re-embodying memory in new ways. Neuroscientist and clinician Dan Siegal has posited that every act of recall is potentially an act of modification (1999). When we remember, we bring the past into the context of the present, and as that past surfaces, it is exposed to the different experiential elements residing in the here and now. If those new elements are safe, calm, welcoming, and relationally secure (i.e., a therapeutic relationship), a painful memory can be consciously worked with on a body level, as a way to re-encode the past situation with new, more regulated associations.

The explicit memory of a difficult event is not forgotten, nor are the emotional and physiological states that occurred with them, but these remembered states can now be associated with a present that is more able to hold and care for the past with equanimity and perspective.

Badenoch puts it this way:

> The very process of directing attention toward a particular memory adds, at a minimum, the energy and information of the present moment to that memory. This is one way that our comforting presence actually may alter our clients' painful past experiences. If we are able to stay in connection with one another, the feeling of comfort – often communicated through the sound of our voice, the position of our body, the look on our face as it reflects our inner experience of compassion – will initiate new neural firings in the neural nets of frightening & repeated childhood events.
> (2008: 8)

Other therapeutic strategies can develop for different memory systems. Neuroscience has shown us, for instance, that nonconscious, motoric habits are not forgotten (they are like riding a bike!). Evidence that habituation is involved in the formation of addiction has been accumulating (Holloway 1991), to the point where not being able to stop taking one more drink or drug has been called a 'programmed reach'. We can also habituate to emotions, a factor likely involved in mood disorders.

Addiction hits the habit formation centers of the brain hard, and results in sensory and motor stereotypy, a state of not being able to feel or enact much that is outside of the addictive habit. In these situations 'unlearning' the programmed body memories has to be very deliberate, using a combination of conscious attention and novel sensory experiences and motoric behaviors in order to create a new option to the old body memory (Caldwell 1996).

Another consideration in psychotherapy involving body memory can be the possibility of false memories. False memories likely form via the interpreter mechanism of the left hemisphere in the brain, that half of our cortex that processes via logic, linearity, and literalness. Siegal (1999) has stated that the left hemisphere gets out into the world with words, and the right hemisphere gets out into the world with movement. The right hemisphere specializes in imagery, emotional processing, and stress regulation. It is thought that false memories arise when the left hemisphere makes up a logical (but potentially incorrect) explanation for what the nonverbal right hemisphere is doing. What this may point us to is the likelihood that by postponing the explanatory narratives of the left hemisphere, and engaging directly with conscious movements that can directly and accurately express the feelings welling up in the right hemisphere, we can avoid the trap of trying to figure out whether a recovered memory is true or not.

Because most processing of sensory input occurs outside of conscious awareness, and only new, important or threat-based information is selectively passed on to the conscious processing of the neocortex, psychotherapy must involve 'waking up to' current sensations and states. This initial therapeutic task could be called the

Awareness Phase of the session, and in this phase the therapist and client attend to the client's embodied experience. Holding current states in nonjudgmental and non-interpretive awareness, often called 'open attention' or body-centered mindfulness, helps to create a safe container for the rest of the session to emerge.

When new inputs are emergent, then a second phase (called Owning Phase) of direct physical engagement might follow, where the client can take empowered ownership of sensation, and allow complex motoric responses to develop in response to direct experiencing. Interestingly, most repetitive movement organizes at a subcortical level, in the basal ganglia or cerebellum. Novel movements, however, tend to depend on the premotor and prefrontal cortex. By enacting the authentic movements that want to emerge as a result of mindful attention to ones current state, the prefrontal functions so crucial to healthy emotional and psychological regulation may be strengthened.

A third stage (called Appreciation Phase) then might organize, one that integrates sensation and movement with viscerally-based feelings of relational safety, comfort, and resolution, as well as self-empathy. This positive affective experience is crucial for the modification of body memory. It cannot be manufactured, but emerges as a natural by-product of the sense of agency that develops as a result of the previous two phases.

Lastly, a fourth stage (called Action Phase) could occur. At this point, because the body needs new actions to consolidate, replicate and remember therapeutic changes, the client might want to physically play with (and from within) new bodily memories. In this phase the client practices and rehearses the application of novel sensorimotor processes to his or her daily life, still within the experiential support of the therapeutic relationship.

Conclusion

Body memories form from sensory experiences, encoded and stored together with emotions, arousal states, relational contexts, and cognitive attitudes, into holistic schema that then organize motor maps. Those in turn plan and execute our bodily behavior. By working with the sensorimotor states of the body directly, we can consciously and carefully attend to, engage with, and hopefully resolve old and outdated body memories, memories that have shaped and driven our thoughts, attitudes, and actions. "At that point, these implicit mental models cease to exert so much covert influence over our relational choices and behaviors because they are no longer non-conscious determinants, but rather just other elements in a flexible decision-making process" (Badenoch 2008: 26).

By seeing human beings as a coherent collection of interdependent systems, most of which share interconnected means of encoding, storing, and retrieving various kinds of information, we can appreciate body memory as a very real and relevant contributor to our self identity and behavior.

References

Badenoch, B. (2008). *Being a brain-wise therapist: A practical guide to interpersonal neurobiology*. New York: W. W. Norton.

Blakeslee, S. & Blakeslee, M. (2007). *The body has a mind of its own: How body maps in your brain help you to do (almost) everything better*. New York: Random House.

Caldwell, C. (2009). Animal models of human trauma. In M. Bekoff (Ed.), *Animal behavior encyclopedia* (pp. 862–868). New York: W.W. Norton.

Caldwell, C. (2002). The moving cycle: A model for healing. In P. Lewis (Ed.), *Integrative holistic health, healing, and transformation* (pp. 273–294). Springfield. IL: C.C. Thomas.

Caldwell, C. (1996). *Getting our bodies back*. Boston, MA: Shambhala Publications.

Calvin, W. (1998). The emergence of intelligence. *Scientific American 9*(4), 44–51.

Cozolino, L. (2002). *The neuroscience of psychotherapy: Building and rebuilding the human brain*. New York: W.W. Norton.

Doyon, J. & Ungerleider, L. (2002). Functional anatomy of motor skill learning. In L. Squire & D. Schacter (Eds.), *Neuropsychology of memory* (pp. 225–238). New York: Guilford Press.

Elzinga, B. M. & Bremner, J. D. (2002). Are the neural substrates of memory the final common pathway in posttraumatic stress disorder (PTSD)? *Journal of Affective Disorders, 70*, 1–17.

Feldman Barrett, L., Niedenthal, P. & Winkielman, P. (Eds.). (2005). *Emotion and consciousness*. New York: Guilford Press.

Fuchs, T. (2004). Neurobiology and psychotherapy: An emerging dialogue. *Current Opinions in Psychiatry, 17*, 479–485.

Gabbard, G. (2000). A neurobiologically informed perspective on psychotherapy. *British Journal of Psychiatry, 177*, 117–122.

Gabrieli, J. (1998). Cognitive neuroscience of human memory. *Annual Review of Psychology, 49*, 87–115.

Gabrieli, J., Fleischman, D., Keane, M., Reminger, S. & Morrell, F. (1995). Double dissociation between memory systems underlying explicit and implicit memory in the human brain. *Psychological Science, 6*(2), 76–82.

Garrett, B. (2009). *Brain and behavior*. Thousand Oaks, CA: Sage Publications.

Holloway, M. (1991). Prescription for addiction, *Scientific American, 264*, 94–103.

Juhan, D. (1987). *Job's body: A handbook for bodywork*. Barrytown, NY: Station Hill Press.

Lambert, K. & Kinsley, C. H. (2005). *Clinical neuroscience*. New York: Worth Publishers.

LeDoux, J. (2002). Emotion, memory and the brain. *Scientific American, 270*, 50–57.

LeDoux, J. (1996). *The emotional brain: The mysterious underpinnings of emotional life*. New York: Touchstone.

Levine, P. (1997). *Waking the tiger: Healing trauma*. Berkeley, CA: North Atlantic Books.

Lyons-Ruth, K. & members of the Change Process Study Group (1998). Implicit relational knowing: Its role in development and psychoanalytic treatment. *Infant Mental Health Journal, 19*, 282–289.

Ogden, P., Minton, K. & Pain, C. (2006). *Trauma and the body: A sensorimotor approach to psychotherapy*. New York: W.W. Norton.

Parson, E. R. (1999). The voice in dissociation: A group model for helping victims integrate trauma representational memory. *Journal of contemporary psychotherapy, 29*, 19–38.

Rothschild, B. (2000). *The body remembers: The psychophysiology of trauma and trauma treatment*. New York: W.W. Norton.

Schore, A. (2001). The effects of early relational trauma on right brain development, affect regulation, and infant mental health. *Infant Mental Health Journal, 22*(1–2), 201–269.

Siegal, D. (1999). *The developing mind: How relationships and the brain interact to shape who we are*. New York: Guilford Press.

Squire, L. (1992). Declarative and nondeclarative memory: Multiple brain systems supporting learning and memory. *Journal of Cognitive Neuroscience, 4*(3), 233–243.

Squire, L. & Schacter, D. (Eds.). (2002). *Neuropsychology of memory*. New York: Guilford Press.

Van der Kolk, B. (1994). Trauma and memory: The flexibility of memory and the engraving of trauma. *Trauma Information Pages*, Articles: 7/8/03 http://www.trauma-pages.com/vanderk4.htm P. 1–21.

CHAPTER 17

Memory, metaphor, and mirroring in movement therapy with trauma patients

Marianne Eberhard-Kaechele
German Sports University, Cologne

This chapter defines trauma and describes some of its long term consequences, in particular traumatic body memory. A model of the formation of traumatic body memory is used as a reference to discuss the potential of dance/movement therapy to address this phenomenon. After a brief reflection on ground rules for trauma-focused therapy, four interrelated approaches in dance/movement therapy with trauma patients are considered. These include (1) the psycho-educational retraining of trauma-based action patterns, (2) the modulation of arousal through the deconstruction of affects, (3) the transformation of the subjective meaning of traumatic experience through experiential movement metaphors, and (4) the development of affect regulation and reflective distance to traumatic memory through interpersonal mirroring.

Keywords: body memory, dance/movement therapy, metaphor, mirroring, trauma

Psychological trauma and its aftermath

Psychologically traumatizing events involve direct or witnessed threats to the personal or physical integrity of an individual. Of those persons who experience a traumatic situation, up to 30% will find their trust in themselves and in the world fundamentally questioned and develop a post-traumatic stress disorder (PTSD). Symptoms include: re-experiencing the traumatic incident on a psychosomatic level, social avoidance, and hyperarousal. In the USA approximately 5 million patients have the disorder in any one year. The magnitude of exposure, prior trauma, and lack of social support appear to be the three most significant predictors for developing chronic PTSD (van der Kolk 1994; Baldwin 2010).

The subjective interpretation of the meaning of traumatic events plays a major role in the development of PTSD (Baldwin 2010). Fischer and Riedesser (2003) describe psychological trauma as an experience of a vitally threatening discrepancy between stressful situational factors and the coping abilities of the individual. If traumatic experiences cannot be processed, survivors live their lives as if a failure of their coping capacities were constantly impending. Neurological damage suffered during and after the traumatic event, years of lost or limited chances for learning and development, and ongoing distorted perception may all lead to true inadequacy in dealing with everyday life events (Wöller 2006; van der Kolk 2006).

Empirical studies show that untreated traumatic stress has devastating consequences for the health and life expectancy of survivors. Childhood trauma leads to chronic depression, suicide, addictions, obesity, and many secondary or tertiary illnesses such as diabetes, hypertension, heart disease and skin ailments many decades later (Egle, Hardt, Nickel, Kappis & Hoffmann 2002; Felliti 2002). One reason for the perseverance of traumatic stress is that it results not only from traumatic events themselves but also from traumatic memories that continuously invade the daily life of survivors, even many years after a traumatic event has passed. Particularly problematic are so-called body memories that present themselves on a pre-verbal level, detached from biographical memory, in the form of physical sensations, postures or movement sequences (Young 1992).

This chapter will describe a model of the formation of traumatic body memory and discuss the potential of dance/movement therapy to address this phenomenon by promoting the awareness of the body and movement, as well as offering alternative experiences on a sensory, aesthetic, and relational level.

Traumatic body memory

According to Tschacher (2006) remembering is not a process of retrieving an accurately preserved set of information. Modern theories see memory as the productive process of actively generating patterns according to generalized previous experiences. Therefore, memories are a simplified, condensed, more pronounced and biased version of what was once reality, comparable to metaphors. These metaphors are subjective interpretations of the meaning of the traumatic event which influence subsequent life processes just as strongly, if not more so, than the factual reality of the event (Fischer & Riedesser 2003).

Memory is also embodied: The emotions and physical sensations experienced during the formation of a memory and those experienced during its recall play a major role in generating the version of an event produced in memory (Damasio 1994; van der Kolk 1994). As mentioned above, memories are not confined to mental images or thoughts, but may also appear as sensory perceptions such as temperature or tension changes, or they may take the form of physical symptoms such as pain, rapid heartbeat, or breathing problems and further, they may occur as action patterns such as fleeing, self-grooming, or freezing (van der Kolk 2006; Herman 1992). Such implicit or procedural memories develop at a preverbal stage of life or under traumatic

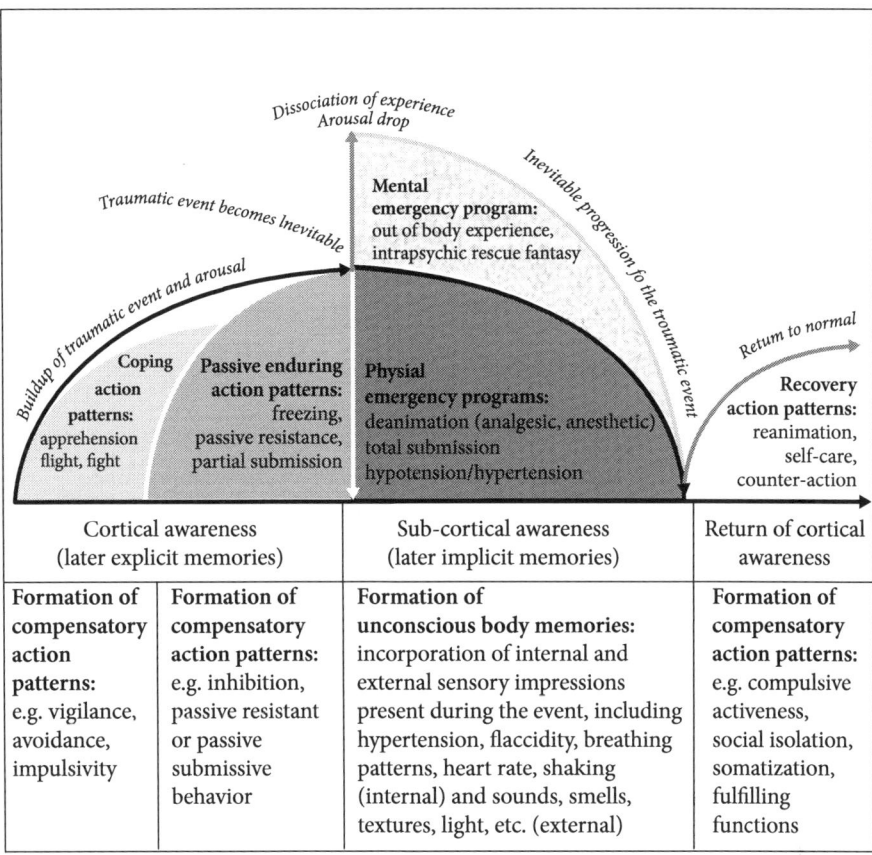

Cortical awareness (later explicit memories)		Sub-cortical awareness (later implicit memories)	Return of cortical awareness
Formation of compensatory action patterns: e.g. vigilance, avoidance, impulsivity	**Formation of compensatory action patterns:** e.g. inhibition, passive resistant or passive submissive behavior	**Formation of unconscious body memories:** incorporation of internal and external sensory impressions present during the event, including hypertension, flaccidity, breathing patterns, heart rate, shaking (internal) and sounds, smells, textures, light, etc. (external)	**Formation of compensatory action patterns:** e.g. compulsive activeness, social isolation, somatization, fulfilling functions

Note. Modified from Hochauf (2007), with additions from Nijenhuis et al. (2004), and Rothschild (2002).

Figure 1. The formation of traumatic body memory and action patterns

circumstances, as will be explained in Figure 1 (Nijenhuis, Van der Hart & Steele 2004; Rothschild 2002).

Both psychodynamic (Hochauf 2007) and behavioral (Nijenhuis, Van der Hart & Steele 2004) perspectives on trauma agree on the following model for the process of the formation of traumatic body memory illustrated in Figure 1. The primary concept of the model is that individual action patterns originate at specific points before, during, and after a traumatic event and can therefore be understood as purposeful survival strategies. The models main features are as follows: In the upper part of the diagram, the progression of a traumatic event, indicated by arrows, is described in italics. On the second level, within the shaded areas, the action patterns that emerge during particular stages of a traumatic process are listed. On the third level, we see the mode of brain functioning active during the various phases of the process, which will determine the kind of memories accessible to the person at a later time. On the fourth level, we find compensatory behaviors that echo the trauma-related action patterns (in the shaded areas) and remain active long after an event has past. In a later section of this article, I will describe how the various action patterns are addressed in treatment.

As shown in Figure 1, under the extreme stress of trauma, a person may involuntarily separate or dissociate their thoughts or imaginations from body sensations and emotions, in order to survive the intolerable situation. Traumatic body memories arise later, when triggered by sensory stimuli that are similar to those present during the traumatic event. In turn, body memories activate significant physical sensations and behavior patterns (see Figure 1) transposing the survivor into the experience of a traumatic situation. This perception is unmediated by cortical capacities such as language symbols which could put the threatening event at a distance (e.g., I feel *as if* I am in danger.). Instead the incident is immediate, physical and emotional, an "experiential metaphor" (Begy 2010: 51) (e.g., I feel *it is* dangerous here and now.).

A spontaneous experiential metaphor is the association of one experiential psycho-somatic configuration with another (Rusch 2009). For example, a person caught in the pressure of people trying to exit and enter an elevator at the same time might find themselves suddenly reminded of the pressure they feel when caught between the demands of their job and family. In the case of a trauma survivor, the person might feel transposed into a situation of domestic violence. Body psychotherapies such as dance/movement therapy draw on constructed experiential metaphors as a form of intervention, involving the physical realization of abstract ideas such as emotional processes or mental states.

If the physical symptoms of attacks on the body and or psyche of a person are not processed and regulated, they will reappear with increasingly overwhelming intensity. This causes the cycle of dissociation of memory, emotion, and body awareness to further escalate (Ogden & Minton 2000). A major reason to ban body awareness from consciousness, or to control it excessively, is the fact that the implicit body memory is active during a traumatic event and preserves the traumatic experience. In contrast, the explicit or verbal memory is deactivated and seemingly free of devastating memories, as illustrated in Figure 1 (Rothschild 2002).

In Table 1 below, the features of explicit, declarative memory are compared with those of implicit, procedural memory. This comparison shows practitioners which modalities of communication are appropriate when dealing with body memory and reveal why interventions that solely access the explicit memory are less successful (Rothschild 2002; Briere 2002).

A final facet of body memory discussed in the next section refers to the meaning of the traumatic event.

Table 1. Comparison of explicit and implicit memory

Feature of memory	Explicit/declarative memory	Implicit/procedural memory
mode of awareness	conscious	unconscious/conscious
type of information	cognitive facts temporal spatial mental verbal/semantic descriptions of operations descriptions of procedures	emotional conditions ever-present atmospheric physical sensory automatic capabilities automatic procedures
mediated by (neural structure)	Hippocampus	Amygdala, basal ganglia cerebellum
age of maturation	approx. third year of life	from birth
activity during trauma, flashbacks, dissociation	suppressed	activated
means of expression/ access	verbal, narrative, symbolic, scenic, explicit metaphor	somatic, atmospheric, motor, experiential metaphor, image schemata

Note. Modified from Rothschild (2002), with additions from Johnson (2007), Hantke (2006), and Clancey (2001).

The central theme of the traumatic situation

Persons suffering from complex post-traumatic stress disorder (PTSD) develop a subjective interpretation of the meaning of the traumatic experience in relation to their self-concept and their worldview. This interpretation is known as 'Zentrales traumatisches Situationsthema (ZTST)' or *central theme of the traumatic situation* (CTTS) (Fischer & Riedesser 2003). Briere explains the phenomenon as follows: "For example, the young child who is being maltreated often infers negative self- and other-characteristics from such acts. He or she may conclude that he/she must be intrinsically unacceptable or malignant to deserve such "punishment" or neglect, or may come to see himself or herself as helpless, inadequate, or weak. As well, the abused child may come to view others as inherently dangerous, rejecting, or unavailable" (Briere 2002: 176).

As opposed to discrete cognitions or episodic memories, the CTTS is embodied. It is the result of a recurring pattern of sensorimotor experience which congeals over time into what Johnson (2007) calls a *body-based image schema*. Possible examples are verticality, source-path-goal, center and periphery, container and contained, link, positions in space such as above, below, behind, or in front. The formation of image schemata, however, is a natural part of cognitive development and not of itself a symptom of trauma.

For example, the repeated association of emotional sadness with the sensory-motor experiences of gravity such as the downward motion of the body through the loss of muscular tension or the falling of tears, activate the image schema of verticality across various domains of experience. Verticality is the basis used to create the conceptual metaphor "emotional sadness is a downward motion". Conceptual metaphor theory postulates that "abstract concepts are defined by systematic mappings from body-based, sensorimotor source domains onto abstract target domains" (Johnson 2007: 177). The metaphor is reflected in our speech: we understand the statement "I'm feeling down." not only semantically, but also on a sensorimotor level. Any sensory stimulus with a downward tendency such as falling leaves in autumn (visual), successively deepening musical notes (acoustic), or the pull of a heavy bag on our shoulder (haptic) can (re-)activate the association of sadness.

Conceptual metaphors combine subjective experience and judgment with sensorimotor experience to create images that are almost universally valid across many cultures (Lakoff & Johnson 1999). The fate of traumatized individuals, however, transforms universally positive images into the central theme of their traumatic situation. Table 2 shows examples of conceptual metaphors and typical deformations through traumatic experiences.

Table 2. CTTS as image schemata projected onto metaphors

Commonplace metaphors	Traumatic metaphors
Closeness is warmth	Closeness is pain
A link is an aid	A link is a siphon
My body is a temple	My body is a dump
Behind me is support (backing)	Behind me is danger
Vitality is joy	Vitality is guilt

Clinical practice has shown that "These core beliefs and assumptions are often relatively nonresponsive to superficial verbal reassurance or the expressed alternate views of others later in life, since they are not, in fact, verbally-mediated" (Briere 2002: 177). According to van der Kolk (2006), the effective treatment of trauma on the basis of neurobiological research must be body-based, and entail the facilitation of affect, tolerance and interoception, the modulation of arousal, and the regulation of self-esteem through engaging in effective action after confrontation with physical or emotional helplessness. One method that fulfills all of these criteria is dance/movement therapy.

Dance/movement therapy

Dance/movement therapy is considered as one of the expressive arts therapies as well as a form of body psychotherapy. Developed as a clinical treatment in the USA in the 1940s and 1950s, DMT is based on the assumption of the interrelation of somatic, emotional, cognitive, and social processes (Levy 2005). It can be defined as the psychotherapeutic use of dance and movement in an interactional process aimed at the treatment of illness and the facilitation or maintenance of physical and psychological health and quality of life (ADTA American Dance Therapy Association 2009; Eberhard-Kaechele 2009c). The method addresses the healthy aspects of the individual and supports a developmental process that is as self-determined as possible. Bernstein (1995:42) writes with regard to traumatized patients: "In dance therapy the body becomes at once the vehicle for change and the focus of change, so that the client can begin to reclaim her body as an ally in her struggle toward health."

Dance therapy uses specific methods which originated in dance art and are particularly appropriate for the treatment of traumatized individuals, for example:

- The movement analysis of the posture and movement of a person decodes information regarding inner processes of cognition and emotion. Corresponding interventions address the body or movement to encode positive experiences, expand the patient's movement repertoire and increase their influence upon cognitive, emotional, social, and physical functioning (Goodill 2005).
- Artistic processes of composition and symbolization create a safe distance to traumatic events and at the same time build a bridge between fragmented components of experience such as cognition, emotion, sensory perception, and behavior. Artistic activity aids in the formulation of a verbal narrative of traumatic events, embedding them in a temporal and spatial orientation, which is the essence of trauma recovery. Composing experiential movement metaphors empowers the individual with control over a situation, transforming inner meanings of events and allowing for the discovery and practice of alternative coping strategies (Schedlich 2003). Creative improvisation develops problem-solving abilities and offers experiences of self-efficacy vital for transforming trauma induced negative self-judgments (Meekums 2002).
- The therapeutic movement relationship offers a way to discover and further develop or change patterns of interpersonal relating. These patterns develop on a body level in early childhood and determine central aspects of the personality and the behavior repertoire of adults. Dance therapists are trained in a great number of modalities of the nonverbal choreography of relationships, including kinesthetic empathy and the mirroring of affect and intention in movement (Levy 2005; Stanton-Jones 1992).

I will proceed to focus on four interrelated approaches to the treatment of traumatic body memories, based on these specific aspects of dance therapy and tested in 18 years of clinical practice with patients with complex PTSD. These approaches are (1) the psycho-educational retraining of trauma-based action patterns, (2) the modulation of arousal through the deconstruction of affects, (3) transforming the meaning of traumatic experience through movement metaphors, and (4) interpersonal mirroring.

Trauma treatment

The general rules of trauma-specific therapeutic treatment have been discussed at length elsewhere, for example by Herman (1992) or Rothschild (2010). However, before I go on to describe specific dance therapy methods, I would like to mention the most important rules of trauma-adapted therapy from these sources.

- The therapeutic situation, including the therapeutic relationship, need to be transparent, safe, and controllable for the patient (and the therapist) at all times.
- Therapy should focus on establishing safety within the life situation of the patient, on establishing psycho-physical stability and on discovering and strengthening resources, before any kind of trauma exposition takes place.
- Therapists need to consider the individuality of each patient when they choose, form, and perform interventions.
- Body memories are phenomena that emerge in the process of therapy by themselves. They can promote development, when the patient feels strong enough to give up the protection of dissociation. It is not effective or advisable to try to forcibly "uncover" traumatic memories using body techniques. Forced remembrance may further cement dissociation processes, producing no result, or may end in a re-traumatizing flood of uncontrollable affects.
- The treatment of traumatic memories always involves maintaining a solid connection to the present moment through sensory input and awareness of the supportive therapeutic alliance. The patient may then deal with memories by oscillating their attention between past and present in individually appropriate intervals.

Deconstructing and modulating affects

At the beginning of the 20th century, Rudolf von Laban revolutionized the scholarship of dance with a new approach to movement which was later called Laban Movement Analysis (LMA). He rejected the traditional complex steps and positions as the basis of dance, and in their place he put the abstracted, physical elements of movement such as space, time, weight, shape, body parts, and social interaction. These parameters are the building blocks of LMA (Laban 1980) and are similar to the concept of vitality affects of Daniel Stern (1992). Laban's perspective opened up a myriad of combinations that can be used to describe or facilitate all types of movement, not just dance. Laban's goal was to increase the adaptability of a person's movement while respecting their individual physiognomy and movement preferences. He also studied the correlations between particular movements and emotional and cognitive processes (Davies 2001).

In the same way that Laban deconstructed dance, LMA allows therapists and patients the deconstruction of affects, so that the latter can work on the mastery of regulation without being upset by categorical affects such as anger or fear. By differentiating and gaining control over the movement attributes of emotions separately and only then combining them into categorical affects, patients may gain control over their emotions and physical sensations. By this means, the body is no longer a threat but a source of security. For example, it is possible to work separately on the mastery of the regulation of tension, speed, intensity, distance, or directions in space in a co-vert way through exercise, dance, or sports. When these abilities have been mastered and a tolerance for higher intensity levels has been attained, the elements can be combined to an emotional expression such as striking out in anger, slumping in sorrow, or cringing with shame.

The basic forms of movement addressed in LMA are not only the "alphabet" we use to express emotional "words" and "sentences". They are also the vehicle for embodying protective action patterns which emerge during traumatic processes.

Recognizing and expanding action patterns

According to Van der Kolk (2006) the medical treatment of PTSD through psycho-therapy and psychopharmacology tends to narrowly focus on neurochemistry or cog-nitive and emotional states. For lack of adequate solutions, little attention is paid to disruptions in the experience of physical sensations and the automatic activation of trauma-related action patterns, triggered by language or sensory input. These behav-iors, outlined in Figure1, unfold automatically, usually inappropriate to the immediate situation, fortifying the person's feelings of inadequacy. Here is brief example: *Ellen is a secretary working in an open office. Every time she senses someone standing behind her chair, she must jump up and leave the room, constantly interrupting her work.* Self-rein-forcing cycles of experience and behavior conserve and perpetuate these patterns. For example, the awareness of muscle tension in the body evokes fear, fear causes more tension, more tension evokes more fear, and so on (Sander & Schedlich 2006).

Due to the neurobiological suppression of the brain regions responsible for speech production during traumatic experiences, verbal therapies are limited in their ability to access or change fixed action patterns. Cognitive self-management may redirect arousal from the sensorimotor and emotional levels for a short time, but this will not achieve the processing and assimilation of sensorimotor reactions to the trauma (Ogden & Minton 2000).

Dance therapists deal directly with the physical and psychological aspects of movement patterns, bringing them to consciousness in a safe environment. Rather than eliminating these patterns from the repertoire of the patients, interventions sup-port a transformation of the meaning of the behavior pattern to the patient. This is achieved through psychoeducation and movement exploration.

Psychoeducation is the systematic practice of informing patients, to help them to access and learn strategies to deal with mental illness and its effects (Winkler 2008). Understanding the science and logic behind seemingly "crazy" behaviors relieves a patient's burdensome feelings of fear, shame, and guilt or of the danger of being pathologized by others. She takes on a position of control and efficacy that counteracts traumatic experiences of powerlessness and lack of orientation. Traumatization may destroy a person's sense of living in a coherent world, where things make sense. By contrast, working on an ordered process with a theoretical model can help restore that sense of coherence (Antonovsky 1979). Finally, becoming an expert on one's own symptoms dissipates fears of dependency upon professional help and supports active self-responsibility (Wöller 2006).

In my work with action patterns, I first offer patients an introduction to the model discussed in the chapter on traumatic body memory, in which symptomatic behavior is explained as a remnant of protective or recovery actions (Nijenhuis, Van der Hart & Steele 2004; Fischer & Riedesser 2003). Then we experiment with the appreciation of the effectiveness of the various action patterns, beginning with the most basic emergency systems and working our way towards the most challenging forms. While the personal preferences of patients may vary, the system shown in Figure 2 provides a suggestion for the order of interventions, based on a reversal of the trauma process.

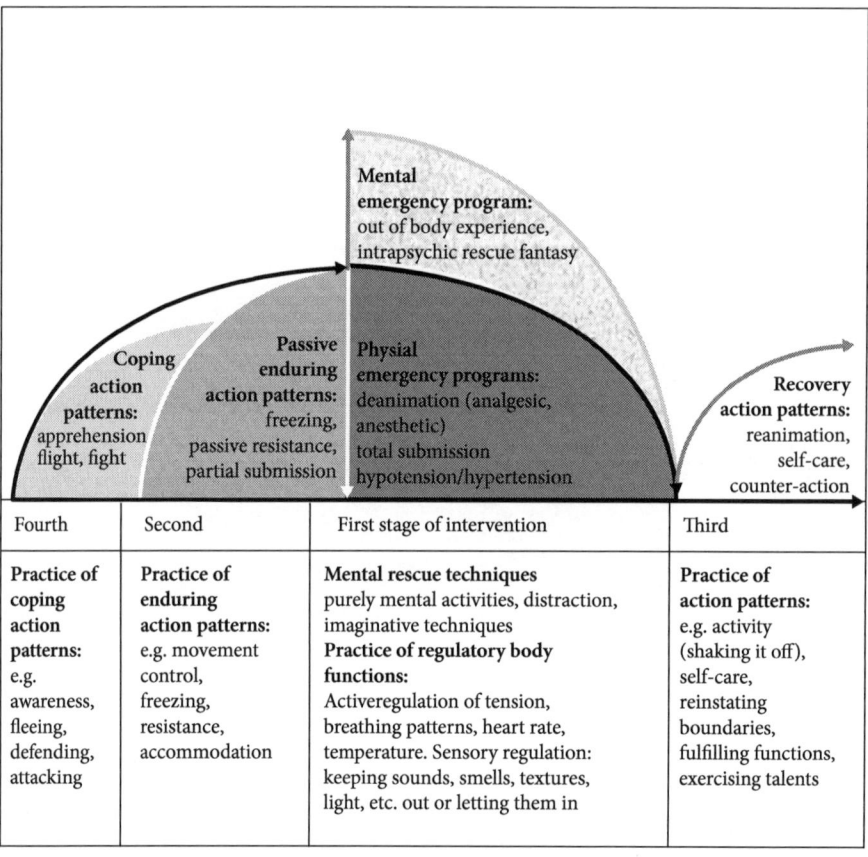

Fourth	Second	First stage of intervention	Third
Practice of coping action patterns: e.g. awareness, fleeing, defending, attacking	**Practice of enduring action patterns:** e.g. movement control, freezing, resistance, accommodation	**Mental rescue techniques** purely mental activities, distraction, imaginative techniques **Practice of regulatory body functions:** Activeregulation of tension, breathing patterns, heart rate, temperature. Sensory regulation: keeping sounds, smells, textures, light, etc. out or letting them in	**Practice of action patterns:** e.g. activity (shaking it off), self-care, reinstating boundaries, fulfilling functions, exercising talents

Figure 2. Sequence of interventions for the validation of defensive action patterns

Together with the patients we construct movement sequences in which their action pattern is a competence. For example, a "stop-dance", in which the ability to stay completely still is recognized as an achievement, validates the action pattern of freezing. Consciously using movements that once took their course automatically boosts feelings of self-control and self-trust. Coupled with the resolution of the trauma-induced distortions of self-image (see the section on experiential metaphors) patients can learn to guide their urge to move toward behavior more suited to the current situation and to leave the past behind.

To this end, the patients must overcome their conditioned response to trigger stimuli and develop first a tolerance for these. Triggers are not just atmospheric conditions such as lighting, temperature, smells, or the shape of a room (narrowness, low roof, etc.) related to the trauma. They may also involve particular forms of self-movement or the movement of other persons, such as: movement or stillness, changes in muscle tension (towards relaxation or tensing), body positions (open, closed, leaning forward), traveling or staying on one spot, the intensity of movement (high/low), speed of movement (acceleration/deceleration), certain directions or spatial orientations (forwards, backwards or above, beside, behind), places in the given space (facing the door etc.) and the intensity of pressure on body parts (strong/light) (Eberhard-Kaechele 2007; Lewis 1999). As with the action patterns we encourage the patients to consciously use the trigger modalities under safe conditions in order to gradually neutralize their effect and later even to bestow a positive valence on these movements. Alternately to the focus on the more or less problematic behaviors, we actively seek out action patterns that are associated with self-efficacy and pleasurable sensorimotor experiences to support the resources of the patient (Sander & Schedlich 2006; Grawe 2000). To focus exclusively on these positive aspects, however, would leave many patients with the feeling that they are being left alone with their troublesome symptoms and emotions. For this reason, the individual ratio of focusing on positive compared to negative experiencing that works for each patient must be explored.

Experiential metaphors and image schemata

In order for the therapeutic reprocessing of traumatic experiences to take place on a neural level, significant body memories must be activated to an optimal degree of arousal. Experiences stored in explicit memory can be activated by verbal intervention. However, experiences stored in implicit, emotional memory must be activated on a perceptual level, by means of sensorimotor stimuli (van der Kolk 2006; Grawe 2000). Experiential metaphors projected from body-based image schemata are examples of such stimuli. The characteristics of image schemata make them particularly useful tools for the creation of interventions. According to Johnson (2007) and Gibbs (2005), body-based image schemata

- pertain to many levels of experience and allow for the cross-modal transference of information between sensory systems and contexts, based on their origin in the neural co-activation of motor, affective, and cognitive brain regions.
- are image-like, in that they conserve a perceived structure as a whole. By this virtue, they can represent complex phenomena in a simple aesthetic expression such as a movement, a visual object, or a musical phrase that can become a vehicle for therapeutic exploration. For example, a forward movement can stand for the complex process of development and healing, a backward movement for the complex phenomenon of a relapse into a drinking problem.
- consist of structures with a minimal number of elements and relations between these, such as *source, path, and goal or center-periphery.* Through metaphoric projection, image schemata help us to understand the structures and common themes of various therapeutically relevant situations. For example, with respect to the center-periphery schema, in how far am I the center of attention at my workplace, in my family, or in the healthcare system, etc.?
- are dynamic, as they imply not only states but also processes. (e.g. the balance schema implies not only the state of balance but also associated activities such as seeking and finding a balance, losing balance and falling etc.)
- generate meanings and consequences that are helpful for problem solving. Working with image schemata, patients discover problem solving *principles* on a higher level of abstraction, not just solutions for *individual situations.* For example, "What options are there in dealing with hierarchy?" rather than "What shall I say to my boss next week?".
- are a form of experiential abstraction: at once mental and physical (Clancey 2001), thereby addressing both sides of the brain at once.

In dance/movement therapy we encourage the patients to choreograph experiential metaphors using image schemata, which they can subsequently transform. Returning to the prior example of the conceptual metaphor "sadness is a downward movement", we may use downward movements as a way of reconnecting split-off affects and physical sensations. Slowly letting parts or the whole of the body sink downward, lowering a scarf from a high held position, or letting the petals of a flower fall, are all possibilities of creating an experiential metaphor to explore sadness. Later, by adding the opposite direction to the choreography, joy and its metaphoric upward movement can be introduced. The following examples describe some further metaphors particularly relevant in the treatment of trauma.

The image schema 'container' is often projected onto the metaphor of a hole, which swallows and destroys everything positive. Pitman and Orr (1990) first coined the phrase "the black hole of trauma" (p. 469), for this phenomenon that recurs in the imagery of many traumatized patients. When patients are able to give this hole a concrete form in an experiential metaphor, their creative potential to deal with the phenomenon can be released. For example, they may want to fence it off, put a lid on it, or learn to keep a good distance to it and resist its magnetic attraction.

Another example of the container schema is the metaphor of the violation of boundaries. When asked to draw a boundary around themselves or a symbolic object of value using props such as ropes, chairs or cushions, trauma survivors will often create a piece meal line upon the floor representing their fragmented boundaries. A person who challenges the function of the boundary as a limitation is usually allowed to pass with little resistance. We can interpret this behavior as a protective strategy that prevents the escalation of a threat by the motto; "If you give in, the bad situation is over sooner." After confirming the adaptive purpose of the former behavior, the therapist can encourage the patient to experiment with building more solid (and therefore more confrontation-provoking) boundaries. Patients are supported in taking on challengers with active defense behaviors when appropriate, and in learning to judge when fleeing is more advisable than putting up a fight.

The metaphor of the broken link between parts of the self, self and others, even between self and the world that traumatized persons experience, is often represented by ropes, scarves or threads of wool that are let go of or torn. Feeling the abrupt change from tension to its' lacking during the rupture and sensing the real pull of a connection to another person (the image schema of attraction), when the rupture has been repaired, is often the first step to healing the inner disconnection and to feeling whole at last.

Destructive relationships can also find expression with the metaphor of a link, as seen in the example of one patient who choreographed her familial situation together with fellow patients using ropes as props to represent "family ties" as follows: *The patient was connected to her mother by a rope ending in a noose around the mother's neck. The mother was tied closely to the father with another rope. Any attempt of the daughter to escape her abusive father had the result of strangling her mother. In the moment when the patient could experience this metaphor on the sensory level, she instinctively let go of the rope and with it the responsibility for her mother. She remarked that she had been told that she must learn to differentiate between her own and her mother's life, but this thought had not "sunken in" on an emotional or behavioral level until this moment.*

In this example, we see the effect of the performance of an experiential metaphor. It generates an immediate reality in the body and psyche of the patient, not just an imaginary reality, which enables her to access problem-solving potential that may not have been available otherwise (Fischer-Lichte 2004; van Oers 2001).

It is important when composing experiential metaphors with image schemata, that we first construct a metaphor for the current state of the patient, which is a protective (albeit anachronistic) strategy. The act of choreography heightens the patients understanding of their conflicts as they must study the situation exactly in order to give it a form. The communicative and regulative functions of the current protective patterns must be acknowledged and valued in the context of the patient's biography by the therapist but more importantly by the patient. This positive regard for the current state can initiate a positive experience of competency that challenges the self-image installed by the traumatic events. Under this impression of ability, the pathway to new solutions for old problems is opened. Moving on to choreograph the target state of seemingly healthy action patterns may be very threatening to patients and should be treated with appropriate caution.

Image schemata are developed through everyday experiences on three levels which can be replicated in body psychotherapy. The first level is the process of experiencing one's own body in action, exerting influence on the environment and on oneself. The second level is the process of experiencing impressions and influences through the environment. The third level is the process of manipulating and observing objects and substances. A great advantage of the work with experiential metaphors and image schemata is that they can be composed with any type of medium, and work with any of the three levels mentioned above. Keeping in mind the fact that relationships can be extremely threatening for traumatized individuals, I have found the following progression of interventions helpful, and will exemplify it with the image schema of *support*:

1. *Objects interact with objects*: The patient experiments with the interaction between two sponges, leaning one against the other, discovering principles helpful for her problems with support.
2. *People interact with objects*: The patient can experiment with supporting a sponge leaning on her body or she leans on the wall and feels its support.
3. *People interact with people*: The patient experiments with supporting and being supported with the therapist or with other patients.
4. *People interact with themselves*: The patient experiments with her possibilities of supporting herself, for example, resting her head on her knees in a curled up position sitting on the floor. While in this position she focuses her awareness alternately on the supporting and the supported parts of her body, integrating the separate roles she practiced in phase 3. (Eberhard-Kaechele 2009)

The example of support demonstrates one of the most important tasks of trauma therapy: to develop or restore the ability to engage in safe and satisfying relationships. The following section is devoted to this facet of treatment.

Trauma recovery through mirroring

Traumatic experiences are either of themselves social events, or they are embedded in a social environment. The quality of a person's early attachment experiences determines whether they will be prone to developing trauma-related disorders. Negative attachment experiences result in the insufficient development of affect regulation and the conditioning of maladaptive patterns of social regulation. These result in a predisposition for victimization and the inability to cope with trauma, should it occur (Schore 2003). The aforementioned central theme of the traumatic situation (CTTS) often pertains to the attachment relationship, not just to the trauma. It is the combined experience of a perpetrator *and* an inadequate protector, or worst of all, the event of a designated protector acting as a perpetrator, that is most likely to give rise to post-traumatic symptoms.

Wöller (2006) observed that the long term impacts of childhood trauma typically involve the destruction of all sense of self-efficacy and self-esteem, the disruption of the ability to form relationships, and the frequent misinterpretation of interpersonal situations as threatening, as well as difficulties with emotion regulation. Seen from this perspective, treatment involves the completion of interrupted developmental tasks and skills and the creation of positive memories of competence and supportive relationships.

Crucial to the development of social competence and affect regulation is the successful interpersonal attunement or mirroring between children and their caregivers. Traumatized individuals often lack the experience of being attuned to. As a result, they may themselves be unable to attune to others or mentalize their inner states but rely solely upon the sensory information they can pick up externally, with a tendency to relate everything they see (negatively) to themselves (Huber 2009; Fonagy, Gergely, Jurist & Target 2004). A patient might interpret the angry expression on the therapists face, resulting from a prior phone call with the landlord, as an expression of dissatisfaction with her and react to this interpretation with fear or opposition.

Other trauma survivors may be unable to differentiate between the feelings, intentions, and beliefs of others and their own, having learned to enter into the mental states of others as a survival strategy. Through structural dissociation processes, patients may lose their cognitive ability to process verbal instructions and be forced to rely on learning by imitation (van der Hart, Nijenhuis & Steele 2006). In all of these cases, therapeutic intervention based on the recapitulation of the development of mentalization and affect regulation through mirroring processes can be very effective. To begin with, the therapist interactively assists the patient in regulating dysregulated states. With time, the patient (re-)acquires the skills of self-regulation and reflection (van der Hart, Nijenhuis & Steele 2006).

The history of the use of mirroring techniques or kinesthetic empathy in dance therapy is as old as the method of dance/movement therapy. In the 1940's particularly the American dance therapist Marian Chace applied the multimodal mirroring of the affects of her patients, by means of her own movements, voice, props, and music as a medium of treatment for psychiatric patients (Sandel 1993).

Chace's goals in respect to affects were self-acceptance, the externalization of emotions, the intensification of expression, the expansion of the symbolic expressive repertoire, access to memories important for the understanding of feelings, and finally the integration of physical activity, emotional experience, and verbal reflection (Chaiklin & Schmais 1979). While the theoretical discussion of mirroring and attunement in psychotherapy meanwhile has been informed by new disciplines such as infant or embodiment research, the goals mentioned above remain much the same.

In Table 3 I offer my own attempt to develop a taxonomy of interaction modalities in ontological order. This system allows clinicians to diagnose the level at which a

Table 3. Modalities of interpersonal mirroring in dance therapy

No.	Modality	Characteristics of movement and affect regulation	Development of mentalisation
1	initiation	The ability to initiate, continue and terminate movement/attention processes (gazing towards something, keeping it in view, diverting one's gaze). Primary self-efficacy and pre-requisites for regulation.	Discovering contingency,[1] self-discovery, causal thinking.
2	medial/ oceanic mirroring	Totally simultaneous movement between partners or play with controllable objects. Enables interpersonal transcendence, or it is a sign of merging and a lack of differentiation between self and others, or a sign of non-personal perception of people as inanimate objects.	"Perfect" contingency, self-exploration, taking control.
3	concordant mirroring		
3a	modal mirroring	Mirroring in the literal sense, egocentric, along a common axis of movement. Affect attunement, learning from others, and sense of agency.	High level but not perfect contingency, exploration of the social world.
3b	cross modal mirroring	Dynamic/shape is mirrored by voice, another expressive medium or another body part. Facilitation of exploration.	Medium level contingency, exploring the environment.
3c	parallel mirroring	Side by side = solidarity, one behind the other = support or leading and following. Joint attention toward a third entity. Shared interest. Social referencing.	Joint attention, teleologic/goal-oriented thought.
3d	counter movement	Anti-phasic coordination of cyclic movements, e.g. open-close vs. close-open, up-down vs. down-up.-Precursor of intersubjectivity, alter-centric vs. egocentric, each participant has their own axis of movement.	Perspective taking, differentiation of perspectives.
4	deferred imitation	Deferred imitation, retention and recall of movement, memory development, identification processes. Replacing one object with another in the repetition of a situation marks the beginning of symbolization and the pretend modality.	Intentional thought, symbolization.

---

1.   Contingency in this case means the more or less simultaneous occurrence of two events which suggest a dependency between the two, such as the gesture of a hand and the movement of a toy. The greater the control of the actor over the reaction, or put differently, the more exact the matching of the movements, the higher the level of contingency (Fonagy et al. 2004).

5	contrasting	The main intention of the movement is reversed, e.g. speed: quick vs. slow, shape: round vs. jagged, direction: up vs. down etc. Ambivalent: doing the opposite serves differentiation, while the common theme/the friction serves connection.	Conceptual thought, e.g. opposites, directions, positions, forms, intentional thought II differentiation of self/others beliefs.
6	variation	Simultaneously maintaining contact and serving individuation and expansion of abilities. Self-regulation of affects through "tuning" the dynamics/forms of movement. Adaption to various situations.	Adaptivity, representational thought.
6a	marked variation	Differentiation of one's own and others affects. Regulation of arousal through mild and possibly humorous exaggeration, containment. Externalization of affects in play or artistic activity, uncoupled from the consequences of reality.	Representational thought, pretend play with mental elements (feelings, intentions, beliefs).
7	complementary interaction	The partner's roles are interdependent and constitute one another, e.g. the carrier & the carried, the hunter & the hunted, the protector & the protected, the victim & the perpetrator etc. Integration of reality and fantasy, self/others abilities, regulation of other people's affects (comforting, provoking etc.)	Complete representations and theory of mind, understanding deception. Reflecting mode of thought.

Note. This table integrates information from Eberhard-Kaechele (2010), Schneider and Büttner (2008), Sodian (2008, 2005), Klöpper (2006), Fonagy et al. (2004), Fonagy and Target (2002), Grossmann and Grossmann (2005), Trevarthen (2004), Schore (2003), Kestenberg Amighi et al. (1999), Sandel (1993), Stern (1992), Lewis-Bernstein (1972/1981), Kestenberg and Sossin (1979), and Kestenberg (1965).

patient is functioning and to appropriately address them at this level. It also provides a rational for the progression of interventions in the course of therapy.

With respect to the justified mistrust of patients with PTSD, dance therapists see mirroring as a complex form of interacting that involves more than the imitation of the *external form* of the movement. Great attention is paid to the empathetic reflection of the *affective state* of the patient in movement. Also, the *intentions* of the patient are reflected back to them through the process of picking up on their intentional themes and structuring these in subsequent movement sequences.

For example, a patient laid out a circle on the floor with a rope, intending to create a space of the size of her body. Unconsciously, she created a space far too small, and when she attempted to lie down in the space, many body parts were crossing the boundary into general space. Subsequently, the therapist picked up the themes of "How much space do I allot myself?" and "Boundary crossing" and created movement opportunities to explore these intentional themes with the patients.

In order to reduce anxiety and concentrate on the strengths of the patient, the mirroring modalities may be applied to any kind of expression, whether motor, musical/phonological, visual art, or verbal. Affect synchronizing actions generate and amplify positive affects, which not only have a pleasant and strengthening effect in their own right, they also have the effect of absorbing and neutralizing negative affects and decreasing depressivity (Schore 2003). Also, synchronizing movement enhances group cohesion and the sense of security in a group (Marsh, Richardson & Schmidt 2009), a sorely needed experience for most trauma survivors.

Conclusion

Trauma is in one way or another ingrained in the body of the survivor. Through embodiment research we can better understand how phenomena like body memory come to be, and discover how we can empower patients to escape the repetitive cycle of arousal and dissociation. By addressing symptoms on the level at which they occur, we can foster appreciation for the wonder that is the human being and human body's central role in mediating emotion and cognition.

Still, it is important to remember that the "Resolution of the trauma is never final; recovery is never complete. The impact of a traumatic event continues to reverberate throughout the survivor's lifecycle" (Herman 1997:211). Therefore, our goal cannot be to eliminate all traces of a trauma. Instead, we can aim to help the patient to understand and appreciate their former patterns of behaving and feeling, to accept themselves as they are now, and to add new memories and create new metaphors that affirm their dignity, worth, and self-efficacy in the face of adversity.

References

American Dance Therapy Association. (ADTA) (2009). *Who we are*. Retrieved on January 6 2009 from American Dance Therapy Association: http://www.adta.org/about/who.cfm.

Antonovsky, A. (1979). *Health, stress, and coping: New perspectives on mental and physical well-being*. San Francisco: Jossey-Bass.

Baldwin, D. (2010). *About trauma*. Retrieved on October 12 2010 from http://www.trauma-pages.com/trauma.php.

Begy, J. (2010). *Interpreting abstract games: The metaphorical potential of formal game elements*. Retrieved on October 12 2010 from Massachusetts Institute of Technology: http://cms.mit.edu/research/theses/JasonBegy2010.pdf.

Bernstein, B. (1995). Dancing beyond trauma: Women survivors of sexual abuse. In F. Levy (Ed.), *Dance and other expressive therapies* (pp. 41–58). London: Routledge.

Briere, J. (2002). Treating adult survivors of severe childhood abuse and neglect: Further development of an integrative model. In J. Myers, L. Berliner, J. Briere, C. Hendrix, T. Reid & C. Jenny (Eds.), *The APSAC handbook on child maltreatment*, 2nd edition (pp. 175–203). Newbury Park: Sage.

Chaiklin, S. & Schmais, C. (1979). The Chace approach to dance therapy. In P. Lewis Bern-stein (Ed.), *Eight theoretical approaches in dance/movement therapy* (pp. 15–30). Dubuque, Iowa: Kendall/Hunt.

Clancey, W. (2001). Is abstraction a kind of idea? or How conceptualization works. A commen-tary. *Cognitive Science Quarterly, 1*, 390–419.

Damasio, A. (1994). *Descartes' error: Emotion, reason, and the human brain.* New York: Avon Books.

Davies, E. (2001). *Beyond dance. Laban's legacy of movement analysis.* London: Brechin Books.

Eberhard-Kaechele, M. (2007). The regulation of interpersonal relationships by means of shape flow: A psychoeducational intervention for traumatised individuals. In S. Koch & S. Bender (Eds.), *Movement analysis. The legacy of Laban, Bartenieff, Lamb and Kestenberg* (pp. 203–211). Berlin: Logos.

Eberhard-Kaechele, M. (2009). Die Bedeutung des Containerschemas in der Körperpsychothe-rapie bei traumabedingten Ekelempfindungen [The importance of the container schema in body therapy treatment of trauma-based contempt]. In R. Vogt (Ed.), *Ekel als Folge traumatischer Erfahrungen. Psychodynamische Grundlagen und Studien, psychotherapeu-tische Settings, Fallbeispiele* [Contempt as a consequence of traumatic experience. Psycho-dynamic background, psychotherapeutic settings and case descriptions] (pp. 141–155). Gießen: Psychosozial.

Eberhard-Kaechele, M. (2010). Spiegelungsvorgänge in der Tanztherapie / Körperpsychothera-pie [Mirroring in dance therapy / body psychotherapy]. In S. Bender (Ed.), *Bewegungsana-lyse von Interaktion* [Movement-analysis of interaction] (pp.193–212). Berlin: Logos.

Egle, U., Hardt, J., Nickel, R., Kappis, B. & Hoffmann, S. (2002). Long-term effects of adverse childhood experiences – Actual evidence and needs for research. *Zeitschrift für Psychoso-matische Medizin und Psychotherapie, 48,* 411–434.

Felliti, V. (2002). The relationship of adverse childhood experiences to adult health: Turning gold into lead. *Zeitschrift für Psychosomatische Medizin & Psychotherapie, 48,* 359–369.

Fischer, G. & Riedesser, P. (2003). *Lehrbuch der Psychotraumatologie* [Textbook of Psychotrau-matology]. München: Ernst Reinhardt.

Fischer-Lichte, E. (2004). *Ästhetik des Performativen* [Aesthetics of the performative]. Berlin: Suhrkamp.

Fonagy, P. & Target, M. (2002). Neubewertung der Entwicklung der Affektregulation vor dem Hntergrund von Winnicotts Konzept des "falschen Selbst" [Re-appraisal of affect regu-lation processes on the background of Winnicotts concept of the "false self"]. *Psyche, 56* (9/10), 829–862.

Fonagy, P., Gergely, G., Jurist, E. & Target, M. (2004). *Affektregulierung, Mentalisierung und die Entwicklung des Selbst* [Affect regulation, mentalization and the development of the self]. Stuttgart: Klett-Cotta.

Gibbs, R. (2005). *Embodiment and cognitive science.* New York: Cambridge University Press.

Goodill, S. (2005). *An Introduction to Medical Dance/Movement Therapy. Health Care in Mo-tion.* London : Jessica Kingsley.

Grawe, K. (2000). *Psychologische Therapie* [Psychological therapy]. Göttingen: Hogrefe.

Grossmann, K. & Grossmann, K. (2005). *Bindungen – das Gefüge psychischer Sicherheit* [At-tachment – the structure of psychic safety]. Stuttgart: Klett-Cotta.

Hantke, L. (2006). Vom Umgang mit Dissoziationen und Körpererinnerungen [How to address dissociation and body memory]. In M. Zobel (Ed.), *Traumatherapie – eine Einführung* [Trama therapy an introduction] (pp. 112–134). Bonn: Psychiatrie-Verlag.

Herman, J. (1992). *Trauma and recovery. The aftermath of violence – from domestic abuse to political terror.* New York: Basic Books.

Hochauf, R. (2007). *Frühes Trauma und Strukturdefizit. Ein psychoanalytisch-imaginativ orientierter Ansatz zur Bearbeitung früher und komplexer Traumatisierungen* [Early trauma and structural deficit. A psychanalytic-imaginative appraoch for the treatment of early and complex traumatization]. Kröning: Asanger.

Huber, M. (2009). *Wege der Traumabehandlung. Teil 2* [Pathways to trauma treatment. Part 2]. Paderborn: Junfermann.

Johnson, M. (2007). *The meaning of the body. Aesthetics of human understanding.* Chicago: The University of Chicago Press.

Kestenberg, J. (1965). The role of movement patterns in development, I: Rhythms of movement, II: Flow of tension and effort. *Psychoanalytic Quarterly, 34,* 517–563.

Kestenberg, J. & Sossin, M. (1979). *The role of movement pattems in developement* (Vol. 2). New York: Dance Notation Bureau.

Klöpper, M. (2006). *Reifung und Konflikt. Säuglingsforschung, Bindungstheorie und Mentalisierungskonzept in der tiefenpsychologischen Psychotherapie* [Maturation and conflict. Attachment theory and mentalization concept in psychodynamic therapy]. Stuttgart: Klett-Cotta.

Lakoff, G. & Johnson, M. (1999). *Philosophy in the flesh. The embodied mind and its challenge to western thought.* New York: Basic Books.

Levy, F. (2005). *Dance/movement therapy – A healing art.* Reston, Virginia: The American Alliance for Health, Physical Education, Recreation and Dance.

Lewis Bernstein, P. (1972/1981). *Theory and methods in dance/movement therapy.* Dubuque, Iowa: Kendall/Hunt.

Lewis, P. (1999). Healing early child abuse: The application of the Kestenberg Movement Profile and its concepts. In J. Kestenberg Amighi, S. Loman, M. Sossin & P. Lewis (Eds.), *The meaning of movement: Development and clinical perspectives of the Kestenberg Movement Profile* (pp. 235–247). New York: Brunner-Routledge.

Marsh, K., Richardson, M. & Schmidt, R. (2009). Social connection through joint action and interpersonal coordination. *Topics in Cognitive Science, 1,* 320–339.

Meekums, B. (2002). *Dance movement therapy.* London: SAGE.

Nijenhuis, E., Van der Hart, O. & Steele, K. (Januar 2004). *Trauma-related structural dissociation of the personality.* Retrieved on May 3rd, 2005 from Trauma Information Pages: http://www.trauma-pages.com/nijenhuis-2004.htm.

Ogden, P. & Minton, K. (Oktober 2000). *Sensorimotor psychotherapy: One method for processing traumatic memory.* Available at: Traumatology, Volume VI, Issue 3, Article 3: http://www.fsu.edu/~trauma/v6i3/v6i3a3.html (Accessed 9 September 2007).

Pitman, R. & Orr, S. (1990). The black hole of trauma. *Biological Psychiatry, 27,* 469–471.

Rothschild, B. (2002). *The body remembers – The psychophysiology of trauma and trauma treatment.* New York: W.W. Norton.

Rothschild, B. (2010). *8 keys to safe trauma recovery: Take-charge strategies to empower your healing.* New York: W.W. Norton.

Rusch, D. (2009). Mechanisms of the soul: Tackling the human condition in videogames. In *DiGRA 2009: Breaking new ground: Innovation in games, play, practice, and theory.* London: Brunel University. Available at: http://www.digra.org/dl/db/09287.01371.pdf (Accessed: 12 July 2010)].

Sandel, S. L. (1993). The process of empathetic reflection in dance therapy. In S. L. Sandel, S. Chaiklin & A. Lohn (Eds.), *Foundations of dance/movement Therapy: The life and work of Marian Chace* (pp. 98–111). Columbia, Maryland: The Marian Chace Memorial Fund of the American Dance Therapy Association.

Sander, E. & Schedlich, C. (2006). Trauma-adaptierte Tanz- und Ausdruckstherapie [Trauma-adapted dance and expressive therapy]. In S. Trautmann-Voigt & B. Voigt (Eds.), *Körper und Kunst in der Psychotraumatologie* [Body and art in psychotraumatology] (pp. 223–242). Stuttgart: Schattauer.

Schedlich, C. (2003). Material zum Einführungskurs zur Ausbildung zum Fachberater für Psychotraumatologie [Introductory materials for the psychothraumatology specialist]. *Unpublished Manuscript*. Cologne: University of Cologne.

Schneider, W. & Büttner, G. (2008). Entwicklung des Gedächtnisses bei Kindern und Jugendlichen [Memory development in children and adolescents]. In R. Oerter & L. Montada (Eds.), *Entwicklungspsychologie* [Developmental psychology] (6., completely revised edition; pp. 480–501). Weinheim: Beltz.

Schore, A. (2003). *Affect regulation and the repair of the self.* New York: Norton.

Sodian, B. (2005). *Kognitive Entwicklung in der Kindheit* [Cognitive development in childhood]. Stuttgart: Kohlhammer.

Sodian, B. (2008). Entwicklung des Denkens [Development of thinking]. In R. Oerter & L. Montada (Eds.), *Entwicklungspsychologie* [Developmental psychology] (6th completely revised edition, pp. 436–479). Weinheim: Beltz.

Stanton-Jones, K. (1992). *An introduction to dance movement therapy in psychiatry.* London: Tavistock/Routledge.

Stern, D. (1992). *The interpersonal world of the infant.* New York: Basic Books.

Trevarthen, C. (2004). Learning about ourselves from children: Why a growing human brain needs interesting companions. Retrieved December 12, 2009 from Perception in Action: http://www.perception-in-action.ed.ac.uk/ publications.htm.

Tschacher, W. (2006). Wie Embodiment zum Thema wurde [How embodimnet became a topic]. In M. Storch, B. Cantieni, G. Hüther & W. Tschacher, *Embodiment* [Embodiment] (pp. 13–34). Bern: Huber.

van der Hart, O., Nijenhuis, E. & Steele, K. (2006). *The haunted self. Structural dissociation and the treatment of chronic traumatisation.* New York: W.W. Norton.

van der Kolk, B. (2006). Clinical implications of neuroscience research in PTSD. *Annals of the New York Academy of Sciences, 1071,* 277–293.

van der Kolk, B. (1994). The body keeps the score: Memory & the evolving psychobiology of post traumatic stress. *Harvard Review of Psychiatry,* 1994, 1(5), 253–265.

van Oers, B. (2001). Contextualisation for abstraction. *Cognitive Science Quarterly 1,* 279–302.

Winkler, M. (5 November 2008). *Psychoeducation.* Retrieved November 1, 2010 from Web-4Health: http://web4health.info/en/answers/psy-therapy-education.htm.

Wöller, W. (Ed.). (2006). *Trauma und Persönlichkeitsstörungen* [Trauma and personality disorder]. Stuttgart: Schattauer.

Young, L. (1992). Sexual abuse and the problem of embodiment. *Child Abuse & Neglect, 42* (1), 89–100.

CHAPTER 18

Body memory as a part of the body image

Päivi Pylvänäinen
Clinical Outpatient Program, Tampere, Finland

First outlining body memory from a phenomenological perspective, this chapter then relates that view with the information offered by neurosciences, especially with the work of Kandel (2007), and makes efforts to understand, what is the nature of connections between body memory and the body-self; is something one just experienced part of body memory immediately after the lived moment; and how body memory influences the responses and actions the body-self expresses. Through vignettes from a clinical dance/movement therapy (DMT) group, it is explored how patients encounter body memory related issues in DMT.

Keywords: body image, body memory, neuroscience, dance/movement therapy, psychiatric outpatients

This chapter explores body memory in relation to the tri-partite model of body image (Pylvänäinen 2003, 2006, 2008). The tri-partite model of body image differentiates the body image into the elements of body-self, body memory and image properties. The body-self is an active, responsive element in the body image, the body's quality of being present and in interaction with the environment. The body-self is actualized in the present through connectedness with the sensory, kinesthetic and perceptual information in the body. The image-properties are perceptions, thoughts, judgments, and values related to the physical appearances of the body. The image-properties evoke emotional responses in the person and these are experienced through the body-self. Body memory is the name for the embodied information storage function of the body.

A phenomenological view on body memory

Body memory on a phenomenological level has three spheres: habitual, traumatic and erotic body memory (Casey 1987). Habitual body memory is defined as the active presence of the individual's past in the body. Habitual body memory contains the embodied experiences of everyday routine activities and movement repertoire. This essentially builds the sense of coherence, continuity and familiarity. It supports orientation in the present situation. The habitual body memory, as it carries our movement repertoire and embodied ways of coping, can foster a sense of safety, mastery, and agency (Pylvänäinen 2003). Traumatic body memory, according to Casey, holds sensations and kinesthetic responses from moments of trauma and pain, whether emotional or physical. These moments may have been personally lived, or observed in others. In traumatic body memories the integration of the body is violated and the experience of embodiment becomes fragmented. The third sphere of body memory, erotic body memory, is the storage of embodied experiences of pleasure. Casey suggests that erotic body memories are essentially interpersonal. As secure and attuned interactions are nurturing and empowering to us, they also bring pleasure which is experienced in the body and is then stored there. This has a positive impact on the general state of the body-self.

In an interdisciplinary exchange on the concept of body memory (Pylvänäinen 2010), the shared consensus was that body memory is a bodily resonance in relation to some lived experience. However, as the nervous system and the brain integrate information, body memories may become associated with olfactory information, visual imagery, sounds and/or words that are related to the situation. Body memory is a hybrid of time, space and kinesthesia. It has potential to make the past present through embodied reminiscence, and yet it also may enable the person to recognize that the present moment is distanced from the past. Body memory influences the state of the body as it has an impact on how the present moment is experienced. Importantly, body memory shapes the person's perception of his/her window of tolerance; what s/he feels s/he can hold in his/her body and not to break. The contents of body memory arise from how we are in relation with the other – how the body-self interacts with the other and what kind of imprint that leaves into the body. Not only is body memory shaped by the interactions with the other and our experiences of ourselves, it is also shaped by our interactions with nature and environment. The patterns that the body repeats in the tension cycles and body-attitudes in its relation to space and environment are contents of body memory (Shahar-Levy 2009:275). Body memory stores our experiences; what we have learnt through our experiences on the embodied level. The contents of body memory are created through the interactive body-self.

Body memory perceived through the neurosciences

Kandel, a Nobel Prize winning neuroscientist, whose molecular biological approach has revolutionized human understanding of how information received by our senses becomes hard-wired, is an inspiring source of knowledge also when deepening the understanding of body memory. In the year 2000 Kandel received the Nobel Prize in Physiology and Medicine for his contributions to the study of memory storage in the brain. Kandel differentiates two kinds of memory: implicit and explicit memory, both of which can function in either short-term or long-term storage of information. He defines conscious memory as explicit or declarative memory: conscious recall of people, places, objects, facts, and events. Unconscious memory refers to implicit or procedural memory: habituation, sensitization, classical conditioning, perceptual and motor skills (Kandel 2007: 132). Implicit memory guides us through well-established routines that are not consciously controlled (ibid.: 279). This unconscious, implicit memory seems to equal with the content that has been related to body memory. Kandel notes, "that constant repetition can transform explicit memory into implicit memory. Implicit memory often has an automatic quality. It is recalled directly through performance, without any conscious effort or even awareness that we are drawing on memory" (ibid.: 132). This is particularly true for habitual body memory, but also for traumatic and erotic body memory. Implicit memories of skills, habits, and conditioning are stored in the cerebellum, striatum, and amygdala (ibid.: 130).

Body memory on a cellular level is manifest in how the neural pathways are shaped to store information relating to sensations and kinesthetic responses in the body. Information processing patterns and response patterns on the neural level are shaped by experience. In his scientific work, Kandel's particular interest has been around what actually goes on at the level of the synapse when behavior is modified by learning and how different forms of learning and memory relate to each other on the cellular level. He studied these phenomena on the cellular level in a fairly simple snail-like animal, Aplysia, and was able to show what changes happen in neurons, when the animal learns through habituation, sensitization, and conditioning. He also studied how this learning becomes stored in implicit memory. Even though we like to think that humans are different from snails, a biological fact is that different organisms – and different types of cells – are made from the same material. Half of the genes expressed in the human genome are present in much simpler invertebrate animals, such as the snail Aplysia (Kandel 2007: 245). Thus the neural phenomena Aplysia demonstrates also essentially apply to humans.

At the core of the lessons from Aplysia is the unfolding of the fact, that the living body and its nervous system learn from the sensations received from the environment. There are many kinds of learning, and one kind of learning – and eventually memory – is mediated by sensory neurons, interneurons, and motor neurons. Kandel (2007: 66–67) sums Cajal's early findings on the nervous system:

> Sensory neurons, which are located in the skin and in various sense organs, respond to specific type of stimulus from the outside world – mechanical pressure (touch), light (vision), sound waves (hearing), or specific chemicals (smell and taste) – and send this information to the brain. Motor neurons send their axons out of the brain stem and spinal cord to effector cells, such as muscle and gland cells, and control the activity of those cells. Interneurons, the most numerous class of neurons in the brain, serve as relays between sensory and motor neurons.

By increasing the amount of glutamate a sensory cell sends to a motor cell, sensitization strengthens the synaptic potential elicited in the motor neuron, thus making it easier for that neuron to fire an action potential and cause the response pattern (ibid.:222). Thus there is a response pattern that is created by the living body and its nervous system: initiated by sensory information received by the sensory neurons, and executed by the motor, kinesthetic activity. The motor, kinesthetic action is related to a sensory perception, and the information from the sensory perception is transmitted by the intermediary neurons. The serotonin-releasing interneurons are called modulatory interneurons because they do not mediate behavior directly; rather, they modify the strength of response (the gill-withdrawal reflex in *Aplysia*) by enhancing the strength of the connections between sensory and motor neurons (ibid.:223). The organism has, and indeed needs, an integration of sensory, tactile, proprioceptive, and motor efferent information; it is the essence of its ability for intelligent action, which can be shaped by information from the environment and the organism's own state. Going to synaptic level, Kandel and his colleagues found that in implicit memory

> ... the same synaptic connections between sensory and motor neurons that are altered in short-term habituation and sensitization are also altered in long-term habituation and sensitization. Specifically, in long-term habituation the number of presynaptic connections among sensory neurons and motor neurons decreases, where as in long-term sensitization sensory neurons grow new connections that persist as long as the memory is retained. There is in each case a parallel set of changes in the motor cell. (ibid.:213)

The learning and its storage in memory thus shape the nervous system. In relation to body memory, some fascinating and also baffling questions arise: Is something I just experienced part of my body memory immediately after the lived moment? What is the nature of connections between body memory and the body-self? How dominant is the role of body memory in the choice of responses and actions the body-self expresses? Pondering on these questions can organize the understanding of body image and body memory. In Kandel's work, some perspectives on these questions may be found. He discovered a clear pattern in the changes that take place in a single sensory and motor cell for short- and long-term memory. A modulatory interneuron is activated by a sensory cell, which receives information from a body part. The way of signaling the modulatory neuron uses is the transmission of serotonin to the sensory neuron that is directly connected to a motor neuron (Kandel 2007:224). Kandel discovered in his experiments that one brief pulse of serotonin strengthened the synaptic connection between the sensory and motor neuron for a few minutes by enhancing the release of glutamate from the sensory cell. Glutamate is a major excitatory neurotransmitter. A functional change happens as the synapse is strengthened via this enhanced release of glutamate. At this stage, the nucleus of the cell is not involved. According to Kandel, this is the phenomenon under short-term memory. Anatomical change happens after several (5) pulses of serotonin: the synthesis of proteins in the nucleus is activated and new synaptic connections grow, as well as the release of glutamate is enhanced (ibid.:255–256). If we boldly try to apply this information on the level of body memory, we would have to ask, how strong is the impact of an experience – is it just "one pulse of serotonin" or "several pulses of serotonin", which would make the nucleus of the neuron change, and thus lead to a long-term storage of the information? This is quite an abstract and technical question, but it does guide us toward acknowledging, that experiences are sensed in varying intensity by our sensory system. The stronger or more repetitive the stimulus, the stronger the signaling and the more happens in the neurons, which increases the possibility that the neurons may become transformed by the signaling for a shorter or even longer period of time.

Could we assume then, that the body-self, i.e. our sensory and motor systems, act and respond, and when some more permanent transformation happens in the configuration of the connections between the neurons in these systems, then a new body-memory trace has settled into the system? It may be very relevant to recognize that the nervous system is in a state of constant change in its almost infinite connections. The human brain contains about 100 billion neurons (Kandel 2007: 443), and some of them function as sensory neurons. The amount of connections between the nerve cells is huge: Kandel shares Bailey's and Chen's finding that a single sensory neuron has approximately 1300 presynaptic terminals with which it contacts about 25 different target cells – motor neurons, excitatory interneurons, and inhibitory interneurons (ibid.: 214). So a change in one connection is a very minor change in this network of connections, and yet it has some impact on the way the nervous system and the brain process information. Kandel states: "The cellular mechanisms of learning and memory reside not in the special properties of the neuron itself, but in the connections it receives and makes with other cells in the neuronal circuit to which it belongs (ibid.: 142)". In the constant processes of experiencing and acting, the neurons make connections, indeed struggle to make connections with each other. The connectedness defines the survival and development of a neuron (Cozolino 2002); the integration of the nervous system defines the survival and development of an organism; and this pattern is repeated in the significance of connectedness and interaction between individuals. There must be some stability in the connections to enable and organize the functioning, and there must be some changes in the connections as live processes take place.

In a lived experience, it is clear that the body-self and body memory are closely connected. The body-self responds and acts in the here and now, and in its responses it is informed by information stored the body memory: the habits, the learnt thresholds and response patterns. But, in our actions, do we only repeat what we have already learnt? If we place the functions of sensitivity, kinesthesia and attention to the body-self, there opens up an option for choice and the creation of new activity. I propose that the body-self creatively shapes the response from the information body-memory offers and on the basis of the present sensations and information from the environment. It becomes essential, what is the focus of attention, and how much consciousness plays in. Kandel (2007: 302) quotes Mountcastle:

> ... sensory nerve fibers, (are) our only information channels, our lifelines to re-
> ality. They provide also what is essential for life itself; an afferent excitation that
> maintains the conscious state, the awareness of self. Sensations are set by the
> encoding functions of sensory nerve endings, and by the integrating neural me-
> chanics of the central nervous system.

Kandel (2007: 313) reminds us, that in the field of psychology already one of the original thinkers, William James pointed out that there is more than one form of attention.
Involuntary attention is supported by automatic neural processes and it is particularly
evident in implicit memory. Involuntary attention is activated by a property of the
external world. Voluntary attention is a specific feature of explicit memory and arises
from the internal need to process stimuli that are not automatically salient. I propose
the body-self holds both involuntary and voluntary attention. The coupling of consciousness with attention defines whether the attention is involuntary or voluntary.

According to Kandel (2007: 374), "consciousness is a state of perceptual awareness, or selective attention writ large. At its core, consciousness in people, is an awareness of self, an awareness of being aware, ability to experience and attend to and
reflect upon those experiences." The ability for attention and consciousness that the
body-self holds enables the channelling of some of the contents of body memory into
our conscious processing. I propose the body-self holds the ability for consciousness
and attention because we need to be attentive to and conscious about something:
initially that something would be our sensory perceptions which can be perceived
only through the body. Kandel (ibid.: 383) makes an interesting reference to the work
of Crick and Koch, who proposed that in the brain, claustrum may be a population
of nerve cells that mediates the unity of consciousness. Claustrum is a sheet of brain
tissue that is located below the cerebral cortex. Claustrum connects to and exchanges
information with almost all of the sensory and motor regions of the cortex as well as
the amygdala, which plays an important role in emotion. It is significant, that all of
the neural networks relating also to implicit learning and memory – sensory and motor networks and amygdala – are areas that the claustrum is connected to as it makes
consciousness emerge. This, I propose, indicates that the body-self is involved with
the creation and maintenance of consciousness and attention. And yet, in the present
moment, for these functions, the body-self needs the connections to body memory.

Fascinating in this regard is the finding, which Kandel brings up from studies by
Kornhuber and Libert (Kandel 2007: 389–390). Kornhuber found in his experiment,
that invariably, each movement of the right index finger his study subjects executed
was preceded by a little blip in the electrical record of the activity in the brain. He
called this potential in the brain the "readiness potential" and found, that it occurred
one second before the voluntary movement. Later Libert found that the readiness
potential appeared 200 milliseconds before a person consciously felt an urge to move
his/her finger. Libert proposes that the process of initiating a voluntary action occurs
in an unconscious part of the brain, but that just before the action is initiated, consciousness is recruited to approve or veto the action. The body-self may start some

activity unconsciously, and at some point of the process, the activity may become conscious.

The body-self is active and responding in the present. The brain actually has a more limited capacity for processing sensory information than what is the capacity for measuring environment in the body and receptors (Kandel 2007: 311). Attention acts as a filter, selecting some objects for further processing, and yet, attention does not necessarily imply consciousness. For example, studies have shown, that the neural system stores both unconscious, emotionally charged memories and conscious, explicit memories of feelings. They are stored because unconsciously or consciously, attention was paid to the stimuli that evoked the emotions and feelings. In the neurological research of emotion processing in humans, the unconscious recall of emotional memory has been shown to involve implicit memory storage, whereas conscious remembrance of the feeling state has been shown to involve explicit memory storage and therefore to require the hippocampus (ibid.: 342). Using the perception of fearful faces as the setting in which to study the unconscious and conscious perception of emotional information, Kandel and his colleagues (ibid.: 387) found out, that in the unconscious perception of fearful faces neural activation takes place in the basolateral nucleus of amygdala, which receives the most of incoming sensory information and is the primary means by which amygdala communicates with the cortex. In the conscious perception of fearful faces the neural activation is located in the dorsal region of amygdala, which contains the central nucleus, sending information to the regions of the brain that are part of the autonomic nervous system – concerned with arousal and defensive responses. In both instances, body-self mediated information is needed and processed. This again gives ground to the understanding, that body-self can be functioning both consciously and unconsciously.

The connections and exchange between the body-self and body memory are fundamental; they enable each other and function in an orchestrated way. In the study about the perception of fearful faces (Kandel 2007: 387), it was also discovered, that the higher the person's background anxiety, the greater the person's response. People with low background anxiety had no response at all in the case of unconscious perception of fearful faces. Unconsciously perceived threats disproportionally affected people with high background anxiety, where as consciously perceived threats activated fight-or-flight response in all volunteers in Kandel's and colleagues' study. Background anxiety is presumably developed in connection with earlier experiences, and that information is stored in body memory. Another interesting view to the interconnectedness of the body-self and body memory appears in the neural phenomenon that in the unconscious perception of an emotional signal, the signal goes to those parts of the amygdala which communicate with the cortex, whereas in the conscious perception the signal is sent onwards to the autonomic nervous system, which shapes the state of arousal and defensive responses (ibid.: 387). What happens then, when the state of arousal changes and some defensive responses are activated? Defensive responses may be perceived as information stored in body memory, particularly in habitual and traumatic body memory. Through these changes in the responsive body-self, the person has more embodied information and more time and chances to attend to it. In doing this the body-self is actively involved, again combining the information from body memory and from the present situation.

If the understanding is, that body memory influences the state of the body-self in the present moment, how does it do it? The tension patterns, for example the background anxiety, are one channel for body-memory to shape the state and responses of the body-self. Koch (2007) reports some interesting results from experiments on how movement in the present moment influences person's affect or cognitive evaluations. She had participants move the arms in either fighting or indulgent movement qualities. The results showed that when movement had a quality of fighting rhythms, it caused higher negative affect (tense, aggressive, nervous, etc.). The quality of indulgent rhythms caused higher positive affect (relaxed, joyful, playful, etc.). In two other experiments she studied the influence of movement rhythms (indulgent versus fighting movement rhythms) and movement shape (approach versus avoidance arm movement) on attitudes toward initially valence free Chinese ideographs (cf. Cacioppo, Priester & Berntson 1993). These studies indicated that when movement was indulgent in rhythm and approaching in shape it evoked the most positive attitudes toward the initially valence-free Chinese ideographs. The quality combination of indulgent rhythm and avoidance shape produced the least positive attitudes. The combination of fighting rhythm with either approaching or avoidance shape caused fairly similar impact on attitudes, and in both instances the attitudes were significantly less positive than in the condition of indulgent rhythm and approaching shape. However, when the combination was congruent, i.e. fighting rhythm was combined with avoidance shape, the attitudes where more positive than when the combination was clashing, i.e. the indulgent rhythm was combined with avoidance shape. I find it very interesting to consider these results in relation to body memory: what kind of experiences and learning have previously related to these rhythm and shape combinations? It seems, that the activation of positive body memories – indulgence signaling safety and approaching signaling connection and gratifying encounter – has the most positive impact on the present state of the body-self and the experienced affect and attitudes. The fighting quality combined with either approaching or avoidance shape produces somewhat positive attitudes. This could echo the experiences of successful use of own strength, which may activate a sense of agency and sense of control. The least positive impact on attitudes arises from the clashing combination of indulging rhythm and avoidance shape, which in combination may relate to experiences of displeasure, the loss of volition and sense of agency. In these ways, the qualities of our interactions, which become stored in the body memory, return to influence the responses the body-self creates in the present moment.

Encountering the body memory in a dance/movement therapy group

In my work as a psychologist in a psychiatric outpatient clinic, facilitating a dance/ movement therapy (DMT) group, it is fascinating to explore how the concept of body image is reflected in the experiences the patients have in a DMT process. The source of the vignettes presented in the following is a 15-session DMT group for eight women, aged 21–59 years. The group members have signed a consent form allowing the sharing of the material from the group in this text in a manner that protects each individual's privacy. The information about the group is stored in written process notes that I kept in order to support the containment and understanding of the process. There is no video material about the sessions. Consequently, all the information about the embodied, sensory experiences that evolved in the sessions has had to be transformed into words for the purpose of communicating about them in this text.

The patients in the group had various diagnoses: depression (moderate or severe), bi-polar disorder (depressive phase), ADD, eating disorder and social anxiety disorder. Several of the patients had a challenging life situation, e.g. a chronically demanding family situation, burn-out from work, significant changes in relationships or personal roles. Many of the patients had traumatic experiences in their life-history. Two of the patients had gone through an individual psychotherapy (2.5 and 3 yrs), one had received individual psychophysical physiotherapy for a year, one had participated in a group for patients with eating disorders and one had studied expressive therapy. All of the patients had received individual counseling or supportive therapy at the clinic prior to this group. Thus, all of the patients had some experience and skills in reflecting on their experiences. Most of them used medication to support their recovery.

The patients were chosen for participation in this group on the basis of their own interest in doing movement based work and their willingness to participate in a group. In an initial interview the patient's situation was discussed. Mostly the focus was in the present, screening also the patient's experience and thoughts about her body: how she has moved recently, what preferences she has in movement, what her opinions or concerns in relation to her body were. Often the narrative about one's body connected with the mood, the level of the sense of agency and with self-appraisal, i.e. how content or discontent the patient was with herself.

One of the goals of the initial interview was to discuss the personal themes and/ or goals for the patient's participation in the group. The patients (with their avatar names) are here in the order of age, the eldest first:

> Amalia: To continue the exploration of embodiment and the development of regulation skills for the state of tension one holds in the body.

> Birgitta: Exploring the tensions one carries in one-self. Patient also noticed she needs to develop her skill to recognize and describe and differentiate what is one's bodily experience and what is the feeling.

Carla: Exploring the fact that one is middle-aged and lives in a certain way. As her life situation was challenging, the patient expected the DMT group to function as a refueling place. At the start of the group she also thought that the verbal sharing about one's experiences in the group could be a positive and supportive element of the work.

Dora: To explore embodiment, to improve body awareness and the ability to be attentive to the body in everyday life, to deepen one's understanding about the connections between body and mood. Patient was also interested in exploring gentleness and interaction through movement.

Eva: To continue to reflect on one's bodily responses; this patient had already made significant notions about her response patterns which were built on her experiences in earlier interactions in her life. She wanted to maintain the possibility to be engaged with moving and physical activity. Participating in a group therapy was new for her, and she was curious about it. One theme in the process was coming to terms with one's expectations and with what one does in reality. The patient had experienced several disappointments of placing hard expectations on herself and then finding the situation impeding.

Fanni: To strengthen one's sense of self, to develop stress management skills and the ability to relax. The patient was interested in developing her own way of doing, her own space, and her own tempo in her sense of agency. This related to her work and also to her way of participating in social interaction. Since the patient was pregnant at the start of the group, the DMT group would also allow her to encounter her changing body and her path into motherhood in movement interactions.

Gail: The patient had noticed her body image as unstable; sometimes she would be content, sometimes discontent with it. She would like to develop a skill to orient towards her body and movement from an internal rather than external perspective. She also would like to develop her body image towards being able to tolerate the changes that in her future may come along with pregnancy and motherhood.

Hanna: As the patient had recognized her body image was distorted, she wanted to explore it. She had undergone a psychotherapy and wanted to embody the learning she had achieved there: to talk about herself, to be gentle and merciful towards one-self. She found relaxing difficult and was interested in developing the ability to relax. For her, the weekly routine and structure provided by the group was also welcome. She wished the DMT group to be a place to listen to one-self.

The body image related themes came up in various ways in the patients' individual themes. Most of them related to the body-self: developing skills to recognize and

regulate the state of the body-self, the sensations and tensions in the body-self, bringing the body-self into interaction, differentiating between sensations and emotions.
The exchange between body-memory and the body-self become apparent when a patient acknowledged the impact of her past life events on her typical ways of reacting
and responding with her body-self. No-one in the group placed her themes or expectations directly in the image-properties, but rather, the image-properties topics were
filtered through the body-self, e.g. in Gail's theme of learning to relate to her body
through internal experience instead of the perspective of an external gaze.

When the group worked together for the first time in the first session, the goals
the group as a unit held were explored. The group members chose a postcard with an
image which had something that interested them. Later, after a movement warm-up,
we returned to these cards with a question "what do these images contain that expresses something one wants to bring into the group as a quality in interaction or as a
theme to work on?". This was first expressed verbally, and we then improvised movement holding in consciousness the themes that emerged in the verbal sharing. In this
indirect and creative way the patients shaped some goals for the group:

> secure space
> physicality
> trust, safety – feeling – happiness, joyfulness – calming down
> caring – there is support – helping each other – sharing joys and sorrows
> together
> being different, going into the same direction – there is space for each person
> it does not matter even if one's wing was hurt – freeing one-self from old
> dependencies
> adventure – something forms, ripens – nourishment for the soul

Grouped in this way, the goals actually unfold a theme of a developmental process:
sense of safety, physicality, emotion, gratifying interaction, tolerance of difference,
acceptance and change, and adventuring into something unknown, which can be
nourishing. Even though the group did not present its goals in this grouping order,
it molded its essential nature through this list of words. All these words relate to secure and attuned interaction which enables the individual to explore and integrate
the experiences. In particular, these words describe a physical, emotional, and social
environment which allows the body-self to be fully engaged. The patients described it
spontaneously, initially orienting with their sense of interest.

In the therapy process that unfolded over the 15 sessions approximately half
of the time was spent in movement and half in discussing the experiences. Central
themes were group formation, exploring moving in the group and exploring one's
own kinesthesia. At some points, an educational approach was utilized and the patients received information about body image, body memory, embodiment, the significance of the non-verbal in interaction and about mindfulness. This information
supported the patients in getting a cognitive perspective on and understanding of the

movement work, and also in developing an accepting and non-judgmental attitude towards one's embodied experiences. The group was committed to this work. As the trust in the group developed, also the troubles and difficulties in relation to one's body and in interaction started to emerge in the sharing. In its interactions, the group created support to the members. Through the creative process of moving and verbalizing, the group members had several meaningful insights into their situation, which helped them to understand themselves and their ways of coping in their everyday lives. In this process, the body image changed: there was more respect, consciousness, and compassion in relation to one's body image.

The process brought up body memory related issues with varying nuances. Sometimes a *movement pattern* activated body memory. For example Carla, in the middle of a confusing and rushed life situation, in session three, found a rolling movement on the floor, which gave her an embodied experience of being carried by the floor, relaxation and trust. The movement also reminded her of her childhood plays, where rolling was a sort of releasing and letting go. This made her note that now in adulthood one can also let go, ease, and enjoy it; that it is important to acknowledge both the strong, fighting side and the indulging side in oneself.

Sometimes it was a *movement quality* that activated a body memory. In one interaction situation, Carla and Amalia felt that the interaction was uncomfortable, unsatisfying. When talking about this experience and reminiscing on what was the trouble, a mismatch in their tempos was discovered. Carla had felt the tempo of the shared movement was rushed, too quick. Her immediate response was unwillingness to join this, a desire to take her own space and tempo. Simultaneously, she was reminded that in her professional and family life she had for years been going along the tempos and needs the others brought in. She remembered the repeated situations with her mother who was always rushing her when it was time to get going, controlling her in this way. Carla observed that these childhood and work-life memories of forced tempos activated in her stomach a tight, pressing, squeezing sensation, which was radiating into the back.

Sometimes the elicited patterns of body memory were acknowledged specifically as *a coping mechanism*. For Amalia, in the above mentioned interaction with Carla, the mismatch of connection and tempos brought a notion about her way of coping over the years: when in an uncomfortable and non-motivating situation, she has tried to use quickness as a way to get through the moment. This had also meant shutting off the sensing, just performing. This interaction made her notice and pay attention to this often used coping pattern. In the discussion, the option of a more sustained tempo was connected with the possibility of sensing more, when it is safe to sense. In this way, the old, body memory based coping pattern received some new input for the future.

Like in the previous example of Carla's and Amalia's experience, it quite often was *the social, interactional situation*, which was the key to activate the surfacing of the body memory. In some moments the history of interactions was alluded to through self-reflections. For example, Birgitta commented in one session, that it is very

difficult to find one's own movement when for the whole life-time one had to always do what others told to. In an other session Birgitta experienced again something
which was deeply connected with her body memories. The theme was to move with
a cotton cloth. These cotton cloths were differently patterned. Birgitta had quickly
picked up the cloth with a pattern she desired, and someone remarked, she would
also have wanted that cloth. This had made Birgitta to feel guilty, and she shrinkingly
curled under the cloth, becoming invisible, in a small shape and feeling she no longer
exists. She noticed, that the old traumas of moments when feeling "I am not existing"
joined into the present experience. Quietly she pulled and pressed the cloth into her
fist and then threw it away, with a genuine feeling of disgust and rejection. After a little
while she stood up, walked after the cloth, picked it up and folded it into her hands,
squeezed it with full strength, and felt hatred towards the cloth. At the same time she
collected herself into an upright, handsome stance, and then felt clearly she was existing. It was also fascinating, that in the cloth Birgitta chose for herself, the pattern was
small dots, which Birgitta described as a representation of her feelings of smallness
(inferiority). She thought a large pattern might have been attractive to her as well, but
she would have been unable to take it. At the end of her movement, her own body
shape was a large pattern.

Quite frequently, body memory emerged in a subtle way, intertwined with the
body-self in the present, reflecting *life history and the way of being in one's body, that
has been shaped by the past experiences*. In these moments, there was not necessarily
a sense of dealing with a memory nor of dealing with the past. The body memory
entered the present moment through habitual patterns of sensing, moods, and bodily
states. At the first glance one might have thought the patient's response is solely arising
from the present situation, but as similar patterns kept returning in slightly different
situations, it gradually became possible to perceive the impact of body memory in the
responses. For example Eva, in a long phase of depression, at the start of the therapy
process said that she felt, metaphorically speaking, a difficulty in going through her
own birth, she felt a need of nurturance and a sense of not being alone. In the second
session, in her movement she discovered that she is able to do movement by receiving good support from the ground. In the fifth session, through a theme of moving
a picture drawn to represent one's mood, Eva discovered a squatting position, where
she begun to feel sleepy. She surrendered into her bodily desire to rest, lay on her
back on the floor, and in so doing, realized this was possible: she continued to exist
even though she felt tired or even fell asleep. The curiosity about movement did not
escape from her even if she allowed herself to sense her tiredness. In the middle of the
therapy process, she frequently sensed her bodily heaviness, agitation, tightness in the
muscles and breathing, and tiredness. Occasionally her sensory perceptions about her
body brought to her attention that she was feeling comfortable as she engaged with
movement: it was easier to breathe when standing than when sitting, self-touch clarified the body boundaries and a smile eased her state in another session. One day she
noticed moving felt easy and free-flowing. In session ten she noted, that even though
her situation in her everyday life was much improved now, her body could not let go

of the sense of a struggle, which stayed inside her, while on the outside she seemed calm. The discomfort, that "was" her in the middle phase of the therapy, now started to emerge as something she could consciously and deliberately observe and reflect on. The old patterns of being in the body, shaped by her body memory, had been repeatedly encountered in the activity of the body-self in the present, and the reflection on these sensations gradually allowed a more conscious relationship to them. In a later session, Eva's discomfort and restlessness in the moment significantly eased as she played with dropping down and picking up a cotton cloth. In this movement, she said she was exploring the idea that she could release her own controlling and let things settle on their own. At the end of this movement exploration, she sat down and loosely entwined the cloth around her own ankles. She thought the entwining contained her restlessness, but she wondered how it could do so, as the binding was not tight at all. I suggested, perhaps the contact, just the resting in contact with something, was helpful. As a movement metaphor, this action in an implicit way echoed the patient's need to experience nurturance and to not be alone. The next session she did not feel restless.

The lived experience in the body is the base

In the group process, it was central to take time for the development of the sense of the group, familiarizing with moving in a group, and with the motility and sensory information in one's own body. The participants were exploring and encountering their own body image in the process through movement and reflection. At the start of the process, the participants spontaneously brought up themes that shaped safety and a sense of connectedness in the group. This is the base, a setting for the body-self to be encountered. The more we moved and observed ourselves in movement, the more information we had, which also opened the path for facing the contents of body memory. This process elicited different kinds of responses, emotions, and thoughts. The written feedback from the group members at the end of the group process demonstrated this as follows:

> Amalia: DMT brought to her an experience that *her body is releasing tensions and burdens*. She frequently felt good and relaxed after the sessions. She felt a relief in her body every time she noticed emotional tensions were released. Often after the sessions Amalia felt energetic and wanted to talk (often about past events), *to pour out her thoughts also verbally*. She found her physical and mental well-being had improved.

> Birgitta: She found DMT to be fun. She discovered new sides of herself and her body. *She did not like to take a leadership role in Chacian circles* (an improvisational movement method of DMT). Her experience was that she gained more self-confidence and acceptance towards her body in the group. After the process, she also felt proud of herself since she always made herself come to the sessions.

Carla: Moving in the group made Carla to *learn about her body and its rhythms. She also found different personal meanings to small and large movements.* For her, moving was refreshing and it gave her strength. In the group setting, she learnt to focus on herself even though there were others around. She came to appreciate her body as her most precious and unique possession.

Dora: The experience of the DMT process allowed Dora to connect with her embodied sensations and feelings that might have otherwise been hidden or differently understood on the verbal level. She was several times surprised by what she found her body telling in movement and dance. She was able to live emotional states as she focused on movement. Moving helped to *release tensions* that easily accumulate in the body. For her, the process was an expedition into the body. She found the body to hold wisdom and truthfulness. She developed the skill of perceiving the messages of the body in herself. "Reading" the other's body was a challenge, and she noticed one often makes conclusions based on what one perceives in one's own body. She felt the group became familiar during the process, it was easy to be in it and sharing felt good, it was possible to be what one is. Hearing the experiences of others gave help and brought new ideas. In group, she also noticed *which feelings were easy to share and which she tended to hide from others, for example tears.*

Eva: In DMT group, Eva noticed she longs for moving since moving brings her pleasure and allows her to connect with her sensations in her body. She noticed she tends to pay a lot of attention to strains and other unpleasant sensations in the body. For her, the movement tasks first felt complicated or difficult to enter, but in most occasions, she found into the movement and it did reflect her state in the moment. *She had found reinforcement to what kind of movements and being were typical of her, and also insights to why this was so.* Eva discovered her body as being curious also about new kinds of movement – and whether she experienced them difficult or positive, depended on her mental condition.

Fanni: Participating in the group helped Fanni *to alleviate social anxiety.* She discovered it felt good to concentrate and listen to others – opening up to the shared communication instead of withdrawing into an internal dialogue. The alternation of conversation and moving felt good to her. Through movement and touch it was easy, or easier, to work with themes that were difficult for her. She made a notion that facing and accepting one's self-centeredness was hard.

Gail: In the beginning it was difficult for her to move when others were present and could see her, but gradually her *trust strengthened, timidity eased, and moving became less of an act of performing.* Through the DMT process she found a new way of relating to *the unpleasant sensations in her body: she could take a more observing and reflective stance toward them which made her less anxious about her embodied sensations.* She felt her relationship to her own body became slightly more friendly and accepting.

Hanna: DMT was often a puzzling experience: while moving, she felt she did not get enough out of it, but after a few days or weeks, she noticed that *something from the movement exercise and experience had stayed in her mind and adhered in to her daily life.* After the DMT process she listened more to her body, wondering what her sensations might mean. She felt able to describe her physical experiences in words and to connect them with what was going on in her mind. One of the most significant experiences in the DMT group for Hanna was the concretization of her body image. She had hoped to learn to perceive her real physical boundaries, and after the DMT process she perceived and felt them more clearly than before. She found a new kind of appreciation toward embodiment.

How was body memory involved in what the group members consciously recognized of their DMT experience? Generally, the release of tension relates to body memory, as the body often is a container of tension. Amalia's experience of feeling an urge to also verbally release her stories after having had an experience of a body-based release of tensions, seems to indicate, that there are connections between body memory and explicit, narrative memory. Body memory appears in some patients' feedback in the context of old, social behavioral patterns, such as in Birgitta's comment about the difficulty to take a leadership role. In her life experience she had learnt an opposite role, and in her body memory the response patterns of trying to be invisible and compliant were dominating. Her efforts of trying out new roles and new ways of responding could be understood as her body-self creating new alternatives in the present moment, negotiating between the old patterns drawn from the body memory and the present potentials. Also, the patterns of social withdrawal vs. engagement, which appeared in Fanni's experience, are rooted in body memory. Dora's comment about the differences in how she expressed socially different emotions also relates to learnt interaction patterns, which have much to do with body memory. Trust, an aspect that Gail's text referred to, is to a large extent shaped by very early body memory. Carla's experience of learning about the rhythms in her body and the meanings associated with small and large movements was clearly connected with body memory, as in the DMT process she recollected her life-history relating to these qualities. Here the connecting with the contents of body memory supported her body-self to create new patterns and ways of relating to the environment.

The DMT process clearly elicited new discoveries and learning in the group members. It added new contents to their body memory, new response patterns for interaction situations. One essential aspect seemed to be the change in thresholds; Gail phrased it clearly when she described she could take a more observing and reflecting stance at the sensations she perceived in her body, which made her less anxious. A sensation from then on was not so much of an alarm for her but something that could be neutrally observed. This kind of change helps the body-self to maintain more tolerable levels of tension or vigilance, which echoes in the state of the whole nervous system.

In their own words, patients do not talk about body memory. They talk about their lived experience. The lived experience in the body is the base. This experience could be examined on a microscopic level, which would reveal the constant work of the neurons. In the human experience the firing of nerve cells truly remains on an implicit level, and we can only connect to what the firing activates: sensation, movement, emotion, imagery, words. Yet it is valuable to acknowledge the neurological level, as it has scientifically demonstrated the fantastic nature of a living organism, the miracle that a material, living body is sensitive, responsive, creative, learning, and remembering. This exploration indicates the relevance of paying attention to the information in the body.

Summary

First outlining the body memory from a phenomenological perspective, this chapter then related that view with the information offered by the neurosciences, equaling body memory with implicit memory. Referring to research by Kandel, it was suggested that the living body and its nervous system learn from the sensations received from the environment and from the body itself. The organism needs to integrate the sensory, tactile, proprioceptive and motor efferent information as it is the basis of its ability for intelligent action, which can be shaped by information about the environment and the organism's own state. The ability for attention and consciousness that the body-self maintains, enables the channeling of some of the contents of body memory into our conscious processing. The tension patterns are one channel for body-memory to shape the state and responses of the body-self.

In a clinical dance/movement therapy (DMT) group, facilitated at a psychiatric outpatient clinic, it was possible to observe how patients encounter body memory related issues in DMT. Most of the personal goals the patients had for the DMT group were related to the body-self: developing skills to recognize and regulate the state of the body-self, bringing the body-self into interaction, differentiating between sensations and emotions. In the DMT process, body memory related issues were activated by movement patterns or qualities, or by the social situation. Body memory also appeared in the process through coping patterns and in the ways the patient related to her sensations. The experience of the DMT group process produced new contents to patients' body memory, new response patterns for interaction situations, and more observing and neutral ways of relating to the sensations in the body.

References

Casey, E. S. (1987). *Remembering: A phenomenological study.* Bloomington, IN: Indiana University Press.

Cacioppo, J. T., Priester, J. R. & Berntson, G. (1993). Rudimentary determinants of attitudes II: Arm flexion and extension have differential effects on attitudes. *Journal of Personality and Social Psychology, 65,* 5–17.

Chaiklin, S. & Wengrower, H. (Eds.). (2009). *The art and science of dance/movement therapy. Life is dance.* New York: Routledge.

Cozolino, L. (2002). *The neuroscience of psychotherapy. Building and rebuilding the human brain.* New York: W.W. Norton & Co.

Kandel, E. R. (2006). *In search of memory. The emergence of a new science of mind.* New York: W.W. Norton & Co.

Koch, S. C. (2007). Basic principles of movement analysis: Steps toward validation of the KMP. In S. C. Koch & S. Bender (Eds.), *Movement analysis – Bewegungsanalyse* (pp. 235–248). Berlin: Logos.

Pylvänäinen, P. (2003). Body image: A tri-partite model for use in dance/movement therapy. *American Journal of Dance Therapy, 25,* 39–56.

Pylvänäinen, P. (2006). The tri-partite model of body image and its application to experiences in butoh. In S. C. Koch & I. Bräuninger (Eds.), *Advances in dance/movement therapy. Theoretical perspectives and empirical findings* (pp. 40–51). Berlin: Logos.

Pylvänäinen, P. (2008). A dance/movement therapy group as a community outreach for intercultural women in Tokyo. *Body, Movement and Dance in Psychotherapy, 3*(1), 31–44.

Pylvänäinen, P. (2010). Conference review: Movement – embodiment – body memory, Heidelberg, Germany, 6–8 October 2008. *Body, Movement and Dance in Psychotherapy, 5 (1),* 95–100.

Shahar-Levy, Y. (2009). Emotorics: A psychomotor model for the analysis and interpretation of emotive motor behavior. In S. Chaiklin & H. Wengrower (Eds.), *The art and science of dance/movement therapy. Life is dance* (pp. 265–297). New York: Routledge.

CHAPTER 19

The embodied word

Heidrun Panhofer,* Helen Payne,** Timothy Parke**
and Bonnie Meekums#
*University Autònoma Barcelona, Spain / **University of Hertfordshire,
England / #University of Leeds, England

During the last decades a narrative outlook has become very popular in many disciplines, including psychotherapy whose central model is based on the exteriorisation of inner worlds through verbalisation. The following chapter assesses the narrative tradition from an embodiment perspective and explores the extent to which the embodied experience can and needs to be worded. Stemming from the discipline of Dance Movement Psychotherapy (DMP), a psychotherapeutic approach which makes use of embodied perceptual practices such as movement, play and dance, it draws on a recent study (Panhofer 2009) which shows some of the limitations of language. Supporting a psycho-corporeal integration, it emphasizes other possible ways of communicating the embodied experience, such as through metaphors, images, and poetry. Where it is difficult to communicate an inner experience through verbal narration, such as practiced in verbal psychotherapy, metaphors, images and poetry may offer a useful alternative, alongside the embodied perceptual practices such as play, movement, and dance.

Keywords: narrative tradition, embodiment, languaging movement, wording the essence of the therapeutic process, embodied metaphors

The narrative tradition

> Silence, solitude, what is more essential to the human condition? 'Maternal silence' is what I like to call it. Life before the coming of language. That place where we begin to hear the voice of the inanimate. Poetry is an orphan of silence. The words never quite equal the experience behind them. (Simic 1985)

Throughout the last decades a narrative outlook has become very popular not only in psychotherapy, but also in other disciplines such as philosophy, theology, anthropology, sociology, political theory, literary studies, religious studies, and even medicine

(Strawson 2004). In psychotherapy, externalizing the internal world through verbalisation is the traditional model (Strupp & Binder 1984; Tomm 1988; White & Epston 1990; Angus & Hardtke 1994) and has led to the development of "narrative therapy", a psychotherapeutic approach which organizes and structures psychological activity through the construction of narratives. This chapter assesses the narrative tradition from an embodiment perspective and explores the extent to which the embodied experience can and needs to be worded.

The word "narrative" derives from the Latin word *gnarus* and the Proto-Indo-European root *ghnu*, "to know." As an interpretation of some of the characteristics of the world that is historically and culturally grounded and formed by human personality (Fisher 1984), narratives are used in daily communication as a means of sense making, or to better understand events, people, places, etc.

In psychotherapy literature, the term "narrative" has come to have different connotations and usage. Narratives can be real or imagined events that involve the client or others outside therapy (Stiles et al. 1999). Narrative therapy, as an approach to psychotherapy, counseling, and community work, seeks to build on the positive impact of writing on self-understanding and sense of identity. It offers a way of working that is interested in history and the broader context that is affecting people's lives.

Narrative therapy centers on people as being the experts on their own lives, assuming that they have many abilities, competencies, beliefs, values, responsibilities, and skills that will assist them to view their problems from a separate, different perspective and eventually help to integrate and resolve them. The word 'narrative' refers to the emphasis that is placed upon the stories of people's lives and the differences that can be made through particular ways of telling and retelling these stories. The narrative approach looks at diverse approaches of understanding the stories of people's lives, and ways of re-authoring these stories as a collaboration between client and therapist or counselor. It may aid to re-member and re-author past experiences through stories, trace the history, name and situate the problem in a context and discover unique outcomes (Bruner 1986a; White 1988; Parry & Doan 1994; Eron & Lund 1996; Pennebaker & Seagal 1999; Crossley 2000; Gersie 2000; Morgan 2000; Hunt & Samspon 2002; Hieb 2005; Meekums 2005; Schauer, Neuner & Elbert 2005; Gersie & King 2006; Payne 2006).

Richert (2006) draws attention to four fundamental assumptions which are common in narrative psychotherapies. The first assumption elucidates the existence of "first order" and "second order" realities (Watzlawick 1996). Even though a first order reality probably exists and limits our mental constructions, it cannot be known exactly. The typical postmodernist view considers what is real to be a by-product of a socially constructed world (Gergen 2001).

Based on this critical constructivist tradition, the second assumption is that second order realities are built in a narrative structure. Narrative therapists claim that, in order to make sense of their experience, people create narratives and live "in" and "through" their stories (Freedman & Combs 2000; White & Epston 1990). The third assumption is that different people create different stories, and as a result different realities. The concept of a single reality is replaced, acknowledging several realities that depend on the individual and his surrounding social and temporal features. The forth assumption is that a connection is made between "broken stories" and psychological dysfunction: where individuals sees themselves as incompetent and feeble, limiting options make them helpless and ineffectual (Richert 2006).

In Angus and Heineke's (1994) critical review of research literature on narratives in psychotherapy, a suggestion of three conceptualizations of narratives is put forth: "narratives," "the narrative", and "narrative process." Descriptions of single actions or individual stories that clients disclose during their therapy sessions are referred to by them as "narratives." Once several diverse story lines are interwoven into a coherent whole, Angus and Heineke (1994) talk about "the narrative." This can be the beginning of the development of an overall picture, a larger perspective and an important organisation of inter- and intrapersonal themes. Cognitive and emotional processes that aid clients to understand themselves and their interpersonal relationships in a more comprehensive way are called "narrative processes."

According to Meier (2002) a more comprehensive definition and description of narratives still remains to be developed. She also criticizes the lack of published research evaluating narrative therapy and its characteristics and effectiveness.

> Although postmodernist thinking has heightened the awareness of psychologists to the linguistic and cultural structuring of human experiences and problems, it has failed to provide a balanced and holistic view of the same conditions.
> (Meier 2002: 240)

The narrative type versus the non-narrative

The English philosopher Strawson (2004) not only argues against narrative therapy approaches, but also against the fashion for a narrative outlook amongst many disciplines. He challenges the widespread argument that human beings typically experience their lives as a narrative, stating that a good life does not necessarily need to involve a kind of self-telling. He opposes what is often claimed by narrative therapists, namely the concept that all people are essentially storytellers and that storytelling is seen as one of the oldest and most universal forms of communication (Fisher 1984). This "narrative paradigm", a theory proposed by Fisher (1984), indicates that all meaningful communication is a form of storytelling or reporting of events, and therefore human beings live and understand life as a series of continuing narratives, each with its own quality, controversy, characters, beginnings, middles, and ends.

Strawson (2004: 430) on the contrary, argues that by no means are all human beings essentially storytellers: he distinguishes a non-narrative type of individual which he calls the "episodic", and identifies himself with this category, and its opposite, the narrative or "diachronic" type. "Diachronic" considers themselves in the past and in the future, projecting each way in time. Past actions are relevant for the present; they shape the present and will be there in the future. "Diachronics" typically see, live, or experience their lives as a narrative of some sort, or at least as a collection of episodes and stories. Conversely, "episodics" are characterized by their lack of projection in either the past or the future, and are likely to have no particular tendency to tell their life in narrative terms.

> One has little or no sense that the self that one is was there in the (further) past and will be there in the future, although one is perfectly aware that one has long-term continuity considered as a whole human being.   (Strawson 2004: 430)

Whereas Strawson defends the "episodic", non-narrative life as a normal and as a positive, non-pathological form of human being, others claim that a narrative orientation is essential for a successful, healthy life: "Narrative is the primary scheme by means of which human experience is rendered meaningful" affirms Polkinghorne (1988: 11) as if an *episodic*, non narrative view had no meaning, and "People's capacities to tell coherent stories about themselves is a consequence of good childhood experiences," states Launer (2006: 342), as if those who have not had a happy childhood would be incapable of a narrative outlook. A similar position can also be perceived in the Adult Attachment Interview (George, Kaplan & Main 1985, 1996), a semi-structured interview based on attachment theory conducted along the lines of a psychotherapy assessment (Holmes 2001). Rather than looking at the content itself, the way how the stories are told is assessed in order to evaluate an individual's type of attachment.

Identity and the narrative tradition

A German proverb states: "*Gesichtslos ist geschichtslos*" – no face, no history. Pondering on this saying, one may come to the conclusion that those who have no history do not know who they are. Therefore, it claims, a coherent sense of one's personal story is vital for one's identity. Strawson cites Campbell (1994) and reflects on his wish to be a "Mr. Nobody" like the "*Mann ohne Eigenschaften*" (Man without traits) in Robert Musil's work. Born in very poor circumstances, Musil (1880–1942) witnesses the last days of the Austro-Hungarian monarchy. A long lasting empire, with a clear set of rules and conventions falls apart, and Musil, himself married to a Jewish woman, emigrates to Switzerland where he dies in 1942 in complete poverty. Musil's analysis of the vanishing monarchy of the emperor Franz Joseph is portrayed in the protagonist of the book, Ulrich, a man from high society, good-looking and rich. Musil emphasizes how all of Ulrich's clothes are embroidered with the capital letters of his name, as if he wanted to highlight the strong sense of identity that once had been experienced in Ulrich's life. Despite these outer signs of a clear character Ulrich lives in a time where all values have become irrelevant and, at 32 years of age, he cannot recognize a global order any more. Disillusioned and frustrated, he decides to take a holiday from his own life in order to understand its secret mechanisms. He retreats into passivity, a mere reflective attitude, where as a "man without traits" he is no more man but mere matter. Musil's novel, *"Roman einer Endzeit"* (novel of a terminal epoch) portrays the clear loss of identity, the end of an area, its belief systems, order and integrity.

Accordingly, Strawson opposes strongly Campell's wish to become such a "Mr. Nobody," underlining the importance of identity and his own clear sense of personality. Yet for him, "…it is only the present shaping consequences of the past that matter, not the past as such" (Strawson 2004: 438). In fact, he agrees that some aspects of the past are indeed important. But what defines these "present shaping consequences of the past that matter" (Strawson 2004: 438)? Considering the work of the neurologist Antonio Damasio and his somatic marker hypothesis, a new light can be shed on Strawson's critique. Somatic Markers, according to Damasio (1994), form the basis of human consciousness. They are the way in which cognitive representations of the external world interact with cognitive representations of the internal world – where perceptions interact with emotions. Emotions are cognitive representations of body states, therefore the body is considered an important container for these past and present moments. Perhaps the *episodic type*, as described above, is not necessarily unable to tell a coherent story of his life, but processes, accesses, and communicates his cognitive representations of body states in a different, rather corporeal way.

Barsalou's (1999) perceptual symbol system theory would support this view: It shows clearly that cognition is inherently perceptual, and integrates the positive contributions of the different existing approaches to knowledge, namely, according to him (ibid) representation, statistical processing, and embodiment. Atkins furthermore, demands that

> (…) philosophies of personal identity must be broadened away from the current alternatives of either psychological or bodily continuity and embrace psycho-corporeal holism. (2008: 9)

He argues for an intersubjective conception of selfhood which originates in human embodiment.

The narrative approach and its clinical implications

Strawson (2004) further asserts that the aspiration to explicit narrative self-articulation seems natural for some, but in others it is highly unnatural and ruinous, he argues. The more they recall, retell, and narrate themselves, the further they move away from an accurate self-understanding (Strawson 2002). Lyubomirsky et al. (2006) support and specify this view with their study of different ways of processing negative and positive experiences. They find that narrative procedures such as writing and speaking are very beneficial when it comes to articulating stressful, unhappy, or traumatic life events, but may be harmful when applied to happy incidents. In contrast, repetitive circular replaying – as it occurs in private thought – is more useful when the target is processing a happy life event, but may be damaging when dealing with a negative experience.

It is indeed assumed that traumatic memories being characterized by their fragmentation, failure of memory, and disorganisation differ from other types of memories. Numerous studies have explored the relationship between trauma narratives during therapy and post traumatic stress disorder severity (Minnen et al. 2002; Foa et al. 1995). Whereas a lot of research to date has focused on narrative content itself, Foa, Molnar and Cashman (1995) explore the process of narrative organization during post traumatic stress disorder treatment. Their findings and more recent results from trauma therapy (e.g., Minnen et al. 2002) suggest that successful therapy and organization in trauma narratives are indeed related. In other words, in order to overcome trauma, the traumatic events need to be remembered and de-fragmentized. They need to be put into a new, coherent order and, as stressed by Meekums (2005) need to be embodied again. This also seems to be the case for other types of crises. An externalized construction of the problem reduces the likelihood of debilitating guilt and self-blame for the "defect" in the person, and invites active coping on the part of the problem-affected person or family (Tomm 1988).

However, Lyubomirsky's (2006) findings show us on the other hand that the helpful effect of writing or speaking about negative life events does not pertain when considering positive life events. In their study, they distinguish between a more structured approach such as writing and talking which tends to involve organizing, integrating, and analyzing one's problems with a focus on solution generation or at least acceptance, and a more disorganized and even chaotic approach such as circular thinking or rumination. However, they have not investigated what impact processing through embodied perceptual practices such as movement, play, and dance would have, and whether, according to Lyubomirsky (2006), these belong to the narrative, rather organizing approach or to the more disorganized stance, similar to thinking.

The limitations of language

The approaches of the psychotherapy process researchers Angus, Levitt and Hardtke (1994) and Angus and Hardtke (1994) suggest that all forms of successful psychotherapy entail the articulation, elaboration, and transformation of the client's self-told life story or macro-narrative. Nevertheless, similar to Lyubomirsky they do not incorporate an understanding of embodied practices. The concept of tacit, bodily knowing could perhaps add to their narrative approach, which is so far rather language-dependent.

Atkins (2008) refers to Gabriel Marcel, a contemporary but less well-known colleague of Merleau-Ponty who points out the ambiguity of not just *having a body* but also *being a body*, which makes it extremely difficult to speak about the embodied experience. Sheets-Johnstone (2007) also brings our attention to the limitations of language, especially concerning the early stages of life:

> We usually think of thinking as being language-dependent – that language, thinking and rationality are an inviolate triumvirate of some kind or other. And we don't remember having thought in movement in terms of our early life, and having learned how to navigate in the world by way of movement, which is the way we learn in the beginning.   (Sheet-Johnstone 2007:3)

Stern starts from a similar view:

> (…) language is a double-edged sword. It …makes some parts of our experience less shareable with ourselves and with others.   (Stern 1985:162–163)

According to Stern (1985), the most fundamental parts of a human being need to be learned and understood by the baby in a primarily nonverbal way: In order to navigate the world, babies accumulate representations of objects, are able to anticipate, recall, have memories of events and repeat them. Interactional patterns such as the duration of the eye-contact, quality of touch, distance between people and others are being laid down without the use of language. Stern states:

> (…) I think nature decided that you don't want language when you're learning all that stuff because language would actually screw it up, and you could never learn it. (…) I know you know all this because it's kinesthetic concepts and corporeal concepts.   (reported in Sheets-Johnstone 2007:4)

Gallagher talks of "language as a modality of the human body" (2005:107) which is generated out of movement and refers to Merleau-Ponty: "the body converts a certain motor essence into vocal form" (1962:181). Glenberg et al. (2008) in their study of processing abstract language confirm that embodied mechanisms are an integral part of the comprehension process.

"Body knowledge is the basis on which language can rest," affirms Stern (reported in Sheets-Johnstone 2007:4) but this is not taken into account by so many of the narrative theorists. Lakoff and Johnson (2003) equally underline the connection between bodily existence and cognition. In their view, language structures are built on the basis of bodily experiences which create images and symbols and therefore also language metaphors.

"To describe the dynamics, one must first actually experience them", insists Sheets-Johnstone (2009:436). And in actually experiencing them, one readily finds that "For all this, names are lacking" (Husserl 1964:100). Husserl does not simply point out an insufficiency in language, but calls attention to an experience that cannot be named in the first place.

Damasio's (1994, 1999) contributions further highlight that it is difficult to access somatic markers which are at the same time crucial for a narrative organisation of the client by the use of mere verbal techniques. He postulates that "the mind is embodied, in the full sense of the term, not just embrained" (Damasio 1994:93).

There have also been calls from a purely verbal psychotherapeutic perspective to expand clinical attention towards an inclusion of the embodied experience. For

Knoblauch (2005), a trainer in psychoanalysis, the process of symbolization is limited in the communication of clinical work as a "talking cure". He criticizes the displacement effect of language and the futility that language meets, as a description of lived experience. The dance/movement therapist Dosamantes-Beaudry (2007) assesses critically the analytic tradition:

> Though today psychoanalysts consider patients' expressive nonverbal behavior to be an integral part of psychoanalytic treatment, the focus of psychoanalytic treatment continues to be maintained upon verbally communicated content and the verbal interpretations made by the therapist are still considered to be the most effective form of therapeutic intervention.   (ibid.: 79)

Dance Movement Psychotherapy[1] and the different body oriented psychotherapies offer a specific approach which goes beyond words. "All memories, significant and insignificant, are represented in the body, therefore, one can access those memories through body or movement work," states Penfield (1992: 168). Expressive body movement is one way to give form to the unconscious (Jung 1916), lending itself as a natural medium to further emotional integration. By playing and moving, people find ways to organize their material and history into a manageable form. They come to master the processes of remembering and internalizing through the use of symbolism in movement and play (Panhofer 2005), a vital act for the construction of narratives. It is for that reason that the relationship between movement and narration has been further investigated in Panhofer's (2009) study, drawing from both traditions in order to look into their connections and possible limitations and to explore the possibility of wording the embodied experience (Parviainen 2002, 2003; Ylönen 2003, 2004).

Languaging the embodied experience

Sheets-Johnstone (2007: 1) addresses the question of whether, and to what extent, movement and verbal language can be connected referring to the "challenge of languaging the experience." Using a mixed methodological strategy influenced by the heuristic tradition (Douglas & Moustakas 1985; Moustakas 1961, 1968, 1988, 1990) the procedures of Panhofer's study had its roots in an artistic inquiry approach (McNiff 1986, 1992, 1993, 1998; Wadsworth 2000; Hannula 2004; Nevanlinna 2004), using movement and dance as a method of inquiry (Csordas 1993; Koltai 1994; Smith 2002; Riley 2004), and writing as a form of analysis (Reason & Hawkins 1988; Coffey & Atkinson 1996; Wolcott 1994, 2001; Sparkes 2002, 2003).

---

1. The original term in the UK used to be Dance Movement Therapy (DMT) prior to June 2008. Whereas most European countries have remained with this term the UK has changed the term to Dance Movement Psychotherapy (DMP), emphasising the psychotherapeutic approach: This study will mainly refer to the new term DMP.

In Panhofer's study (2009), a group of co-researchers, all of whom fully trained DMPs and members of the Spanish Professional Dance Movement Therapy Association, created a written narrative on a significant moment in therapy.[2] After this first process of writing, they explored the same theme through movement, creating a short movement sequence which they concluded with yet another expressive response through writing. This threefold process of writing, moving, and writing was repeated several times based on numerous different significant moments, allowing hence a wide-ranging exploration of how the essence of what has been experienced physically could be communicated in words.

The findings showed that the character of the narratives, before and after the movement, changed greatly: Sentences showed to be shorter, narratives were more emotive, spontaneous, expressive, chaotic, and poetic. It was furthermore shown that narratives diminished after the movement. It seemed as though the movement sequences in themselves had to some extent replaced the words, suggesting that much of the embodied experience cannot or does not need to be worded at all. A particular high use of movement metaphors was found after the movement. This could mean that moving brings the therapists closer to their metaphors from the body, showing that the embodied word needs to be linked to a personal, emotive vocabulary. Developing this point further, it is possible that once things have been worded for a first time, and then embodied, a subsequent wording will take a different, less explicit form, richer in allusion and thus transcend the movers experience pointing into the wider world. Whereas the first wording may have been more internal, a preliminary making sense and a coding more inwardly directed, the second wording may be more directed to the outside world and a more outgoing form of communication, however with a strong inner connection to the internal world of the experiencer.

Relation to body memory

The findings also illustrated that body memory (all five types of body memory as defined by Fuchs 2004) can be accessed through movement. An understanding of the lived experience can be reached through the process of moving, without the necessity for further verbalisation. Much of the knowing remains in the body, building on the early basis of primary intersubjectivity (Trevarthen 1977), or intercorporeity (Merleau-Ponty 1973).

Other publications (Panhofer et al. 2011a; Panhofer et al. 2011b) have concentrated on the importance of non-languaged ways of knowing and how these can be accessed through movement. The following discussion will therefore mainly focus on

---

2. A significant moment in this research was defined as that part of the therapy session "where the therapist believed there was an event which significantly developed the therapeutic relationship or pushed the therapy forward in some way" (Campbell et al. 2003:420), or as a moment in therapy where some "insight" was reached (Elliott et al. 1994:450).

the embodied word, looking in particular at the use of poetic language, metaphors, and images. The study showed clearly how the emerging ways to communicate the embodied experience changed from a linear description with little personal involvement to an inner dialogue, rich in images, and metaphors. It appeared as though the process of engaging in embodied perceptual practices such as movement, play, and dance transformed the style of narrating into shorter sentences that were more chaotic and expressive, more like poems with lines and verses than linear accounts.

The "singing of the things" – the use of poetic language

Many writers of the 19th and 20th century doubted already that an objectively recognizable reality could be presented through linguistic or literary means and questioned the traditional role assigned to language in this respect. As a leading figure in German poetry Rainer Maria Rilke claimed that only through a poetic language can a "higher truth" be expressed. In his poem from 1899 "*Ich fürchte mich so vor der Menschen Wort*" (I am so afraid of the word of man) he comments on the inadequacy of language for expressing basic human perceptions:

Ich fürchte mich so vor der Menschen Wort

Ich fürchte mich so vor der Menschen Wort. Sie sprechen alles so deutlich aus:
Und dieses heißt Hund und jenes heißt Haus, und hier ist Beginn,
und das Ende ist dort.
Mich bangt auch ihr Sinn, ihr Spiel mit dem Spott, sie wissen alles, was wird und war;
kein Berg ist ihnen mehr wunderbar; ihr Garten und Gut grenzt grade an Gott.
Ich will immer warnen und wehren: Bleibt fern. Die Dinge singen hör ich so gern.
Ihr rührt sie an: sie sind starr und stumm. Ihr bringt mir alle die Dinge um.
(Rilke 1899: 23)

I am so afraid of the word of man

The words of humans fill me with fear. They name all the things with articulate sound:
so this is called house and that is called hound, and the end's over there
and the start's over here.
Their thinking is scary, with scorn they have fun; they know what will come
and what came before; and even the mountain is sacred no more: their property ends
just where God's has begun.
I'm meaning to warn them and stop them: Stay clear! It's the singing of things
I'm longing to hear. You touch them and stiff and silent they turn. You're killing
the things for whose singing I yearn!
(Rilke 1899)[3]

---

3. Translation by Walter A. Aue, http://myweb.dal.ca/waue/Trans/Rilke-Wort.html.

Resisting the factual realism of the time Rilke claims that human-kind kills the nature of things and that only the lyrical, poetic can still perceive the "singing of the things". It is interesting that after the movement sequences the co-researchers returned to this poetic way of expressing themselves as they tried to communicate the essence of their experience. Taking a distance from a linear, factual description they found it easier for their emotions to be represented in a lyrical form, communicating the "hard-to-be-worded" through poetry.

Bracegirdle (2007) points out how poetry, as a representation in words and the interpretation of those words has been discussed for centuries. In her research, she proposed to her clients that they use poetic forms of writing such as lines and stanzas, and in doing so provided them with a containing structure. Her findings highlight how that which cannot be spoken can indeed be represented through the use of allegory, symbols, and metaphor. In Panhofer's study (2009), through the process of moving, words had been reduced but also become more concise; they had taken shape and also gained containment through image and metaphor (Lago 2004).

The use of metaphors and images

The postmodernist viewpoint allows us to move beyond the understanding of language as the bearer of truth but rather as a by-product of human interchange that gains its meaning not from its mental or subjective underpinnings but from its use (Wittgenstein 1953; Gergen 2001). In psychotherapy, the principal goal is the successful communication of profound inner experiences from one human being to another. Where verbal language seems limited, the use of movement and metaphor offers new possibilities. Bearing in mind Lakoff and Johnson's approach (1980/2003: 5) who talk about metaphor as "experiencing one thing in terms of another" it becomes evident that if the embodied experience is the "one thing" words do not necessarily have to be the other, but this may also be music, drawing, sculpting, etc. One may focus on movement and use it as a metaphor to "carry over" embodied meanings.

In one of the initial narratives of the present study, a co-researcher mentioned her patient/client using the expression of not being sure 'whether this was the right suit to wear'. This verbal metaphor would be classified as an *image metaphor* by Lakoff (1987) and Lakoff and Turner (1989) as it maps an image, rather than more general knowledge. Probably with this image in mind, the co researcher must have gone into the movement sequence, immediately associating it with another image, the one of a Venetian carnival. She then developed this image herself in the course of the account, talking about "representing different characters" and reflecting on her client who "could slip into different personalities." The co-researcher interpreted the idea of the different roles one is playing in life with the vital question for this particular patient who was facing issues concerning his sexual identity.

The *image metaphor* is understood as an image mapping in which the mental image of "wearing the right suit" is mapped onto the mental image of the client, a process which is brilliantly documented with the example of André Breton's love poem "Free Union" by Gibbs and Bogdonovich (1999), and Lakoff (1987): "My wife whose hair is brush fire, whose thoughts are summer lightning, whose waist is an hourglass, …" (Gibbs & Bogdonovich 1999: 37). This poem illustrates several examples of *image metaphors* which, instead of providing concrete knowledge, create more new mental images and thus more metaphors to carry over the meaning.

The *image metaphor* from one co-researcher's final narrative had a similar effect. She mentioned a 'stream of words of such horrible things', repeating Breton's surrealistic use of images where several images are mapped on the target model. A stream of words does not exist in reality; however, it conveys its characteristics of flow, strength, magnitude, and movement. "A stream of words of such horrible things" is mapped over the verbal communication of the client, turning it into dangerous water one could easily drown in and conveys most perfectly the sheer horror the co-researching therapist must had been feeling when listening to the client's story.

According to Lakoff and Johnson (2003, 1999), metaphors are shaped by the sense of us as embodied beings, and this is the basis for understanding all sorts of concepts. Gibbs et al. (2004: 2) agree that "the poetic value and the communicative expressiveness of metaphoric language partly arises from its roots in people's ordinary, felt sensations of their bodies in action." They defend a direct link between recurring patterns of embodied experience, metaphor, conventional, and poetic language. The guiding assumption that movement and meaning are reciprocally connected to each other and mutually determined by each other is also shared by Skilters and Böger (2010). For them, meaning is bodily grounded and one way of analyzing it is through movement execution.

Kövecses (2003), concentrating on metaphors and emotion ("happy is up", "love is fire", "sad is dark", "shame is a burden", etc.), provides further confirmation. He shows how metaphors connected with emotions derive directly from embodied experience and, given cross-cultural evidence, argues how man's actual physiology may well be universal – for example anger does indeed go together with objectively measurable bodily changes such as a rise in skin temperature, blood pressure, pulse rate, and deeper respiration in most cultures:

> The universality of actual physiology might be seen as leading to the similarities (though not equivalence) in conceptualized physiology (…), which might then lead to the similarity (though again not equivalence) in the metaphorical conceptualization of anger and its counterparts.   (Kövecses 2003: 160)

Whereas physiological responses do not automatically produce metaphor, Kövecses highlights how a particular embodiment of, for example, anger, limits the choice of available metaphors for anger. These findings are of particular interest for the present study, since the metaphors and images used have been produced by Spanish, Portuguese, Dutch, and Austrian individuals but have been assessed in a UK university context and therefore indeed embrace a wide range of cultural variety within the European scope.

Gibbs et al. (2004) support these conclusions when examining the metaphor "ANGER IS HEATED FLUID IN A CONTAINER". Although it may be argued that the knowledge about "heated fluid in containers" comes from observation only, it is a matter of fact that people acquire this source domain knowledge through their experiences of their own bodies.

> Once more, the recurring aspects of these sensory and full-bodied kinesthetic experiences give rise to image-schematic source domains that get projected to form conceptual metaphors. (Gibbs et al. 2004: 1195)

Conceptual metaphors, referring to the understanding of one idea or concept in terms of another (time is "money", sad is "down", love is "patient", love is a "journey", etc.), have been defined as "a mapping of the structure of a source model onto a target model" (Ungerer & Schmid 1996: 120). These metaphors involve understanding one domain of experience (for example "sad") in terms of a very different and more concrete experience (down). Numerous source domains of many *conceptual metaphors* reflect significant patterns of bodily experience. "In this way, part of how people make sense of and understand different linguistic expressions is grounded in embodiment" (Gibbs et al. 2004: 1196).

The findings of the study of Panhofer (2009) clearly show a limitation of literal language when accessing inner worlds, and (instead) suggest that possible ways of communicating the embodied experience may be through symbolic language using metaphors, images, and poetry. Where it is difficult to communicate an inner experience through verbal narration with narrative, such as practiced in verbal psychotherapy, metaphors, images, and poetry may offer a useful alternative, alongside the embodied perceptual practices such as play, movement, and dance.

Conclusions

> *In my book of Genesis, poetry is the orphan of silence.*
> *Maternal silence.*
> *That in all of us which belongs to the universe.*
> *The mother's voice calls its name over the roofs of the world.*
> *Whoever hears it turns toward his ancestral home.*
> *A hallowed moment.*
> *Timeless presence which has no language.*
> *Whoever senses himself existing has no need to say much*
> (Simic 1985: 113)

Like the Serbian-Austrian poet Simic, the Austrian-English philosopher Wittgenstein (1889–1951) had already challenged the limits of language in his early work *Tractatus*

Logico-Philosophicus (1922). When searching for a publisher for this book he wrote to the editor Ludwig von Ficker in 1919:

> I once wanted to give a few words in the foreword which now actually are not in it, which, however, I'll write to you now because they might be a key for you: I wanted to write that my work consists of two parts: of the one which is here, and of everything which I have not written. And precisely this second part is the important one.   (Wittgenstein 1922:133)

We do not know whether Wittgenstein should be classified as an "episodic" or "diachronic" type, according to Strawson's (2004:430) definition, but his comment confirms some of the drawbacks of verbal language. When putting the narrative tradition into the light of the newly emerging embodiment approaches, its strengths and limitations become evident, highlighting the necessity of an embodied, holistic perception of human beings and their lived experience. Bearing this concept in mind, the use of embodied, perceptual practices seem to be a vital contribution for any type of psychotherapy that tries to get in contact and process the inner worlds of individuals.

Gallagher sums up this personal, embodied link as follows in an interview at Bochum University for German radio "Deutschlandfunk":

> For me there is nothing which is not embodied, I do not even exclude theories. Narratives are certainly put into language. But if you ask me: what is language? In a certain sense, language is a motor performance of the body. There is the vocal language, hand-signals, gestures, but these are most of all bodily movements. The fully developed language does elevate this onto a higher level but the linguistic statements which arise therefrom have their roots in bodily experiences and I am convinced that one never really detaches from these.   (Hubert 2009)

With this statement Gallagher proposes a bridge of the gap between language and experience, as pointed out by Simic when calling poetry the "orphan of silence". Even though language cannot produce a mirror image of the experience, as Simic regrets (Mijuk 2002:15), the bodily experience allows a bridge between the two: "Whoever senses himself existing has no need to say much" Simic (1985:113) points out, an argument that seems of great value for those psychotherapeutic traditions that are based upon an intersubjective conception of selfhood. "Sensing oneself", getting in touch with one's bodily self and the memory of the body through the use of embodied perceptual practices needs to be an integral part for any psychotherapeutic approach that tries to access the knowledge of the body, reaching beyond words.

References

Angus, L. & Hardtke, K. (1994). *Narrative processes in psychotherapy*. Canadian Psychology, 35, 190–203.

Angus, L., Levitt, H. & Hardtke, K. (1999). The narrative processes coding system: Research applications and implications for psychotherapy practice. *Journal of Clinical Psychology. 55*(10), 1255–1270.

Atkins, K. (2008). *Narrative identity and moral identity. A practical perspective*. London: Routledge.

Böger, C. (2010, in press). Formgenese und metaphorische Instruktion: zur Wechselwirkung von Bedeutung und Bewegung [Form-genesis and metaphorical instruction: On the interplay of meaning and movement]. In J. Bietz & M. Roscher (Eds.), *Form und Bewegung – Prozesse der Ordnungsbildung und ihre wirklichkeitskonstituierende Bedeutung* [Form and movement – Processes of order formation and their reality-constituting meaning]. Berlin: Lehmann.

Bracegirdle, C. (2007). *Beauty and the Beast: Clients' experience of counselling within a narrative framework, considering concepts of containment and freedom*. Unpublished doctoral thesis, submitted in partial fulfillment of the requirements of the University of Hertfordshire for the Degree Doctor of Philosophy, University of Hertfordshire Library.

Bruner, E. (1986a). Ethnography as narrative. In V. Turner & E. Bruner (Eds.), *The anthropology of experience*. Chicago: University of Illinois Press.

Campbell, J. (1994). *Past, space, and self*. Cambridge, MA: MIT Press.

Coffey, A. & Atkinson P. (1996). *Making sense of qualitative data: Complementary research strategies*. Thousand Oaks: Sage.

Crossley, M. (2000). *Introducing Narrative Psychology. Self, Trauma and the construction of meaning*. Buckingham: Open University Press.

Csordas, T. (1993). Somatic modes of attention. *Cultural Anthropology, 8*(2), 135–156.

Damasio, A. (1994). *Descartes' Error: Emotion, reason and the human brain*. London: Harper Collins.

Damasio, A. (1999). *The Feeling of what happens: Body and emotion in the making of consciousness*. London: Harcourt.

Dosamantes-Beaudry, I. (2007). Somatic transference and countertransference in psychoanalytic intersubjective Dance/Movement Therapy. *American Journal of Dance Therapy, 29*(2), 73–89.

Douglas, B. C. G. & Moustakas, C. (1985). Heuristic inquiry: The internal search to know. *Journal of Humanistic Psychology, 25*(3), 39–55.

Elliot, R., Saphiro, D. Firth-Cozens, J., Stiles, W., Hardy, G., Llewelyn, S. & Margison, F. (1994). Comprehensive process of insight events in cognitive-behavioural and psychodynamic-interpersonal psychotherapies. *Journal of Counselling Psychology, 41*(4), 449–463.

Eron, J. B. & Lund, T. W. (1996). *Narrative solutions in brief therapy*. New York: The Guildford Press.

Fisher, W. R. (1984). Narration as a human communication paradigm: The case of public moral argument. *Communication Monographs, 52*, 347–367.

Foa, E. B., Molnar, C. & Cashman, L. (1995). Change in rape narratives during exposure therapy for posttraumatic disorder. *Journal of Traumatic Stress, 8*, 657–690.

Freedman, J. & Combs, J. (2000). *Narrative therapy. The social construction of preferred realities*. London: WW. Norton & Company Ltd.

Fuchs, T. (2003). The memory of the body. [Online] URL: http://www.klinikum.uniheidelberg.de/fileadmin/zpm/psychatrie/ppp2004/manuskript/fuchs.pdf [accessed 8th December 2008].

Gallagher, S. (2005). *How the body shapes the mind*. New York: Oxford. University Press.

Gergen, K. J. (2001). Psychological science in a postmodern context. *The American Psychologist, 56*(10), 803–813.

Gersie, A. (2000). *Story making in bereavement*. Dragons Fight in the Meadow. London: Jessica Kingsley Publishers.

Gersie, A. & King, N. (2006). *Story making in education and therapy*. London: Jessica Kingsley Publications.

George, C., Kaplan, N. & Main, M. (1985, 1996). Adult attachment interview. Unpublished protocol (3rd ed.). Department of Psychology, University of California, Berkeley.

Gibbs, R. W. & Bogdonovich, J. (1999). Mental imagery in interpreting poetic metaphor. *Metaphor and Symbol, 14*(1), 37–44.

Gibbs, R. W. (2003). Embodied experience and linguistic meaning, *Brain and Language, 84*, 1–15.

Gibbs, R. W., Lenz, P. C. L. & Francozo, E. (2004). Metaphor is grounded in embodied experience. *Journal of Pragmatics, 36*, 1189–1210.

Glenberg, A. M., Sato, M. Cattaneo, L. Riggio, L., Palumbo, D. & Buccino, G. (2008). Processing abstract language modulates motor system activity. *The Quarterly Journal of Experimental Psychology*. Psychology Press.

Hieb, M. (2005). *Inner journeying through art-journaling. Learning to see and record your life as a work of art*. London: Jessica Kingsley.

Hannula, M. (2004). River low, mountain high. Contextualizing artistic research. In A. W. Balkema & H. Slager (Eds.), *Artistic research*. Amsterdam: Rodopi.

Holmes, J. (2001). *The search for the secure base. Attachment theory and psychotherapy*. East Sussex: Brunner-Routledge.

Hubert, M. (2008). Körper im Kopf. Wissenschaft im Brennpunkt [The body in the head. Science in focus] [Online]. http://www.dradio.de/dlf/sendungen/wib/722397/ [accessed 4th June 2009].

Hunt, C. & Samspon, F. (Eds.). (2002). *The self on the page. Theory and practice of creative writing in personal development*. London: Jessica Kingsley Publishers.

Husserl, E. (1964). *The phenomenology of internal time consciousness* (trans. James S. Churchill). Bloomington: Indiana University Press.

Jung, C. G. (1916). The transcendent function. *Collected Works 8*. Princeton: Princeton University Press, 1975, 67–91.

Knoblauch, S. H. (2005). Body rhythms and the unconscious. Toward an expanding of clinical attention. *Psychoanalytic Dialogues, 15*(6), 807–827.

Koltai, J. (1994). Authentic Movement: The embodied experience of text. *Canadian Theatre Review, 78*, 21–5.

Kövecses, Z. (2003). *Metaphor and emotion. Language, culture, and body in human feeling*. Cambridge: Cambridge University Press.

Lago, C. (2004). "When I write I think," personal uses of writing by international students. In G. Bolton, S. Howlett, C. Lago & J. Wright (Eds.), *Writing cures. An introductory handbook of writing in counselling and therapy*. London: Routledge.

Launer, J. (2006). New stories for old: Narrative-based primary care in the United Kingdom. *Families, Systems & Health, 24*, 336–344.

Lakoff, G. & Johnson, M. (1980/2003). *Metaphors we live by*. London: University of Chicago Press.

Lakoff, G. & Johnson, M. (1999). *Philosophy in the flesh: The embodied mind and its challenge to Western thought*. New York: Basic Books.

Lakoff, G. & Turner, M. (1989). *More than cool reason: A field guide to poetic metaphor.* Chicago: The University of Chicago Press.

Lakoff, G. (1987). Image metaphors. *Metaphor and Symbol, 2*(3), 219–222.

Lyubomirsky, S., Sousa, L. & Dickerhoof, R. (2006). The costs and benefits of writing, talking, and thinking about life's triumphs and defeats. *Journal of Personality and Social Psychology, 90*(4), 692–708.

McNiff, S. (1986). Freedom of research and artistic inquiry. *The Arts in Psychotherapy, 13*(4), 279–284.

McNiff, S. (1992). *Art as medicine.* Boston: Shambhala Books.

McNiff, S. (1993). The authority of experience. *The Arts in Psychotherapy, 20,* 3–9.

McNiff, S. (1998). *Art-based research.* London: Jessica Kinglsey.

Meier, A. (2002). Narrative in psychotherapy theory, practice, and research: a critical review. *Counselling and Psychotherapy Research, 2*(4), 239–251.

Meekums, B. (2005). Creative writing as a tool for assessment: implications for embodied writing. *The Arts in Psychotherapy, 32,* 95–105.

Merleau-Ponty, M. (1973). *The prose of the world* (Transl. by J. O'Neil). Evanston, IL: Northwestern University Press.

Minnen, A., Wessel, I., Dijkstra, T. & Roëlofs, K. (2002). Changes in PTSD patients' narratives during prolonged exposure therapy: A replication and extension. *Journal of Traumatic Stress, 15*(3), 255–258.

Mijuk, G. (2002). *Orphan of slence: The poetry of Charles Simic.* Unpublished Dissertation to fulfill the requirements for the doctorate in the Faculty of Letters of the University of Fribourg in Switzerland. [Online]. URL: http://ethesis.unifr.ch/theses/downloads.php?file=MijukG.pdf [accessed 16th August 2010].

Morgan, A. (2000). *What is narrative therapy? An easy-to-read introduction.* Adelaide: Dulwich Centre Publications.

Moustakas, C. (1961). *Loneliness.* Englewood Cliffs, NJ: Prentice-Hall.

Moustakas, C. (1968). *Individuality and encounter.* Cambridge, MA: Doyle.

Moustakas, C. (1972). *Loneliness and love.* Englewood Cliffs, NJ: Prentice-Hall.

Moustakas, C. (1988). *Phenomenology, science, and psychotherapy.* Sydney, Nova Scotia: Family Life Institute, University College of Cape Breton.

Moustakas, C. (1990). *Heuristic Research. Design, methodology, and applications.* London: Sage.

Nevanlinna, T. (2004). Is artistic research a meaningful concept? In A. W. Balkemaand & H. Slager (Eds.), *Artistic Research* (pp. 80–83). Amsterdam: Rodopi.

Panhofer, H. (2005). Come back, come back! Apegos rotos y sus implicaciones clínicas en Danza Movimiento Terapia [Come back, come back! Broken attachments and their clinical implications in Dance/Movement Therapy]. In H. Panhofer (Ed.), *El cuerpo en psicoterapia. La teoría y práctica de la Danza Movimiento Terapia* [The body in psychotherapy. Theory and practice of Dance and Movement Therapy] (pp. 99–130). Barcelona: Gedisa.

Panhofer, H. (2009). *New approaches to communicate the embodied experience in Dance Movement Psychotherapy.* Unpublished thesis submitted in partial fulfillment of the requirements for the degree doctor of philosophy, University of Hertfordshire.

Panhofer, H., Payne, H., Meekums, B. & Parke, T. (2011a). The space between body and mind: Two models for group supervision. In S. Scoble (Ed.), *The Space between: The potential for change. European Consortium for Arts Therapies Education: Selected Proceedings of the 10th European Arts Therapies Conference, London, September 2009.* Ecarte e-publication http://www.ecarte.info/. Plymouth: University of Plymouth Press.

Panhofer, H., Payne, H., Meekums, B. & Parke, T. (2011b). Dancing, moving and writing in clinical supervision? Employing embodied practices in psychotherapy supervision. *The Arts in Psychotherapy, 38*, 9–16.

Parviainen, J. (2002). Bodily knowledge: Epistemological reflections on dance. *Dance Research Journal, 34*(1), 1123.

Parviainen, J. (2003). Dance techne: Kinetic bodily logos and thinking in movement. *Nordisk Estetisk Tidskrift, 27*, 8, 159–175.

Parry, A. & Doan, R. (1994). *Story re-visions. Narrative therapy in the postmodern world.* New York: Guildford Press.

Payne, M. (2006). (2nd ed). *Narrative therapy. An introduction for counsellors.* London: Sage.

Penfield, K. (1992). Individual movement psychotherapy. In H. Payne (Ed.), *Dance movement therapy: Theory and practice.* London: Tavistock/Routledge.

Pennebaker, J. W. & Seagal, J. D. (1999). Forming a story: The health benefits of narrative. *Journal of Clinical Psychology, 55*, 1243–1254.

Polkinghorne, D. E. (1988). Narrative knowing and the human sciences. Albany: State University of New York Press.

Reason, P. & Hawkins. P. (1988). Storytelling as inquiry. In P. Reason (Ed.), *Human inquiry in action* (pp. 79–101). Thousand Oaks: CA: Sage.

Richert, A. J. (2006). Narrative Psychology and Psychotherapy. *Journal of Psychotherapy Integration, 16*(1), 84–110.

Riley, S. R. (2004). Embodied Perceptual Practices: Towards an embrained and embodied model of mind for use in actor training and rehearsal. *Theatre Topics, 14*(2), 445–471.

Rilke, R. M. (1899). *Mir zur Feier. Gedichte* [To celebrate me. Poems]. Berlin: Meyer Verlag.

Schauer, M., Neuner, F. & Elbert, T. (2005). *Narrative exposure therapy. A short-term intervention for traumatic stress disorders after war, terror, or torture.* Göttingen: Hogrege & Huber.

Sheets-Johnstone, M. (2007). Dance, movement, and bodies: Forays into the non-linguistic and the challenge of languaging Experience: Evening II. [Online]. URL: http://www.youtube.com/watch?v=-pTxptDPQzI [accessed 21th July 2009].

Sheets-Johnstone, M. (2009). *The corporeal turn: An interdisciplinary reader.* Exeter: Imprint Academic.

Simic, C. (1985). *The uncertain certainty: Interviews, essays, and notes on poetry.* Ann Arbor: University of Michigan Press.

Skilters, J. & Böger, C. (2010, in press). Embodied semantic structures in movement execution and language. In J. Luchjenbroers & M. Aldridge (Eds.), *Conceptual structure and linguistics research, Vol. 1: Grammar, blending and metaphor.* Amsterdam/Philadelphia: John Benjamins.

Smith, M. L. (2002). *Moving self: The thread which bridges dance and theatre.* Research in Dance Education, 3(2), 123–141.

Sparkes, A. (2003). Bodies, identities, selves: Autoethnografic fragments and reflections. In T. Denison & P. Markula (Eds.), *Moving writing: Crafting movement in sport and research* (pp. 51–76). New York: Peter Lang.

Sparkes, A., Nilges, L., Swan, P. & Dowling, F. (2003). Poetic representations in Sport and Physical Education: Insider Perspectives. *Sport, Education and Society, 8*(2), 153–177.

Stern, D. (1985). *The interpersonal world of the infant: A view from psychoanalysis and developmental psychology.* New York: Basic Books.

Stiles, W. B., Honos-Webb, L. & Lani, J. A. (1999). Some functions of narrative assimilation of problematic experiences. *Journal of Clinical Psychology, 55*, 1213–1226.

Strawson, G. (2004). Against Narrativity. *Ratio (new series)* XVII December.

Strupp, H. & Binder, J. (1984). *Psychotherapy in a new key: A guide to time-limited dynamic psychotherapy*. New York: Norton.

Tomm, K. (1988). Interventive interviewing: Part III. Intending to ask lineal, circular, strategic, or reflexive questions? *Family Process, 27*, 1–15.

Trevarthen, C. (1977). Descriptive analyses of infant communicative behaviour. In H. R. Schaffer (Ed.), *Studies in mother-infant interaction*. London: Academic Press.

Ungerer, F. & Schmid, H. J. (1996). *An introduction to cognitive linguistics*. London: Wesley Longman Ltd.

Wadsworth, L. (2000). *Artistic inquiry in Dance/Movement Therapy. Creative alternatives for research*. Springfield: Charles C. Thomas Publisher.

Watzlawick, P. (1996). The construction of "clinical realities." In H. Rosen & H. T. Kuehlwein (Eds.), *Construction realities: Meaning-making perspectives for psychotherapies* (pp. 55–70). San Fransisco: Jossey-Bass.

White, M. (1988, Winter). The process of questioning. A therapy of literary merit? *Dulwich Centre Newsletter*.

White, M. & Epston, D. (1990). *Narrative means to therapeutic ends*. London: W.W. Norton & Company.

Wittgenstein, L. (1922). *Tractatus Logico-Philosophicus*. Frankfurt: Suhrkamp Verlag.

Wittgenstein, L. (1953). *Philosophical investigations*. Transl. by G. E. M. Anscombe. New York: Macimillan.

Wittgenstein, L. (1990). *Über Gewißheit*. Frankfurt/Main: Suhrkamp. Engl. Transl. *On Certainty*. In G. E. M. Anscombe and G. H. von Wright (Eds.) (1975). Transl. by Denis Paul and G. E. M. Anscombe. Oxford: Basil Blackwell.

Wolcott, H. (1994). *Transforming qualitative data: Description, analysis, and interpretation*. London: Sage.

Wolcott, H. (2001). *Writing up qualitative research*. London. Sage.

Ylönen, M. (2003). Bodily flashes of dancing women: Dance as a method of inquiry. *Qualitative Inquiry, 9*(4), 554–568.

Ylönen, M. (2004). A dance by mother and daughter. *The Arts in Psychotherapy, 3*, 11–17.

CHAPTER 20

Emotorics

Development and body memory

Yona Shahar-Levy
Free Researcher

This chapter is not a scientific discourse based on erudite quotations. Its purpose is rather (a) to present the typological model of Emotorics, a theory I have developed for the purpose of tentative reconstruction of the subjective meaning embedded in the evoked memory fragments, and (b) to share with my readers selected episodes in which obscure body behavior suddenly comes to the surface presenting entries from my personal professional diary. The basic premise of Emotorics is that motor behavior patterns and emotive body language develop from core biological-relational prototypes. I present selected episodes in which early memories were first "replayed" by obscure body behavior which seems out of any present context. Each episode will be followed by some personal reflections about their possible meaning in light of Emotorics' typology.

Keywords: implicit emotive body memory clusters, emotive-relational body language, typological perspective of relational space (the parental envelope space and the open interpersonal space), core motor-prototypes of emotive body language

The process of memory retrieval in the clinic brings to therapy a personal drama of anxiety and hope, of pleasurable and painful memories. The only visible part in this drama is the moving body. I see body shapes and movement patterns, but I cannot see the patient's inner world. My aim is to uncover hidden emotions, conflicts, and developmental deficits which have been bound in the muscles. It is for this purpose that I developed the psychodiagnostic tool I labeled *Emotorics* (see below). *Emotorics* enables me to resonate with the person's feeling and to offer meaningful interpretations when needed. While verbal expressions of the person's narrative can certainly produce clues to forgotten, significant events (as typical of more traditional psychotherapies), I nonetheless look also in the direction of the moving body, specifically at implicit, non-verbal expressions as they are revealed in early body memories. The term body does not imply a narrow physiological approach. Rather, it emphasizes the fact of multiple dynamic levels which are included in the term (as they are contained in the actual body). Before relating excerpts from my professional journal, I wish to clarify certain assumptions and concepts essential to the body model I have developed in my clinical work and which I have elaborated in my prior writings (Shahar-Levy 2001, 2004, 2009). Essential premises are:

1. The motor system functions as an archive of emotive-motor memory clusters. By definition, a body memory cluster contains bodily, emotive, perceptual, and relational elements.

    Emotive-motor memory clusters (Shahar-Levy 1994, 2001) are blocked action impulses often manifested in unexplained, anachronistic patterns of pain and chronic ("remembered") muscle tension, the original context of which has been lost. These patterns are expressed in body postural attitudes which have been severed from their original context. They are inner structures which contain a rigid core of incomplete emotive-motor impulses, blocked emotional expression, or somatic substitutes for either of these. In addition, they store fragments of the original subjective body behavior and the subjective impressions of the other bodies. In this respect they store qualities of more than one body and represent a degree of non-differentiation between self-body and the other significant bodies. In such emotive-memory clusters, the past is entangled with the present. The body feels as if remote past experiences are happening at the present moment.

    Memory clusters are often manifested in chronic ("remembered") muscle tension, postural shapes, and/or body attitudes whose original context has been lost. In some cases, these blocked impulses to action are explicitly connected with specific events or persons. In other cases their original situational and/or relational contexts remain obscure. A memory cluster contains both the original subjective emotion and the response of the environment (the other). This is what makes it a cluster rather than just a simple memory.

2. Body memories clusters contain a wide range of emotions, such as anger, longing, and aggression. In theory, these can be either positive or negative. In the reality of the clinic, the dominant emotive coloring of memory clusters is that of longing, failure and impotence. This may be because it is an *incomplete* action impulse that leaves its mark, whereas completed action flows on and becomes integrated with consecutive experiences.

In the course of the past thirty-five years I have developed a theoretical model which I call *Emotorics* (Shahar-Levy 1994, 2001.) It delineates the dynamic and developmental links between emotional and motor processes.

Basic premises of emotorics

Early infant-parent physical space and boundaries develop from two core-prototypes

> Prototype P-0: The Parental Physical Envelope body organization in which the infant's body is being held and encircled in flexed postures
>
> Prototype P-1: The vertical-individuated Body-self in face-to-face relations

Prototype P-0 is the initial stage of human development characterized by a parental physical envelope in which the infant's tiny body is held and handled by bodies of parenting adults.

This is the physical/relational condition in which the infant's body surface is subject to various types of kinesthetic parental care. If all goes well, the empathetic, parental envelope will result in a beneficial course of development. However, if there is empathic failures within the inescapable space of the parental envelope, many types of cumulative traumata may evolve.

The concept of the parental envelope reflects the specific nature of the motor potentials at the beginning of life. In this stage the infant's tiny selfbody is dependent totally on the handling of parenting others, whose bodies, voices, smells, muscle tension, rhythms, and motions form a closed space. In this physical condition of diffused body boundaries a unique psychophysical mechanism prevails namely, *kinesthetic introjective identification*. This mechanism is based on diffuse boundaries which creates implicit kinesthetic links between the body of the infant and the bodies of its surrounding parenting figures. The infant is likely to adopt body qualities and symptoms from its parents as a way of storing the feeling of implicit connectedness to its parent's body.

Since the parental envelope is the earliest relational structure, coinciding with the developmental stage in which the motor and postural skills have not yet reached full maturation, it leaves its mark on the deepest foundations of the body-mind systems. At this stage possibilities for detaching and withdrawing from the parental body are few. The only way to achieve these states is through postural manipulations within the infant selfbody.

In its pure form, the parental envelope setting does not last more than a few months. However its psychophysical marks are stored forever in implicit body memories. An empathic envelope will assure a beneficial course of development. In the course of healthy development Prototype P-1 patterns are added and integrated into a rich, individual repertoire. However, parental empathic failures (Kohut 1977) and impingement (Khan 1974) within the inescapable space of the parental envelope may create traces of emotive frustration and rage which in turn may crystallize into various forms of pathological behavior.

The complementary Prototype P-1, *face-to-face* body alignment is the type of body organization in which the potentials of muscle movement and vigor enable the child to stand on his feet and maintain vertical anti-gravity postures. The Prototype P-1 is the physical basis for vigor motor actions and postural choices in relation to objects and situations.

Emotive body language develops from two types of sensory-motor patterns: Type-0 which consists of circular, low-energy undulation and Type-1 vigor, ballistic, boundary breaking movements. The qualities of Type P-0 differ significantly from the qualities of Type P-1 in regard to space, time, objects, and body parts.

A person's body behavior contains significant diagnostic keys. Qualities of these early prototypes are embedded in one's implicit memories. Thus body memories provide points of reference for deciphering an individual psychomotor history. This gives us a typological grid for tentative assessment of emotive body language and of emotive body memories clusters.

Basic typology of emotive body language

In the present context, emotive body language is a collective expression for motor patterns which contains emotional attitudes such as drives, emotions, motivations, and relations to space, time, and other bodies. From a paradigmatic point of view each relational prototype is served by a specific core-prototype of motor behavior:

The parental envelope prototype
The parental envelope prototype is served by the P-0 motor prototype, i.e. the *attachment* motor type. The infant's tiny selfbody is held by parenting others, whose bodies, voices, smells, muscle tension, rhythms, and movements form a physical parental envelope. Its body is characterized by flexed, round body shapes, immature spinal support, and high plasticity. It contains potentials which are compatible with the physical conditions inside the parental envelope and the maturity level of a motor system which is not yet able to maintain spinal supported, upright postures.

The face-to-Face prototype
The face-to-Face prototype is served by **the** P-1 motor prototype, characterized by *forceful ballistic-projective movements and vertical postures*. Its seeds appear in the second half of the first year of life and it develops gradually with the increased maturation of motor and postural skills. These qualities give the young baby motor tools to build his spine and limbs in preparation for the process of separation-individuation (Mahler et al. 1975). They also contain the potential for positive and negative aggression.

The developmental roots of these early prototypes are intertwined from this early point in time on in one's body. In therapy, one of the therapist's tasks is to meet the challenge of disentangling past memory fragments from present experiences and to reintegrate past memory clusters into therapy and real life.

If the assumption that emotive body language of Prototype P-0 differs significantly from emotive body language of Prototype P-1 is correct, the moving body contains significant diagnostic keys. By combining attunement to the individual narrative with the perspective of the typological grid of the core-prototypes we gain additional perspective for interpretation.

Markers of hidden emotive memory clusters
The emotive body carries implicit, seemingly out-of-context early memory clusters. Since they are often detached from present life they are not easily discerned. Repetitive clinical phenomena indicate the presence of hidden memory fragments or clusters.

1. *Fixation of an archaic stage of development, reflecting implicit mechanisms for preserving the presence of a lost object in the self's body*
2. *Dysfunctional emotive motor cycles*
3. *The transition from primary to secondary emotions is hampered*
4. *Regression to infantile movement patterns and posture*
5. *Archaic body image*
6. *Unresolved conflicts and repressed emotions reflected in rigid non-adaptive psychomotor strategies of avoidance and withdrawal*
7. *Non-flexible postural contours*
8. *Constriction or dissociation of a specific body part accompanied by chronic muscle contraction in the same body parts*
9. *Splits in body functioning: selective activation or suppression of body parts as markers of memory cluster*
10. *Somatic reactions: shallow breathing, general muscle contraction, generalized muscle contraction, skin pathologies, shallow or interrupted breathing, nausea, dizziness, anxiety, insomnia, eating disorder*
11. *Stagnation of motor development at a primary level of organization*

In the clinic, retrieval of memory clusters often does not follow its original chronological order. Fragments of body behavior appear senseless until they are connected to the person's past or present experiences. I have found it helpful to formulate a basic catalogue of common markers of memory evocation, the most important of which are listed here:

Markers of memory fragment evocation
1. *Unexpected appearance of anxiety and pain*
2. *Sudden outburst of unexpected tears and intense emotions*
3. *Unexpected regressed postures and sounds accompanied by intense emotions*
4. *Motor constriction and patterns of avoidance and withdrawal for which there is no visible reason. In such cases, the spontaneous movement improvisation leads to spontaneous freezing. It takes meticulous attunement to find out the deep psychological meaning of this body strategy and to find ways to defreeze.*

5. *Unexpected appearance of ballistic movements seemingly dissociated from a coherent cognitive view of what is happening. Sometimes what is happening looks like the enactment of a drama in which one partner is visible while the other is implied only by the movement of the person whom we can see.*

Developmentally some of these markers reflect the level of body somatic dominance, while others reflect later phases of body muscular maturation. I use these signs as additional keys to a person's verbal accounts and general behavior.

Body memory clusters in reference to the typological grid

Illustrative episodes from my diary

Since much of the unfolding dramas were not known to either of us until some obscure fragments of memory was unexpectedly retrieved, I often felt like a detective gathering details on a person's secrets and hopes, as these would be revealed in newly evoked memories. When fragments of memory clusters came to the surface, I would see more and more clues that enabled me to fill in the gaps in the person's implicit emotive body narrative. My empathy would grow, as together we engaged in a joint examination of memory details.

I would like now to illustrate some of these concepts by referring to several, brief episodes. These episodes focus on emotive movement narratives which illustrate how implicit memory clusters are first unknowingly "played out" in the body and then become objects of cognitive scrutiny (i.e., implicit becomes explicit). I will also show how individual body phenomena reflect universal typological aspects of emotive movement.

Memory clusters which reflect body qualities from Type [P-0]
developmental phase

Episodes reflecting the condition of kinesthetic introjective identification in the parental envelope phase.

Episode 1. Martin – A body enveloped by generalized muscle contraction
Martin is a professional, 53 years of age, who suffered from lingering depression, fatigue, and an on-going sense of failure. His body showed generalized muscle contraction and shallow or interrupted breathing. I understood these as somatic reactions to repression of self-vigor (designated as aggressive behavior). Following is a description of a recurrent behavior in therapy:

Martin is lying on his back turning gently from side to side. Suddenly his movement stops. He raises his arms in front of his face as though reaching out toward an invisible object. Tears burst out. He cries and murmurs: "I am lying on my back, weeping, yelling and crying out – but no one comes. I see nothing. Anxiety engulfs me. My chest contracts with pain and panic. I am afraid I shall never be able to inhale again."

Another memory: "I am in my bed and my mother is in her room. I cry for her. She is sitting in the kitchen with her friends." His breaths looked like internal convulsions. He is aware of them and says: "I tried to overcome my panic by "overloading" all parts of my body, especially the nerves. I have taught myself to apply 'local anesthesia' to most of my body parts. As a result I do not feel my body as complete. Now I feel how all my muscles are contracted so as not to feel the anxiety."

My reflections (from my professional journal):

* Emotive movement improvisation evokes both sides of the conflict: the incomplete aggressive impulse and the fear of pending punishment. This fear had been trapped in his muscles along with his memories of the conflict around those same movement patterns.

** Chronic generalized muscle contraction is an indicator of blocked self-vigor or of chronic generalized anxiety. In many cases, chronic generalized anxiety is the result of vigor suppression by the environment. Chronic generalized muscle contraction (tension) serves as a physiological screen against the frightening sensation of anxiety. Seen from another vantage point, generalized muscle contractions may serve as a substitute for the protective shield that should have been provided by the patient's mother. As a result his body became a prison, in which he moved in circles of infantile rage.

Episode 2. Yally – A state of chronic fatigue
Yally lost her mother at the age of five. Time and again she returns to her memory with tears.

She sits with her back against the wall, facing me. She reminisces how her mother lay on the sofa and complained about her helplessness and fatigue. Yally lies on her belly and turns her body horizontally from side to side. As she does this she cries softly and says: "All my life I feel wrapped by unexplained fatigue" …She sobs and whispers intermittently: "I miss my mother's soft stomach. I close my body in a turtle-like shell. The crust of the shell is hard creating a wall between me and the world. But inside the turtle-shell my stomach is soft like the stomach of my mother."

Following this episode she turns to her back and stretches her arms from her body up towards an invisible object. "I want to reach out and touch her face but my arms feel fragile like a baby's arms."

My reflections:

1. When we think of body memory, whose body do we have in mind, the mother's or the reminiscing child? Is the general fatigue her own or that of her sick mother?
2. The dominance of horizontal postures in a body memory seems to indicate that this memory had been crystallized in the P-0 phase of body relations.

3. Drawing from years of clinical experience, I have come to assume that body memories from the parental envelope phase are based on a special mechanism, which can be referred to as *kinesthetic introjective identification* (which I now have re-discovered as *incorporate body memory*; Fuchs this volume). This mechanism is based on the early psychophysical condition of diffused boundaries between the body of the infant and its parents within the parental envelope. This condition creates kinesthetic links which bring with it the potential for *introjective identification* of parental behavior and emotive positions. The infant is likely to adopt body qualities and symptoms from its parents as a way of storing the feeling of implicit connectedness to the parent's body.

4. Yally's feeling that her arms are fragile may resonate with earlier feelings of helplessness which had been evoked and merged with later experiences of similar feeling tones.

Episode 3. Beth's mother – The queen of ice

Beth's mother lost her first born child to severe sickness. Beth was born one year later. Her mother was still mourning the loss of her dear, little girl and could not attend to her newborn baby. Each session started the same way. Beth would lay on her stomach motionless for about twenty minutes.

"My mother was like a mother of ice" said Beth. In my imagination my mother was the queen of ice. I felt that I must impersonate my dead sister by numbing my own body. I made it a surrogate body for her lost child. My body was a stage on which my mother played her bereavement. She dressed me with her tears and loneliness and the clothes which she had bought for her dead little baby."

As she talked her body was behaving like that of a little baby. It looked as if she wanted to embody the helpless, hypotonic dead sister through infantile movement patterns, such as for example, lying down, making soft hand motions, etc. I felt as though she was turning herself into a surrogate baby for her mourning mother. Repeatedly she would whisper: "I am so frightened" … "I do not understand what is going on around me." … "My body is frozen" … "I feel dead – like my sister". "I am afraid that I shall die like her".

My reflections:

I was not sure whether I should intervene or not. Then a thought crossed my mind:

* Here is another example of kinesthetic introjective identification which functions as an implicit means to preserve a virtual connection with a lost object (the dead sister). She kept her late sister "alive" in her own body by adopting body qualities and symptoms similar to those of that person. Through kinesthetic introjective identification with the motionless dead body of her sister, she made herself into a surrogate baby who would fill the vacuum left in her bereaved mother's heart. At the same time she hoped to attract her mother's attention to her but without success.

Memory clusters which reflect body qualities from Type [P-1]
developmental phase

The following episodes belong to Type [P-1] developmental phases, in which the body
reached physical separation, but there was no emotionally mature separation.

Episode 4. Lynn – Repressed motor impulse displaced into somatic reactions
Lynn (age 24) played with a ball. She threw it at the wall. After two or three throws
she stopped. Her body froze. Her forcefulness dissipated into a meek posture and faint
voice as she murmured: "I feel so helpless, so nauseous and dizzy. My mother beat me
frequently. Her anger petrified me. It still does. I am still emotionally like I'm an extension of hers." ..."I am so afraid. I feel my arms are blocked." Then she reminisced:
until I was five years old, I was a tomboy. I climbed trees, was wild and acted out in
class; and then they transferred me to another kindergarten. There, they had iron discipline. I was punished for practically every little movement and twitch and learned
very quickly to be afraid of virtually any movement at all." ... "There are moments
when I hate my mother." She speaks of hatred and rage in a timid tone of voice.

Episode 5. Sara – Emotional conflict locked in the muscles
Sara (36) suffers from mild arthritis. Her fingers are twisted and deformed, and her
arms weak. She reports "My hands hurt all the time especially when I feel anger." She
alternates between a passive meek posture and outbursts of aggressive motions aimed
at an invisible object. In one session, she sees a doll at a corner of the room. Hesitat-
ingly, she goes toward it and grabs it aggressively, hitting it and screaming: "I hate you.
I hate you. I hate you." She then explains that she feels a strong need to hurt her mother by pinching her skin as the mother did to her. "No, not to pinch, I want to hit her,
but I am afraid my hand will hurt even more." Suddenly her body collapsed and she
whispered: "You did not love me. Why did you not love me?" Her aggressive motions
turned into a soft hug. She embraced the doll and said, "I am so confused. I love you,
mommy. I want you to love me. I want to embrace you and be embraced by you."

> My reflections:
> Could Sara's arthritis be a sort of *somatic-emotive confusion* between conflict-
> ing love-anger impulses which pull the sensory-motor system to contradictory
> directions?
> Based on my clinical experience Emotorics' and the physiology of motor emotive
> discharge I put forward in the Hebrew book a hypothesis according to which
> when emotive feelings are blocked from active motor discharge they might be
> converted to somatic channels and be transformed to somatic illnesses such as
> asthma, dermatitis, visceral illnesses, headaches, to name but few.

For young infants and children who are unable to exert the motor vigor nausea, dizziness, and headaches are the last possible bodily defensive maneuvers. In some cases,

they are the result of displaced fight-or-flight energy from the motor system to somat-ic/visceral organs (Shahar-Levy 2001, 2004). I came to this working hypothesis after several therapeutic experiences in which the opposite had occurred. When during the process of dance/movement therapy persons who had suffered from somatic illnesses such as dermatitis or psoriasis, or digestive problems dared to evoke forceful move-ments in conjunction with relevant memory clusters and their condition improved tremendously.

Episode 6. Shelly – Infantile emotive patterns as a "magic" device to stop time
at a moment prior to the loss of harmony due to catastrophe
Shelly (age 10) was four years old when her parents divorced. Although she was very bright and well adjusted in school, she was often ridiculed by her peers because of her infantile behavior. In the clinic, Shelly wobbled around the room, aimlessly protrud-ing her tongue while moving her head from side to side. "I enjoy feeling silly. I want to be silly. I do not want to understand what goes on around me". The discrepancy between her real age and her emotive motor behavior puzzled me. Not only did she move like a toddler she also talked like one, using soft high pitched voice and broken sentences. Silly behavior or perpetuation of an archaic stage of development can be motivated by an implicit wish to stop the progress of time at a point prior to what the person experienced as "a catastrophe" which destroyed the family harmony.

My reflections:

Repetition of infantile emotive patterns sometimes seemed like an implicit body device to restore the time when an imagined harmonious life prevailed before a painful change (a "catastrophe") ruined it all. In Shelly's case her parents divorced when she was a toddler yet they continued to live in the same community. Her life became like a virtual King Solomon's Verdict: She was literally divided be-tween her mother's and father's new families. Her solution was to preserve her "old body" unchanged by perpetuation of infantile behavior and manner of talk. Unfortunately this behavior caused alienation and ridicule from her peers in spite of her high intelligence and academic achievements. I noted to myself that in therapy we shall have to work on bridging the gaps between Type-0 and Type-1 behavioral qualities as well as between her body level and her high intelligence.

Episode 7. Daniela – Kinesthetic introjective identification as a basis
for self-assurance
Daniela (32) came to therapy at the age of thirty-two. She describes her life as quite satisfactory. Daniela looked much younger than her real age. Her body was thin and bent forward. When she spoke there was a contrast between the soft, hesitant voice, and the clear-cut, well articulated use of words. She told me that she lost her mother when she was two years old and does not remember her at all. She was married and held an interesting position in a successful corporation. After the birth of her first child, she started to feel unexplained sadness when nursing. "No one had ever told

me anything about my mother. Nobody mentioned her name. I did not dare to ask because I was afraid to hurt my father's or my stepmother's feelings."

A repetitive body memory:

> Daniela stays on the rug and moves her fingers in front of her face. She watches how they move. As time passed, she would move her mouth in sucking movements. She looked calm and happy. She says: *"When I am like this, I feel connected to my innermost self. I don't know why"*. Daniela's body is curved, looking like a baby lying in the arms of a grown-up person. In this position she remains for a long time and whispers:
> "For a moment I felt the touch of my mother's skin. I felt held by her. But it is only when I am in this position that I can feel her closeness." Suddenly, Daniela sits up. She says: "I feel a burning sensation at the back of my neck". Gradually the sensation turns to a vague feeling of obscure longing. She rubs her neck vigorously then rises up and rubs her arms. These movements were followed by stepping forward and stretching her arms to the sides.

My reflections:

* The neck is the area in which one feels the mother's inner arm muscle as one sucks at mother's breast. It seems that Daniela "kinesthetically remembered" her mother's arm and that this kinesthetic memory constituted in Daniela's body a bridge to her mother's body.

In our last session Daniela said:

> I feel that I received my mother back. When I came to therapy, I said that I want to connect to my true self. I know now that I did so by reconnecting to the memory of my mother. "In my imagination I felt as if I was dancing with my mother." I felt with her that it was a moment of grace beyond words.

My reflections:

* Forgotten memories came to the surface and brought Daniela to a new awareness of how her body-self is forever intertwined with memories of her mother. This realization brought to life the good qualities of her lost mother and the awareness that these qualities were part of her emotive body memories and would always be with her. They would be an accessible source of inner nourishment.

Discussion

The activity of the motor system creates a dynamic link between the past and the present. When a submerged body memory cluster of implicit memories is partially lifted, the past speaks to the self through movements and body sensations in the present. Thus, new opportunities are created to confront and re-experience unresolved feelings and movement. In the process, fixated memory clusters and the stereotyped movement patterns which accompany them become more flexible.

The diagnostic value of the typological grid

According to Emotorics the activity of the motor system is seen as the underlying common denominator of diverse psychophysical phenomena and a central aspect of the motor system activity is the dynamic interplay between universal/paradigmatic qualities and personal/biographic ones.

I chose to focus here on the typologies elaborated upon in the *Emotorics Two-Prototype Grid*... The fact that body memory clusters stemming from the original experience with space, time and "remembered" significant others reappear in therapy enables therapist and client to decipher together the psychological meanings underlying fixated or spontaneous body behavior. I have been astonished to see how body typological similarities and differences between people enable me to formulate tentative answers to certain basic questions, such as: At what age did the trauma occur? Which body parts were most damaged? Which body parts carry the burden of the defensive efforts? Which body parts store traumatic memories? To what degree did these traumatic body memories impair future development and pleasurable body experiences?

A typological grid provides a common basis as well as a magnifying glass for the examination of certain "faults", such as rigidity, excess, and deficit in the self's individual psychomotor style. This opens the way to possible reconstruction of subjective narratives. The typological grid is not meant to replace other diagnostic models but to shed light on the body aspects of early infant-parent relations. It is meant to provide the therapist with an additional tool for amplifying empathy and understanding the moving person.

Within the special conditions created by DMT, emotive movement improvisation can facilitate a change of consciousness which enables "forgotten" sensations, images and reflections to come to the surface. These are often first enacted through seemingly out-of-context *body patterns*, entirely incongruent with the person's present age and situation in life. In fact, these patterns are not at all related to the present, but stem from original, long-forgotten experiences.

Sometimes it seems that an enactment is occurring in the therapy room, a drama in which one partner is visible but the other can only be implied through the movement. In this process boundaries between past and present, self and others, and situational conditions are dissolved into a particular, emerging experience. This is accompanied by changes in the expression of face, posture, and muscle tone. Even the voice may be transformed to that of a helpless child. It is as though the body clock stopped just at the point at which anxiety and helplessness first took their appearance, as though a short cut to the infantile phase has opened up. The body of the grown person has been taken over by primitive patterns, displaying early emotive physical attitudes, unresolved issues, and unfulfilled impulses.

I asked myself why in the case of Daniela unlike in most other cases the retrieved memories contained positive emotions in spite of the fact that she lost her mother so early? Can the preponderance of negative feelings in evoked memory clusters be the result of the fact that traumatic experience leaves a more powerful and long-lasting impression in the organism than benevolent experience? In the case of Daniela, there was fortunately an inner core of beneficial support. In the other cases, there were clusters of difficult, inhibiting feelings, such as sadness, anger, and helplessness.

Retrieval of body memories can bring about changes in feeling states. Blocked impulses, which had been dormant for years, may come to the surface in a blend of implicit and explicit memories, opening up new possibilities for insight and growth. In this process, new opportunities are created for exploring archaic, inner feeling states as well as body posture in relation to space, time, energy, and objects.

Initially, movement may evoke painful memories. But, as therapy progresses, the mover's healthy resources are released and become increasingly prevalent. Thus the body can become a source of self empowerment leading to insight, embodied alternatives, and alleviation of pain.

References

Fuchs, T. (this volume). The phenomenology of body memory. In S. C. Koch, T. Fuchs, M. Summa & C. Müller (Eds.), *Body memory, metaphor and movement*. Amsterdam: John Benjamins.

Khan, R. M. (1974). *The privacy of the self*. New York: International University Press.

Kohut, H. (1977). *The restoration of the self*. New York: International University Press.

Mahler, M. S., Pine, F. & Bergman, A. (Eds.). (1975). *The psychological birth of the human infant*. New York: Basic Books.

Panksepp, J. (2003). At the interface of affective, behavioral, and cognitive neurosciences: Decoding the emotional feelings of the brain. *Brain and Cognition, 52,* 4–14.

Shahar-Levy, Y. (2004). *The visible body reveals the secrets of the mind* (in Hebrew). Jerusalem: Author's Edition.

Shahar-Levy, Y. (2001). The function of the human motor system in processes of storing and retrieving preverbal, primal experience. *Psychoanalytic Inquiry 21*(3). New Jersey: The Analytic Press.

Shahar-Levy, Y. (2001, 2004). *The visible body reveals the secrets of the mind: A body-movement-mind paradigm (BMMP) for the analysis and interpretation of emotive movement* (in Hebrew). Jerusalem: Author's Edition.

Shahar-Levy, Y. (2005). Typology of emotive movement. *Dialogues: Journal of Clinical Psychology Israel* (in Hebrew).

Shahar-Levy, Y. (2009). Emotorics: A psychomotor Model for the Analysis and Interpretation of Emotive Motor Behavior. In S. Chaiklin & H. Wengrower (Eds.), *The art and science of Dance Movement Therapy* (pp. 256–297). New York: Routledge / Taylor & Francis Group.

Shahar-Levy, Y. & Trautmann-Voigt, Sabine (2009). Das body movement mind paradigm (BMMP) [The body movement mind paradigm (BMMP)]. In S. Trautmann-Voigt & B. Voigt (Eds.), *Grammatik der Körpersprache* [The grammar of body language]. Stuttgart: Schattauer.

CHAPTER 21

The emergence of body memory in Authentic Movement

Ilka Konopatsch and Helen Payne
University of Hertfordshire

The re-discovery and integration of body and bodily-felt experience as well as the connection between different levels of processing are essential parts of the practice of Authentic Movement (AM). Memories and regression can be experienced as more "whole" by adding formerly unconscious or forgotten bodily-felt aspects. Embodying metaphors may lead to a direct experience of their structure. The integration of different levels of experience can be furthered through metaphors which support a holistic understanding of the body-mind process as well as the communication between mover and witness. The BodyMind Approach (BMA) facilitates the connection and sense-making between body movement, sensation, imagination, feeling and cognition for patients suffering Medically Unexplained Symptoms (MUS) (Payne 2009a, 2009b).

Keywords: Authentic Movement, memory, metaphor, body-mind experience, body-mind approach

Invisible bodies

When Johnson (2007) is talking about "bodily disappearance" the "recessive body" or "background disappearance", he is arguing that many of our bodily processes, our perceptive organs, much of our sensory-motor system and our internal organs, are vital to making experience possible, consciously accessible. Thus we rely on the body functioning without necessarily feeling how this function is taking place. Johnson concludes that "*The principal result of these forms of bodily disappearance is our sense that our thoughts, and even our feelings, go on somehow independent of our bodily process*" (Johnson 2007:6).

Zitt (2008) describes another kind of body disappearance contrasted by the ever growing attention on body appearance in the media and personal lives. "*The body ... is getting a great amount of attention in Western society and culture ... while at the same time the sensual perception of body sensations and basic bodily needs seem to disappear*" (Zitt 2008: 39, translated by author).

Under this influence, the body is presented with a new set of expectations to fit the standards of health and beauty promoted by mass media. At the same time it appears to have lost its meaning as a working body, and the awareness of one's physical well-being is increasingly ignored. The sensitive, feeling and knowing body is rarely taken into account on either the grounds of natural condition or cultural reality. Nevertheless, a large number of people are seeking a different approach to their bodies through sports, yoga, meditation etc. In the therapies, this seeking is reflected by a growing attention paid to the arts and body-based therapies.

There, the feeling and sensing body returns to the focus of attention. We are eager to re-learn focussing and relying on the resource of the body's natural knowledge.

> Trusting the experience of the body is the hardest because most of us don't feel the body. I think that's why we keep being more and more removed from the body because it's not seeable in a way that is valued in our culture.
>
> (Sullwold 2007: 49)

Authentic Movement, as an approach to self-exploration, intends to create a space for hidden, unconscious and sensitive personal themes to be explored. By being movement-based, it is creating a space for the "hidden" body. In the process of allowing the mover to connect to body sensations, thoughts, feelings and needs equally, some of the above effects of the 'appearance emphasised' pre-occupation with the body might be reduced.

Authentic Movement

Authentic Movement (AM) aims to "*increase connections between body, mind and spirit*" (Payne 2006: 161). The approach, originally named 'moving from within' (Whitehouse 1979), was first developed by American dance therapist, dancer and teacher Mary Whitehouse. Her own Jungian analysis and interest in Jungian studies influenced her work, so Authentic Movement is closely associated with Jung's concept of active imagination. Due to it's reliance on spontaneous movement and self-directness it can also be viewed as a form of free association in movement (Payne 2006).

The ground form of Authentic Movement involves two people, termed 'mover' and 'witness', who usually meet in a studio or an other safe and quiet environment offering enough space for movement. The movement part of the practice involves no use of music or props other than a cushion to sit on and some blankets if they should be needed.

The role of the mover is to descend into a process that is comparable to active imagination or free association. After a warm up and agreement on time frame, she is closing her eyes and turns her focus inward to any body sensation, feeling, thought or image arises. There is no instruction or thematic aim to a movement sequence. On the contrary, movers are encouraged to stay congruent to their experience and let the body take the lead in exploring upcoming themes. These threads can then be followed or dismissed whenever it feels appropriate, in movement or stillness (Payne 2006) with the eyes kept closed. Stillness can be experienced just as meaningful as movement in this context, dismissing an impulse as important as following it.

One mover describes her descent into the process like this:

> *Hm, it's always different. Sometimes I have reacted to inner images, sometimes there was nothing, just emptiness. Sometimes there was at twitch of muscles or the arm just suddenly started to move. That can be very different.*
> (Interviewee FC, Konopatsch 2005: 56, translation by author)

A movement sequence can last between just a few minutes up to half an hour or more. In group settings, longer sequences are used frequently. Consequently, usually more than one theme emerges in a session. As the process is not shaped by expectation or direction, it could be best described as an ongoing stream of sensations and ideas that, just like in active imagination, might lead to unexpected insights "*that means, I embody these images, then this is not right anymore. Then I let go. It's an ongoing trying 'Where am I' without losing myself*" (Interviewee FA, Konopatsch 2005: 58, translation by author).

The role of the witness is usually taken by the facilitator/teacher. In a group setting participants also act as witnesses for other group members. The witness sits in stillness in the presence of the mover's experience. She follows the mover's physical movements as well as her own inner process in response to what she is seeing. She is also keeping the time, signalling the beginning and end of a movement sequence, so that the mover can slowly return and open her eyes.

From a witness's notes:

> *One mover on her belly, tapping a rhythm with her hands. Clicking a rhythm with her fingers. Then she stretches one arm out, directed towards me. I imagine she is saying, come on, join!*   (Extract from personal journal)

After moving, transition is an optional part of an Authentic Movement session. It is a time where neither mover nor witness speak yet, but may individually engage in writing, drawing or other creative expression. Some movers also use this time to meditate. The witness can take notes while still attending to her task as time-keeper and facilitator. The mover can use this time to reflect within creative expression which can facilitate her personal processing. Material from transition can be taken into the verbal sharing if the mover wishes to do so.

After moving, mover and witness sit together to speak. The mover has the opportunity to share significant elements of the movement experience as she speaks first about her specific remembered movements, connecting them then with images, feelings etc. that accompanied the movement.

Then witness speaks with unconditional positive regard (Rogers 1973), carefully selecting those aspects of her own experience that respond to the elements already mentioned by the mover. Adler refers to the importance of a witness who is aware of her own personal history and her boundaries (Adler 2002). Great care is also taken in the way experiences are put into words, especially by the witness who speaks in the present tense and owns her projections and interpretations by a strict discipline regarding the verbal format. Staying in the present tense and other verbal structures help to ensure emotional safety for the mover. In consequence, processes of transference and counter-transference become transparent for both mover and witness, furthering the understanding of their individual process.

Authentic Movement is mostly used in a group setting. Within the group, participants can take on a set of different roles and change from being a mover to becoming witness for another one in the group, while the facilitator remains meta-witness for the group as a whole. The number of movers or witnesses for a set movement sequence may vary, allowing the group to explore the effects of these variations on communication, responsibility and verbal exchange.

Body-mind experience in Authentic Movement

Closing their eyes at the beginning of a movement session, movers exclude visual input and turn their focus inward. By turning away from the dominant levels of conscious every-day experience, space and attention is given to what we may call "body wisdom" to unfold.

Beginners in Authentic Movement practice start by learning how to pay attention to their body sensations, feelings or thoughts that may eventually turn into an impulse to move. Authentic Movement is suitable for participants with a strong sense of self and probably some former experience of therapy or self-exploration. In applied approaches, such as the BodyMind Approach, teaching body awareness can be a vital part of the work alongside the mover-witness experience. Practicing inner listening is promoting a new focus on body experience. The mover is becoming aware of the body in connection to emotional states. The emerging movement is not restricted by any frame, technique or purpose. Movers are encouraged to follow their own individual impulses, whether these are visible in movement or not. Tracking one's movement without planning or generating it creates a new state of being in the body and the mind while at the same time being aware of one's body in space. While letting go and following free flowing movement, movers are at the same time responsible for ensuring that they move safely for their own benefit and for others in the group. When moving strongly and fast they are asked to open their eyes slightly and briefly to be sure of their position in space and that of others around them. They develop an increasing awareness of spatial boundaries and of the body's natural ability to sense others in the room. In fact, interruption between movers or between mover and object occur very rarely. By the heightened sensibility to sound, temperature and other senses, participants learn to adjust their movements accordingly. The witness, sitting in stillness, is a constant reference point for the mover's spatial and emotional journey.

Self-exploration and change are sometimes experienced purely in the body, without the need for verbalisation. The why and how of an action is not necessarily available to the conscious mind, yet it can clearly be experienced in the body, often accompanied by a feeling of deep satisfaction. The endpoint of a process is often more apparent to mover and witness. For example, after a long period of heaviness and working on the floor, a mover might get up and jump. After months of activity, another mover may finally lie down. Clearly the body in AM is not a mere pathway to explore a problem or discover hidden conflicts. Much rather, if followed, it may offer pathways and solutions by its own means. The body itself may facilitate change.

> We need to trust that the body has its own wisdom, that it is enough for the experience just to stay in the body. The body wants to tell its own story by moving. Movement is the body's story.   (Sullwold 2007:49)

While some movement sessions evolve purely around body sensations, more often movers experience a connection between the body and other levels of experience. With practice, following and tracking one's movement becomes easier, and movers become more aware of accompanying thoughts and images. Simultaneity creates new meaning experiences complement, change and contradict each other.

The surrender to a movement impulse, awareness of different levels of experience and the meta-perspective of tracking one's own movement together result in a state of "moving and being moved" (Whitehouse 1979).

Memory and regression: Body-mind connections to the past

> Because of the natural wisdom of the body and its capacity to store every memory at 'bone level'.   (Adler 1999:146)

We are entering into Authentic Movement with a physical history and we may connect to it through our body. Memories can be triggered through a certain movement, a body position, at other times a memory can be the initial impulse to move. Either way, the cognitive recollection is connected to the body experience, which points out the body-mind aspect of Authentic Movement. A memory can even evolve completely around a bodily-felt sensation such as in the following example:

> *Having lost my great aunt who was very dear to me some months earlier, I moved without the intention to focus on this event. After a while of moving around and searching, I found myself in a position where one of my hands lay in the other. Suddenly and vehemently I remembered an event that happened two or three years before. I had visited my aunt in hospital for some minor illness and was holding her hand, me sitting in a chair, her sitting on her bed wearing a*

nightdress. I realised how the hand I was holding now in the movement session, my own, was so similar to the one I was holding then, my great aunt's. At this moment all my held-back grief for the recent loss broke through as well as a deep gratitude for the memory of closeness that I was given in that moment. To this day I have access to the memory of my aunt's hand by recalling the movement session.   (Extract from personal journal)

The mover's memory in this narrative was triggered by a body position, i.e. holding her own hand. Experiencing the recollection in a body-mind-state added an additional, formerly unnoticed aspect to the memorised event, the feeling of her aunt's hand in hers at the event a few years ago. The bodily-felt aspect also promoted a new insight, the similarity of the two hands, thus making a connection to the lost person. Emotions of loss and of gratitude were firmly set in the present time, the movement session. The memory, by being directly experienced in the body is connecting past experience to the present process. By sharing the experience with her witness verbally, this mover was enabled to further process the event and make a connection with the future through the lasting body-mind-memory of her aunt.

The amount of simultaneous input, cognitive recollection, body sensation, insight and emotion may sound much to deal with. Nevertheless it is usually experienced as a natural flow of impressions and sensations in a state of heightened attentiveness. The complexity of tasks is easily addressed within movement. Unravelling and integrating experiences are happening at the same time, integration furthered and deepened in transition and in verbalisation with the witness.

Authentic Movement and metaphor

The emergence of metaphors and the conscious dealing with them are important factors in the integrative process, and integral parts of Authentic Movement. Due to their multi-modal nature, metaphors are especially useful in accessing themes otherwise too complex to grasp.

Metaphors and symbols evolve throughout the Authentic Movement process. During the movement experience they can emerge directly out of the bodily movement or be initiated by a thought or image. Just like the memories described above, they are felt and moved in, and by, the body not thought about or reflected upon, but directly experienced in movement. According to Samaritter, metaphors have different sources: personal, cultural and archetypal (Samaritter 2009). Personal metaphors she claims, represent individual body experience that can also be represented in spoken language. Conceptual metaphor theory roots the genesis of metaphorical thinking in body experience so that abstract conceptualizations are linked back to body process (Johnson 2007). Regarding Authentic Movement, one could possibly say that the mover experiences "being" both the embodied and the abstract meaning of a metaphor by accessing the physical sensation at the same moment as the abstract idea thus consciously experiencing the source domain and the target domain connected in the same instance.

Lackoff (2008) describes the emergence of primary metaphor through the simultaneous occurrence of experiences. A body sensation, such as warmth, and an emotion, such as affection, can be connected on a neuronal level. He says "*Thus, Affection is Warmth arises from experiencing affection while being held by one's parents and simultaneously experiencing their body warmth*" (Lackoff 2008: 187).

Those most basic connections, reflecting the structure of some of our metaphorical thinking, can potentially be experienced in movement. Similar to the experience of regression, various levels of processing are active at the same time. A body sensation experienced in Authentic Movement is receiving metaphorical meaning of affection or positive energy. In the following example, for the mover, the different experiences in the flow of the movement sequence are held together by the metaphoric meaning and the personal sense making resulting from it. A mover reports:

> ... *at some point my hand came to this sun and I felt this warmth and a huge amount of pain swelled up, many tears, but I was THERE, I had arrived. And this was a key moment in Authentic Movement that I would have experienced in a completely different way in verbal therapy. So this warmth then came through the hand and through the whole body and that was as if, also here, I can receive the sun I need to survive.*
>
> (Interviewee FA, Konopatsch 2005: 63, translation by author)

Just as metaphors have the potential to integrate different levels of processing and connect them to a holistic experience, metaphors can also help to further reflect movement experience thus enhancing the mover's ability for change. In movement metaphors first evolve in their embodied form. The mover can literally 'move on' with them and process and change are facilitated in the body experience, as described above. After the movement in transition time the same metaphor is processed or other, new complementary images may be found. In addressing a new level of processing through different media such as writing, drawing and clay work, a different quality or aspect is added to the experience through the different medium and integration of the movement experience into cognitive awareness may be reached.

In verbal sharing, the communicative value of metaphors becomes especially apparent. The witness, may already have seen perceived the embodied metaphor already in sitting with the mover, present with empathy, throughout the movement sequence. Now she has the opportunity to learn about the mover's experience through the words and metaphors offered by the mover. The mover speaks about the experience and name a metaphor or may show a picture etc. If she resonates with it, the witness can respond with an image or metaphor that evolved in the presence of the mover's experience. Both these metaphors are rooted in the body. Firstly, in the mover's body – the one who is expressing the embodied metaphor. Secondly, in the witness's body that is responding to this expression with sensation, image etc. For the understanding and communication between mover and witness this is of particular value.

> ... the importance of metaphor conveying complexity and facilitating a deep understanding between client and therapist or between group members, allowing those individuals to provide the kind of silent "not-knowing" (yet deeply understanding) witness that conveys far more than words, and also allowing for the transformative qualities of the metaphor to reveal themselves.
> (Meekums 2008: 27)

In the following example, one metaphorical image is guiding the mover through the entire Authentic Movement process:

> *One mover is going down on her knees. She is suddenly in a jungle, surrounded by huge plants. A tiger, moving slowly, looking out for prey she is feeling the energy and power in her body.*
> *In transition she draws a tiger's head in strong colours with piercing eyes. A sense of satisfaction is present, having put this feeling into a visual expression. In the verbal exchange she talks about the experience and shares the picture with her witness. The witness, in turn reports having seen a big cat moving around the room. She in turn, offers to show her picture drawn in transition time. The mover accepts to see the picture and finds not a tiger's but a leopard's pattern – a rather delicate drawing that she feels connects and adds another quality to her own interpretation of her experience, making it more complete. When mover and witness put the drawings on the wall they realize, that their drawings indeed connect in two touching lines at the bottom of the tiger's head and the top of the witness's more abstract drawing.*   (Extract from personal journal)

A web of connections was made visible in the process described above. The mover was fully involved in a body-mind-experience embodying the image of the tiger in movement, exploring different qualities of the image such as strength and power. She then transferred some of this experience into drawing and speaking to her witness.

Witness and mover connected through sharing a similar metaphor, then silently reflecting on it individually in transition, and finally by sharing visual and verbal references to the experience. Similar or matching metaphors, especially when experienced non-verbally can be deeply touching for both mover and witness.

> *Such a feeling of inner strengthening and support. To be seen in this moment. And that the image was the same as my witness's image. That was so incredible for me! I felt so much strengthened and supported. In a way I hadn't known before.*   (Interviewee FC, Konopatsch 2005: 71, translation by author)

Contradicting metaphors may also be shared by the witness, especially since the process is not focused on the mover but on the movement experience. In this way it offers an opportunity to explore differentiation (rather than unity), witness perceptions and transference in relation to their own individual experience.

Implications for clinical application: The BodyMind Approach

The BodyMind Approach (BMA) derives from Dance Movement Psychotherapy with a strong emphasis on Authentic Movement. It, too, *"engages the fundamental inter-relationship between body and mind"* (Payne 2009a) and is especially used in a group setting for patients suffering from Medically Unexplained Symptoms (MUS).

Authentic Movement's main feature, the relationship between witness and mover is an essential part of the BodyMind Approach (BMA), together with a set of more structured techniques such as body awareness and relaxation exercises. Participants are encouraged to write a diary and set goals for their personal development. The aim is to integrate verbal and non-verbal medium and to enhance the patient's self-reflective process in order to improve well-being and symptom-distress (Payne 2009a). Patients with MUS are different compared to the population featured above. In contrast to the above mentioned background disappearance of the body, they are painfully aware of their bodies. Nevertheless, chronic pain is only one symptom amongst others such as musculo-skeletal aches and pain, tinnitus, skin conditions, headaches, dizziness and panic attacks. Whereas in AM movers usually go into a movement sequence without a set goal, patients attending BMA groups have an interest and intention to reduce or control the symptoms from which they suffer. Even though attention is forced on their body by physical distress, the sensitive, feeling and "knowing" body remains hidden unless addressed in the BMA process and in Authentic Movement. Structured exercises offer the first positive engagement these patients have had with their bodies in a long while and at the same time support coping strategies that are applicable outside the group setting.

In a pilot study carried out between 2005 and 2007 researchers found that participants reported an increased awareness of the close connection between emotions and physical reactions (Payne 2009a). Further findings from both quantitative (Payne & Stott 2010) and qualitative studies (Payne 2009b) showed an increased level of well-being, self-esteem and self-reflection. Doctor visits and medication were often reduced and generally activity levels, the symptom distress and stress management were improved. Some participants were able to identify cause and effects in the body-mind relationship and by stopping the cause as a consequence, were able to inhibit or reduce the symptom.

In BMA, as in AM, physical expression is met with unconditional positive regard. The symptom, which might or might not act as a symbol or metaphor for some of the participants' emotional situations, is initially accepted as one part amongst others in the mover's overall bodily-experience and physical history. By slowly making connections between body and other processes, attention is opened to all kinds of physical experience including body-learning, increased self-understanding and changes in life-style.

Moving in the collective

Authentic Movement is mostly used in group settings. Experience is different than in the ground form of the mover-witness dyad. Different themes can be explored as a member of a group. The evolving of memories and metaphors is influenced by other movers' processes. Movers can also change perspective and become witness for another member of the group. By attending to their process in the service of their mover, and in resonance with the other's experience, or the inter-relatedness of experiences, transference and compassion become more present and are, again, related to the actual bodily experience during witnessing.

As a mover in a group of many, people meet. They touch, they hear each other, avoid or welcome each other. Even without contact movers are aware of being in a group and the individual experience is put into perspective with this reality. Memories and regression can change in so far as other bodies and sounds might be either included in the triggering of the memory, or in the embodiment and "moving with" the memory. For example, when a mover leaning against another mover's leg, remembers leaning against her mother as a little child.

Making contact with another mover often involves images and metaphors. Two movers often share a similar story or image, sometimes they each move within their own individual fantasies. On occasion, an entire group can become involved in a shared story. "*I mean, there are other people, there is sound, there are voices, maybe with these voices the fantasy of a choir in Greece, sometime, a thousand years ago emerges*" (Interviewee FA, Konopatsch 2005: 57, translated by author). A witness becoming aware of such a story or image can share this with the group a piece of 'collective witnessing'.

Conclusion

In Authentic Movement different levels of experience are present at the same time. Thinking, sensing and imagining are related to the body in movement. By making conscious connections, experiences can gain new meaning and further personal insight. Memories recalled in movement may be triggered by thoughts, images, movement or body sensation. The bodily-felt aspect of a memory can be added to the recollection of a meaningful event. Integration and understanding are furthered by embodied metaphors. While these can change and "be moved with" further processing takes place in clay-work, writing, drawing and verbalization. Metaphors also facilitate communication and understanding between mover and witness and thus support the development of their relationship. In the BodyMind Approach, the principle of becoming aware, and of connecting and integrating different levels of experience is applied for those suffering from MUS. The combination of verbal and non-verbal techniques, together with moving and witnessing supplements participant's sense-making and symptom-management and often lead to the symptom's disappearance or reduction. Practicing Authentic Movement in a group setting is changing and enriching the mover's experience of herself and others, also by taking on the role of the witness for other group members. This unique way of sharing the process of self-exploration in movement creates a sense of belonging in the group. The basic underlying principle of "both-and" (Whitehouse 1979), of discovering and connecting, of differentiation, unity and integration is mirrored in the group, where each is attending to their own process whilst being part of the collective.

As Janet Adler describes it:

> This unrehearsed, synchronous unfolding of events creates a village story. Movers and witnesses participate within the complexity of their own individual personalities, doing what they each must do. It is the story of a collection of people bringing unconscious material into consciousness, through embodiment, because of each other. It is not unlike a cluster of cells, like the heart, in which each cell is doing what it must do, resulting in a pumping heart.
>
> (Adler 1999:199)

References

Adler, J. (1999). The collective body. In P. Pallaro (Ed.), *Authentic movement* (pp. 190–204). Philadelphia: Jessica Kingsley.

Adler, J. (2002). *Offering from the conscious body*. Vermont: Rochester.

Johnson, M. (2007). *The meaning of the body*. Chicago: University of Chicago Press.

Konopatsch, I. (2005). *Warum Authentische Bewegung?* [Why Authentic Movement?] Unpublished Masters Thesis, Technical University, Berlin.

Lackoff, G. (2008). The neuroscience of metaphoric gestures. In A. Cienki & C. Müller (Eds.), *Metaphor and gesture* (pp. 283–289). Amsterdam/Philadelphia: John Benjamins.

Meekums, M. (2008). Spontaneous symbolism in clinical supervision. In H. Payne (Ed.), *Supervision of Dance Movement Psychotherapy* (pp. 18–32). London: Routledge.

Payne, H. (2006). The body as container and expresser. In J. Corrigall, H. Payne & H. Wilkinson (Eds.), *About a body: Working with the embodied mind in psychotherapy*. London: Routledge.

Payne, H. (2009a). Pilot study to evaluate Dance Movement Psychotherapy (the BodyMind Approach) in patients with medically unexplained symptoms: Participant and facilitator perceptions and a summary discussion. *Body, Movement and Dance in Psychotherapy*, 4(2), 77–94.

Payne, H. (2009b). Medically unexplained conditions and the BodyMind Approach. *Counselling in Primary Care Review*, 10(1), 6–8.

Payne, H. & Stott, D. (2010). Change the moving bodymind: Quantitative results from a pilot study on the use of the BodyMind approach (BMA) to psychotherapeutic group work with patients with medically unexplained symptoms (MUS). *Counselling and Psychotherapy*, 10(4), 1–12.

Rogers, C. R. (1973). *Die klient-bezogene Gesprächstherapie* [Client-centered therapy]. München: Kindler.

Samaritter, R. (2009). The use of metaphors in dance movement therapy. *Body, Movement and Dance in Psychotherapy, 4*(1), 33–43.

Sullwold, E. & Ramsay, M. (2007). A dancing spirit: Remembering Mary Starks Whitehouse. In P. Pallaro (Ed.), *Authentic Movement*. Volume Two (pp. 45–49). London: Jessica Kingsley.

Whitehouse, M. (1979). C. G. Jung and dance therapy. In P. Pallaro (Ed.), *Authentic Movement* (pp. 73–101). Philadelphia: Jessica Kingsley.

Zitt, C. (2008). *Vom medialen Körperkult zum gesellschaftlichen Krankheitsbild* [From the media-related body cult to the societal model of illness]. Wien: Praesens Verlag.

CHAPTER 22

Nakedness, hunger, hooks and hearts

Embodied memories and movement psychological processes in dance therapy and movement pedagogy

Helle Winther
University of Copenhagen

In spite of many different theoretical approaches, there is today substantial agreement that body and psyche must be regarded as a coherent dynamic and organic system with innate cultural and social significance, some of which may be observed directly in the body and movement of the individual. This article is based on this often primarily theoretically grounded observation, and reveals, through narratives from movement pedagogic and dance therapeutic contexts, a need for regarding the multidimensional meanings of not just the body, but also of movement. The narratives in the article about embodied memories concern emotional nakedness, existential hunger, felt "hooks" and wounded hearts. The question is whether investigations of body and movement may create a counterweight to the pervasive focus on verbalization, and give occasion to examine problems and possibilities for solutions through concrete and direct access to the body's basic expressivity, rooted in embodied experience.

Keywords: embodied memory, multidimensionality of the body, narrative research, embodied experience, change processes

My heart has been torn out

I miss you, Mother.
It hurts indescribably.
It's like my heart has been torn out of my chest.
I feel so open and vulnerable.
It's like my legs cannot really carry me and move me forward – I feel a constant unrest and cramps in my legs, they feel so tense.
My back almost always hurts – it's like I can't straighten up, my back feels both tense and loose in its joints at the same time.

I'm almost always surrounded by kind, obliging, loving people whom I
appreciate and am fond of, still I feel alone.
It's so difficult for me to see the future without you.
It's like I have lost a part of myself.   (Asta)

The body experience cited above was written by Asta shortly after her mother's death. Thus Asta opens this article, in which phenomenologically inspired narratives attempt to put into words, exemplify and reflect on embodied memories and movement psychological processes in dance therapy and movement pedagogy.

This article reveals, through narratives and embodied memories from movement pedagogy and dance therapy contexts, a need for considering the multidimensional significance of not just the body, but of movement of the body.

Practitioner research and narrative methods

This presentation originates from a research project entitled "Movement Psychology: The Language of the Body and the Psychology of Movement Based on the Dance Therapy Form Dansergia" (Winther 2009).

In this multidisciplinary research project, the author explores her own practice in the fields of both movement pedagogy and dance therapy (Winther 2009, 2010). Exploration of own practice is inspired by what Jarvis (1999) and Payne (1993) term *practitioner research*. This position brings with it an inevitable subjectivity. Thus the practitioner researcher oversteps especially the positivistic research tradition's inherent criteria of objectivity and validity, which on the one hand may be regarded as a serious point of criticism. On the other hand, the practitioner researcher, besides having a challenging double role, has the possibility, as Jarvis (ibid.) writes, to catch and register nuances in various situations in practice which are able to be noticed only by experience-based and qualitative involvement. The practitioner researcher is, exactly because he/she is involved in practice, able to describe aspects of situations with a depth and empathic and bodily understanding that traditional forms of research would not be able to maintain (ibid.: 36).

Embodied memories are by their very nature sensual and complex, and thus not readily available for verbalization. Therefore, research on bodily experiences is also a methodological challenge. The richness of embodied memories and bodily experiences and movement expression is found solely in the immediate experience itself. In a process of reflection, we are challenged to work with only certain aspects of the whole experience, but nevertheless, as researchers in the field of movement we are aiming to find methods that may capture a living, expressive complexity. Therefore, it may be important for researchers to take the challenge seriously, and dare to venture away from a one-dimensional writing position thus striving for a multi-dimensional writing process (Sparkes 2003).

Therefore, this article builds on narrative method sources, inspired by phenomenological, narrative and autoethnographic research methods, among others (Merleau-Ponty 1962/2004; Tordres 2007; Sparkes 2002, 2003; Winther 2009, 2010). It is based on poetic autoethnographically inspired narratives from the fields of both movement pedagogy and dance therapy. The narratives are written by Max, Asta, Karen, and Signe, and the author has been present in all of the situations described in the article. Max is a 25 year old student. Asta, Karen and Signe are women between the ages of 30 and 48 years old. Signe is new to dance therapy, while Karen and Asta have worked with dance therapy for several years.

Max, whom the reader will meet in a moment, has completed an education with a professional focus on developing both practical and teaching competence in dance.[1] Asta, Karen, and Signe, whom we will meet later, have worked with personal change processes through the dance therapy form Dansergia.[2] For ethical reasons, their names have been changed here.

Because the article is inspired by phenomenology and focuses on meeting what is living and respecting the bodily narratives as a foreground, its structure is a constant dialogue between narratives and theory. In order to "get closer to" the body, the narratives will often be presented before relevant theory.

Therefore, we shall now go into Max's learning process in a movement pedagogical context. In connection with his education, Max is to create his own personal dance solo. He chooses to create a dance about identity.

On identity, feelings, and body

> *The overriding theme of the solo was identity. I got the energy from the frustration I felt when I try to change and develop myself, and discover that I just end up where I started anyway. I think we all, from time to time, would like to be different, or maybe even worse, be someone else entirely. That we feel stuck in a role, or that a given situation makes the development you want impossible. It was that feeling, that frustration that I tried to express in my solo.* (Max)

---

1. At the Department of Exercise and Sport Sciences, University of Copenhagen, Denmark.

2. Dansergia, which has been developed on the basis of the body therapeutic theories and methods of LEP (Life Energy Process), is based on a combination of Western and Eastern interpretations of the concept of life energy understood as a basic dynamic life force (Zoetler et al. 2001; Sabetti 1986). The therapeutic work in Dansergia builds on a wholeness-oriented view of the body, and focuses, as do other forms of dance movement therapy "(…) more on being moved by life energy than on trying to move it. We understand that the life force in all things is already in motion. We only need to discover how it moves, where it moves and why" (Sabetti 2001: 13).

Max chose to create a dance solo about identity, a dance that is based in the feeling of being stuck without the possibility of changing. Being "stuck" is a metaphor, which immediately may bring to mind an inner image of something or someone who wishes to, but cannot move.

At the same time, Max describes almost the same image at the start of his creative process, on the basis of a concrete body and emotional experience:

> I had feared that perilous Friday for a long time, the day of my solo performance. I have not really been afraid of performing in front of the others, or of not being able to find something to perform. I think that in secret, I have feared doing what I had wanted to do the most – trying to express my feelings with my body. During the idea and practice phases, I was never successful in giving into it and feeling it. My body danced away, but 'I' wasn't there.   (Max)

Also in this situation, in which there is a conflict between "my body" and "me," between the physical movement and the psychological and emotional state, may be characterized as "stuck."

When Max isn't successful at "giving into" and "feeling" in the above situation, he is confronted with the fact that he, if he wishes to express his feelings through the body, *cannot* in this context be satisfied with working with the body as an instrument or an object that he can exercise, direct, and control. Perhaps he is used to this, and it is this understanding of the body that is being shaken:

> I have always thought that I had a good body consciousness. My body has been practical and goal-directed, and has always solved a given task very satisfactorily, whether it has been a dive, a long pass in handball, or running short or long distances.   (Max)

If Max chooses to work with practical, goal-directed quality in this dance context, he will only meet a body that "dances away" without identification with the movement.

Thus his description, rich as it is in experience, goes to the heart of a discussion about various ways of regarding the body, in which the landscape of theory shifts significantly before the waves of change role in over realities that are closer to practice.

In research on body culture – and, one might add, implicitly in the various body cultures – two seemingly contradictory pairs of concepts appear repeatedly. Most deeply, they concern the contrast between the apparently controllable idealized image and felt experience, between the "the others" or perhaps what the individual sees and wishes to see, and what can be felt or not felt: the contrast between, on the one hand, *having a body*, and on the other hand, *being a body*; the contrast between, on the one hand, having a body that we can use, form, master, repair, and consciously present on the basis of our self-image, and on the other hand, being an alive and experienced body with senses, feelings, and sometimes an uncontrollable inner life. These opposite pairs of concepts describe dualistic struggle about the body as culture or nature, and is often termed *body construction* or *body experience* (Damasio 1994; Csordas 1999;

Totton 2010). The core of the discussion itself reflects its dualism. Western culture is still characterized by the legacy of Descartes, which separates body and mind thought and feeling, nature and culture. This has taken many years to change into a more nuanced and multidimensional view. This dualism splits up the world into things which do not immediately lend themselves to unification, and at the same time provides the foundation for viewing things as separate, which undeniably also has colored the practice of many body cultures (Winther 2009).

However, in research on the body in various cultures there is now a widespread tendency to see that this is not about an either-or choice, but an inclusive both point of view. It opens for the possiblity to see the body as an eternally moving and changeable process (Csordas 1999; Lowen 2006; Merleau Ponty 1962/2004).

According to phenomenology, bodily recognition supersedes thought and intellect. Bodily direction is the most original form of recognition, and according to phenomenological thinking, a prerequisite for consciousness of any kind. Thus "the lived body" may be regarded as humans' most basic condition of existence (Merleau-Ponty ibid.). According to Merleau-Ponty, our immediate existence is an anonymous and pervading body-ness with an expressive presence, which is moved by the individual's life experiences (ibid.).

> Psychological motives and bodily occasions may overlap because there is not a single impulse in a living body which is entirely fortuitous in relation to psychic intentions, not a single mental act which has not found at least its germ or its general outline in physiological tendencies. It is never a question of the incomprehensible meeting of two causalities, nor a collision between the order of causes and that of ends.   (Merleau-Ponty 1962/2004: 101)

Thus, it may well be that we in the body, because it is alive, have inherent bodily patterns which have been influenced by both cultural, societal, and life historical differences; and at the same time, we have inherent universal and biological similarities (Koch & Bräuninger 2006; Sabetti 1986; Tordres 2007; Winther 2009).

Life "is in the blood." We are present in and with our body throughout life. Sense experiences and hurt feelings, childhood, the culture, and the current norms of upbringing and interaction between people become a part of our bodily, emotional, and acting disposition and our way of relating to life and each other. Our lived body carries this, regardless of whether we are conscious of or apparently unknowing about the treasure chest of embodied memories. We are influenced by the past at the same time as we influence both our present and future life.

In the reality of movement, it may be, especially for adults such as Max, a huge challenge to approach the feeling of an expressive presence and a basic feeling of existence. It may mean going beyond boundaries when feelings are given bodily expression in a solo dance, even if this is, in the deepest sense in relation to a wholeness-oriented view of the body, an obvious connection.

Dance movement therapy, which is the therapeutic use of movement to further the emotional, cognitive, physical, spiritual, and social integration of the individual, is based on just this: a wholeness-oriented view of the body, and focuses on personal development through the body (Koch & Bräuninger 2006). Exactly because it works so concretely with wholeness in therapeutic processes, the practical work may contribute to nuance the concept, and at the same time give insight into the wisdom of the body through embodied memories. In the following paragraphs, a fight against and with the body in relation to Karen's lived experience is described. Paradoxically enough, lived experience may be embedded as a kind of dualism in the individual's body experience. It may have gotten so stuck that it shows itself as a painful conflict between doing and being, between control and needs, between what is inner and outer. For Karen, whom we now shall meet, the acceptance and recognition of how things really are is an important step in a fruitful and healing change process. Karen too is afraid of feeling, but it is anxiousness for a far more deep-seated problem than we have seen in Max's more situational experience. Karen's body experience and embodied memories are connected with a longstanding attempt to control her body's volume. This attempt has also left deep marks in her self-concept. She is now looking at this through a dance therapeutic process in Dansergia.

The body starves – On the need for a multidimensional view of the body

> When I look at myself in the mirror
> I see a tall girl with long legs and long arms,
> but I cannot feel my hands.
> I feel that my body is much too long.
> When I walk slower and sink down in my knees, I begin to feel substance.
> A feeling of strength.
> But it doesn't reach further than my knees.
> It feels hard to walk around with a body that I don't inhabit.
> The others see this long body.
> They can't see that I only reach to my knees.
> The feeling of mismatch between big/tall outer/inner
> but also the feeling of being afraid at the thought of filling my body out.
> I am not in doubt that if I let my body's need for food direct what I eat
> and not, as now, that it's always the control that directs that too
> then I would weigh more/have more volume.
> My body is always hungry for both food, physical contact, sexual contact and
> caring. And it is afraid to feel.
> This hunger is so strong and seems insatiable.   (Karen)

The body starves and is insatiable. Karen's body is not just hungry for food. It is hungry for "physical contact, sexual contact" and "caring." Karen's body is, even though she would prefer not to feel it, both *lived* and living, and contains meanings that are woven together by virtue of the many-faceted complexity of hunger. Karen's description thus also points to a need for a multidimensional view of the body which may house the many condensed dimensions. Here it becomes necessary to open up for the body psychological perspectives which are described by Boadella (2006), Lowen (2006), Pierrakos (1990) and Sabetti (1986, 1993), among others. All of these express in slightly different ways that the body's experiences, due to different life situations, may entrench themselves as concrete physical traces, for example, as a state of muscular tension, in the body's physical structure, in the quality of movement, in breathing rhythm, or in typical – often body language – patterns of action. In research on body and dance therapy as well, done by for example Young (2010), and Halprin (2003), it becomes apparent how life affixes itself in very concrete ways that are both noticeable and visible in our bodies.

> Just as the physical body gives us a literal and concrete structure that expresses who we are, so every part and function of the body can also be understood as metaphors for expression of our being. We feel and observe our life experiences through our bodies. All the stresses of our lives are stored in and affect the body, often creating distress and imbalance, which are reflected in our emotional and mental states. Our bodies contain our life stories just as they contain bones, muscles, organs, nerves and blood. (Halprin 2003: 17)

Even though life entrenches itself in the physical structure as well, it is not a sign of immobility. From conception to death, the human body is in constant movement and change (Winther 2009).

We shall now meet Signe, who has started a dance therapy process. In her professional and personal life, she is afraid to take space, and admits that she often draws back.

Movement psychology

> *The breath in my chest.*
> *I sort of stand better on my legs today,*
> *can move my weight and breathe fully at the same time......*
> *Weight transfer.*
> *My chest moves, my arms begin to sort of want to participate.*
> *The movement gets bigger and bigger.*
> *All the time, the same, from side to side, from leg to leg.*
> *It feels wonderful.*
> *I cannot find that hole in my chest today, it's gone.*
> *Filled out? With air? It feels whole. I feel whole.* (Signe)

"The breath in my chest." In most forms of body and dance therapy, the breath is an essential point of focus (Boadella 2006; Lowen 2006; Sabetti 2001). The word psychology comes etymologically from the Greek word psyche, which means "breath", "spirit", or "soul", and *logia*, which means "study of." The meaning of the word itself thus contains, through its focus on breath, a fusion of body and soul, body and psyche. The movement necessary for life, which we see in its most basic expression in the inhalation and exhalation of the breath – taking something in, and letting something out – is essential to the concept of psychology, and thus also may be taken quite literally.

Through a movement examination, in Signe's case with focus on the breath, her contact with her feet and the repetitive movement from side to side, a process of body acknowledgment opens up, which is rooted in the connection between movement and psychology.

Movement psychology, which is in development, seeks a deeper understanding of the connection between the language of the body, the psychology of movement, and human emotional dynamics.[3]

Movement psychology is inspired by body psychology (Lowen 2006), phenomenology (Merleau-Ponty 1962/2004), and energy psychology (Sabetti 1986, 1993, 2001), and takes as it starting point a wholeness-oriented view of the human organism in which body, soul, thoughts, and feelings are regarded as a coherent system in constant exchange with cultural, societal, and universal movements.[4]

While Max and Signe describe momentary impressions of feelings, acknowledgment and embodied memories, which change or tell of their feeling of identity, Karen expresses a more permanent bodily based feeling of identity. We shall now proceed to Asta, who will tell about how her existential meeting with her mother's death and how her ensuing dance therapeutic mourning process created change and freedom in her body and a feeling of identity.

Hooks and hearts

> *I miss you mother.*
> *It is indescribably painful.*
> *It feels like my heart is torn from my chest.*
> *I feel so open and vulnerable.*
> *It feels like my legs can't really support me and carry me forward.*   (Asta)

---

3.   In the international literature there is extensive material on the relationship between body and psyche, as well as on dance as therapy (Boadella 1985; Lowen 1988; Meekums 2002; Koch 2006; Sabetti 1986, 1993; Sparkes 2002).

4.   http://www.idrottsforum.org/articles/winther/winther070606.html#_ftn1%23_ftn1.

These are the words with which Asta opened this article. Even though Asta was prepared for her mother's death, standing face to face with the confronting finality of death is a process which deeply affects her experience of self (Winther 2010).[5] Thus she chooses to go into a dance therapeutic process in order to have the possibility to meet her grief and say goodbye through a deep body process. Here are excerpts from Asta's ten page long account of one process.

> *I tried to notice why I am so attached to my mother, and I noticed a feeling of mutuality. The movement was a rocking from side to side, beginning in my ankles and knees, my arms and hands followed and created a wavy movement that expressed togetherness and this mutuality. I acknowledged that my mother and I understood each other, we knew each other's needs, feelings and thoughts, and understood each other's actions.*
>
> *It hurt so much, and I called out to her, while knowing that she would not be coming.*
>
> *I most of all wanted to collapse, but found support by noticing my feet and the floor, my legs shook.*
>
> *I cried and cried, it was as if the tears wouldn't stop. At the same time weighted down by grief and pain, but also relieved. A relief I couldn't immediately define. But after a while I felt it on the back side of my body and on my neck and shoulders. Earlier in therapy I've had the feeling of a lot of hooks sitting in my back. In the hooks there are lines, and on each of the lines there are things attached, episodes, relationships and feelings which try to draw me backwards, resulting in a split between my front and back sides. I have also worked on letting go of the muscles in my neck and shoulders – I used them to hold on with. In the work today, I felt that some of the hooks had lost their grip in my back, and that my neck had become more free, thus leading to a feeling of relief. It became a dance and I got the feeling of there being room for something new.*
>
> *My mother loved me, I miss her love and pray with all my heart that she is all right wherever she is, because I don't understand the end of her life. I am alive, and I feel that I am alive, and that I am where I am with my body.* (Asta)

The bodily and emotional relationship between mother and child is one of the strongest interpersonal connections (Ylönen 2004). Therefore, it follows that also the embodied memories about especially this relationship have set deep traces in the individual's body and feelings (Winther 2010).

---

5. Asta's earlier dance therapeutic processes in Dansergia are described in other articles (Winther & Stelter 2008; Winther 2010).

To my very dearest mother
In a strange way, there is also something that feels lighter after your death. It
feels as though a heavy and a light energy are playing a melody. The melody is
a little disharmonic because the heavy part takes most space for the time being.
Maybe the lighter one comes from the recognition that I have to let my feelings
go, notice them, acknowledge them and learn from them. With your death I got
time. The time can be used for working through in a process which in the short
run is about your death and saying farewell to you. And then … Simultaneously,
with my grief and my need to hide and collapse, I have an enormous desire for
freedom and a wish to change.
I want to dance and experience new things, … I want to live: I want a new
wardrobe, buy new shoes. I want to be seen. I want to sense and be sensed. I just
don't quite know how this will happen.

It is only when Asta gives herself the possibility to see and meet her grief, at the same
time acknowledging the "hooks in her back" that Asta took the first steps toward also
being able to give space to new life.

Also Max had to take new steps in his process.

I was dancing – Movement and energy
When I finally stood there with everyone's eyes turned toward me, there were
still many things that I had not planned, or had not practiced. … I had firmly
decided to let the music creep into me and try to express the feelings that
streamed through me. I let myself be led, and noticed that I was one hundred
percent focused on my dance. I was dancing … All my thoughts, all my feelings
and all my energy were brought together as one, I was concentrated, but still at
ease – was it perhaps an experience of flow?   (Max)

In the moment Max let himself be "led," he experienced that "all my energy was
brought together as one." The conflict which earlier had been characterized by contradictory physical, psychological, and emotional movements loosened up, and therefore he was finally "dancing."

Max himself refers to "energy," and movement in its simplest form may be characterized by the concept of energy. Energy is a relative concept which transcends the
dualistic division of body and soul. Energy may be regarded as the vital and dynamic
expression of fundamental life energy which, unless it is unbalanced or controlled,
runs through the organism as a constant stream and a strong flow (Sabetti 1986;
Pierrakos 1990). In this connection, Sabetti describes how body and energy psychology understands the body as a multidimensional unit (Sabetti 2001). The body's movements may be understood as multidimensional as well, with inherent

Physical
Mental
Psychological
Emotional
Social
Cultural
Spiritual

qualities and levels of meaning (Sabetti 2001). Even though every movement in principle, as previously mentioned, contains several qualities and levels of meaning, this does not mean that every movement is *in contact with* all of these levels.

At the same time, this multidimensional view of movement may explain how either conflicts may occur on either the personal or interpersonal, or in principle, cultural level, when, as we have seen with Max and Karen, movements occur in opposite directions between the various levels of meaning; or how connection and change may occur as when Asta, by letting her body show the way into and through grief, meets a new freedom. At the same time, conscious work with an energetic and multidimensional perspective may be fruitful in both a movement pedagogic and dance therapeutic context. When the levels, as in Max's description, begin to go together, great intensity of movement may occur. This intensity will often – in a therapeutic context, as in Asta's case – also entail emotional expression. Signe also meets her tears on the way to herself:

> *Continue the movement.*
> *Then the tears come.*
> *Try to stop them, but then let go, let them flow.*
> *After all, it's just me who's in there – all of me and that's good enough.*
> *I can be just like this.*
> *I feel filled up, filled out, relieved.*
> *With my eyes open…….*
> *Remember that I was going to pull myself together in order to say, in an unclear voice – That I found myself.*
> *And the tears?*
> *Joy is the answer. My body is quiet.* (Signe)

In many contexts, there is no distinction made between the concepts *feeling* and *emotion* (Bjerg 2004). In an energy-based and movement psychological context, feelings are understood as an inner, experienced movement with a certain direction and intensity, which often start as sensing and then grow into a feeling (Sabetti 2001). The word *emotion* comes from the same linguistic root as the word *motion*, that is, movement, here understood as being in the mind (Bjerg 2004). Emotion is described by Sabetti (1986) and Reich (1972) as a movement outward: *e-motion* (from Latin ex, out, movere, to move), and is thus connected with the *expression* of feelings, as for example laughter, crying, and expressions of anger.

In a usual dance exercise, it would probably not have been a challenge for Signe to move either her chest or her arms, but the movements in a dance therapeutic process may be regarded as being connected with several levels of movement. Therefore, they are also more intense, and develop via sensing and feeling, to emotional expression as well, which in this case is expressed by tears of joy, connected with the acknowledgment of "finding herself."

Both Max's dance process, Karen's description of the hunger in her body, Asta's experience of hooks and hearts, and Signe's experience of finding herself illustrate how body experiences manifested through body language and movement may be connected with either healthy or somewhat frail self-esteem and experienced identity, which is underneath the idealized image, everyday consciousness and body presentation.

Such complex problems are not solved from one day to the next. In a dance therapeutic context too, this is a process that takes a while, if it is at all possible to slowly recover or newly discover such bodily confidence.

The multidimensional view of the body and movement respecting body memories and the lived body with it, may provide the necessary developmental potential also for movement pedagogy in an educational context.

In all learning contexts involving the body, there will be personal development and thus elements of boundaries that have to be surmounted. Therefore, this article will close with accounts of Signe's, Asta's, and Max's experiences of going beyond boundaries, and change.

Nakedness, liberation, abundance and change

> *I am allowed to be here.*
> *It's ok that I take space.*   (Signe)

Signe, who was afraid of taking space, professionally and personally, reaches through movement an acknowledgment of having to take space. The question is: where is "here"? Is "here" in her own body and feelings? Is "here" in the dance therapeutic room she moves at the time? Is this about her relationship to her life history and social relationships? Is it also a culturally and societally challenging "here," and/or an existential "here" on earth?

Or is it perhaps just by virtue of the body's living and multidimensional complexity, all of this at once? So too Asta, who felt that her heart had been torn out of her chest and felt that she had lost a part of herself, must now cope with the also body-based acknowledgment of the loss and liberation of hooks in her back; she must find her legs anew, her own identity and perhaps her heart.

It's now up to me
to find
my own identity.

I think my mother will always
be
with
me,

She is after all part of
my world,
but I'm now free
to let go of –
if I dare, and want to –

the hooks

that are also a part of
identifying
with my mother.   (Asta)

For Max as well, acceptance and going beyond boundaries are both important for his change process, anchored in the body, which he expresses as a nakedness in relation to the concrete social context.

> *Naked and vulnerable, unsure of the reaction, mine and theirs, that's how I stood there. The time waiting felt like an eternity, and when I was finally in the middle of it, it disappeared, eternity, time, or at least the feeling of it. There were no laughing faces, no mocking, but openness, friendliness, and respect. I expressed myself, my thoughts and feelings, and it was totally fine. I was ok…*

Both Signe, Max, and Karen express the importance of acceptance and trust. If in closing we reflect on these themes for a moment in the macro-perspective of society, and relate these to the typical identity problem complex of postmodernity, it is precisely trust and the subjectively experienced right to be "here" which has become scarce. The modern individual must learn to live with what Giddens (1991) terms an ontological insecurity.

Therefore, basic security, which is built up through early significant relationships, most often those between parents and children, as Jørgensen (2002) points out, is decisive for the individual's ability to navigate through and thrive in the complexity of postmodernity. This security may also, as shown, be supported through, paradoxically enough, challenging and insightful processes which unavoidably and on totally different levels open up for embodied memories in movement pedagogical and dance therapeutic work. This article has illustrated some of these processes through the eyes of the practitioner researcher, and with the voices of Asta, Max, Karen, and Signe.

They have all written on the basis of their deep involvement; this may be criticized on the background of traditional scientific criteria, and at the same time be a challenge in the direction of new research methods which dare to get closer to the body, identity experiences, and emotional dynamics. The aim of the article has not been to reflect an objective truth. It has attempted to get behind the mirror reflection and into other dimensions of reality. Respecting and seeing sensual and present embodied memories.

References

Boadella, D. (1985). *Bio-Energie und Körpersprache* [Bio-energy in the body language]. In H. Petzold (Ed.), *Die neuen Körpertherapien* [The new body therapies] (pp. 14–51). Paderborn: Junfermann Verlag.

Boadella, D. (2006). Soma-Semantik- Bedeutungen des Körpers. In G. Marlock & H. Weiss (Eds.), *Körpertherapien* (pp. 14–51). Paderborn: Junfermann Verlag.

Bjerg, J. (2004). *GADs psykologi leksikon* [GADs lexicon of psychology]. København: G. E. C. Gads Forlag.

Csordas, T. J. (1999). Embodiment and cultural phenomenology. In G. Weiss, & H. F. Haber (Eds.), *Perspectives on embodiment* (pp. 143–165). New York: Routledge.

Giddens, A. (1991). *The Consequences of Modernity*. Cambridge: Polity Press.

Halprin, D. (2003). *The expressive body in life, art and therapy*. London/Philadelphia: Jessica Kingsley Publishers.

Jarvis, P. (1999). *The practitioner researcher. Developing theory from practice*. San Francisco: Jossey-Bass.

Jørgensen, C. R. (2002). *Psykologien i senmoderniteten.* [Psychology in late modernity]. København: Hans Reitzels.

Koch, S. C. (2006). Interdisciplinary embodiment approaches. Implications for creative art therapies. In S. C. Koch & I. Bräuninger (Eds.), *Advances in Dance/Movement Therapy. Theoretical perspectives and empirical findings* (pp. 17–29). Berlin: Logos.

Koch, S. C. & Bräuninger, I. (Eds.). (2006). *Advances in Dance/Movement Therapy. Theoretical perspectives and empirical findings*. Berlin: Logos.

Lowen, A. (2006). *The language of the body. Physical dynamics of character structure*. Alachua: Bioenergetic Press.

Merleau-Ponty, M. (1962/2004). *Phenomenology of perception*. New York: Routledge Classics.

Payne, H. (1993). From practitioner to researcher. Research as a learning process. In H. Payne (Ed.), *Handbook of inquiry in the arts therapies: One river, many currents* (pp. 16–40). London: Jessica Kingsley.

Pierrakos, J. (1990). *Core energetics*. Mendocino: LifeRhythm Publications.

Reich, W. (1972). *Character Analysis*. New York: Farrar, Straus and Giroux.

Sabetti, S. (1986). *The wholeness principle*. Sherman Oaks: Life Energy Media.

Sabetti, S. (1993). *Waves of change*. Sherman Oaks: Life Energy Media.

Sabetti, S. & Freligh, L. (Eds.). (2001). *Life energy process, forms – dynamics – principles*. Munich: Life Energy Media.

Sparkes, A. (2002). *Telling tales in sport and physical activity. A qualitative journey*. Leeds: Human Kinetics.

Sparkes, A. (2003). Bodies, identities, selves: Autoethnografic fragments and reflections. In T. Denison & P. Markula (Eds.), *Moving writing: Crafting movement in sport and research* (pp. 51–76). New York: Peter Lang.

Todres, L. (2007). *Embodied enquiry: Phenomenological touchstones for research, psychotherapy and spirituality*. Basingstoke, UK: Palgrave Macmillan.

Totton, N. (2010). Being, having, and becoming bodies. *Body, Movement and Dance in Psychotherapy, 5*(1), 21–31.

Winther, H. (2009). Movement psychology: The language of the body and the psychology of movement based on the dance therapy form Dansergia. University of Copenhagen: Akademisk Online.

Winther, H. (2010). The mothers life and death in dance therapeutic processes in Dansergia. *Body, Movement and Dance in Psychotherapy, 5*(2), 171–184.

Ylonen, M. E. (2004). A dance by mother and daughter. *The Arts in Psychotherapy, 31*(1), 11–17.

Young, C. (2010). The history and development of body-psychotherapy: European Diversity. *Body, Movement and Dance in Psychotherapy, 5*(1), 5–21.

CHAPTER 23

Dance/movement therapy with traumatized dissociative patients

Sabine C. Koch and Steve Harvey

Heidelberg University / Taranaki District Health Board, New Plymouth

In this chapter, we describe dissociation and dissociative identity disorder (DID) and the value of dance/movement therapy (DMT) with traumatized dissociative child and adult patients. Most patients with dissociative states have suffered trauma during childhood and have recurring traumatic memories, loss of time (dissociative amnesia), and physical stress (i.e., stress on the sensorimotor level often relieved by self-harm on the bodily level). In order to address trauma that occurred on the body level, we consider therapy on the body level to be an important part of a multidisciplinary approach. The first part of the chapter contains some general thoughts on the phenomenon of dissociation and how to address it in DMT. The second part of the chapter provides a case vignette of an abused child experiencing dissociation and five adult group therapy case vignettes in the context of a clinical DMT session designed to help DID patients. In the end, we present principles of movement therapy from work with dissociative children and adults.

Keywords: dissociative identity disorder, dissociation, body memories, grounding, mirroring, dance/movement therapy

Approaching dissociation

Dissociation is the ability to exit one's body when something harmful occurs to it. Such "out-of-body states" belong to the normal capacity of human beings. Dissociation literally means to be disconnected or to lack connection. Dissociative experiences are not integrated into the usual sense of self. They can occur at the level of consciousness, memory, identity, or perception. Dissociation is often accompanied by the experience of being "taken over" as if one was a passenger in one's body rather than the driver. If dissociation impairs the life of the self or others in harmful ways, therapeutic treatment is indicated.

According to DSM IV, there are four main categories of a dissociative disorder:

1. *Dissociative Amnesia* is characterized by an inability to recall important personal information, usually of a traumatic or stressful nature that is too extensive to be explained by ordinary forgetfulness. The duration of disorder varies from a few days to a few years (the latter can be found, for instance, in holocaust survivors).
2. *Dissociative Fugue* is the sudden, unexpected travel away from home or one's place of work, accompanied by an inability to recall one's past and confusion about one's personal identity or the assumption of a new identity. The person is generally unaware of the amnesia.
3. *Depersonalization Disorder* is characterized by a persistent or recurrent feeling of being detached from one's own mental processes or body as if "watching oneself from outside" or as if "watching a movie."
4. *Dissociative Identity Disorder* (DID; previously known as Multiple Personality Disorder; MPD) is the most severe and chronic manifestation of dissociation, characterized by the presence of two or more distinct identities or personality states that recurrently take control of the individual's behavior, accompanied by an inability to recall important personal information that is too extensive to be explained by ordinary forgetfulness. Usually there is a host personality (identified by the person's official name) and a number of alters, with different identity states remembering different aspects of autobiographical information (Kluft 1999). Cues in the environment usually trigger a sudden shifting from one personality to another. There is an estimated prevalence rate of .01% to 1% (Coons 1984) of genuine DID patients in the general population.

Dissociative amnesia is an important diagnostic criterion, and often refers to an auto-biographical event that is forgotten, such as abuse, a troubling incident, or a block of time, from minutes to years. It can occur in the middle of a conversation. Most commonly, repetitive childhood physical and/or sexual abuse and other forms of trauma are associated with the development of dissociative disorders (Kluft 1985; Putnam 1985).

Dissociation usually develops as a healthy mechanism in an unhealthy environment. The ability to temporarily "leave" their bodies helps victims of severe psychological, physical, or sexual abuse to survive and continue with their lives (Kluft 1985). In childhood trauma, dissociation can be considered adaptive because it reduces the overwhelming distress created by trauma. However, if dissociation continues to be used in adulthood, when the original danger no longer exists, it can be maladaptive. DID patients are most often hospitalized because they are a danger to themselves with self-harm or self-mutilation as common symptoms; however, one might wonder why there are not more male DID patients in the hospitals. To address this, Putnam (1989) reported that DID is not necessarily more rare in men, but that DID men are more often found in prisons because they tend to direct their aggression outwardly instead of inwardly.

We consider it important to address trauma that occurred on the body level with therapy on the body level (Koch & Weidinger von der Recke 2009). Dance/movement therapy (DMT) provides grounding and reality testing opportunities on the body level for DID patients. DMT can also provide a way for patients to rehearse important interpersonal actions as well as to re-inhabit their bodies. With children, movement might be the central way in which they can understand trauma and change since verbal processing is often too abstract. Also, children are more influenced by their interactions with adults. Attachment security with a significant caretaker is often vital to the change process.

In this chapter, we will present a DMT approach to working with dissociative children and adults. The similarities and differences in the manifestation of dissociation in children and adults will be addressed. Case illustrations and a vignette from an expressive therapy approach as well as from a clinical group session with adult women are used to illustrate the application of physically oriented expression to facilitate positive change.

The role of movement therapy with dissociative children: A case vignette

Some years ago, the second author was working primarily with children who had experienced significant abuse. He used a DMT approach involving physical play (Harvey 1990, 2011). Much of this work included work with children who had been removed from their parents' homes due to significant care and protection issues. During one session with a 10-year old, the boy became trancelike and engaged in an enactment in which he picked up a teddy bear and began to strangle it. The session had initially been set up to help the boy develop an appropriate way to express his aggression as he was engaging in explosive outbursts of violence regularly in the residential center where he was living. The therapist originally had provided several stuffed animals and had suggested he begin a wrestling match as he had stated he was very interested in wrestling on TV. In this scenario, the therapist had taken the role of an announcer providing verbal comments on a wrestling match between the boy and teddy bear. Applying these roles, the announcer described the boy's movement quality while the boy spontaneously engaged in a vigorous series of moves such as picking up the teddy bear (cast in the role of his opponent), spinning the bear over his head, and slamming the bear onto a mat that had been set up as the wrestling ring.

At first, the boy was quite responsive to the therapist's verbal comments, which were not only about the physical action but also reflected the emotional states the boy was expressing in his physically oriented play. After a few minutes, the boy became very focused on the bear, looking only directly into the toy's eyes, using high intensity bound flow as he began to enact killing the bear by squeezing the animal's throat. During this time, the boy became totally unresponsive to the verbal comments of the therapist and became very absorbed in his physical action. He was not able to stop despite the therapist's efforts at verbal redirection. The activity lost the playful intention present at the beginning of the action, and the boy continued until the strangulation had finished some several minutes later.

When the boy stopped, he had no memory of what had taken place and his emotional state was unaffected by the intense action he had been involved in only moments before. The boy had entered the expressive playroom in a positive mood and he left in the same state, saying he had enjoyed being able to play. The next week, when asked by the therapist what he remembered of the last session, the boy again had no memory of the events from the previous week and proceeded to develop more expressive physically oriented playful actions such as a tug-of-war when given the opportunity. These sessions were stopped shortly afterwards due to the boy's transfer to another facility many miles away. The administrator of the original center reported that the boy had been removed from his birth family's home due to his father's extreme violence toward his children. A police investigation had revealed that a younger sibling had been murdered by strangulation in the home some years before. However, no further details about the specifics of the violent events were known.

Whereas it would have been very interesting and perhaps useful for the boy to somehow connect his enactment of his emotional states – in particular, his physical experience of fear and vulnerability – to the events that he most certainly was exposed to in his earlier years, no further follow up occurred due to the transfer of the boy's placement. From a Dance Therapy point of view, it would have been very helpful for the boy to have been provided or to have created an alternative way to process his past; perhaps using a more playfully constructed improvised physical play had therapy been consistent over a period much longer than a few sessions.

In reviewing the boy's unusual play several years later, it is clear that he had a dissociative episode in which he re-experienced a real event from his early family life in some way in which he was unable to process and remember in a normal fashion. It is likely that the ongoing extreme violence he was exposed to led into a bodily felt experience of high levels of fear/anxiety in combination with his young age in a way that he was unable to use language or more age-level-appropriate imagery to recognize and understand the aggressive events in a meaningful manner. When he later became involved with the physical actions of wrestling with the stuffed animals, his body became activated without his normal sense of language, metaphor making, and play. He also didn't appear to experience any of the physical emotion related to the violence of his early life in a more conscious way. Both prior to and following the enactment of the strangulation of the teddy, the boy presented with a positive mood. In this way, his experience of the death of the sibling seemed to have become fragmented from the boy's understanding of himself and his life history. He was relatively well adjusted except for his ongoing highly aggressive behaviors that had led him to a referral.

Terr (1990), James (1994), Harvey (2003), and Gil (2006) have presented case material regarding how the expressive play of children who have experienced significant psychological trauma is impacted. Such impacts include dissociated play enactment, repetitive play actions, and play that is characterized by hyper- or hypo-arousal and agitation (Perry 2000; van der Kolk 2006). Such play is related to the neurological changes that occur from a child's experience of abuse, especially severe experiences of violence in combination with a lack of comforting and soothing from parental attachment figures.

As illustrated in the case example above, dissociative play is particularly characterized by episodes that are significantly fragmented and separate from the rest of a child's expression. In this vignette, the child shifted into a state of experience that had little connection to his usual physical expressive characteristics, and the play metaphors had no relation to the thematic development or the play narrative. As the research on the neurological impacts of trauma suggests, the boy's lower brain functioning likely became predominant and led to a lack of integrated functioning of higher and lower brain centers. In children who have experienced severe abuse, this lack of integration contributes to strange and often bizarre segments of expression. In the example above, the play changed from a playful game of wrestling into an intense enactment of strangulation that had several real-life characteristics of which the boy had no recall.

Both Perry (2006) and van der Kolk (2006) have suggested that interventions and treatment strategies need to incorporate movement and somatic experiences. James (1989) advocated the use of body activities in the treatment of traumatized children, whereas Gil (1994) stressed the need to include parenting figures in therapy activities. Harvey (1992, 2003, 2006) reported using both spontaneous and structured movement interactions and high intensity physical play involving positive emotion with parents and children as being of primary importance in situations involving trauma of young children. Taken together, the principles of DMT treatment of children who experience dissociation include the use of playful physical expression, guided participation of parent/caretaker interactions with their children that access feelings of secure attachment and attunement to the child, and spontaneous therapist and parent involvement within the metaphors generated during dissociation. The overall goal of these interventions is to integrate the child's overwhelming physical experiences of fear with the experience of security and attuned expression within playful metaphor making.

A general scenario that has emerged from the second author's family oriented dance therapy with abused children is that of the "death" scene. This scene has usually occurred during mother/child dyad sessions. Approaches to working with this scene illustrate the application of interventions with children during dissociation. At times during co-created physical play with their adult caregivers, some children stop all activity by lying or falling down, becoming literally frozen and limp. This behavior appears to have no connection with prior physical activity or play action. The freeze also stops any further expression. The children are not able to speak or generate play metaphors. These episodes are an example of the fragmented experiences described above. At this time, a strategy that has been useful is for the therapist to bring the child's parent close to the child's body and wait for the child to begin to move. The parent is then coached to join her child's movement, matching the child's rhythms no matter how small or subtle. Typically the mutual movements develop into dances that are quite playful. However, the development of such dance interactions is not instantaneous and may take time. This mutual movement can then be developed into metaphorical "coming alive" dances (see Harvey 2003, for a more complete case presentation). The next section of this chapter will show a typical DMT session with adult DID patients.

The role of DMT for adults with Dissociative Identity Disorder: A treatment method and clinical case vignettes

In the clinical group setting described here, at one of the oldest psychiatric hospitals on the East Coast of the United States, dance/movement therapy is a core therapy in the treatment of DID patients. The hospital followed an integrative treatment concept of dynamic psychoanalytic treatment combined with cognitive-behavioral therapy and complementary therapies such as dance/movement therapy (Baum 1991). The therapy session was conducted by dance/movement therapist Edith Baum. Edith Baum, no longer with us, has left a suitable method regarding how to work with groups of Dissociative Identity Disorder patients and dissociation in DMT in the following, referred to as the *Baum-circle*. The session was designed for DID outpatients, that is, patients staying in the hospital during the day, but going to their own homes at night. The first author, then in DMT training, co-led the session with Edith Baum, who was the main therapist. The session was videotaped for educational and supervision purposes with the patients' consent.

In the group, there were seven patients: five women and two men. The women were all diagnosed with Dissociative Identity Disorder; the men had other diagnoses (major depression; and dementia due to HIV). Most of the women in the group had suffered severe abuse with an early onset of either a physical or sexual nature. The integration of men into the group was important for the female DID patients to gain trust and to lessen their anxiety about sharing emotions not only with other women affected by similar trauma, but also with men.

When the patients arrived in the light wooden-floored room on the top floor of the renaissance building, they chatted in a lively fashion with one another. After everybody was there and the session started, they became serious and one could sense the concentrated attention in the group. The patients knew that this complementary therapy format could provide much relief and progress to them as they had participated in several previous sessions. In the movement warm-up initiated by the therapist, going in a circle, each patient contributed one movement that was then joined by the entire group. In this way, all participants became aware of their active and egalitarian role in the group therapy session and could begin to say something to the group without using words.

The main part of the DMT session consisted of the free improvisation of single patients following the principles of *authentic movement,* but by adapting them to short-term group therapy sessions. The mover was encouraged to bring her own music to the session to help her express her feelings. When beginning her improvisation, she then tried to follow her inner movement impulses as authentically as possible, being true to her perceptions, sensations, feelings, and thoughts.

The method

In this format of DMT, the *Baum-circle*, free improvisation is used by one mover who is followed by the entire group. Following Jungian thought, the movement improvisation can be understood as a chain of free associations that can be used in the therapeutic process. Positive as well as negative body memory content can arise. The positive body memories can be understood and used as resources, working on the strengths and skills of the patient. The negative ones can be further addressed in group therapy or in single therapy sessions working on a nonverbal narrative of the trauma. The group's role is to try to follow the movement quality of the initiating patient. This means that group members do not need to go into movements that are too complicated or fast for them to follow, but that the important thing is to pick up the quality of movement and to resonate with that quality in order to get a sense of the emotional message the mover conveys.

This process of mirroring has therapeutic implications similar to those of verbal mirroring in client-centered therapy (Rogers 1951). It serves the goal of establishing rapport and empathy (using emotional contagion); it conveys respect, acceptance without conditions, and reality testing opportunities to the participants. Generally, the group serves as a corrective for personal experiences of the past.

An important goal of the movement therapy sessions, especially with DID patients, is to express one's own feelings in the presence of others without becoming a danger to the self or to others. A major part of the work with DID patients consists of the development of the ability to direct one's own anger not to the inside, but to the outside, imagining that it is addressed at the person who has caused the trauma. This "punching out, instead of punching in" is a difficult issue for most of the patients. A major step is taken when they are ready to do it, and again when they are doing it with the actual effort of strength that it affords. The problem (and the potential) of the expressive movement and particularly the use of the movement quality of strength is that it can evoke body memories that are often painful, bringing to consciousness disordered body perceptions that have been neglected for a long time. Specific movements are connected to specific traumatic experiences and have therefore been suppressed in everyday life. The body parts implied are held and numbed, and the affected movement is no longer displayed.

In the *Baum-circle*, as in most other DMT methods, after the main part of the session (the movement part), the group comes together to exchange their experiences while moving (the verbal processing part). The patients who moved initiate the reporting of their experiences. The other group members then provide feedback on

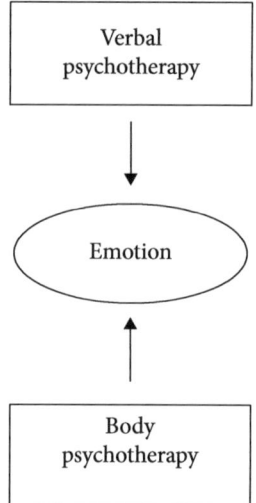

Figure 1. Complementary effects of verbal and body psychotherapy in the process of approaching emotion (Koch 2011)

what they saw and experienced while they moved together with them. The therapist emphasizes that the feedback is to be conveyed in a nonjudgmental fashion and encourages the exchange of images and metaphors that arose for the group members. The session provides the opportunity for the mover to express traumatic content that cannot – or is not yet ready to – be expressed in words in a nonverbal symbolic fashion in movement. Since the trauma contains many bodily aspects, the body needs to be included in the therapeutic process. In this process, a patient regains control over his or her body and learns to appreciate it as a source of strength, pleasure, and as a positive health resource.

DMT in clinical treatment can provide an alternative way to address the patients' emotions. Whereas verbal therapies address the emotions from the top down, movement therapy addresses them from the bottom up. In this way, both forms of therapy have complementary and cross-fertilizing effects on the healing process.

The patients in the group

Amber:[1] *Being caught in different parts of the brain*
Amber was a patient whose entire body expressed helplessness. Her voice was soft, her hands and legs were always in a tremor. Her body was always in distress. While she was very dependent and almost child-like, at the same time, she had an aura of natural wisdom about her. She was open to sharing and learning and was a rational

---

1.   All patient names are pseudonyms.

thinker. Amber had a history of alcohol abuse and a history of long-term hospitalizations in psychiatry. Three years prior to the group session, she had a manic episode.
During the last weeks before this group session, she was symptom free. Despite of
her being away from alcohol and being symptom free, it was obvious that she had no
resources available to participate in a regular everyday work life. Amber shared her
thoughts on her DID. For her it was like "being in one part of my brain, without access to another, and then being in another part of my brain, without being able to get
back to the first."

Amber was able to use the dance therapy sessions to support her autonomous ego
functions. When she started to move, her tremor always went away immediately. On
this day, she chose to move to a song from Peter Gabriel "Hold On." Her movements
were slow, solemn, and controlled. In the beginning, she lifted her hands to the ceiling as if to say "My god, please can you help me?" She searched for something to hold
on to, she reached out, and she grabbed an imaginary tow-rope and pulled it down
with strength. In the second verse, she knelt down with her hands behind her back
in chains. Then she struggled with this situation and finally got up on her feet. At the
climax of her performance, she broke these chains and then just stood there with her
arms spread out to the side, her face conveying pride and liberation.

In the feedback circle at the end of the session, Amber verbalized the negative
parts of her performance: "I felt like a prisoner, very restrained within a small area…
and I needed to get out of there…"; then she interrupted herself: "actually, I do not
have many feelings about it" and signaled to the group that she felt that she had not
expressed her feelings well. The group members reflected back that they had experienced her as particularly expressive of much emotion and personal struggle. Group
members reflected that she had shown a liberation from the chains and pain, as well as
shown her potential through her use of strength. She was able to accept this feedback
and to see the positive aspects of what she had expressed in movement.

Barbara: Lost in bodyless space

Barbara was a DID patient who had an additional diagnosis of borderline personality disorder. She chose a song entitled "I don't know what I am looking for," and her
movement to the chorus of the song conveyed helpless searching movements from
side to side with the upper part of the body using middle reach space with many head
shakes and shoulder shrugs as signals of resignation. At the end of the chorus, there
was a part of the music that went harder with more rhythmic beats. Barbara used this
part to "punch out." She practiced punching out and imagining her perpetrator while
doing so in order to express her aggression toward a more appropriate place. While
she tried, her effort of strength was not well developed at this point in time and the
therapist knew that it would take her several more movement sessions to get to the
point where she would be able to use strength with more authenticity.

In Barbara's performance, the conflict between anger and sadness became prevalent and the fear of her own strength could be seen in her movement efforts. She tried
to use *strength* when her anger arose, but in fact she used *vehemence* – a precursor of

strength in movement development (Kestenberg, Amighi et al. 1999). This could have indicated (a) that she was still in the process of learning how to use strength, and/or (b) that she used vehemence as a defense mechanism in order not to sense the feelings that were associated with her rage (fear, helplessness, sadness, grief). She was quite conscious of this conflict when she brought it to the feedback circle: "I wasn't really all connected. Part of me felt angry and part of me felt sad. The ultimate wish is 'I want to go home,' but the song says 'you can never go home.' When I felt the anger, I was afraid of losing it."

Sarah: Primal needs split the self

Sarah was a relatively high-functioning patient working at the University level in research and teaching. She also was diagnosed with DID after experiencing an episode of severe abuse. However, this episode had not occurred in early childhood and the psychological impacts were not as extreme as in the other patients.

Sarah came to the outpatient program only when she was in a crisis. She had almost no limitations concerning her movement. She had remarkable flexibility of her torso and lower body for a patient with DID. In DMT, the torso is regarded as the seat of the emotions, and most DID patients hold it quite stiff. Movement is often initiated more from the periphery than from the center of the body. Sarah had no problems initiating movement from her torso. However, she had some difficulty participating in relaxation exercises. Her perpetrator had used soft spoken hypnotic words in ways that are often employed in relaxation sessions.

Sarah picked a rhythmic piece of drum music with only percussion and no melody or voice for her movement presentation. She started sitting on the floor with rhythmic movement of the upper body getting stronger with each repetition. She crawled on the floor and shook her long hair to the beat. Hardly anyone in the group was able to follow this primal performance and most participants almost gave up. Sarah moved with her eyes closed, so she did not see the other's reactions. She later stated in the feedback circle: "I was a bit closed off because of the camera. I thought of the universe and being connected with it."

Leila: Victim of occultist ritual

Leila was one of the patients who suffered severely and was very fragile. She was constantly rehospitalized because of self-harm and distress due to frequent amnesias (losses of time). At the same time, she could readily use movement as a resource because she had studied ballet continuously since childhood. She had told the group that her mother had also been a DID patient. She reported that her mother was involved in a circle of witches and had followed other occultist traditions. Leila revealed that she had received a brand mark on the back of her head when she was 4 years old to indicate that she too was a member of this cult. She stated that when she was 13 years old, she has been admitted to a circle of 13 witches.

Leila suffered from prolonged periods of lost time and would frequently find herself in situations in which she had no understanding of how she had gotten there. In addition to these psychological difficulties, she also had multiple physical symptoms. One such problem included a significant asymmetry of her body. Her left side was the one that had been constantly harmed and her movements showed this impact in a visible one-sidedness. She was additionally diagnosed with a histrionic personality disorder.

In this group session, she selected a piece of music from a film soundtrack with mostly slow sad instrumental pieces. She entered into a state of inwardness quite early into the piece of music. The group was able to follow her quick anxious pull backs and her cautious approaches directed to the center of the circle formed by the group. Halfway into the performance, Leila knelt down on the floor as if she was back against a wall in fear. Then, the fingers of her left hand crawled like small animals from her lap to the outside world, moving forward to the center of the circle, yet her right hand pushed them back. Every time the fingers of the left hand carefully crawled out, the right hand came and pushed them back. Then she retreated even deeper into herself and became almost motionless for an extended period of time.

The therapist approached her, sitting very close in front of her calling out her name. Leila reported later that this call of her name (of the name of the main personality) seemed to come from the other end of a very long corridor – but that she was unable to return. She reported that quite early in her performance she had switched to another personality. This personality was totally unknown to her and quite threatening. When "the little people" (her childhood selves in the form of the crawling fingers) tried to come out, she was still there and tried to protect them. But then the new personality totally took over and pulled her into a dark place full of fear. Only when her neighbor Anna called a helper-self (a 2-year old called "Twoy") was she able to switch back and reappeared as "Twoy." At this time, she suddenly fell to a sitting position with her legs stretched out. When her face reappeared behind her hair, she had a totally different facial expression, muscle tone, voice, and body movement than before, or than we had ever seen from her. She began to interact with us with the facial expression, voice, and body movement of a 2-year old (e.g., pronounced twisting rhythm). The entire group was puzzled by this extreme switch. The therapists then began speaking with her and Leila was able to indicate that she was settled by nodding to the therapist's inquiry. In the course of the next patient's performance, Leila was able to switch back to her organizing personality "Leila." In the feedback circle, she said that she "could not remember much" about the switch that had just occurred. She indicated that it would be difficult to bring up the issues in the group setting, stating that she would bring the event to her individual therapy session later that day. She then began to cry and questioned her ability to trust the group. However, the therapist confirmed that it had taken a large amount of trust for Leila to allow the authentic movement to happen in the group and that she could be proud of herself to have taken such a risk.

Catherine: Dissociated lower body half

Catherine suffered sexual abuse during her childhood and later from her supervisor when she was in the navy. She never seemed to be able to take herself seriously. Her outer appearance was quite masculine. She had no breasts or hips and appeared as one slim line from top to bottom. Catherine likely had the most severe body schema disorder of the women in the group. Whenever she followed others or initiated her own movement, she was unable to open her legs. This led to her placing herself in very awkward postures during the sessions. However, Catherine appeared to be entirely unaware of this. Her lower body was in neural flow such that she was unable to allow sensations in this part of her body.

For her performance, Catherine chose a quiet and calm song. She moved her upper body only. She used some uplifting gestures directed to the ceiling. However, she initiated these movements from the periphery rather than her torso, indicating little emotional involvement. Her movement qualities expressed much indecisiveness, passivity, and helplessness. Even when she moved her upper body, her legs and hips remained in neutral flow and did not swing with her arm movements in a natural manner. Her pelvis was held in one position much like a child might. Her knees were held straight and stiff. In this position, it was hard to achieve grounding because she could not sense the floor well. Children under the age of 6 move their bodies in one unit. After that age, they begin to differentiate the movement of upper and lower body.

Catherine was also treated in individual dance/movement therapy due to the severity of her body schema disorder. Such treatment included grounding exercises, sensory integration, work on developing her strength effort, and therapy to teach her to give in to the pull of gravity. The main goal of the work was to help her develop more natural movements of her hips, pelvis, and the lower half of her body without the fear of releasing traumatic body memories. The goal of these interventions was to help Catharine counteract the physical aspects of the victim role and to allow the anxiety-free reoccurrence of the natural flow of movement and with it the re-inhabitation of the body.

In the feedback circle, Catherine noted that she could not remember anything from her performance, but that it had something to do with "things in my life going too soon." She then started to talk about her multiple losses. She ended her verbal report by saying "I am reaching for serenity and peace of mind…". This desire was clearly perceived by other patients in the group, who provided feedback on this aspect. Leila noted "you looked like you were reaching for a castle… you stood on tiptoes… and then just dropped." Barbara added "It reminded me of my own performance, and I felt desperate with you, but I liked the part with the 'rainbow' where you went up with your arms because it conveyed hope."

Generally, patients affected by dissociative symptoms appreciate the possibilities that movement therapy offers to them. The patients in the DMT group described here regarded dance/movement therapy as a treatment modality that centrally contributed to their process of recovery. Then, what are the principles of movement therapy with dissociative patients?

Principles of DMT with dissociative adults

On the basis of the assumption that trauma caused on the body level needs to be treated on the body level, the main principles that are helpful in working with DID patients with dance/movement therapy are summarized below:

1. *Grounding*: The self needs to (re-)inhabit the body and to be able to stay bodily present in order to not dissociate in social situations. Dissociation, once a functional mechanism, has become dysfunctional in everyday life and needs to be addressed by more appropriate coping strategies. Work on movement repertoire and particularly on efforts – the movement qualities – directly furthers the development of an array of coping mechanisms in the patient's movement.
2. *Mirroring*: Mirroring of others' movement furthers empathy and the use of one's own body for interpersonal resonance. Being mirrored promotes the feeling of being validated the way one is by the group. Verbal and nonverbal feedback also have the important function of facilitating reality testing, helping to counteract perceptual biases, helping to reintegrate fragmented body parts, and providing an avenue for patients who experience dissociation with a more realistic evaluation of their own skills, strengths, and weaknesses.
3. *Building strength and resources*: The work on building one's own movement qualities of strength and the ability to address aggression at the appropriate place instead of toward oneself is an important skill that can have an impact on patients' bodily, affective, and cognitive aspects. The work on the patients' strength in their movement assists in the process of changing the role of the victim and helps strengthen a sense of agency and self-efficacy. On the body level, it facilitates the reduction of tension and helps patients to direct aggression outwardly instead of inwardly. These physical developments assist with the processes of self-assertion and grounding that counteract dissociation. On the ego level, DMT serves the development of ego strength and positive self-feelings, to counteract the "regressive pull," and to discover and develop the strong, active, and resourceful parts of the self. It should be noted, however, that care needs to be taken with relaxation exercises because such activities can cause feelings of helplessness and further dissociative reactions.
4. *Work with body memories*: DMT should facilitate a stepwise going through painful and disturbing body memories to help the patient to create a nonverbal as well as a verbal narrative in order to overcome trauma. Most predominantly in individual movement therapy, sessions that guide the patient through their life story of trauma can be successful (Caldwell 2010; Hofmann 2005; Rothschild 2000). Next to being the container for negative memories, the body is also a reservoir

for positive memories. These positive body memories need to be re-accessed in order to experience the body as a resource. DMT works on disentangling the association of body and trauma and (re-)establishing previously owned, as well as new positive body feelings.

5. *Use of metaphors*: Free associations in movement bring about images and metaphors of symbolic expression of material too painful to be verbalized. The use of creativity and higher level integration via metaphors can be helpful for and timesaving in the healing process. Movement analysis, as a method of diagnosis and intervention planning, helps to generate hypotheses about the time and circumstances of the trauma (Eberhard-Kaechele this volume; Eberhard-Kaechele 2007).

6. *Authenticity*: The body and its expressions can be experienced within a safe, non-threatening environment. By the testimony of the other group members, the patient experiences that she can be validated just the way she is within the group of others. The value of authenticity emphasizes being true to oneself and helps avoid dissociative tendencies such as escaping into false roles or alters.

7. *Working with resistance*: For many dissociative patients, the conscious experiencing of the body is initially extremely threatening and one reason for the dissociation. Certain movements with idiosyncratic meaning for the patient are well-suited for triggering traumatic memories. People who have experienced severe trauma can develop a tendency to neglect or even hate their bodies. Often traumatic events leave people with a fragmented experience of their bodies. The body is the sphere where women in particular attempt to solve interpersonal conflicts in an intrapersonal way. Major reasons for the admission of female patients to psychiatry are self-mutilation and suicide attempts. Exercises oriented at the needs and strengths of the patients can create positive connotations with the body and its movements. They can decrease feelings of being controlled from some external force or being a passive subject to one's own body and increase a positive and natural experience of body parts and body rhythms formerly associated with fear and anxiety (Schedlich & Sander 2008).

8. *Working with touch*: The therapist needs to always check with the patient first regarding whether it is acceptable for them to use methods that imply touch. Some authors recommend the avoidance of any kind of touch in therapy. Others recommend the presence of a second therapist when the main therapist is going to use touch. In some countires, therapists are not allowed to work with touch right from the start. Developmentally, it is precisely the haptic affection that is responsible for the positive valence of the body (Bowlby 1988; Strauss 2006). Touch is important in the development of the differentiation of self and the world of objects, individuation, and mere survival (Montague 1971; Spitz 1946). In DID patients, because the trust in "good" touch is often destroyed, a therapeutic building process is necessary in order to re-establish this lost trust. In this process, when working with touch, the patient needs to be subjectively in control.

Principles of DMT with dissociative children

All of the principles named above can be applied to children as well. The following adoptions can be helpful:

In grounding, the use of props can help to generate the movement qualities the children need to be working on developmentally. In mirroring, children love games of leading and following. The therapists should choose significant scenes and problems for mirroring, let the child initiate, and mirror possible solutions. When developing solution scenarios in joint play, the strengths of the child ought to be built upon. Positive memories connected to bodily activity need to be identified. In working with metaphors, instead of verbalizing, the therapist can have the child draw a picture or create a song. It is important to build the child's sense of agency and self-efficacy by focusing on their resources. To achieve authenticity, the child should be asked to express what he or she really wants. Resistance should be integrated into play. And touch needs to be carefully introduced.

Enhancing physical play that has intrinsic pleasure is perhaps the single most important way to help children build strength and provide coping. Normally children play easily and generate a spirit of "fun" as they create metaphors, games, and narratives spontaneously. Natural play helps build resilience and adaptability. Such play produces positive physical states. This kind of playful engagement can be very problematic, however, for children who have been traumatized. A portion of any intervention with children who show dissociation needs to encourage the development of spontaneous physically oriented creative play in which the therapist initially recognizes a child's play initiatives to build extended playful interactions. Parents are then taught to attune to their children in this way as well.

Conclusions

It is notable that dissociative children and adults both express fragmented episodes during physically oriented expressive interventions. During severe abuse, children's neurological functioning becomes segmented: Language and even metaphor making become separated from the emotional states of fear and the need for security. This segmentation continues into adulthood. Both children and adults have experiences in which their past overwhelms them. Children require real-life relationships (e.g., parents) to produce a bodily felt sense of security (attachment), whereas adults seem to be capable of gaining this security in a holding environment of a group or strong therapeutic alliance. For both children and adults, the use of physical action can facilitate the therapeutic process. Physical action helps the body to rehabituate.

Body work with traumatized dissociative patients can be initially difficult because the history of the patients in most cases is one of trauma, pain, and hurt on the body level. After initial resistance to body work is overcome, however, it can decisively contribute to the healing process. Physical play, especially with a protective parent, can help children re-establish their own natural sense of pleasure in playful movement and to generate feelings of security in interactions. In adults, an integration of the disturbed body image can frequently be achieved, and the positive valence of the body and its memories can be strengthened. By experiencing their own strength in a realistic way, dissociative patients can address their aggression toward the outside (the perpetrator) instead of toward the inside, can leave behind the role of the victim, accept and integrate their own good and bad aspects, take on a more active role, and move on with their lives.

References

Baum, E. Z. (1991). Movement therapy with multiple personality disorder patients. *Dissociation, 4*(2), 99–104.

Bowlby, J. (1988). *A secure base: Parent-child attachment and healthy human development.* London: Routledge.

Caldwell, C. (2010). *Personal communication.*

Coons, P. M. (1984). The differential diagnosis of multiple personality: A comprehensive review. *Psychiatric Clinics of North America, 7,* 51–65.

Eberhard-Kaechele, M. (2007). The regulation of interpersonal relationships by means of shape flow: A psychoeducational intervention for traumatised individuals. In S. C. Koch & S. Bender (Eds.), *Movement analysis – Bewegungsanalyse. The legacy of Laban, Lamb, Bartenieff and Kestenberg* (pp. 203–212). Berlin: Logos.

Eberhard-Kaechele, M. (this volume). Memory, metaphor, and mirroring in movement therapy with tauma patients. In S. C. Koch, T. Fuchs, M. Summa & C. Müller (Eds.), *Body memory, metaphors, and movement.* Amsterdam: John Benjamins.

Gil, E. (1994). *Play in family therapy.* New York: Guilford Press.

Gil, E. (2006). *Helping abused and traumatized children: Integrating directive and nondirective approaches.* New York: Guilford Press.

Harvey, S. A. (1990). Dynamic play therapy: An integrated expressive arts approach to the family therapy of young children. *The Arts in Psychotherapy, 17*(3), 239–246.

Harvey, S. A. (2003). Dynamic family play with an adoptive family struggling with issues of grief, loss, and adjustment. In D. Weiner & N. Oxford (Eds.), *Action methods in conjoint therapy.* Washington, D.C.: American Psychological Association Books.

Harvey, S. A. (2006). Dynamic play therapy. In C. Schaefer & H. Kaduson (Eds.), *Contemporary play therapy.* New York: Guilford.

Harvey, S. A. (2011). Physical play with boys of all ages. In C. Haen (Ed.), *Working with boys.* London: Routledge.

Hofmann, A. (2005). *EMDR – Therapie psychotraumatischer Belastungssyndrome* [EMDR – Therapy of post-traumatic stress syndrome]. Stuttgart: Thieme.

James, B. (1989). *Treating traumatized children.* Boston: Lexington Books/Macmillan.

James, B. (1994). *Handbook for treatment of attachment-trauma problems in children.* Boston: Lexington Books/Macmillan.

Kluft, R. P. (1985). *Childhood antecedents of multiple personality*. Washington, D.C.: American Psychiatric Press, Inc.

Kluft, R. P. (1999). An overview of the psychotherapy of Dissociative Identity Disorder. *American Journal of Psychotherapy, 53*(3), 289–319.

Koch, S. C. & Weidinger von der Recke, B. (2009). Traumatized refugees: An integrated dance and verbal therapy approach. *The Arts in Psychotherapy, 36*, 289–296.

Montague, A. (1971). *Touching: The human significance of the skin*. New York: Columbia University Press.

Perry, B. (2000). The neurobiology of childhood maltreatment: The neurodevelopment cost of adverse events childhood events. In K. Franey, R. Geffner & R. Falconer (Eds.), *The cost of maltreatment: who pays? We all do*. San Diego: Family Violence and Sexual Assault Institute.

Perry, B. (2006). Applying principals of neurodevelopment to clinical work with maltreated and traumatized children. In N. B. Webb (Ed.), *Working with traumatized youth in child welfare*. New York: Guilford Press.

Putnam, F. W. (1985). Dissociation as a response to extreme trauma. In R. P. Kluft (Ed.), *Childhood antecedents of multiple personality* (pp. 63–97). Washington, D.C.: American Psychiatric Press.

Putnam, F. W. (1989). *Diagnosis and treatment of multiple personality disorder*. New York: Guilford Press.

Rogers, C. (1951). *Client-centered therapy: Its current practice, implications and theory*. London: Constable.

Rothschild, B. (2000). *The body remembers: The psychophysiology of trauma treatment*. New York: Norton.

Schedlich, C. & Sander, E. (2008). Stabilisierung in der Traumaadaptierten Tanz- und Ausdruckstherapie – TATT [Stabilization in trauma-adapted dance and expressive therapy – TATT]. In G. Fischer & P. Schay (Hrsg.), *Psychodynamische Psycho- und Traumatherapie: Konzepte-Praxis-Perspektiven [Psychodynamic psycho- and trauma-therapy: Theory-practice perspectives]*. Wiesbaden: VS-Verlag.

Spitz, R. A. (1946). Hospitalism. A follow-up report. *The Psychoanalytic Study of the Child, 1*, 113–117.

Strauss, K. (2006). *Bonding Psychotherapie – Grundlagen und Methoden* [Bonding psychotherapy – foundations and methods]. München: Kösel.

Terr, L. (1990). *Too scared to cry*. New York: Haper & Row.

van der Kolk, B. (2006). Clinical implications of neuroscience research in PTSD. *Annuals of the New York Academy of Science, 1071*(IV), 277–293.

CHAPTER 24

Focusing, felt sensing and body memory

Elmar Kruithoff
Focusing Institute, Denmark

Our bodies implicitly contain our entire life context. While continuously inter-acting with their environment, our bodies are our past experiences and implied next steps at the same time. Past and future are inseparable in the present bodily process, which is capable of generating highly organized meanings and behav-ior. "Body memory" is part of what is called "felt sensing" in Focusing terms.

Keywords: focusing, felt sense, body memory, Gendlin, philosophy of the implicit, phenomenological sense

> Living bodies have their history written all over them.
> (Richard Dawkins, *The Greatest Show on Earth*)

The first experiential practice (Gendlin 2004b) derived from Eugene T. Gendlin's phi-losophy of the implicit (Gendlin 2009b) is called Focusing. Focusing describes how to utilize a bodily felt, phenomenological sense (Gendlin 2004b) of one's life in order to access its implied next steps (Gendlin 1992b).

Throughout our individual history, our bodies continuously feel themselves[1] while acting and breathing. They function as our sense of each situation, which is more than mere (Gendlin 1992a) perception through our five senses: The body is on-going interaction with its environment and we are able to directly feel its way of living (Gendlin 1992a) as a whole. Gendlin calls this kind of feeling a "Felt Sense"; and, as he puts it, the Felt Sense actually is (Gendlin 2003) our situation. A Felt Sense has always a direction; it is at, about, for or in a specific context. It implicitly contains the world we live in including all that has been done and said till now.[2]

From a Focusing point of view, we are able to experience a flow (Gendlin 1966) of Felt Senses, which implicitly contains the entire life context in form of past events

---

1. "Much vitally important knowledge comes from studying the living body as if it were a machine. But other approaches reveal other dimensions of the body" (Gendlin 2004a).

2. "... the environment, our perceptions, the context of all that has been done and said till now, what is being gotten at, the purpose, the definitions, and a very great deal more" (Gendlin 1966).

and perceptions as well as demanded non-logical (Gendlin 1985) sequences and steps (Gendlin 1992b) of their own accord: speech, action, understanding, memories, ideas, knowledge, feeling, and so forth. Sequences of body movement are regarded as especially powerful if developed from a Felt Sense.[3] Moreover, in order to initiate change instead of repeating the same patterns over again, expressing and felt sensing are to be combined, allowing them to mutually influence and change each other.[4]

Gendlin sees the individual's past as a sum total of life experience[5] present in the body; and because our bodies *are* in fact our past experiences, they also *are* the implied next step. Past and future melt together in the present ongoing bodily process, which is an always unfinished, single entity.[6]

> I can now use the word "is" to include both the now-ongoing behaving and the implying. I don't want to say "the body is this, and implies that"; I want to say "it is this and is the implying of that," for it is both. I want to overcome the old model according to which everything is a perfectly actual entity which has no past or future in its "is." The body's "is" is always also an implying.   (Gendlin 1973)

As we see here, "body memory" is an inseparable facet of the body's ongoing felt sensing. Being this kind of living texture (Gendlin 1966) of environmental interaction the body is capable of generating highly organized meanings[7] and behavior. Here is an

---

3. "More powerful than letting words come from a felt sense may be letting body movement come" (Gendlin 1981a).

4. "Ideally there would be a felt sense first, a movement (or image, or words, etc.) would come from the felt sense. Then, sensing again afterwards, one would find the felt sense changed or new, as a result of the expression that has occurred. (...) The same kind of "zig zag" between expression and felt sense, back and forth, characterizes any therapy or change process, in my opinion. An expression can lead to a changed whole-body sense, from which, in turn, a new expression can arise. To skip that zig-zag process usually leads to repetitiveness rather than change. Therapeutic change consists of new whole body formations" (Gendlin 1981a).

5. "An individual's sum total of life experiences, including traumatic events, saturates every part of his or her physical body. A person is much more than the thin, shifting attention or consciousness" (Gendlin 2010).

6. "We have to change the inner assumptions of our basic concepts. The entities with which we begin need to be both body and environment as single events rather than today's usual concepts that present them as separate. And they need to be not only what plain "is," but also that more finely organized but unfinished kind of order which I call 'implying.' Every bit of body is its environment and implies its next further eventing. Our concepts need to be restructured so that what is, is always also an implying" (Gendlin 2004a).

7. "(...) anything 'has meaning' in the sense that it affects a living system ... and affects it therefore always in complexly organized respects. Because the body is a completely organized interaction, therefore, anything that impinges on it has a complex meaning" (Gendlin 1966).

example, in which Gendlin makes clear among other things how memories are subtly present and necessary in order to generate a next step or sequence:

> In itself, what happens may only be a falling pebble, but when it hits the skin of an animal it may create an impact in the animal which is not only a powerful feeling, but highly organized meanings … that is to say, the pebble may stir the animal to complex reactions, of intense listening, of utterly still run-ready tensed muscles, of complex felt knowledge of the possible nearness of some foe, of hiding places, of its young to be protected, of pathways to run, of scents to seek, of the direction of wind and oncoming weather, and much more. All this is what I call "implicit" in that first felt impact which the falling pebble stirred.   (Gendlin 1966)

Almost any experience can be used to access or invite a Felt Sense. Whether it is a thought, an emotion, an action, a posture, facial expression, gesture, movement,[8] the trick is always to be with the experience in such a way that it can develop and unfold on its own. Empty repetitions on the contrary are a sign of stuck process, such as for instance perpetuating thoughts and emotions, chronic tension, or recurrent micro-movements: An issue keeps showing up in the body, like a bodily held "self-remind-ing" memory, implying what is still missing.

An additional stance of "I know this already" which often comes with clear labeling, neatly packaged in old conceptual boxes can be a major problem in helping the process to find its solution. By contrast, the phrase "Focus freshly on it instead, let it come freshly again" (Gendlin 1969) captures the idea of bringing a conceptu-ally vague, implicit level of the currently stuck issue into awareness[9] and allowing it to find new steps or sequences *by itself*. With this kind of open attention, the issue becomes able to differentiate itself rather than stay fixed in its first version. On this level, even seemingly old, repeated or bodily "remembered" behavior is always new, alive and interactive (which makes clear why a therapist's body also already is a strong intervention).

> Behavior forms freshly each time, both when it is new, and when it has happened before. (…) A behavior sequence stops the moment the feedback doesn't enable the next bit to form.   (Gendlin 2009a)

---

8. "Focusing fits almost always, because any thought, image, feeling, interaction, or action-step can be used to lead to the implicitly sensed edge, and from that edge any of these kinds of human experience can arise" (Gendlin 1981b).

9. "Please note that 'explicit' and 'implicit' meanings are both in awareness. What we con-cretely feel and calf inwardly refer to is certainly 'in awareness' (though the term 'awareness' will later require some reformulations). 'Implicit' meaning is often confusingly discussed as if it were 'unconscious' or 'not in awareness.' It should be quite clear that, since the direct referent is felt and is a direct datum of attention, it is 'in awareness.' Anything termed 'implicit' is felt in awareness" (Gendlin 1964).

Also, it is interesting that our bodies – with more or less help – are able to find their next *right* step through the implicit level.[10] But Focusing is not at all restricted to psychotherapy; in fact, it has proven to be an open, generic, culturally adaptable,[11] and possible unifying (Gendlin 1969) process; both common ground and method of methods (Gendlin 1974). In psychotherapy, the feeling process (made accessible through Focusing) has shown to be essential for change (Hendricks 2001).[12] Nowadays, Focusing is taught in many different fields (Gendlin 2009c), such as Focusing based staff training in schools (school development award 2010)[13] or hospitals; Focusing training for quality of life in women with breast cancer (Alice Ladas outstanding research award in body psychotherapy for 2010; Klagsbrun, Lennox, Summers & Lauren 2010); Focusing in Community Psychosocial Wellness in Afghanistan, El Salvador and Pakistan; Overcoming poverty in Ecuador (Hernández 2009); War zones (Rojas De Knaus 2003); Medical Decision-Making (Grindler Katonah 1999); Business Corporations (Mineyama, Tsutsumi, Soshi, Nishiguchi & Kawakami 2007) etc.

Focusing is an application of Eugene Gendlin's philosophy of the implicit ready to be integrated into other methods, concepts (like *body memory*) or theories by showing how to employ them experientially (Hendricks 2007).

References

Gendlin, E. T. (2010). *On focusing and trauma.* URL: http://www.focu-sing.org/trauma.html.

---

10. "The language is part of culture and history, but the body is always freshly here again, and can say 'no', even when culture and reason say 'yes'. If you enter there, you find a finely ordered cluster of strands, far more intricate than culture" (Gendlin 2004b).

11. This was most impressively demonstrated in Afghanistan, where the Focusing Intitute in cooperation with Nina Joy Lawrence and Dr. Patricia Omidian created a public health, community based approach based on Inner Relationship Focusing training. The same is true for any kind of adaptation to specific language used by different professions or in different fields of expertise. And: "Focusing has been proved to effectively reduce collective and individual psychological suffering in globally diverse cultures and nations. It facilitates community building and helps shape a more coherent, fair and just society across ethnic, cultural and gender lines. (…) The Focusing process is designed to be simple to teach, inexpensive, adaptable to different cultures and locally sustainable" (Gendlin 2005).

12. Hendricks, Marion N. (2001). Focusing-Oriented/Experiential Psychotherapy. In D. Cain & J. Seeman (Eds.), *Humanistic Psychotherapy: Handbook of Research and Practice*, American Psychological Association. From http://www.focusing.org/research_basis.html.

13. Focusing staff training was one of the decisive factors for awarding our client school with the School Development Award 2010 (Kruithoff 2010).

Gendlin, E. T. (2009a). *A changed ground for precise cognition. Unpublished manuscript* (35 p. 28), URL: http://www.focusing.org/gendlin/pdf/gendlin_a_changed_ground_for_precise_cognition.pdf.

Gendlin, E. T. (2009b). *Directory to the philosophy of entry into the Implicit.* URL: http://www.focusing.org/philo.html.

Gendlin, E. T. (2009c). *Vision statement for Focusing action steps and projects.* URL: http://www.focusing.org/social_issues/vision_statement_for_focusing.html.

Gendlin, E. T. (2005). *Afghanistan Psychosocial Wellness/Women's Project.* URL: http://www.focusing.org/projects/tfiafsc.html.

Gendlin, E. T. (2004a). Five philosophical talking points to communicate with colleagues who don't yet know focusing. Staying in Focus. *The Focusing Institute Newsletter, 4*(1), 5–8. URL: http://www.focusing.org/gendlin/docs/gol_2187.html.

Gendlin, E. T. (2004b). The new phenomenology of carrying forward. *Continental Philosophy Review, 37*(1), 127–151. URL: http://www.focusing.org/gendlin/docs/gol_2228.html.

Gendlin, E. T. (2003). Beyond postmodernism: From concepts through experiencing. In Roger Frie (Ed.), *Understanding experience: Psychotherapy and postmodernism* (pp. 100–115). Routledge. URL: http://www.focusing.org/gendlin/docs/gol_2164.html.

Gendlin, E. T. (1992a). The primacy of the body, not the primacy of perception [Excerpt from pages 343–353, slightly revised]. *Man and World, 25*(3–4), 341–353. URL: http://www.focusing.org/gendlin/docs/gol_2162.html.

Gendlin, E. T. (1992b). The wider role of bodily sense in thought and language. In M. Sheets-Johnstone (Ed.), *Giving the body its due* (pp. 192–207). Albany: State University of New York Press. URL: http://www.focusing.org/gendlin/docs/gol_2067.html.

Gendlin, E. T. (1985). Some notes on the "self". *The Focusing Folio, 4*(4), 137–151. URL: http://www.focusing.org/gendlin/docs/gol_2107.html.

Gendlin, E. T. (1981a). Movement therapy, objectification, and focusing. *The Focusing Folio, 1*(2), 35–37. URL: http://www.focusing.org/gendlin/docs/gol_2016.html.

Gendlin, E. T. (1981b). The whole process is more natural than the divided pieces. *The Focusing Folio, 1*(3), 18-23. URL: http://www.focusing.org/gendlin/docs/gol_2132.html.

Gendlin, E. T. (1974). Client-centered and experiential psychotherapy. In D. A. Wexler & L. N. Rice (Eds.), *Innovations in client-centered therapy* (pp. 211–246). New York: John Wiley & Sons. URL: http://www.focusing.org/gendlin/docs/gol_2118.html.

Gendlin, E. T. (1973). A phenomenology of emotions: Anger. In D. Carr & E.S. Casey (Eds.), *Explorations in phenomenology: Papers of the Society for Phenomenology and Existential Philosophy* (pp. 367–398). The Hague: Martinus Nijhoff. URL: http://www.focusing.org/gendlin/docs/gol_2095.html.

Gendlin, E. T. (1969). Focusing. *Psychotherapy: Theory, research and practice, 6*(1), 4–15. URL: http://www.focusing.org/gendlin/docs/gol_2048.html.

Gendlin, E. T. (1966). The discovery of felt meaning. In J. B. McDonald & R. R. Leeper (Eds.), *Language and meaning. Papers from the ASCD Conference, The Curriculum Research Institute* (Nov. 21–24, 1964 & March 20–23, 1965) (pp. 45–62). Washington, D.C.: Association for Supervision and Curriculum Development. URL: http://www.focusing.org/gendlin/docs/gol_2039.html.

Gendlin, E. T. (1964). A theory of personality change. In P. Worchel & D. Byrne (Eds.), *Personality change* (pp. 100–148). New York: John Wiley & Sons. URL: http://www.focusing.org/gendlin/docs/gol_2145.html.

Grindler Katonah, D. (1999). *Medical decision-making*. Presentation at the 6th International Congress on Cancer, Hong Kong University, Hong Kong. URL: http://www.focusing.org/doralee_med_decision-making.htm.

Hendricks, M. N. (2007). The role of experiencing in psychotherapy: Attending to the "Bodily Felt Sense" of a problem makes any orientation more effective. *Journal of Contemporary Psychotherapy, 37*(1), 41–46.

Hendricks, M. N. (2001). Focusing-oriented/experiential psychotherapy. In D. Cain & J. Seeman (Eds.), *Humanistic psychotherapy: Handbook of research and practice*. Washington, D.C.: American Psychological Association. URL: http://www.focusing.org/research_basis.html.

Hernández, W. (2009). *Focusing and overcoming extreme poverty in Ecuador*. URL: http://www.focusing.org/docs/fotconfppt/Descongelamiento-de-la-Pobreza-3-eng.pdf.

Klagsbrun, J., Lennox, S. L. & Summers, L. (2010). Effect of "clearing a space" on quality of life in women with breast cancer. *USABPJ, 9*(2), 48–53. URL: http://www.focusing.org/medicine/effect-of-clearing-a-space.pdf.

Kruithoff, E. (2010). *Focusing für Lehrerinnen und Lehrer*. [Focusing for teachers]. URL:http://www.focusing.org/fot/focusing_f%C3%BCr_lehrerinnen_und_lehrer.pdf.

Mineyama, S., Tsutsumi, A., Soshi, T., Nishiguchi, K. & Kawakami, N. (2007). Supervisor's attitudes and skills for active listening with regard to working conditions and psychological stress reactions among subordinate workers. *Journal of Occupational Health, 49*, 81–87.

Rojas De Knaus, L. (2003). *Teaching focusing in war zones*. URL: http://www.focu-sing.org/social_issues/rojas_kos.

CHAPTER 25

Mindfulness, embodiment, and depression

Johannes Michalak,* Jan M. Burg* and Thomas Heidenreich**
*University of Hildesheim, Germany / **University of Applied Sciences,
Esslingen, Germany

During the past decade, Mindfulness-Based Cognitive Therapy (MBCT) aiming
at relapse prevention in depression has been developed and empirically tested.
All exercises taught during MBCT are based on the development of a heightened awareness of one's body. The important role of the body is also stressed
in a recently emerging interdisciplinary field of research termed 'embodiment'.
This research program focuses on the interactions between bodily, cognitive,
and emotional processes. Based on the obvious role of the body in MBCT and
on the theoretical and empirical evidence highlighting the role of the body in
emotional processes, we argue that considering embodied processes might be
a useful perspective for research on the etiology of depression and on mechanisms of action in MBCT.

Keywords: embodiment, major depression, mindfulness, cognitive therapy,
relapse prevention

Mindfulness is a principle rooted in eastern mediation practice. It refers to a state of
mind characterized by a nonjudgmental awareness of the present moment. In addition, it is the process that leads to this mental state (Bishop et al. 2004; Kabat-Zinn
2003). Teachers of mindfulness stress the importance of practice to attain a deeper
and experience-based understanding of what is meant by mindfulness. A conceptual
approach to mindfulness might be of help for a first look at the territory of mindfulness; however, the lifelong task of mindfulness practitioners is to *embody* this principle. And indeed, one fundamental characteristic of mindfulness exercises is their
focus on the *body*. For example in breathing meditation, one of the fundamental practices in most meditation traditions, people practice being aware of their breathing.
The instruction is not to *think* of their breathing but instead to be *bodily aware* of
the entire process of inhalation and exhalation. These mindfulness practices enable
people to more and more 'inhabit' their body, transforming the 'Körper' (the body as
a tool or object) into a 'Leib' (the body as the place of being; i.e., awareness and experience; Plessner 1982). Moreover, by coming into contact with this embodied existence,

one can intensify the living connectedness with oneself and with the world, and thus change very basic 'existential feelings' (Fuchs & Schlimme 2009).

During the past two decades, a growing interest in the integration of mindfulness into the treatment of patients with psychological or physical disorders has emerged. Several treatment approaches that focus on training patients in mindful awareness to enhance their coping with severe physical and psychological suffering have been developed (see Bishop 2002; Grossman, Niemann, Schmidt & Walach 2004; Baer 2003; Heidenreich & Michalak 2009; Hofmann, Sawyer, Witt & Oh 2010). One of the disorders in which mindfulness has been integrated into treatment is depression. Mindfulness-Based Cognitive Therapy (MBCT; Segal, Williams & Teasdale 2002) was especially developed for relapse prevention in depression. In several methodologically sophisticated studies, MBCT has been shown to substantially reduce the risk of relapse of formerly depressed patients with a history of at least three previous depressive episodes (e.g., Kuyken et al. 2008; Ma & Teasdale 2004; Teasdale et al. 2000).

Several theories have been developed to explain the beneficial health-related consequences of practicing mindfulness (see Baer 2003). Most of these theories explain the effects of mindfulness either on a cognitive level (e.g., heightened meta-cognitive awareness – the ability to see cognitions as mental events instead of self-evident truths; Teasdale, Moore, Hayhurst, Pope, Williams & Segal 2002) or on a behavioral level (e.g., exposure to adverse internal experiences, leading to desensitization; Kabat-Zinn 1982). However, given the fact that mindfulness-based approaches stress the importance of experientially coming into contact with the body, one might speculate whether complementing cognitive and behavioral theories with elements highlighting the role of the body might deepen our understanding of the effects of mindfulness-based approaches.

In recent years, an interdisciplinary field of research has emerged, focusing especially on the complex interactions between bodily, cognitive, and emotional processes (Niedenthal 2007; Niedenthal, Barsalou, Winkielman, Krauth-Gruber & Ric 2005). Theoretical approaches and research findings from this embodiment perspective on emotions might be especially suitable to refine our models of psychopathological phenomena such as depression and the way mindfulness might play a role in deescalating dysfunctional processes, which, unchallenged, might lead to relapse and recurrence of this debilitating disorder.

The major aim of the present chapter is to elaborate the relationship between mindfulness and an embodied conception of depression. We will first give an overview of mindfulness and its clinical application in MBCT. Then we will present some basic tenets of the embodiment perspective on emotion with special emphasis on embodiment and depression. In the final section of this chapter, we will focus on the question of why mindfulness-based approaches stress the importance of the body. Interweaving these new developments within basic and clinical research is a challenging task; thus, much that is said here will remain speculative. However, whenever possible we will present empirical evidence supporting our approach.

Mindfulness and Mindfulness-Based Cognitive Therapy (MBCT)

Mindfulness can be defined as a mental state characterized by nonjudgmental aware-ness of the present moment (Bishop et al. 2004; Kabat-Zinn 2003). It can emerge when we *pay attention* in a particular way: *on purpose, in the present moment and non-judgmentally* (Kabat-Zinn 2003).

A good way to clarify what this definition is about is to look at the opposite of its defining characteristics: In everyday life, our mind is rarely in the *present moment*. Instead it is very often busy with daydreaming, planning the future, or thinking about past events. When we drive a car or climb stairs, for example, we are seldom in contact with the here-and-now reality of these activities. We can be busy planning the next meeting or thinking about a conversation we had an hour ago. In this situation, one could say, we are functioning in an automatic-pilot mode – our mind is doing one thing while our body does another thing. One of the results of being on automatic pilot is that we lose contact with the richness every moment holds.

Anyone who had tried to be mindful of the present moment knows how difficult it is to stay present. Because of the tendency of the mind to wander and the ease with which we enter into a half-conscious, automatic-pilot state, someone who wants to develop mindfulness will be immediately confronted with this tendency to drift away. But in practicing mindfulness, we do not shy away from this fact. Rather one learns to *purposely* bring back the awareness to the present moment each time one notices it has wandered away. In fact, in mindfulness practice, we say that noticing when one is not present is a sign that one is practicing mindfulness. The task in mindfulness prac-tice is to 'come home' to the present *each time* one notices that the mind has drifted away. Thus, the invitation of mindfulness practice is to live every situation in direct contact with the here-and-now – whether the situation seems to be positive, negative, or neutral.

Another characteristic of our minds is that we tend to immediately *judge* our experiences and label them as good or bad. Or we want them to last longer, if they are pleasant, or to disappear, if they are unpleasant. Being mindful means to try – as best we can – to be aware of when we judge and then not to engage in the judging activity. By turning our awareness to the present moment and all its qualities, we lessen the hold of the judging mind which obscures our perception.

During the last decade, several approaches integrating training in mindfulness into clinical treatment have been developed (e.g., Mindfulness-Based Stress Reduc-tion, MBSR, Kabat-Zinn 1990; Dialectical Behavior Therapy, Linehan 1993). These ap-proaches share the assumption that mindfulness is a healthy quality of mind that can help people to cope even with severe physical and psychological suffering. Mindfulness might reduce the tendency to become overly identified with dysfunctional cognitions, it might help to deliberately decide one's course of action in the here-and-now instead of being driven by a habitual patterns of thinking or behaving (autopilot-modus), and it might help to turn towards experiences rather than escaping or avoiding them (for an overview of ideas about why mindfulness helps see Baer 2003).

One mindfulness-based approach targeted for depression is MBCT (Segal et al. 2002). Originally, it was developed specifically for *relapse prevention* in depression. Its development was motivated by strong and accumulating evidence that even after successful pharmacological or psychotherapeutic treatment of an acute episode of Major Depression (MD), relapse and recurrence are common phenomena (Vittengl et al. 2007; Westen & Morrison 2001). The risk of relapse for patients with more than two previous episodes of MD exceeds 70% (Consensus Development Panel 1985). Especially because of its recurrent nature, MD is associated with a high burden of disease (Lopez & Mathers 2006) as well as substantial social costs (Donohue & Pincus 2007; Mintz et al. 1992).

Research has shown that relapse and recurrence are predicted by the number of earlier episodes, degree of remission and comorbid disorders (Burcusa & Iacono 2007; Sullivan et al. 2000). While critical life events are believed to play a major role in first episodes of depression, there is evidence that this strong link does not apply to recurrent depression (Sullivan et al. 2000).

In MBCT, it is assumed that vulnerability to relapse and recurrence of depression arises from repeated associations between depressed mood and patterns of negative, self-devaluating, hopeless thinking during episodes of major depression. This repeated association leads to heightened levels of cognitive reactivity to dysphoric mood in individuals who have recovered from MD, making them more vulnerable to depressive relapse (see Segal et al. 1999; Segal et al. 2006).

The authors of MBCT postulate that the core skill that MBCT aims to teach is the ability, at times of potential relapse, to recognize and disengage from mind states characterized by self-perpetuating patterns of ruminative, negative thought (Teasdale, Moore, Hayhurst, Pope, Williams & Segal 2002). In MBCT, intensive mindfulness training is used to support patients in recognizing and disengaging from negative modes of mind.

The group-based MBCT-program (Segal et al. 2002) consists of 8 weekly sessions of approximately 2.5 hours duration. It combines elements of Mindfulness-Based Stress Reduction (Kabat-Zinn 1990) with components of cognitive-behavioral therapy.

The main part of each session consists of learning/practicing and giving and receiving feedback about *formal mindfulness exercises*. The first formal mindfulness exercise taught is the 'body scan'. In this exercise participants learn to sequentially attend to each section of the body – beginning with the toes of the left foot and moving systematically through each body part, ending with the top of the head. The instruction is to pay attention to all sensations in the various body parts mindfully. Thus, the entire body is mindfully scanned.

The second formal practice is sitting meditation, in which participants mindfully follow their breathing. When they notice that their attention has shifted away from their breathing (for example to thinking, daydreaming, or focusing on a sensation), participants learn to gently direct their attention back to their breathing. After several sessions in which mindfulness of breathing is stabilized, other objects such as sensa-tions, sounds, cognitions, and emotions are added to the sitting meditation.

The third formal mindfulness practice consists of a sequence of gentle yoga exer-cises that allow patients to practice mindfulness in movement. To participate in the MBCT program, patients must commit to practicing formal mindfulness exercises 45 minutes per day during the eight week course. Participants receive detailed in-structions each week on which exercises are to be practiced as homework. CDs are provided for each of the exercises.

The *informal mindfulness exercises* foster the transfer of mindfulness into daily life. In the first week of the course, for example, patients choose a routine activity such as washing dishes, climbing the stairs or taking a shower, which they perform with moment-to-moment awareness, thus connecting body and mind during the activities (e.g., being aware of the body-movements while climbing the stairs). During the eight weeks of the course, patients are encouraged to practice daily activities mindfully so that mindfulness gradually influences all daily routines. The 'breathing space' is a brief (three-minute) exercise in which patients are asked to attend to their breathing three times a day. The major aim of the breathing space is also the transfer of mindfulness to daily life.

In addition to the mindfulness exercises, *elements of cognitive-behavioral therapy* (CBT) are integrated into the MBCT program. However, unlike CBT, there is little emphasis in MBCT on changing the content of thoughts. Instead, it is proposed that changing the *relationship* to depressive thought is a critical skill patients need to learn or strengthen. Within MBCT, patients should learn to recognize that thoughts and feelings are *events in the mind* and not self-evident truths or aspects of the self. Cor-respondingly, MBCT tries to facilitate "decentered" views on cognitions and feelings (i.e., "Thoughts are not facts" and "I am not my thoughts") by means of a systematic training in mindfulness. Mindfulness makes it possible to 'turn towards' experiences rather than escaping or avoiding them (e.g., dysphoric mood) without "getting lost" in ruminative, negative thought (Segal et al. 2002).

Moreover, by turning our awareness to the present moment and all its qualities, mindfulness can facilitate a living connectedness with the richness every moment holds, which is a valuable resource for enhancing well-being (Brown & Ryan 2003) and coping with depressive mood (Astin 1997; Shapiro et al. 1998).

Several studies have shown that MBCT reduces the risk of relapse in formerly depressed patients with a history of at least three previous episodes of depression. The first study on MBCT was conducted by Teasdale et al. (2000). They randomized 145 recovered recurrently depressed patients to continue with treatment as usual (TAU) or, in addition, to receive MBCT. In the 60-week study period, MBCT significantly reduced the risk of relapse in patients with three or more previous episodes of depres-sion (77% of the sample). Rates of relapse/recurrence were 66% in the TAU group and 37% in the MBCT group. However, for patients with only 2 episodes (23% of the sam-ple), MBCT did not reduce relapse/recurrence. This pattern of findings was replicated in another trial with 73 patients conducted by Ma and Teasdale (2004): Relapse rates were reduced by more than 50% in patients with three or more previous episodes, but there was no reduction for patients with two previous episodes. In a recent study, Godfrin and van Heeringen (2010) could also demonstrate substantially reduced rates of relapse for MBCT patients with three or more previous episodes of MD. Bondolfi et al. (2010) could not demonstrate reduced rates of relapse in the MBCT group. However, they found that time to relapse was substantially prolonged in the MBCT group compared to the TAU group. Moreover, Kuyken et al. (2008) found MBCT to be at least as effective in reducing relapse/recurrence in MD as maintenance pharmacological treatment based on the British 'National Institute for Clinical Excellence' guidelines, which can be regarded as the 'gold standard' of evidence-based relapse prevention in MD (NICE 2004).

In several small-scale studies, preliminary evidence has been gathered for the effectiveness of MBCT in treating patients with chronic forms of depression (Barnhofer Crane, Hargus, Amarasinghe, Winder & Williams 2009; Eisendrath, Delucchi, Bitner, Fenimore, Smit & McLane 2008; Kenny & Williams 2007), severe sleep disorders (Heidenreich, Tuin, Pflug, Michal & Michalak 2006) or generalized anxiety disorder (Evans, Ferrando, Findler, Stowell, Smart & Haglin 2008).

Embodiment

Theoretical background

Some recent theories of emotion converge in the idea of the *embodied* nature of emotion (e.g., Damasio 1994; Niedenthal 2007; Niedenthal et al. 2005; Teasdale & Barnard 1993). The term *embodiment* is used by researchers in psychology (Barsalou 1999; Glenberg & Robertson 2000), philosophy (Clark 1997; Fuchs 2006; Varela, Thomson & Rosch 1991), artificial intelligence (Pfeifer & Bongrad 2006), and linguistics (Lakoff & Johnson 1999) to express the notion that knowledge is embodied or grounded in bodily states and in the brain's modality-specific systems (for a review see Niedenthal 2007; Niedenthal et al. 2005). Correspondingly, embodiment theories of emotion suppose a complex reciprocal relationship between the bodily expression of emotion and the way in which emotional information is processed. The notion that the bodily expression and emotional processes are closely interconnected can be traced back to the early days of academic psychology (James 1884). Early critics of embodied emotion argued that bodily feedback is too undifferentiated and too slow to represent emotional experience (Cannon 1929). However, since then research has shown that in fact the motor system can support extremely subtle distinctions (Niedenthal 2007).

As Goldman and de Vignemont (2009) and Wilson (2002) have pointed out, there are different ways of using the term embodiment in the literature. Let us briefly introduce two of the most central conceptions of embodiment:

1. Bodily activity interpretation: one's bodily actions or body anatomy (e.g., posture) have an important causal role in cognition and emotion. A seminal study that can be interpreted on the background of this embodiment interpretation was conducted by Strack, Martin and Strepper (1988). They required their participants to hold a pen in their teeth, which unobtrusively creates a contraction of the zygomaticus major muscles, the muscles involved in the production of a human smile. They found support that participants in the pen-in-teeth condition rated humorous cartoons as being funnier than subjects in the control condition in which zygomaticus contractions were inhibited.

2. Bodily format interpretation: In cognitive science it is proposed that information is processed in different formats of mental representation (e.g., a visual format, an auditory format; see Jackendoff 1992). For example, the memory of a situation is stored in different formats (e.g., visual information in a visual format; position and movements of the body in a bodily format; by analyzing information from these sensory formats, higher-order meaning structures can be gathered that use more abstract and symbolical/verbal formats). Moreover, when executing actions, different systems using different formats contribute to the regulation of the action. Bodily format interpretations of embodiment assume that mental representations in various bodily formats or codes have an important causal role in cognition. Not actual bodily actions or bodily anatomy are central for this interpretation but the fact that that cognitive and emotional processes are influenced by information encoded in a bodily format. Research on mirror neurons is an example of this type of embodiment interpretation. Mirror neurons are neurons in the premotor cortex which not only send movement instructions to the hand or other effectors but also echo instructions for the same movements when one merely observes another person executing that movement (Buccino et al. 2001; Gallese, Fadiga, Fogassi & Rizzolatti 1996; Gallese, Keysers, C. & Rizzolatti 2004; Rizzolatti & Sinigaglia 2007). In empathy, for example, the output of the mirror neuron system might inform an individual about the state or the goals of another individual by allowing him or her to feel the state of the other person from 'the inside', because the mirror neuron system provides information in a bodily format (i.e., during interaction with another person one literally feels the physical or emotional pain the other person is experiencing because similar pain-processing brain structures are activated in the empathizer which process information in a bodily and not merely in a verbal or symbolic format).

In the following section, we will review some clinical research indicating the relevance of embodied processes for depression. It will be shown that both types of embodiment interpretations are relevant in this field.

   One example of a clinical theory that stresses the importance of bodily information in depression is the Interacting Cognitive Subsystems (ICS) approach (Teasdale 1999; Teasdale & Barnard 1993). One assumption of this complex theory is that that sensory input (e.g., in a bodily format) makes a direct and important contribution to emotional states which distinguish them from more intellectual and rational processes. It is only when cognitive (e.g., thematic semantic context of a situation) information and sensory (e.g., proprioceptive) information are interlocked that the person will, for example, *feel* sad or hopeless instead of just thinking about sadness or hopelessness. In the so called 'depressive interlock configuration,' bodily and cognitive feedback loops can become established that 'lock' subsystems into a self-perpetuating configuration that maintains depression.

Empirical findings on the relevance of the body in depression

Empirical research on the embodiment of depression is relatively sparse. Some indirect evidence for the significance of the body in depression comes from studies on processing emotional material in *non-clinical populations*. Several studies have shown that the processing of emotionally negative and positive material can be influenced by bodily manipulations. For example, as mentioned above, Strack et al. (1988) demonstrated that manipulation of the facial expression impacts the degree to which cartoons were rated as funny. In a study on the retrieval of unpleasant autobiographical memories, Riskind (1983) could show that different postures and facial expressions modulated the latencies in retrieving positive vs. negative life experiences. More specifically, an erect posture and smiling in contrast to frowns and a slumped posture decreased latencies for the retrieval of pleasant autobiographical memories relative to the speed of retrieving unpleasant autobiographical memories. In another study by Riskind (1984), a slumped vs. upright sitting posture affected levels of depression and behavior (i.e., persistence in insolvable tasks) of individuals following failure or success. Duckworth, Bargh, Garcia and Chaiken (2002) demonstrated that instructions to push a lever away from their body (i.e., avoidance movement) or pull it toward their body (i.e., a consumption movement) have profound effects on processing emotionally positive or negative pictures. Moreover, in a series of experiments Koch (2009) demonstrated that different movement qualities had an influence on mood. Smooth in contrast to sharp transitions in movement rhythms produced more positive affect.

Taken together, this evidence from basic research indirectly supports the notion that bodily processes might be relevant for the onset and maintenances of depressive states because they subtly biases emotional processes.

Research on gait patterns of *clinically depressed patients* has also highlighted the complex interactions between bodily and emotional processes. Some earlier studies have analyzed gait patterns in depressed patients (Bader, Bühler, Endras, Klippstein & Hell 1999; Lemke, Wendorff, Mieth, Buhl & Linnemann 2000; Paleacu, Shutzman, Giladi, Herman, Simon & Hausdorff 2007; Sloman, Berridge, Homatidis, Hunter & Duck 1982; Sloman, Pierynowski, Berridge, Tupling & Flowers 1987). In sum, the results of these studies showed that currently depressed patients evidence reduced gait velocity, stride length, increased standing phase and gait cycle duration (Wendorff, Linnemann & Lemke 2002). However, these studies have certain methodological limitations: they restrict their analysis to the lower limbs and to forward and backward limb movements – that is, to one (the sagittal) dimension.

In a recent study, Michalak, Troje, Fischer, Vollmar, Heidenreich and Schulte (2009) used a motion capture system equipped with nine CCD video cameras to measure the gait patterns of 14 currently depressed inpatients and 14 matched never-depressed control participants with a high temporal and spatial resolution. The system tracks the position of 41 markers attached to the participants' bodies and allows a comprehensive three-dimensional analysis of the whole body while walking. Gait patterns of currently and never depressed participants showed considerable differences: currently depressed patients walked more slowly and showed smaller arm swings than healthy participants. Remarkably, depressed patients show larger amplitudes than never depressed people in lateral body sway. This means that when a depressed patient approaches the observer, the observer would see pronounced swaying lateral movements of the upper body. Moreover, the gait of depressed patients was characterized by a slumped posture and reduced vertical up-and-down movements of the upper body. An animation visualizing this function can be viewed at http://biomo-tionlab.ca/Demos/BMLdepression.html.

Moreover, Michalak et al. (2009, Study 2) could show that a convergent gait pattern characterizes sadness in a non-clinical population. Utilizing a within-subject design, sad and happy mood was induced in a sample of 23 undergraduate students by a musical mood induction procedure. Again, the analyses revealed that speed, arm swing, lateral body sway, posture of the upper body, and the amplitude of vertical movements of the upper body were discriminating features. An animation of the gait pattern associated with sad and happy mood can also be found at http://biomotionlab.ca/Demos/BMLdepression.html.

In a further study, Michalak, Troje and Heidenreich (2010) examined whether formerly depressed patients with a high risk of depressive relapse show gait patterns that resemble those of the currently depressed and sad individuals. It was proposed that deviant gait patterns might be a trait-marker of depression and thus not only apparent in currently but also in formerly depressed individuals. In this study, the gait patterns of 23 formerly depressed outpatients with a history of at least three previous episodes were compared to those of 29 never-depressed control participants. The effect size of the differences between formerly and never depressed participants were considerably smaller than those reported for currently depressed inpatients. However, the gait of formerly depressed participants still differs in some parameters from normal gait. Specifically, formerly depressed participants displayed reduced walking speed and reduced vertical movements of the upper body.

In summary, these studies on gait patterns of depressed and formerly depressed individuals show that emotional processes and the motor system are closely interconnected. The exact nature of this embodiment of depression has yet to be clarified. The experimental design of the mood induction study (Michalak et al. 2009; Study 2) allows us to infer that mood states can have causal effects on the way people walk. However, embodiment theories of emotion assume more complex interactions between bodily and emotional processes. As described above, the Interacting Cognitive Subsystems (ICS; Teasdale 1999; Teasdale & Barnard 1993) approach proposes that proprioceptive information causally influences the emotional state of individuals.

Preliminary evidence for effects of changes in proprioceptive information on depression was gathered in a study Koch, Morlinghaus and Fuchs (2007). Thirty-one currently depressed patients were assigned to one of three conditions: (1) a dance condition in which participants performed a traditional upbeat circle dance characterized by pronounced up-and-down movements for 3 minutes, (2) a conditions in which participants just listened to the music without dancing, and (3) a condition in which participants rode a home trainer bike (ergometer) for the same time and up to the same level of arousal as the dance group. Depression scores most strongly decreased and vitality scores most strongly increased in the dance condition. These results indicate that even short changes of movement patterns might causally influence depressive mood. Moreover, the basic research on the influence of posture, facial expression, and movement on emotional processing in non-clinical populations, which we reported above, lends strong support for the existence of bodily feedback loops affecting emotions. In future research, further studies investigating the causal effects of body manipulations on depression are needed.

Why is the body important in Mindfulness-Based Cognitive Therapy for depression?

In this section, we will link mindfulness and embodiment research to argue that the body is an important focus of MBCT. Starting from early Buddhist texts (Satipatthana Sutta), focusing on bodily sensations such as breathing has been the basis for all meditative practice.

The body as an anchor of mindfulness

In every formal mindfulness exercise taught in MBCT, the body is the anchor of mindfulness. In breathing meditation for example, the direct, experiential contact with breathing is used as a reference point of awareness. This reference point makes it easier to realize when the mind wanders away from this present-moment experience into the past, the future or diffuse states of mind-like daydreaming or fantasizing. Practitioners are instructed not to think of their breathing, but instead to be aware of the body during the entire process of breathing out and breathing in.

In two recent studies, Burg and Michalak (2011) and Burg and Michalak (in press) investigated the clinical relevance of staying in contact with one's body during mindful breathing. Specifically, they examined the associations between a mindful breathing exercise (MBE) and depression-related variables, namely rumination, depressive symptoms, self-esteem, and self-esteem stability. Rumination, as defined in the Response Styles Theory (RST), means responding to sadness by focusing re-petitively and passively on the meaning, causes, and consequences of one's mood, and is considered to be a central risk factor for depression relapse (Michalak, Hölz & Teismann, in press; Nolen-Hoeksema 1991; Nolen-Hoeksema, Wisco & Lyubomirsky 2008). A sample of 42 undergraduate psychology students was asked to complete the MBE and measures of rumination, depressive symptoms, self-esteem, and self-esteem stability. In the MBE, participants are instructed to observe and sense their breathing for about 18 minutes and to return to their breathing whenever they lose the mindful sensation of it. Within this time period, participants are prompted 22 times at ir-regular intervals to indicate whether they have lost mindful contact with their breath-ing as a result of mind wandering. Moreover, they are requested to indicate states of mindlessness every time they noticed them on their own during inter-signal intervals. This made it possible to calculate the sum of all phases in which the participant's mind never wandered (no click within a phase and a 'mindful'-response at the end upon a signal) and stayed in contact with the bodily sensation of breathing. The close alignment of the MBE with one of the most central mindfulness exercises, namely breathing meditation, might enhance the ecological validity of assessing mindfulness in comparison with self-reports. The results showed negative correlations between the MBE and measures of rumination and depressive symptoms, as well as positive correlations between the MBE and self-esteem and self-esteem stability. Thus, people who were more able to stay mindfully in contact with their body during breathing meditation reported less rumination und fewer depressive symptoms, but higher and more stable self-esteem.

Moreover, further evidence for the importance of the ability to mindfully stay in contact with one's body is demonstrated by a new questionnaire (Body Mindful-ness Questionnaire, BMQ), focusing specifically on body-related mindfulness (Burg, Heidenreich & Michalak, submitted). The questionnaire comprises two factors: ex-periencing body awareness and appreciating body awareness. The first factor, body-related mindfulness, captures the extent to which the respondent remains mindfully in contact with his or her body in everyday life. More precisely, the negatively worded items measure how often respondents lose the awareness of their body in everyday activities, as a result, for example, of slipping into automatic pilot, mind wandering, ruminating, and so on. For example, items include, "I'm so absorbed in my thoughts that I no longer pay attention to my body," and "I forget my body in everyday stress." Results show moderate positive associations of this factor with other mindfulness questionnaires (convergent validity) and negative correlations with clinical variables such as perceived stress, neuroticism, rumination, as well as depressive and dissocia-tive symptoms. Thus, there is evidence for the healthy quality of being bodily aware in one's life.

Mindfulness of one's emotions

a. *Early detection of escalating emotional patterns*
As the ICS approach and other embodiment theories propose, the body plays a central role in emotions. Correspondingly, mindfully coming into contact with one's body also means coming into contact with one's emotions. This might help people with emotional vulnerabilities to realize very early when dysfunctional emotional processes escalate. Individuals with a history of depression very often report that they became aware of their negative mood only after their mood had grown to a full-blown episode of depression. When mood states have fully escalated, it is very difficult to take steps for a healthy de-escalation. Training in mindfulness might assist formerly depressed individuals to be aware at an early stage of more or less subtle bodily signs of depressive mood such as lethargy, tension in the neck, or a lump in the throat. This might help them to react to this escalation with awareness and to take deliberate steps to care for themselves, instead of acting out dysfunctional automatic reactions to their mood states (negating or suppressing the current state, excessive rumination, panic because of the dysphoric mood etc.).

Moreover, as Fuchs and Schlimme (2009) have pointed out, psychological disorders such as depression affect a prereflective embodied sense of self. This means that psychological disorders affect the person's being-in-the-world, or, in systems terms, cause disturbances in the ecological interactions of an individual with his or her environment. From this perspective, psychological disorders always manifest themselves in particular disturbances of embodied existence, even if only in the way of very basic 'existential feelings'. These 'existential feelings' are forms of *body memory* resulting from condensed past experiences of interactions with other persons and with the non-social environment (see chapter by Fuchs, this volume). As mindfulness shapes the awareness of these 'existential feelings' (i.e., the prereflective sense of self as connected with the environment), it could be expected that mindfulness training can help patients to identify these subtle forms of disturbances very early. Moreover, as mindfulness 'opens' the mind and furthers an experiential and living contact with the body and with its connection with the environment, it might reduce tendencies to disembodiment and existential feeling of encapsulation often found in psychological disorders. Evidence for the reciprocal nature of Mindfulness and Depersonalization (a condition characterized by subjective experiences of unreality in one's sense of self) was found by Michal, Beutel, Jordan, Zimmermann, Wolteres and Heidenreich (2007). In a sample consisting of patients suffering pain syndromes and students, a substantial negative correlation between mindfulness and depersonalization was found.

b. *Mindful body-awareness as an antidote to emotional avoidance*
Of course, coming into contact with one's emotions is often challenging, especially when these emotions are negative. All of us have the tendency to avoid inner experiences such as sadness, shame, jealousy, or anger. However, excessive and inflexible

experiential avoidance has been shown to be a key transdiagnostic factor leading to the escalation and persistence of various psychological disorders (Hayes, Strosahl & Wilson 1999; Hayes, Wilson, Gifford, Follette & Strosahl 1996; Hayes et al. 2004; Kashdan, Barrios, Forsyth & Steger 2006). Mindfulness brings us into contact with the here-and-now experiences of emotions on a bodily level. Instead of ruminating or thinking about emotions or the situations that elicited these emotions, practitioners learn to attend to the 'bodily manifestation' of emotions in the here-and-now. They are invited to let go of the 'mental film' in their heads (e.g., "Why did this happen to me?"; "What are the consequences, if I cannot control these feelings?") and to 'turn towards' experiences on a bodily level. The task is to allow the bodily 'felt sense' (Gendlin 1981) to unfold in the present moment and to feel how, for example, the sadness or anxiety becomes manifest in the chest or in the stomach. This should be done with a gentle and curious stance and in a way that is not defensive, but rather acknowledges one's limits.

Empirical evidence for the notion that mindfulness might reduce experiential avoidance and related forms of dysfunctional ways of dealing with emotions (i.e., rumination, worry, thought suppression, Segal et al. 2002; Borkovec & Inz 1990) stems from different strands of research. Studies assessing mindfulness with self-report measures have consistently shown that trait mindfulness is negatively associated with experiential avoidance, dissociation, rumination, thought suppression, and worry (e.g., Baer, Smith, Hopkins, Krietemeyer & Toney 2006; Brown & Ryan 2003; Hayes & Feldman 2004; Ströhle, Nachtigall, Michalak & Heidenreich 2010). More specifically, as reported above, Burg, Heidenreich and Michalak (submitted) found a negative correlation between body-awareness assessed with the BMQ and rumination.

Moreover, various studies on the effects of MBCT and MBSR have demonstrated that mindfulness-based approaches reduce the tendency to ruminate (Eisendrath, Delucchi, Bitner, Fenimore, Smit & McLane 2008; Jain et al. 2007; Kingston, Dooley, Bates, Lawlor & Malone 2007; Michalak, Hölz & Teismann 2010; Ramel, Goldin, Carmona & McQuaid 2004). In addition, in a study with functional MRI, Farb, Mayberg, Bean, McKeon, and Segal (2010) could show that training in mindfulness (i.e., MBSR) results in a greater recruitment of brain regions associated with body sensations (i.e., right-lateralized recruitment, including visceral and somatosensory areas) after induction of sadness. The greater somatic recruitment during evoked sadness was associated with decreased depression scores. This finding supports the notion that (a) mindfulness training indeed increases body-awareness and (b) that heightened body-awareness has beneficial effects on depression.

c. Intuitive insight into the interplay between the body and emotional processes
By means of mindfulness practice, individuals might increase the awareness of the complex interaction of body states with cognitive and emotional processes. This heightened awareness might not only assist people in recognizing and disengaging from negative cognitive states (as cognitive theories of mechanisms in MBCT postulate) but also in recognizing and disengaging from negative bodily patterns (e.g.,

posture or movement patterns) that increase the risk of escalating negative emotional states. For example, when an individual mindfully realizes that a certain posture (e.g., a slumped posture) or a certain style of movement (e.g., walking in sluggish way) has deleterious effects on mood and well-being, he or she might be able to change this bodily pattern into one that is more beneficial.

In support of this notion, Michalak, Troje and Heidenreich (2010) found that depressive gait patterns changed during a course of MBCT. In an uncontrolled study with 23 formerly depressed patients, they could show that patients trained in mindful body-awareness during MBCT showed normalized walking speed and lateral body sway. While walking speed increased, lateral body sway was reduced. In addition, vertical head movements showed a marginally significant increase toward normalization. Even though the sizes of these changes were small, formerly depressed patients approximately halved the discrepancy between their performance and that of normal controls with regard to speed and vertical head movements. Since the changes were not simply attributable to changes in levels of depression, this finding might indicate that MBCT increases a 'feeling' for the effects of the body on emotion and might help patients to change dysfunctional movement patterns. This is another example of the way mindfulness might affect *body memory*. A certain habitual posture or style of movement might be the result of repeated non-verbal interactions with the social environment during development (see chapter by Fuchs, this volume). This intercorporeal memory is implicitly and unconsciously present in every encounter. Mindfulness might help us to be aware of this subtle form of body memory and might give us the possibility to make new experiences with a new style of embodied interaction.

Embodied compassion and the body as the place of bliss

Mindful contact with the body is not just a means of coming into contact with avoided and negative emotional patterns. Perhaps more importantly, the body is or can be a valuable positive resource and – while practicing mindfulness – the place where people can experience deep states of calmness and joy. It would be a misunderstanding of mindfulness practice to equate mindfulness with exposure and habituation to negative and unwanted internal feelings. Even though it is important to be experientially open to all experiences that become manifest in the field of awareness, this should not be done in a cold or detached way. Instead, people are invited to cultivate a sense of compassion for themselves and others. And because of the bodily focus of mindfulness, the kind of compassion cultivated in mindfulness practice is not abstract or diffuse, but has to be manifested within the concrete bodily experience. Of course this is a subtle dimension of mindfulness practice and can only be learned on an experiential basis.

Some indirect support for the notion that mindfulness is embodied through a compassionate stance comes from findings that trait mindfulness is associated with self-compassion (Baer et al. 2006). More specifically, the second facet of the BMQ

(Burg et al., submitted), appreciating body awareness, which assesses appreciation of one's bodily experience (for example, "It is enriching for me to experience my body consciously," "I value experiencing a strong connectedness with my body"), showed substantial positive correlations with established mindfulness questionnaires. These positive associations are consistent with the notion that the body can be a valuable positive resource within the cultivation of mindfulness. At the same time, Burg et al. (submitted) reported negative associations between body appreciation, perceived stress and depressive symptoms.

Contact with organismic needs and limits

We often lose contact with our organismic needs and limits when we are entangled in an inflexible 'doing-mode.' We are so preoccupied with striving for goals that we do not realize that we are hungry or thirsty or that we are exhausted and tired. The important capacity of humans to act intentionally towards long-term goals detached from current need states can have detrimental consequences if this capacity is used inflexibly and by default. Mindful contact with the body can bring people into touch with their current needs. Thus, people can decide more flexibly and deliberately how they want to react to the current need state in concert with their long-term aspirations.

Vivid contact with the other persons in interactions

If a person is in contact with his or her own inner states, this familiarity with him- or herself might help to bring about empathic contact with another person in interactions. The mirror neuron system might be a basis template for knowing the other person from 'the inside'. As soon as we come into contact with another person, our bodies interact and cause subtle sensations in one another. The sensations triggered during the interaction are caused by *body memories* of the interaction-histories of the people who interact. Mindfulness might be a valuable resource for making one *aware* of the reactions to the other person and for deepening our understanding of the other person. In line with this argument, Safran and Muran (2000) recommend mindfulness practice for therapists to come to a deeper understanding of the implicit relationship patterns in the interaction between therapist and clients. This is the basis for identifying so called 'alliance ruptures' during the therapeutic process and entering into a meta-communication process with the client to resolve such alliance ruptures.

Support for the notion that mindfulness training of the therapist is beneficial stems from a study of Grepmair, Mitterlehner, Loew, Bachler, Rother, and Nickel (2007). Utilizing a randomized controlled design, they could show that mindfulness training of psychotherapists had positive effects on their patients' treatment outcome. However, it should be noted that the specific role of mindfulness of the body was not addressed in this study.

Conclusion

In the present chapter, we argued that the body is highly relevant in mindfulness and mindfulness-based treatment approaches. On the basis of the theoretical proposals and empirical findings on the embodiment of emotions, we assume that bodily processes are relevant in many psychological disorders since the body may be relevant in dysfunctional escalation of emotional processes and as the medium for existential feelings of connectedness or disconnectedness with the social and material world. The experiences we have collected during our history manifest themselves via body memory in every situation, they are our *lived past*. One specific characteristic of mindfulness-based interventions is that they systematically train practitioners to come into contact with their body, to inhabit their body with awareness and correspondingly to transform the '*Körper*' into a '*Leib*'. Conscious attention toward the body might help us to be aware of the memories our bodies mediate, but also to be aware of the fact that every moment is fresh and new, providing us with the freedom from being determined by our past experiences.

As we pointed out above, in clinical settings, this might help patients to cope with their emotional vulnerability in an aware, self-caring, and deliberate way. On a fundamental level, therapists who stay mindfully in contact with their own body and with the embodied here-and-now reality of their patients implicitly express their respect and esteem for their patients and their own existence, and for the endeavor of the therapeutic enterprise.

References

Astin, J. (1997). Stress reduction through mindfulness meditation: effects on psychological symptomatology, sense of control, and spiritual experience. *Psychotherapy and Psychosomatics, 66,* 97–106.

Bader, J. P., Bühler, J., Endrass, J., Klipstein, A. & Hell, D. (1999). *Muskelkraft und Gangcharakteristika depressiver Menschen* [Muscle force and the gait characteristics of depressive individuals]. *Nervenarzt, 70,* 613–619.

Baer, R. A. (2003). Mindfulness training as a clinical intervention: A conceptual and empirical review. *Clinical Psychology: Science and Practice, 10,* 125–143.

Baer, R. A., Smith, G. T., Hopkins, J., Krietemeyer, J. & Toney, L. (2006). Using self-report assessment methods to explore facets of mindfulness. *Assessment, 13,* 27–45.

Barnhofer, T., Crane, C., Hargus, E., Amarasinghe, M., Winder, R. & Williams, J. M. G. (2009). Mindfulness-based cognitive therapy as a treatment for chronic depression: A preliminary study. *Behaviour Research and Therapy, 47*(5), 366–373.

Barsalou, L. W. (1999). Perceptual symbol systems. *Behavioral and Brain Sciences, 22,* 577–660.

Bishop, S. R. (2002). What do we really know about mindfulness-based stress reduction? *Psychosomatic Medicine, 64,* 71–84.

Bishop, S. R., Lau, M., Shapiro, S., Carlson, L., Anderson, N. D., Carmody, J., Segal, Z. V., Abbey, S., Speca, M., Velting, D. & Devins, G. (2004). Mindfulness: A proposed operational definition. *Clinical Psychology: Science and Practice, 11*, 230–241.

Buccino, G., Lui, F., Canessa, N., Patteri, I., Lagravinese, G., Benuzzi, F., Porro, C. A. & Rizzolatti, G. (2001). Neural circuits involved in the recognition of actions performed by non-conspecifics: an fMRI study. *Journal of Cognitive Neuroscience, 16*, 114–126.

Bondolfi, G., Jermann, F., Van der Linden, M., Gex-Fabry, M., Bizzini, L., Weber Rouget, B. et al. (2010). Depression relapse prophylaxis with Mindfulness-Based Cognitive Therapy: Replication and extension in the Swiss health care system. *Journal of Affective Disorders, 122*, 224–231.

Borkovec, T. D. & Inz, J. (1990). The nature of worry in generalized anxiety disorder: A predominance of thought activity. *Behaviour Research and Therapy, 28*, 153–158.

Brown, K. W. & Ryan, R. M. (2003). The benefits of being present: Mindfulness and its role in psychological well-being. *Journal of Personality and Social Psychology, 84*, 822–848.

Burcusa, S. L. & Iacono, W. G. (2007). Risk for recurrence in depression. *Clinical Psychological Review, 27*, 959–985.

Burg, J. M., Heidenreich, T. & Michalak, J. (submitted). *The development of the body mindfulness questionnaire (BMQ)*. Manuscript submitted for publication.

Burg, J. M. & Michalak, J. (2011). The healthy quality of mindful breathing: Associations with rumination and depression. *Cognitive Therapy and Research, 35*, 179–185.

Burg, J. M. & Michalak, J. (submitted). Achtsamkeit Selbstwert und Selbstwertstabilität [Mindfulness, self-esteem, and self-esteem stability]. *Zeitschrift für Klinische Psychologie und Psychotherapie.*

Cannon, W. B. (1929). *Bodily changes in pain, hunger, fear, and rage* (2nd ed.). New York: Appleton.

Clark, A. (1997). *Being there. Putting brain, body, and the world together again.* Cambridge, MA: MIT Press.

Damasio, A. R. (1994). *Descartes' error. Emotion, reason, and the human brain.* New York, NY: Avon Books.

Donohue, J. M. & Pincus, H. A. (2007). Reducing the social burden of depression. *Pharmacoeconomics, 25*, 7–24.

Duckworth, K. L., Bargh, J. A., Garcia, M. & Chaiken, S. (2002). The automatic evaluation of novel stimuli. *Psychological Science, 13,* 513–519.

Eisendrath, S. J., Delucchi, K., Bitner, R., Fenimore, P., Smit, M. & McLane, M. (2008). Mindfulness-based cognitive therapy for treatment-resistant depression: A pilot study. *Psychotherapy and Psychosomatics, 77*, 319–320.

Evans, S., Ferrando, S., Findler, M., Stowell, C., Smart, C. & Haglin, D. (2008). Mindfulness-based cognitive therapy for generalized anxiety disorder. *Journal of Anxiety Disorders, 22*, 716–721.

Farb, N. A. S., Mayberg, H., Bean, J., McKeon, D. & Zindel, V. S. (2010). Minding one's emotions: mindfulness training alters the neural expression of sadness. *Emotion, 10*, 25–33.

Fuchs, T. & Schlimme, J. E. (2009). Embodiment and psychopathology: a phenomenological perspective. *Current Opinion in Psychiatry, 22*, 570–575.

Gallese, V., Fadiga, L., Fogassi, L. & Rizzolatti, G. (1996). Action recognition in the premotor cortex. *Brain, 119*, 593–609.

Gallese, V., Keysers, C. & Rizzolatti, G. (2004). A unifying view of the basis of social cognition. *Trends in Cognitive Sciences, 8*, 396–403.

Gendlin, E. T. (1981). *Focusing*. New York, NY: Bantam.

Glenberg, A. M. & Robertson, D. A. (2000). Symbol grounding and meaning: A comparison of high-dimensional and embodied theories of meaning. *Journal of Memory and Language, 43*, 379–401.

Godfrin, K. A. & van Heeringen, C. (2010). The effects of mindfulness-based cognitive therapy on recurrence of depressive episodes, mental health and quality of life: A randomized controlled study. *Journal of Affective Disorders*.

Goldman, A. & de Vignemont, F. (2009). Is social cognition embodied? *Trends in Cognitive Sciences, 13*, 154–159.

Grepmair, L., Mitterlehner, F., Loew, T., Bachler, E., Rother, W. & Nickel, M. (2007). Promoting mindfulness in psychotherapists in training influences the treatment results of their patients: A randomized, double-blind, controlled study. *Psychotherapy and Psychosomatics, 76*, 332–338.

Grossman, P., Niemann, L., Schmidt, S. & Walach, H. (2004). Mindfulness-based stress reduction and health benefits: A meta-analysis. *Journal of Psychosomatic Research, 57*, 35–43.

Hayes, S. C., Strosahl, K. & Wilson, K. G. (1999). *Acceptance and commitment therapy: An experiential approach to behavior change*. New York: Guilford Press.

Hayes, S. C., Strosahl, K., Wilson, K. G., Bissett, R. T., Pistorello, J., Toarmino, D. et al. (2004). Measuring experiential avoidance: A preliminary test of a working model. *The Psychological Record, 54*, 553–578.

Hayes, S. C., Wilson, K. G., Gifford, E. V., Follette, V. M. & Strosahl, K. (1996). Experiental avoidance and behavioral disorders: A functional dimensional approach to diagnosis and treatment. *Journal of Consulting and Clinical Psychology, 64*, 1152–1168.

Hayes, A. M. & Feldman, G. (2004). Clarifying the construct of mindfulness in the context of emotion regulation and the process of change in therapy. *Clinical Psychology: Science and Practice, 11*, 255–262.

Heidenreich, T., Tuin, I., Pflug, B., Michal, M. & Michalak, J. (2006). Mindfulness-based cognitive therapy for persistent insomnia: A pilot study. *Psychotherapy and Psychosomatics, 75*, 188–189.

Heidenreich, T. & Michalak, J. (2009). Achtsamkeit [Mindfulness]. In J. Margraf & S. Schneider (Eds.), *Lehrbuch der Verhaltenstherapie [Textbook of behavior therapy]* (Vol. 2, pp. 569–578). Berlin: Springer.

Hofmann, S. G., Sawyer, A. T., Witt, A. A. & Oh, D. (2010). The Effect of Mindfulness-Based Therapy on Anxiety and Depression: A Meta-Analytic Review. *Journal of Consulting and Clinical Psychology, 78*, 169–183.

Jackendoff, R. S. (Ed.). (1992). *Languages of the mind: Essays on mental representation*. Cambridge, US: The MIT Press.

Jain, S., Shapiro, S. L., Swanick, S., Roesch, S. C., Mills, P. J., Bell, I. et al. (2007). A randomized controlled trial of mindfulness meditation versus relaxation training: Effects on distress, positive states of mind, rumination, and distraction. *Annuals of Behavioral Medicine, 33*, 11–21.

James, W. (1884). What is emotion? *Mind, 19*, 188–205.

Kabat-Zinn, J. (1982). An outpatient program in behavioral medicine for chronic pain patients based on the practice of mindfulness meditation: Theoretical considerations and preliminary results. *General Hospital Psychiatry, 4*, 33–47.

Kabat-Zinn, J. (2003). Mindfulness-based interventions in context: past, present, and future. *Clinical Psychology: Science and Practice, 10*, 144–156.

Kabat-Zinn, J. (1990). *Full catastrophe living: The program of the Stress Reduction Clinic at the University of Massachusetts Medical Center.* New York: Delta.

Kashdan, T. B., Barrios, V., Forsyth, J. P. & Steger, M. F. (2006). Experiential avoidance as a generalized psychological vulnerability: Comparisons with coping and emotion regulation strategies. *Behaviour Research and Therapy, 44,* 1301–1320.

Kenny, M. & Williams, M. (2007). Treatment-resistant depressed patients show a good response to Mindfulness-based Cognitive Therapy. *Behaviour Research and Therapy, 45,* 617–625.

Kingston, T., Dooley, B., Bates, A., Lawlor, E. & Malone, K. (2007). Mindfulness-based cognitive therapy for residual depressive symptoms. *Psychology and Psychotherapy: Theory, Research and Practice, 80,* 193–203.

Koch, S. C., Morlinghaus, K. & Fuchs, T. (2007). The joy dance – specific effects of a single dance intervention on psychiatric patients with depression. *The Arts in Psychotherapy, 34,* 340–349.

Kuyken, W., Byford, S., Taylor, R. S., Watkins, E., Holden, E., White, K. et al. (2008). Mindfulness-based cognitive therapy to prevent relapse in recurrent depression. *Journal of Consulting and Clinical Psychology, 76,* 966–978.

Lakoff, G. & Johnson, M. (1999). *Philosophy in the flesh: The embodied mind and its challenge to western thought.* New York, NY: Basic Books.

Lemke, M. R., Wendorff, T., Mieth, B., Buhl, K. & Linnemann, M. (2000). Spatiotemporal gait patterns during over ground locomotion in major depression compared with healthy controls. *Journal of Psychiatric Research, 34,* 277–283.

Linehan, M. (1993). *Cognitive-behavioral treatment of borderline personality disorder.* New York: Guilford Press.

Lopez, A. D. & Mathers, C. D. (2006). Measuring the global burden of disease and epidemiological transitions: 2002–2030. *Annals of Tropical Medicine & Parasitology, 100,* 481–499.

Ma, S. H. & Teasdale, J. D. (2004). Mindfulness-based cognitive therapy for depression: Replication and exploration of differential relapse prevention effects. *Journal of Consulting and Clinical Psychology, 72,* 31–40.

Michal, M., Beutel, M., Jordan, J., Zimmermann, M., Wolters, S. & Heidenreich, T. (2007). Depersonalization, mindfulness and childhood trauma. *Journal of Nervous and Mental Disease, 195,* 693–696.

Michalak, J., Troje, N., Heidenreich, T., Fischer, J., Vollmar, P. & Schulte, D. (2009). The embodiment of sadness and depression – Gait patterns associated with dysphoric mood. *Psychosomatic Medicine.*

Michalak, J., Hölz, A. & Teismann, T. (in press). Rumination as a predictor of relapse in mindfulness-based cognitive therapy for depression. *Psychology and Psychotherapy: Theory, Research and Practice, 84*(2), 230–236.

Michalak, J., Troje, N. F. & Heidenreich, T. (2010). Embodied effects of mindfulness-based cognitive therapy. *Journal of Psychosomatic Research, 68,* 312–313.

Mintz, J., Mintz, L. I., Arruda, M. J. & Hwang, S. S. (1992). Treatment of depression and the functional capacity to work. *Archives of General Psychiatry, 49,* 761–768.

National Institute for Clinical Excellence. (2004). *Depression: Management of Depression in Primary and Secondary Care. Clinical Guideline, 23.* London: NICE.

Niedenthal, P. M. (2007). Embodying emotion. *Science, 316,* 1002–1005.

Niedenthal, P. M., Barsalou, L. W., Winkielman, P., Krauth-Gruber, S. & Ric, R. (2005). Embodiment in attitudes, social perception, and emotion. *Personality and Social Psychology Review, 9,* 184–211.

Nolen-Hoeksema, S. (1991). Responses to depression and their effects on the duration of depressive episodes. *Journal of Abnormal Psychology, 100,* 569–582.

Nolen-Hoeksema, S., Wisco, B. E. & Lyubomirsky, S. (2008). Rethinking rumination. *Perspectives on Psychological Science, 3,* 400–424.

Paleacu, D., Shutzman, A., Giladi, N., Herman, T., Simon, E. S. & Hausdorff, J. M. (2007). Effects of pharmacological therapy on gait and cognitive function in depressed patients. *Clinical Neuropharamcology, 30*(2), 63–71.

Pfeifer, R. & Bongard, J. C. (2006). *How the body shapes the way we think. A new view of intelligence.* Cambridge, MA: MIT Press.

Plessner, H. (1982). *Mit anderen Augen. Aspekte einer philosophischen Anthropologie [With different eyes: Aspects of a philosophical anthropology].* Stuttgart: Reclam.

Ramel, W., Goldin, P. R., Carmona, P. E. & McQuaid, J. R. (2004). The effects of mindfulness meditation on cognitive processes and affect in patients with past depression. *Cognitive Therapy and Research, 28,* 433–455.

Riskind, J. H. (1983). Nonverbal expressions and the accessibility of life experience memories: A congruence hypothesis. *Social Cognition, 2,* 62–86.

Riskind, J. H. (1984). They stoop to conquer: Guiding and self-regulatory functions of physical posture after success and failure. *Journal of Personality and Social Psychology, 47,* 479–493.

Riskind, J. H. (1983). Nonverbal expressions and the accessibility of life experience memories: A congruence hypothesis. *Social Cognition, 2,* 62–86.

Rizzolatti, G. & Sinigaglia, C. (2007). *Mirrors in the brain. How our minds share actions and emotions.* Oxford: University Press.

Safran, J. D. & Muran, J. C. (2000). *Negotiating the therapeutic alliance.* New York, NY: Guilford Press.

Segal, Z. V., Gemar, M. C. & Williams, J. M. G. (1999). Differential cognitive response to a mood challenge following successful cognitive therapy or pharmacotherapy for unipolar depression. *Journal of Abnormal Psychology, 108,* 3–10.

Segal, Z. V., Williams, J. M. G. & Teasdale, J. D. (2002). *Mindfulness-based cognitive therapy for depression: a new approach to preventing relapse.* New York, NY: Guilford Press.

Segal, Z. V., Kennedy, S., Gemar, M., Hood, K., Pedersen, R. & Buis, T. (2006). Cognitive reactivity to sad mood provocation and the predication of depressive relapse. *Archives of General Psychiatry, 63,* 749–755.

Shapiro, S. L., Schwartz, G. E. & Bonner, G. (1998). Effects of mindfulness-based stress reduction on medical and premedical students. *Journal of Behavioral Medicine, 21,* 581–599.

Sloman, L., Pierrynowski, M., Berridge, M., Tupling, S. & Flowers, J. (1987). Mood, depressive illness and gait patterns. *The Canadian Journal of Psychiatry, 32,* 190–193.

Strack, F., Martin, L. L. & Stepper, S. (1988). Inhibiting and facilitating conditions of the human smile: A nonobtrusive test of the facial feedback hypothesis. *Journal of Personality and Social Psychology, 54,* 768–777.

Ströhle, G., Nachtigall, C., Michalak, J. & Heidenreich, T. (2010). Die Erfassung von Achtsamkeit als mehrdimensionales Konstrukt: Die deutsche Version des Kentucky Inventory of Mindfulness Skills (KIMS) [The assessment of mindfulness as a multidimensional construct: The German version of the Kentucky Inventory of Mindfulness Skills (KIMS)]. *Zeitschrift für Klinische Psychologie und Psychotherapie, 39,* 1–12.

Sullivan, P. F., Neale, M. C. & Kendler, K. S. (2000). Genetic epidemiology of major depression: Review and meta-analysis. *American Journal of Psychiatry, 15,* 1553–1562.

Teasdale, J. D. & Barnard, P. J. (1993). *Affect, cognition and change: Remodeling depressive thought*. Hove: Lawrence Erlbaum Associates.

Teasdale, J. D. (1999). Emotional processing, three modes of mind and the prevention of relapse in depression. *Behaviour Research and Therapy, 37*, 53–77.

Teasdale, J. D., Segal, Z. V., Williams, J. M. G., Ridgeway, V. A., Soulsby, J. & Lau, M. A. (2000). Prevention of relapse/recurrence in major depression by mindfulness-based cognitive therapy. *Journal of Consulting and Clinical Psychology, 68*, 615–623.

Teasdale, J. D., Moore, R. G., Hayhurst, H., Pope, M., Williams, S. & Segal, Z. V. (2002). Meta-cognitive awareness and prevention of relapse in depression: Empirical evidence. *Journal of Consulting and Clinical Psychology, 70*, 275–287.

Varela, F. J., Thompson, E. & Rosch, E. (1991). *The embodied mind: Cognitive science and human experience*. Cambridge, MA: MIT Press.

Vittengl, J. R., Clark, L. A., Dunn, T. W. & Jarrett, R. B. (2007). Reducing relapse and recurrence in unipolar depression: A comparative meta-analysis of cognitive-behavioral therapy's effects. *Journal of Consulting and Clinical Psychology, 75*, 475–488.

Wendorff, T., Linnemann, M. & Lemke, M. R. (2002). Lokomotion und Depression. [Locomotion and depression]. *Fortschritte der Neurologie, Psychiatrie, 70*, 289–296.

Westen, D. & Morrison, K. (2001). A multidimensional meta-analysis of treatment for depression, panic, and generalized anxiety disorder: A empirical examination of the status of empirically supported therapies. *Journal of Consulting and Clinical Psychology, 69*, 875–899.

Wilson, M. (2002). Six views of embodied cognition. *Psychonomic Bulletin & Review, 9*, 625–636.

PART IV

Conclusions

CHAPTER 26

Body memory

An integration

Michela Summa,* Sabine C. Koch,* Thomas Fuchs*
and Cornelia Müller**
*Heidelberg University / **Viadrina University, Frankfurt/Oder

In this final chapter, we summarize the state of the art concerning the research on body memory in phenomenology, in the cognitive sciences, and in embodied therapies. Thereby, we show the impact of the studies collected in this volume for the development of the research in these three fields. Firstly, we consider the contributions from the cognitive sciences and from embodied therapies from a phenomenological standpoint. Secondly, we show how the present volume contributes to the current debate on memory in the cognitive sciences. Thirdly, we discuss the relevance of body memory with selected populations from the perspective of embodied therapies. And finally, we conclude with the most important points of this book.

Keywords: body memory, phenomenology, cognitive sciences, embodied therapies, transdisciplinary approach

> The violinist Itzak Perlman, in trying to play a difficult note, raises his eyebrows (if it is a high note) and keeps them raised until the note has been played… it is generally believed that these motions are secondary and ancillary. But suppose that a good part of musical memory is in fact lodged in these peculiar movements. Suppose that they are significant.
>
> (Zajonc & Marcus 1984: 83–84)

In this final chapter, we will attempt an integration of what we have learned about body memory through the work on and around this edited volume. We will start with a phenomenological contribution, continue with a discussion on the role of body memory in the cognitive sciences, and conclude with the clinical and therapeutic perspective. We would like to thank all the contributors of this volume, who additionally sent short definitions of body memory from their disciplinary perspectives, and all the colleagues who sent case examples from personal and clinical experiences.

Body memory in phenomenology

The studies collected in this volume have approached body memory from the per-spectives of phenomenology, of the cognitive sciences, and of embodied therapies. The integrative approach, which ultimately defines the overall project of the book, reveals itself fruitful for both the theoretical definition of body memory in its different forms, and the evaluation of therapeutic work on body memory with patients affected by different pathologies.

Enriching previous theoretical and empirical work on body memory, the descriptions provided by the different contributions in this volume allow us to formulate a comprehensive definition of body memory, as resulting from a dialogue between phenomenology and the cognitive sciences. Assuming the distinction between explicit and implicit memory, originally formulated in cognitive psychology (e.g. Schacter 1987, 1996; Jansen this volume) and insisting on the bodily character of subjectivity, which has been emphasized by both phenomenology and embodiment theories,[1] we can describe body memory as the most concrete determination of implicit memory. In other words, body memory coincides with implicit memory insofar as the latter is lived through by a bodily subject.[2] Body memory, thus, embraces the totality of our subjective perceptual and behavioral dispositions, as they are mediated by the body. As such, body memory can be phenomenologically addressed as a form of "operative intentionality" (Fink 1966; Merleau-Ponty 1945): rather than being a re-presenting or presentifying act of recollection, body memory designates the pre-thematic impact of preceding bodily experiences on the meaningful, and yet implicit, configuration of our actual experience.

This general definition, however, entails many further specifications, which are correlated to the different domains of lived experience. Let us examine some of these specifications from a phenomenological point of view and seek to show in what sense they may enable us to gain a richer understanding of the role of body memory in giving shape to our lived experience.

As theoretical background for the following considerations, we particularly assume the work of Husserl, Bergson and Merleau-Ponty. Even if Husserl does not explicitly adopt the notion of body memory, in both his published and unpublished texts we can find some important clues to address this phenomenon (Summa 2011).

---

1. See, notably, Fuchs (2000, 2008a, 2008b, this volume); Husserl (1952); Jung and Sparenberg (this volume); Legrand (2006); Merleau-Ponty (1945); Pylvänäinen (this volume); Waldenfels (2000).

2. For a clear formulation of conceptual distinction between embodied and bodily self, see Legrand (2006). The author convincingly adopts the term 'embodied self' to designate a self whose mental states would only be accidentally correlated with bodily states. The notion of bodily self, instead, implies that embodiment is a non-accidental, constitutive character of subjectivity and selfhood. For the relevance of this distinction with respect to the relationship between implicit memory and body memory see Summa (2011).

More exactly, Husserl shows that body memory plays a role in both perceptual constitution and the formation of bodily, pre-reflective self-awareness. In both cases, body
memory allows us to get acquainted with perceptual and experiential patterns, and to
acquire familiarity with our bodily capacities. Moreover, body memory is responsible
of the formation of an individual style of perceiving and moving, and more generally
of experiencing the world. As such, body memory is the condition for the formation
of the bodily "I can". The phenomenological inquiry into the synthetic accomplishments implied in body memory is based on the phenomenology of time-conscious-
ness and of passive synthesis, in particular association and affection (Husserl 1966a,
1966b, 2001, 2006).

In almost the same years as Husserl, and yet following an independent path, the
French philosopher Henri Bergson developed a complex theory of memory, which
was also based on the analysis of lived experience. Most relevant for our discussion
is his distinction between *souvenir-image* ("image-memory") and *mémoire-habitude*
("habit-memory"), which, in a way, mirrors the above mentioned distinction between
explicit and implicit memory. Whereas the so-called *souvenir-image* representative-
ly reproduces episodes of our lives, *mémoire-habitude* is an implicitly enacted kind
of memory that is particularly operative in the formation of practical dispositions
(Bergson 2007: 87).

Merleau-Ponty's contribution to the definition of body memory is particularly
related to the role of motor intentionality in the formation of bodily habitualities
(Merleau-Ponty 1945: 166). Considering the cases of professional typists and instru-
mentalists, Merleau-Ponty insists on the peculiar, implicit "knowledge" that allows
them to arrive at successfully performing their respective activities of typing and playing as complex and integrated unities. The process of formation of such an implicit
knowledge, of course, can be extended to all our complex and articulated performances, e.g. reading or dancing. As a result of individually regulated learning processes,
during which the single phases and movements must be consciously controlled in
their succession and articulation (so, for instance, the single steps of a dance or the
finger placement corresponding to each single note), we progressively become able
to dance, to play an instrument etc. in a spontaneous or habitual way. At this point,
we are even unable to explicitly recollect or to list the single movements required to
properly actualize the performance. This becomes *in principle* impossible, because
the whole of the performance entails more than the mere sum of the single movements. It has become the unity of a style. Rather than being directed to the single and
fragmented steps of the performance, thus, our attention can now be oriented toward
the final goal of the action: to the text we are writing or reading, to the melody we are
playing, or to the dance we are embodying. What we once have learned has become
part of our fund of experiences; it has built a store of implicit and bodily knowledge.
This is primarily a form of practical, non-objectivating knowledge. It permeates as it
were the bodily limbs and comes forth by means of bodily efforts.

Following Polanyi (1967), and restating what we said above concerning implicit
memory, we can appropriately call this form of cognition "implicit knowing", mostly

operating within a "tacit dimension". It is worthwhile stressing that such perceptual and kinaesthetic habitual memory at the same time opens up and limits our experiential possibilities, and this is the reason why it gives shape to an individual style of experiencing. This clearly emerges if we think about the difficulties we encounter when trying to remove some of our typical practical mistakes, e.g. in playing an instrument. Yet, the ambiguous, both opening and limiting, character of habitual body memory also concerns our successful performances: by learning how to play the clarinet, I will progressively develop a unique style, which I will certainly be able to enrich and maybe modify, but which will also affect all my performances and have an impact on them, thus becoming part of my individual way of approaching the instrument.

Even if we can find some clues for a more specific distinction of the different forms of body memory in the work of the three just mentioned authors, the previous discussion shows that their inquiry is mainly devoted to what we now call habitual body memory. The main focus, indeed, remains on the formation of certain patterns of experience and movement, which become in a way inscribed in one's lived-body. Recently, Edward Casey and Thomas Fuchs have developed a more differentiated approach to body memory, the fruitfulness of which clearly emerges from different contributions in this volume. Casey (2000) distinguishes and describes three forms of body memory: habitual, traumatic, and erotic. In doing so, he stresses that "body memory" cannot be simply equated with the "memory of the body", if by the latter the body is conceived as the objective correlate of memory acts. Rather, body memory in its different forms is considered to be "intrinsic to the body, to its own ways of remembering: how we remember in and by and through the body" (Casey 2000: 147).

Quasi providing a neuroscientifically based pendant to this phenomenological discourse, Caldwell (this volume) shows how emerging work in neuroscience currently stresses the role of the whole body in the formation of body memory, thereby particularly considering the moving, sensing, feeling, and emoting body. This approach, as the author points out, challenges the traditional neurocentric approach to body memory from within.

In his phenomenological studies on body memory, Fuchs (2000, 2008a, 2008b, this volume) proposes an articulated categorical differentiation, developing a descriptive taxonomy that includes six forms of body memory. These can be schematically defined as follows:

> *Habitual or procedural memory* refers to the habitualization of the sensorimotor capacities of the lived-body. It allows us to acquire sensorimotor skills and attitudes, to get acquainted with perceptual and movement patterns, and to develop an individual style of interaction with the world.
>
> *Situational memory* extends into the spatio-temporal situation in which we bodily participate. As such, it entails the involuntary emergence of memory-images and impressions that are related to the atmosphere of certain (mostly affectively charged) lived situations. Moreover, situational body memory

makes possible both the feeling of familiarity with some situations and the feeling of alienness with respect to others, thus allowing us to "get involved in" or to "be touched from" peculiar situations.

Intercorporeal memory is related to the most basic, pre-thematic and bodily contact with other subjects. This form of memory makes possible the pre-thematic and implicit interaction with the other, itself mediated by bodily experience and skills. As such, intercorporeal memory makes possible the basic formation of dyadic and more generally intersubjective patterns of interaction.

Incorporative memory is mainly based on the phenomenon of bodily imitation or identification, and implies the reshaping of one's own primary bodily schemata of expression and behavior in social contexts. Thus, it makes possible the development of specific bodily attitudes and the assumption of embodied social roles. As such, this form of body memory is based in particular on the "interiorisation" of the gaze of the other.

Pain memory refers to the impact that painful experiences still have on our present. This impact manifests itself, for instance, in the unreflected and spontaneous caution that our fingers, as it were, assume in handling knives, if we once got injured.

Traumatic memory – referring to the impact traumatic experiences still have on the present – is the most severe form in which implicit memory impinges on our experiences. Traumatic memories may emerge as displaced or in the form of bodily symptoms, without any explicit awareness of the connection between the past and the present experience. The traumatic event in its violence in many cases withdraws from any explicit representation.

Commenting on Fuchs's early approach, Gendlin (this volume) points out that the inquiry into body memory shall not consider exclusively the past dimension. Otherwise, one might take the chance of considering actual behavior and performances as quasi-deterministically following from previous experiences or from acquired habits. Instead, Gendlin proposes to underscore the capacity of the body to shape something new on the basis of previous and sedimented experience. The notion of 'felt sense', particularly, is intended here as synthesizing (1) the impact of past experiences that are sedimented in body memory and (2) the open future implications, or the capacity to create something new.

In a recent study, Koch (this volume) empirically tested and validated Fuchs's taxonomy. Empirical and phenomenological evidence for the validity of these differentiations can be found in different studies collected in the present volume, which have more or less explicitly contributed in developing and enriching the account of the different forms of body memory.

Different from what Sheets-Johnstone (this volume) suggests, we do not believe that the attempt to differentiate the modalities in which body memory experientially manifests itself coincides with the mere pursuit of oppositional dichotomies, as if such dichotomies could be considered to be an end in and of themselves. On the contrary, these differentiations, which are grounded in the description of lived experiences, are meant to pursue the Aristotelian and then phenomenological aim of the possibly richest and most complete description of experiential givenness. Even admitting that there is some concrete overlap between the different morphological types mentioned above, it is only through such differentiation that we can investigate the specificity of the phenomena that fall under the general category of body memory. The risk, otherwise, is a monolithic account of body memory, which can maybe capture some of its general features, and yet does not properly consider how these features are concretely actualized in the different situations, and how they dynamically differentiate in order to cope with the different situations. Consequently, far from neglecting the central role that movement plays in the formation and the unfolding of body memory, the descriptive and differential approach we have just presented seeks to shed light on the irreducible specificities of the many forms that this very dynamics may assume. So for instance, the dynamics of life (and of body memory) obviously assumes a different configuration when we learn to dance and develop this very peculiar "habituality" (Alarcon this volume), or when we move along the double vector of the form of traumatic memory that Behnke calls "enduring", that means, "simultaneously enacting a centripetal move (pulling back inward) and a centrifugal move (pushing outward)" (Behnke this volume, p. 196).

Besides deepening the theoretical insights into the nature, the structure and the dynamics of body memory, and besides providing some quantitative evidence for the differentiations elaborated from a phenomenological perspective, the contributions in this volume have obtained important results regarding two other points. On the one hand, the role of body memory meaning formation and in giving shape to our cognition has been highlighted (Bermeitinger & Kiefer; Jansen; Jung & Sparenberg; Kolter, Ladewig, Summa, Koch, Müller & Fuchs; Suitner, Koch, Bachmeier & Maass; Summa this volume). On the other hand, the relevance of the work on body memory with patients affected by different pathologies has been demonstrated (Eberhard-Kaechele; Koch & Harvey; Kolter et al.; Konopatsch & Payne; Michalak, Burg & Heidenreich; Pylvänäinen; Shahar-Levy; Winther this volume).

We will now assess how these studies contribute to the research on memory in the cognitive science and in the clinical domain. Besides providing further empirical evidence for the centrality of body memory in our lived experience, these lines of research further enrich the phenomenological inquiry into body memory by adding new differentiations and new facets to the previous descriptions and open up the field for a fruitful dialogue between theoretical research and therapeutic practice.

Body memory in the cognitive sciences

> Body memory is the long-term representation of body sensations, external per-
> ceptions, and actions that form the basis for our knowledge about the internal
> and external world.   (Bermeitinger & Kiefer 2011)

> From a cognitive psychology point of view, theories of memory are concerned
> with the structure of memory as well as the processes which operate within this
> structure. Concerning this structure, body memory can be considered as im-
> plicit, which means that cognitive psychologists have to construct tests where the
> participants are not aware that their body memory is being retrieved. Establish-
> ing "Body Memory" as an empirical concept will be one of the challenging tasks
> in the future.   (Jansen 2011)

Why do we speak of body memory in the cognitive sciences?

Interdisciplinary embodiment approaches advance a view of the body and the mind
as one integrated system, though differing in perceptual vs. conceptual processing
(Koch 2010). From this perspective, the person is understood as an embodied agent
and as a living, organismic system as opposed to an information processing system
(Semin & Smith 2008; Smith & Semin 2004). Thought and emotion are conceptualized as embodied, based on the integration of bodily states in the brain (Barsalou
1999; Damasio 1999).

In cognitive psychology, a theory of embodied memory has been put forward
by Arthur Glenberg (1997). Glenberg states that memory developed the way it did
for its role in perception and action, and that "conceptualization is the encoding of
patterns of possible physical interaction with a three-dimensional world (...) determined by the types of bodies we have" (Glenberg 1997: 1). Starting from the question
how language conveys meaning, he suggests that linguistic meaning is grounded in
bodily activity. Persons, then, understand language by creating embodied conceptualizations of the situations the language refers to (e.g. spatial representations as shown
by Tversky 2008). This seems to be a plausible account of how individuals process
language referring to experiences of the real world. Metaphor would be a way to make
abstract knowledge experientially accessible; however there remains a broad array
of linguistic meaning which is neither metaphorically nor metonymically related to
lived experience.[3]

---

3. The role of body memory in conceptualization and meaning formation has been considered
by Summa (this volume) from a phenomenological standpoint. Even if the phenomenological
approach cannot be said to converge with Glenberg's (for the reasons discussed in the mentioned
chapter, phenomenologists, for instance, would not consider conceptualization as determined
by the types of body we have), the two perspectives agree in considering conceptualization as a

Traditional psychological theories have been treating memory in terms of internal representations, i.e. arbitrary symbols for the encoding of features. Accordingly, empirical research has been limited to laboratory studies providing arbitrary word lists, measuring memory with recall and recognition tests, or with priming tests, mostly using reaction time measures, hits, and errors as dependent variables. Yet these methods of measurement are not indicated if memory is conceptualized as embodied and in the service of the interaction with a three-dimensional environment. Glenberg's embodiment perspective provides an insight into meaning-making considering the constraints of the environment and the body that memory is bound to. By doing so, Glenberg's perspective overcomes the abstractions and the exclusive focus on cognitive processes that characterized previous laboratory studies. Taking this perspective seriously, new studies have been developed, which adopt more appropriate methods of measurement (Koch & Hentz 2011; Koch & Kasper 2009; Suitner et al. this volume).

The body remembers in a life-long learning history. Even the earliest pattern of how we are held, comforted, guided and reacted to by our care-givers remains imprinted in the body, in our later actions and our entire habitus. These forms of memory have been described by phenomenologists as intercorporeal [*zwischenleibliches*] body memory and as incorporative [*inkorporatives*] body memory (Fuchs this volume). They are meaningful in the individual's development and can become important in therapeutic treatment of disturbances, but have not been treated by cognitive science as forms of memory in their own right. Based on life-long learning processes, they cannot be easily accessed in laboratory situations. Besides intercorporeal and incorporative memory, Fuchs' descriptive taxonomy also includes situational body memory, traumatic body memory, and procedural body memory (skill-related) (Fuchs this volume). In psychological research, these different types of memory have been touched upon under the names of state-dependent memory, trauma-related memory, and procedural or implicit memory. These experientially detected and descriptively categorized forms of body memory are waiting for empirical testing.

Empirical and phenomenological research on body memory contributes to fill a void in memory research and has the potential to reconcile classical and embodied memory approaches. Methodological possibilities to assess body memory resulting from the contributions in this edited volume are summarized in the following paragraph, before a closer look at possible future experimental research on body memory is taken.

---

dynamic process of meaning formation, which, at least as far as empirical concepts are considered, has its roots in the most basic, bodily and perceptual, layers of experience.

The contribution of research on body memory to cognitive psychology

Memory contributes to the formation of our spatial-, temporal- and self-coherence. In cognitive psychology, explicit or declarative memory is considered to entail anything we can keep in mind and consciously recall (Schacter 1987, 1996; Squire 2004). More exactly, it comprises both autobiographical memory (recollection of facts and episodes related to one's own life, e.g. my eighteenth birthday) and semantic memory (recollection of data or facts acquired from written or oral sources, e.g. the storming of the Bastille on July, 14th 1789). On the contrary, implicit memory embraces all procedures, skills, and processes that we have once learned and that have progressively become habituated through repeated performance (skill learning, habit formation, classical conditioning, emotional learning, and priming; Roediger 1990; Schacter 1987, 1996).

As mentioned above, the concept of body memory derives from the encounter of the psychological differentiation of memory forms and systems with the phenomenological account of bodily subjectivity. The notion of body memory can be considered equivalent with the notion of implicit memory, if the latter is not merely assumed as referring to one or more systems of the brain, but rather more holistically refers to the lived body. Body memory, thus, is a form of lived experience, which is constantly re-actualized and implicitly lived through by a bodily subject.

In his seminal article, Roediger (1990) argues that the dissociation of results in implicit and explicit memory research in cognitive psychology is mainly due to the different methods that we use to measure these two types of memory: Explicit memory is measured by deliberate, meaning-related recall and recognition tests that require deeper processing, whereas implicit memory is measured by data-driven priming experiments (repetition priming or semantic priming, using techniques such as word-stem completion or word completion etc.; more superficial processing) or by skills tests with amnesic patients. Roediger argues against a multiple-systems approach of memory (Schacter 1987) and in favor of a processing approach.[4]

Nevertheless, empirical evidence has been found in favor of both the multiple memory systems and the different modes of processing approach. In fact, both approaches need not be mutually exclusive and can explain certain aspects of the empirical data in a more appropriate way (highlighting either the more distinct or the more overarching cognitive aspects). However, it is still a challenge to fill the empty cells in Table 1.

Starting from Table 1, we will now try to place body memory as understood in this book into the cognitive sciences conceptualizations. Research on body memory would tap into the cell of measuring implicit memory data-driven as well as with meaning-related procedures. The skills aspect of body memory would fall into the

---

4. We may ask ourselves whether the discussion about the memory systems in the brain really helps us in defining the problem at the experiential level. Even if it would be shown that we only have one memory system, we would still have different kinds of memory experiences.

Table 1. A graphic demonstration of Roediger's argument: The empirically found dissociation of memory systems may be due to the differences in measurement or processing (Roediger 1990)

	Implicit memory	Explicit memory
Data-driven measures	Priming Experiments Skills Learning/Retention	
Meaning-related measures		Recall Recognition

data-driven processing measures, since we are testing an acquired skill that is non-deliberate for the person. The interpersonal aspect of body memory is also data-driven (even though it can become meaning-related such as in counter-transference phenomena). The habitus aspect of body memory and incorporative body memory fall into the meaning-related cell: while one's body attitude may be totally implicit and not consciously accessible – it was and is shaped by specific interactions with one's parents, significant others, and other possible role models. The situational aspect of body memory is likewise meaning-related (e.g. the familiarity with the house of my childhood; or the feeling of a certain arousal state such as in skiing). And finally, probably the most obviously meaning-related aspect of body memory is the traumatic one. A trauma in one's personal history, maybe even in one's preverbal history, deeply impacts one's emotional well-being throughout life. In the case of trauma, it is relevant to investigate techniques of integrating the implicit in the course of one's life, in order to overcome suffering, the role of the victim, and the feeling of "stuckness".

Reder, Park and Kieffaber (2009) recently challenged the division between implicit and explicit memory systems in the human brain. Arguing that some implicit and explicit tasks share the same memory representations and stressing the role of the formation of new associations to distinguish implicit- and explicit-memory tasks, the authors suggest considering memory as a more integrated system. At the same time, they show that with the repetition priming paradigm (as the main experimental method) we have only been looking at one form of "implicit memory". More diverse methods and broader concepts are considered necessary. Phenomenology also addresses this need for a broader conceptualization of implicit memory, while embodiment research addresses its empirical investigability (see next section).

The operationalization of body memory

How can we empirically investigate body memory? Where are the constraints to body memory? Do they lie in the nature of our bodies, of the environment, or rather in the interaction of both? What are the methodological options to investigate body memory?

Body memory can be investigated on several methodological levels.

1. Firstly, we can conduct interviews (Koch this volume), and in addition to the classical interview setting, we may use techniques suited to evoke the implicit content to access the unconscious and the preconscious. Some of these techniques are relaxation and free association, hypnosis, mindfulness, meditation, focusing, and movement improvisation such as in authentic movement (Koch & Kasper 2009; Konopatsch & Payne this volume). Focusing, for instance, seems particularly suited to make connections between somatic reactions, emotions and cognitions (Gendlin 1996). Because it is a "sitting technique" with immediate verbal feedback, it may be also easier to employ and less threatening to client and therapist than some of the other body-mind techniques. Data collected from this or similar settings can then be empirically analyzed in a content analysis (Koch this volume).

2. Secondly, we can use the body-based techniques described here for direct exploratory investigation into body memory (Kolter et al. this volume). Based on behavioral observation and a cognitive-linguistic analysis of movement improvisation and of spontaneous movements in connection with verbalization (for instance in a dance class context), we can follow the processes of explication of the implicit through movement and words. By tracing how body movements turn into experiential source domains for multimodal metaphors, and how metaphors emerge and are successively activated and foregrounded, we can determine different degrees of implicitness and explicitness of memory (Kolter et al. this volume; Müller 2008a, b; Müller & Tag 2010). Drawing on Müller's approach to metaphorization as a dynamic process ranging from sleeping to waking metaphors, we can empirically reconstruct the path of a fully implicit type of memory (e.g. as executed in spontaneous and unreflected gesturing) to an increasingly explicit type of memory (when gestures become sources for multimodal metaphors), to a fully explicit form of memory (when body-movement receives meta-communicative awareness) (Kolter et al. this volume; Müller 2008a, b; Müller & Tag 2010).

   Tracing bodily movements from speechless contexts to contexts encompassing both body movement and speech allows us to empirically document the transition from implicit body memory to explicit verbalized memory, i.e. from the felt qualities of bodily experience, through the transformation of movement into an experiential source domain of a multimodal metaphor, up to explicit meta-reflection.

   As a result of our analyses (Kolter et al. this volume; Summa this volume), we suggest that not only may implicit memory be conceived as body memory, but sleeping metaphors incorporate implicit experiential memory too. Implicit memory, in other words, has a direct impact on meaning and concept formation. This becomes particularly clear if we consider the cognitive and experiential operativity of sleeping metaphors, and the process making their activation possible. Only when metaphoricity has been activated, the implicit bodily quality of the metaphoric source domain turns into an explicit one and the metaphor is considered waking (Müller 2008a, b; Müller & Tag subm.).

These observations indicate that body memory informs communication and is fundamentally dynamic in nature. The suggested empirical procedure, moreover, offers an alternative to word-based approaches of languaging movement, such as approaches that consider a metaphor exclusively as a linguistic concept. On the contrary, the cognitive-linguistic and sequential analytical method that we have applied (Kolter et al. this volume; Müller & Tag subm.) shows that metaphors have a stronger and larger cognitive potential, which has its grounds in bodily experience. Through the process of metaphorization, based on the realm of embodied experience, empirical concepts are constituted. These observations are in harmony with Vygotsky's and Hörmann's assumption of a continuum between meaning in movement and meaning in language (Vygotsky 1969; Hörmann 1976), with movement as the more basic and developmentally earlier concept, both serving a communicative purpose (*Verständigung*).

3.   Thirdly, we can investigate body memory in experimental designs. We can conceptualize body memory either as independent or as dependent variable. In our case, where movement (kinesthetic memory; Koch this volume; Sheets-Johnstone this volume) is of particular interest, studies were conducted regarding three main foci:
   –   the influence of movement on body memory, such as in body feedback effects (Hatfield, Cacioppo & Rapson 1994; Koch 2011a; Suitner et al. this volume);
   –   the influence of body memory on movement, such as in the influence of stereotypes on movement (Bargh, Chen & Burrows 1996), but also in dance instructions, metaphoric instructions (Böger this volume; Kolter et al. this volume), imaging, or authentic movement (Adler 2002; Konopatsch & Payne this volume; Pallaro 2007);
   –   the effects of the coupling of movement and meaning on reaction times and memory (motor congruency effects such as in spatial bias research, where movement is neither the independent nor the dependent, but a conditional independent variable (Casasanto & Dijkstra 2010; Koch, Glawe & Holt 2011).

   Movement, thus, can serve as an independent, as a dependent and as a conditional dependent variable. Barsalou, Niedenthal, Barbey and Ruppert (2003) distinguish four types of embodiment effects that can be empirically investigated and related to the taxonomy of body memory of Fuchs (this volume; see Table 2).

Starting with movement as a dependent variable, we can particularly investigate the previously introduced category of incorporative body memory (cf. Fuchs this volume). Firstly, we can do so by focusing on how perceived social stimuli cause bodily states (the first of four embodiment effects identified by Barsalou et al. 2003; see Table 2). A classic example for such a design is the study of Bargh et al. (1996) where the researchers subliminally primed their participants with the stereotype of old people (using words such as "Florida", "Bingo", etc. vs. no prime in the control group) causing

Table 2. System of reference displaying how embodiment effects (Barsalou et al. 2003) relate to body memory categories (Fuchs this volume); BM = body memory

#	Type of embodiment effect	Type of body memory
1.	Perceived social stimuli cause bodily states (e.g. Bargh et al. 1996)	incorporative/intercorporeal
2.	The perception of bodily states of others causes own bodily imitation (e.g., Bavelas, Black, Lemery & Mullett 1986)	incorporative/intercorporeal (traumatic: identification with the aggressor)
3.	Own bodily states cause affective states (e.g. Laird 1984; Riskind 1984)	habitual, situational (+instrumental use of BM)
4.	The congruency of bodily and cognitive states modulates the efficacy of the performance (e.g. Förster & Strack 1996)	habitual, situational

the primed group to walk more slowly to the elevator after the experiment than the control group (for a review of such effects see Dijksterhuis & Bargh 2001).

Secondly, we can investigate how the perception of bodily states of others causes own bodily imitation (the second of four embodiment effects identified by Barsalou et al. 2003). An example for this category would be an experiment by Bavelas et al. (2000), who had their participants watch a video where somebody had a heavy object fall on his fingers and found an empathic facial reaction in their participants, including intercorporeal and components of pain-related traumatic body memory (for other mapping experiments see Wilson & Knoblich 2005). This and the next category go beyond incorporative body memory and also allow us to investigate intercorporeal body memory (Fuchs this volume), since the mapping aspect in most cases refers to other bodies (and not objects). We can further investigate the effects of instruction on movement, and thus for example identify metaphors that are helpful for participants to embody specific movement qualities (e.g. Böger this volume), for example, to broaden their movement repertoire in dance therapy (Eberhard-Kaechele this volume).

In order to investigate procedural body memory (Fuchs this volume) designs employing movement as an independent variable would be appropriate. All investigations of the influences of own bodily states on affective or cognitive states (the third category of the system of Barsalou et al. 2003) make up the first category of this research. Research on body feedback effects fall into this category (Adelman & Zajonc 1989; Koch 2011a; Rossberg-Gempton & Poole 1992; Suitner et al. this volume) investigating proprioceptive afferent feedback from the body periphery to the central nervous system. Body feedback research allows us to assess both procedural and situational body memory. Priming experiments are the classical way to assess procedural body memory. There are different forms of priming, semantic priming, repetition priming, sentence completion tasks, etc. Priming effects are classically measured by reaction time measures.

Situational body memory is more environmentally anchored and would best be investigated with the classical state-dependent memory experiments of cognitive psychology. Findings from this line of research suggest that the same bodily state in the learning situation and in the situation of recall causes a more successful performance than a different state (e.g. if I study X after a glass of wine, my recall of X after a glass of wine on the next day should also be better). Beyond the effects on a successful performance each of the situations also contain an emotional, a "somatic marker" (Damasio 1999), or a "felt sense" component (Gendlin 1996) that plays on memory.

Interestingly, the first three types of embodiment effects have been already described by Theodor Lipps (1903), a German psychologist at the turn of the last century, as part of the empathy process. The last category, encompassing that the congruency of bodily and cognitive states modulates the efficacy of the performance, employs movement as part of the independent variable (Förster & Strack 1996). According designs allow us to assess procedural and situational body memory. Designs in this line have been recently employed by Casasanto and Dijkstra (2010), and by Koch, Glawe and Holt (2011). The researchers in both studies used a Stroop task to create congruent and incongruent movement – meaning pairs, employing directional movements and words related to the vertical (up – happy/powerful; down – sad/powerless) or the sagittal movement axis (forward – future; backward – past). Research employs this congruency of movement and word meaning as an independent variable (Suitner et al. this volume) to show the relatedness of movement and meaning by reaction time and recognition measures, thus addressing procedural body memory.

Body memory in clinical perspective[5]

> Body Memory is a non-conscious and non-cognitive form of recall that occurs in the context of bodily actions. In body memory, remembering is doing; remembering is a form of present-moment enactment that has nonetheless been aroused and organized from previous bodily experiences.   (Caldwell 2011)

> Body memory comprises certain bodily actions/postures, or representations in a bodily format that are associated with past experience and are activated by stimuli associated with past situations in which the experience occurred.
> (Michalak, Burg & Heidenreich 2011)

In therapeutic work, it is important to track the different forms of implicit memories, which are reactivated by sensing and moving, and to assist the patient in the process of integrating these implicit experiences. In creating a nonverbal narrative, individuals

---

5.   Particular thanks go to Marianne Eberhard-Kaechele who contributed to this subsection of the chapter.

may become aware of how their implicit memories fit into the narratives of their life, an awareness that can constitute an important step in the healing process.

Embodied access to memory

Body memory is a central topic in body-based clinical methods such as dance/movement therapy, focusing, and mindfulness approaches. In an embodied conceptualization of memory, it is assumed that positive as well as negative experiences are stored in sensorimotor format (Barsalou 1999; Niedenthal, Barsalou, Winkielman, Krauth-Gruber & Ric 2005). Movement can evoke experiences and facilitate healing processes, as many of the chapters in the third part of the book highlight. The dynamics of movement also include stillness, where listening inwardly and making use of the so called 'felt sense' can take place (Gendlin; Kruithoff; Michalak et al. this volume). By meditative sitting or lying, the body can be prepared to become conscious of the most subtle and basic movements of life, such as growing and shrinking in breathing. By listening inwardly, important issues can be separated from unimportant ones, priorities can be identified (Kruithoff this volume) and organismic needs and limits can be experienced (Michalak et al. this volume). By moving, activation of the memory content stored under similar encoding conditions can be facilitated, memories can be worked with, and action can be rehearsed from the starting point of the embodied situation (e.g. Caldwell; Eberhard-Kaechele; Koch & Harvey; Kolter et al.; Konopatsch & Payne; Panhofer, Payne, Parke, Meekums; Pylvänäinen; Winther this volume).

An interesting question for clinical body work is whether and how specific memories can be evoked by specific body interventions. Next to basic research on body memory, it is necessary to conduct applied studies in therapy- and close-to-therapy contexts. First findings from such studies indicate that congruency of movement and emerging memory content can be expected (Koch & Hentz 2011; Koch & Kasper 2009) in terms of *valence congruency*, that means, positively valenced movement (e.g. skipping, jumping, twisting) can give rise to positive memories. In our studies, movement in strong vs. light qualities caused differential affect and memories: strong movement caused more fighting affect and more memories of negative life events, light movement caused more playful affect and more memories of positive life events. In addition, the same studies show that congruency of movement and emerging memory content can be expected in form of *quality congruency*: movement in a light fashion motivated memories of situations where one moved in the same light quality, movement in a strong fashion aroused memories related to that same quality of strength.

The vital aspects of body memory for the recovery of learned content with the help of kinesthetic situational memory (Koch this volume) – the memory from proprioceptive movement feedback – are conveyed in the following example of dance/movement therapy student Teresa from Spain:

I was talking to my colleague about the workshop I took in Munich. I did not remember so much in the beginning, but when I did the movement, we started from inside my pelvis – we worked on weight – the memories began to come back to me and not only was I able to remember the succession of movements but also the concept she tried to teach to us behind the movements. I believe I would not have recovered my memories in such detail without the help of the movement.

(Bas 2010)

Body memory and trauma: Nonverbal narratives complement and correct verbal narratives

Verbal narrative has been recognized by trauma experts as an integral part of a successful trauma treatment (e.g. van der Kolk 1994). However, a characteristic of traumatic memory is that the explicit, declarative memory is deactivated during the climax of a traumatic event, while the implicit, procedural memory is activated (Eberhard-Kaechele this volume; Rothschild 2002). Therefore, verbal narrative is in a sense a goal and not the starting point for therapy. Instead, nonverbal narrative (Caldwell this volume; Trevarthen & Delafield-Butt 2011, for nonverbal narrative in early interaction) can facilitate, complement or sometimes replace verbal narrative in therapy. Panhofer et al. (this volume) delineated the limitations of language and argued that the patient's non-verbal narrative deserves greater understanding, which may be achieved in the safe setting provided by movement therapy.

Embodied therapies can help trauma survivors since they need not directly verbalize traumatic contents they cannot express in words, whether emotional or factual, due to the neurobiological suppression of the brain regions responsible for speech production during traumatic experiences. Some also may not be at ease with verbalization in general, due to developmental deficits, and may feel safer in expressing their feelings nonverbally as given in movement therapy and other arts therapies.

In such therapeutic contexts, traumatized patients can safely search for a metaphor emerging from movement that acts as a vehicle for the processing of traumatic experience, and the patient's subjective interpretation of its meaning, on a sensorimotor and neural level (Eberhard-Kaechele this volume). Most core beliefs and assumptions concerning a trauma do not respond to verbal intervention because they are not verbally but procedurally mediated (Briere 2002). In addition, the metaphor can put the patient back in relation with a more general human experience. This awareness of a common experiential theme can help the patient overcome the feelings of loneliness and isolation that trauma can bring with it and increases the communicability of the experience.

Moreover, embodied therapies may also help persons with cognitive disturbances or those who are verbally over-defended and move away from an accurate self-understanding the more they talk about themselves. Remembering is not a process of retrieving an accurately preserved set of information. It is rather the productive process of actively generating patterns according to generalized previous experiences (e.g. Tschacher 2010).

As Caldwell (this volume) suggests, false memories can arise when we need to make up cognitive explanations for experiences that feel completely wrong or seem to be simply impossible within our "understanding" of the world, for instance, when a family member believed to be good causes severe harm to one's integrity. In these situations, the verbal narrative can go completely erroneous ways, whereas the bodily experience may remain intact and, if carefully followed up, can guide us to an accurate understanding of the situations in question.

> It is thought that false memories arise when the left hemisphere makes up a logical (but potentially incorrect) explanation for what the nonverbal right hemisphere is doing. What this may point us to is the likelihood that by postponing the explanatory narratives of the left hemisphere, and engaging directly with conscious movements that can directly and accurately express the feelings welling up in the right hemisphere, we can avoid the trap of trying to figure out whether a recovered memory is true or not. (...) By enacting the authentic movements that want to emerge as a result of mindful attention to ones current state, the prefrontal functions so crucial to healthy emotional and psychological regulation may be strengthened. (Caldwell this volume, p. 230)

Caldwell suggests Authentic Movement as a road to the nonverbal narrative. Authentic Movement can be carried out in a dyad, in a group or alone; further processing can take place in clay-work, writing, drawing, and verbalization. Metaphors facilitate communication and understanding between mover and (inner) witness and thus support the development of the relationships level (Konopatsch & Payne this volume). While the clinicians contributing to this edited volume account for the neurophysiological underpinnings of body memory (Pylvänäinen this volume), they remain critical to a "reductionistic neurocentrism" (Caldwell this volume) and rather ground their contributions in phenomenology or genuine embodied therapy approaches.

A case example of Caldwell illustrates the work with the nonverbal narrative:

> I worked ... with a woman who survived the tsunami in Indonesia, doing several sessions with her less than two months after the catastrophe. This was a very healthy and resourced woman, who was vacationing there with her family. Her verbal narrative of this horrific event and its aftermath was very coherent – she was able to talk calmly and sequentially about it. But she asked for sessions because she reported that her body was still suffering from shock symptoms, as well as a leg injury incurred when she was tumbled around under the water. She had come very close to dying, and even when she knew she was going to live, she spent another horrifying hour amongst the chaos, first clinging to a tree and then searching for her family, not knowing if they were dead or alive.

The work proceeded on several levels, where we needed to both protect and inquire into the leg injury, as well as help to unravel the conflict between her understandably intense emotionality and the sense of immobilizing shock held in her body. Her psychological health and cognitive resources had helped her to make a 'left-hemisphere', verbal language narrative of the event, but because the trauma had been so incredibly and overwhelmingly physical, her body could not yet form its own coherent narrative of the event. During the tsunami, her body could not do anything to help itself – it could not construct any movement sequences that might help her to survive – it was pushed and tossed by forces so massively large that there was nothing she could do but hold her breath. After the initial wave, there was a hour where she didn't know if she would survive, or if she had the strength to fight another wave. She reported feeling an alternation of frozen shock and extreme fear at the time, and that the feeling was still in her body now, "creeping around like a zombie." It would be crucial to help her body to construct its own experiential narrative, a 'right-hemisphere' coherency between emotion, images, sensation, breath, and most of all, movement.

We first worked with what happened physically, allowing her body to slowly and carefully approximate some of the shapes it was pushed into in the waves. She could only do this for a few moments before overwhelming emotion would begin to arise, and we would exit the shapes, and just let the feelings emerge. I call this 'entering and relieving the symptom,' and under different names it is a feature of any responsible trauma therapy. What is important here is that I became very directive when the emotions got too strong, because much like the tsunami waves themselves, the overwhelming affect took away the capacity for her body to find the narrative, to shape itself adaptively. There are actually very observable signs in the body when it is ready to enter or to relieve an experience. I call them movement tags. By observing these bodily signals, the therapist can be directive not from his or her own beliefs about regulation, but from a body to body relational attunement, where the tags/signals become very visible and poignant.

I externally regulated her by using touch and voice to make sure that any feeling that emerged could be 'held' by either myself (via holding her, especially her leg), or by her own body (via finding movements that allow the emotions to be expressed coherently, within precise and conscious movement sequences). Her arousal was never permitted to exceed or overwhelm her body's ability to move adaptively through the experience.

By entering and relieving the bodily events and the emotions that were aroused with them now that she (and her family) was safe, her body began to gradually, on its own, create a coherent narrative of what happened, largely independent of the very different coherency demands of the left hemisphere. We did not try to create specific movements that either of us might assume would be optimal (such as creating a body narrative where she heroically pushed and swam her way through the event). This would not be true, and a bullying imposition of left hemisphere beliefs onto the right hemisphere processing. What emerged were very precise actions – centimeters of difference could make a movement feel not right – that were attended to very potently by both of us.

What her right hemisphere implicit processing of the body memory involved was the construction of some very complex and precise movement sequences that were creative and authoritative beyond the capacity of either her or my left hemisphere's to dictate. These highly spontaneous and consciously executed movements helped her body to make its own 'sense' of the event, and therefore make left and right hemisphere integration possible, a hallmark of recovery. The movements evolved into a very graceful 'dance' with the event, during which my body's implicit processing (touch, breath, voice tone and prosody, bodily attunement) helped hers to weave together emotion, conscious movement, sounds, images, and breath. Interestingly, her leg injury also got better, likely because she deeply listened to how *it* wanted to unwind the strains and impacts via careful conscious movements, sometimes with my holding and supporting her leg as she did so.

Healing this type of event in a high functioning client involved accessing her body memory, helping it to become regulated on its own terms, and then allowing her body to generate a physical narrative, without the dictates of the left hemisphere. By privileging and centralizing the right hemispheric, nonverbal movement memory for a time, coherence can then meet coherence, left can work with right, implicit can weave together with explicit, and healing can unfold in an organic way.   (Caldwell 2011)

Finally, we briefly wish to mention further applications for working with body memory beyond the population of traumatized individuals focused upon in this volume. Therapeutic work with body memory and metaphor is very powerful with elderly and demented populations as well as with psychotic patients. The following example of Dianne Dulicai, dance/movement therapist from the US, conveys one possibility to use body memory in therapy with severely mentally impaired patients.

I worked on a unit with long term hospitalized patients, mostly schizophrenic with multiple hospitalizations. One gentleman I will call Will always came to the session but rarely communicated with me or the other men. He moved into the room with his usual shuffle, retreated upper body, head lowered and no eye contact. I had seen this man for three months with very small changes. This day in the group movement therapy session, one of the gentlemen initiated a movement in which it looked as if he was shoveling dirt and throwing it over his shoulder. I was concerned the image may be disturbing to others so I changed the shovel-like action to a forward horizontal action like carrying a flag. Will changed his posture to erect, slowed the action and said, "I used to be a baker. You put the spatula in the oven and bring out the fresh bread". It was the first time anyone had heard him speak in three months. The rest of the men supported his statement and continued a conversation.

> I believe that the movement struck an important body memory and he was
> able to retrieve a self he had lost contact with. I tell the story in teaching as an ex-
> ample of body memory especially when teaching the concept of allowing process
> to evolve in a movement session.   (Dulicai 2008)

Such examples show us the indwelling power of remembering when we hit a vital
body memory in a movement session. The possibility of the implicit evocation of
memory has implications for the work with severely disturbed and demented populations. In dementia, while explicit memory is distorted, implicit memory remains
intact and can be utilized in movement therapy: Positive affect, contentment, and
resilience can be evoked and even developed by working with intact body memories
of elderly and severely disturbed clinical populations. This is a hopeful perspective in
light of the demographic trends western societies are facing.

In sum, embodied therapies help to access an individual's memory (Caldwell,
Eberhard this volume), emotion (Shahar-Levy this volume), compassion (empathy,
sympathy, encounter), organismic needs and limits, and enable vivid contact with
others and the environment (Michalak et al. this volume). They help to establish
and surmount intra- and interpersonal boundaries (Winther this volume), support
steps toward self-regulation and self-efficacy, and afford access to individual sources
of resilience and strength (Koch & Harvey this volume). Embodied therapies can
provide reality testing in psychosis and progress as well as integrity in dementia and
related diseases.

A translational model

Multiple translational processes between movement, language, and meaning influence the healing process. In embodied therapies they are often bridged by verbal and
nonverbal metaphors. The symbolic character of movement becomes particularly
relevant in artistic and psychotherapeutic processes.[6] When verbal methods fail or
do not suffice, treatment can proceed almost entirely nonverbally from diagnosis to
healing. Treatment progress is then scientifically hard to trace. However, since this is
a crucial case of the densification of the unspoken into metaphors and memories that
search for an eruption into the verbal, this is a well-suited domain to investigate and
document translational processes from implicit to explicit memory.

The body and the interpersonal space are the loci of these translations. Their
resonance is the condition for experiencing qualities and empathy. The expressive

---

6. In the joint research project "Body Language of Movement and Dance" (research grant
from the Federal Ministry of Education and Research, Germany, BMBF) we investigate the
multiple translational processes between body, dance, movement, language and meaning with
the methods of phenomenology, psychology and cognitive linguistics. An important goal of
the project is the development of theoretical and practical knowledge for the applied field of
dance/movement therapy and dance training.

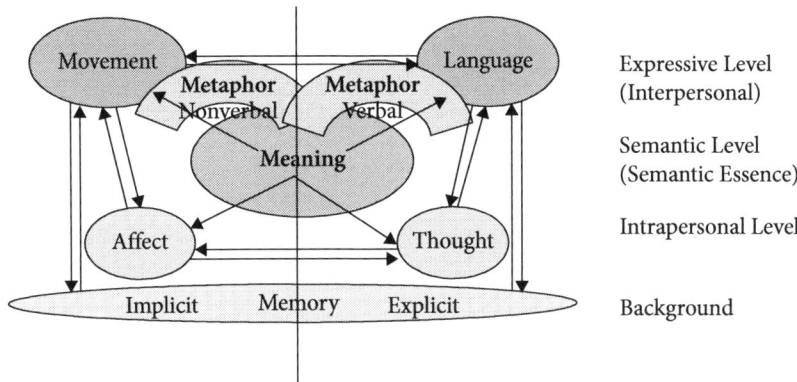

Expressive Level
(Interpersonal)

Semantic Level
(Semantic Essence)

Intrapersonal Level

Background

Figure 1. Multiple translational processes between movement, language, and meaning on the background of affect, cognition, and memory (Koch 2011); the midline separates more right hemispheric (left side) from more left-hemispheric (right side) processes

level has functional and symbolic-representative aspects. Both play an important role in communication. While in everyday movement and language the functional aspect predominates, the symbolic-representational level plays a more important part in cultural forms such as dance and improvisation. In many psychosomatic diseases the symbolic-representational level also predominates. This is one of the reasons why body- and art-centred nonverbal approaches have such an important meaning in the healing process.[7]

Conclusions

Without summarizing into detail all the results of the different studies collected in this volume, we wish to conclude these remarks by discussing what we believe to be the most important outcomes of the book as an integrative work, and meanwhile open up the field for future research. One of the substantial credits of this volume is to provide not only an interdisciplinary, but more properly a transdisciplinary approach to body memory. The different perspectives are not merely juxtaposed, they are not assumed as self-enclosed and respectively independent disciplines. Rather, each of them has profited from the encounter with the others in the attempt to give shape to a common vocabulary and to promote a deeper understanding of the set of phenomena labeled

---

7.   Conversely, healing can occur independently of symbolic processes in diseases, such as dementia, where the patients have lost the ability to symbolize and express themselves in a metaphorical way. All left-hemispheric processes and functions (including explicit memory and the others on the left side of the diagram in Figure 1) are impaired and patients can foremost be reached via movement, affect, and implicit memory for successful treatment or stabilization.

as body memory. Body memory, indeed, has been described as to the different forms of its experiential manifestation. Fuchs's typological differentiation is particularly relevant in this sense, since it shows that body memory reaches far beyond the formation of bodily habitualities, and embraces the different modalities of our situational and intersubjective being in and interacting with the world.

The three main perspectives under which body memory has been considered in this book (phenomenology, the cognitive sciences and embodied therapies) converge in considering body memory as an inherently dynamic phenomenon. As such, body memory unfolds itself in time and space; it is something we constantly enact in our relation with the world and with others. Similarly, the transition from body memory into language, i.e. the transition from implicit to explicit memory, is to be considered as inherently dynamic. This becomes visible, for instance, in the process of emerging multimodal metaphors from source domains, which are embodied in movement.

The essentially dynamic character of body memory, however, still needs further investigation, and this is more generally true for the role of bodily movement in embodiment research (see Koch 2011a, b). That movement is one of the central feature of human experience is particularly shown by the following evidences: (1) the earliest categories we can developmentally distinguish have to do with movement (the distinction of moving, living animated beings from non-moving, artificial, non-animated objects; Pauen & Träuble 2009); (2) movement and the perception of intentions through movement help us with intelligent solutions that are relevant for our survival, e.g. in everyday traffic situations or when we stand face-to-face with a dangerous wild animal such as a bear or a mountain-lion (Blythe, Todd & Miller 1999).

The integrative approach promoted in this volume not only allows us to more appropriately describe the phenomenon of body memory in its different forms, but also offers the basis to rethink body memory within a complex and stratified theory of experience. Phenomenologically, this theory is fundamentally based on the correlation between subjectivity and the world. The different contributions in this volume have provided further evidence for this correlation by particularly stressing the connection between body memory and the sensorimotor, kinesthetic, affective, and emotional aspects of lived experience. In doing so, they have shed new light on the complex articulation of the most basic layers of lived experience. In other words, they have been able to show how body memory is an essential moment of our basic, pre-reflective self-experience, and how it operates in shaping experiential configurations starting from these most basic layers. Yet, the self being open toward the world and toward other subjects, body memory cannot but be considered in relational terms, as well. And indeed, all the memory forms that have been considered in these studies bear witness to this relational character.

To stress such relational character implies the re-evaluation of the meaningfulness of experience, starting from its most basic layers and comprehending both its "normal" and "pathological" moments. The analysis of the connection between body memory and therapy provided by some of the studies in this volume have further contributed to determine in what sense psychopathology itself should be considered as experience of meaning, rather than being merely labeled as epiphenomenon of physical processes or as totally deprived of meaning.

The relation between body memory and the experience of meaning also emerges with respect to the formation of empirical concepts and metaphorical meaning. As it is testified by our pre-reflective use of sleeping metaphors, body memory, which also assumes in this case a remarkable socio-cultural character, is operative in linguistic and bodily communication, even if it does not receive explicit attention. These sleeping metaphors can be further reflected upon and thematized, thus becoming 'awake'. Memory, movement, and metaphor, thus, are intrinsically related within the dynamic transitions that articulate the implicit (pre-reflective, pre-thematic) and the explicit (reflective, thematic) moments of our experience. The integration of body memory within a bodily related theory of knowledge shows how the meaningful (yet pre-categorial) configurations that are developed within the basic layers of lived experience affect the development of more complex conceptual formations, contributing to give shape to our higher order cognitive processes.

This book has laid the groundwork for investigating a core phenomenological topic in a transdisciplinary and interdisciplinary way. Phenomenologists have prepared the ground by describing the different forms in which implicit body memory operates and gives shape to our experience and added empirical data. Cognitive scientists have contextualized the topic within an embodiment framework. Clinical practitioners have been adding additional theoretical perspectives, empirical data, and applied questions resulting from clinical practice. It will take time to further investigate and unfold the rich aspects provided by the theories contained within the phenomena of body memory. Yet, it will be a worth while endeavor.

References

Adelman, P. K. & Zajonc, R. B. (1987). Facial efference and the experience of emotion. *Annual Review of Psychology, 40,* 249–280.

Adler, J. (2002). *Offerings from the conscious body. The discipline of authentic movement.* Rochester: Inner Traditions.

Alarcon, M. (this volume). Body memory and dance. In S. C. Koch, T. Fuchs, M. Summa & C. Müller (Eds.), *Body memory, metaphor and movement.* Amsterdam: John Benjamins.

Bargh, J. A., Chen, M. & Burrows, L. (1996). Automaticity of social behavior: Direct effects of trait construct and stereotype activation on action. *Journal of Personality and Social Psychology, 71,* 230–244.

Barsalou, L. W. (1999). Perceptual symbol systems. *Behavioral & Brain Sciences, 22,* 577–609.

Barsalou, L. W., Niedenthal, P. M., Barbey, A. K. & Ruppert, J. A. (2003). Social embodiment. In B. H. Ross (Ed.), *The psychology of learning and motivation,* Vol. 43 (pp. 43–92), San Diego, CA: Academic Press.

Bas, T. (2010). Personal communication.

Bavelas, J. B., Black, A., Lemery, C. R. & Mullett, J. (1986). "I show you how I feel": Motor mimicry as a communicative act. *Journal of Personality and Social Psychology, 50*, 322–329.

Behnke, E. (this volume). Enduring. In S. C. Koch, T. Fuchs, M. Summa & C. Müller (Eds.), *Body memory, metaphor and movement*. Amsterdam: John Benjamins.

Bergson, H. (2007). *Matière et mémoire. Essai sur la relation du corps à l'esprit.* [Matter and memory. Essay on the relation of body and spirit] Paris: PUF.

Bermeitinger, C. & Kiefer, M. (2011). Personal communication.

Bermeitinger, C. & Kiefer, M. (this volume). Embodied concepts. In S. C. Koch, T. Fuchs, M. Summa & C. Müller (Eds.), *Body memory, metaphor and movement*. Amsterdam: John Benjamins.

Blythe, P. W., Todd, P. M. & Miller, G. F. (1999). How motion reveals intention. In G. Gigerenzer, P. Todd & the ABC Research Group (Eds.), *Simple heuristics that make us smart* (pp. 256–285). Oxford: Oxford University Press.

Böger, C. (this volume). Metaphorical Instruction and Body Memory. In S. C. Koch, T. Fuchs, M. Summa & C. Müller (Eds.), *Body memory, metaphor and movement*. Amsterdam: John Benjamins.

Briere, J. (2002). Treating adult survivors of severe childhood abuse and neglect: Further development of an integrative model. In J. E. B. Myers, L. Berliner, J. Briere, C. T. Hendrix, T. Reid & C. Jenny (Eds.), *The APSAC handbook on child maltreatment*, 2nd edition (pp. 175–202). Newbury Park, CA: Sage.

Casasanto, D. & Dijkstra, K. (2010). Motor action and emotional memory. *Cognition, 115*(1), 179–185.

Casey, E. (2000). *Remembering. A phenomenological study*. Bloomington: Indiana University Press.

Caldwell, C. (2011). Personal communication.

Caldwell, C. (this volume). Sensation, movement, and emotion: Explicit procedures for implicit memories. In S. C. Koch, T. Fuchs, M. Summa & C. Müller (Eds.), *Body memory, metaphor and movement*. Amsterdam: John Benjamins.

Damasio, A. R. (1999). *The feeling of what happens: Body and emotion in the making of consciousness*. New York: Harcourt Brace.

Dijksterhuis, A. & Bargh, J. A. (2001). The oerception-behavior expressway: Automatic effects of social perception on social behavior. *Advances in experimental social psychology, 33*, 1–40.

Dulicai, D. (2008). Personal communication.

Eberhard-Kaechele, M. (this volume). Memory, metaphor, and mirroring in movement therapy with trauma patients. In S. C. Koch, T. Fuchs, M. Summa & C. Müller (Eds.), *Body memory, metaphor and movement*. Amsterdam: John Benjamins.

Fink, E. (1966). *Studien zur Phänomenologie 1930–1939* [Phenomenological studies 1930–1939]. Den Haag: Martinus Nijhoff.

Förster, J. & Strack, F. (1996). Influence of overt head movements on memory for valenced words: A case of conceptual-motor compatibility. *Journal of Personality and Social Psychology, 71*, 421–430.

Fuchs, T. (2000). Das Gedächtnis des Leibes [The memory of the body]. *Phänomenologische Forschungen, 5*, 71–89.

Fuchs, T. (2008a). *Leib und Lebenswelt. Neue philosophisch-psychiatrische Essays* [The body and the life-world. New philosophical-psychiatric essays]. Kusterdingen: Die Graue Edition.

Fuchs, T. (2008b). Leibgedächtnis und Lebensgeschichte [Body memory and life history]. In
F. A. Friedrich, T. Fuchs, J. Koll, B. Krondorfer & G. M. Martin (Eds.), *Der Text im Körper.
Leibgedächtnis, Inkarnation und Bibliodrama* [The text in the body. Body-memory, Incar-
nation and bibliodrama] (pp. 10–40). Hamburg: EB-Verlag.

Fuchs, T. (this volume). The phenomenology of body memory. In S. C. Koch, T. Fuchs,
M. Summa & C. Müller (Eds.), *Body memory, metaphor and movement*. Amsterdam: John
Benjamins.

Gendlin, E. T. (1996). *Focusing-oriented psychotherapy. A handbook of the experiential method.*
New York: Guilford.

Gendlin E. T. (this volume). Comment on Thomas Fuchs: The time of the explicating process.
In S. C. Koch, T. Fuchs, M. Summa & C. Müller (Eds.), *Body memory, metaphor, and movement*. Amsterdam: John Benjamins.

Glenberg, A. M. (1997). What memory is for. *Behavioral and Brain Sciences, 20*, 1–55.

Hatfield, E., Cacioppo, J. T. & Rapson, R. L. (1994). *Emotional contagion*. Paris: Cambridge
University Press.

Hörmann, H. (1976). *Meinen und Verstehen. Grundzüge einer psychologischen Semantik*
[Meaning and understanding. Outline of a psychological semantics]. Frankfurt am Main:
Suhrkamp.

Husserl, E. (1952). *Ideen zu einer reinen Phänomenologie und phänomenologischen Philosophie.
Phänomenologische Untersuchungen zur Konstitution* [Ideas pertaining to a pure phenomenology and to a phenomenological philosophy. Studies in the phenomenology of consti-
tution]. Den Haag: Martinus Nijhoff.

Husserl, E. (1966a). *Zur Phänomenologie des inneren Zeitbewusstseins (1893–1917)* [On the
phenomenology of the consciousness of internal time]. Den Haag: Martinus Nijhoff.

Husserl, E. (1966b). *Analysen zur passiven Synthesis* [Analyses concerning active and passive
synthesis]. Den Haag: Martinus Nijhoff.

Husserl, E. (2001). *Die Bernauer Manuskripte über das Zeitbewusstsein (1917–1918)* [The Ber-
nau manuscripts on time consciousness]. Dordrecht/Boston/London: Kluwer.

Husserl, E. (2006). *Späte Texte über Zeitkonstitution 1929–1934. Die C-Manuskripte* [Later texts
on the constitution of time]. Dordrecht: Springer.

Jansen, P. (this volume). Implicit body memory. In S. C. Koch, T. Fuchs, M. Summa & C. Müller
(Eds.), *Body memory, metaphor and movement*. Amsterdam: John Benjamins.

Jansen, P. (2011). Personal communication.

Jung, C. & Sparenberg, P. (this volume). Cognitive perspectives on embodiment. In S. C. Koch,
T. Fuchs, M. Summa & C. Müller (Eds.), *Body memory, metaphor and movement*. Amsterdam: John Benjamins.

Koch, S. C. (2010). Bewegung und Bewusstsein [*Movement and consciousness*]. In R. Hampe
& P. Stalder (Eds.), *Multimodalität in den Künstlerischen Therapien* [Multimodality in the
arts therapies] (pp. 41–57). Berlin: Frank & Timme.

Koch, S. C. (2011a). Basic body rhythms and embodied intercorporality: From individual to
interpersonal movement feedback. In W. Tschacher & C. Bergomi (Eds.), *The implications
of embodiment: Cognition and communication* (pp. 151–171). Exeter: Imprint Academic.

Koch, S. C. (2011b). *Embodiment. Der Einfluss von Eigenbewegung auf Affekt, Einstellung und
Kognition* [Embodiment: The influence of movement on affect, attitudes and cognition].
Berlin: Logos.

Koch, S. C. (this volume). Testing Fuchs' taxonomy of body memory – A content analysis. In S. C. Koch, T. Fuchs, M. Summa & C. Müller (Eds.), *Body memory, metaphor and movement*. Amsterdam: John Benjamins.

Koch, S. C. & Harvey, S. (this volume). Dance therapy with traumatized dissociative patients. In S. C. Koch, T. Fuchs, M. Summa & C. Müller (Eds.), *Body memory, metaphor and movement*. Amsterdam: John Benjamins.

Koch, S. C., Glawe, S. & Holt, D. (2011). Up and down, front and back. Movement and meaning in the vertical and sagittal axis. *Social Psychology, 42*(3), 193–203.

Koch, S. C. & Hentz, E. (2011). The influence of light and strong movement on affect and memories. Poster at the conference "Body memory and therapy", 31.03.–02.04.2011, Heidelberg, Germany.

Koch, S. C. & Kasper, D. (2009). Body memory. An empirical investigation of a phenomenological concept. Poster at the conference "Herbstakademie 2009: Embodiment", 06.–08.10.2009, Bern, Switzerland.

Kolter, A., Ladewig, S., Summa, M., Koch, S. C., Müller, C. & Fuchs, T. (this volume). Body memory and the emergence of metaphor in movement and speech. An interdisciplinary case study. In S. C. Koch, T. Fuchs, M. Summa & C. Müller (Eds.), *Body memory, metaphor and movement*. Amsterdam: John Benjamins.

Konopatsch, I. & Payne, H. (this volume). The emergence of body memory in Authentic Movement. In S. C. Koch, T. Fuchs, M. Summa & C. Müller (Eds.), *Body memory, metaphor and movement*. Amsterdam: John Benjamins.

Kruithoff, E. (this volume). Focusing, felt sensing, and body memory. In S. C. Koch, T. Fuchs, M. Summa & C. Müller (Eds.), *Body memory, metaphor and movement*. Amsterdam: John Benjamins.

Laird, J. D. (1984). The real role of facial response in the experience of emotion: A response to Tourangeau and Ellsworth, and others. *Journal of Personality and Social Psychology, 47*, 909–917.

Legrand, D. (2006). The bodily self: The sensori-motor roots of pre-reflective self consciousness. *Phenomenology and the Cognitive Sciences, 5*, 89–118.

Lipps, T. (1903). Die Einfühlung [*Empathy*]. In *Leitfaden der Psychologie* [In guide through psychology]. (Kap. 14, 187–201). Leipzig: Wilhelm Engelmann.

Merleau-Ponty, M. (1945). *Phénoménologie de la perception* [The phenomenology of perception]. Paris: Gallimard.

Michalak, J., Burg, J. & Heidenreich, T. (2011). Personal communication.

Michalak, J., Burg, J. & Heidenreich, T. (this volume). Mindfulness, embodiment, and depression. In S. C. Koch, T. Fuchs, M. Summa & C. Müller (Eds.), *Body memory, metaphor and movement*. Amsterdam: John Benjamins.

Müller, C. (2008a). *Metaphors. Dead and alive, sleeping and waking. A dynamic view*. Chicago: University of Chicago Press.

Müller, C. (2008b). What gestures reveal about the nature of metaphor. In A. Cienki & C. Müller (Eds.), *Metaphor and gesture* (pp. 219–245). Amsterdam: John Benjamins.

Müller, C. & Tag, S. (2010). The dynamics of metaphor. Foregrounding and activating metaphoricity in conversational interaction. *Cognitive Semiotics, 16*.

Niedenthal, P. M., Barsalou, L. W., Winkielman, P., Krauth-Gruber, S. & Ric, F. (2005). Embodiment in attitudes, social perception, and emotion. *Personality and Social Psychology Review, 9*, 184–211.

Pallaro, P. (2007). Somatic countertransference: The therapist in relationship. In P. Pallaro (2007), *Authentic Movement: Moving the body, moving the self, being moved* (pp. 176–193). London: Jessica Kingsley.

Panhofer, H., Payne, H., Parke, T. & Meekums, B. (this volume). The embodied world. In S. C. Koch, T. Fuchs, M. Summa & C. Müller (Eds.), *Body memory, metaphor and movement*. Amsterdam: John Benjamins.

Pauen, S. & Träuble, B. (2009). How 7-month-olds interpret ambiguous motion events: Category-based reasoning in infancy. *Cognitive Psychology, 59*(3), 275–295.

Polanyi, M. (1967). *The tacit dimension*. London: Routledge & Kegan.

Pylvänäinen, P. (this volume). Body memory as a part of the body image. In S. C. Koch, T. Fuchs, M. Summa & C. Müller (Eds.), *Body memory, metaphor and movement*. Amsterdam: John Benjamins.

Reder, L. M., Park, H. & Kieffaber, P. (2009). Memory systems do not divide on consciousness: Reinterpreting memory in terms of activation and binding. *Psychological Bulletin, 135*(1), 23–49.

Riskind, J. H. (1984). They stoop to conquer: Guiding and self-regulatory functions of physical posture after success and failure. *Journal of Personality and Social Psychology, 47,* 479–493.

Roediger, H. L. (1990). Implicit memory. Retention without remembering. *American Psychologist, 45*(9), 1043–1056.

Rossberg-Gempton, I. & Poole, G. D. (1992). The relationship between body movement and affect: From historical and current perspectives. *The Arts in Psychotherapy, 19,* 39–46.

Rothschild, B. (2002). *The body remembers: The psychophysiology of trauma and trauma treatment*. New York: Norton.

Schacter, D. L. (1987). Implicit memory: History and current status. *Journal of Experimental Psychology: Memory, Learning and Cognition 13*(3), 501–518.

Schacter, D. L. (1996). *Searching for memory. The brain, the mind, and the past*. New York: Basic Books.

Semin, G. R. & Smith, E. R. (2008). *Embodied grounding*. Cambridge University Press.

Shahar-Levy, Y. (this volume). To move, to re-member, to re-connect. In S. C. Koch, T. Fuchs, M. Summa & C. Müller (Eds.), *Body memory, metaphor and movement*. Amsterdam: John Benjamins.

Sheets-Johnstone, M. (this volume). Kinesthetic body memory. In S. C. Koch, T. Fuchs, M. Summa & C. Müller (Eds.), *Body memory, metaphor and movement*. Amsterdam: John Benjamins.

Smith, E. R. & Semin, G. R. (2004). Socially situated cognition. Cognition in its social context. In M. P. Zanna (Ed.), *Advances in experimental social psychology* (Vol. 36, pp. 53–117). Amsterdam: Elsevier.

Squire, L. (2004). Memory systems of the brain: A brief history and current perspective. *Neurobiology of learning and memory, 82,* 171–177.

Suitner, C., Koch, S. C., Bachmeier, K. & Maass, A. (this volume). Dynamic embodiment and its functional role: A body feedback perspective. In S. C. Koch, T. Fuchs, M. Summa & C. Müller (Eds.), *Body memory, metaphor and movement*. Amsterdam: John Benjamins.

Summa, M. (2011). Das Leibgedächtnis. Ein Beitrag aus der Phänomenologie Husserls [Body memory. A contribution from Husserl's phenomenology]. *Husserl Studies, 27*(3), 173–196.

Summa, M. (this volume). Body memory and the genesis of meaning. In S. C. Koch, T. Fuchs, M. Summa & C. Müller (Eds.), *Body memory, metaphor and movement*. Amsterdam: John Benjamins.

Trevarthen, C. & Delafield-Butt, J. (2011). Personal communication.

Tschacher, W. (2010). Wie Embodiment zum Thema wurde [How Embodiment became an issue]. In M. Storch, B. Cantieni, G. Hüther & W. Tschacher (2010, 2. erweiterte Auflage), *Embodiment. Die Wechselwirkung von Körper und Psyche verstehen und nutzen* [Embodiment. Understanding the interplay of body and psyche] (pp. 11–34). Bern: Hogrefe/Huber.

Tversky, B. (2008). Embodied spatial cognition. Presentation at the "XXIX International Congress of Psychology", Berlin, Germany, July 20–25, 2008.

van der Kolk, B. (1994). The body keeps the score: Memory and the evolving psychobiology of post traumatic stress. *Harvard Review of Psychiatry, 1*(5), 253–265.

Vygotsky, L. S. (1969). *Denken und Sprechen* [Thought and speech]. Frankfurt a.M.: Fischer.

Waldenfels, B. (2000). *Das leibliche Selbst. Vorlesungen zur Phänomenologie des Leibes* [The bodily self. Lectures on the phenomenology of the body]. Frankfurt a. M.: Suhrkamp.

Wilson, M. & Knoblich, G. (2005). The case for motor involvement in perceiving conspecifics. *Psychological Bulletin, 131*, 460–473.

Winther, H. (this volume). Nakedness, hunger, hooks, and hearts. Embodied memories and movement. Psychological processes in dance therapy and movement pedagogy. In S. C. Koch, T. Fuchs, M. Summa & C. Müller (Eds.), *Body memory, metaphor and movement*. Amsterdam: John Benjamins.

Zajonc, R. B. & Markus, H. (1984). Affect and cognition: The hard interface. In C. Izard, J. Kagan & R. B. Zajonc (Eds.), *Emotions, cognition and behavior* (pp. 73–102). Cambridge: Cambridge University Press.

Authors notes

Prof. Dr. Thomas Fuchs, psychiatrist and philosopher, M.D. in History of Medicine and Ph.D. in Philosophy, Jaspers professor and head of the section "Phenomenological Psychopathology and Psychotherapy" at the Dept. of Psychiatry in Heidelberg, chairman of the section "Philosophical Foundations of Psychiatry" of the German Psychiatric Association (DGPPN), fellow of the Marsilius-Kolleg (Center for Advanced Interdisciplinary Studies) University of Heidelberg. Major research areas: phenomenological psychopathology, psychology and psychotherapy, coherence and disorders of self-experience, phenomenology and cognitive neuroscience, history and ethics of medicine and psychiatry.

Dr. Michela Summa, graduated in Philosophy at the University of Pavia in 2004 and obtained her Ph.D. in Philosophy from the Universities of Pavia and Leuven in 2010 with a dissertation on Husserl's phenomenology of time and space. Currently, she has a post-doc position at the Psychiatric Clinic in Heidelberg. Her main interests include phenomenology, transcendental philosophy and theory of knowledge, the debate regarding phenomenology and the cognitive sciences, phenomenological psychopathology.

Dr. Maxine Sheets-Johnstone, Ph.D. In her first life, Maxine Sheets-Johnstone was a dancer/choreographer, professor of dance/dance scholar. In her second and ongoing life, she is a philosopher whose research and writing remain grounded in the moving body. She is affiliated with the Department of Philosophy at the University of Oregon. Her publications include *The Phenomenology of Dance* (1966), *Illuminating Dance: Philosophical Explorations* (1985), *The Roots of Thinking* (1990), *The Roots of Power: Animate Form and Gendered Bodies* (1994), *The Roots of Morality* (2008); *Giving the Body Its Due* (1992), *The Primacy of Movement* (1999), *The Corporeal Turn: An Interdisciplinary Reader* (2009). She was awarded a Distinguished Fellowship at the Institute of Advanced Study at Durham University in the UK in the spring of 2007 for her research on xenophobia.

Dr. Elizabeth A. Behnke is the coordinator and senior research fellow of the Study Project in Phenomenology of the Body. Her current research uses the transcendental-phenomenological methods of Edmund Husserl to investigate kinaesthetic consciousness and styles of interkinaesthetic comportment, with special emphasis on the relevance of the research findings to body/movement awareness practices such as restorative embodiment work.

Dr. Mónica E. Alarcón Dávila is an independent scholar in the field of philosophy and is founding member of mBody, an artistic research group. She is currently assistant lecturer at the Hochschule Furtwangen, Faculty of Digital Media and is working on several interdisciplinary and multicultural projects focusing on the question of the constitution of identity in a multicultural society. Her special fields of interest are phenomenology of dance, phenomenology of the body, artistic research, interculturality, and media.

Dr. Eugene T. Gendlin, an American philosopher and psychologist, received his Ph.D. in Philosophy from the University of Chicago, where he taught for many years. He has developed a "philosophy of the implicit," which changes basic assumptions, and he is well known for "Focusing" and "Thinking at the Edge," two procedures for thinking with the implicit as well as with logic. Dr. Gendlin has published many articles, most of which are available (also in translation) at the Gendlin Online Library (http://www.focusing.org/gendlin/). Among his many publications are the books *A Process Model* (1997) and. *Experiencing and the Creation of Meaning* (1962/1970). The central issues in Gendlin's thought are discussed by leading philosophers in *Language Beyond Post-Modernism: Saying and Thinking in Gendlin's Philosophy, Comments by Fourteen Philosophers* (1997).

Prof. Dr. Petra Jansen studied Anthropology, Ethnology, Psychology and Mathematics at Mainz University. She got her Ph.D. in Experimental Psychology in 1999 from Duisburg University. In 2005, she finished her habilitation in psychology at Düsseldorf University. Since 2008 she is Head of the Institute of Sport Science at Regensburg University. Her main research interest is the relation between motor functions, emotion, and cognition. Her studies are conducted from a developmental perspective and make use of neuroscientific methods.

Prof. Dr. Christina Bermeitinger studied Psychology (2001–2005) and Sports Science (2003–2005) at the University of Göttingen. She received her Diploma in Psychology in 2005 and moved then to the Saarland University where she worked in the research group of Prof. Dr. Dirk Wentura. In 2009 she received her Ph.D. In the same year she went as W1-professor (Juniorprofessor) for general psychology to the University of Hildesheim.

PD Dr. Markus Kiefer studied Psychology at the University of Mannheim until 1995, received his Ph.D. from the University of Heidelberg in 1998 and his lecturing qualification (Habilitation) in Psychology from the University of Konstanz in 2004. He is head of the section for Cognitive Electrophysiology at the Department of Psychiatry of the University of Ulm and Senior Lecturer (Privatdozent) at the Department of Psychology of the University of Konstanz. His research is focused on the cognitive psychology and cognitive neuroscience of memory, language and consciousness.

Dr. Christina Jung (née Jäger) graduated in Psychology at the Christian-Albrechts-University in Kiel in 2006. In her diploma thesis she investigated the influence of stimuli with emotional content on event related brain potentials. She then joined the group of Prof. Dr. Wolfgang Prinz at the Max Planck Institute for Human Cognitive and Brain Sciences in Leipzig and obtained her Ph.D. on intra- and interpersonal bimanual coordination. From 2007 to 2008 she worked as a fulltime researcher and EEG laboratory manager at the MPI in Leipzig. At present she is a fellow of the Max Planck International Research Network on Aging (MaxnetAging).

Dr. Peggy Sparenberg (née Tausche) graduated in Psychology at the Otto-von-Guericke University of Magdeburg in 2007. Her diploma thesis investigated the neuronal correlates of audiovisual speech integration. After that she worked at the Max Planck Institute for Human Cognitive and Brain Sciences in Leipzig and obtained her Ph.D. in 2011, investigating the mechanisms and representations involved in the mental simulation of temporally occluded actions.

Dr. Caterina Suitner is a social psychology researcher at the University of Padova. Her main research area focuses on the role of writing direction in social targets' representations from an embodied perspective (i.e., Spatial Agency Bias). She is also interested in cross-cultural psychology and stereotyping. Her research has been published in journals such as Journal of Experimental Social Psychology, European Journal of Social Psychology, and Social Cognition. She has also contributed to several edited books and has edited a special issue for Social Psychology.

PD Dr. Sabine C. Koch, Psychologist, Dance/Movement Therapist, M.A., BC-DMT, is researcher and lecturer at the University of Heidelberg, Germany. Specialized in Kestenberg Movement Profiling (KMP), movement analysis and dance/movement therapy. Ph.D. on microanalysis of gender communication. Present work on "Embodiment: The Influence of Movement on Affect, Attitudes and Cognition" (2011). She coordinates the National Research Project on "Language of Movement and Dance", financed by the German Ministry of Education and Research (BMBF). Her research interests include embodiment, personality and social psychology, psycholinguistics, nonverbal communication, gender, health, phenomenology, body psychotherapy, movement analysis, and creative arts therapies.

Dipl.-Psych. Katharina Bachmeier is a psychology student at the University of Jena. She is currently writing her diploma thesis in organizational psychology about the support of international students. During her studies she focused on intercultural and social psychology. She is part of a research project on the relations between the directionality of written language, gender stereotypes and directional bias in person perception (Spatial Agency Bias) at the University of Padova.

Prof. Dr. Anne Maass is Professor of Social Psychology at the University of Padova. She received her MS at the University of Heidelberg and her Ph.D. at Florida State University. She has been associate editor the Journal of Personality and Social Psychology and is currently editor of the European Journal of Social Psychology. Her past and current research interests include: minority influence; eyewitness testimony; sexual harassment; stereotyping and stereotype threat; language and social cognition; embodiment. She has published over 100 publications, including 70 articles in international peer-reviewed journals. She has received the Gordon Allport Intergroup Relations Prize (together with Carnaghi et al.) in 2007 and the Henri Tajfel Award in 2011.

Dr. phil. Claudia Böger is currently working as a lecturer at the Universität der Bundeswehr, Munich. Research interests in sport's education and motor research with the special focus on philosophical anthropology.

Astrid Kolter studied Psychology and Peace & Conflict Studies at the University of Marburg, Germany, she is student of Dance/Movement Therapy (DMT) at the Frankfurter Institut für Tanztherapie, researcher at the University of Heidelberg, Germany, and lecturer at the international Master of Arts Therapies at the Catholic University of Freiburg, Germany & HAN University, Netherlands. She is teacher for ballet, modern-, jazz-, tapdance and free dance. Current research foci are indication, counterindication and description of methods of DMT.

Dr. des. Silva H. Ladewig studied Linguistics and Anglistics at the Freie Universität Berlin. Researcher in the projects "Language of Movement and Dance" (BMBF) and "Towards a grammar of gesture: evolution, brain, and linguistic structures" (Volkswagen Stiftung) at the European University Viadrina. Dissertation on the "Syntactic and semantic integration of gestures into speech. Structural, cognitive, and conceptual aspects". Research foci include gesture studies, multimodal grammar, embodiment, sign language linguistics.

Prof. Dr. Cornelia Müller is Professor of Applied Linguistics at the Faculty of Social and Cultural Sciences Academics at the European University Viadrina Frankfurt (Oder), Vice-president for Research and Young Academics at the European University Viadrina Frankfurt (Oder). Current projects are "Towards a grammar of gesture: evolution, brain and linguistic structures" (VolkswagenStiftung), "Gesture and Alexithymia" and "Mulitmodal Metaphors and Expressional Movement" (Cluster of excellence "Languages of Emotion", Freie Universität Berlin). "Language of Movement and Dance" (BMBF). Research areas include: gesture studies; cognitive metaphor theory; multimodality (attention, embodiment); language use (cognition and emotion).

Prof. Dr. William S. Sax is Professor and Head of the Department of Anthropology at the South Asia Institute, University of Heidelberg, Germany. He teaches and conducts research on the ethnography of South Asia, performance theory, ritual studies and medical anthropology. He is the author of numerous articles on these topics, along with several books including *God of Justice: Ritual Healing and Social Justice in the Central Himalayas* (2009) and *Dancing the Self: Personhood and Performance in the Pandav Lila of Garhwal* (2002) both published by Oxford University Press, New York.

Dr. Karin M. Polit is Research Associate at the Collaborative Research Centre 'Ritual Dynamics' and lecturer at the Institute for Ethnology, University of Heidelberg, Germany. Her main interests lie in the fields of performance studies, medical anthropology and the anthropology of youth. She is the author of *Good Women: Reflections of Gender and Agency among Dalit Women of Garhwal*.

PD Dr. Ralf P. Meyer, molecular medical scientist, is a lecturer in Molecular Medicine at the University of Freiburg, Germany, and a teacher for biotechnology and chemistry at the Merian School for Biotechnology in Freiburg. Ralf P. Meyer studied chemistry in Freiburg, Germany, and made his doctoral degree in Neurobiochemistry. After some years as research fellow at the Karolinska Institute, Stockholm, Sweden, and the Biozentrum of the University of Basel, Switzerland, Ralf P. Meyer went back to the University of Freiburg as leader of a working group dealing with the "drug-hormone crosstalk of the brain". This includes strong interest in cell development and cell memory. Since 2010 Ralf P. Meyer acts as teacher at the Merian School of Biotechnology in Freiburg (http://omnibus.uni-freiburg.de/~rm83).

Dr. Christine Caldwell, Ph.D., BC-DMT, LPC, NCC, ACS, is the founder and former director of the Somatic Counseling Psychology Department at Naropa University in Boulder, where she currently teaches coursework in somatic counseling theory and skills, clinical neuroscience, research, and developmental psychology. Her work began over thirty years ago with studies in anthropology, dance therapy, bodywork and Gestalt therapy, and has developed into innovations in the field of dance therapy and body-centered psychotherapy. She calls her work the Moving Cycle. The Moving Cycle spotlights natural play, early physical imprinting, the transformational effect of fully sequenced movement processes, the practice of dying, the opportunities in addiction, and a trust in personal essence. She has taught at the University of Maryland, George Washington University, Concordia, Seoul Women's University, Southwestern College, and Santa Barbara Graduate Institute, and trains, teaches and lectures internationally. Her books include *Getting Our Bodies Back* (1996) and *Getting In Touch* (1997) and she has published over 30 articles and chapters on dance therapy and body psychology.

Dr. Marianne Eberhard-Kaechele, Dance/Expressive Arts Therapist, is researcher and lecturer at the German Sports University Cologne, institute of Clinical Movement Science and Health Promotion, department for Neurology, Psychosomatics and Psychiatry. She is registered as a trainer and supervisor by the German National Association for Dance Therapy and holder of the European Certificate of Psychotherapy. Current research foci are interpersonal coordination, mentalization, embodiment, metaphor and their implications for clinical practice. Current clinical practice with trauma, personality disorders, affective disorders, psychosomatic and eating disorders.

Päivi Pylvänäinen is a licensed psychologist and a dance therapist. She completed her DMT degree at MCP Hahnemann University (Drexel), Philadelphia, as a Fulbright scholar. In Finland she currently works as a clinical psychologist applying DMT in a public healthcare psychiatric outpatient clinic and in her private practice. She has published articles on body image and DMT applications with adult populations.

Dr. Heidrun Panhofer, Ph.D., MA DMT, senior registered member DMT of the Spanish Dance Movement Therapy Association, is coordinator and lecturer of the Master and Postgraduate Programme of Dance Movement Therapy at the Department of Psychology, Universitat Autònoma de Barcelona, Spain. Originally Austrian, she edited the first book on Dance Movement Therapy in Spanish *El cuerpo en psicoterapia: La teoría y práctica de la Danza Movimiento Terapia* (2005; The body in psychotherapy – Theory and practice of Dance Movement Therapy). As a co-founder, she served as the president of the Spanish Association for Dance Movement Therapy, ADMTE, for four years. She lectures in DMT at different universities and institutes in Europe and her clinical practice includes group and individual work with children, adolescents and adults in special educational institutions, different psychiatric settings and private practice in the UK, Germany, and Spain.

Prof. Dr. Helen Payne, is a UKCP accredited psychotherapist; fellow ADMT, UK and Sen. Reg. dance movement psychotherapist who helped to pioneer DMT in the UK starting the professional association, training, research and publications. She conducts research, supervises PhDs and examines nationally and internationally. Trained in Laban Movement; Person-Centered Counselling and Group Analysis, Helen Payne also has a private practice offering her own form of Authentic Movement with groups and individuals.

Dr. Tim Parke has worked as a language teacher and researcher in many types of institution, most recently in higher education in the UK. His principal academic interest is the different ways in which languages develop in people, whether through acquisition or through conscious teaching and learning. His publications are in the areas of language-learner narratives, bilingualism, and language teaching methodology.

Dr. Bonnie Meekums is an honorary fellow and senior practitioner of the Association for Dance Movement Psychotherapy (DMP) UK. She lectures in counselling and psychotherapy for the University of Leeds and also teaches DMP in several countries. Author of two books including Dance Movement Therapy (Sage, 2002), she is also Symposium Co-Editor for the British Journal of Guidance and Counselling. Her research interests lie in embodiment and transformational/arts based methods.

Yona Shahar-Levy is a teacher of Introductory and Advanced Courses in Dance-Movement Therapy Academic Programs, Israeli Dance/Movement Therapist and supervisor, 1985–1993; chairperson of the Israeli Association of Creative-Expressive Therapies (ICET); creator of an Innovative Model for Psychomotor Assessment of Emotive Movement (Emotorics: Body-Movement-Mind Paradigm). Emotorics is based on integration between body-movement dynamics and developmental paradigms, Continued Education in Group Analysis, Somatic Experiencing (SE) with Peter Levine and EMDR. Publications include *The Visible Body Reveals the Secrets of the Mind: A Body-Movement-Mind Paradigm (BMMP) for the Analysis and Interpretation of Emotive Movement* (2001, 2004; in Hebrew).

Dipl.-Psych. Ilka Konopatsch, psychologist and Authentic Movement practitioner, trained in BodyMind Approach, Dance Pedagogics. Her psychological and movement work in Germany, Turkey and the UK includes personal development and dance groups – especially aimed at immigrant women, depressed or psychotic patients and their families and special needs children. Research interest evolves around embodiment in Authentic Movement and the BodyMind Approach as well as Transcultural Psychotherapy.

Dr. Helle Winther, Ph.D., is an Associate Professor at the University of Copenhagen, Section of Human and Social Sciences, Department of Exercise and Sport Sciences. Dance- and body psychotherapist in the dance therapy form Dansergia. Research and teaching in the area of dance, movement, body language and communication, dance therapy and movement psychology. Co-author and editor of four books and anthologies, and author of many articles in journals and books.

Dr. Steve Harvey, Ph.D.., BC-DMT, RPT/S, is currently the Senior Consultant Psychologist with the Taranaki District Health Board in New Plymouth, New Zealand. He has practiced as a child and family psychologist, dance therapist, and play therapist of rover thirty years. Steve Harvey helped pioneer family play therapy and has published extensively in this area.

Elmar Kruithoff is a certified psychologist, focusing teacher and heads the Focusing Kompetenz Zentrum (www.focusing-center.de) in Hamburg and Copenhagen. He worked as assistant professor at University of Hamburg's Department of Psychology as well as research associate at the University Hospital. He lectures in schools, hospitals and companies.

Prof. Dr. Johannes Michalak is a professor of clinical psychology at the University of Hildesheim. After his diploma in Psychology (1994), he finished his Ph.D. (1999) and worked at the Ruhr-University Bochum (Department of Clinical Psychology and Psychotherapy). He was an acting professor at the Universities of Heidelberg (2006–2007) and Bochum (2009–2010) and a visiting professor at Queen's University Kingston (Canada). He is a licensed behavior therapist and supervisor. Research interests include mindfulness-based approaches, depression and personal goals of patients.

Dipl.-Psych. Jan Michael Burg is Ph.D. student at the Ruhr University Bochum (since 2008). He studied Psychology at the Wilhelms-University Münster (2003–2008) and acquired his diploma in 2008. Research interests include affective disorders, as well as mindfulness-based interventions and body-related processes in clinical psychology.

Prof. Dr. Thomas Heidenreich is Professor of Psychology at the faculty Social Work, Health and Nursing at the University of Applied Sciences in Esslingen (since 2006). After his diploma in psychology (1994), he finished his Ph.D. (2000) and worked as a scientific assistant at the University of Frankfurt (Department of Psychology and Clinic for Psychiatry and Psychotherapy). Also, he is a trained behavior therapist and supervisor. Research interests include cognitive-behavioral approaches to mental disorders (social phobia, depression) as well as mindfulness-based approaches.

Addresses for correspondence

Prof. Dr. Dr. Thomas Fuchs
Klinik für Allgemeine Psychiatrie
Sektion Phänomenologische Psychopathologie und Psychotherapie
Universitätsklinikum Heidelberg
Voßstr. 2, D-69115 Heidelberg
E-mail: thomas.fuchs@med.uni-heidelberg.de

Dr. Michela Summa
Klinik für Allgemeine Psychiatrie
Sektion Phänomenologische Psychopathologie und Psychotherapie
Universitätsklinikum Heidelberg
Voßstr. 2, D-69115 Heidelberg
E-mail: michela.summa@med.uni-heidelberg.de

Dr. Maxine Sheets-Johnstone
Department of Philosophy
1295 University of Oregon
Eugene, OR 97403-1295, USA
E-mail: msj@uoregon.edu

Dr. Elizabeth Behnke
PO Box 66, Ferndale WA 98248, USA
E-mail: sppb@openaccess.org

Dr. Mónica Alarcón
Hansjakobstr. 93
79117 Freiburg, Germany
E-mail: tanzphil.alar@yahoo.de
Web page: www.monica-alarcon.de and www.mbodyresearch.de

Dr. Eugene Gendlin
c/o The Focusing Institute
34 East Lane
Spring Valley, NY 10977

Prof. Dr. Petra Jansen
Universität Regensburg, Institut für Sportwissenschaften
Universitätsstr. 31
93053 Regensburg, Germany
E-mail: Petra.Jansen@psk.uni-regensburg.de

Prof. Dr. Christina Bermeitinger
University of Hildesheim, Institute for Psychology
Marienburger Platz 22, D-31141 Hildesheim
E-mail: bermeitinger@uni-hildesheim.de

PD Dr. Markus Kiefer
University of Ulm, Department of Psychiatry
Section for Cognitive Electrophysiology, Leimgrubenweg 12, D-89075 Ulm
E-mail: Markus.Kiefer@uni-ulm.de

Dr. Christina Jung (ehemals Jäger)
Max-Planck-Institut fuer Kognitions- und Neurowissenschaften, Arbeitsbereich Psychologie
Stephanstr. 1a, D-04103 Leipzig

Dr. Peggy Sparenberg (ehemals Tausche)
Max-Planck-Institut fuer Kognitions- und Neurowissenschaften, Arbeitsbereich Psychologie
Stephanstr. 1a, D-04103 Leipzig

Dr. Caterina Suitner
Dipartimento di Psicologia dello Sviluppo e della Socializzazione (DPSS)
Universita' di Padova
Via Venezia, 8
35139 Padova, Italy
E-mail: caterina.suitner@unipd.it

PD Dr. Sabine C. Koch
University of Heidelberg, Department of Psychology
Hauptstr. 47–51
69117 Heidelberg, Germany
E-mail: sabine.koch@urz.uni-heidelberg.de

Dipl.-Psych. Katharina Bachmeier
Dipartimento di Psicologia dello Sviluppo e della Socializzazione (DPSS)
Università di Padova, Via Venezia, 8
35139 Padova, Italy

Prof. Dr. Anne Maass
Dipartimento di Psicologia dello Sviluppo e della Socializzazione (DPSS)
Università di Padova, Via Venezia, 8
35139 Padova, Italy
E-mail: maass@psico.unipd.it

Dr. Claudia Böger
Institut für Sportwissenschaft und Sport, Bundeswehr University of Munich
Werner-Heisenberg-Weg 39
85577 Neubiberg
E-mail: claudia.boeger@unibw.de

Dipl. Psych. Astrid Kolter
University of Heidelberg
Department of Psychology
Hauptstr. 47–51
69117 Heidelberg, Germany
E-mail: astrid.kolter@psychologie.uni-heidelberg.de

Dr. des. Silva H. Ladewig
European University Viadrina
Department of Cultural Studies
Große Scharrnstraße 59
15230 Frankfurt (Oder), Germany
E-mail: mail@silvaladewig.de

Prof. Dr. Cornelia Müller
European University Viadrina
Professor of Applied Linguistics
Department of Cultural Studies
Große Scharrnstraße 59
15230 Frankfurt (Oder), Germany
E-mail: Sekretariat-CMueller@europa-uni.de

Prof. Dr. William Sax
Heidelberg University, South Asia Institute
Im Neuenheimer Feld 330
69120 Heidelberg, Germany
E-mail: sax@asia-europe.uni-heidelberg.de

Dr. Karin Polit
University of Heidelberg, Institute for Ethnologie
Sandgasse 7
69117 Heidelberg, Germany
E-mail: kpolit@sai.uni-heidelberg.de

PD Dr. Ralf P. Meyer
Merian Schule Freiburg
Rheinstraße 3
D-79104 Freiburg, Germany
E-mail: ralf.meyer@klinikum.uni-freiburg.de

Dr. Christine Caldwell
Somatic Counseling Psychology
Naropa University
2130 Arapahoe Avenue
Boulder, CO, 80302, USA

Dr. Marianne Eberhard-Kaechele
German Sports University
Institute of Health Promotion and Clinical Movement Science Department of Neurology,
Psychosomatics and Psychiatry
Am SportparkMüngersdorf 6
50933 Köln
E-mail: m.eberhard-kaechele@dshs-koeln.de

Päivi Pylvänäinen
Makasiininkatu 14 B 21
FIN-33230 Tampere, Finland
E-mail: paivi.pylvanainen@tanssiterapia.fi; paivi.pylvanainen@tampere.fi

Dr. Heidrun Panhofer
Universitat Autònoma de Barcelona (UAB)
Coordinadora del MA y PG en Danza Movimiento Terapia, Edifici d'estudiants
Plaça Civica, 08193 Bellaterra (Barcelona), Spain
E-mail: info@en-e-mocion.com

Prof. Dr. Helen Payne
University of Hertfordshire
Meridian House, 32 The Common
Hatfield, Herts, AL10 0NZ, UK

Dr. Timothy Parke
University of Hertfordshire
School of Humanities, Faculty of Humanities Law and Education
Hertfordshire, Herts
E-mail: T.Parke@herts.ac.uk

Dr. Bonnie Meekums
NEW ROOM 3.09
School of Healthcare, University of Leeds
Woodhouse Lane, Leeds, LS2 9JT, UK

Yona Shahar-Levy
26 Gelber St. Jerusalem
96755 Israel
E-mail: zviyon@gmail.com

Dipl.-Psych. Ilka Konopatsch
Görlitzer Str. 50
10997 Berlin

Dr. Helle Winther
University of Copenhagen, Department of Exercise and Sport Sciences
Section of Human and Social Sciences
Nørre Allé 51
2200 Copenhagen N, Denmark
E-mail: hwinther@ifi.ku.dk

Dr. Steve Harvey
23 Gilbert Street
New Plymouth
New Zealand 4610

Elmar Kruithoff
Athensvej 2 B
DK 2300 Kopenhagen S

Prof. Dr. Johannes Michalak
University of Hildesheim
Department of Clinical Psychology
Marienburger Platz 22
31141 Hildesheim, Germany
E-mail: johannes.michalak@uni-hildesheim.de

Dipl.-Psych. Jan M. Burg
Universität Bochum
GAFO 03/926
D-44780 Bochum

Prof. Dr. Thomas Heidenreich
Hochschule Esslingen
Flandernstraße 101
73732 Esslingen

Index

A

action patterns   257, 267–270, 273, 275–277, 280

action prediction   142, 144–145

action simulation   141–142, 147

action understanding   142, 144–145, 150

activated metaphoricity   4, 201, 205, 212, 215

activation of metaphors   201–202, 207, 221

Adler, Janet   220, 224, 344, 351, 428, 439

Alarcón Davila, Mónica E.   3, 105, 109–110, 422, 446

amodal   2, 121, 124–127, 132

anthropology   4, 6, 111, 184, 187–189, 197–198, 227–228, 307, 321, 412

anxiety   18, 284, 295–297, 303, 327, 331, 333, 338, 372, 374, 380, 382, 398, 405, 409–410, 413

arts therapies   272, 323, 366, 432, 442

attachment   255, 259–260, 280, 285–286, 310, 322, 330, 371, 373, 383–384

attention   5, 12, 15, 17, 43, 45, 47, 51, 53, 60, 68–69, 98, 133, 153, 155, 172, 191, 203, 213, 221, 228, 259, 261–263, 274–275, 278, 282–283, 293–295, 300–301, 303, 305, 308, 312–313, 321–322, 334, 341–342, 344, 349, 374, 389, 395–396, 403, 408, 419, 433, 439

Authentic Movement   5, 263, 322, 341–352, 433, 442–443

B

background   18, 23–24, 27, 34, 36, 38, 44, 60

Bachmeier, Katharina   3, 155, 164, 184

Barsalou, Lawrence   2, 6, 126, 130–133, 139–140, 155–158, 168–169, 188, 190, 194, 196, 311, 394, 398, 408, 411, 423, 428–429, 431, 440, 443

basic-level categories   23, 25–26, 30, 33–34, 37–38

Baum, Edith   192, 197

behavioral matching   148

Behnke, Elizabeth A.   3, 83, 85, 90, 92, 94–95, 97–99, 101–102, 422, 440

Bergson, Henri   10, 21, 68–69, 112, 171, 184, 418–419, 440

Bermeitinger, Christina   3, 121, 126–127, 132, 134, 422–423, 440

beyond words   314, 320, 337

body as a resource   382

body   1–5, 6, 9–25, 27–30, 32–33, 36–41, 43–47, 49–51, 53, 56–71, 73–81, 83–87, 90, 97, 99–103, 105–112, 115, 117–122, 129–130, 141–143, 145–148, 151, 153, 155–162, 164, 166–167, 169–174, 176–189, 194, 196–199, 201–213, 216, 221–230, 232–233, 240–241, 243–245, 249, 255–264, 267–280, 282–287, 289–306, 311–315, 320–323, 327–367, 369–373, 375–385, 387–391, 393–397, 399–409, 412, 417–444

body [lived]   1, 3, 9, 14–15, 17, 19, 22, 86, 172, 357, 364, 425

body feedback   4, 155–162, 166–167, 177, 179–182, 184, 428–429, 444

body image   47, 58–59, 61–65, 70–71, 118, 120, 289, 292, 297–300, 302, 304, 306, 331, 384, 443

body knowledge   11, 313

body language   4, 30, 327, 330–331, 340, 359, 364, 366

body memory   1–6, 9–14, 16–20, 22–25, 28, 30, 32–33, 36–41, 43–44, 46, 67–69, 73, 83, 105–107, 111–112, 115, 117–119, 155–158, 160–162, 164, 169, 171–174, 176–189, 201–206, 210, 216, 221–230, 240, 243–244, 249, 255–256, 258–263, 267–270, 276, 284–285, 289–297, 299–302, 304–306, 315, 327–328, 332–334, 337–339, 341, 375, 384, 387–388, 390, 404, 406, 408, 417–433, 435–436, 438–444

body memory, auditory   178, 182

body memory, habitual / traumatic / erotic (Casey)   267–269, 276, 289–291, 295

body memory, gustatory   178, 182

body memory, haptic   178, 182

body memory, incorporative   118, 173, 178, 180, 426, 428–429

body memory, intercorporeal   172, 178, 180, 429

body memory, kinesthetic   443

body memory, olfactory   178, 182

body memory, pain-related   178, 180

body memory, procedural   118, 172, 178, 180, 424, 429–430

body memory, situational   118, 172, 178–183, 420, 424, 429–430

body memory, tactile   43
body memory taxonomy   3,
   171, 183
body memory, visual   178, 182
body-mind approach   341
body-mind experience   341,
   344
body psychology   360
body psychotherapy   167, 173,
   272, 280, 285, 376, 390
body rhythms   6, 158, 169, 184,
   322, 382, 442
body-self   289–290, 292–296,
   298–299, 301–302, 304–305,
   329, 337
body scan   396
body schema   47, 61–65, 70–71,
   118, 120, 380
Böger, Claudia   4, 187, 189–191,
   195, 318, 428–429, 448
boundary violation   83, 87–88,
   92, 94, 100
brain   2, 17, 22, 25, 28, 30, 39,
   46–52, 61–62, 64, 69, 71–72,
   112, 119, 122, 127–129, 134–139,
   141, 144, 147, 150–152, 168, 177,
   196–197, 199, 226, 243–251,
   255–257, 259, 261–262,
   264–265, 269, 275, 278, 285,
   287, 290–291, 293–295, 306,
   321–322, 339, 373, 376–377,
   398–399, 405, 408–409, 412,
   423, 425–426, 432, 440–441,
   443–444
Bourdieu, Pierre   16, 21, 228–
   229, 232, 241
Buytendijk, Frederik J. J.   189,
   196, 212–222, 224
Burg, Jan M.   5, 393, 402–403,
   405, 407, 409, 422, 430, 442

C
Caldwell, Christine   4, 167–168,
   255, 261–262, 264, 381, 384,
   420, 430–433, 435–436, 440
Casey, Edward S.   5–6, 12, 21,
   23, 38, 67–69, 89, 92, 102, 106,
   111, 205, 224, 232–233, 241,
   289–290, 306, 391, 420, 440

categories   4, 23, 25–26, 30,
   33–34, 37–38, 40, 44, 64, 69,
   122–124, 126–129, 133–140,
   168, 171, 173, 175–179, 182–184,
   186, 204–205, 255, 370, 429,
   438
category representation   121,
   130
case study   4–5, 40, 59, 137,
   201–202, 206, 222, 224, 234,
   442
cell memory   243
Chaiklin, Sharon   202, 225, 281,
   285, 287, 306, 339
change processes   353, 355
classic view   121
clinical implications   287, 311,
   323, 385
clinical practice   1, 182, 272–
   273, 439
cognition   1–4, 6, 24, 28, 33, 36,
   40, 69–70, 72, 78, 119–122,
   130, 133–141, 146, 148–152, 154,
   156–159, 161–162, 166–170,
   184, 187, 189, 196–199, 226,
   243–244, 247, 249–251, 273,
   284, 311, 313, 339, 341, 391, 399,
   409–410, 412–413, 419, 422,
   437, 440, 442–444
cognitive anthropology   4
cognitive linguistics   4, 23, 28,
   38–41, 189, 197, 202, 222, 325
cognitive psychology   11, 115,
   117–119, 121, 126, 138–139, 148,
   150, 153, 183, 205, 418, 423,
   425, 430, 443
cognitive science   3, 28, 39–40,
   43, 123, 133–134, 137–139, 141,
   150–151, 153, 169, 183–184,
   188–189, 196–197, 250, 285–
   287, 399, 413, 422, 424
cognitive semantics   187, 189–
   190, 193–194, 197
cognitive therapy   393–395,
   402, 408–413
collective memory   227, 230,
   232
common coding   143, 148, 153
communication   6, 123,
   130–132, 138, 148, 152, 158–159,

167–169, 183–184, 202, 204,
   214, 244, 270, 303, 308–309,
   314–315, 317–318, 321, 341, 344,
   347, 350, 384, 407, 428, 433,
   437, 439–442, 444
communication, bodily   439
communication, verbal   123,
   131–132, 318
communicability   432
concept   1–5, 25, 30, 32, 34,
   49, 76, 102, 106, 111, 116–119,
   121–125, 127–128, 131–133, 135,
   137, 139, 146, 148, 156–157, 159,
   163, 169, 171, 176–177, 183–185,
   196, 201, 226, 228, 232, 243,
   249, 256–257, 269, 271, 274,
   285–286, 290, 297, 309, 312,
   319–320, 323, 329, 342, 358,
   360, 362, 374, 423, 425, 427–
   428, 432, 436, 442
concept representation   121,
   127, 131
conceptual metaphor theory   1,
   4, 272, 346
consciousness   6, 10–11, 13, 19,
   23–24, 28–30, 35–36, 45, 58,
   60–61, 67, 69–71, 75–76, 79,
   86, 105–106, 109–112, 117, 120,
   133, 138–139, 173, 208, 212,
   215–216, 222, 224–226, 232,
   260, 264, 270, 275, 293–295,
   299–300, 305, 311, 321–322,
   338, 351, 356–357, 364, 369,
   375, 419, 440–443
constraints   2, 127, 142, 156–157,
   164, 424, 426
content analysis   4, 171, 173, 176,
   178, 181–182, 184, 226, 427, 442
converging evidence   162
core motor-prototypes of
   emotive   327
core self (Stern)   66–67
covert imitation   142, 144
Cozolino, Louis   257–258, 264,
   293, 306
creative arts therapies   447
creative processes of body
   memory   73
Csordas, Thomas   232, 241, 314,
   321, 356–357, 366

D

Damasio, Antonio 129, 132, 134, 138–139, 268, 285, 311, 313, 321, 356, 398, 407, 423, 430, 440

dance 1, 3–4, 20, 65–66, 71, 103, 105–112, 149, 169, 174, 198, 201, 204, 206–207, 210, 220, 223–226, 230, 236–240, 267–268, 270, 272–275, 277–278, 281–287, 289, 297, 303, 305–307, 312, 314–316, 319, 321, 323–325, 336, 339, 342, 349, 351–367, 369, 371–374, 377, 380–381, 385, 402, 411, 419, 422, 427–429, 431, 435, 437, 439, 442, 444

dance movement psychotherapy (DMP) 198, 226, 307, 314, 323, 349, 351

dance/movement therapy (DMT) 20, 201, 204, 210, 220, 223–226, 267–268, 270, 272–273, 278, 281, 285–287, 289, 297–298, 302–306, 321, 323, 325, 336, 338, 366, 369, 371, 373–376, 378, 380–383, 431

dance therapy 225–226, 273–274, 281–282, 284–285, 287, 306, 321, 352–355, 359–360, 367, 372–373, 377, 429, 442, 444

dementia 20, 53, 138, 223, 243, 374, 436

denial 17

depression 5, 224, 268, 297, 301, 332, 374, 393–394, 396–406, 408–413, 442

development 5, 14–15, 17, 48, 66, 69, 72–75, 78–80, 88, 103, 120, 169, 176, 190, 194, 221, 225, 243–247, 250, 260, 264–265, 267–268, 271, 274, 278, 280–282, 284–287, 293, 297, 302, 308–309, 322, 327, 329, 331, 336, 338, 349–350, 355, 358, 360, 364, 367, 370, 373–375, 378, 381–384, 390–391, 393, 396, 406, 409, 417, 421, 424, 433, 439–440

dichotomies of long-term memory systems 116

dichotomy of explicit and implicit memory 115

differentiation of body memory categories 179, 429

dynamics 4, 15, 24, 35–36, 43–45, 47, 49–57, 59–66, 72, 93, 172, 204–205, 226, 283, 313, 360, 366, 422, 431, 443

DMT group 297–298, 303–305, 380

dissociation 116, 119–120, 137–138, 244, 264, 270–271, 274, 281, 284–287, 331, 369–371, 373–374, 381–385, 405, 425–426

dissociative identity disorder (DID) 5, 369–371, 374–375, 377–378, 381–382, 385

dualism 11, 45, 75, 88, 241, 357–358

dynamic aspects of the body 1, 3, 155–156, 168

dynamic body feedback 4, 155, 157–158, 162, 167

dynamic embodiment 4, 155, 165–167, 184, 444

E

Eberhard–Kaechele, Marianne 4, 267, 273, 277, 280, 283, 285, 382, 384, 422, 429, 431–432, 440

either/or contraries 43

embodied approach 133, 137–139, 141, 162, 196

embodied cognition 1–3, 24, 36, 130, 137, 139, 148, 150, 154, 156, 167–168, 170, 187, 413

embodied emotion 145–146, 398

embodied experience 96, 188, 197–198, 226–228, 232, 240, 263, 300, 307–308, 312–319, 322–323, 353, 428

embodied intercorporeality 6, 169, 184, 442

embodied memory 156, 227, 230, 232, 234, 353, 423–424

embodied metaphors 307, 350

embodied therapies 1, 4, 417–418, 432, 436, 438

embodied view 121

embodiment 1, 3–4, 6, 25, 27–30, 34, 36, 38, 41, 71, 83–84, 93, 96, 101, 118–119, 121, 125, 130, 132–133, 138, 141, 150, 155–158, 162–163, 165–170, 184, 187–189, 193–194, 196–197, 231, 257, 261, 281, 284–285, 287, 290, 297–299, 304, 306–308, 311, 318–320, 350–351, 366, 393–394, 398–402, 404, 408–409, 411, 418, 423–424, 426, 428–430, 438–444

embodiment premise 189

emergence of metaphors 4–5, 202, 346

emotion 3–4, 6, 15, 75, 78, 132–133, 135, 138–139, 141, 145–147, 150–152, 154, 168–169, 177, 243, 247–250, 255, 258–259, 264, 270, 273, 281, 284–285, 294–295, 299, 305, 318, 321–322, 328, 346–347, 363, 372–373, 376–377, 389, 394, 398–399, 401, 406, 409–411, 423, 434–436, 439–440, 442–443

emotion simulation 147

emotive-relational body language 327

emotorics 5, 306, 327–329, 335, 338–339, 450

enduring 3, 21, 83–87, 90–97, 100–101, 229, 422, 440

epigenetics 4, 243, 249

experience 2, 6, 9, 11–15, 17, 19, 22–40, 43–44, 47, 49, 54–62, 65–66, 73–74, 79, 83, 85–88, 90–98, 100–101, 103, 105–107, 109–110, 112, 115–118, 120, 122, 125–127, 133, 136, 141, 146–147, 150, 152, 155–157, 168–169, 172–173, 177, 180, 182–183, 185, 188–190, 193–195, 197–198, 201–205, 208–209, 212, 216, 219–228, 230, 232–233, 240, 246, 249, 255, 257–263, 267, 270–273, 275, 278–281, 284–285, 290–291, 293–294, 297, 299–305, 307–324,

334–335, 338–339, 341–351,
353–354, 356, 358, 361–362,
364, 369, 372–373, 381–382,
387–389, 391, 393, 398, 402,
406–408, 412–413, 418–423,
425, 427–428, 430, 432–434,
438–439, 442
experientialism   23–25, 27–28,
34, 36, 38
experiential metaphor   270–
271, 278–279
explication   9, 19, 68, 86, 201–
202, 210–212, 214, 216–217,
220–223, 427
explicating process   73, 441
explicit memory   11, 19, 23, 44,
74, 106, 116, 119–120, 201–203,
205–207, 222–223, 262, 270,
277, 290–291, 294–295, 425–
426, 436–438

F
father   47, 179–180, 239, 260,
279, 336–337, 372
felt sense   5, 20, 52–53, 76, 79,
218, 260, 383, 387–389, 392,
405, 421, 430–431
fight or flight   91, 295, 336
focusing   1, 3–6, 20–21, 79, 81,
102, 127, 134, 148, 155, 188, 206,
277, 383, 387, 390–392, 394,
396, 402–403, 410, 427–428,
431, 441–442
formation   3, 10, 14, 23–26,
28–30, 33–38, 46, 48–50, 58,
80, 95, 137, 156–157, 162, 166,
176, 179, 196, 199, 205, 214,
219, 246–247, 250, 257, 260,
262, 267–269, 271, 299, 321,
419–422, 425–427, 438–439
free recall   116, 147, 162
from implicit to explicit memory
201, 222, 437–438
Fuchs, Thomas   1, 3–4, 6, 9, 12,
15, 21–23, 36, 38–40, 44–45,
67, 70, 73–78, 80–81, 106,
111, 118, 120, 171–173, 175,
177, 181–184, 188, 197, 201,
205, 221–222, 225–226, 264,
315, 321, 334, 339, 384, 394,
398, 402, 404, 406, 409, 411,

417, 420–422, 424, 428–429,
438–444
functional embodiment   156

G
gait   10, 171, 400–401, 406, 408,
411–412
Gallagher, Shaun   37–38, 39–41,
47, 58, 61–64, 66, 70–71, 313,
320–321
Gallese, Vittorio   26, 28, 39,
130, 135, 144, 151–153, 190, 197,
399, 409
Gendlin, Eugene T.   3, 5–6,
20–21, 73, 75–77, 81, 88, 93,
102, 387–391, 405, 410, 421,
427, 430–431, 441
gesture   6, 13, 45, 56, 83, 85–87,
92–101, 202–203, 207, 209,
211–215, 223–226, 282, 351,
389, 443
Gibbs, Raymond W. Jr.   35, 39,
131, 135, 189–190, 193–194,
196–197, 225–226, 277, 285,
318–319, 322
Gindler, Elsa   97
Glenberg, Arthur   122–123,
130–131, 135, 142, 151, 155–158,
162, 166, 168, 190, 195,
197–198, 313, 322, 398, 410,
423–424, 441
grounding   38, 41, 62, 133–134,
137–138, 140, 151, 166–168, 170,
197, 199, 369, 371, 380–381,
383, 410, 443
group case study   5
group psychotherapy   5
gustatory body memory   179,
181–182, 186

H
habit(s)   9–13, 15, 43–44, 46–47,
56–59, 61, 64–66, 68, 73, 77,
106, 163–165, 171, 239, 257,
262, 291, 293, 419, 421, 425
habitual memory   68, 172, 176,
420
habitus   16, 173, 184, 228, 230,
232–233, 424, 426
Hanna, Thomas   47, 70, 92, 102,
298, 304

haptic body memory   109, 171,
179, 181–182, 186, 246, 382
Harvey, Steve   5, 369, 371–374,
384, 422, 431, 436, 442
Hatfield, Elaine   158, 169, 181,
184, 428, 441
healing   1, 5, 202, 226, 232, 241,
256, 259, 261, 264, 278–279,
286, 358, 376, 382, 384, 431,
435–437
Heidenreich, Thomas   5,
393–394, 398, 401, 403–406,
409–412, 422, 430, 442
hermeneutics of the body   227
Husserl, Edmund   3, 6, 11–12,
22–25, 29–37, 39–41, 46, 49,
52, 67, 69–70, 77, 83–84,
89–92, 96–98, 100, 102–103,
105, 107, 109–112, 184, 204,
225–226, 313, 322, 418–419,
441, 444

I
ideomotor theory / principle
143, 148
image   10, 16, 18–19, 23, 25,
33–41, 47, 58–59, 61–65, 70–71,
118, 120, 187, 190, 194–195, 197,
220, 223, 271–272, 277–280,
289, 292, 297–300, 302, 304,
306, 317–320, 323, 331, 343,
346–348, 350, 356, 364, 384,
419, 436, 443
image schema   34–35, 194–195,
271–272, 278–280
imitation   16, 141–144, 151,
153, 173, 229, 243, 247–249,
281–283, 421, 429
implicit emotive body memory
clusters   327
implicit body memory   3,
23–25, 30, 32–33, 115, 118–119,
201, 210, 221, 223, 270, 427,
439, 441
implicit memory   1, 3–4, 9,
11, 13, 19, 22, 33, 44, 46, 74,
106, 115–117, 119–120, 201,
205–208, 215, 220, 222–223,
255, 257–258, 260–261, 264,
271, 291–292, 294–295, 305,

332, 418–419, 421, 424–427, 436, 443
implicit memory typology   9
implicit processes   73, 208
incorporative memory   15, 184, 421, 424
India   227, 233, 240–241
instrumental use of body memory   177–181, 429
integration   3, 74, 118, 121, 176, 202, 205, 221, 223, 245, 281, 283, 290, 292–293, 307, 314, 324, 341, 346–347, 350–351, 357, 373–374, 380, 382, 384, 394, 417, 423, 435, 439
integrative model of the trauma process   4
interaction modalities   281
interaction   14–15, 34–36, 53, 74, 78–79, 123, 132, 141, 148, 150–151, 153, 155–157, 159, 162, 164, 166, 172, 187, 190, 194, 196, 203, 208, 210, 213, 220, 226, 246, 258, 274, 280–281, 283, 285, 289, 293, 298–300, 304–305, 325, 357, 387–388, 399, 405–407, 420–421, 423–424, 426, 432, 443
intercorporeal memory   14–15, 18, 75, 118, 406, 421
intercorporeality   6, 9, 14–15, 169, 184, 442
interdisciplinary   1, 4, 23, 40, 70–71, 199, 201–202, 204, 207, 220, 222–223, 249, 290, 324, 366, 393–394, 423, 438–439, 442
interview   171, 173–176, 178, 181–185, 206, 220, 224, 297, 310, 320, 322, 427
interview on body memory   171, 174

J
Jacoby, Heinrich   97
James-Lange theory of emotion   146, 150
James, William   13, 22, 45, 143, 146, 150, 152, 294, 322, 372–373, 384, 398, 420

Jansen, Petra   3, 115, 119, 418, 422–423, 441
Johnson, Marc   3–4, 6, 24–30, 34–37, 40, 93, 101, 103, 122, 130, 136, 189–190, 193–194, 198, 271–272, 277, 286, 313, 317–318, 322, 341, 346, 351, 398, 411
Jung, Christina   3, 141, 314, 322, 342, 352, 422, 441
joint action   148, 150–151, 153, 286

K
Kandel, Eric   5, 106, 112, 289–295, 305–306
Kestenberg, Judith S.   159–160, 169, 202–204, 225–226, 283, 285–286, 378, 384
Kiefer, Markus   3, 121–123, 125–132, 135–136, 139, 422–423, 440
kinesthetic   33, 44, 48–49, 51, 54, 60, 83–87, 89–96, 98–100, 171, 178–179, 182, 186, 420
kinesthesia   1, 43, 45–50, 53, 55, 57–61, 64, 68–69, 111, 290, 293, 299
kinesthetic body memory   443
kinesthetic empathy   273, 281
kinesthetic memory   1, 3, 43–44, 47, 49, 51–54, 56–62, 64–67, 69, 71, 337, 428, 443
kinesthetically-informed neuropsychology   47
kinesthetic/kinetic melodies   43–44, 47–51, 55–59, 62–63, 65
kinetic dynamics   43, 47, 49, 51, 53–54, 57, 60–61, 63–64
Kirkengen, Anna Luise   87–88, 90, 93, 101, 103
knowing how/knowing that   11, 46, 91, 116, 119, 171, 205, 221, 223, 240, 361
knowledge   2–3, 9–11, 14, 24, 29–31, 33–34, 37, 39–41, 45–46, 49, 57, 63, 66, 78, 116, 122–128, 131–139, 152, 156, 162, 182, 197–198, 205, 208, 223, 229–230, 233–234, 240, 290,

311, 313, 317–320, 324, 342, 388–389, 398, 419, 423, 439
Koch, Sabine   1, 3–6, 36, 39–40, 134, 147, 155, 159, 161, 167, 169, 171, 176, 181, 183–184, 201, 204, 225–226, 285, 294, 296, 306, 339, 357–358, 366, 369, 371, 376, 384–385, 400, 402, 411, 417, 421–424, 427–431, 436–444
Kolter, Astrid   4, 36, 40, 201, 422, 427–428, 431, 442
Konopatsch, Ilka   5, 341, 343, 347–348, 350–351, 422, 427–428, 431, 433, 442
Kohut, Heinz   329, 339
Kruithoff, Elmar   5, 387, 392, 431, 442

L
Laban, Rudolf von   103, 109, 112, 159, 161, 169, 185, 204, 226, 274, 285, 384
Ladewig, Silva   4, 36, 40, 201, 422, 442
Lakoff, George   3–4, 6, 24–30, 34–36, 38–40, 122, 124, 130, 133, 135–136, 188, 190, 193–194, 197–198, 272, 286, 313, 317–318, 322–323, 398, 411
language   4, 6, 30, 40–41, 55, 65, 69, 71, 98–99, 105, 116, 131, 133–135, 138, 140–141, 146, 150–151, 158, 163–165, 168, 170, 187–190, 193–199, 215, 220, 222, 226–230, 232, 240, 247, 257, 270, 275, 307, 312–314, 316–320, 322, 324, 327, 330–331, 340, 346, 354, 359–360, 364, 366–367, 372, 383, 391, 410, 423, 428, 432, 434, 436–438
languaging movement   307, 428
learning   4–6, 12–13, 15, 44, 46, 49, 52, 54–55, 57–58, 61, 66, 70, 75, 79, 95, 108, 115–116, 119–120, 133–137, 139, 143, 151–152, 187–189, 194, 196–199, 214, 216–217, 219, 229, 243, 248–249, 255–256, 258, 260,

264–265, 268, 279, 281–282, 287, 291–294, 296, 298–299, 304–305, 313, 322, 344, 349, 355, 364, 366, 376, 378, 396, 419–420, 424–426, 430, 440, 443–444
learning of movements 188
learning process 187–188, 219, 355, 366
limbic system 243, 247–250
limitations of language 307, 312, 432
lived body 3, 9, 14–15, 17, 19, 22, 86, 172, 357, 364, 425
living present 91–92, 95, 240
Lohmar, Dieter 22, 32, 39–40, 103, 225
loss of time 369

M
Maass, Anne 3, 155, 163–164, 169–170, 184, 422, 444
Mahler, Margaret 330, 339
major depression 374, 393, 396, 411–413
meaning 3, 5, 12, 20, 23–26, 29–31, 33, 35, 37–41, 87, 100–101, 121–123, 130–131, 137, 139, 148, 156, 158, 160–161, 169, 172, 187–190, 193–198, 202–203, 205, 207–208, 210, 212–215, 217, 219–221, 223–229, 233, 241, 248, 257–259, 267–268, 270–271, 273, 275, 286, 310, 316–318, 321–322, 325, 327, 331, 342, 345–347, 350–351, 360, 363, 382, 391, 399, 403, 410, 422–428, 430, 432, 436–437, 439, 441–442, 444
meaning determination 194
Meekums, Bonnie 5, 273, 286, 307–308, 312, 323–324, 348, 351, 431, 443
memory 1, 3–4, 9, 11–15, 17–19, 22–23, 33, 44, 46, 67–68, 74–75, 106, 115–120, 171–172, 176–178, 182–184, 201–203, 205–208, 215, 220, 222–223, 255, 257–258, 260–262, 264, 267, 270–271, 277, 286, 290–

292, 294–295, 305, 332, 406, 418–422, 424–427, 430–432, 436–438, 443
memory, explicit 11, 19, 23, 44, 74, 106, 116, 119–120, 201–203, 205–207, 222–223, 262, 270, 277, 290–291, 294–295, 425–426, 436–438
memory, habitual 68, 172, 176, 420
memory, implicit 1, 3–4, 9, 11, 13, 19, 22, 33, 44, 46, 74, 106, 115–117, 119–120, 201, 205–208, 215, 220, 222–223, 255, 257–258, 260–261, 264, 271, 291–292, 294–295, 305, 332, 418–419, 421, 424–427, 436, 443
memory, incorporative 15, 184, 421, 424
memory, intercorporeal 14–15, 18, 75, 118, 406, 421
memory, procedural 11–12, 14, 44, 171–172, 183, 270–271, 291, 420, 432
memory, situational 13, 171, 178, 182–183, 420, 431
memory clusters 327–328, 330–332, 335–336, 338–339
memory – implicit, explicit 1, 3–4, 9, 11, 13, 19, 22–23, 33, 44, 46, 74, 106, 115–117, 119–120, 201–203, 205–208, 215, 220, 222–223, 255, 257–258, 260–262, 264, 270–271, 277, 290–292, 294–295, 305, 332, 418–419, 421, 424–427, 436–438, 443
memory research 3, 115, 119, 183–184, 424–425
memory structure and processes 115
memory systems 11, 19, 115–117, 120, 172, 255, 257, 260–262, 264, 425–426, 443–444
mentalization 281, 285–286
Merleau-Ponty, Maurice 1, 6, 10–12, 14–15, 22–23, 40–41, 47, 56–61, 63–66, 68, 71, 102, 112, 159, 169, 184, 188–189,

198, 204, 226, 228, 230, 241, 312–313, 315, 323, 355, 357, 360, 366, 418–419, 442
metaphor 1–2, 4, 6, 36, 39–40, 92, 135, 169, 184, 188–190, 193–194, 197, 199, 201, 203, 208–218, 220–221, 223, 225–226, 267, 270–272, 278–279, 302, 317–319, 322–324, 339, 341, 346–349, 351, 356, 372–373, 383–384, 423, 427–428, 432, 435, 439–444
metaphor, sleeping and waking 217, 223
metaphor and body memory 4, 224
metaphoric instruction 4, 188, 190, 196
Michalak, Johannes 5, 393–394, 398, 401–403, 405–406, 409–412, 422, 430–431, 436, 442
mindfulness 5, 263, 299, 393–397, 402–413, 427, 431, 442
mindfulness-based cognitive therapy 393–395, 402, 408–413
mirroring 5, 145, 147, 169, 267, 273, 280–285, 369, 375, 381, 383–384, 440
mirroring, theory of 5
mirror neurons 141, 144, 147–148, 150, 248, 399
mother 180, 239, 260, 279, 300, 319, 325, 333–337, 339, 350, 353–354, 360–362, 365, 367, 373, 378
motor contagion 148
motor intentionality (Merleau-Ponty) 47, 56–58, 419
movement 1–2, 4–6, 10–12, 15–16, 20, 25, 29, 35–36, 39–40, 43–73, 83–84, 94, 97–99, 101, 103, 107–112, 117–118, 132, 139, 141–145, 147, 149–150, 152, 155–162, 166–167, 169–171, 173–174, 176, 178, 180, 183–191, 193–196, 198–199, 201–221, 223–226, 255, 257–258,

261–263, 267–268, 270, 272–275, 277–278, 281–287, 289–290, 294, 296–307, 312–319, 321–325, 327, 330–336, 338–357, 359–367, 369, 371, 373–384, 388–389, 391, 397, 399–400, 402, 406, 420, 422, 427–444
inclusion of   3
spatio-temporal-energic qualites of   47, 51–54, 65
pointillist conception of   47, 63–65
qualitatively structured dynamics of   45
movement analysis   2, 159–160, 169, 183, 202, 208, 210, 226, 273–274, 285, 306, 382, 384
movement level   219
movement patterns   189, 206–207, 218, 225, 275, 286, 305, 327, 331, 333–334, 338, 402, 406, 420
movement pedagogy   353–355, 364, 444
movement psychology   354, 359–360, 367
movement quality   159–162, 212, 216, 300, 371, 375
movement rhythms   155, 159–161, 296, 400
movement therapy   1, 4–5, 20, 173, 201, 204, 210, 220, 223–226, 267–268, 270, 272, 278, 281, 285–287, 289, 297, 305–306, 315, 321, 323–325, 336, 339, 352, 357, 366, 369, 371, 374–376, 380–381, 384, 391, 431–432, 435–436, 440
Müller, Cornelia   1, 4, 6, 36, 161, 174, 201–203, 207, 209–210, 221, 417, 422, 427–428, 448
multidimensionality of the body   353
multimodal metaphors   36, 201–202, 207, 215, 427, 438
multiple personality disorder (MPD)   369–370, 384–385
see dissociative identity disorder

N
narrative research   5, 353
narrative therapy   308–309, 321, 323–324
narrative tradition   307–308, 310, 320
neurobiology   28, 137, 243–244, 249, 251, 264, 385, 444
neuronal network   243, 249
neuroscience   4, 26, 28, 43, 55, 69, 119, 121, 133–136, 138, 150–153, 249–251, 255, 262, 264–265, 287, 289, 306, 351, 385, 409, 420
Niedenthal, Paula   2, 6, 132, 138, 146, 152, 155–156, 158, 169, 259, 264, 394, 398, 411, 428, 431, 440, 443

O
occultist   378
off-line Embodiment   155–158
olfactory body memory   171, 178–179, 181–182, 290
on-line Embodiment   156–157

P
pain memory   16–17, 180, 186, 421
panic   18, 89, 180, 260, 333, 349, 404, 413
Panhofer, Heidrun   5, 188, 198, 220, 226, 307, 314–315, 317, 319, 323–324, 431–432, 443
Parke, Timothy   5, 307, 323–324, 431, 443
parental envelope   327, 329–330, 332, 334
Payne, Helen   5, 307–308, 323–324, 341–343, 349, 351, 354, 366, 422, 427–428, 431, 433, 442–443
perception   6, 10, 12–14, 16, 20, 22, 25–26, 29, 33–35, 38–41, 62, 65, 68, 71, 73, 79, 110, 112, 117, 119–122, 127, 129–131, 133–136, 138, 140–146, 149–153, 156, 160–162, 169, 171–172, 178, 188–190, 193–199, 226, 241, 243, 247, 249, 259, 268, 270, 273, 282, 287, 290, 292,

295, 320, 342, 366, 369, 387, 391, 395, 411, 423, 429, 438, 440, 442–443
perceptual practices   307, 312, 316, 319–320, 324
perceptual priming   118–119
performance   4, 11, 16, 48–50, 53, 73–74, 76, 107, 115–117, 120, 143–144, 146, 148–149, 152–154, 172, 190, 206–207, 211, 218, 221, 227–231, 233, 239–242, 245, 279, 291, 320, 356, 377–380, 406, 419, 425, 429–430
perpetrator   280–281, 283, 377–378
phenomenological experience   190
phenomenological sense   96, 100, 387
phenomenology   2–6, 9–10, 22–25, 28–36, 38–41, 62–63, 70–72, 81, 83, 96, 99, 102, 105–107, 109, 111–112, 118, 169, 171, 184, 198, 201–202, 204, 208, 222, 225–226, 241, 322–323, 339, 355, 357, 360, 366, 391, 417–419, 426, 433, 438, 441–442, 444
philosophical anthropology   4, 6, 187–188, 198, 412
philosophy of the implicit   387, 390
play therapy   384
pointillist conceptions of movement   43, 47, 63–65
Polit, Karin   4, 227, 235, 238, 241, 449
possession   4, 227, 230–233, 241, 303
possibilizing   94
practice   1, 21, 48, 51, 64, 66, 84, 96–98, 102, 133, 160, 171, 182, 223, 226–230, 232–233, 241, 272–273, 275, 286, 321–324, 341–342, 344–345, 354, 356–357, 366, 385, 387, 391–393, 395–397, 402, 405–411, 422, 439
practitioner research   354

practitioner researcher 354, 365–366

prediction 141–142, 144–145, 164

presentification 205

preverbal memory 2, 426

procedural memory 11–12, 14, 44, 171–172, 183, 270–271, 291, 420, 432

process of meaning articulation 195

protention [protention, protentional, protentionally] 52, 65, 91, 95, 102, 109

Proust, Marcel 9, 19–22

psychiatric outpatients 289

psychiatric outpatient clinic 297, 305

psychoeducation 275, 287

psychology 2–4, 6, 11, 13, 22, 26, 39–40, 72, 115, 117–121, 123, 126, 133, 136–140, 148, 150–153, 166, 168–171, 174, 183–184, 190, 196–197, 199, 203, 205–206, 224–225, 255, 264, 287, 294, 306, 320–324, 339, 354, 359–360, 362, 366–367, 398, 403, 408–413, 418, 423, 425, 430, 439–444

psychopathology 1, 3, 172, 184, 409, 439

psychotherapy 5–6, 93, 102, 157, 167, 169–170, 173, 198, 226, 255–256, 259, 261–262, 264, 272, 275, 280–281, 285–286, 297–298, 306–310, 312, 314, 317, 319–325, 349, 351–352, 367, 376, 384–385, 390–392, 408–411, 441, 443

PTSD (Post Traumatic Stress Syndrome) 5, 247, 260–261, 264, 267, 271, 273, 275, 283, 287, 323, 385

Pylvänäinen, Päivi 5, 289–290, 418, 422, 431, 433, 450

R

reactivation 17, 32–33, 89, 121, 132

reaction time 143, 157, 424, 429–430

recognition 19, 21, 33, 37, 48, 54, 64, 85, 105, 116, 131, 135–137, 143–144, 150–152, 157, 164, 223, 357–358, 362, 409, 424–426, 430

relapse prevention 393–394, 396, 398, 411

relational 15, 17, 46, 78, 92, 95, 139, 172, 183, 189, 194, 259–260, 263–265, 268, 327–330, 434, 438–439

recollection 9–11, 17, 19–21, 23, 44, 65, 171, 173, 177, 345–346, 350, 418, 425

remembering 4, 6, 21, 38, 47, 67–69, 102, 111, 224, 241, 255–259, 268, 305–306, 314, 352, 370, 420, 430, 432, 436, 440, 443

reminiscence 290

representation 3, 35, 50, 60, 117, 121, 123–124, 127, 129–131, 135–138, 142–143, 147, 149–150, 153, 163–164, 169, 301, 311, 317, 399, 410, 421, 423

resource 177–179, 182, 184, 191, 342, 376, 378, 382, 397, 406–407

restorative embodiment work 93, 96

retention 52, 65, 91, 105–106, 109, 119, 258, 282, 426, 443

rhythms – smooth, sharp 159–161

ritual 4, 227–230, 232–234, 237, 239–242, 378

ritual journey 4

ritual possession 4, 232

Rizzolatti, Giacomo 144, 151, 153, 248, 251, 399, 409, 412

Roediger, Henry L. 425–426, 443

Rogers, Carl 177, 181, 192, 197

Rosch, Eleanor 34, 123–124, 138–139, 398, 413

Rothschild, Barbara 261, 264, 269–271, 274, 286, 381, 385, 432, 443

rumination 312, 402–405, 409–412

S

Sax, William 4, 227, 230–232, 241, 448, 455

Schacter, Daniel L. 11, 22, 46, 69, 115–116, 120, 205, 226, 256, 264–265, 418, 425, 443

Schore, Allan N. 259–260, 265, 280, 283,–284, 287

sedimentation 32–33, 65, 92, 99

self 5, 9, 16, 21, 41, 51, 54–55, 57–60, 62–63, 65–67, 69–72, 74, 78, 81, 87–88, 92, 95, 100, 103, 107, 109–112, 145, 148, 151, 157, 170, 173, 181, 191, 196, 201, 210, 214–216, 219, 222, 224–225, 232, 241, 246, 249, 260, 263, 268, 271–273, 275–277, 279, 281–285, 287, 289–290, 292–305, 308–312, 320–322, 324, 328–329, 331–333, 336–339, 342, 344–345, 349, 351, 356, 358, 361, 364, 369–370, 375, 378–379, 381–383, 389, 391, 394, 396–397, 400, 402–406, 408–409, 412, 419, 425, 432, 436, 438, 442–444

self-congruent 5

sensibility 59, 96, 344

sensory and motor reenactment 121

sensorimotor simulation 2

separation / individuation 19, 213, 283, 330, 335, 382

sexual abuse 103, 284, 287, 370, 380

Shahar-Levy, Yona 5, 202, 273, 290, 327–328, 336, 422, 436, 450

shared representations 148, 151

Sheets-Johnstone, Maxine 1, 3, 6, 43–45, 50–51, 57, 67, 71, 112, 132–133, 139, 159, 170, 202, 226, 312–314, 324, 391, 422, 428, 443

simile 208–209, 211

situation 10, 14, 18, 20, 30, 33, 37, 49–50, 52, 59, 64, 79–80, 89, 91, 93, 95, 115–116, 118–119, 131–133, 146, 157–158, 160–162, 164, 166–167, 174, 179–180, 182–183, 186, 191, 194–195,

207–209, 258–259, 261, 267,
270–275, 277, 279–280, 282,
290, 296–298, 300–301, 305,
338, 355–356, 377, 387, 395,
399–400, 408, 420, 430–431
situational dependency   121,
126, 130
situated cognition   130, 133,
135–136, 138–139, 157, 166,
199, 443
situated memory   155
situational body memory   118,
172, 178–183, 420, 424,
429–430
situational memory   13, 171, 178,
182–183, 420, 431
social embodiment   6, 440
social facilitation   148, 154
social interaction   141, 148, 151,
274, 298
somaesthetic   84, 86, 94
somatic osmosis   92–93
somatic psychology   255
Sparenberg, Peggy   3, 141, 422,
441
space   3, 6, 9, 13, 21, 35, 39, 57,
59, 64, 75, 77–78, 97–98, 103,
105, 107–112, 128, 139, 148, 169,
174, 182, 188, 197, 233–234, 271,
274–275, 277, 283, 290, 298–
300, 321, 323, 327, 329–330,
338–339, 342, 344, 359, 362,
364, 377, 392, 397, 437–438
spatio-temporal   3, 47, 50–54,
65, 420
spatial agency bias   4, 155,
162–163, 169–170
sports education   187, 198
sport science   4, 115, 187–188,
198
state-dependent memory   424,
430
Stern, Daniel   15, 46, 66–67, 72,
78, 172, 184, 202, 226, 274, 283,
287, 313, 324
steroid hormones   243, 245,
248, 250
subjective determination   190
Summa, Michela   1, 3–4, 6, 23,
36, 39–41, 183–184, 201, 205,

221, 226, 339, 384, 417–418,
422, 427, 439–444
symbol   158, 168, 196, 311,
322–323, 349, 408, 410, 440

T
tactile-kinesthetic/affective
bodies   43, 66–67
taxonomies of memory   43,
46, 67
temporality [temporality,
temporal]   3, 12, 19, 21,
28, 31, 33, 36, 47–48, 50–54,
61–62, 64–65, 68–69, 74, 77,
83, 87–91, 95, 99–100, 106–
108, 127–129, 132, 144, 157, 198,
217, 234, 243, 247–250, 271,
273, 309, 401, 420, 425
therapy process   5, 299, 301, 359
Thompson, Evan   47, 70, 72, 413
time   2–3, 13, 18–19, 21–22,
45, 51–53, 57–58, 60, 64, 66,
68, 70, 72–75, 77, 83, 89–90,
95–96, 100, 105, 107–112,
116–117, 123, 127–128, 130, 134,
136, 142–145, 148–149, 155,
157, 166, 168, 172, 177, 180,
183, 190–192, 199, 202, 206,
210–211, 213, 220, 224–225,
228, 230, 233–235, 239, 245–
246, 248, 256–261, 269–271,
273–275, 281, 290, 293, 296,
299–302, 309–310, 313, 315,
317, 319, 322, 325, 330, 333–339,
342–344, 346–350, 353,
355–359, 361–366, 369–371,
373–379, 382, 387, 389, 395,
398, 402–403, 407, 419–420,
424, 426, 429–430, 434–436,
438–439, 441
touch   10, 13, 69, 110, 150, 152,
186, 291, 301, 303, 313, 316, 320,
333, 337, 350, 382–383, 407,
434–435
transdisciplinary approach   417,
438
trauma   1, 4–5, 9, 17–18, 88,
100, 167, 173, 177, 182, 256, 258,
260–261, 264–265, 267–281,
284–287, 290, 312, 321, 338,

369–376, 381–385, 390, 411,
424, 426, 432, 434, 440, 443
trauma therapy   182, 261, 280,
312, 434
traumatic   1–3, 9, 12, 17–18,
67–68, 83–84, 87–92, 96, 106,
118, 171, 173, 177–178, 180–181,
184, 186, 205, 247, 257,
260–261, 267–277, 279–281,
284–287, 289–291, 295, 297,
311–312, 321, 323–324, 338–339,
369–370, 375–376, 380, 382,
384, 420–422, 424, 426, 429,
432, 444
traumatic body memory   3, 83,
173, 178, 180, 205, 267–269,
276, 290, 295, 424, 429
traumatic body memory
formation   267–269
traumatic memory   1, 9, 12,
17–18, 67, 106, 118, 177, 267,
286, 421–422, 432
Trevarthen, Colwyn   283, 287,
315, 325, 432, 444
trigger stimuli   277
tripartite model of the body   5,
289
Tversky, Barbara   133, 139, 423,
444
typological perspective of
relational space   327
typus-typoi   3, 23, 25, 30–38

U
unintentional synchronization
148–149
unconscious [implicit, non-
deliberate]   13, 22, 27–30,
35–37, 39, 44, 46, 52, 136,
146, 148, 151, 159, 167, 190,
204–205, 208, 210, 212, 222,
225, 257, 271, 291, 294–295,
314, 322, 341–342, 351, 427

V
validation   4, 208, 220, 276, 306
Van der Kolk, Bessel   259–261,
267–268, 272, 275, 277, 372,
432
Varela, Francisco J.   98, 102,
398, 413

verbalizability   5, 205

W
Waldenfels, Bernhard   107,
   112, 444
Western metaphysics   47
Whitehouse, Mary S.   342, 345,
   351–352

Winther, Helle   5, 353–355, 357,
   359, 361, 367, 422, 431, 436,
   444
word fragmentation /
   completion task   115, 118
wording the essence of the
   therapeutic process   307
working memory   46, 115–116,
   119

Z
Zahavi, Dan   27–28, 39, 41,
   47, 72
Zajonc, Robert B.   148, 154, 156,
   168, 170, 202, 206, 417, 429,
   439, 444